THE PUBLIC PAPERS AND ADDRESSES

OF FRANKLIN D. ROOSEVELT

THE PUBLIC PAPERS AND ADDRESSES OF

FRANKLIN D. ROOSEVELT

WITH A SPECIAL INTRODUCTION

AND EXPLANATORY NOTES BY

PRESIDENT ROOSEVELT

Volume Five

THE PEOPLE APPROVE

1936

RANDOM HOUSE · NEW YORK · 1938

The material in these volumes has been

compiled and collated by

SAMUEL I. ROSENMAN

Counsel to the Governor during the ad-

ministration of Franklin D. Roosevelt

as Governor of the State of New York

1929-1932

Contents

Contents

Contents

Contents

Contents

Contents

Contents

Contents

Contents

Contents

Contents

Contents

Contents

Contents

Contents

Contents

Contents

Contents

The People Approve

Introduction

As the nation advanced into the year 1936, the coming presidential campaign became of increasing importance in the development and exposition of national policies. Through the spring every effort was made by the opposition to attack individuals, to magnify minor errors of administration, to misrepresent actual facts, and at the same time to give lip service to the cause of social betterment and elimination of ancient abuses, without offering any specific proposals alternative to the methods we were following.

This attitude indeed may be said to epitomize the whole tenor of the later campaign of the opposition, both before the party conventions and during the succeeding months up to election day.

About 85 percent of the press of the Nation supported the opposition. Many newspapers and magazines went to the length of coloring, distorting, or actually omitting important facts in the news columns as well as in the editorial pages. This is obviously not written in a spirit of bitterness, because of the simple fact that the attitude of these opposition leaders and newspaper owners or editors actually helped the Administration. In other words, the voting public quickly grasped the situation, resented it, and gave the obvious tactics no further consideration. From the point of view of votes, the New Deal gained. From the point of view of public confidence, the opposition leadership and the majority of the press lost.

The major opposition party was handicapped from the start by the impossible attempt at their Cleveland Convention to run with the hares and hunt with the hounds. They sought in their platform to write one paragraph in vaguely progressive terms in order that it might appeal to the more liberal West, and in the next paragraph to repeat some ancient truism which would sound well in the stately mansions of the East.

I was but echoing the general public understanding of the

Republican platform and of the conduct of the campaign of Republican leaders, when in my speech in Denver (Item 159, this volume) I compared them to the ancient Roman god Janus who had two faces, looking east and west at the same time.

Furthermore the financial and economic and social comments and suggestions on the Republican side of the campaign were so vague and so contradictory that they could not be termed even proposals or offers of definite legislation.

From the outset of the campaign, it was my object to make the issues as broad and as clear as possible. In so doing, there was no effort to concentrate on the elements of undisputed material recovery, or to omit reference to the clear accomplishments in the correction of abuses or to objectives of further specific reform.

Again and again during the campaign, we brought out the importance and desirability of those great purposes of economic and social reform which the Supreme Court had struck down through its decisions during 1935 and in the spring of 1936.

Again and again we stressed the need of developing and spreading the purchasing power of all economic groups in the Nation through agricultural and wage legislation. Again and again we promised continuation of the policy of checking the domination over national economics exercised by a few closely integrated financial and industrial interests. Repeatedly we reaffirmed our determination to continue our efforts to protect our natural resources and plan for their proper use, and to continue our struggle in behalf of human security.

All of our broad objectives were, of course, definitely related to the position which at that time had been assumed by the Supreme Court of the United States. Its current decisions were not only delaying specific steps, but, in prevailing opinions, were serving notice on the country that no law framed to obtain our social and economic objectives would be sustained.

As to the choice of a specific remedy to meet the undeniable fact that the majority of the Supreme Court was in fact legislating on the desirability rather than the constitutionality of laws, none was made during the campaign. There were several possible alternatives of method. Emphasis in the campaign was therefore properly placed on the goal of a Government which, through the cooperation of all its branches, would make democracy work.

It was hoped that, in the election, a great popular majority would express itself in favor of the New Deal objectives. This hope was abundantly fulfilled. The overwhelming popular and electoral approval followed the clear-cut statement of our objectives in our platform and in many of my campaign speeches, especially in my Madison Square Garden speech where I made a definite promise that the fight for them would go on with unabated vigor. (See Item 206, this volume.) The election results permitted no doubt whatsoever to remain that, so far as the policies and goal of the New Deal were concerned, *The People Approve.*

The influence of election day and of this verdict of the people began to manifest itself on Court decisions in the spring of 1937.

Looking back on the year 1936, I consider it a period in which the American people began to think more than before in specific terms. In the three previous years, with the impelling desire for recovery and reform, there was general acceptance of broad policies and broad legislation. We had been thinking rather generally in terms of "business," "agriculture," "industry," and "labor."

In 1936, however, we commenced to discriminate in our public thinking, especially in regard to our continuing efforts to end specific evils or unwholesome practices in many fields. The public generally recognized this, and was thus able to discriminate between the good and the bad, when the promises of 1936 came to be fulfilled in 1937 and 1938. For example, the public began fully to understand that the efforts of the Administration and the Congress to close loopholes in the tax laws which had been taken advantage of by a few rich men and corporations, were not an attack on all rich men and corporations; and, in the same way, that efforts to end abuses perpetrated by some public utilities were not a campaign against successful private ownership of utilities.

Inevitably, growing thought on specific details began to bring
with it certain natural forms of selfishness. Preferences and benefits were bound, during such a period, to be tinged with local or
regional considerations or with the special aspects of particular
occupations or businesses. This unfortunately necessitated a
temporary clouding of the national point of view. It is perhaps
an inevitable phase. But I believe most deeply that it is a phase
preparatory to the final stage when, having finally learned the
lesson of the interdependence of all groups, the American public
will return more firmly than ever to the understanding that local
or sectional or group interests cannot interfere with national
action for national needs.

The good-neighbor policy, which I declared in my first Inaugural Address, and its implications and practical expressions during my first term of office, including the reciprocal trade agreements, were submitted to the electorate for approval in the election of 1936. The overwhelming verdict at the polls encouraged
me in that purpose.

I felt that the policy of the good neighbor had also been so
widely approved throughout the twenty-one American Republics, that early in 1937 I consulted with the twenty other Presidents, looking toward the holding of a special conference — not
merely to receive pledges of good-will from one another but to
devise consultative methods for the settlement of inter-Republic
problems or disagreements, and through consultation to provide
defense against aggression spreading from other continents.

In the foreign field, especially in Europe, there were unmistakable evidences in increased frequency of a disposition among
Nations to disregard solemn treaty obligations — a precedent for
an even more serious situation in 1937. The race of armaments
was accelerated, and no effort to establish more permanent ways
toward peace succeeded anywhere except on this continent.

With the hope of helping the fulfillment of the great ideals of
peace and the good neighbor for the American Continent, I visited Brazil, the Argentine Republic and Uruguay late in the
autumn. The Secretary of State and the representatives of all the

American Republics subsequently drew up and approved with entire unanimity a series of agreements which placed the Americas far in the lead in the quest for international peace. (See Items 17, 211, 222-227 of this volume.) Here was another great objective of our Government which the verdict of November, 1936, indicated that *The People Approve*.

Franklin D. Roosevelt

Washington, D. C.
January 17, 1938

1 ❡ Annual Message to the Congress. January 3, 1936

Mr. President, Mr. Speaker, Members of the Senate and of the House of Representatives:

WE ARE about to enter upon another year of the responsibility which the electorate of the United States has placed in our hands. Having come so far, it is fitting that we should pause to survey the ground which we have covered and the path which lies ahead.

On the fourth day of March, 1933, on the occasion of taking the oath of office as President of the United States, I addressed the people of our country. Need I recall either the scene or the national circumstances attending the occasion? The crisis of that moment was almost exclusively a national one. In recognition of that fact, so obvious to the millions in the streets and in the homes of America, I devoted by far the greater part of that address to what I called, and the Nation called, critical days within our own borders.

You will remember that on that fourth of March, 1933, the world picture was an image of substantial peace. International consultation and widespread hope for the bettering of relations between the Nations gave to all of us a reasonable expectation that the barriers to mutual confidence, to increased trade, and to the peaceful settlement of disputes could be progressively removed. In fact, my only reference to the field of world policy in that address was in these words: "I would dedicate this Nation to the policy of the good neighbor — the neighbor who resolutely respects himself and, because he does so, respects the rights of others — a neighbor who respects his obligations and respects the sanctity of his agreements in and with a world of neighbors."

In the years that have followed, that sentiment has remained the dedication of this Nation. Among the Nations of the great Western Hemisphere the policy of the good neighbor has happily prevailed. At no time in the four and a half centuries of modern civilization in the Americas has there existed—in any year, in any decade, in any generation in all that time—a greater spirit of mutual understanding, of common helpfulness, and of devotion to the ideals of self-government than exists today in the twenty-one American Republics and their neighbor, the Dominion of Canada. This policy of the good neighbor among the Americas is no longer a hope, no longer an objective remaining to be accomplished. It is a fact, active, present, pertinent and effective. In this achievement, every American Nation takes an understanding part. There is neither war, nor rumor of war, nor desire for war. The inhabitants of this vast area, two hundred and fifty million strong, spreading more than eight thousand miles from the Arctic to the Antarctic, believe in, and propose to follow, the policy of the good neighbor. They wish with all their heart that the rest of the world might do likewise.

The rest of the world—Ah! there is the rub.

Were I today to deliver an Inaugural Address to the people of the United States, I could not limit my comments on world affairs to one paragraph. With much regret I should be compelled to devote the greater part to world affairs. Since the summer of that same year of 1933, the temper and the purposes of the rulers of many of the great populations in Europe and in Asia have not pointed the way either to peace or to good-will among men. Not only have peace and good-will among men grown more remote in those areas of the earth during this period, but a point has been reached where the people of the Americas must take cognizance of growing ill-will, of marked trends toward aggression, of increasing armaments, of shortening tempers—a situation which has in it many of the elements that lead to the tragedy of general war.

On those other continents many Nations, principally the smaller peoples, if left to themselves, would be content with their boundaries and willing to solve within themselves and in cooperation with their neighbors their individual problems, both economic and social. The rulers of those Nations, deep in their hearts, follow these peaceful and reasonable aspirations of their peoples. These rulers must remain ever vigilant against the possibility today or tomorrow of invasion or attack by the rulers of other peoples who fail to subscribe to the principles of bettering the human race by peaceful means.

Within those other Nations — those which today must bear the primary, definite responsibility for jeopardizing world peace — what hope lies? To say the least, there are grounds for pessimism. It is idle for us or for others to preach that the masses of the people who constitute those Nations which are dominated by the twin spirits of autocracy and aggression, are out of sympathy with their rulers, that they are allowed no opportunity to express themselves, that they would change things if they could.

That, unfortunately, is not so clear. It might be true that the masses of the people in those Nations would change the policies of their Governments if they could be allowed full freedom and full access to the processes of democratic government as we understand them. But they do not have that access; lacking it they follow blindly and fervently the lead of those who seek autocratic power.

Nations seeking expansion, seeking the rectification of injustices springing from former wars, or seeking outlets for trade, for population or even for their own peaceful contributions to the progress of civilization, fail to demonstrate that patience necessary to attain reasonable and legitimate objectives by peaceful negotiation or by an appeal to the finer instincts of world justice.

They have therefore impatiently reverted to the old belief in the law of the sword, or to the fantastic conception that they, and they alone, are chosen to fulfill a mission and that all the others among the billion and a half of human beings in the world must and shall learn from and be subject to them.

I recognize and you will recognize that these words which I have chosen with deliberation will not prove popular in any Nation that chooses to fit this shoe to its foot. Such sentiments, however, will find sympathy and understanding in those Nations where the people themselves are honestly desirous of peace but must constantly align themselves on one side or the other in the kaleidoscopic jockeying for position which is characteristic of European and Asiatic relations today. For the peace-loving Nations, and there are many of them, find that their very identity depends on their moving and moving again on the chess board of international politics.

I suggested in the spring of 1933 that 85 or 90 percent of all the people in the world were content with the territorial limits of their respective Nations and were willing further to reduce their armed forces if every other Nation in the world would agree to do likewise.

That is equally true today, and it is even more true today that world peace and world good-will are blocked by only 10 or 15 percent of the world's population. That is why efforts to reduce armies have thus far not only failed, but have been met by vastly increased armaments on land and in the air. That is why even efforts to continue the existing limits on naval armaments into the years to come show such little current success.

But the policy of the United States has been clear and consistent. We have sought with earnestness in every possible way to limit world armaments and to attain the peaceful solution of disputes among all Nations.

We have sought by every legitimate means to exert our moral influence against repression, against intolerance, against autocracy and in favor of freedom of expression, equality before the law, religious tolerance and popular rule.

In the field of commerce we have undertaken to encourage a more reasonable interchange of the world's goods. In the field of international finance we have, so far as we are concerned, put an end to dollar diplomacy, to money grabbing, to speculation for the benefit of the powerful and the rich, at the expense of the small and the poor.

As a consistent part of a clear policy, the United States is following a twofold neutrality toward any and all Nations which engage in wars that are not of immediate concern to the Americas. First, we decline to encourage the prosecution of war by permitting belligerents to obtain arms, ammunition or implements of war from the United States. Second, we seek to discourage the use by belligerent Nations of any and all American products calculated to facilitate the prosecution of a war in quantities over and above our normal exports of them in time of peace.

I trust that these objectives thus clearly and unequivocally stated will be carried forward by cooperation between this Congress and the President.

I realize that I have emphasized to you the gravity of the situation which confronts the people of the world. This emphasis is justified because of its importance to civilization and therefore to the United States. Peace is jeopardized by the few and not by the many. Peace is threatened by those who seek selfish power. The world has witnessed similar eras — as in the days when petty kings and feudal barons were changing the map of Europe every fortnight, or when great emperors and great kings were engaged in a mad scramble for colonial empire.

We hope that we are not again at the threshold of such an era. But if face it we must, then the United States and the rest of the Americas can play but one role: through a well-ordered neutrality to do naught to encourage the contest, through adequate defense to save ourselves from embroilment and attack, and through example and all legitimate encouragement and assistance to persuade other Nations to return to the ways of peace and good-will.

The evidence before us clearly proves that autocracy in world affairs endangers peace and that such threats do not spring from those Nations devoted to the democratic ideal. If this be true in world affairs, it should have the greatest weight in the determination of domestic policies.

Within democratic Nations the chief concern of the people is to prevent the continuance or the rise of autocratic institutions that beget slavery at home and aggression abroad. Within our borders, as in the world at large, popular opinion is at war with a power-seeking minority.

That is no new thing. It was fought out in the Constitutional Convention of 1787. From time to time since then, the battle has been continued, under Thomas Jefferson, Andrew Jackson, Theodore Roosevelt and Woodrow Wilson.

In these latter years we have witnessed the domination of government by financial and industrial groups, numerically small but politically dominant in the twelve years that succeeded the World War. The present group of which I speak is indeed numerically small and, while it exercises a large influence and has much to say in the world of business, it does not, I am confident, speak the true sentiments of the less articulate but more important elements that constitute real American business.

In March, 1933, I appealed to the Congress of the United States and to the people of the United States in a new effort to restore power to those to whom it rightfully belonged. The response to that appeal resulted in the writing of a new chapter in the history of popular government. You, the members of the Legislative branch, and I, the Executive, contended for and established a new relationship between Government and people.

What were the terms of that new relationship? They were an appeal from the clamor of many private and selfish interests, yes, an appeal from the clamor of partisan interest, to the ideal of the public interest. Government became the representative and the trustee of the public interest. Our aim was to build upon essentially democratic institutions, seeking all the while the adjustment of burdens, the help of the needy, the protection of the weak, the liberation of the exploited and the genuine protection of the people's property.

It goes without saying that to create such an econmic constitutional order, more than a single legislative enactment was called for. We, you in the Congress and I as the Executive, had to build upon a broad base. Now, after thirty-four months of work, we contemplate a fairly rounded whole. We have returned the control of the Federal Government to the City of Washington.

To be sure, in so doing, we have invited battle. We have earned the hatred of entrenched greed. The very nature of the problem that we faced made it necessary to drive some people from power and strictly to regulate others. I made that plain when I took the oath of office in March, 1933. I spoke of the practices of the unscrupulous money-changers who stood indicted in the court of public opinion. I spoke of the rulers of the exchanges of mankind's goods, who failed through their own stubbornness and their own incompetence. I said that they had admitted their failure and had abdicated.

Abdicated? Yes, in 1933, but now with the passing of danger they forget their damaging admissions and withdraw their abdication.

They seek the restoration of their selfish power. They offer to lead us back round the same old corner into the same old dreary street.

Yes, there are still determined groups that are intent upon that very thing. Rigorously held up to popular examination, their true character presents itself. They steal the livery of great national constitutional ideals to serve discredited special interests. As guardians and trustees for great groups of individual stockholders they wrongfully seek to carry the property and the interests entrusted to them into the arena of partisan politics. They seek — this minority in business and industry — to control and often do control and use for their own purposes legitimate and highly honored business associations; they engage in vast propaganda to spread fear and discord among the people — they would "gang up" against the people's liberties.

The principle that they would instill into government if they succeed in seizing power is well shown by the principles which many of them have instilled into their own affairs: autocracy toward labor, toward stockholders, toward consumers, toward public sentiment. Autocrats in smaller things, they seek autocracy in bigger things. "By their fruits ye shall know them."

If these gentlemen believe, as they say they believe, that the measures adopted by this Congress and its predecessor, and carried out by this Administration, have hindered rather than promoted recovery, let them be consistent. Let them propose to this

14

Congress the complete repeal of these measures. The way is open to such a proposal.

Let action be positive and not negative. The way is open in the Congress of the United States for an expression of opinion by yeas and nays. Shall we say that values are restored and that the Congress will, therefore, repeal the laws under which we have been bringing them back? Shall we say that because national income has grown with rising prosperity, we shall repeal existing taxes and thereby put off the day of approaching a balanced budget and of starting to reduce the national debt? Shall we abandon the reasonable support and regulation of banking? Shall we restore the dollar to its former gold content?

Shall we say to the farmer, "The prices for your products are in part restored. Now go and hoe your own row?"

Shall we say to the home owners, "We have reduced your rates of interest. We have no further concern with how you keep your home or what you pay for your money. That is your affair?"

Shall we say to the several millions of unemployed citizens who face the very problem of existence, of getting enough to eat, "We will withdraw from giving you work. We will turn you back to the charity of your communities and those men of selfish power who tell you that perhaps they will employ you if the Government leaves them strictly alone?"

Shall we say to the needy unemployed, "Your problem is a local one except that perhaps the Federal Government, as an act of mere generosity, will be willing to pay to your city or to your county a few grudging dollars to help maintain your soup kitchens?"

Shall we say to the children who have worked all day in the factories, "Child labor is a local issue and so are your starvation wages; something to be solved or left unsolved by the jurisdiction of forty-eight States?"

Shall we say to the laborer, "Your right to organize, your relations with your employer have nothing to do with the public interest; if your employer will not even meet with you to discuss your problems and his, that is none of our affair?"

Shall we say to the unemployed and the aged, "Social security lies not within the province of the Federal Government; you must seek relief elsewhere?"

Shall we say to the men and women who live in conditions of squalor in country and in city, "The health and the happiness of you and your children are no concern of ours?"

Shall we expose our population once more by the repeal of laws which protect them against the loss of their honest investments and against the manipulations of dishonest speculators? Shall we abandon the splendid efforts of the Federal Government to raise the health standards of the Nation and to give youth a decent opportunity through such means as the Civilian Conservation Corps?

Members of the Congress, let these challenges be met. If this is what these gentlemen want, let them say so to the Congress of the United States. Let them no longer hide their dissent in a cowardly cloak of generality. Let them define the issue. We have been specific in our affirmative action. Let them be specific in their negative attack.

But the challenge faced by this Congress is more menacing than merely a return to the past — bad as that would be. Our resplendent economic autocracy does not want to return to that individualism of which they prate, even though the advantages under that system went to the ruthless and the strong. They realize that in thirty-four months we have built up new instruments of public power. In the hands of a people's Government this power is wholesome and proper. But in the hands of political puppets of an economic autocracy such power would provide shackles for the liberties of the people. Give them their way and they will take the course of every autocracy of the past — power for themselves, enslavement for the public.

Their weapon is the weapon of fear. I have said, "The only thing we have to fear is fear itself." That is as true today as it was in 1933. But such fear as they instill today is not a natural fear, a normal fear; it is a synthetic, manufactured, poisonous fear that is being spread subtly, expensively and cleverly by the same people who cried in those other days, "Save us, save us, lest we perish."

I am confident that the Congress of the United States well understands the facts and is ready to wage unceasing warfare against those who seek a continuation of that spirit of fear. The carrying out of the laws of the land as enacted by the Congress requires protection until final adjudication by the highest tribunal of the land. The Congress has the right and can find the means to protect its own prerogatives.

We are justified in our present confidence. Restoration of national income, which shows continuing gains for the third successive year, supports the normal and logical policies under which agriculture and industry are returning to full activity. Under these policies we approach a balance of the national budget. National income increases; tax receipts, based on that income, increase without the levying of new taxes. That is why I am able to say to this, the Second Session of the 74th Congress, that it is my belief based on existing laws that no new taxes, over and above the present taxes, are either advisable or necessary.

National income increases; employment increases. Therefore, we can look forward to a reduction in the number of those citizens who are in need. Therefore, also, we can anticipate a reduction in our appropriations for relief.

In the light of our substantial material progress, in the light of the increasing effectiveness of the restoration of popular rule, I recommend to the Congress that we advance; that we do not retreat. I have confidence that you will not fail the people of the Nation whose mandate you have already so faithfully fulfilled.

I repeat, with the same faith and the same determination, my words of March 4, 1933: "We face the arduous days that lie before us in the warm courage of national unity; with a clear consciousness of seeking old and precious moral values; with a clean satisfaction that comes from the stern performance of duty by old and young alike. We aim at the assurance of a rounded and

17

permanent national life. We do not distrust the future of essential democracy."

I cannot better end this message on the state of the Union than by repeating the words of a wise philosopher at whose feet I sat many, many years ago.

"What great crises teach all men whom the example and counsel of the brave inspire is the lesson: Fear not, view all the tasks of life as sacred, have faith in the triumph of the ideal, give daily all that you have to give, be loyal and rejoice whenever you find yourselves part of a great ideal enterprise. You, at this moment, have the honor to belong to a generation whose lips are touched by fire. You live in a land that now enjoys the blessings of peace. But let nothing human be wholly alien to you. The human race now passes through one of its great crises. New ideas, new issues —a new call for men to carry on the work of righteousness, of charity, of courage, of patience, and of loyalty. . . . However memory bring back this moment to your minds, let it be able to say to you: That was a great moment. It was the beginning of a new era. . . . This world in its crisis called for volunteers, for men of faith in life, of patience in service, of charity and of insight. I responded to the call however I could. I volunteered to give myself to my Master—the cause of humane and brave living. I studied, I loved, I labored, unsparingly and hopefully, to be worthy of my generation."

2 ❰ The Annual Budget Message. January 3, 1936

To the Congress:

PURSUANT to provisions of law I transmit herewith the Budget of the United States Government for the fiscal year ending June 30, 1937, together with this message, which is definitely a part thereof. The estimates have been developed after careful analysis of the revenues, obligations, and reasonable needs of the Government, and I recommend appropriations for the purposes specifically detailed.

PART I

No mortal is permitted unfailingly to predict the future. This is particularly true of estimates which relate to the money values of property and services in a world of Nations torn by dissension, by violent price fluctuations, and by forebodings of the future.

It is, therefore, a cause for congratulation within our own Nation to realize that a consistent, broad national policy, adopted nearly three years ago by the Congress and the President, has thus far moved steadily, effectively, and successfully toward its objective.

In March, 1933, in spite of substantial increases in tax rates during the preceding Administration, Federal tax receipts had fallen to such a low level that even normal expenses of Government could not be carried on without creating a mounting deficit. In addition to normal expenses the problem of millions of starving unemployed called for a relief program which obviously would greatly increase that deficit.

The national policy which we then adopted sought to stop the downward economic spiral by taking simultaneous action along a dozen fronts. The chief objectives were: To make bank deposits secure, to save farms and homes from foreclosure, to start public works on a large scale, to encourage home building, to increase farm crop values, to give useful work instead of a dole to the needy unemployed, to reduce all interest rates, to increase foreign trade in both exports and imports, to extend Government credit to railroads and other privately owned activities, to reduce unsound and generally disastrous speculation, to eliminate starvation wages, to seek a higher level of values, and then to maintain those values.

On the part of the Federal Government the many legislative acts creating the machinery for recovery were all predicated on two interdependent beliefs. First, the measures would immediately cause a great increase in the annual expenditures of the Government—many of these expenditures, however, in the form of loans which would ultimately return to the Treasury. Second, as a result of the simultaneous attack on the many fronts I have indicated, the receipts of the Government would rise definitely and sharply during the following few years, while greatly increased expenditure for the purposes stated, coupled with rising values and the stopping of losses, would, over a period of years, diminish the need for work relief and thereby reduce Federal expenditures. The increase in revenues would ultimately meet and pass the declining cost of relief.

This policy adopted in the spring of 1933 has been confirmed in actual practice by the Treasury figures of 1934, of 1935, and by the estimates for the fiscal years of 1936 and 1937.

There is today no doubt of the fundamental soundness of the policy of 1933. If we proceed along the path we have followed and with the results attained up to the present time we shall continue our successful progress during the coming years.

To state it even more concisely, we can look forward today to a continued reduction of deficits, to increased tax receipts, and to declining expenditures for the needy unemployed. Let it be remembered that the major part of the increase in tax receipts anticipated in 1937 over 1936 from comparable sources is coming from old tax schedules. The only changes made last year in the tax schedule were, first, the elimination of the tax on checks and, second, slight increases in taxes on large incomes, on large estates, and on large corporations and in capital stock and excess profits taxes. By the elimination of the tax on checks we lost forty million dollars in revenue and the slight increases on estates and on personal and corporate incomes will add only about 222 million dollars to Government receipts this coming year. I emphasize that the great bulk of increased Government income referred to above results from increased earning power and profits throughout the Nation and not from the new taxes imposed by the Revenue Act of 1935.

Final success will depend, of course, on the strength of the efforts put forth by the employers of the United States greatly to increase the number of persons employed by them. The finances of the Government are in better condition than at any time in the past seven years. I say this because starting with the autumn of 1929, tax receipts began a steady and alarming decline while, at the same time, Government expenditures began a steady rise; today, tax receipts are continuing a steady climb which commenced in the summer of 1933, whereas Budget estimates for the next fiscal year will show a decreased need for appropriations.

The credit of the Government is at its highest. The average of the business men of the Nation stand ready to do their share. It is to be hoped that motives and attacks which spring only from the desire for political or financial power on the part of a few will not retard the steady progress we are making.

Our policy is succeeding. The figures prove it. Secure in the knowledge that steadily decreasing deficits will turn in time into steadily increasing surpluses, and that it is the deficit of today which is making possible the surplus of tomorrow, let us pursue the course that we have mapped.

In my Budget message of January, 1935, I said, "I am, however, submitting to the Congress a Budget for the fiscal year 1936 which balances except for expenditures to give work to the unemployed. If this Budget receives approval of the Congress, the country will henceforth have the assurance that with the single exception of this item, every current expenditure of whatever nature will be fully covered by our estimates of current receipts. Such deficit as occurs will be due solely to this cause, and it may be expected to decline as rapidly as private industry is able to reemploy those who now are without work."

In looking at the revised estimates for the fiscal year 1936, I am more than pleased to find that we have not only accomplished what I said we would in my Budget message of a year ago but that the results with respect to both expenditures and receipts have surpassed expectations.

1. My Budget message of January, 1935, forecast that the expenditures for the fiscal year 1936 would be $8,520,000,000. Our most recent estimate shows that our expenditures will be $7,645,-000,000, or $875,000,000 less than originally forecast.

2. Receipts were estimated in January, 1935, at $3,992,000,000. At the present time it appears that they will be $4,411,000,000, or an increase of $419,000,000.

3. The message of January, 1935, forecast a gross deficit of $4,528,000,000, and the most recent figures show that the deficit will be $3,234,000,000, or a decrease of $1,294,000,000.

This great improvement of the fiscal outlook during this present year has been brought about through policies which the Congress and the President initiated in 1933 and which we have since maintained.

Now let us look at the Budget for the fiscal year 1937:

To run all the regular activities of the Government I shall need a total of $5,069,000,000. These regular activities include interest on the public debt, major public works, operations of the Civilian Conservation Corps, and agricultural benefit payments, but do not include strictly work relief items. I expect to pay for these regular activities with estimated receipts of $5,654,000,000, leaving an excess of receipts of $585,000,000. Out of this $585,000,000 I shall need $580,000,000 for debt retirement, which will still leave $5,000,000 of excess receipts over expenditures after having paid for all of the regular expenditures of the Government plus debt retirement.

The item for relief remains. Without that item the Budget is in balance. To make today a formal Budget estimate of the amount necessary for work relief would be of necessity a difficult task. We have too recently reached our goal of putting three and one-half million people to work; and the beneficial effects from this program and from increasing expenditures on public works cannot be foretold as accurately today as they can two months from now. Furthermore, employment by private industry continues to show substantial gains over the figures of a year ago. It is reasonably certain that the total appropriations for work relief during the fiscal year 1937 will be far less than during the current fiscal year. It is estimated in this Budget that expenditures for recovery and relief out of unexpended balances of previous emergency appropriations will amount to $1,103,000,000. Including these expenditures the gross deficit for 1937, without an estimate for additional work relief, is less than the gross deficit for 1936 by $2,136,000,000. I do not anticipate that the need for additional relief funds will be as great as that sum.

To state the case even more precisely, the gross deficit of the Government in 1934 was $3,989,000,000; in 1935, $3,575,000,000; in 1936 (estimate), $3,234,000,000; and in 1937 (estimated but not including any new appropriations for work relief), $1,098,-000,000. Therefore, it is clear: First, that since June 30, 1934, the gross deficit of the Government shows a steady decrease during the fiscal years 1935 and 1936. Second, that if work relief appropriations by this session of the Congress were made up to a total of $2,136,000,000, the total gross deficit for the fiscal year 1937 would not exceed that of 1936, which was the lowest gross deficit of the past three years. Therefore, it follows that by whatever amount the appropriation for work relief at this session is less than $2,136,000,000, the gross deficit for 1937 will be less than the deficit for 1936 by the same amount.

With this limitation and this excellent prospect clearly in mind, I am not including in this Budget estimates for additional relief appropriations. I shall transmit such estimates with far greater knowledge and, therefore, with greater accuracy in sufficient time before the adjournment of this session to give the Congress full opportunity to examine into the subject and to make the necessary appropriations.

The credit of the Government is in sound condition. On October 15, 1933, war-time issues of First and Fourth Liberty Bonds were outstanding in the aggregate amount of $8,200,000,000, bearing interest at an average rate of about $4\frac{1}{8}$ percent. Today this entire amount has been refunded, of which about $5,000,-000,000 was exchanged for long-term bonds bearing interest at rates ranging from $2\frac{3}{4}$ to $3\frac{1}{4}$ percent per annum; $1,900,000,000 was exchanged for Treasury notes bearing interest from $1\frac{1}{2}$ to $2\frac{1}{2}$ percent per annum, and the balance was paid in cash. The average rate on the securities issued to refund the Liberty Bonds is less than $2\frac{3}{4}$ percent per annum, a saving of approximately $1\frac{3}{8}$

percent a year, or an annual reduction in interest payments of more than $100,000,000 on these particular securities.

The average rate on the interest-bearing debt was, on June 30, 1934, approximately 3.18 percent, whereas on November 30, 1935, it had been reduced to 2.575 percent.

If the Congress enacts legislation at the coming session which will impose additional charges upon the Treasury for which provision is not already made in this Budget, I strongly urge that additional taxes be provided to cover such charges. It is important as we emerge from the depression that no new activities be added to the Government unless provision is made for additional revenue to meet their cost.

PART II

RECOMMENDATIONS

The following recommendations are offered:

APPROPRIATION TRANSFER PROVISIONS. — The text accompanying a number of the estimates of appropriations has been drafted to include provision for transfer between appropriations within the same department. This provision will add a measure of administrative flexibility and will tend to promote economical execution of the program as a whole, and approval thereof by the Congress is recommended.

REPEAL AMENDMENT TO AGRICULTURAL ADJUSTMENT ACT. — During the first session of the Seventy-fourth Congress the Agricultural Adjustment Act was amended so as to appropriate a sum equal to 30 percent of customs receipts to the Secretary of Agriculture to encourage exportation and domestic consumption of agricultural commodities. No estimate of expenditure for account of this legislation is included herein; and repeal of the amendment is recommended for the following reasons:

By appropriating directly instead of authorizing an appropriation the amendment denies to the President the opportunity to consider the need and include appropriate estimates in the Budget; and it denies to the Congress the opportunity to review such estimates in their relation to the whole program of the Government. The amendment violates the principles of the Permanent Appropriation Repeal Act of 1934, and of the Budget and Accounting Act of June 10, 1921. It is in conflict with sound administration in that it provides in advance for large annual expenditures without any attempt to coordinate income and expense. The amendment was passed in the last days of the session as a result of conference agreement and without the debate and consideration by the Congress which the import of the measures clearly justifies.

APPORTIONMENTS OF APPROPRIATIONS. — Within the last few months control of the administrative expense of twenty emergency agencies has been vested in the Bureau of the Budget which after a general survey of all of them has effected substantial reductions in proposed expenditures for administrative purposes. Allowances for administrative expenses are subject to such adjustment as the status of the agency warrants.

The 20 agencies brought under the Budget are the Agricultural Adjustment Administration; Commodity Credit Corporation; Electric Home and Farm Authority; Export-Import Banks (2); Farm Credit Administration; Federal Coordinator of Transportation; Federal Deposit Insurance Corporation; Federal Emergency Administration of Public Works; Federal Emergency Relief Administration; Federal Farm Mortgage Corporation; Federal Home Loan Bank Board; Federal Housing Administration; Federal Savings and Loan System; Federal Savings and Loan Insurance Corporation; Federal Surplus Relief Corporation; Home Owners Loan Corporation; National Recovery Administration; Reconstruction Finance Corporation; and Tennessee Valley Authority.

It is recommended that Section 3679 of the Revised Statutes be amended so as to bring all agencies of the Government, including Government-owned and Government-controlled corporations, within the authority of the Director of the Budget with respect to apportionments of appropriations and of other funds available to them.

PART III

REVIEW OF THE FISCAL YEARS 1935 AND 1936 AND THE FISCAL PROGRAM OF 1937

This review concerns itself with cash actually received and paid out by the Treasury in the fiscal year 1935; and with the estimates of receipts, appropriations, and expenditures for the fiscal years 1936 and 1937. As elsewhere stated herein the program of regular activities for 1937 includes activities under the Agricultural Adjustment Act and the Civilian Conservation Corps (Emergency Conservation Work), heretofore classed as emergency. Therefore the figures used herein for 1934, 1935, and 1936 have been adjusted to a comparable basis.

FISCAL YEAR 1935

RECEIPTS. — Treasury receipts for the year ended June 30, 1935, were in excess of estimates prepared a year ago. Considering all sources except postal revenues, total receipts amounted to $3,800,-467,202, or $89,000,000 above the estimate. Internal revenue, including processing taxes on farm products, produced $3,277,-690,028, exceeding the estimate by $80,000,000. Customs receipts amounted to $343,353,033, an increase over the estimate of $56,-000,000. Miscellaneous receipts, including realization upon assets, estimated at $227,184,181, fell short of the estimate by $48,-000,000; the amount actually received under this item was $179,-424,140.

EXPENDITURES. — While actual receipts for the year were greater than anticipated, actual expenditures were less than the amount estimated by $1,205,000,000. The aggregate of all expenditures was $7,375,825,166, against an estimate of $8,581,069,026. Approximately a billion dollars of this difference related to recovery and relief, and the regular agencies accounted for the remainder.

The total spent for recovery and relief was $3,068,803,053, whereas the 1936 Budget estimate was $4,068,541,852, exclusive of expenditures made under the Agricultural Adjustment Act and made by the Civilian Conservation Corps. This difference is partly due to this fact:

When the Budget for 1936 was prepared it seemed probable that the Reconstruction Finance Corporation, in all accounts except relief, would close the year with an excess of loans over repayments; and the amount of the net expenditures was estimated at $556,000,000. However, because of improved business conditions, the demands for Corporation assistance were so much less than estimated and the repayments of loans so much greater, that the Corporation actually closed the year with net receipts of $107,-000,000. Therefore, the net difference between the estimated expenditure and the actual result amounted to $663,000,000. Other agencies spent for recovery and relief $337,000,000 less than estimated.

For the operation and maintenance of regular departments and establishments of the Government, including the Agricultural Adjustment Act and the Civilian Conservation Corps, actual expenditures were $2,912,537,509, against the estimate of $3,104,-961,174.

For statutory debt retirements there was expended $573,558,-250, and for interest on the public debt $820,926,353, whereas the amounts budgeted for these items were, respectively, $572,-566,000 and $835,000,000.

DEFICIT AND PUBLIC DEBT. — The year closed with a gross deficit of $3,575,357,964 instead of the estimate of $4,869,418,338. After deducting the amount paid out for statutory debt retirement the net deficit was $3,001,799,714. The increase in the total outstanding gross public debt was $1,647,751,210, which figure is properly obtained by subtracting from the net deficit the decrease in the general fund balance, the excess of receipts from trust funds, increment on gold, et cetera, over expenditures from the same accounts, and the amount of retirement of national-bank notes from the gold increment. As of June 30, 1935, the total outstanding gross public debt was $28,700,892,624, while on June 30, 1934, it was $27,053,141,414.

BY drawing upon the experience of the first six months of the current year it is possible to forecast with a fair degree of accuracy the results of financial operations for the whole 1936 fiscal period.

Receipts.—The same sources of income (excluding postal revenues) which a year ago were expected to produce receipts aggregating $3,991,904,639 are now expected to produce a total of $4,410,793,946.

Of the items comprising the whole, income taxes will develop $1,434,112,000, or $246,000,000 more than the 1936 Budget estimate.

Miscellaneous internal revenue exclusive of processing taxes is now estimated at $1,873,091,000, an increase of $187,000,000. Receipts from customs are expected to reach a total of $353,191,000, exceeding the original estimate by $55,000,000. Other changes, some upward and some downward, result in the new estimate of total receipts at a figure of $419,000,000 higher than shown in the Budget for 1936 which was presented a year ago.

The present estimate for processing taxes in 1936, included in the above total, is in round figures $529,000,000, as against the original estimate of $570,000,000. Actual receipts for the five months ended November 30, 1935, totaled $56,000,000, while up to that date approximately $148,000,000 of due payments had been impounded directly as the result of preliminary court action.

It is pertinent to repeat here a statement appearing in the Summation of the 1936 Budget: "Estimates of receipts contemplate continued collection of processing taxes. If the attack which has been made upon this act is sustained we will have to face the problem of financing existing contracts for benefit payments out of some form of new taxes."

Two new taxes, namely, the bituminous coal tax and the taxes upon carriers and their employees, both representing recent legislation, will contribute $39,000,000 not included in the original estimate of receipts for 1936. New taxes imposed by the Social

Security Act and the Revenue Act of 1935 will not produce any income until the fiscal year 1937.

EXPENDITURES. — Indications are that expenditures including debt retirement during the present fiscal year will not reach the amount budgeted by approximately $875,000,000; the total now foreseen is $7,645,301,338, against the original estimate of $8,-520,413,609. Exclusive of debt retirement the total of expenditures is now estimated at $7,093,276,338, while the original comparable figure was $7,883,979,609. For recovery and relief the revised estimate of expenditures for the fiscal year 1936 is less than the original Budget estimate by $738,000,000, and expenditures for all regular purposes, including Agricultural Adjustment Act and Civilian Conservation Corps, will be less by $137,000,000. Debt retirement will require $84,000,000 less than was budgeted and interest payments will be $133,000,000 less. All regular expenditures, excluding service on the public debt, will be greater than the original Budget estimate by about $80,000,000.

The reduction in interest payments from the amount budgeted, as referred to above, was due largely to the refunding of First and Fourth Liberty Loan bonds aggregating $8,200,000,000, at substantially lower rates of interest.

DEFICIT AND PUBLIC DEBT. — The revised estimates as set out herein show a gross deficit for the current fiscal year of approximately $3,234,000,000, instead of the original Budget forecast of $4,529,000,000. After deducting the amount of statutory debt retirement the net deficit will be, in round figures, $2,682,000,000. The gross public debt as at June 30, 1936, should not be greater than $31,000,000,000. This estimate assumes that the working balance in the Treasury on June 30, 1936, will be approximately the same as it was on June 30, 1935, namely, $1,001,142,951. Obviously, if the working balance is less, the gross debt will be less; and if it is greater, the gross debt will be greater.

The foregoing figures are set out in the following table for ready comparison between Budget estimates of a year ago and what are now considered probable.

Comparison of original and revised estimates, fiscal year 1936, adjusted to classification of expenditures in 1937 Budget

	Budget estimate, January, 1935	Revised estimate
1. Receipts (excluding postal):		
Income tax............................	$ 1,188,000,000	$ 1,434,112,000
Miscellaneous internal revenue..........	1,685,900,000	1,873,091,000
Processing taxes on farm products........	570,000,000	529,042,000
Customs..............................	298,000,000	353,191,000
All other.............................	250,004,639	221,357,946
Total receipts.......................	3,991,904,639	4,410,793,946
2. Expenditures:		
Regular, including A.A.A. and C.C.C.	3,402,351,134	3,482,208,151
Interest on the public debt..............	875,000,000	742,000,000
Recovery and relief....................	3,606,628,475	2,869,068,187
Total expenditures...................	7,883,979,609	7,093,276,338
3. Net deficit............................	3,892,074,970	2,682,482,392
Statutory debt retirements..............	636,434,000	552,025,000
Gross deficit........................	4,528,508,970	3,234,507,392
4. Gross public debt.......................	34,238,823,656	30,933,375,017

Postal revenues for the fiscal year 1936 are now estimated at $670,000,000, which is $25,000,000 over the original estimate.

THE FISCAL PROGRAM OF 1937

There is presented here a brief factual résumé of the principal features of the Budget for the fiscal year 1937, the details of which appear in subsequent text and tables. A few high points stand out and justify emphasis.

Without impairing the ability of the Government to carry on its normal functions and to prosecute those activities essential to continued recovery, the Budget reflects a substantial decrease in the spread between income and outgo. This is consistent with the prediction made in the Budget message a year ago and is possible because of progressive improvement in the economic status of the people. The state of national recovery is such that receipts from prevailing tax sources on the basis of present rates appear adequate for financing the ordinary operations of the Government in 1937, including service on the public debt; and no new or additional taxes are proposed.

Legislation enacted by the first session of the 74th Congress makes it necessary to provide in the 1937 estimates new appropriation items aggregating $667,000,000. This total will become approximately $767,000,000 should the Congress reject the recommendation, hereinbefore offered, for repeal of that part of the Agricultural Adjustment Act which appropriates to the Secretary of Agriculture a sum equal to 30 percent of customs receipts.

Legislation enacted by the first session also permits including in these estimates a total of $769,000,000 of additional receipts, of which about 70 percent will accrue under the Bituminous Coal Conservation Act, the act levying taxes upon carriers and their employees, and the Social Security Act. It is worthy of note that but slightly less than 30 percent of this increase will be derived under the Revenue Act of 1935. This act, it will be recalled, slightly increased taxes on individuals whose net incomes exceed $50,000 per year; slightly increased estate taxes on larger fortunes with a corresponding increase in gift taxes; and in respect of corporations, decreased taxes on net earnings of small corporations while increasing in relative ratio the taxes on net income of larger corporations. The act also provided for an increase in taxes on capital stock and on excess profits of corporations. The effect of the excess-profits tax was to increase taxes on corporations which earned in excess of certain percentages of their adjusted declared value of capital stock.

The total revenue expected to be produced by these taxes in the fiscal year 1937 will be only $222,000,000, or 11 percent, over the income, estate, gift, capital-stock, and excess-profits taxes under the old law. Since collections in the fiscal year 1937 from income taxes and the estate tax only partially reflect the Revenue Act of 1935, the above amount will be somewhat larger on a full year basis.

A Federal public works program of $405,000,000 is recommended to meet in part the development and improvement requirements of the Government, and as a proper Federal contribution to work opportunity. While this program represents an increase of about $187,000,000 over the amount for similar purposes for which the Congress made specific appropriations for the current fiscal year, it is $333,000,000 less than the total amount made available for Federal public works in 1936, considering allotments made from emergency funds.

The success attending the operations of the Civilian Conservation Corps and the Agricultural Adjustment Administration under emergency status justifies taking them into the Budget and program for 1937 as regular activities, and the estimates of appropriations and expenditures have been prepared accordingly. The appropriation recommended for Civilian Conservation Corps is for the period March 31, 1936, to March 31, 1937, and amounts to $246,000,0000, while the appropriation for the Agricultural Adjustment Administration is for the full year and amounts to $499,054,985.

The table on page 33 gives a clear picture of the main figures proposed in this Budget and shows how they compare with similar figures for previous years.

Directing attention to a comparison between fiscal operations proposed for 1937 and now estimated for 1936, as set forth in the table, the following comment is pertinent:

RECEIPTS. — Receipts in 1937 (exclusive of postal revenues and processing taxes and also, for purposes of comparison, exclusive of taxes imposed under the Social Security Act, the Bituminous Coal Conservation Act, and the act levying taxes upon carriers and their employees) are expected to reach a total of $4,559,817,650, an increase of $716,665,704 over similar receipts for 1936 now estimated at $3,843,151,946, and $1,280,730,319 over 1935. It should be pointed out here that this increase is due largely to increased collections anticipated under the old schedules. As has been stated, only about $222,000,000 will be col-

[In millions of dollars]

	Actual		Estimated	
	1934	1935	1936	1937
I. RECEIPTS:				
Income taxes........................	818	1,099	1,434	1,943
Miscellaneous internal revenue...........	1,470	1,657	1,873	2,103
Processing taxes......................	353	521	529	547
Customs.............................	313	343	353	354
Miscellaneous.......................	162	180	183	160
Taxes under the Social Security Act, the act levying taxes upon carriers and their employees, and the Bituminous Coal Conservation Act......................	....	....	39	547
Total receipts....................	3,116	3,800	4,411	5,654
II. Expenditures:				
1. Regular:				
Operation and maintenance of regular departments and establishments	1,086	1,083	1,568	2,586
Veterans' pensions and benefits.......	556	605	718	790
Interest on national debt...........	757	821	742	805
Tax refunds (exclusive of processing taxes)........................	63	45	47	49
Agricultural Adjustment Act.........	290	743	621	619
Civilian Conservation Corps.........	332	436	528	220
Statutory debt retirements..........	360	573	552	580
Total regular.................	3,444	4,306	4,776	5,649
Excess of receipts over regular expenditures......................	....	....	....	5
Excess of regular expenditures over receipts.........................	328	506	365	....
2. Recovery and relief..................	3,661	3,069	2,869	1,103[1]
Gross deficit...................	3,989	3,575	3,234	1,098
Gross public debt.............	27,053	28,701	30,933	31,351

[1] Represents estimated expenditures from unexpended balances of previous emergency appropriations.

lected in 1937 as a result of new schedules in the Revenue Act of 1935.

From processing taxes the sum anticipated is $547,300,000, against the estimate of $529,042,000 for the current year, an increase of $18,258,000. Other taxes recently authorized by the

Congress under the Social Security Act, the Bituminous Coal Conservation Act, and the act levying taxes upon carriers and their employees will produce $547,100,000 in 1937 and $38,600,-000 this year, an increase of $508,500,000.

Thus 1937 receipts from all sources, except postal revenues, are estimated at $5,654,217,650, against the revised estimate of $4,410,793,946 for the current fiscal year. The increase in total receipts from stated sources is, therefore, $1,243,423,704.

Postal receipts for the coming year are estimated at $705,-000,000, an increase of $35,000,000 over $670,000,000 anticipated in 1936. This is further evidence of the upward trend in economic conditions.

An examination of the detailed estimates of receipts for 1937 indicates a gain over 1936 in income tax of $508,488,000, the figures for the two years being respectively $1,942,600,000 and $1,-434,112,000. Similarly, estimated receipts from miscellaneous internal revenue, exclusive of processing taxes, are up from $1,-873,091,000 to $2,103,114,000, a gain of $230,023,000. Customs receipts are forecast at $354,000,000, substantially the same as anticipated for 1936. The reduction of $22,654,296 in probable miscellaneous receipts, from $182,757,946 to $160,103,650, brings the net increase in the estimates of these four classes of receipts to $716,665,704, as stated.

The provisions of the Social Security Act, the Bituminous Coal Conservation Act, and the act levying taxes upon carriers and their employees are such that receipts during the fiscal year 1936 will be comparatively small while revenues from these sources in the next fiscal year will show substantial increases. The amounts estimated for 1937 from such new taxes in the order named are $433,200,000, $12,300,000, and $101,600,000.

EXPENDITURES. — The expenditures for 1937 contemplated under this Budget will total $6,752,606,370, or approximately $893,000,000 less than is now estimated for 1936.

Of the two major categories of expenditure, namely, regular and recovery and relief, allowances for regular activities, including the Agricultural Adjustment Act and Civilian Conservation Corps, amount to $5,649,781,738 as compared with $4,776,233,-151 for 1936, an increase of $873,548,587. For recovery and relief, expenditures listed herein are those which will be made from unexpended balances, practically all of which will have been obligated prior to June 30, 1936, and practically all of which have been allotted. The total of such expenditures in 1937 is estimated at $1,102,824,632, which is a decrease of $1,766,243,555 from the figure of $2,869,068,187 for 1936.

In regular expenditures there is included $805,000,000 for interest on the public debt, an increase of $63,000,000 over the same item for the current year; and $580,125,000 for statutory debt retirements, an increase of $28,100,000. The cost of service on the public debt in 1937, therefore, will exceed that for 1936 by $91,100,000.

Excepting debt retirement and interest, the net increase in expenditures for regular activities is $782,448,587 as compared with 1936. The major part of this increase is accounted for as follows: (*a*) For financing activities under the Social Security Act, the act levying taxes upon carriers and their employees, and the Bituminous Coal Conservation Act, $485,000,000; (*b*) for other new legislation, $125,000,000; (*c*) for increased public works, transferred from emergency appropriations, $228,000,000; (*d*) for the veterans' adjusted-service certificate fund in order to bring the annual contribution of the Government nearer its actual liability under existing law, $60,000,000; and (*e*) for national defense, to meet the policy of the Congress and the Executive in making up for the delay by the United States in bringing the Navy up to the strength contemplated by the naval treaties of 1922 and 1930, and to provide replacement and improved equipment and additional personnel for the Army, $193,000,000.

In the War Department Appropriation Act for the fiscal year 1935, the Congress adopted a policy of increasing the average enlisted strength of the Army from 118,750 to 165,000 men and toward accomplishing such purpose appropriated an additional $20,000,000 for expenditure during that year. These funds are sufficient to maintain an *average* enlisted strength during 1936 of approximately 147,000 men. The estimates of expenditure included in this Budget are sufficient in amount to maintain this average during the fiscal year 1937, with the purpose in view of providing in the 1938 Budget the funds necessary to recruit the Army to such strength by the close of that year as will produce an average enlisted strength of 165,000 throughout the fiscal year 1939, the maximum indicated by the Congress. It is felt that this is as fast as the Government should proceed in this matter in the light of the present forecast of fiscal affairs.

The contemplated expenditures for the Civilian Conservation Corps show a decrease of $308,383,000 as against estimated comparable expenditures for 1936.

DEFICIT AND PUBLIC DEBT. — The gross deficit for the fiscal year 1937 is estimated at $1,098,388,720, including $580,125,000 for statutory debt retirement, or a net deficit of $518,263,720. It is estimated that the gross public debt on June 30, 1937, will amount to $31,351,638,737, as compared with an estimated debt on June 30, 1936, of $30,933,375,017. The figure for 1937 does not include such amounts for work relief during the coming year as may be determined upon by the Congress.

APPROPRIATIONS.—Appropriations recommended in this Budget aggregate $6,400,000,000, including probable supplemental items estimated at $600,000,000, while the appropriations already made and prospective supplemental items for the fiscal year 1936, exclusive of the appropriation of $4,000,000,000 for recovery and relief, amount to $5,146,000,000, an increase of $1,-254,000,000 required for the fiscal year 1937 over the fiscal year 1936.

This increase is due to (1) additional appropriations amounting to approximately $610,000,000, including supplementals to be submitted later, required to finance new legislation enacted at the last session of Congress; (2) an appropriation of $246,000,000 to continue the operations of the Civilian Conservation Corps from March 31, 1936, to March 31, 1937; (3) an increase in specific appropriations of $187,000,000 on account of general public works; and (4) increases in the general departmental requirements aggregating approximately $211,000,000, due largely to the increases in the Army, Navy, and the Department of Agriculture.

Existing authorizations for the Federal-Aid Highway System provide for appropriations of $125,000,000 for each of the fiscal years 1936 and 1937. Under these authorizations $40,000,000 have previously been appropriated for the fiscal year 1936. Toward the balance of $85,000,000 authorized for that year there is provided under the item "General Public Works Program" an estimate of $60,000,000, which it is believed will be sufficient to meet commitments maturing during 1937. As to the authorization of $125,000,000 for the fiscal year 1937, language is included in this Budget having for its purpose the cancelation of this authorization for 1937 and making it applicable to the fiscal year 1938. This course appears fully justified in view of the fact that during the fiscal years 1933 to 1936, inclusive, there has been made available from emergency funds a total of approximately $1,192,-000,000 for the construction of highways and the elimination of grade crossings, and that from these funds there will be available for expenditure during the fiscal year 1937 a total of more than $250,000,000 in addition to the $60,000,000 provided for in the General Public Works Program, previously referred to. Moreover, roads of secondary classification and farm-to-market roads are being constructed under allotments of emergency funds in amounts approximating $115,000,000.

The following table shows the approximate estimate of appropriations required to administer new legislation enacted during the last session of Congress, and also shows the amount of receipts anticipated in 1937 from new general tax provisions.

	Estimated appropriations, 1937
Social Security Act	$479,689,840
Railroad Retirement Act	47,645,000
Bituminous Coal Conservation Act	1,155,000

Amendments, pension laws	45,581,132
Postal 40-hour week	27,326,420
Elimination diseased cattle	17,500,000
Soil conservation	27,500,000
Agricultural research and extension	11,000,000
Reduction interest rate, Federal land banks	10,065,075
Total	667,462,467

Estimated receipts from taxes under the Social Security Act,
the act levying taxes upon carriers and their employees,
and Bituminous Coal Conservation Act 547,100,000

Because there has not been sufficient time to plan the organization and methods required, no detailed estimates are included in the Budget for expense to be incurred by the Social Security Board, and by the Bureau of Internal Revenue for collecting taxes authorized by the three new acts heretofore referred to. However, the probable expense has been approximated and is included in the total lump sum of $600,000,000 estimated to cover 1937 supplementals. The necessary estimates covering the remainder of the current year will be transmitted during the early days of the session, together with complete details for 1937. Likewise no estimate for administering the Potato Act has been prepared since it is believed this act should be amended along lines to be recommended by the Secretary of Agriculture, and a supplemental estimate can then be transmitted.

3 (Address at the Jackson Day Dinner, Washington, D. C., Broadcast to 3,000 Similar Dinners Throughout the Nation. January 8, 1936

Mr. Chairman, my friends:

ON OUR dinner cards tonight is a medallion portrait of a man who gave a memorable toast, "The Federal Union, it must be preserved."

This meeting tonight, in the City of Washington, is one of many hundreds being held throughout our forty-eight States and territorial possessions and even on board ships at sea, in honor of the memory of a great General, a great President, Andrew Jackson. To all of you I extend my most sincere and heartfelt greetings.

I am happy to stand here tonight and declare to you that the real issue before the United States is the right of the average man and woman to lead a finer, a better and a happier life. And that was the same issue, more than a hundred years ago, that confronted Andrew Jackson.

I speak tonight to this Democratic meeting, to these Democratic meetings throughout the Nation, in the same language as if I were addressing a Republican gathering, a Progressive gathering, an Independent gathering, a Farmer-Labor gathering, a gathering of business men or a gathering of workers or farmers. There is nothing that I say here tonight that does not apply to every citizen in the country no matter what his or her political affiliations may be.

It is true that we Americans have found party organizations to be useful, and indeed necessary, in the crystallization of opinion and in the demarcation of issues. It is true that I have received many honors at the hands of one of our great parties. It is nevertheless true that in the grave questions that confront the United States at this hour, I, as President of the United States, must and will consider our common problems first, foremost and preeminently from the American point of view.

To most of us, Andrew Jackson appropriately has become the symbol of certain great ideals. I like best to think of him as a man whom the average American deeply and fundamentally understood. To the masses of his countrymen, his purposes and his character were an open book. They loved him well because they understood him well—his passion for justice, his championship of the cause of the exploited and the downtrodden, his ardent and flaming patriotism.

39

Jackson sought social justice; Jackson fought for human rights in his many battles to protect the people against autocratic or oligarchic aggression.

If at times his passionate devotion to this cause of the average citizen lent an amazing zeal to his thoughts, to his speech and to his actions, the people loved him for it the more. They realized the intensity of the attacks made by his enemies, by those who, thrust from power and position, pursued him with relentless hatred. The beneficiaries of the abuses to which he put an end pursued him with all the violence that political passions can generate. But the people of his day were not deceived. They loved him for the enemies he had made.

Backed not only by his party but by thousands who had belonged to other parties or belonged to no party at all, Andrew Jackson was compelled to fight every inch of the way for the ideals and the policies of the Democratic Republic which was his ideal. An overwhelming proportion of the material power of the Nation was arrayed against him. The great media for the dissemination of information and the molding of public opinion fought him. Haughty and sterile intellectualism opposed him. Musty reaction disapproved him. Hollow and outworn traditionalism shook a trembling finger at him. It seemed sometimes that all were against him—all but the people of the United States.

Because history so often repeats itself, let me analyze further. Andrew Jackson stands out in the century and a half of our independent history not merely because he was two-fisted, not merely because he fought for the people's rights, but because, through his career, he did as much as any man in our history to increase, on the part of the voters, knowledge of public problems and an interest in their solution. Following the fundamentals of Jefferson, he adhered to the broad philosophy that decisions made by the average of the voters would be more greatly enduring for, and helpful to, the Nation than decisions made by small segments of the electorate representing small or special classes endowed with great advantages of social or economic power.

40

He, like Jefferson, faced with the grave difficulty of disseminating facts to the electorate, to the voters as a whole, was compelled to combat epithets, generalities, misrepresentation and the suppression of facts by the process of asking his supporters, and indeed all citizens, to constitute themselves informal committees for the purpose of obtaining the facts and of spreading them abroad among their friends, their associates and their fellow workers.

I am aware that some wise-cracking columnist will probably say that good old Jackson no doubt realized that every red-blooded American citizen considered himself a committee of one anyway. Nevertheless, Jackson got his ideas and his ideals across not through any luxurious propaganda, but because the man on the street and the man on the farm believed in his ideas, believed in his ideals and his honesty, went out and dug up the facts and spread them abroad throughout the land.

History repeats—and I am becoming dimly conscious of the fact that this year we are to have a national election. Sometimes at the close of a day I say to myself that the last national election must have been held a dozen years ago—so much water has run under the bridge, so many great events in our history have occurred since then. And yet but thirty-four months, less than three years, have gone by since March, 1933.

History repeats—in those crowded months, as in the days of Jackson, two great achievements stand forth—the rebirth of the interest and understanding of a great citizenry in the problems of the Nation, and an established Government which by positive action has proved its devotion to the recovery and well-being of that citizenry.

Whatever may be the platform, whoever may be the nominee of the Democratic Party—and I am told by the Chairman that a Convention is to be held to decide these momentous questions—the basic issue, my friends, will be inevitably the retention of popular Government—an issue fraught once more with the difficult problem of disseminating facts and yet more

41

facts, in the face of an opposition bent on hiding and distorting facts.

And that, my friends, is why organization, not party organization alone — important as that is — but organization among all those, regardless of party, who believe in retaining progress and ideals, is so essential.

That is why, in addition to organization, I make this specific recommendation — that each and every one of you who are interested in obtaining the facts and in spreading those facts abroad, each and every one of you interested in getting at the truth that lies somewhere behind the smokescreen of charges and countercharges of a national campaign, constitute yourself a committee of one. To do this you need no parchment certificate, to do this you need no title. To do this you need only your own conviction, your own intelligence and your own belief in the highest duty of the American citizen.

To act as such a committee of one you will need only your own appointment, an appointment which carries with it some effort, some obligation on your part to carry out the task you have assigned to yourself. You will have to run down statements made to you by others which you may believe to be false. You will need to analyze the motives of those who make assertions to you. You will need to make an inventory in your own community, in order that you may check and recheck for yourself and thereby be in a position to answer those who have been misled or those who would mislead.

After my Annual Message to the Congress last Friday evening, I received many appreciative letters and telegrams from all over the country, and I think it will interest you to know that within a few hours I received more of these than at any time since the critical days of the spring of 1933. I have carefully read those letters and telegrams and I found two facts that I think are worthy of repeating to you tonight. The first is that out of the many, many hundreds, a very large number were sent to me by families who evidently heard my Message while grouped together in the family home. "My wife and I want you to know how much we appreciate," and so forth — or "The Jones family, gathered tonight with our friends, sends you this message of confidence." In other words, as greatly as and perhaps even more greatly than on any other occasion since I have been in the White House, I have the definite feeling that what I have said about the great problems that face us as a Nation has received a responsive, an appreciative and an understanding answer in the homes of America. This means a lot to me.

The other interesting fact about these letters and telegrams is the very great number of them that come from business men, from storekeepers, from bankers and from manufacturers. The gist of their messages to me is that they are grateful, that they appreciate my statement that it is but a minority of business and finance that would "gang up" against the people's liberties. I reiterate that assertion tonight. By far the greater part of the business men, industrialists, and other employers of the Nation seek no special advantage; they seek only an equal opportunity to share in the common benefits, the common responsibilities and the common obligations of their Government.

I am naturally grateful for this support and for the understanding on their part that the Government of the United States seeks to give them a square deal and a better deal — seeks to protect them, yes, to save them from being plowed under by the small minority of business men and financiers, against whom you and I will continue to wage war.

We can be thankful that men and women in all walks of life realize more and more that Government is still a living force in their lives. They understand that the value of their Government depends on the interest which they display in it and the knowledge they have of its policies.

A Government can be no better than the public opinion which sustains it.

I know that you will not be surprised by lack of comment on my part tonight on the recent decision of the Supreme Court. I

43

cannot and will not render offhand judgment without studying, with the utmost care, two of the most momentous opinions, the majority opinion and the minority opinion, that have ever been rendered, in any case before the Supreme Court of the United States. The ultimate results of the language of these opinions will profoundly affect the lives of Americans for many years to come. It is enough to say that the attainment of justice and the continuance of prosperity for American agriculture remain an immediate and constant objective of my Administration.

Just as Jackson roused the people to their fundamental duties as citizens, so must the leadership of this era do its utmost to encourage and sustain widespread interest in public affairs. There was something of eternal youth in the spirit of Andrew Jackson. The destiny of youth became the destiny of America.

Tasks immediately before us are as arduous as the conquest of the frontiers a century ago. The Nation is still young, still growing, still conscious of its high destiny. Enthusiasm and the intelligence of the youth of the land are necessary to the fulfillment of that destiny.

As I understand the temper of the people, particularly the temper of youth, no party of reaction, no candidates of reaction can fulfill the hope and the faith of that everlasting spirit. It is the sacred duty of us who are vested with the responsibility of leadership to justify the expectations of the young men and women of the United States.

We are at peace with the world; but the fight goes on. Our frontiers of today are economic, not geographic. Our enemies of today are the forces of privilege and greed within our own borders.

May a double portion of Old Hickory's heroic spirit be upon us tonight. May we be inspired by the power and the glory and the justice of his rugged and fearless life.

The people of America know the heart and know the purpose of their Government.

They and we will not retreat.

4 ❡ The Two Hundred and Sixty-fifth Press Conference (Excerpts). January 10, 1936

(Conference following adverse decision of the Supreme Court on A.A.A. — Land use and soil conservation — Soil fertility.)

Q. Mr. President, do you still stand on your statement of last October 25th, relative to agriculture?

THE PRESIDENT: What was that?

Q. A permanent program.

THE PRESIDENT: Yes. If you want a lead about agriculture, I think probably it would be worth while to bring out certain responsibilities that necessarily devolve on me.

I have to think of agriculture from the point of view of forty-eight States, not separately, but as a part of the Nation. In other words, there is no question as to what my duty as President is, and that is to view agriculture as a national problem.

The reason I am saying this is that, at the present time, as a result of the decision *(United States* v. *Butler,* 297 U.S. 1), many of the old suggestions that were made back as far as the earlier days of President Coolidge's Administration are being revived. There are, for instance, much discussion and a good deal of suggestion that we should subsidize the export of certain crops. Of course, if you once begin to subsidize the export of certain crops, you will subsidize the export of a great many crops and eventually of all crops. And because I have to think of agriculture nationally, rather than think of it as a local problem, I have to think of the implications of what would happen if, by an export subsidy of some kind, we encouraged the growing of a very vastly increased total of agricultural production.

You can take any number of examples. For instance, wheat. We never had very much of a problem in wheat until, well, the past generation, when dry farming came in, and with the advent of dry farming, the old buffalo

45

grass was plowed up. It was not plowed up in one county or township, it was plowed up in a great many States; and we all know the result of that.

With the advent of modern machinery and a certain amount of capital, you could go in and drive a furrow in buffalo-grass country ten miles long before you turned around. The result was what we all know, that a very light soil was turned up, the grass was plowed under and disappeared, and farmers started in to raise wheat. Because of the great area in which each farm could be cultivated, the yield per acre was not the main consideration. A man could make money on wheat at a reasonable price if he got a yield of only ten or twelve bushels to the acre. Of course ten or twelve bushels an acre is nothing, but nevertheless it paid to do it if wheat was paying a big price.

What was the result of this plowing up of land that had never been plowed up before in all history? Dust storms began, and they have been getting steadily worse year by year. The result is that we have in this country an area which is subject to dust storms. This was caused solely by the fact that we have been using land for the wrong purpose. Instead of using it for pasture, we are using it for wheat.

Now, what is the area? It isn't just one State, it is the Panhandle of Texas, Western Oklahoma, Western Kansas, Western Nebraska, Western South Dakota—just speaking from memory—Western North Dakota, a large portion of Montana, Eastern Wyoming and Colorado and Northern New Mexico.

Now, the area in square miles I don't know; I never figured it out. But, thinking of it in terms of the map, that area is probably as large as all of New England and all of New York and all of New Jersey and all of Pennsylvania put together. That is a tremendous national area.

If we go in for a national agricultural policy that encourages the plowing up of that land again—and we are

46

trying to take it out from being plowed — it means that people will go in with modern machinery and, because of some kind of an export subsidy, it will pay them to plow it up again. And the dust storms will continue and we shall approach much more quickly what we have all been worrying about — making that area a desert on which nobody can live.

Now, the same thing is true of cotton. If we were to give an export subsidy, it would mean that people would say, "Domestic prices are all right, the export prices are all right, too; the more I grow the more money I make," and the average cotton farmer in the Southeast, let us say, will increase his land, and start going up on the hilltops, and will begin planting again land that ought to be in pasture or in woods. The result will be that all through the cotton area you will have an increase in the amount of soil that runs off in waste to the ocean.

In other words, to put it the most simple way, we must avoid any national agricultural policy which will result in shipping our soil fertility to foreign Nations. I think probably that is the best way of putting it.

Q. Can we put that in quotes?

THE PRESIDENT: Yes, you can put that in quotes. We must avoid any national agricultural policy that will result in shipping our soil fertility to foreign Nations. We have had so many lessons in that in the past that it seems perfectly clear.

Of course, it is very easy and attractive to say, "We can go ahead and raise any quantity at all of any crop with a certain definite export market caused by a Congressional subsidy." A lot of people will be for it, but not the thinking farmer; and more and more of them are thinking all the time.

The people who probably are most actively for it are, first, the transportation companies, the railroads, because, of course, it means more business for them. It is very human that they should think about the railroads ahead of soil

47

fertility or the future of the Nation. That is perfectly human. To the steamship companies also it means carrying more. It is perfectly reasonable and natural that they should think in terms of more bulk agricultural freight than about the future of this country. And it is very reasonable that the warehouse people, too, should seek greater crops. It means that they will have more crops to put into their warehouses. It is very natural that commission merchants should also think of greater crops, because the bigger the crop the bigger the commission. And it is reasonable also that the commodity exchanges should be in favor of bigger crops.

In other words, the pocketbook, naturally, has a very definite influence on people who are engaged in some particular line of handling farm products, so that is one of the things we have to think of.

I think that covers the thing pretty well. I have tried to say it in as simple terms as possible.

My position is that I have to think of the future of the country. It seems pretty clear from the teachings of history that absolutely unlimited production — not merely in two or three crops, because if you start with two or three you will eventually get a subsidy on all crops — will result in the loss of American soil fertility in a generation or two; and I believe that we have to think ahead.

Q. That seems to point to something in the nature of the allotment plan or . . .

THE PRESIDENT: No, I was just thinking out loud. We haven't come to any plan yet. We are still talking it over, as you know. Undoubtedly we shall try to get some legislation at this session which will carry out in some way the general thought of seeking to maintain or perhaps to retain and regain soil fertility because we have lost an awful lot of it and, at the same time, keep the price for American agricultural crops up to a high level.

Q. You do not agree that the equalization feature would elimi-

nate the objection to the subsidy idea? Some of the advocates
seem to think so.

THE PRESIDENT: That is a question of opinion. They are all talking about it.

Q. Do you think you can do this by an Act in Congress?

THE PRESIDENT: That is what we are trying to do.

Q. Have you found a loophole in the Supreme Court decision
which would permit you to make payments to farmers?

THE PRESIDENT: We are really discussing the whole thing. It
really, honestly, is in the discussion stage. . . .

Q. This is in line with what you gave us on the national farm
problem. Doesn't it come down to this, that no national or
Federal plan of getting the price up to the farmers is possible
without crop control? Isn't that stating the same thing in
another way?

THE PRESIDENT: Practically, yes; in some form.

Q. In other words, you have got to compel a farmer to cooperate?

THE PRESIDENT: Unless you go to the theory of subsidizing exports
and having unlimited production.

Q. Would farm machinery manufacturers be among those that
would like to see as large production as possible?

THE PRESIDENT: I doubt it; I don't know. I have never asked.
Farm machinery manufacturers have come to the conclusion,
I think, that the more permanent agricultural prosperity is,
the better it is for them. It keeps their business running at a
more stable rate, year in and year out. They are opposed to
tremendous fluctuations in farm purchasing power. They
would like to see a farmer buy a gang plow with a certain
knowledge that three years or five years from now, if it is
worn out, he could buy another one.

Q. If we subsidize exports, wouldn't foreign Nations be apt to
regard that as dumping and restrict imports?

THE PRESIDENT: Most of them do restrict at the present time,
nearly all.

Q. That would make the plan impracticable, if they put re-
strictions of that sort on?

49

THE PRESIDENT: I think it would be well worth your while to find out the number of European Nations that import our farm products today that have definite quotas. I think you will find out that a very large number of European Nations have them. . . .

Q. Can the program of soil fertility you describe be made applicable to the 1936 crop?

THE PRESIDENT: I hope so.

Q. Are there any more of these agricultural matters that are going to be announced in here today?

THE PRESIDENT: No, just Cabinet meeting today, that is all.

(See Introduction to Volume IV for further discussion of this decision; also Items 6, 11, 28 and 39 of this volume. For material on A.A.A. see Vol. II, Items 20, 54, 83, 92; Vol. IV, Items 113, 152.)

5 ❨A Greeting in Behalf of a Campaign for Trained Personnel in Government Service. January 16, 1936

My dear Mrs. Gellhorn:

I DO not need to tell you, as a leader among the public-spirited women of America, that it is most difficult, if not impossible, for a Government to raise and maintain in any field a standard higher than the public will support. This is why it is essential that national organizations of the character and strength of the National League of Women Voters should secure and disseminate accurate information on vital questions which have implicit within them not alone principles of efficiency and economy of interest to taxpayers, but above that the principles of good government.

It matters not what political party is in power by the elective will of the people. The Government functions for all. And there can be no question of greater moment or broader effect than the maintenance, strengthening and extension of the merit system established in the competitive principles of the Civil Service Act, whose fifty-third birthday is being celebrated this month.

The National League of Women Voters has chosen wisely in conducting a campaign for securing trained personnel in the Government service through the open competition provided only by the merit system; and I am glad to assure your great organization of my support in this effort.

Very sincerely yours,

Mrs. George Gellhorn,
National League of Women Voters,
St. Louis, Missouri.

6 ❬ The Two Hundred and Sixty-seventh Press Conference (Excerpts). January 17, 1936

(Bonus Bill — Soil erosion and conservation — Proposed legislation for soil conservation.)

THE PRESIDENT: What is the news?

Q. That is what we would like to know.

Q. What is the handout?

THE PRESIDENT: There isn't any. I have to work it out.

Q. There is still a lot of speculation on your attitude toward the bonus.

THE PRESIDENT: I suppose there is. There was last year and there was the year before. This is the third year.

Q. What is the reply?

THE PRESIDENT: There was speculation last year and there was speculation the year before. This is the third year.

Q. Shall we guess the same way we did last year? (*Laughter*)

THE PRESIDENT: You are too obvious, Stevie (*Mr. Stephenson*). . . .

Q. Do you care to discuss the breakdown of the London Naval Conference for background?

THE PRESIDENT: I don't think I can. I think you have practically.

51

everything there was; the various statements made by the British and by the Americans and the Japanese cover it pretty well. There is not anything much which can be added. It is quite clear. . . .

Q. Mr. President, would you care to talk on farm relief if we point out that you are not replying to Mr. Hoover?

THE PRESIDENT: Yes, I would just as soon do that. As a matter of fact what I was reading over when you came in were two things: first, the Soil Erosion Act of 1935 and, second, the statement I made and gave out on October 25th of this past year. (See Item 152, Vol. IV.) I think probably the easiest thing to do is to read the statement of October 25th over, because that gives you a pretty good picture, a pretty good lead as to what the objective has been for a long time. In other words, this isn't anything new.

This statement of October 25th last year referred to the broad policy in relation to agricultural adjustment; and of course on that I want to point out again that adjustment does not mean only adjustment downward, it means adjustment upward as well. If a man takes a quarter of his acreage out of one crop and puts it in another crop, he is adjusting one crop downward and adjusting another crop upward. It is an adjustment that works both ways.

I said there were two points and, mind you, this was away back in October.

The first was to carry out the gains already made, thereby avoiding the danger of a slump back into the conditions brought about by our national neglect of agriculture. The second, to broaden present adjustment operations so as to give farmers increasing incentives for conservation and efficient use of the Nation's soil resources.

(Reading) "The time may come when the Triple A will prove as important in stimulating certain kinds of production as it has been in removing recent burdensome surpluses.

"Tens of millions of acres have been abandoned because of

erosion. This jeopardizes both consumer and producer. Real damage to the consumer does not result from moderate increases in food prices but from collapse of farm income so drastic as to compel ruthless depletion of soil. That is the real menace to the Nation's future food supply and has caused farmers to lose their homes. It has hastened the spread of tenancy. It lies at the root of many serious economic and social problems besetting agriculture.

"Already the adjustment programs have made important gains in conservation and restoration of soil fertility. Many millions of acres which farmers have signed contracts to divert from surplus production" — this, of course, was when the contracts were legal — "are being devoted to legumes, pastures, hay and other crops which fertilize the soil and protect it from blowing and washing away.

"The long-time and more permanent adjustment program will provide positive incentives for soil conservation."

And then I spoke of the more simplified and more flexible program of the future and how it can serve to iron out the succession of extreme market gluts and shortages which in the past have wrecked the structure. And I said further, "I can think of nothing more important to the permanent welfare of the Nation than long-time agricultural adjustment carried out along these lines."

That was true last October and it is true today with the exception of the contract method of soil conservation.

The Soil Conservation Act seems to point out a way to carry out the broad purposes; so we are proceeding on that theory.

Q. Does that not also contain a contract method?

THE PRESIDENT: No.

Q. Doesn't that permit the Government to lease land?

THE PRESIDENT: Yes.

Q. And thereby withdraw it from production?

THE PRESIDENT: The bill says at the beginning, "It is hereby

recognized that the wastage of soil and moisture resources of farm, grazing and forest lands resulting from soil erosion is a wastage of national welfare, etc. The Secretary of Agriculture is authorized to conduct surveys relating to the character of soil erosion, the preventive measures needed, to carry out preventive methods, including but not limited to engineering methods, changes in use of land, to cooperate and enter into agreements with and to furnish financial or other aid to any agency, Government or otherwise, or any person subject to the conditions necessary, to acquire lands or rights or interests therein by purchase, gift, condemnation or otherwise, whenever necessary for the purposes of the Act."
The rest is administration. . . .

Q. Does the present statute provide you with sufficiently broad legislative . . .

THE PRESIDENT: It may be necessary to amend very slightly to clarify one or two of the provisions. It would be a very simple amendment.

Q. How do you raise the money for this?

THE PRESIDENT: On that we haven't anything as yet.

Q. Do you propose to amend the Act to provide for additional payments to farmers?

THE PRESIDENT: You mean this Act?

Q. Yes.

THE PRESIDENT: As I said, very, very slight amendments.

Q. If you lease the land from the farmer and thereby withdraw production, the rental money you pay to the farmer would be about the same thing as the benefit payment under the A.A.A.?

THE PRESIDENT: That would depend entirely on the character of the land. It would not be in every case.

Q. Any estimate of the cost of this program?

THE PRESIDENT: No.

Q. In case a man had any submarginal land on his farm at all, this would not give you the means for leasing it?

54

THE PRESIDENT: Yes, but his land might be running out. It might not be submarginal today, but it might be tomorrow.

Q. Or some time in the future?

THE PRESIDENT: Yes. One of the things that needs clarification, speaking about amendments: Obviously the purpose of this is to prevent the loss of soil fertility. Now, of course, very few of you know anything about farming (*laughter*) but you can imagine perfectly well a field — let us bring it down to a field — where there isn't erosion in the sense that the soil is running off of the field into the creek. In other words, it is not something that, when it dries, you can pick up in your hand. Nevertheless, that same field may be having a condition where the chemicals in the soil are being carried away. You can't pick up those chemicals in your hand.

So, soil erosion, when you come down to a matter of actual fact, may be in one of two forms, the tangible thing that you can pick up in your hand, such as a handful of mud, or it may be the chemicals that are being washed out of the land. For instance, you take Hyde Park: It is an entirely different proposition from down in Georgia. In Warm Springs, Georgia, the soil itself actually washes off the cultivated fields and eventually you get these great furrows, gullies. At Hyde Park we don't get any gullies except on some of the higher hills. But if I don't rotate crops at Hyde Park, if I keep on planting corn year after year in the same field, after a while I don't get any corn crop. There are two causes, the first being that the corn itself takes the minerals out of the soil, and the second is that when that land is never put back into pasture, the chemicals in that particular field run off with the rains. That does not make a gully because chemicals are almost intangible; you cannot pick them up in your hand.

That is one of the questions with respect to this bill — whether it clearly enough states that soil erosion is not limited to the physical running off of the soil in the form of ground. Is that clear?

55

Q. On the other basis of interpretation, there would be erosion on every farm in the country.

THE PRESIDENT: Yes, possible erosion.

Q. Wouldn't it be actual, because you can't keep growing the same crop on any land without having it deteriorate?

THE PRESIDENT: That is perfectly true.

Q. As a practical proposition, who will determine, and how, what land is eroding and what is running away?

THE PRESIDENT: Oh, the same people who are doing it now, the county agents helped by the State colleges of agriculture. Put the entire system under the Department of Agriculture.

Q. Would you care to state whether you believe this program would be better in the long run than the original A.A.A.?

THE PRESIDENT: If you read the October 25th statement you will see that this is carrying out what A.A.A. started to do, which was supplemented by the Soil Erosion Act. It is nothing new; no new policy. It is carrying out what we started two years ago.

Q. Have you any estimate of the number of acres of crop land which will be taken out of commercial production?

THE PRESIDENT: Probably not any. In other words, as I said before, if you have a hundred acres all planted to one thing and if you take twenty-five acres and devote them to something else, that does not take them out of production. If you put a field into pasture, that does not take it out of commercial production.

Q. With the exception of these minor amendments to the Soil Erosion Act, you do not expect to ask for legislation on the subject?

THE PRESIDENT: On the farm end of it. I am not talking about the tax end. That is a different thing. I think we can probably get by with these small amendments and with appropriations.

Q. You will have to ask for new taxes?

THE PRESIDENT: That is an entirely different subject.

(On the matter of the Bonus Bill see Item 12 of this volume. On Soil Conservation see Items 4, 11, 28 and 39 of this volume.)

7 ❡ Informal Extemporaneous Remarks to the New Jersey State Emergency Council. January 18, 1936

Governor Hoffman, Mr. Mayor:

I SUPPOSE the most correct term for all of you people is to say, "My fellow workers."

I have been wanting to come to one of these meetings for a long time, to see how they are conducted; and when I heard of the first meeting you attended under the chairmanship of Charley Edison, I wanted to see how New Jersey works. And I am very proud of New Jersey.

You have been one of the first States in the Union to carry through the coordination, the tying together of all of our Government activities. You have pointed a lesson that is being followed out in every other State in the Union, with the objective within a very short time of having an excellent organization similar to this one operating in all of the other States.

It is tremendously important, of course, especially in view of the fact that a lot of this work is comparatively new, that we step on each other's toes as little as possible. That can be avoided principally through information, through knowledge of what people are doing in other branches of this big, broad program.

That is why I think that all of you, in addition to your own individual work within your own offices and agencies, have still another duty, and that is to become walking encyclopedias.

Somebody in the Housing Administration is going to be asked about the operation of the C.C.C. camps. Of course, he cannot become letter-perfect on it, but it is very distinctly up to him to know something about the general purpose and the general operation, not only of C.C.C. camps, but of all other governmental agencies.

In that connection we have two duties or obligations. The first is to seek, through this information about what everybody else is doing, every reasonable means for a greater efficiency of the whole. That was the primary objective of the National Emergency Council—to see that we were not duplicating work, to see how in an administrative way we could improve the administrative machinery. The National Emergency Council, through its directors in all the States of the Union, is working with extraordinary efficiency toward this end.

Your other duty, along the same line, is your relationship with the public. I do not suppose that I am any exception to the rule. The number of fool questions and the number of fool stories that come to me in Washington are duplicated in the experience of every one of you here today.

Of course, let us be charitable, those statements and those questions result from a lack of information. It is our duty to correct that lack of information on the part of the public.

People who come around saying all sorts of things that you and I know are not true indicate in most cases just plain lack of information. And so each and every one of you has that further duty to explain what it is all about to the public as a whole. I have been interested in several of the questions asked today. One of them, for example, was as to how the employment service was working out, whether the employers knew of the operations of the employment service, not only the Federal Employment Service but its sister that works hand and hand with it, the State Employment Service. There are a great many cases in almost every branch of your work and mine, where we have an opportunity to make our work more useful by giving greater information about it. That is true of housing; it is true of Home Owners Loan; it is true of W.P.A.; it is true of Public Works; it is true of all the relationships in which you stand to the public as a whole.

I want to say just one word about the usefulness of what we are doing. There is a grand word that is going around, "boondoggle." It is a pretty good word. If we can "boondoggle" ourselves out of this depression, that word is going to be enshrined in the hearts of the American people for many years to come.

The point, of course, is that all of these projects, all of this work that we are doing, spring from a necessity, a definite human need, a need of this generation, a need of the year in which we live and of last year, and the year before. In carrying out this work, we are filling a current need, but, in addition to that, we are trying to do it in such a way that it is going to be useful in some way to the community next year and the year after and for generations to come.

Speaking of projects, where do they originate? Does anybody have an idea that there is sitting in Washington some individual locked in a room, tapping his forehead and saying, "Let me think up something new for Newark, New Jersey?" Or Hackettstown or any other place? Why, of course not.

The projects arise in the first instance, in ninety-nine cases out of a hundred, from the local authorities, the officers who have been duly chosen, the Governors of States, the departments of State Governments, the mayors of cities, the supervisors of counties. We have gone to them and asked, "What is the most useful thing on which the Federal Government can help out in this locality?" And in ninety-nine cases out of a hundred, the origin is in the local governing authorities of every State and every community throughout the land.

And I believe that people appreciate the fact that the overwhelming majority of the things that we are doing are useful; and that, strangely enough, in doing them, the liberties of self-government have remained unimpaired. I have not heard Mayor Ellenstein or any other mayor in this great country of ours say, "Don't do that; we don't want to do that; your projects are mad; your projects are useless." No, they are cooperating with the Federal Government, and in the process no mayor in this country has been shorn of any of the responsibilities of his office. In other words, as we all know, we are still carrying out the principles of home rule.

I am particularly happy to see the exhibits around these walls. A great many citizens do not know of the many ramifications of this work. The new agencies and many of the old agencies that are almost as old as the Government of the United States, tied in together, are working in a harmonious whole. It is a very heartening thing to realize that the older departments of the Government, the ones that go back fifty, one hundred, and one hundred fifty years, have taken in the younger brethren and sisters in the Federal work.

To you I want to say just one personal word. I have always had faith that when a job had to be done there would be a great many public-spirited men and women who would come forward and offer their services.

That has been true not only among the experts, not only in the professions—and they have been magnificent—but also among men and women in general who have stepped forward, and at great personal sacrifice in many, many cases have helped their Government to carry on this work in an efficient and very admirable way.

To you who are representing in the State of New Jersey all of these great agencies, working cooperatively with the State of New Jersey, with the counties, and with the cities, I want to extend to you my thanks for what you are doing. I am very, very proud of you.

I am glad to have had this opportunity. I wish I could have been with you through all the meetings, this morning's session and the whole of this afternoon's session. I have learned a good deal by just looking at the program, and I wish that everybody who is a visitor here today would read that program. It might give them a broader and a more American point of view.

I have something like this meeting every day; not everybody together, but in the course of the average day in Washington I suppose I come in contact with the representatives of about half of all the Federal agencies that there are, personally, or by telephone, or by correspondence. I try to keep in touch with the coordinating of all of our work as much as is humanly possible. So, though I may seem to be a long way off down there in Washington, you have no idea of the many details of all your work that actually come across my own personal desk. I have a fellow feeling for your work. I not only want you to work with me, but I am going to do the best I can to work with you.

8 ⟨ Address at the Dedication of the Theodore Roosevelt Memorial. January 19, 1936

Mr. Chairman, Governor Lehman, Mayor LaGuardia, Trustees of the New York State Roosevelt Memorial, Trustees of the American Museum of Natural History, ladies and gentlemen:

THIS memorial, the cornerstone of which I laid some years ago, and in the dedication of which I am privileged to participate this afternoon, is typical of Theodore Roosevelt. It reflects the universality of his mind and of his interests. Its decorations—in place or in planning—tell part of the story of his life, the story of his work, and the story of his play; they depict the construction of the Panama Canal in which he was the dominating spirit; the Treaty of Portsmouth, which ended the Russo-Japanese War; the quest for scientific knowledge which carried him into the African jungle; symbolic figures of fauna and flora to tell generations to come of his interest in nature and in conservation—all these bear witness to his intense vitality and to his varied contributions to our national culture. The Roosevelt Memorial Commission has been faithful in executing its high trust.

The quotations on these walls, too, bring us their message out of the rich storehouse of his written words.

"Conservation means development as much as it does protection"—a text which ought to be emblazoned in every treatise on the care and perpetuation of America's national resources.

Or this: "The Nation behaves well if it treats the natural resources as assets which it must turn over to the next generation increased, and not impaired, in value."

From his writings in the realm of statecraft we find this: "A great democracy must be progressive or it will soon cease to be great or a democracy." It is his warning to us of this day, to us of this generation that eternal progress is still the price of liberty.

It is fitting that this memorial perpetuating the life and work of one who stirred such great interest in the field of natural history should itself be an adjunct of the American Museum of Natural History. My friend, the late Professor Henry Fairfield Osborn, so long the head of this noble institution for the increase and diffusion of scientific knowledge, and for many years a devoted colleague of him in whose honor we are gathered today, advocated this memorial soon after Theodore Roosevelt's death.

Each and every one of us feels a sadness today that Professor Osborn could not have lived to take part in this, the culmination of his great desire; we know that his spirit is with us.

This memorial of such noble architectural proportions is withal intimate and vital. Above all things, it is useful. There was an intimate quality about Theodore Roosevelt which all of us who knew him recall at this hour. We think of him not as an abstract being dwelling apart on the heights, but rather as a friendly soul, pervading this very hall which we are dedicating to his memory.

Theodore Roosevelt possessed talents and abilities which we know today were unusual even among leaders of men. Whatever he did, he did with all of his might.

With that spirit of vital activity, be it also remembered that he also received the Nobel Peace Award. In him was combined a passion for righteousness and for that strong sense of justice which found expression in the "Square Deal." Race, creed, color were not determining factors with him. He took a man for what he was.

"A man who is good enough to shed his blood for his country," said he at Springfield, Illinois, on a Fourth of July, "is good enough to be given a square deal afterwards. More than that no man is entitled to, and less than that no man shall have."

In his first Message to Congress he had written: "The most vital problem with which this country, and, for that matter, the whole civilized world, has to deal, is the problem which has for one side the betterment of social conditions, moral and physical, in large cities, and for another side the effort to deal with that tangle of far-reaching questions which we group together when we speak of 'labor.' "

This creed for social justice may be found in many quotations from later messages. He said:

"In the vast and complicated mechanism of our modern civilized life, the dominant note is the note of industrialism, and the relations of capital and labor, and especially of organized capital and organized labor, to each other, and to the public at large, come second in importance only to the intimate questions of family life.

"The corporation has come to stay, just as the trade union has come to stay. Each can do and has done great good. Each should be favored as long as it does good, but each should be sharply checked where it acts against law and justice."

You and I still remember how those whom he denounced with righteous wrath winced under the stigma of such fighting epithets as "malefactors of great wealth," "the wealthy criminal class" and the "lunatic fringe." He had a gift for pungent phrase, boiling down his whole political philosophy into homely and popular maxims as "Speak softly but carry a big stick." And it is no wonder that John Morley said in 1904: "The two things in America which seem to me most extraordinary are Niagara Falls and President Roosevelt."

With clearness of vision, with energy, with unfaltering faith, he labored through his entire strenuous career to transform politics from a corrupt traffic to a public service. With a very passion for justice and equality before the law he sought with voice, with pen, with every resource at his command, to obtain for men everywhere their constitutional guarantee of life, liberty and the pursuit of happiness.

I have purposely emphasized the many-sidedness of his character. That extraordinary range of interests makes difficult the task of anyone who would adequately summarize his career and his achievements. Varied as were his political activities, the scope of his literary interests was no less extended. His volumes on American history, on current problems, and on his own experiences as a hunter and explorer, captured and retained the interest of the American people.

We know how he loved the great outdoors. He loved the life of the boundless plains which he had known as a rancher in the West. He found strength in the wilderness. He knew the birds and animals and trees and plants and flowers.

And so he worked, so he wrought, so he wrote. His familiarity with all literature, with history, and with biography, was reflected alike in his private writings and in his public utterances. Who but he could have given Bunyan's "Man-with-the-Muck-rake" an emphasis which he gave it thirty years ago, so that the term "muckraker" passed into the language and is current with us even to this day?

He enriched, he enlarged and extended our American cultural horizon. Out of the rich experiences he had known, his mind received a cast which later was reflected when he infused action and life and color into what before his time had been a somewhat dull and drab statecraft.

Everything about him was big and vital and, above that, national. He was able to see great problems in their true perspective because he looked at the Nation as a whole. There was nothing narrow or local or sectional about him. It is not for me here today to speak of the final place which history will accord to Theodore Roosevelt; but we know and the Nation knows, and the world knows, that Theodore Roosevelt was a great patriot and a great soul.

When he died, the Secretary of his class at Harvard, in sending to his classmates a notice of his passing, added at the end this quotation from *Pilgrim's Progress*:

"After this it was noised abroad that Mr. Valiant-for-truth was taken with a summons by the same post as the other, and had this for a token that the summons was true, 'That his pitcher was broken at the fountain.' When he understood it, he called for his friends and told them of it. Then he said, 'I am going to my Father's, and though with great difficulty I have got hither, yet now I do not repent me of all the trouble I have been at to arrive where I am. My sword I give to him that shall succeed me in my pilgrimage, and my courage and skill to him that can get it. My marks and scars I carry with me, to be a witness for me that I have fought His battles who now will be my rewarder.'"

9 ❲ Message of Condolence on the Death of King George V. January 20, 1936

It is with deep sorrow that I learn of the death of His Majesty, your father. I send to you my profound sympathy and that of the people of the United States, in whose respect and affection he occupied a high and unique place.

I had the privilege of knowing His Majesty during the war days and his passing brings to me personally a special sorrow.

His Majesty the King,
Sandringham Palace,
Norfolk, England.

Mrs. Roosevelt and I extend to Your Majesty and to the members of your family our heartfelt sympathy and join you in mourning the loss of one whose high qualities of kindness and wisdom have been so powerful an influence for universal peace and justice.

Her Majesty Queen Mary,
Sandringham Palace,
Norfolk, England.

The President also sent messages to the Governor General of Australia, the Governor General of the Dominion of Canada, the Governor General of the Irish Free State, the Governor General of New Zealand and the Governor General of the Union of South Africa.

10 ❡ Congratulations to Carrie Chapman Catt on a Half Century of Public Service. January 22, 1936

My dear Mrs. Catt:

Our old friendship, dating back to the days when I was a very young State Senator in 1911, would be sufficient reason for me to write you on your completion of half a century of public service. But there is a greater reason — because the whole country applauds you and your very great contributions to our well-being.

The many years of devoted work which you gave to the cause of woman's suffrage have long since been justly rewarded not only by the passage of the Nineteenth Amendment to the Constitution in our own country, but also by marked improvement in the status of women throughout the world.

Those of us who are directly concerned with the maintenance and encouragement of peace between Nations are also grateful to you for the splendid leadership you give to the cause of peace and the furtherance of the prevention of war.

May you continue for many years to come as the strong and active captain in these noble objectives of a better civilization.

With my warm regards,
Always sincerely,

Mrs. Carrie Chapman Catt
New York City

11 ❡ Excerpt from a Press Conference Release on the Proper Use of Land. January 24, 1936

So TO manage physical use of land in the United States that we will not only maintain soil fertility, but will hand on to the next generation a country with better productive power and a greater permanency of land use than the one we inherited from the previous generation — that is the broad objective.

We have got to go a long way to catch up with the mistakes of

66

To the House of Representatives:

I return herewith, without my approval, H. R. bill 9870, entitled "An Act to provide for the immediate payment of World War adjusted service certificates, for the cancellation of unpaid interest accrued on loans secured by such certificates, and for other purposes."

On May 22, 1935 in disapproving a bill to pay the bonus in full immediately instead of in 1945, I gave in person to a joint session of the Congress complete and explicit reasons for my action.

The bill I now return differs from last year's bill in only two important respects: first, it eliminates the issuance of unsecured paper currency to make the payments required and substitutes interest bearing bonds, which, however, may be converted into cash for face value at any time; second, it adds $263,000,000. to the total payments by forgiving interest after October 1, 1931, on amounts borrowed.

In all other respects, the circumstances, arguments and facts remain essentially the same as those fully covered and explained by me only eight months ago.

I respectfully refer the members of the Senate and of the House of Representatives to every word of what I said then.

My convictions are as impelling today as they were then. Therefore I cannot change them.

Franklin D Roosevelt

The White House
January 24, 1936

the past, so as to make the United States, as a whole, as productive as it was a hundred years ago.

12 ❡ The President Vetoes for a Second Time the Soldiers' Bonus. A Message Written in Longhand. January 24, 1936

To the House of Representatives:

I RETURN herewith, without my approval, H.R. bill 9870, entitled "An Act to provide for the immediate payment of World War adjusted service certificates, for the cancelation of unpaid interest accrued on loans secured by such certificates, and for other purposes."

On May 22, 1935, in disapproving a bill to pay the bonus in full immediately instead of in 1945, I gave in person to a Joint Session of the Congress complete and explicit reasons for my action.

The bill I now return differs from last year's bill in only two important respects: first, it eliminates the issuance of unsecured paper currency to make the payments required and substitutes interest-bearing bonds, which, however, may be converted into cash for face value at any time; second, it adds $263,000,000 to the total payments by forgiving interest after October 1, 1931, on amounts borrowed.

In all other respects, the circumstances, arguments and facts remain essentially the same as those fully covered and explained by me only eight months ago.

I respectfully refer the members of the Senate and of the House of Representatives to every word of what I said then.

My convictions are as impelling today as they were then. Therefore I cannot change them.

13 ❡ A Tribute to Abraham Lincoln to Be Read on His Birthday. January 25, 1936

My dear Mr. Maresh:

THE Association over which you preside is fortunate in the possession of a "Lincoln Shrine"; and I congratulate you and the citizens of your State upon having within your borders a symbol which serves to make more real the memory of him to whom you this day pay homage.

Abraham Lincoln was not a son of the North or of the South. Born in Kentucky and nurtured in the very heart of our land, the scope of his intellect and of his sympathies was co-extensive with the length and breadth of our domain. Nor could Abraham Lincoln have come from any class that did not know, through daily struggle, the grim realities of life. Self-sustained, self-educated, and grounded in common sense through contact with his fellow man, he developed that homely philosophy with which we have come to associate his name and with which he was to solve the problems of a distraught Nation.

From such an origin and from such a school, there emerged a character destined to transfuse with new meaning the concepts of our constitutional fathers and to assure a Government having for its broad purpose the promotion of the life, liberty, and happiness of all the people.

Very sincerely yours,

A. L. Maresh,
Lincoln Association,
Cleveland, Ohio.

14 ❡ White House Statement on Expediting the Payment of the Soldiers' Bonus. January 27, 1936

IN VIEW of the fact that Congress has enacted the law authorizing the exchange of Adjusted Service Certificates for bonds, the President indicated today to the Veterans Administration and the Treasury Department that he desired the provisions of the new law carried out as expeditiously as accuracy will permit. The President also indicated that the magnitude of the administrative task of carrying the provisions of the new law into effect was so great that patience should be exercised in the matter.

The President was advised that more than seven million interest calculations will be necessary and that it will require between 2,500 and 3,000 additional personnel working for approximately six months to do this job. It should be remembered that the amount due each individual veteran must be separately worked out for each case. The additional personnel to handle this enormous figuring and clerical job must, under the law, come from the civil service rolls.

Application blanks will be available in all regional offices of the Veterans Administration and in the hands of Service Organizations within the next two or three days. If the veterans will keep in mind that the bonds are to be issued dated June 15, 1936, and after filing their applications will refrain from writing follow-up letters, they will greatly assist in the prompt administration of the new law.

15 ❡ White House Statement on the Advisability of Preserving Soldiers' Bonus Bonds. January 27, 1936

The National Commanders of the three major ex-service organizations called upon the President today to assure him that they would do everything within their power to persuade veterans to retain the bonds issued to them in lieu of their Adjusted Service Certificates, unless they expected to use the cash for some permanently useful purpose.

The President, as well as the Commanders of the ex-service organizations, feel that the veterans should consider first of all the protection of their families.

Immediate and urgent need for funds offers, of course, a valid reason for cashing the bonds.

In the same way, the paying off of indebtedness is wholly reasonable, just as using the cash for something of permanent value such as a new home or the definite improvement of an existing home, would be reasonable.

What the President and the Commanders were fully agreed on, however, is that every effort should be made by the veterans, by their organizations and by all who have their welfare at heart, to prevent the frittering away of cash obtained from the bonds. Permanent advantage as opposed to wholly temporary pleasure should be the criterion.

Those who keep the bonds or any part of them not only can get ready cash at any time if necessary, but while they hold these non-transferable bonds they will receive 3 percent interest on the safest imaginable investment. They are true "Thrift Bonds."

The President and the Commanders feel confident that very many veterans will keep these Government bonds in whole or in part for long-range protection of themselves and their families.

16 ⟨ A Message to the Congress on a Plan for the Control and Proper Use of Our Water Resources. January 30, 1936

To the Congress:

I TRANSMIT herewith for the information of the Congress a letter from the Chairman of the National Resources Committee with the accompanying report entitled: "Little Waters: a Study of Headwater Streams and Other Little Waters: Their Use and Relations to the Land."

This report treats of a subject with which the physical well-being of our people is intimately bound up, yet to which, in the past, too little attention has been paid. We have grown accustomed to dealing with great rivers, with their large problems of navigation, of power and of flood control, and we have been tempted to forget the little rivers from which they come. The report points out that we can have no effective national policy in those matters, nor in the closely related matter of proper land uses, until we trace this running water back to its ultimate sources and find means of controlling it and of using it.

Our disastrous floods, our sometimes almost equally disastrous periods of low water, and our major problems of erosion, to which attention has been called by the reports of the National Resources Board, the Mississippi Valley Committee, the Soil Erosion Service, and other agencies, do not come full-grown into being. They originate in a small way in a multitude of farms, ranches and pastures.

It is not suggested that we neglect our main streams and give our whole attention to these little waters, but we must have, literally, a plan which will envisage the problem as it is presented in every farm, every pasture, every wood lot, every acre of the public domain.

The Congress could not formulate, nor could the Executive carry out the details of such a plan, even though such a procedure were desirable and possible under our form of government. We can, however, lay down certain simple principles and devise means by which the Federal Government can cooperate in the common interest with the States and with such interstate agencies as may be established. It is for the Congress to decide upon the proper means. Our objective must be so to manage the physical use of the land that we will not only maintain soil fertility but will hand on to the next generation a country with better productive power and a greater permanency of land use than the one we inherited from the previous generation. The opportunity is as vast as is the danger. I hope and believe that the Congress will take advantage of it, and in such a way as to command the enthusiastic support of the States and of the whole public.

(See Items 8 and 73 of Vol. IV.)

17 ❮ The President Suggests to All the American Republics an Inter-American Conference at Buenos Aires to Advance the Cause of American and World Peace. January 30, 1936

My dear Mr. President:

THE agreement by the Governments of Bolivia and Paraguay upon the peace protocols recently negotiated at Buenos Aires has afforded the Government and people of the United States the deepest gratification, since it has led them to hope that there is now every prospect of a permanent and equitable solution of this tragic controversy, which has continued for so long a period; which has caused the sacrifice of so many lives; and which has placed so crushing a burden of expenditure upon the citizens of the two belligerent Nations. I know well with what intimate concern the Government and people of Argentina have followed the course of these hostilities, and their happiness at the termination of the conflict is fully shared by the Government and people of the United States.

I cherish the sincere conviction that the moment has now arrived when the American Republics, through their designated representatives seated at a common council table, should seize this altogether favorable opportunity to consider their joint responsibility and their common need of rendering less likely in the future the outbreak or the continuation of hostilities between them, and by so doing, serve in an eminently practical manner the cause of permanent peace on this Western Continent. If the tragedy of the Chaco can be considered as having served any useful end, I believe such end will lie in our joint willingness to profit from the experience learned and to exert our common endeavors in guarding against the repetition of such American disasters.

It has seemed to me that the American Governments might for these reasons view favorably the suggestion that an extraordi-

See Items 35 and 222-227 of this volume for further material on this subject and for addresses made by me on my visit to this Conference.

18 ❡ Radio Address on the Occasion of the President's Third Birthday Ball for the Benefit of Crippled Children. January 30, 1936

TONIGHT, on my fifty-fourth anniversary, I am very happy because Colonel Doherty, Carl Byoir and Keith Morgan tell me that their reports indicate that this year's celebration, in the interest of continued efforts against infantile paralysis, will exceed our fondest hopes of success. Tonight in every State and in every outlying territory of our Nation many millions of people are enjoying themselves at all kinds of local parties. They have resolutely aligned themselves to carry on the fight against infantile paralysis until this dread and costly disease is brought under definite and final control.

Ten years ago it was made possible for me, with the support of many personal friends, to start the work of the Warm Springs Foundation in Georgia and I dedicated it to one purpose — to apply itself to the task and to keep everlastingly on the job, not by itself alone but with the cooperation of the doctors, the orthopedic hospitals and those thousands of individuals on whose shoulders falls the brunt of caring for several hundred thousands of the afflicted.

No single agency, whether it be the doctor, the hospital or the research laboratory, can cope individually with this great problem; we can do it only by joining our efforts.

Without your local committees the National Committee could not function. You tonight who are attending these celebrations, and you who are in your homes, have greatly helped to make a reality of what was once only a hope. In nearly seven thousand communities you are helping to produce concrete results by making it possible for large numbers of those who suffer from physical handicap caused by infantile paralysis to receive aid and assistance. The lives of these people, young and old, will be made easier. Through rehabilitation by far the greater part of them will become more mobile and will take their places in active life once again with their heads lifted high and their courage unabated.

I am confident that each local committee will work out, with the best medical advice, plans for the wise administering of the 70 percent of the funds which, as a result of this year's Birthday parties, will remain in your community for expenditure.

The 30 percent of the funds which you will send to the National Committee will be used by the Foundation to intensify the national part which it is playing in building up the national fight. I take this opportunity to thank Mr. Jeremiah Milbank, Dr. Paul de Kruif and the other members of the Research Commission, and all those who with them are administering the research activities in connection with the work.

With full confidence and faith in the success we are already attaining. I rededicate the Foundation to the task which lies ahead.

I wish I could look into your faces tonight. You have made me very happy, more happy than I can express in words. Though I cannot be with you, I want each and every one of you to know and feel that I deeply and sincerely appreciate all that you have done for the cause, all of the inspiration which you have applied to it. I am especially grateful not only to the National Committee but to the local chairmen of the local committees who have worked so hard, and also to the press, to the radio, and to the newsreels which have visualized for the whole country the need and the reasons for this great national campaign.

To several hundred thousand victims of infantile paralysis I send very personal greetings, especially to the youngsters among them whose lives lie ahead of them. It is on their behalf that I thank you once more.

(See note to Item 14, Vol. III.)

19 ❴A Greeting to the North American Wildlife Conference. February 3, 1936

To the North American Wildlife Conference:

I REGRET my inability to extend a personal welcome to you or to participate personally in your discussion. Because this is impossible, I have asked Secretary Wallace to convey my best wishes for a most successful and profitable meeting.

It has long been my feeling that there has been a lack of full and complete realization on the part of the public of our wildlife plight, or the urgency of it, and of the many social and economic values that wildlife has for our people. This, and the firm belief in the ability of the American people to face facts, to analyze problems, and to work out a program which might remedy the situation, impelled me to call the North American Wildlife Conference.

Our present wildlife situation is more than a local one. It is national and international. I sincerely hope that with the help of good neighbors to the north and south of us, your Conference will unite upon a common purpose and a common program.

You have been told that this Conference is an open forum; that it is entirely autonomous; that its future is subject to its own decisions. This is as it should be, for it makes it possible for you as representatives of thousands of wildlife organizations with millions of interested and zealous members to make effective progress in restoring and conserving the vanishing wildlife resources of a continent.

NOTE: The North American Wildlife Conference which was called pursuant to my recommendation (see Item 182, Vol. IV) resulted in the organization of the General Wildlife Federation. The Federation now has headquarters in Washington and is represented by state-wide organizations in thirteen regions throughout the United States. Each region is headed by an outstanding wildlife conservationist. The purpose of regional organization is to solidify sentiment for the conservation of wildlife resources and to lend all possible assistance to Federal and State authorities striving toward the same end.

The foregoing greeting was read at the opening session of the Conference by Secretary of Agriculture Wallace.

20 ❪ A Greeting to the National Education Association. February 4, 1936

My dear Miss Samuelson:

YOUR letter of January thirteenth is a very cogent defense of a well-established American principle. I appreciate its candor and I am glad to assure you that I am not in disagreement with it.

If some activities of the Government during recent years have seemed to some persons in the field of education to violate the principle defended in your letter, the reason is that these activities have not concerned education alone. Always there has been the element of relief. In fact, it has been the relief feature which has justified the Federal Government's supplying funds for programs so largely educational as have been the emergency education program, the emergency aid to rural schools, the program of college student aid, and, in fact, the whole National Youth Administration. Had these programs been wholly educational and had they represented essentially a Federal plan to aid in the support of education, it would have been my policy to use only the regularly constituted agencies of education to administer them.

Relief, however, is a problem with which educational people are not generally well acquainted. It is even doubtful whether educational authorities would wish to administer the relief phases of the combined program of education and relief involved in such an enterprise as the emergency education program. Cooperation, therefore, between relief agencies and educational agencies was imperatively necessary.

Will you not accept my assurance that if and when the Federal Government enters into any program of Federal participation in education where the sole, or even the primary, consideration is the advancement of the Nation's educational system, it shall be

78

my purpose to avoid all division of responsibility and to expect the educational agencies, Federal, State and local, to have charge of such a program?

Very sincerely yours,

Miss Agnes Samuelson,
President, National Education Association,
Washington, D. C.

(This letter was read at an annual meeting of the Association in St. Louis, Mo., on February 23, 1936.)

21 ❡ A Letter of Appreciation to an "Understanding Friend." February 8, 1936

My dear Mr. Stancourt:

THOUGH we have not met, your letter makes me believe that I can call you a friend — an understanding friend.

It is not alone because you as a soldier of the late war have thought of me as your Commander-in-Chief.

It is not alone because you, like me, feel a hurt when people who do not know hold up to ridicule our efforts to do useful things with the public moneys.

It is not alone because you tell me that the American Guide is going to be a useful fact-book for our whole country.

It is most of all because you give me the blessings of the unknown men whose voices seem never to be heard, because you rightly believe that I do try, as best I may, to understand the human and the spiritual problems of the millions in our great land who are loyal to our common ideals and who want to hold their heads high.

I am grateful to you. You have helped me.

Faithfully yours,

Louis Stancourt, Esq.,
Roosevelt, Long Island,
New York.

79

22 ❡ A Statement on the Death of Former Vice President Charles Curtis. February 8, 1936

I AM deeply distressed to learn of the sudden passing of my old friend, Charles Curtis. Whether they knew him as a Senator, as the Vice President of the United States, or as the man he was in his own right, his legion of friends will remember him, always affectionately, and will mourn his passing.

23 ❡ "The Truth Is Found When Men Are Free to Pursue It"—Address at Temple University, Philadelphia, on Receiving an Honorary Degree. February 22, 1936

Governor Earle, President Beury, friends of Temple University, and, I am glad to be able to say now, my fellow alumni:

I HAVE just had bestowed upon me a twofold honor. I am honored in having been made an alumnus of Temple University; and I am honored in having had conferred upon me for the first time the Degree of Doctor of Jurisprudence.

It is a happy coincidence that we should meet together to pay our respects to the cause of education not only on the birthday of the Father of this Nation, but also in the halls of a very great institution that is bringing true education into thousands of homes throughout the country. I have always felt certain that in Washington's wise and kindly way, he deeply appreciated the importance of education in a Republic—I might say throughout a Republic—and also the responsibility of that thing known as Government to promote education. Let this simple statement stand by itself without the proof of quotation. I say this lest, in this year of 1936, if I quoted excerpts from the somewhat voluminous writings and messages of the first President of the United States, some captious critic might search the Library of Congress to prove by other quotations that George Washington was in favor of just the opposite! Therefore, on this anniversary of his birth I propose to break a century-old precedent. I shall not quote from George Washington on his birthday.

More than that, and breaking precedent once more, I do not intend to commence any sentence with these words — "If George Washington had been alive today" or "If Thomas Jefferson" or "If Alexander Hamilton" or "If Abraham Lincoln had been alive today — beyond peradventure, beyond a doubt or perhaps the other way around, etc., etc., etc."

Suffice it to say this: What President Washington pointed out on many occasions and in many practical ways was that a broad and cosmopolitan education in every stratum of society is a necessary factor in any free Nation governed through a democratic system. Strides toward that fundamental objective were great, as we know, in the first two or three generations of the Republic, and yet you and I can assert that the greatest development of general education has occurred in the past half century, indeed, within the lives of a great many of those of us who are here today.

As literacy increases people become aware of the fact that Government and society form essentially a cooperative relationship among citizens and the selected representatives of those citizens.

When we speak of modern progress, it seems to me that we place altogether too much emphasis upon progress in material things — in invention, in industrial development, in growth of national wealth.

But progress in the things of the mind has been even more striking in these past fifty years. In my childhood a high-school education was an exceptional opportunity for an American boy or girl; a college education was possible only to an exceedingly small minority. Professional schools had hardly come into existence. And yet since 1900, thirty-six years ago, while the Nation's population has increased by about 70 percent, the enrollment in all branches of institutions of higher learning has increased well over 400 percent, and that tells the story.

At the beginning of this century the total enrollment in our colleges and universities was just one student short of 168,000.

I think it is too bad that the enumerators and college presidents did not get that other one student; it would have been so much easier for the statisticians and enumerators in this year.

Today, instead of 168,000, less one, over a million students are seeking degrees in our colleges and universities and more than 700,000 are enrolled in extension courses and summer schools. I think that we of Temple University — and you see I am exercising my right now to speak as an alumnus — can take special pride in the part that our institution has taken in this growth, for Temple has carried in practice the basic ideal of its great founder, Doctor Russell Conwell. I am very happy to think back to the days when I was in college and heard him deliver that famous lecture which almost every man, woman and child knew. Doctor Conwell believed that every young person should be given a chance to obtain a good education, and he founded Temple University to meet the needs of those who might not be able to afford a college education in other halls. He believed that education should respond to community needs and fit itself into the many-sided and complex life that modern conditions have imposed upon us.

I shall watch with the keenest interest the working out of the plan recently adopted by Temple for carrying even further the practical application of this practical guiding ideal. I refer to the plan for forming an organization to be known as the "Associates of Temple University," and to be composed of representatives of the various commercial, industrial, financial and professional interests of the community outside the University's walls. As I understand it — and this is something that every other university can well afford to emulate — as I understand it, this organization will be far more than a mere advisory body, set up to meet on special and infrequent occasions and to draft recommendations of a general character. The "Associates of Temple University" will be an integral and organic part of the University's structure; the individual Associates will have clearly defined duties and re-

82

sponsibilities, which they will carry out according to a definite plan, and their purpose will be to serve as the "eyes and ears" of the university throughout the community, constantly alert to the changing social and economic needs, and continuously interpreting these needs to the university itself.

I am proud to be the head of a Government which tries to think along similar lines, a Government that has sought and is seeking to make a substantial contribution to the cause of education, even in a period of economic distress. Through the various agencies of the national Government, we have been helping educational institutions not only to maintain their existence, but to add to their equipment and to their offerings to the youth of the country. Since 1933 the Government has made, through the various governmental agencies of the Administration, allotments of various kinds to communities for schools, colleges and library buildings, amounting to more than $400,000,000. I shall not go into higher mathematics and tell you the man-hours of work that that has created, but you can work it out for yourself, and you will agree with me that that expenditure of money has served at least two purposes. In addition to bricks and mortar and labor and loans, we are also providing through the Works Progress Administration educational courses for thousands of groups of adults wherever there are competent unemployed teachers; and, through the National Youth Administration, funds for part-time employment to help deserving young people to earn their way through accredited colleges and universities in every part of the United States.

We have rightly taken the position that in spite of the fact that economic adversity through these years might impose upon the youth of the country distressing and unavoidable burdens, the Government owed it to the future of the Nation to see that these burdens should not include the denial of educational opportunities for those who were willing and ready to use them to advantage.

Educational progress in the past generation has given to this country a population more literate, more cultured, in the best sense of the word, more aware of the complexities of modern civilized life than ever before in our history. And while the methods of spreading education are new, the lessons of education are eternal. The books may be new, but the truth is old.

The qualities of a true education remain what they were when Washington insisted upon its importance.

First among these qualities is a sense of fair play among men.

As education grows, men come to recognize their essential dependence one upon the other. There is revealed to them the true nature of society and of Government which, in a large measure, culminates in the art of human cooperation.

The second great attribute of education is peculiarly appropriate to a great democracy. It is a sense of equality among men when they are dealing with the things of the mind. Inequality may linger in the world of material things, but great music, great literature, great art and the wonders of science are, and should be, open to all.

Finally, a true education depends upon freedom in the pursuit of truth. No group and no Government can properly prescribe precisely what should constitute the body of knowledge with which true education is concerned. The truth is found when men are free to pursue it. Genuine education is present only when the springs from which knowledge comes are pure. It is this belief in the freedom of the mind, written into our fundamental law, and observed in our everyday dealings with the problems of life, that distinguishes us as a Nation, the United States of America, above every Nation in the world.

In our ability to keep pure the sources of knowledge, in our mind's freedom to winnow the chaff from the good grain, in the even temper and in the calmness of our everyday relationships, in our willingness to face the details of fact and the needs of temporary emergencies—in all of these lie our future and our children's future.

"On your own heads, in your own hands, the sin and the saving lies!"

24 ❧ Radio Address on Brotherhood Day. February 23, 1936

I AM happy to speak to you from my own home on the evening of a Sabbath Day which has been observed in so many of your home communities as Brotherhood Day. The National Conference of Jews and Christians has set aside a day on which we can meet, not primarily as Protestants or Catholics or Jews but as believing Americans; a day on which we can dedicate ourselves not to the things which divide but to the things which unite us. I hope that we have begun to see how many and how important are the things on which we are united. Now, of all times, we require that kind of thinking.

There are honest differences of religious belief among the citizens of your town as there are among the citizens of mine. It is a part of the spirit of Brotherhood Day, as it is a part of our American heritage, to respect those differences. And it is well for us to remember that this America of ours is the product of no single race or creed or class. Men and women — your fathers and mine — came here from the far corners of the earth with beliefs that widely varied. And yet each, in his own way, laid his own special gift upon our national altar to enrich our national life. From the gift that each has given, all have gained.

This is no time to make capital out of religious disagreement, however honest. It is a time, rather, to make capital out of religious understanding. We who have faith cannot afford to fall out among ourselves. The very state of the world is a summons to us to stand together. For as I see it, the chief religious issue is not between our various beliefs. It is between belief and unbelief. It is not your specific faith or mine that is being called into question — but all faith. Religion in wide areas of the earth is being confronted with irreligion; our faiths are being challenged. It is because of that threat that you and I must reach across the lines between our creeds, clasp hands, and make common cause.

85

To do that will do credit to the best of our religious tradition. It will do credit, also, to the best in our American tradition. The spiritual resources of our forbears have brought us a long way toward the goal which was set before the Nation at its founding as a Nation.

Yet I do not look upon these United States as a finished product. We are still in the making. The vision of the early days still requires the same qualities of faith in God and man for its fulfillment.

No greater thing could come to our land today than a revival of the spirit of religion — a revival that would sweep through the homes of the Nation and stir the hearts of men and women of all faiths to a reassertion of their belief in God and their dedication to His will for themselves and for their world. I doubt if there is any problem — social, political or economic — that would not melt away before the fire of such a spiritual awakening.

I know of no better way to kindle such a fire than through the fellowship that an occasion like this makes possible. For Brotherhood Day, after all, is an experiment in understanding; a venture in neighborliness.

I like to think of our country as one home in which the interests of each member are bound up with the happiness of all. We ought to know, by now, that the welfare of your family or mine cannot be bought at the sacrifice of our neighbor's family; that our well-being depends, in the long run, upon the well-being of our neighbors. The good-neighbor idea — as we are trying to practice it in international relationships — needs to be put into practice in our community relationships. When it is we may discover that the road to understanding and fellowship is also the road to spiritual awakening. At our neighbor's fireside we may find new fuel for the fires of faith at our own hearthsides.

It would be a fitting thing for an organization such as the National Conference of Jews and Christians to undertake this kind of project in neighborliness. I should like to see Associations of Good Neighbors in every town and city and in every rural community of our land. Such associations of sincere citizens like-minded as to the underlying principles and ideals would reach across the lines of creed or of economic status. It would bring together men and women of all stations to share their problems and their hopes and to discover ways of mutual and neighborly helpfulness. Here perhaps is a way to pool our spiritual resources; to find common ground on which all of us of all faiths can stand; and thence to move forward as men and women concerned for the things of the spirit.

NOTE: During my Administration, I have made several speeches and sent several messages of greeting to this Conference. They have not all been included in these volumes.

25 ⟨ The President Vetoes a Bill for Crop Production Loans. February 26, 1936

To the Senate:

I RETURN herewith, without my approval, S. 3612, a bill entitled "To provide loans to farmers for crop production and harvesting during the year 1936, and for other purposes."

This bill authorizes an appropriation of $50,000,000 from the general fund of the Treasury for loans to farmers during the year 1936 for production of crops—principally seed loans.

In approving the bill providing $40,000,000 for crop production loans for 1934, I stated that I did so on the theory that it was proper to taper off the crop loan system, which had been initiated on a large scale as early as 1931, rather than to cut it off abruptly, particularly since such loans would serve a useful purpose in aiding certain farmers unable to qualify for crop production loans through the newly established farmers' production credit associations, and that the 1934 loan by the Government should thus be considered as a tapering-off loan.

It is true that I gave my approval to a $60,000,000 crop production loan for 1935, but this loan was primarily for relief purposes principally in the drought-stricken areas, and I recommended to the Congress that the cost of such loans should properly be defrayed from the appropriation for relief purposes. Accordingly $60,000,000 was reappropriated from unobligated balances under allocations from the appropriation of $525,-000,000 for relief in stricken agricultural areas contained in the Emergency Appropriation Act passed the previous year.

In my budget message, transmitting the 1937 Budget, I stated:

> "If the Congress enacts legislation at the coming session which will impose additional charges upon the Treasury for which provision is not already made in this Budget, I strongly urge that additional taxes be provided to cover such charges."

No provision was made in the financial program for the fiscal year 1936, or the fiscal year 1937, for additional crop loans, and, notwithstanding my budget statement, quoted above, the Congress by this bill authorizes an additional draft upon the Treasury for $50,000,000 for new crop loans, without making provision for any revenue to cover such loans.

However, while I am returning this bill without my approval, I recognize that there still exists a need for crop production loans to farmers whose cash requirements are so small that the operating and supervisory costs, as well as the credit risk, make credit unavailable to them at this time through the usual commercial channels and who, unless extended assistance of this character, would no doubt find it necessary to seek some other form of relief from the Government. This is particularly true with respect to those areas in which unusual conditions prevail because of drought, dust storms, floods, rust and other unforeseen disasters.

I fully agree with the Congress that provision should be made for such borrowers during the year 1936, but I feel that other borrowers should seek credit elsewhere.

I am convinced that the immediate and actual needs to which

88

I have referred can be met during the year 1936 by an expenditure of funds materially less than that proposed in the bill under discussion.

Furthermore, these needs can be met, without the necessity of enacting authorizing legislation, through an allocation of funds by me from the appropriation provided in the Emergency Relief Appropriation Act for 1935, which appropriation, I am informally advised by the Comptroller General of the United States, can be utilized for such loans as I might indicate by Executive Order to be desirable and necessary for relief measures.

I believe, therefore, that a special appropriation by the Congress at this time is both inadvisable and unnecessary. That being so, and in the absence of such legislation, I proposed in order to meet this need to issue an Executive Order within the next few days.

NOTE: The foregoing veto message gives the history of emergency crop and feed loan legislation during my Administration (see Item 29, of Volume III, and Item 18, of Volume IV).

On February 28th, 1936, I issued Executive Order No. 7305, as set forth in the foregoing veto message. The amount loaned pursuant to that Executive Order was $16,629,-000, among 188,944 loans, or an average loan of $88; of this sum $9,260,000 was loaned to farmers in States affected by the droughts of 1934 and 1936. The total amount of principal collected on loans under this Order up to October 31, 1937, has been $12,569,000, making an average loss per loan of $21.49. In other words, 75 percent of this principal has been collected.

26 ❧ A Presidential Statement Renewing His Appeal against Profiteering in the War between Italy and Ethiopia. February 29, 1936

By THE Resolution approved August 31, 1935, a definite step was taken toward enabling this country to maintain its neutrality and avoid being drawn into wars involving other Nations. It provided that in the event of the Executive proclaiming the existence of such a war, an embargo would attach to the exportation of arms, ammunition and implements of war destined to any belligerent country. It also authorized the Executive to warn citizens of this country against traveling as passengers on the vessels of any belligerent except at their own risk.

By the Resolution I have just signed, the operation of the August Resolution is extended and strengthened until May 1, 1937. A new and definite step is taken by providing in substance that, when an embargo becomes effective, obligations of any belligerent Government issued after the date of the proclamation shall not be purchased or sold in this country, and no loan or credit extended to such Government, but with authority to the Executive, if our interests require, to except from the prohibition commercial credits and short-time loans in aid of legal transactions. In addition, it in general exempts the other Republics of this hemisphere from the operation of the law.

Following the August enactment promptly on October 5, 1935, I issued a proclamation which made effective the embargo with respect to exportations to Italy and Ethiopia, and I have now issued a new proclamation in order to meet the requirements of the new enactment.

The policies announced by the Secretary of State and myself at the time of an subsequent to the issuance of the original proclamation will be maintained in effect. It is true that the high moral duty I have urged on our people of restricting their exports of essential war materials to either belligerent to approximately the normal peace-time basis has not been the subject of legislation. Nevertheless, it is clear to me that greatly to exceed that basis, with the result of earning profits not possible during peace, and especially with the result of giving actual assistance to the carrying on of war, would serve to magnify the very evil of war which we seek to prevent.

This being my view, I renew the appeal made last October to the American people that they so conduct their trade with belligerent Nations that it cannot be said that they are seizing new opportunities for profit or that by changing their peace-time trade they give aid to the continuation of war.

NOTE: The original neutrality legislation (Joint Resolution No. 173, 49 Stat. 1081, approved by me August 31, 1935, see Item 117, Vol. IV) expired, so far as the provisions relating to arms embargoes were concerned, on February 29, 1936.

As soon as the Congress reassembled in January, 1936, the Administration sponsored a new neutrality bill, known as the Pittman-McReynolds Bill. This bill, in addition to continuing the arms embargo provisions of the expiring law, added a number of new provisions, chief among which were: (1) a prohibition against making loans to belligerent Governments; and (2) a provision authorizing the President to limit the export to belligerents of essential war materials other than arms, ammunition and implements of war, to "normal quantities" — that is, quantities usually exported to such belligerents as averaged during a given period of years before the war.

The Administration vigorously supported this legislation, and the Secretary of State himself appeared before the Committee to urge its adoption.

There was serious opposition to the bill, however. It arose from several groups: from some racial minorities who felt that the countries of their origin might be injured under certain provisions of the bill; from a number of international lawyers who were opposed to our abandoning certain of our so-called "neutrality rights"; and from some sincere persons who conscientiously believed that it would be impossible to administer the provisions of the bill dealing with "normal quantities." As the result of this opposition, the bill did not pass. Instead, on February 29, 1936, the very day on which the arms embargo provisions of the old law expired, a new resolution was hastily enacted and approved which extended the arms embargo provisions until May 1, 1937, and added a new section prohibiting, with certain exceptions, loans and credits to belligerent Governments.

The foregoing statement by me announced the intention of the Administration to adhere to the policies theretofore announced at the time of the issuance of the original proclamations with respect to the war between Italy and Ethiopia (see Item 143, Vol. IV).

I renewed the appeal that I made last October to the American people not to profiteer by taking advantage of the war.

On the same day, I issued Proclamation No. 2159, which was in effect a continuation of the provisions of the arms embargo Proclamation of October, 1935. This Proclamation, with certain deletions, is printed as the following Item.

27 ❨ A Proclamation against the Export of Arms and Ammunition to Italy and Ethiopia. Proclamation No. 2159. February 29, 1936

WHEREAS . . . my proclamation of October 5, 1935, issued pursuant to Section 1 of the joint resolution approved August 31, 1935, declared that a state of war unhappily existed between Ethiopia and the Kingdom of Italy.

NOW, THEREFORE, I, Franklin D. Roosevelt, President of the United States of America, acting under and by virtue of the authority conferred on me by the said joint resolution as amended by the joint resolution of Congress approved February 29, 1936, do hereby proclaim that a state of war unhappily continues to exist between Ethiopia and the Kingdom of Italy; and I do hereby admonish all citizens of the United States or any of its possessions and all persons residing or being within the territory or jurisdiction of the United States or its possessions to abstain from every violation of the provisions of the joint resolution above set forth, hereby made effective and applicable to the export of arms, ammunition, or implements of war from any place in the United States or its possessions to Ethiopia or to the Kingdom of Italy, or to any Italian possession, or to any neutral port for transshipment to, or for the use of, Ethiopia or the Kingdom of Italy.

And I do hereby declare and proclaim that the articles listed below shall be considered arms, ammunition, and implements of war for the purposes of Section 1 of the said joint resolution of Congress:

CATEGORY I

(1) Rifles and carbines using ammunition in excess of caliber .22, and barrels for those weapons;

(2) Machine guns, automatic or autoloading rifles, and machine pistols using ammunition in excess of caliber .22, and barrels for those weapons;

(3) Guns, howitzers, and mortars of all calibers, their mountings and barrels;

(4) Ammunition in excess of caliber .22 for the arms enumerated under (1) and (2) above, and cartridge cases or bullets for such ammunition; filled and unfilled projectiles or forgings for such projectiles for the arms enumerated under (3) above; propellants with a web thickness of .015 inch or greater for the projectiles of the arms enumerated under (3) above;

(5) Grenades, bombs, torpedoes and mines, filled or unfilled, and apparatus for their use or discharge;

(6) Tanks, military armored vehicles, and armored trains.

CATEGORY II

Vessels of war of all kinds, including aircraft carriers and submarines.

CATEGORY III

(1) Aircraft, assembled or dismantled, both heavier and lighter than air, which are designed, adapted, and intended for aerial combat by the use of machine guns or of artillery or for the carrying and dropping of bombs, or which are equipped with, or which by reason of design or construction are prepared for, any of the appliances referred to in paragraph (2) below;

(2) Aerial gun mounts and frames, bomb racks, torpedo carriers, and bomb or torpedo release mechanisms.

CATEGORY IV

(1) Revolvers and automatic pistols using ammunition in excess of caliber .22;

(2) Ammunition in excess of caliber .22 for the arms enumerated under (1) above, and cartridge cases or bullets for such ammunition.

CATEGORY V

(1) Aircraft, assembled or dismantled, both heavier and lighter than air, other than those included in Category III;

(2) Propellers or air screws, fuselages, hulls, wings, tail units, and under-carriage units;

(3) Aircraft engines, assembled or unassembled.

CATEGORY VI

(1) Livens projectors and flame throwers;

(2) Mustard gas (dichlordiethylsulphide), lewisite (chloro-vinyldichloroarsin and dichlorodivinylchloroarsin), ethyldichlorarsin, methyldichlorarsin, ethyliodoacetate, bromobenzyl-cyanide, diphenylchlorarsin, and diphenyl-cyanarsin.

And I do hereby enjoin upon all officers of the United States, charged with the execution of the laws thereof, the utmost diligence in preventing violations of the said joint resolution, and this my proclamation issued thereunder, and in bringing to trial and punishment any offenders against the same.

And I do hereby delegate to the Secretary of State the power of prescribing regulations for the enforcement of Section 1 of the said joint resolution of August 31, 1935, as amended by Section 1 of the joint resolution of Congress approved February 29, 1936, and as made effective by this my proclamation issued thereunder.

And I do hereby revoke my proclamation of October 5, 1935, concerning the export of arms, ammunition and implements of war to Ethiopia and Italy, which was issued pursuant to the terms of Section 1 of the joint resolution of Congress approved August 31, 1935, provided, however, that this action shall not have the effect of releasing or extinguishing any penalty, forfeiture or liability incurred under the aforesaid proclamation of October 5, 1935; and that the said proclamation shall be treated as remaining in force for the purpose of sustaining any proper action or prosecution for the enforcement of such penalty, forfeiture or liability.

28 ❰A Presidential Statement on Signing the Soil Conservation and Domestic Allotment Act. March 1, 1936

IN SIGNING the Soil Conservation and Domestic Allotment Act, I feel that I am approving a measure which helps to safeguard vital public interests not only for today, but for generations to come.

This legislation represents an attempt to develop, out of the far-reaching and partly emergency efforts under the Agricultural Adjustment Act, a long-time program for American agriculture.

The new law has three major objectives which are inseparably and of necessity linked with the national welfare. The first of these aims is conservation of the soil itself through wise and proper land use. The second purpose is the reestablishment and maintenance of farm income at fair levels so that the great gains made by agriculture in the past three years can be preserved and national recovery can continue. The third major objective is the protection of consumers by assuring adequate supplies of food and fibre now and in the future.

The Federal Government, with an annual expenditure far less than the actual yearly wastage of fertility by erosion in the past will make grants of money to farmers, conditioned upon actual evidence of good land use. Thus, in carrying out the soil conservation plan, there will be provided a positive incentive to and protection for those who voluntarily shift from soil-depleting surplus crops, such as cotton, corn, wheat and tobacco, into erosion-preventing and soil-building crops, such as grasses and legumes, of which there is no surplus. This will help to bring about and maintain a healthy supply-and-demand situation from farm commodities, and will have a beneficial effect on farm prices and farm income.

There will be no contracts with farmers. The program does not control individual production of individual farm commodities. The absence of production control may make impracticable

95

the attainment of exact parity prices, as defined in the Agricultural Adjustment Act. Nevertheless, I am confident that the farmers, cooperating with the Government, will work hard within existing legal limitations to achieve the goal of the new law, which is parity not of farm prices, but of farm income. They and we have not abandoned and will not abandon the principle of equality for agriculture.

In general, the new farm act follows the outlines of a long-time policy for agriculture which I recommended in my statement of October 25, 1935. The wise use of land which it seeks to encourage involves sound farm practice and crop rotation as well as soil conservation. The income insurance feature afforded by the conditional payments will help farmers to maintain these beneficial systems of farming without interruption in poor crop years. Long-time adjustments, as I said last October, can be adapted to natural soil advantages of regions and localities.

Sound farming is of direct interest not only to farmers, but to consumers. To the extent that the new plan succeeds in its aim of preserving and improving farm lands, consumers will share substantially in the benefits. In years of surplus, consumers may lightly take for granted the continuance of adequate supplies of food and fibre; but the recurring dust storms and rivers yellow with silt are a warning that Nature's resources will not indefinitely withstand exploitation or negligence. The only permanent protection which can be given consumers must come from conservation practiced by farmers.

For a long time, I have felt that there was need for concerted action to promote good land use. Years ago, as Governor of the State of New York, I took such steps as I could in that direction, and I described them in detail in a speech at French Lick, Indiana, June 2, 1931, on the subject "Acres Fit and Unfit." I said that, having reached a determination as to the best use of land, "we arrive at once at the larger problem of getting men, women and children — in other words, population — to go along with a program and carry it out." I said, "Government itself must take steps, with approval of the governed, to see that plans become realities." (See Item 104, Vol. I.)

As I made that speech, I was thinking in terms of my State, of other States and of the Nation. Now this new Act incorporates a system of Federal aid to function when State cooperation with the Federal Government can be arranged.

The provision for State-Federal cooperation, beginning not later than January 1, 1938, will mark a further application of the principle of shared responsibility. This is in accord with the strong feature of the agricultural adjustment programs which operated in a democratic manner through cooperation with the State land grant colleges, State committees, county associations and county committees, township committees and individual farmers.

The history of every Nation is eventually written in the way in which it cares for its soil. The United States, as evidenced by the progressive public opinion and vigorous demand which resulted in the enactment of this law, is now emerging from its youthful stage of heedless exploitation and is beginning to realize the supreme importance of treating the soil well.

I do not regard this farm act as a panacea or as a final plan. Rather I consider it a new basis to build and improve upon, as experience discloses its points of weakness and of strength. Aiming at justice for agriculture and self-interest for the Nation, the plan seeks to salvage and conserve the greatest values in human life and resources with which this Nation is endowed.

NOTE: The foregoing statute approved February 29, 1936 (Pub. No. 461, 74th Congress; 49 Stat. 1148), set out the following objectives and declared the following policy: (1) preservation and improvement of soil fertility; (2) promotion of the economic use and conservation of land; (3) diminution of exploitation and of wasteful and unscientific use of national soil resources; (4) protection of rivers and harbors against the results of soil erosion in aid of maintaining the navigability of waters and water courses and in aid of flood control; and (5) reestablishment, at as rapid a rate as the Secretary of Agriculture determines to be practicable and in the general public interest, of the ratio between the purchasing power of the net income per person on farms and that

97

of the income per person not on farms that prevailed during the five-year period August 1909-July 1914, inclusive, and the maintenance of this ratio.

See also in this connection Items 4, 6 and 39 of this volume.

I have very often pointed out in messages and speeches that farming practices within the past recent years have been directed primarily toward maintaining or increasing income through increasing production. Rare, indeed, has been the effort to engage in sound soil conserving practices.

The programs carried out under A.A.A. during its operation from 1933 through 1935 were designed to remedy this situation in part. Although they did tend to check soil exploitation by raising prices and by removing the temptation to mine the soil, and although they did encourage shifting of land from intensive use to feed raising uses, the programs were essentially commodity price-raising programs; and agricultural conservation was merely incidental to production control.

The statute referred to in the foregoing statement reversed the situation and made nationwide soil conservation and the proper use of agricultural land resources the prime objectives.

In working out the programs under this statute the chief considerations were the amount of acreage and the kind of farming practices in general. The amount of specific commodities raised is di-

rectly affected only as balanced cropping systems are adopted which require curtailment of the amount of crops produced. The conservation program under this statute deals with the farm rather than with the commodity, as did the production adjustment program under A.A.A.

The material, its arrangement, and some of the phraseology in this note have been taken from the 1936 Report of A.A.A. (Agricultural Conservation 1936) issued by the Department of Agriculture.

The statute provides for economic support and assistance by the Federal Government to the farmers of America in a concerted and co-operative attempt adequately to meet the problem of soil erosion and soil depletion on the farms of the country and at the same time to control the size of crops by following accepted standards of soil conservation.

Just as the Agricultural Adjustment Act and the program to carry it out were developed as a farmers' program, planned in conference with farmers, and administered in great part by farmers or their representatives, the agricultural conservation program was developed by discussion with farmers at open meetings held as soon as possible after the Act was signed. Recommendations and suggestions of farmers and farm organization leaders who attended these meetings provided the basis for the program. College research and extension specialists were also consulted. Actual administration of the agricultural conservation program for 1936 in each community and county was carried on, as in A.A.A., by farmers selected by their neighbors as community and county committeemen. In addition, during the preparation of the 1937 program, meetings of farmers were held in hundreds of communities. The findings and recommendations developed in these meetings were forwarded through the county organizations to the State offices and thence to Washington. Further regional meetings for coordinating and sifting the recommendations from communities, counties, and States have been held, and the entire process culminated in a national program, in the planning of which each region and each type of farming was represented by farmers themselves or by farm specialists.

There are 2,713 county agricultural conservation associations organized in all regions except the Northeast where such associations are being formed for the 1937 program. These organizations are formed under articles of association approved by the Secretary of Agriculture, and have an estimated membership of about 4 1/3 million producers. Through these associations definite administrative, advisory, and other functions with regard to the program in the county, are delegated to officers and committeemen selected by farmers themselves.

The county agricultural conservation associations succeeded the more than 4,000 county agricultural adjustment associations that were formed to assist in administering the commodity-adjustment programs in 1933-35. These commodity-adjustment associations, upon the termination of the production-adjustment programs, were charged with a share of the administrative work in the liquidation of these programs.

Committees of representative farmers in over 2,400 counties worked with the State extension services in analyzing the agriculture in their counties and in working out recommendations for changes in the acreage of crops grown in each county. Specifically these committees were supposed to answer two questions: (1) What acreage and production of crops could be expected, assuming normal weather and prospective prices, but without production-control and marketing-control programs; and (2) What acreage and production of such crops could be expected, assuming normal weather and prospective prices, but with farming systems so adjusted as to maintain soil fertility and control erosion.

The purpose of the survey was to find out the percentage of adjustments of the various products required to maintain soil conservation. Of course, different programs would have to be planned for different crops and different regions, such as the corn belt, the cotton belt,

99

general farming regions, wheat and small-grain regions, dairy regions, tobacco regions, range livestock regions, and other special crop regions. The Act and program were drafted to maintain adequate supplies of food and feed for domestic consumer needs and for profitable foreign outlets without taxing too severely the soil fertility in farm land. It was an attempt to strike a balance of (1) farm income, (2) consumer requirements, and (3) soil requirements. Major emphasis was laid on soil requirements, and the chief objective was to enable farmers to apply on their own farms this nationwide policy designed to conserve soil in a long-range program for the benefit both of producers and of consumers.

The goal originally planned for 1936 was an increase of land devoted to soil-improving and soil-conserving crops which would bring the total up to 130,000,000 acres, as compared with the 1930 figure of 100,000,000 acres. It also aimed at a greater use of the kind of farming practices which would check soil erosion and increase soil fertility. Approximately $470,000,000 was provided by the Congress for this program.

Farmers in every farming area have opportunity to participate, and do participate, in planning the programs carried out by the Agricultural Adjustment Administration, and in determining the provisions of those programs. Participation in the programs themselves is wholly voluntary on the part of farmers, who decide for themselves whether they wish to adopt the soil conserving farm-management system which will qualify them to receive payments under the provisions of the program after it has been adopted.

Briefly, the following steps were taken in working out the program: Farm base acreages were established for each farm voluntarily cooperating in the program. This was the amount of land ordinarily planted on that farm to the crop in question. A soil depleting base was established on each participating farm to provide a standard by which to measure the extent of soil conservation and soil improvement undertaken on each farm, pursuant to the program and to determine the amount to be paid to each individual farmer who cooperated. This base was the amount found to be the total acreage in soil depleting crops on that farm in 1935, modified to take care of unusual situations. Soil depleting crops include the intensive, cultivated row crops such as corn, cotton, tobacco and the small grains such as wheat and oats. The soil conserving crops are, in general, grasses, legumes and green manure crops.

Payments were made only for positive performance by farmers in improving and conserving farm land. Two types of payment were offered to cooperating farmers: a soil-building payment, and a soil-conserving payment.

Soil-building payments were made for planting soil-building crops on regular crop land and for adopting approved soil-building practices. The payments were made at a rate within each State that was based upon recommendations of the State committee approved by the Secretary of Agriculture. Soil-conserving payments were made to farmers for shifting some of their acreage from soil-depleting crops to soil-conserving crops in 1936, with certain maximum protective limits established. Payments in both cases therefore depended upon the number of acres which each participating farmer was willing to remove from regular soil-depleting crop production and turn over to crops which conserved the soil or actually built it up.

The farmers, in this way, received financial help from the Government, which met part of the cost of protecting and conserving their soil and improving and conserving the agricultural resources of the whole Nation.

The appropriations to carry out this Act were approved on March 19, 1936. The program was announced on March 20, 1936. Therefore, time for planning the program for 1936 and for enabling farmers to participate in it was too short for complete results.

Four very definite ends, however, have been and will continue to be served: (1) The rate of exhaustion of soil productivity will be reduced; (2) better adjustment of production to demand for agricultural products will be obtained; (3) more acres of close-growing grasses and legumes have been provided which prevent rapid run-off of water, and which hold the soil in place and lessen flood destructiveness; (4) soil fertility has been and will continue to be improved.

Briefly, as stated in the 1936 Report of A.A.A. (Agricultural Conservation 1936), the immediate practical results of the 1936 soil conservation program were as follows (figures revised):

Sixty-seven percent, or approximately 286,179,000 acres of the total United States crop land were covered by applications for grants under the 1936 program. About 4,321,000 county conservation association members participated in the program. The total acreage diverted from soil-depleting crops amounted to some 31,444,400 acres. Not all of this diversion was the direct result of the soil conservation program. Drought destroyed large acreages of soil-depleting crops. In accordance with sound farm management, farmers replaced these crops where possible with emergency drought-resistant soil-conserving crops. The program placed a limit upon the percentage of his soil-depleting acreage which an individual farmer could be paid for diverting. In the drought-stricken area farmers frequently exceeded this percentage for which they were paid, because of the loss of their original plantings in their desire to produce as much feed and forage as possible.

Of the acreage diverted from soil-depleting crops in the United States, about 68 percent was diverted from the general soil-depleting base, 30 percent from the cotton base, 1 percent from the tobacco base, and 4/10 of 1 percent from the peanut base.

Soil-building practices were carried out on about 52,863,000 acres of land in the Nation. There were approximately 28,458,000 acres of new seedings of legumes alone or in mixtures, and 13,670,000 acres of green-manure crops newly seeded; about 1,779,000 acres of pasture were established or improved. About 3,247,000 acres of land received chemical fertilizers; terracing, contour furrowing, protected summer fallow, and other mechanical erosion controls and miscellaneous soil-building practices were put into effect on about 5,709,000 acres.

Class 1 payments were distributed approximately as follows: 65 percent for diversion from the general base; 27 percent for diversion from the cotton base; 5 percent for diversion from the tobacco base, and 1 percent or less each for diversion of peanut acreage and for participation in the special sugar, rice and flax phases of the program. Of the total payments to farmers, about 15½ percent were for the adoption of soil-building practices. Of the acreage on which these practices were carried out, 83 percent was put into new seedings of soil-improving crops. These new seedings were made on about 43,907,000 acres, of which 65 percent was seeded to legumes alone or in mixtures, 31 percent to green-manure crops, and the remaining 4 percent to grass mixtures designed to establish or improve pastures. Six percent of the land on which payments in connection with soil-building practices were made, received applications of lime, superphosphate or other approved chemical supplements. About 1½ percent of the acreage was terraced, and on 9 percent contour furrowing, protected summer fallow, or other mechanical erosion-control practices were carried out.

29 ❡ A Supplemental Budget Message to the Congress. March 3, 1936

ON JANUARY 3, 1936, in my annual budget message to the Congress, I pointed out that without the item for relief the budget was in balance. Since that time an important item of revenue has been eliminated through a decision of the Supreme Court, and an additional annual charge has been placed on the Treasury through the enactment of the Adjusted Compensation Payment Act.

I said in my budget message:

"... the many legislative Acts creating the machinery for recovery were all predicated on two interdependent beliefs. First, the measures would immediately cause a great increase in the annual expenditures of the Government — many of these expenditures, however, in the form of loans which would ultimately return to the Treasury. Second, as a result of the simultaneous attack on the many fronts I have indicated, the receipts of the Government would rise definitely and sharply during the following few years, while greatly increased expenditure for the purposes stated, coupled with rising values and the stopping of losses, would, over a period of years, diminish the need for work relief and thereby reduce Federal expenditures. The increase in revenues would ultimately meet and pass the declining cost of relief.

"This policy adopted in the spring of 1933 has been confirmed in actual practice by the Treasury figures of 1934, of 1935, and by the estimates for the fiscal years of 1936 and 1937.

"There is today no doubt of the fundamental soundness of the policy of 1933. If we proceed along the path we have followed and with the results attained up to the present time we shall continue our successful progress during the coming years."

If we are to maintain this clear-cut and sound policy, it is incumbent upon us to n..ke good to the Federal Treasury both the loss of revenue caused by the Supreme Court decision and the increase in expenses caused by the Adjustment Compensation Payment Act. I emphasize that adherence to consistent policy calls for such action.

To be specific: The Supreme Court decision adversely affected the budget in an amount of one billion and seventeen million dollars during the fiscal year 1936 and the fiscal year 1937. This figure is arrived at as follows:

Deficit to date (expenditures chargeable to processing taxes less processing taxes collected) in excess of that contemplated in the 1937 budget .... $ 281,000,000

Estimated expenditures to be made from supplemental appropriation approved in the Supplemental Appropriation Act, 1936 296,000,000

Estimated expenditures to be made under the Soil Conservation and Domestic Allotment Act 440,000,000

Total additional deficit 1936 and 1937, due to Supreme Court decision and adjusted farm program $1,017,000,000

For the purposes of clarity, I divide the present total additional revenue needs of the Government into the permanent and the temporary ones.

Permanent Treasury income of five hundred million dollars is required to offset expenditures which will be made annually as a result of the Soil Conservation and Domestic Allotment Act recently enacted by the Congress and approved by me; and an additional sum recurring annually for nine years will be required to amortize the total cost of the Adjustment Compensation Payment Act.

The net effect of paying the Veterans' Bonus in 1936, instead of 1945, is to add an annual charge of one hundred and twenty million dollars to the one hundred and sixty million dollars already in the budget.

We are called upon, therefore, to raise by some form of permanent taxation an annual amount of six hundred and twenty million dollars. It may be said, truthfully and correctly, that five hundred million dollars of this amount represents substitute taxes in place of the old processing taxes, and that only one hundred and twenty million dollars represents new taxes not hitherto levied.

I leave, of course, to the discretion of the Congress the formulation of the appropriate taxes for the needed permanent revenue. I invite your attention, however, to a form of tax which would accomplish an important tax reform, remove two major inequalities in our tax system, and stop "leaks" in present surtaxes.

Extended study of methods of improving present taxes on income from business warrants the consideration of changes to provide a fairer distribution of the tax load among all the beneficial owners of business profits whether derived from unincorporated enterprises or from incorporated businesses and whether distributed to the real owners as earned or withheld from them. The existing difference between corporate taxes and those imposed on owners of unincorporated businesses renders incorporation of small businesses difficult or impossible.

The accumulation of surplus in corporations controlled by taxpayers with large incomes is encouraged by the present freedom of undistributed corporate income from surtaxes. Since stockholders are the beneficial owners of both distributed and undistributed corporate income, the aim, as a matter of fundamental equity, should be to seek equality of tax burden on all corporate income whether distributed or withheld from the beneficial owners. As the law now stands our corporate taxes dip too deeply into the shares of corporate earnings going to stockholders who need the disbursement of dividends; while the shares of stockholders who can afford to leave earnings undistributed escape current surtaxes altogether.

This method of evading existing surtaxes constitutes a problem as old as the income tax law itself. Repeated attempts by the Congress to prevent this form of evasion have not been successful. The evil has been a growing one. It has now reached disturbing proportions from the standpoint of the inequality it represents and of its serious effect on the Federal revenue. Thus the Treasury estimates that, during the calendar year 1936, over four and one-half billion dollars of corporate income will be withheld from stockholders. If this undistributed income were distributed, it would be added to the income of stockholders and there taxed as is other personal income. But, as matters now stand, it will be withheld from stockholders by those in control of these corporations. In one year alone, the Government will be deprived of revenues amounting to over one billion three hundred million dollars.

A proper tax on corporate income (including dividends from other corporations), which is not distributed as earned, would correct the serious twofold inequality in our taxes on business profits if accompanied by a repeal of the present corporate income tax, the capital stock tax, the related excess profits tax and the present exemption of dividends from the normal tax on individual incomes. The rate on undistributed corporate income should be graduated and so fixed as to yield approximately the same revenue as would be yielded if corporate profits were distributed and taxed in the hands of stockholders.

Such a revision of our corporate taxes would effect great simplification in tax procedure, in corporate accounting, and in the understanding of the whole subject by the citizens of the Nation. It would constitute distinct progress in tax reform.

The Treasury Department will be glad to submit its estimates to the Congress showing that this simplification and removal of inequalities can, without unfairness, be put into practice so as to yield the full amount of six hundred and twenty million dollars — the amount I have indicated above as being necessary.

Turning to the temporary revenue needs of the Government, there is the item of five hundred and seventeen million dollars, which affects principally the current fiscal year. This amount must in some way be restored to the Treasury, even though the process of restoration might be spread over two years or three years.

In this case also the formulation of taxes lies wholly in the discretion of the Congress. I venture, however, to call your attention to two suggestions.

The first relates to the taxation of what may well be termed a windfall received by certain taxpayers who shifted to others the burden of processing taxes which were impounded and returned to them or which otherwise have remained unpaid. In unequal position is that vast number of other taxpayers who did not resort to such court action and have paid their taxes to the Government. By far the greater part of the processing taxes was in the main either passed on to consumers or taken out of the price paid producers. The Congress recognized this fact last August and provided in Section 21(d) of the Agricultural Adjustment Act that, in the event of the invalidation of the processing taxes, only those processors who had borne the burden of these taxes should be permitted to receive refunds. The return of the impounded funds and failure to pay taxes that were passed on result in unjust enrichment, contrary to the spirit of that enactment. A tax on the beneficiaries unfairly enriched by the return or nonpayment of this Federal excise would take a major part of this windfall income for the benefit of the public. Much of this revenue would accrue to the Treasury during the fiscal years 1936 and 1937.

The other suggestion relates to a temporary tax to yield the portion of five hundred and seventeen million dollars not covered by the windfall tax. Such a tax could be spread over two years or three years. An excise on the processing of certain agricultural products is worth considering. By increasing the number of commodities so taxed, by greatly lowering the rates of the old processing tax and by spreading the tax over two or three years, only a relatively light burden would be imposed on the producers, consumers or processors.

30 ❪ A Request for Ratification of the Migratory Bird Treaty with Mexico. March 5, 1936

To the Senate:

WITH a view to receiving the advice and consent of the Senate to ratification, I transmit herewith a convention for the protection of migratory birds and game mammals, between the United

States of America and the United Mexican States, signed at Mexico City, February 7, 1936, and an exchange of notes expressing an understanding between the Governments of the two countries that ratifications are to be exchanged in Washington and the convention will come into force on the day on which ratifications are exchanged.

The convention is similar to the treaty for the protection of migratory birds in the United States and Canada signed August 16, 1916. That convention was unquestionably a great step forward toward the restoration and protection of our migratory birds. But inasmuch as numbers of species of the birds whose protection in the United States and Canada has long been provided for, extend their migrations to Mexico and still farther south, and in order to protect other groups of girds which migrate between the United States and the United Mexican States, it is obvious that effective conservation requires further international cooperation. It is for these purposes that the convention with Mexico has been concluded.

The attention of the Senate is invited to the accompanying report from the Secretary of State and the comment of the Secretary of Agriculture presented therein.

NOTE: A migratory bird treaty between the United States and Great Britain for the protection of all species of birds migrating between the United States and Canada was proclaimed on December 8, 1916, and the Act to give it effect was approved on July 3, 1918. The Federal Government, by the treaty, was given authority to control and administer the migratory bird resources, which included all birds migrating between the United States and Canada. Previously they had been administered by the several States. The Migratory Bird Treaty Act provided, however, for full cooperation between the State and Federal agencies concerned. The Secretary of Agriculture is the officer responsible for the execution of the provisions of the Act. The purpose of the treaty is to insure a greater uniformity of administration and protection of these birds by the two countries.

On February 9, 1920, the President was authorized to propose a similar treaty with the Republic of Mexico. The foregoing message sent the proposed convention to the Senate for confirmation. On March 15,

1937, the convention between the United States and Mexico was proclaimed. It, too, affords additional protection to migratory birds and game mammals. The Migratory Bird Treaty Act was amended by the 74th Congress to extend and adapt its provisions to this new convention between the United States and Mexico.

31 ❮ The President Urges Cooperation between the Management and Employees of the Railroads. March 6, 1936

Gentlemen:

I AM concerned by conditions in the railroad industry. With all the other means of transportation which have become so important and are developing so rapidly, the future of the railroads depends on sustained ability to improve service and, in many cases, reduce rates. Much new equipment is and will be needed. Not all that should be done can be done at once, but if the railroads do not progress, they will retrogress. The opportunities for progress are great and will expand. The danger is that these opportunities will be lost.

The country has a vital interest in this matter, but no one has a greater stake than those who own and those who work for the railroads. In many ways their interests are identical, and they ought to be able to work together for a common end. Certainly this is true of better and less costly service which will enable the railroads to lead, or at least keep up with, transportation progress. What disturbs me is the apparent inability of the managements and the men to cooperate in working out such common problems. Issues which ought to be settled by friendly negotiation are being fought out in the battle grounds of Congress and the courts. Legislation has its place. Often it has been necessary for the welfare of labor or capital or both, but it is a remedy to be taken with great caution or it may prove worse than the disease.

A critical situation prompts this letter. It is common knowledge that there is much waste in railroad operation, caused by the great number of railroad companies, and that much of it can be avoided, either by consolidations or by greater cooperation and coordinated use of various facilities. This waste hampers railroad progress and is a burden on the rate-paying public. It ought to be eliminated for the good of all concerned, and conditions favorable to its elimination are now developing. I say this because the tide of traffic is rising. Under such conditions unnecessary and wasteful work can be avoided with least hardship to employees, because new work comes in to take the place of much that goes.

In the long run, the employees will surely gain from maximum efficiency and economy in railroad operation. With competitive conditions what they now are and promise to become, this is the only path to the increased traffic and revenues which the railroad future will require. But sudden steps in this direction may cause temporary hardships. The employees are fairly entitled to protection against such hardships.

The Emergency Railroad Transportation Act, 1933, undertook to promote the elimination of railroad waste and at the same time to protect the employees. This protection is now satisfactory neither to the companies nor to the employees, and by the terms of the Act it will, unless extended, terminate on June 16th, next. It is a matter which is capable of being settled to better advantage by negotiation than by legislation. Given sufficient time, the managements and the men ought to be able to agree, in their common interests, upon a reasonable plan of protection.

If they do not agree and legislation is sought as the only solution, I fear harm to the railroad industry. Both sides will take extreme positions. The effect of such legislation may be to discourage and prevent progress. Litigation will ensue. The courts may strike down what is attempted, so that the battle ground will again shift to Congress. The relations between the managements and the men will be embittered, with unfortunate results in many different ways.

All this can be avoided if the contending parties will confer with each other in a spirit of reasonableness and moderation. The employees ought not to forget what they will gain if the railroads can progress as transportation agencies and what they will lose if the railroads retrogress. They ought to bear in mind that the principle of protecting employees against undue hardship from economy projects is only beginning to gain ground. It is not as yet applied by most industries, nor by the other transportation agencies, nor even by the Government. The railroad industry has always taken the lead in the establishment of good working conditions and labor relations, but it cannot safely get too far in advance of the procession. Nor ought the employees to overlook the fact that if unnecessary railroad costs are not avoided, much desirable work that creates employment may not be undertaken. This has happened in maintenance work especially, and may easily happen again.

On the other hand, the managements ought to bear in mind that the principle of employee protection is steadily finding acceptance among responsible employers. It has been applied on the British railways and utilities. It has been voluntarily applied by certain large industries in this country, including several railroad companies. It is sound and right, and leading railroad executives have so stated. The railroads and their owners have much to hope for employee good-will and morale if an amicable adjustment of this matter can be reached. They have even more to hope for if they are able to develop among themselves the capacity for collective action and a willingness to subordinate pronounced individual views in the interest of effective cooperation.

Convinced, as I am, of the great benefits which will accrue to the railroad industry, to its employees, and to the country if this matter can be adjusted satisfactorily to both parties, I address you, as representatives, respectively, of the managements and the men, to express the hope that no effort will be spared on either side to reach such an adjustment. May I suggest that before you permit such an effort to fail, you confer jointly with me?

The Federal Coordinator of Transportation, acting under the mandate of the Emergency Railroad Transportation Act, 1933, is proposing certain orders directed toward the unification of railroad terminal facilities. As above stated, the protection to railroad employees which that Act affords is now satisfactory neither to the managements nor to the men. In view of the proposed negotiations, I have asked the Coordinator, and he has consented, to defer these proposed orders for a time.

Very sincerely yours,

Mr. J. J. Pelley
President, Association of American Railroads,
Washington, D. C.
and
Mr. J. A. Phillips
Vice Chairman, Association of Railway Labor Executives,
Cedar Rapids, Iowa

NOTE: The Emergency Railroad Transportation Act, 1933, Title I, contained provisions for the protection of railroad labor. (See Item 47, Vol. II.) They were to the effect, among other things, that no railroad employee in service during May, 1933, should be "deprived of employment such as he had during said month of May or be in a worse position with respect to his compensation by reason of any action taken pursuant to the authority conferred by this title." This had the effect of preventing, or greatly limiting, any economies from coordination projects which the railroads might have voluntarily undertaken under the Act, or which the Federal Coordinator of Transportation might have ordered. During his term of office, the Federal Coordinator endeavored to have substituted for these provisions, under legislative authority, a plan of dismissal compensation for employees affected by coordination projects which would afford them reasonable protection, but would be less restrictive than the aforementioned provisions; and a bill was drafted to accomplish this result. However, this bill was not acted upon.

During the third year of the Coordinator's term of office, however, enough employees who had been in service in May, 1933, had died or retired so that there was some opportunity for economies, notwithstanding the restrictive provisions. The Coordinator therefore decided to force the issue by stating that he contemplated, after due opportunity had been given for conferences with and representations from the railroad managements and employees, issuing orders requiring terminal unification at several comparatively small, but typical, places.

Strong protests ensued from both managements and employees. In the circumstances, the foregoing letter of March 8, 1936, was sent by me to Mr. Pelley, President, Association of American Railroads, and to Mr. Phillips, Vice Chairman, Association of Railway Labor Executives. This letter, briefly, pointed out that the labor-protection provisions of the Emergency Act were not then satisfactory either to the companies or to the employees; it showed the desirability of providing reasonable protection by agreement rather than by legislation; it urged the managements and the men to confer on this matter with a view to reaching an agreement; and it stated that I had asked the Coordinator, and he had consented, to defer his proposed orders for a time.

In my statement of March 19, 1936 (see Item 40, this volume), I indicated that the negotiations so inaugurated had reached an impasse, but that I had asked the carriers and the employees to continue the negotiations, and that they had agreed to do so. In the meantime, I had indicated to the Congressional leaders my desire that the continuance of the negotiations be not allowed to interfere with the consideration of pending legislation bearing on the subject of railroad coordinations.

After intervention by me, the negotiations between the representatives of the managements and the employees continued, and an agreement was eventually reached "concerning allowances to railroad employees affected by the joint action of two or more carriers with respect to unification, consolidation, merger or pooling, in part or in whole, through separate railroad facilities or any of the operations or services performed by them through such separate facilities." This agreement was announced in a joint statement issued May 21, 1936, by George M. Harrison, Chairman of the Railway Labor Executives Association, and H. A. Enochs, Chairman of the committee representing the railroad managements.

This agreement was a very constructive step. So far as ultimate results are concerned, however, I regret to say that so far there have been none of importance. It has since been applied in only a very few minor cases. In other words, there has been little progress in coordination projects or consolidations.

32 ❲ A Letter on Allotment of Funds for Crop Production Loans. March 9, 1936

My dear Senator:

THIS is in reply to the letter of March 5, 1936, addressed to me by yourself and other members of the Senate Committee on Agriculture and Forestry, with respect to the allotment of funds under my Executive Order of February 28, 1936, for the purpose of making loans to farmers during the year 1936 for production of crops.

I note that you and your committee members are of the opinion that at least $28,500,000 should be immediately allotted for the making of these loans and are requesting that this be done.

In my Executive Order I set aside, or earmarked, not to exceed $30,000,000 for this purpose, of which $7,000,000 was immediately allotted, and I stated that additional allotments would be made from time to time as might be necessary. I propose to carry out this program. The Governor of the Farm Credit Administration advises me that an additional $13,000,000 will be required on or about March 20th, at which time I shall cause that sum to be made available. He further advises that additional funds may be required on or about April 10th, at which time I shall take the necessary action to see that such amount as may be shown to be necessary is supplied. I cannot see why this arrangement should not be satisfactory to all concerned.

It is not practicable to make an immediate allotment of all of the funds estimated to be required, since it is necessary to follow the routine of drawing in unobligated balances from various allotments of emergency funds and making them available for the making of crop production loans. This will be done, of course, as rapidly as possible and in ample time to meet the needs of the Farm Credit Administration.

I trust that the foregoing will be sufficient to assure you and the members of your committee that adequate provision will be made for providing funds for the making of the loans in question as the need for them becomes necessary.

Sincerely yours,

Honorable E. D. Smith,
Chairman, Committee on Agriculture and Forestry,
United States Senate.

NOTE: On the subject of crop pro-   Item 18, Vol. IV; Item 25, this volduction loans, see Item 29, Vol. III;   ume.

33 ❨A Proposal of a Survey for Possible Outlet for Farm Products Abroad. March 10, 1936

Dear Chester:

As you well know, the fortunes of American agriculture in the next few years are certain to be closely linked with the world economic situation, and particularly that of Europe.

The agricultural industry of this country never could have expanded profitably to its present scope if it had not found substantial markets beyond our own borders. The shrinkage of these markets following the World War, and particularly following the enactment of the Smoot-Hawley tariff of 1930, placed the American farmers in a desperate plight from which only such measures as the Agricultural Adjustment Act and the present Soil Conservation and Domestic Allotment Act could partially rescue them.

Since 1933, there have been extensive changes in the economic policies of foreign countries and in international trade relationships, and further changes are in prospect. Future plans made by farmers of this country will depend in large measure on the extent of their outlets abroad. For that reason, I believe it would be advantageous to them if someone who will have an important part in shaping those plans could survey conditions in Europe at first hand.

115

I am therefore suggesting that you, as Administrator of the Agricultural Adjustment and related Acts, arrange as soon as possible to undertake such a survey.

I feel that during the more than two years that you have administered the farm program, it has been brought through its most critical phases. I believe that it will be not only in your own best interest but in the best interests of the American farmers for you to take a little time away from the arduous duties of active administration, and to size up trade conditions in Europe as I have suggested. And I feel very strongly that your services to the farmers of this country will be more valuable than ever when you return.

Very sincerely yours,

Honorable Chester C. Davis,
Department of Agriculture.
Washington, D. C.

33A ❲ Presidential Statement on the Foregoing Proposed Survey. March 10, 1936

CHESTER C. DAVIS, as Administrator of the Agricultural Adjustment Act and related Acts, has been selected to make a special study for the United States Government of economic conditions in Europe which have a direct bearing upon agricultural programs already undertaken or being planned in this country.

In requesting him to make this study for our Government, Secretary Wallace and I have had in mind the distinguished service Mr. Davis has given American Agriculture, especially during the past two and one-half years. As Administrator, he has been directing governmental efforts which, to a considerable degree, were made necessary by changes in the European outlets for American farm products.

Information to be gathered by him at close hand into the precise nature and extent of these economic changes abroad is expected to assist greatly in developing American farm programs.

Mr. Davis plans to sail for Europe about March 20th. During the absence of Mr. Davis, H. R. Tolley, nationally known agricultural economist, director of the Giannini Foundation and formerly Assistant Administrator, will be Acting Administrator of the Agricultural Adjustment Act, and as such will be in direct charge of the present work of developing the programs under the new Soil Conservation and Domestic Allotment Act.

34 ⟨ The President Reaffirms the Administration's Program for the Development of the Great Lakes–St. Lawrence Seaway and Power Project. March 11, 1936

THE Great Lakes-St. Lawrence Seaway and Power Conference at Detroit is a welcome and significant event. Farm and civic leaders from all sections and official representatives of States and cities are assembling, for a most practical purpose, on the border between Canada and the United States.

The immediate objective of the Conference is the support of constructive measures to utilize the natural resource of the chain of inland seas and connecting rivers which form one of the great frontiers of the world. It has been the historic policy of the two Nations to use this frontier solely as an instrumentality of peace.

Under this policy, an opportunity is now presented to complete a seaway comparable in economic value to the Panama Canal. The public development of St. Lawrence power is inseparably linked with the navigation project.

The improvement of this great resource for the dual purposes of navigation and power is an important part of the program of the present Administration. It will enable us to take the next step to extend to the Northeast benefits already assured from works completed or under construction in the Tennessee Valley in the Southeast, at Boulder Dam in the Southwest, and on the Columbia River in the Northwest.

117

I wish the Conference at Detroit to be assured not only of continued unremitting effort to complete the seaway and power development, but also of my strong conviction that recent events have helped to clear the way for action, upon the broadest lines of public benefit.

In a message to the United States Senate, I pointed out that the construction of dams and locks in the 120-mile stretch of the St. Lawrence River, between Lake Ontario and Montreal, is virtually all that is required to complete the seaway from the head of the lakes to salt water, and that the same works will provide an abundant supply of cheap power in proximity to a great industrial and rural market.

At that time, I stated the belief that this improvement is without any question going to be completed in the near future and that it should be carried forward by both Nations instead of by one. That is my view today.

Such a development as we propose to carry out in the Great Lakes-St. Lawrence Basin unquestionably will result in greater activity for all ports and transportation agencies. This has been the history of all new navigation projects and improvements directed to better commercial communication in this country and throughout the world. The fear that the seaway will result in injury on the lower Mississippi or to our Atlantic ports is groundless.

The use of electric energy is gaining so rapidly today that no sane person would dare to assert that after the seven years required for construction of works, St. Lawrence power would provide a surplus above actual needs. As a matter of fact, careful studies have shown that there will be a serious shortage of electric energy in the Northeast before the project can be completed.

The Tennessee Valley project demonstrates the advantage of unified planning to develop the resources of a great river basin. If the whole of the Great Lakes Basin were all in one country, either in the United States or in Canada, its development would surely have been completed years ago. The mere fact that this natural resource is shared by two countries should not be allowed to hold back an improvement promising the same social and economic gains to both countries.

To expedite action, it is necessary and desirable to adapt existing plans for the improvement of the Great Lakes-St. Lawrence Basin to the mutual interests and respective needs of the two countries. This is obviously required if we are to secure prompt ratification by both Nations.

The Great Lakes-St. Lawrence Treaty of 1932 has not been ratified in either country. Something further than mere submission of a treaty is called for under these conditions.

We are seeking, therefore, a new approach to the problems involved in the many projects for improvements in the Great Lakes-St. Lawrence Basin.

The solid basis of good-will and cooperation which exists between the United States and Canada, their common interest in the development of the Great Lakes-St. Lawrence Basin for navigation and power and the present and future needs of the Province of Ontario and the State of New York for dependable sources of cheap power supply will, I am confident, prove helpful factors. As the result of years of study, and with mutual recognition of well-established rights, it should be unnecessary to enter into lengthy negotiations or to discard thoroughly tested engineering plans.

It is inconceivable that either of the two Nations, bound together by such a tradition of international amity, should stand in the way of the other's utilization of its share of such a great common resource when such use becomes desirable or necessary to its economic progress. It is certain that a plan of development is feasible which, while enabling each Nation to meet its requirements, will not demand of the other any undertaking with which it feels itself unprepared to proceed.

Let us be realistic and frankly face the fact that delays have not been due to any failure of negotiations to reach an accord among the four sovereignties involved: the Federal Government of the United States, the Dominion Government of Canada, the Province of Ontario and the State of New York. Delay has sprung, rather, from fears of economic harm to special localities or to special interests, which I have always believed are grossly exaggerated, and especially from opposition based upon the fact that the power available in these boundary waters is publicly owned and will be generated and distributed, under existing laws, by public agencies in both Canada and the United States.

Provision for the public use of St. Lawrence power was made under a contract between the Dominion Government and the Province of Ontario in 1932. A similar accord, also contingent upon ratification of a treaty, was reached between the United States Corps of Engineers and the Power Authority of the State of New York and upon my recommendation was ratified in 1933 by the United States House of Representatives. Considering all the elements involved, I am more than ever convinced that means can be found to go forward with the development on terms that will serve public requirements.

The Great Lakes-St. Lawrence project is in keeping with the spirit of the times and with the policy of cooperation now firmly established on this continent.

More than one hundred years ago, the United States and Canada set the first successful example in disarmament by withdrawing ships of war from the Great Lakes. Today these Nations, each respecting the complete sovereignty of the other, share an international border of five thousand miles without a single fort along its entire length. Recently the two Nations took prompt action to effect a reciprocal trade agreement by which prohibitive barriers to mutually beneficial commerce across this frontier have been removed.

In the light of these accomplishments, agreement upon the construction of useful works to serve the needs of both countries should present no insuperable difficulties. This is especially true when we consider that these works will enhance the usefulness of the substantial improvements already made by each country as integral parts of a seaway already complete over most of the distance from Duluth-Superior to the Atlantic. And we must remember that equal navigation rights are guaranteed to both Nations over the entire system under treaties which are in force today.

For the United States and Canada to demonstrate the full value of such a policy on a frontier that spans a continent would contribute immeasurably to security and progress in the Western Hemisphere.

With the will to cooperate present, I feel we may look forward confidently to the early undertaking of this project on terms acceptable to the two great neighboring Nations.

NOTE: Since the defeat of the St. Lawrence Treaty in the Senate in 1934 (see Item 7, of Vol. III), several steps have been initiated in preparation for a reconsideration of the entire undertaking as soon as possible.

During July and August, 1934, informal discussions proceeded between Acting Secretary of State Phillips and Prime Minister Bennett of Canada, looking toward the reopening of treaty negotiations, for it was considered advisable to make certain revisions in the treaty before resubmitting it to the Senate. From these preliminary conversations it appeared that circumstances would defer somewhat the reconsideration which I felt necessary.

At my request the New York Power Authority cooperated with the Department of State and with the National Resources Committee insofar as its surveys affected the Great Lakes-St. Lawrence basin.

In my speech at Bonneville Dam August 3, 1934 (see Item 137, Vol. III), I referred to the St. Lawrence project as one of the four outstanding national yardsticks for electric rates.

On August 18, 1934, in connection with a seaway demonstration at the Milwaukee Tercentenary celebration, I sent the mayor a telegram in which I pointed out that I was still greatly interested in the Great Lakes-St. Lawrence seaway, not only as a great international highway for shipping, but also as a fourth yardstick in the power development projects already started by the Federal Government on the Colorado and Columbia Rivers and in the Tennessee Valley.

On November 12, 1934, the Power Authority of the State of New York submitted to me its report on the cost of distribution of electricity (see Item 175, of Volume III). This report showed that for residential use and for small commercial customers the cost of developing and distributing electricity was low enough to warrant very drastic reductions in the rates which were then being charged. The report treated particularly with that part of the United States which would be a potential market for power from the St. Lawrence River, the findings affecting about 7,000,000 customers. A total of twenty-nine cities in six States were included in the survey.

The year following the issuance of this report witnessed the largest aggregate of electric-rate reductions in New York State in recent years, including the establishment of the first promotional rate schedule ever offered to residential customers in New York City.

During December of 1934, the National Resources Board, in its comprehensive reports to the President on public works planning, indicated the availability of the Great Lakes-St. Lawrence development as an important part of the national public works program, including not only the proposed seaway but also the development of power.

During 1935 efforts to prepare the St. Lawrence Treaty for resubmission to the Senate were complicated by a proposal to revive the old treaty between Canada and the United States for development of power on the Niagara River. This Convention had been signed in 1929, but had been rejected unanimously in 1931 by the United States Senate Committee on Foreign Relations, on the ground that it represented a gift of additional power at Niagara Falls to private interests (see Note to Chapter IV and Item 29 in Vol. I).

The imminence of a general election in Canada, involving the possibility of a change in administra-

tion, further complicated the situation in 1935 and delayed further progress in the direction of reopening negotiations between the two Governments. The general election took place in Canada in October, 1935, and as a result, the Rt. Hon. W. MacKenzie King succeeded the Rt. Hon. R. B. Bennett as Prime Minister.

Therefore by this time, on both sides of the border, national administrations responsible for the old treaty which had been defeated in the United States Senate in 1934 had been superseded. A modified treaty, including all problems involved in a planned utilization of the entire Great Lakes-St. Lawrence basin for the benefit of the people on both sides of the water, seemed possible. It was among the subjects of conversation between Prime Minister MacKenzie King and myself when he visited me in Washington on November 9, 1935.

Throughout the year 1935 I conferred numerous times with Chairman Walsh of the New York Power Authority, in order that there might be no delay in taking the matter up after the Canadian elections. Following my conversation with the Canadian Prime Minister, when it had become apparent that a settlement of the problems at Niagara must be associated with any general treaty covering development of the Great Lakes-St. Lawrence basin, I asked Chairman Walsh and Vice Chairman Manly of the Federal Power Commission to prepare a joint informal report on the Niagara situation as a guide to further action in the matter. This report was submitted to me on December 20, 1935.

Between January 1 and March 11, 1936, when the foregoing message was delivered to the Seaway and Power Conference in Detroit, preparations went forward for a new approach to the problem which would take cognizance of the need for including a comprehensive plan for dealing with the Niagara Falls problem. It was felt that the situation was ripe for continuing the objectives of the two international agreements affecting the Great Lakes-St. Lawrence basin which had failed of ratification. In this way the two Nations could cooperate in a constructive settlement of all the major problems of this great boundary resource.

Throughout this period I conferred frequently with Chairman Walsh and other representatives of the Power Authority. Memoranda dealing with important phases of the matter were prepared and given careful consideration. At my request the Power Authority maintained close contact with Secretary Hull and other representatives of the State Department. Informal conversations with the Canadian Government were resumed.

Prime Minister MacKenzie King informed the Canadian Parliament that his Government was prepared to consider the details of plans submitted from Washington with reference to the project. The Seaway and Power Conference adopted a resolution again endorsing the project and calling for the formation of a central organization to coordinate and unify the activities of all the associations, municipalities and other agencies interested. The result was the creation of the National Seaway Council.

Representatives of the National Seaway Council conferred with me on September 16, 1936, presenting a statement outlining their program of action. On December 1, 1936, the National Resources Committee in its report to me recommending a policy for planning, programming, timing and division of costs of public works, included the Great Lakes-St. Lawrence Seaway as part of its plan.

Meanwhile, during the months following the Detroit conference, the activities of the State Department and the Power Authority, in preparation for a reopening of active negotiations, continued. I kept in close touch with these activities and, at my request, as a preliminary to my visit to Canada on July 31, 1936, a series of memoranda was prepared dealing with all important phases of the situation.

Following the election of November 3, 1936, it appeared that these preliminary activities had reached a point at which it would be possible to approach the Canadian Government more formally, with a view to determining the possibility of joint consideration of the broad settlement of the problems of the Great Lakes-St. Lawrence basin which I envisaged. On November 12, 1936, I, therefore, conferred with Chairman Walsh of the New York Power Authority, and arrangements were initiated which led to the conferences in Ottawa on December 4th and 5th, at which representatives of the United States met with Prime Minister MacKenzie King, the members of his cabinet and other representatives of the Dominion of Canada.

The negotiations initiated have continued through the year 1937, including the study of a carefully revised treaty draft. Obstruction continues both in Canada and the United States from the usual two sources — political controversy on both sides of the Niagara and St. Lawrence Rivers, and private power influence in both Nations.

In view of the universal increase in power use and the wide sentiment for a seaway from the Lakes to the Ocean, and because of the generally favorable trend of public opinion in Canada and the United States, I am confident that accord, followed by construction, will not be long delayed.

35 ⟨ White House Statement on the Replies to the President's Suggestion for an Inter-American Conference. March 17, 1936

Replies have now been received from the Presidents of all of the American Republics with the exception of the Republic of Paraguay. The letter addressed by the President to the former President of Paraguay was not received until just after the recent overturn of the Government in Paraguay. Owing to the fact that the new Government has just been recognized by the United States, it has been possible only within the last few days for the President to send a similar letter to the new President of Paraguay. The Government of Paraguay, however, has officially stated to the press that if and when Colonel Franco, the new President of Paraguay, receives such a letter from the President of the United States, he would be glad to reply immediately, expressing his desire to cooperate in the proposed inter-American conference.

All of the replies received have expressed the full and cordial approbation of the President's suggestions and the desire of the American Republics to cooperate enthusiastically in order to assure the successful achievement of the purposes indicated by the President in his recent letter. The majority of the letters received were written within forty-eight hours after the receipt of the President's letter.

Many of the letters contain specific suggestions as to the program which should be undertaken in the proposed conference, and some of the Governments have informed us that more detailed and specific suggestions as to the agenda would be communicated shortly through diplomatic channels.

All of the Governments have expressed their accord with the President's suggestion that the conference be called to convene in Buenos Aires, and the President of Argentina, in his reply, has said:

"I take pleasure in offering Buenos Aires as the seat of the proposed conference, accepting the suggestion which Your Excellency formulated of holding the conference in its midst. I esteem it as a great honor, for which I am deeply grateful."

During the next weeks, there will be continuing communications between this Government and the Governments of the American Republics with a view to obtaining unanimous agreement on the program and agenda for the conference. Until it can be ascertained how long this preparatory period will take, no date can be fixed for the conference.

36 ❦ A Message to the Congress on Appropriations for the Continued Relief of the Unemployed. March 18, 1936

To the Congress:

IN MY budget message of January 3, 1936, I reserved making a recommendation for an appropriation for the relief of unemployment, stating that an estimate and recommendation could be better made at a later date. I am now prepared to submit such a recommendation, and this message should be regarded as supplemental to the budget message.

In asking the Congress for an appropriation to meet the needs of the destitute unemployed during the coming fiscal year, certain facts should be clearly set forth.

(1) Since the spring of 1933, there has been a gain in reemployment in each successive year. At least 5,000,000 more people were at work in December, 1935, than in March, 1933.

(2) In spite of these great gains, there are at present approximately 5,300,000 families and unattached persons who are in need of some form of public assistance — 3,800,000 families and unattached persons on the works program and 1,500,000 on local and State relief rolls. Every thinking person knows that this problem of unemployment is the most difficult one before the country.

(3) These figures, large as they are, do not of course include all those who seek work in the United States. In none of these figures are included the many unemployed who are not on relief but who are experiencing great difficulties in maintaining independent support. Neither are there included many others not on the relief rolls who are content with occasional employment; nor some who are so constituted that they do not desire to work; nor many young people who cannot get work and are obliged to share the livelihood earned by their parents. Because of the impossibility of an exact definition of what constitutes unemployment, no figures which purport to estimate the total unemployed in the Nation can be even approximately accurate.

(4) Nearly all the 1,500,000 unemployable families or unemployable unattached persons are being cared for almost wholly from State or local funds. A very small number of these families or individuals have begun to receive a comparatively small amount of Federal aid under the provisions of the Social Security Act.

The foregoing figures indicate the problem before us. It is a problem to be faced not merely by the Congress and the Executive, not merely by the representatives of Government in the States and localities, but by all of the American people. It is not exclusively the problem of the poor and the unfortunate themselves. It is more particularly the problem of those who have been more fortunate under our system of Government and our economy.

It will not do to say that these needy unemployed must or should shift for themselves. It will not be good for any of us to take that attitude. Neither will it do to say that it is a problem for the States and the localities. If we concede that it is primarily the duty of each locality to care for its destitute unemployed, and that if its resources are inadequate, it must then turn to the State for help, we must still face the fact that the credit and the resources of local governments and States have been freely drawn upon in the last few years and they have not been sufficient.

It has been said by persons ignorant or careless of the truth that Federal relief measures have encouraged States, counties and municipalities to shirk their duty and shift their financial responsibilities to the Federal Government. The fact is that during 1935 State and local governments spent $466,000,000 for emergency relief, which was 13 percent more than these governmental bodies spent in 1934; 49 percent more than they spent in 1933; and 58 percent more than they spent in 1932. Let it also be noted that the great majority of State and local governments are today taking care not only of the 1,500,000 unemployables, but are also contributing large amounts to the Federal works program.

To expect that States and municipalities should at the present time bear a vastly increased proportion of the cost of relief is to ignore the fact that there are State constitutional limitations, and the fact that most of our counties and municipalities are only now emerging from tax delinquency difficulties. Let us further remember that by far the largest part of local taxes is levied on real estate. To increase this form of tax burden on the small property owners of the Nation would be unjustified. It is true that some States, fortunately few, have taken an undue advantage of Federal appropriations, but most States have cooperated wholeheartedly in raising relief funds, even to the extent of amending State constitutions. It is not desired in the next fiscal year to encourage any States to continue to shirk. The Federal Government cannot maintain relief for unemployables in any State.

Relief of the Unemployed

The Federal Government, then, faces the responsibility of continuing to provide work for the needy unemployed who cannot be taken care of by State and local funds.

During the current fiscal year, the cost of relief actually paid out of the Treasury will amount to approximately $3,500,000,000.

During the next fiscal year, 1937, more than $1,000,000,000 will be spent out of the Treasury from prior year appropriations. Practically all of these expenditures will be from allocations made to large projects which could not possibly be completed within this fiscal year. In addition to this amount, the budget contains estimated expenditures aggregating $600,000,000 from appropriations recommended for the Civilian Conservation Corps and various public works.

If to this total of $1,600,000,000 there were added $2,000,000,000 to be expended for relief in the fiscal year 1937, the total for this purpose would just about equal the amount that is being now expended in the fiscal year 1936. An appropriation in this amount would be within the limit set by the budget message, and would in effect provide for the third successive year a reduction in the deficit.

This statement as to the budget program of course depends upon the action of the Congress with respect to the substitute taxes, the reimbursement taxes and the new taxes which I have recommended to replace the lost revenues and to supply the new revenue made necessary by the decision of the Supreme Court invalidating the Agricultural Adjustment Act and by the action of the Congress in appropriating for the immediate payment at the 1945 value of the Veterans' Adjusted Service Certificates. This latter action, as you will recall, requires additional revenue in the amount of $120,000,000 annually for nine years. The agricultural program requires annual substitute taxes of $500,000,000 and there must be raised within the next three years $517,000,000 of revenue to reimburse the Treasury for processing taxes lost in this fiscal year by reason of the Supreme Court's decision.

I am, however, not asking this Congress to appropriate $2,000,000,000.

I am asking only for an appropriation of $1,500,000,000 to the Works Progress Administration. It will be their responsibility to provide work for the destitute unemployed. This request together with those previously submitted to the Congress to provide for the Civilian Conservation Corps and certain public works will, if acted upon favorably by the Congress, give security during the next fiscal year to those most in need, on condition, however, that private employers hire many of those now on relief rolls.

The trend of reemployment is upward. But this trend, at its present rate of progress, is inadequate. I propose, therefore, that we ask private business to extend its operations so as to absorb an increasing number of the unemployed.

Frankly, there is little evidence that large and small employers by individual and uncoordinated action can absorb large numbers of new employees. A vigorous effort on a national scale is necessary by voluntary, concerted action of private industry.

Under the National Recovery Administration, the Nation learned the value of shorter hours in their application to a whole industry. In almost every case, the shorter hours were approved by the great majority of individual operators within the industry. To the Federal Government was given the task of policing against the minority who came to be known as "chiselers." It was clear that "chiseling" by a few would undermine and eventually destroy the large, honest majority. But the public authority to require the shorter hours agreed upon has been seriously curtailed by limitations recently imposed by the Supreme Court upon Federal as well as State powers.

Nevertheless, while the provisions of the anti-trust laws, intended to prohibit restraint of trade, must and shall be fully and vigorously enforced, there is nothing in these or any other laws which would prohibit managers of private business from working together to increase production and employment. Such efforts would indeed be the direct opposite of a conspiracy in restraint of trade. Many private employers believe that if left to themselves they can accomplish the objectives we all seek.

We have learned the difficulties of attempting to reduce hours of work in all trades and industries to a common level or to increase all wage payments at a uniform rate. But in any single industry we have found that it is possible by united action to shorten hours, increase employment, and, at the same time, maintain weekly, monthly or yearly earnings of the individual. It is my belief that if the leaders in each industry will organize a common effort to increase employment within that industry, employment will increase substantially.

In so far as their efforts are successful, the cost to the Federal Government of caring for the destitute unemployed will be lessened, and, if the employment gains are substantial enough, no additional appropriation by the next Congress for the fiscal year 1937 will be necessary.

The ultimate cost of the Federal works program will thus be determined by private enterprise. Federal assistance which arose as a result of industrial disemployment can be terminated if industry itself removes the underlying conditions. Should industry cooperatively achieve the goal of reemployment, the appropriation of $1,500,000,000, together with the unexpended balances of previous appropriations, will suffice to carry the Federal works program through the fiscal year 1937. Only if industry fails to reduce substantially the number of those now out of work will another appropriation and further plans and policies be necessary.

It is the task of industry to make further efforts toward increased output and employment; and I urge industry to accept this responsibility. I present this problem and this opportunity definitely to the managers of private business; and I offer in aid of its solution the cooperation of all the appropriate departments and agencies of the Federal Government.

My appeal is to the thinking men who are assured of their daily bread. However we may divide along the lines of economic or political faith, all right-minded Americans have a common stake in extending production, in increasing employment, and in getting away from the burdens of relief.

Those who believe that Government may be compelled to assume greater responsibilities in the operation of our industrial system can make no valid objection to a renewed effort on the part of private enterprise to insure a livelihood to all willing workers. Those, on the other hand, who believe in complete freedom of private control without any Government participation should earnestly undertake to demonstrate their effectiveness by increasing employment.

NOTE: In my budget message of January 3, 1936 (see Item 2, this volume), I indicated that if relief appropriations were limited to $2,000,000,000, it would be possible to reduce the Federal deficit for the third successive year. However, I did not make a specific recommendation to the Congress at that time as to the emergency relief appropriation for the fiscal year 1937, stating in my message that an estimate and a recommendation could be better made at a later date when the results of current economic trends could be more accurately observed.

By March, 1936, I had decided that the time had come for a reduction in Federal expenditures on the Works Program. All available economic indicators bore out the belief that basic recovery was an established and continuing fact. The Federal Reserve Board's index of industrial production during the early months of 1936 stood at 93 percent of the 1923-25 average, or about 7 percent above the level in March, 1935, and about 55 percent above March, 1933. Reemployment, as indicated by the Bureau of Labor Statistics index of employment in manufacturing industries, had also increased since March, 1935, and, like industrial production, showed signs of further improvement. Works Program employment passed its peak at the end of February, 1936, and a rapid decline in the total was anticipated during the succeeding months.

Accordingly, the foregoing message of March 18, 1936, recommended an emergency relief appropriation of $1,500,000,000 to the Works Progress Administration. I pointed out that an appropriation of this amount, together with appropriations previously recommended for the Civilian Conservation Corps and certain other public works, would take care of the workers in most serious need provided that private employers absorbed an increasing number of the unemployed workers who were on relief or employed on the Works Program during the spring of 1936. As a result, the Congress appropriated the sum of $1,425,000,000 for relief and work relief in the Emergency Relief Appropriation Act of 1936, which I approved on June 22, 1936.

Between the peak in February,

1936, and the end of December, 1936, total employment on the Works Program, including C.C.C. enrollees, decreased from 3,836,000 to 2,988,000. However, during the summer of that year an emergency arose in the midwestern and western States as a result of the drought which made it necessary to provide emergency employment for approximately 350,000 farmers and farm workers. Although industrial production continued to increase, the index reaching a point in January, 1937, about 30 percent above the figure for March, 1935, reemployment in private industry proceeded at a much slower rate. The Bureau of Labor Statistics index of manufacturing employment in January, 1937, was 11.9 percent higher than it had been for the month of March, 1935. As a result of the drought and the failure of reemployment in private industry to absorb a sufficient number of unemployed workers in need, I recommended, in a message to the Congress sent on January 11, 1937 (see Item 240, this volume), an additional appropriation of $790,000,000 for relief and work relief to carry the Works Progress Administration and related programs through June 30, 1937. This recommendation resulted in an appropriation of $789,000,000 for these purposes, which was approved by me on February 9, 1937.

During the winter of 1936-37, the emergency drought sufferers who were still in need of assistance were transferred to the Resettlement Administration which provided them with relief grants and rehabilitation loans. Other Works Program employment continued to decline throughout the winter and at the end of June, 1937, 2,526,000 workers were employed, including C.C.C. enrollees. W.P.A. employment had declined from the maximum of 3,035,000 in February, 1936, to 1,821,000 in June, 1937.

37 ❮ Immediate Steps Taken to Prevent Loss of Life and Destruction of Property by Spring Floods. March 18, 1936

Memorandum for:

> The Secretary of War
> The Secretary of the Treasury
> The Acting Secretary of the Navy
> The Federal Administrator of Works Progress and Relief
> Director of Civilian Conservation Corps
> Chairman of the American Red Cross

I REQUEST that you act as a Committee to determine and to carry out such plans as may be necessary on the part of the Federal Government to prevent loss of life, distress and destruction of property arising from spring floods.

Every necessary agency of the Federal Government should give whatever aid is requested by you.

Your Committee should, of course, keep in close touch with Governors and local officials of the States affected.

Use of Government equipment in such an emergency is hereby authorized.

The Secretary of War will act as Chairman of the Committee.

A copy of this letter is being sent to Rear Admiral Cary T. Grayson, Chairman of the American Red Cross. Please keep in constant touch with him.

NOTE: In the spring of 1936 there were extensive floods in the New England States, Pennsylvania, New York and the States of the Ohio valley, as a result of an unusually early thaw following a severe winter. The foregoing memorandum indicates how the various Government agencies went into action at once to bring relief to flood sufferers.

All of the agencies mentioned in the foregoing memorandum cooperated in the work of flood relief. W.P.A. workers went into action in crews, helping to move families, furniture and valuables from danger zones, spreading warning to persons living in the path of flood waters, and cabling down small buildings to prevent them from washing away. Dikes, sandbag barricades and abutments were built or strengthened to prevent the spread of flood.

Food, bedding and clothing were distributed to refugees. In numerous instances the timely assignment of all W.P.A. workers and C.C.C. workers to emergency operations did much to reduce the loss of life and property. In many localities W.P.A. workers and C.C.C. workers were taken from their regular projects and sent to danger zones before flood crests arrived. Similarly after the flood had passed, thousands of W.P.A. workers were made available to assist in the extensive repair and rehabilitation work necessary throughout the devastated areas.

Working in cooperation with public health authorities, W.P.A. workers were concentrated in flood areas to prevent epidemics of contagious and infectious diseases resulting from the water pollution and unsanitary conditions which always come from flood.

See also Items 38, 41, 42 and 54 of this volume.

38 ❡ A Plea for Contributions to the American Red Cross for the Alleviation of Suffering in the Flood Areas. Proclamation No. 2161. March 19, 1936

FLOOD waters raging throughout eleven States have driven 200,-000 people from their homes, with every indication that this number may be materially increased within the next twenty-four hours. In this grave emergency the homeless are turning to our great national relief agency, the American Red Cross, for food, clothing, shelter and medical care.

To enable the Red Cross to meet this immediate obligation and to continue to carry the burden of caring for these unfortunate men, women and children until their homes are restored and they can return to normal living conditions, it is necessary that a minimum relief fund of three million dollars be raised as promptly as possible.

As President of the United States and as President of the American Red Cross, I am, therefore, urging our people to contribute promptly and most generously so that sufficient funds may be available for the relief of these thousands of our homeless fellow citizens. I am confident that in the face of this great need your response will be as immediate and as generous as has always been the case when the Red Cross has acted as your agent in the relief of human suffering.

(See also Items 37, 41, 42 and 54 of this volume.)

39 ⁅ The President Suggests Cooperation by Farmers in the Soil Conservation Program in Their Individual and National Interest. Presidential Statement. March 19, 1936

THREE weeks ago, when I signed the Soil Conservation and Domestic Allotment Act, I said that this Administration had not abandoned and would not abandon the goal of equality for agriculture. I pointed out that although the Act is addressed primarily to the serious and long-neglected problem of soil conservation, the reestablishment and maintenance of farm income were also a major objective.

Today, as a national soil conservation program is being launched in accordance with the Act by the Agricultural Adjustment Administration, the need for protecting not only the soil, but also farm prices and income appears even greater than when the Act was adopted.

This fact has been made evident by the reports of farmers' intentions to plant compiled by the Department of Agriculture. These reports, announced a few days ago, showed that farmers were planning an increase of 19 percent in their acreage of spring wheat, 6 percent in their acreage of corn, 11 percent in rice, 9 percent in tobacco, and 8 percent in peanuts. These reports are not compiled for cotton, but unofficial reports circulated in the trade and recorded in the press have indicated an increase of around 15 percent in cotton acreage.

In conformance with the Supreme Court's decision, the farmers' production control programs have been stopped, but their chronic surplus problem goes on. Export markets for wheat, pork, and tobacco, lost following the enactment of the Smoot-Hawley Tariff of 1930, have only in small part been regained. The huge carryover of cotton which was accumulated during the years leading up to 1933 has not yet been reduced to normal. Although reduction has progressed well for three years, the carryover is still probably twice as big as it ought to be for the maintenance of a reasonable price in the future.

Although the production control programs have been stopped, farmers are not entirely at the mercy of unbridled competition with their fellow producers, as they were in the years preceding 1933. The new farm act provides for financial assistance by the Government to those farmers who, heeding the warnings contained in the intentions-to-plant reports, wish to shift from the production of unneeded surpluses of soil-depleting crops to the production of needed soil-building crops.

I believe that farmers will find the new program is in the national interest, and in their own individual interest, too. Every farmer takes pride in the productivity of his soil. Every farmer wants to hand on his farm to his children in better shape than he found it. The conservation payments offered by the Government in accordance with the Act will help him to do this.

If farmers for any reason should fail to take advantage of the new Act, and especially if they should carry out their intentions as indicated in the Department of Agriculture reports, the consequent excessive production of such cash crops as cotton and wheat and tobacco might result once more in the wrecking of their prices and the mining of their soil. But if the farmers, in operating the soil conservation program, display the same energy and cooperative spirit which they showed in making the production control programs work, they will go far to protect both their soil and their income. This is an appeal to all farmers to cooperate for their own and the national good to help in preventing excessive production.

Congress has gone as far as it could within judicial limitations to enable farmers to keep the gains they have made in the last three years and to permit their buying power to continue the powerful upward lift it has given to national recovery.

I hope that farmers will not complete their plans for this year's crops until they have had opportunity to study the new Act and that all those to whom it offers advantages may cooperate in the program now being launched.

NOTE: The benefits to the United States from the A.A.A. programs, which were declared in large part unconstitutional by the United States Supreme Court, and which were succeeded by the soil conservation program discussed in the foregoing statement and in Item 28 of this volume, were felt throughout the land almost from the beginning of the programs.

In my message of March 16, 1933, I stated that a new means would have to be found to rescue agriculture. I do not think that it is an exaggeration to say that the means adopted did rescue agriculture.

During the three years between 1932-35 the contribution of agriculture to the national income rose from 5.7 percent to 10.3 percent, equaling the percentage of 1929. Cash farm income rose from its low point of $4,377,000,000 in 1932 to $7,201,000,000. Cash net income above operating expenses, taxes and interest rose from $1,473,000,-000 in 1932 to $3,869,000,000, a rise of 163 percent. On this basis,

although farm population increased by about 830,000 during these three years, the per capita cash net income rose in the same period from $48 to $122.

It is true that this gain was offset in part by an increase in prices of things farmers had to buy. Allowing, however, for an increase of 17 percent in prices farmers paid for all products used by them both in living and in production of their crops, the purchasing power of cash income from farm production was still 41 percent greater in 1935 than in 1932. Allowing for an increase of 15 percent in prices farmers pay for things used only in living, the purchasing power of the cash income of farmers above expenses available for living was still 129 percent greater in 1935 than in 1932.

Farm prices as a whole had moved up during these three years by 66 percent. The greatest gains in price and in income were made in products for which production control measures had been taken — cotton, wheat, corn, hogs, rice, tobacco and peanuts. The price recovery for these products amounted to 120 percent as against 46 percent for prices of other commodities.

Surpluses had come down drastically as production was cut by the adjustment programs and by the 1934 drought. By July 1, 1936, the wheat carryover of July 1, 1933, of 378,000,000 bushels had dropped to 142,000,000 bushels. By August 1, 1936, the United States carryover of American cotton had fallen from 9,600,000 bales in 1932 to 5,300,000 bales. The surplus 386,000,000 bushels of corn in 1933 had fallen by October 1, 1936, to 180,000,000 bushels. The tobacco surplus of 1933 had been cut by a third; the hog surplus had declined by 19,-300,000 head.

This agricultural prosperity which had returned during these three years was reflected also in an upturn in farm real-estate values and a reduction of farm foreclosures and farm bankruptcies. It was accompanied by increased wages to farm laborers. From 80 percent of the pre-war average in 1933, farm-wage rates increased to 98 percent of pre-war average in 1935.

Of equal importance with returned farm income, particularly so far as the future was concerned, were the benefits derived by the soil of the United States from the adjustment program. Increased income removed the pressure upon farmers to destroy the fertility of their soil by continually increasing

their crops. Encouragement was given by the program to farmers to shift parts of their land to feeding crops which improved soil fertility and provided protection against erosion. The adjustment program both encouraged and required a more careful use of land. In 1934, 35,800,000 acres or one-tenth of the Nation's total cultivated acreage was shifted from production of corn, wheat, cotton and tobacco. In 1935 production on 31,000,000 acres was thus shifted. Most of this acreage was put to uses which tended to conserve and maintain its productivity. Only an insignificant percentage was allowed to remain idle.

The recovery of agriculture contributed, of course, to general recovery. Restored purchasing power on the part of the farmers provided a restored market for increased factory production. The extent to which agriculture's recovery helped general recovery in the Nation is reflected not only by the figures of recovery in business and industrial establishments, but more particularly in the marked increase of automobile registrations in rural areas; in the sales of the two largest mail-order houses doing a large proportion of their business with farmers; in the increase in the amount and value of rural retail sales; in the increased sales of fertilizer, gasoline and rural life insurance; in improved rural banking conditions; in increased electricity consumption in the rural districts; and in the great increase in freight shipments into the agricultural areas of the United States.

The decisions of the Supreme Court declaring parts of A.A.A. unconstitutional (see Item 4, this volume and the Introduction to Volume IV) necessitated many changes in fiscal plans and other operations. The decision invalidated the production control activities which had been carried on by A.A.A. by means of voluntary contracts. The decision, however, did not discontinue the following functions which have continued to be exercised by the Department of Agriculture under the original statute and related legislation: establishment and enforcement of marketing agreements and orders; surplus removal operations; loans on agricultural commodities; destruction of diseased animals; the establishment of quotas for the importation of sugar and allotments under such quotas.

The extent of the program executed under the Agricultural Adjustment Act by the end of 1935 is set forth in the note to Item 152, Vol. IV.

Shortly after the Agricultural Adjustment Act was invalidated on January 6, 1936, by the Supreme Court so far as its production-adjustment provisions were concerned, it was estimated that between $250,000,000 and $300,000,000 remained to be paid by the A.A.A. in connection with contracts already entered into.

Funds were appropriated by the Congress (Pub. No. 440, 74th Congress; 49 Stat. 1109, approved February 11, 1936) to complete benefit payments to farmers who had signed product adjustment contracts, where the farmers had complied with the contracts but where funds were unavailable because of the invalidation of the processing taxes.

By the close of 1937 the production-control programs were virtually liquidated. Of the $296,000,000 appropriated by Congress in Public No. 440 some $39,000,000 was used or recommended to be used for other purposes, leaving a net balance of about $257,000,000 for liquidation of the adjustment programs. Through December 31, 1937, some $252,000,000, or 98 percent, of the above net balance, was actually disbursed.

40 ❡ White House Statement on Impasse in Railroad Consolidation Negotiations. March 19, 1936

THE President has been informally advised by the representatives of the carriers and employees who have been negotiating over a proposed railroad consolidation plan that a virtual impasse has been reached in these negotiations.

The President has personally requested both sides to continue the negotiations in an effort to reconcile the differences.

In response to this request from the President the carriers and employees have agreed to continue the negotiations.

In the meantime the President has also indicated to the Congressional leaders his desire that the continuance of these negotiations not interfere with the consideration of pending legislation bearing on the subject of railroad consolidation.

The President has received assurances from the Congressional leaders that they will proceed with consideration of this legislation.

NOTE: For a statement relative to the negotiations referred to in the foregoing statement, the reader is referred to Item 31, this volume.

41 ⟨ The Two Hundred and Eighty-fourth Press Conference (Excerpts). March 19, 1936

(This special Press Conference to discuss emergency measures being taken in connection with flood relief was called by the President subsequent to a conference held by him with Admiral Grayson of the Red Cross, the Secretary of War, Harry Hopkins of W.P.A., Robert Fechner of C.C.C., and others, on the same subject.)

THE PRESIDENT: This is the latest information, not for quotation.

We have had this meeting. The Secretary of War is the Chairman, and all Government departments are completely coordinated in this relief situation. The important thing to stress is, I think, that the Red Cross is principally concerned. I have issued a Proclamation, of which I think you have copies, asking for contributions to the Red Cross in accordance with the usual custom.

This money is absolutely essential to the Red Cross because they handle the problems of clothing, food and lodging and furniture — providing temporary shelter for people and things like that, and medicine. They also cooperate with the municipalities in repairing private houses so that they can be made habitable. There are, of course, a very large number of houses in which the cellars and ground floors have been under water for a day or two.

The second agency is the C.C.C., and they have been doing extraordinarily good work. In that connection there is a rather good human interest feature with respect to this particular flood which is rather new. The Chief of Staff says that one of the outstanding things that has happened in the last forty-eight hours is the information as to exact situations that has been furnished by the C.C.C. amateur radio sets. For instance, on the dam above Johnstown, after the papers had come out with large headlines as to the dam going out, the Army picked up a message from one of the C.C.C. boys who said, "I am sitting on top of the dam and it has not gone out because I am still sitting on it." (*Laughter*) "And it is not going to go out." Of course it did not go out. Now, that kind of information is extremely valuable.

The C.C.C. in every locality where we have camps is providing labor to rescue people and to do patrol work pending the arrival of the militia. They are guarding property, and clearing away the worst part of the debris.

The third agency, the relief workers under Mr. Hopkins, are being used in practically every community. Their task is to clean up and build dikes, as they are doing right here in Washington. Then, as soon as the waters go down, the W.P.A. workers will assist the municipalities and counties and towns in restoring the water supply, restoring the flooded sewers, so that they will work, helping to put the light lines and the telephone lines back into commission, making the highways passable and assisting in building temporary bridge structures, where the bridges have gone out.

And then the fourth phase of it relates to actual rescue work. Of course there is not, at the present time, a very great deal of that. That is being handled by the Coast Guard, and, more or less, under the general direction of the Army, the Chief of Staff. Both the Army and the Coast Guard are participating in that work. The Navy hasn't sent in boats yet because we apparently have enough floating equipment from other sources. It is bringing medical supplies in, cooperating with the health authorities and the Army.

General Markham reports that at Pittsburgh the situation was that the flood reached its crest last night at 9 P.M. at a stage of 46 feet; that at 10:30 this morning it had receded to 39.4 feet and is dropping rapidly.

The power, light and telephone service is out; the water supply south of the Monongahela River is cut off and the central heating is off, but the lights will be resumed tonight. The police and the National Guard are in good and effective control, and the thing seems to be well in hand.

At Sharpsburg, many people were marooned, but all have been gotten out. Apparently twenty persons lost their lives, however, in and around Sharpsburg. The dam near there, which it was feared might go out because it is under construction, is last reported to be okay.

At Johnstown — an Army officer arrived there last night and said this morning that conditions are not as bad as reported. The big dam seems to be safe. There are about 17 feet of water in the downtown section but it is receding quickly. Loss of life has been from 7 to 16. The Red Cross has its relief stations going. Medical supplies are adequate. Food is somewhat deficient, but is beginning to come in in quantity. Selected men from the C.C.C. are in control of policing; and today two thousand W.P.A. workers started to clean up the town. The worst of the crisis is over.

I think that is about all. You will do a service if you will point out that the chief thing we want now is contributions to the Red Cross fund. We will handle this as we have handled other emergencies such as earthquakes and so forth in the past. That is the principal task today.

Q. They ought to put the bee on all the boys today. They collected their expense money. (*Laughter*)

THE PRESIDENT: So far as my plans go, if things are definitely improved tomorrow, we shall go tomorrow, and if not we shall go the next day.

Q. Will you have a Press Conference tomorrow?

THE PRESIDENT: I haven't any other news. If the flood continues, we shall all be pushed on that.

Q. Have you any idea of how much the Red Cross will need for this flood work?

THE PRESIDENT: About three million dollars. Isn't that right, Cary?

ADMIRAL GRAYSON: (*Chairman, American Red Cross*) Yes, sir.

(See also Items 37, 38, 42 and 54 of this volume.)

42 ⟨ White House Statement on Allocation of Funds for Repairs and Replacement of Public Property Damaged by Floods. March 21, 1936

THE President today allocated to the Works Progress Administration $25,000,000 for repairs or replacement of publicly owned property or utilities which have been destroyed or damaged by floods. This sum, which is in addition to an emergency allotment of $18,411,633 made on February 29, will be apportioned to the stricken States as needed.

In making the allocation, the President has given the Works Progress Administration blanket authority to restore roads, streets, bridges, sewers, water and electric plants, and other damaged public properties. The funds previously made available will be used to fight the threat to health which has arisen in many quarters where the waters have receded.

The President pointed out that, with the exception of food and clothing furnished by the Federal Surplus Relief Corporation and from W.P.A. women's projects, direct relief needs were being met by the American Red Cross and by local welfare agencies in the stricken areas. W.P.A. funds generally, he said, would be spent in reestablishment of public improvements. . . .

43 ⟨ White House Statement on the Appointment of a Committee to Formulate a Plan for the Reorganization of the Executive Branch of the Government. March 22, 1936

IT WAS announced at the White House today that the President has appointed a committee to make a careful study of the relation of the Emergency Agencies to the regular organizations of the Executive branch of the Government.

Louis Brownlow of Washington was named chairman of this committee with Charles E. Merriam of Chicago and Luther Gulick of New York as the other members. This committee will serve as an adjunct of the National Emergency Council which will provide the necessary office facilities and such personnel as the committee may require.

The President requested that the new committee present its report to him in time for submission to the 75th Congress of such recommendations as may be based on the report.

The White House also made public a letter from the President to the Vice President asking the Senate to cooperate with the President and with the new committee through a special committee which the Senate has already established to consider certain aspects of the same problem.

A letter from the President to the Speaker of the House was made public at the same time. This letter asks the House to create a committee of a similar character through which the House can cooperate with the President and with the committee just established. There follow the texts of the President's letters to the Vice President and to the Speaker. The letters are identical except for their last paragraphs.

43A ❨ Letters to the Vice President and the Speaker of the House in Reference to the Foregoing Plan. March 22, 1936

My dear Mr. Vice President:

LAST October I began holding some conversations with interested and informed persons concerning what appealed to me as the necessity for making a careful study of the organization of the Executive branch of the Government.

Many new agencies have been created during the emergency, some of which will, with the recovery, be dropped or greatly curtailed, while others, in order to meet the newly realized needs of the Nation, will have to be fitted into the permanent organization of the Executive branch. One object of such a study would be to determine the best way to fit the newly created agencies or such parts of them as may become more or less permanent into the regular organization. To do this adequately and to assure the proper administrative machinery for the sound management of the Executive branch, it is, in my opinion, necessary also to study as carefully as may be the existing regular organization. Conversations on this line were carried on by me during November and December, and I then determined to appoint a committee which would assist me in making such a study, with the primary purpose of considering the problem of administrative management. It is my intention shortly to name such a committee, with instructions to make its report to me in time so that the recommendations which may be based on the report may be submitted to the 75th Congress.

The Senate already has established a special committee to consider certain aspects of this same problem, and I write to you to ask that the Senate, through its special committee, cooperate with me and with the committee which I shall name in making this study, in order that duplication of effort in the task of research may be avoided and to the end that it may be as fruitful as possible.

Sincerely yours,

The last paragraph of the letter to the Speaker read as follows:
The Senate has named a special committee to consider aspects of this general problem, and I respectfully suggest that the House of Representatives also create a special committee of a similar character through which the House of Representatives could cooperate with me and with the committee that I shall name in making this study in order that duplication of effort in the task of research may be avoided and to the end that this study may be made as fruitful as possible.

Very sincerely yours,

NOTE: The report of this committee was submitted by me to the Congress in my Message on Reorganization of the Executive Branch of the Government on January 12, 1937 (see Items 241 and 241A of this volume).

44 ❬ "New Approaches to Old Problems" — Address at Rollins College, Florida, on Receiving Honorary Degree. March 23, 1936

President Holt, ladies and gentlemen:

I DO not need to tell you that I am personally deeply honored in becoming an alumnus of Rollins College, not alone because of my deep interest in the work that is being so splendidly carried on here, but also because of the long-time personal friendship between your President and myself.

And there are two other reasons why I shall never forget the distinction that has been conferred on me by the President of the greatest institution of learning in the State of Florida. They are two reasons that have a lighter touch. It is the first time that I have had the privilege of seeing my better half in cap and gown.

And, finally, I have attained a life-long ambition: At last my literary qualities have been recognized. They have been recognized not because I have published books — and here my friends of the press are going to wiggle and squirm — I am sure it is because in the older days I used to be editor-in-chief of my college paper.

But to come back to Rollins. It is because of the varied culture, the tireless industry and the independent thinking of Doctor Holt that his old friends everywhere in this country were not at all surprised when he substituted new ideas in education for old ideas.

These changes fearlessly inaugurated at Rollins are bearing fruit. They are being watched by educators and literary people all over. The very fact that in some respects they break away from some of the old academic moorings ought not to startle us. In education, as in politics, and in economics and social relationships, we hold fast to the old ideals, and all we change is our method of approach to the attainment of those ideals. I have often thought that stagnation always follows standing still. Continued growth is the only evidence that we have of life.

Yet growth and progress invariably and inevitably are opposed — opposed at every step, opposed bitterly and falsely and blindly. About a week ago I saw a very remarkable film, a picture of the life of Louis Pasteur; and in that film the great English chemist, Lister, said to Pasteur when Pasteur was being denounced as a charlatan and an impostor: "My dear Pasteur, every great benefit to the human race in every field of its activity has been bitterly fought in every stage leading up to its final acceptance."

And if that is true of the sciences, it is true of everything else that enters into our lives — true of agriculture, true of living conditions, true of labor, true of business and industry, and true of politics.

What has taken place at Rollins illustrates what I speak of as new approaches to old problems. If you abolish lectures and recitations and substitute the conference plan of study, you do not abandon the old ideals of culture. An amazing increase in the very number of things which an educated man must know today calls not only for more facts, but calls also for what might be called the third dimension in education — the tying together of all of the subjects and all of the facts into the relationship of their whole with modern life.

Just as you and I, and, indeed, the Faculty and the students in any college throughout the land, reach conclusions individually and collectively, so do the masses of our people individually and collectively approach governmental problems. All of us are greatly influenced by environment, by the people we see every day, by what we might call group association. If we analyze what a group is, we find that the family group is the oldest, the smallest, and yet through all the years of change the most important. And there are other groups to which almost every man and woman is tied, connected in some way. They are connected with some form of association — the church, the social circle, the club, the lodge, the labor organization, the neighboring farmers, the political party. Even business and commerce are almost wholly made up of groups.

The fact of this group existence and resulting group thinking brings forward one of the great problems of orderly Government functioning.

It is the problem of Government to harmonize the interests of these groups which are often divergent and opposing, to harmonize them in order to guarantee security and good for as many of their individual members as may be possible. The science of politics, indeed, may properly be said to be in large part the science of the adjustment of conflicting group interests.

In the community, local government must adjust small groups for community good. In States larger groups must be coordinated for the greater good of all the people within the State. In the Federal Government the problem is to adjust still greater groups in the interests of the largest group of all — a hundred and twenty-five million people in whom reposes the sovereignty of the United States of America. But it is well to remember that the individual citizen contributes most to the good of this largest group only when he or she thinks in terms of the largest group. Only if the spirit of that is carried out can democracy and the republican form of government permanently succeed.

Not long ago two nationally known gentlemen visited me, one in the morning, the other in the afternoon. I asked the opinion of each of them in regard to a suggested new tax to replace a former tax which had been declared unconstitutional. My friend of the morning replied, "I could not approve of that kind of tax. It would cost me many thousands of dollars." My friend of the afternoon said, "Why, a tax like that would, it is true, cost me many thousands of dollars, but I am inclined to think, Mr. President, that it is a fair tax, a tax equitable for the people of the Nation, the people as a whole, and, therefore, I would favor it."

There is the illustration! There is the illustration, and you can multiply it a thousandfold. If I were to write down the opinions of all who come to see me in every walk of life and from every part of the country, I could give you example after example teaching the same lesson — the individual who thinks of himself and the individual who thinks of the Nation.

The development of national understanding as opposed to purely individual or local group domination is growing by leaps and bounds throughout the country. It is the logical development of broader and better education. There is no question that, in every State of the Union, education has made greater strides in this generation than ever before in our history. It still has far to go. You and I are doing all we can to further this progress. And the other objective, the other reason perhaps, for a better understanding along national lines is the logical development of the extension, the moving forward of what I have sometimes called the policy of the good neighbor. The good neighbor is not just the man who lives next door to you. The objective includes the relationship not between you and him alone, but it includes the relationship between your family and his; it extends to all the people who live in the same block; it spreads to all the people who live in the same city and the same county and the same State; and most important of all for the future of our Nation, it must and shall extend to all your neighbors, to your fellow citizens in all the States and in all the regions that make up the Nation.

First of all, your duty and mine is to the Nation. If we perform that duty well — you and I — the policy of the good neighbor will in the long run assert itself so strongly, so victoriously, that it will spread to other peoples and other lands throughout the world. The ideal is there — developed to a greater or less extent among the masses of the people in every Nation. We cannot see it in some places, but, under the surface, the ideal is there. We of the Western Hemisphere are working together to prove the practical value of this great ideal of peace and justice among men and among Nations.

May the good work go on.

45 ⟨ Letters on the Continuation of the C.C.C. Program. March 23, 1936

My dear Mr. Fechner:

IN REVIEWING the Emergency Conservation Work program for the period ending March 31, 1937, at which date the emergency conservation work will terminate according to existing law, I have determined that the present number of Civilian Conservation Corps camps shall be maintained unless such camps are reduced as a result of the completion of the work now being performed by the enrollees of any such camps, or the reduction through discharges, separations, or other causes in the number of enrollees to approximately 163 in any one camp.

I have also determined that the total number of enrollees for the Civilian Conservation Corps should be gradually reduced to about 350,000 and this number maintained through March 31, 1937.

It is appreciated that no hard and fast rule can be laid down. You are therefore authorized to take such measures as may be necessary to carry out this general program as nearly as may be practicable.

Additional funds not to exceed $6,825,000 will be allotted to you as and when needed from the appropriation contained in the Emergency Relief Appropriation Act of 1935 for the balance of this fiscal year, and steps will be taken to secure the necessary funds for the fiscal year 1937.

Very truly yours,

Honorable Robert Fechner,
Director of Emergency Conservation Work,
Washington, D. C.

Dear Mr. Buchanan:

I AM enclosing a copy of a letter which I have today written to Mr. Fechner requesting him to maintain the Civilian Conservation Corps at about 350,000 enrollees up to the time the emergency conservation work ceases on March 31, 1937.

This will probably involve an increase in the estimate of $246,-000,000 contained in the budget for the Civilian Conservation Corps for the period July 1, 1936 to March 31, 1937, on the basis of 300,000 men, of whatever amount is determined to be necessary to care for the increase of the number of enrollees by 50,000. An estimate to cover this amount will be submitted in due course through the usual channels.

Very truly yours,

Honorable James P. Buchanan,
Chairman, Committee on Appropriations,
House of Representatives.

NOTE: For discussion of the C.C.C. see Vol. II, Items 21, 31, 90 and 113; Vol. III, Item 65; and Item 50, this volume.

From March 23 to April 8, I was on a fishing trip in the waters near Cat Island, Great Inagua Island, Caicos Island, Mariguana Island, Crooked Island, Andros Island, and others.

46 (White House Statement on Creation of Committee of Industrial Analysis to Review the Results and Accomplishments of N.R.A. March 26, 1936

THE President by Executive Order has created a Committee of Industrial Analysis to complete the summary of the results and accomplishments of the National Recovery Administration and report thereon.

The Committee is headed by Daniel C. Roper, Secretary of Commerce, and includes Henry C. Wallace, Secretary of Agriculture, and Frances Perkins, Secretary of Labor. Other persons outside of the Government subsequently will be appointed to the Committee by the President.

The President has directed the Committee of Industrial Analysis to bring to a conclusion, and to make available to the public, an analysis of the operations of the N.R.A. codes. Members of the Committee, to be appointed from outside the Government, will be asked to prepare a more general and final survey of the administration of Title I of the National Industrial Recovery Act as a whole.

46A (Executive Order No. 7323, Creating the Committee of Industrial Analysis. March 26, 1936

BY VIRTUE of and pursuant to the authority vested in me by the Emergency Relief Appropriation Act of 1935 (Act of April 8, 1935, c. 48, 49 Stat. 115), it is hereby ordered as follows:

1. There is hereby created a Committee of Industrial Analysis to complete the summary of the results and accomplishments of the National Recovery Administration. The Secretary of Commerce shall be Chairman of the Committee, and the other members shall be the Secretary of Agriculture, the Secretary of Labor,

and such other persons, not now officers of the United States, as the President may hereafter specially appoint.

2. The entire Committee of Industrial Analysis shall—

(a) Assemble and analyze the statistical information and governmental records of experience of the operations of the various trades and industries heretofore subject to codes of fair competition formulated under the authority of Title I of the National Industrial Recovery Act (48 Stat. 195); and

(b) Study the effects of such codes upon trade, industrial and labor conditions in general; and

(c) Make generally available information with respect to industry, particularly hours, wages, child labor and other labor conditions, *provided,* That nothing in this Order shall be construed to authorize the Committee of Industrial Analysis to collect from the general public current statistical information, or to duplicate the statistical work now being performed by any existing agency of Government.

3. Those members of the Committee of Industrial Analysis who are hereafter specially appointed shall prepare for the President an adequate and final review of the effects of the administration of Title I of the National Industrial Recovery Act upon particular industries or problems and as a whole.

4. In order to aid the Committee of Industrial Analysis in carrying out its duties and to furnish employment for and assistance to educational, professional and clerical persons, there is hereby created, in connection with the office of the Secretary of Commerce, a Division of Industrial Economics. This Division of Industrial Economics shall be subject to the general supervision of the Committee of Industrial Analysis and shall assist such Committee in carrying out its functions. . . .

6. The files, records, equipment and property transferred to the Department of Commerce from the National Recovery Administration by the authority of Executive Order No. 7252, dated December 21, 1935, shall be made available to the Committee of Industrial Analysis and the Division of Industrial Economics. The employees transferred by said Executive Order shall be eligi-

ble for, but shall not be automatically entitled to, employment under the authority of paragraph 4 (a) of this Order.

7. This Order shall become effective April 1, 1936.

NOTE: This Committee submitted a report on the operation of the N.I.R.A. prepared by those members who had no official relationship to the Government. This report was submitted by me to the Congress on March 2, 1937. It was based upon an exhaustive study of the work of the N.R.A., and represents the first and most adequate survey by an impartial group of the entire program and work of N.R.A., reviewing the objectives, the successes, the failures and all of its many problems, solved and unsolved. The report and the staff studies upon which it is based are now available for further research by persons interested in the many phases of a proper relationship between Government and industry (House Document No. 158 of the 75th Congress, first session).

I think perhaps the best way to summarize the accomplishments of N.R.A. is to quote as follows from Chapter 20 of that report dealing with general estimates of accomplishment, submitted by this impartial board of review:

"GENERAL ESTIMATE OF ACCOMPLISHMENT

"Fundamentally, of course, the problem of evaluating the N.R.A. is one of determining its effects upon the lives of the people of the country. Many of these effects can be considered in terms of their intermediate stages; but industrial recovery, or price levels, or reemployment are ultimately significant only in their relation to the living conditions of human beings. For certain N.R.A. policies, judgment need not be based upon economic or statistical analyses of intermediate changes. It cannot be doubted that the establishment of minimum wages in the codes went far toward alleviating the hardships of the families of lower paid workers. It cannot be doubted that the increased leisure resulting from shortened hours of work not only lessened the effects of fatigue upon the workers themselves, but also brightened the home lives of millions of people. The child labor provisions of the codes immediately eased the lives of the children taken out of industry and offered them greatly improved prospects for the future. These effects cannot be measured, but they were real, and they are of the kind that should be the primary concern of Government.

"N.R.A. gave jobs to something like 2,000,000 workers by spreading work. The increase in the country's total employment between June and October, 1933, the period in which the President's Reemployment Agreement was put into effect, was estimated at 2,462,000, an increase of 6.8 percent, while the increase within industries operating under the Reemployment Agreement was 11.4 percent. This was apparently due to the shortening of hours, which amounted over the same period to 12.7 percent, rather than to any increase of industrial activity. The Brookings Institution estimates the increase directly traceable to shortening of hours under N.R.A. at 1,750,000.[1] The shorter hours were substantially maintained during the subsequent code period up to the time the codes were terminated, but little further reemployment was observable which could be traced to the hour provisions of the codes.

"Shortened hours in some cases led directly to increased output per man-hour and probably had more general indirect effects in this direction. This made possible a partial avoidance of increased labor costs, within the limits of the shortening of hours which actually occurred. At the same time it reduced the direct work-spreading effect.

"N.R.A. brought about a large increase in total wage distributions, which was at least partly neutralized by increasing prices; but it is impossible to isolate the effects on prices attributable to N.R.A., either as a reflection of wage increases in operating costs or as a reflection of the trade practice price provisions.

[1] The National Recovery Administration: An Analysis and an Appraisal, by Leverett S. Lyon, et al., 1935, p. 833.

The full effect of N.R.A. includes an indeterminate part of the anticipatory rise of prices prior to the codes.

"Average wage increases were moderate, though the minimum rates often meant substantial increases, not only in hourly rates but in weekly earnings, for the lowest paid groups who were directly affected by them and who on the whole received the largest increases. Among the higher paid groups, some merely maintained their weekly earnings and a few suffered a positive decrease. As between industries, those paying the lowest wages showed the greatest increase. The general effect, then, was toward reduction of inequalities.

"N.R.A. also brought much needed aid to some of the most hard-pressed business groups. This aid was temporary in some cases, while in many the effect wore off as competitive pressures overcame particular measures intended to restrain them, and as non-compliance increased.

"The moral and economic value of the N.R.A. child labor provisions, which took out of industry a considerable number of persons below proper working age, is clear. The codes also had a clearly beneficial effect in reducing the number of home workers and in improving the condition of the remainder, but without raising their wages to code levels or in general securing satisfactory compliance in this field.

"The public support given by

N.R.A. to the principle of the freedom of labor to organize and bargain collectively was of great and probably lasting importance, out of proportion to the immediate and tangible results secured. A national stand had been taken on a question involving the essential rights of labor. Immediately, the N.R.A. resulted in a large increase in regular union membership and also in the number and membership of company unions. There was a large increase in collective bargaining or similar activity, with some progress toward mutual understanding and adjustment, and also much friction and dispute. The net effect was probably a step forward (though not in all cases) in the long and slow process of adjusting human rights in industry. More specifically Section 7 (a), in requiring the codes to provide that employees should have the right to organize and to designate bargaining representatives free from interference, restraint, or coercion of employers, undertook to define and prohibit the violation of a right that had previously been recognized but for which there had not been any generally applicable legal sanction.[1] The task faced great difficulties, and the attempt to embody the formula of Section 7 (a) in specific working arrangements failed to resolve the peculiarly stubborn conflicts between what different parties considered to be their rights and legitimate interests, and therefore failed to achieve satisfactory results.

"In the opinion of the Committee it is not possible to answer statistically the question whether N.R.A. did or did not contribute to the industrial recovery, which did make evident progress during the N.R.A. period. This is a particular instance of the general fact stated above that the attempt to isolate statistically the effects of N.R.A. from those of other economic factors faces insuperable difficulties.

"It is clear, however, that N.R.A. made a definite contribution toward changing the prevailing mood of the country from apprehension to hopeful effort, and this was vastly important in itself. Business gained confidence, which was no less real because it may have been partly based on exaggerated expectations of what the codes would do. This led, quite definitely in some cases, to forward buying and more liberal production policies, without that urge to dump the product on the market and so to wreck prices, which would have followed the same accumulation of inventory prior to N.R.A. There was, of course, reaction — prompt in respect to the anticipatory boom of 1933, and slower in other instances. But some cumulative effects had been set in motion, and when disillusionment arrived as to the expected effects of particular code

[1] It had been recognized, and supported within limited fields, in the Railway Labor Act of 1926, the Anti-Injunction Act of 1932, and the Interstate Railroad Bankruptcy Act of 1933.

provisions, there was a more solid basis of demand to fall back on.

"Some of the trade practice provisions intended to raise prices, to stabilize prior price increases or to reduce accumulation of inventory, failed to accomplish their intended effect; but some of these 'failures' may really have been moderate successes from the standpoint of general national recovery. This is a commentary on the inadequacy of our knowledge of how to treat the disease of industrial depressions.

"In so far as the anticipatory rise in prices in the early summer of 1933 was maintained, there was probably an incidental contributory recovery factor in inventory profits on goods made under pre-code conditions.

"The general or aggregate effect of code trade practice provisions on prices is impossible to isolate, by means of the available statistics, from the effects of other conditions prevailing at the same time. Mention has already been made of the importance of the general change in the mood of business and of the boom of May-July, 1933, which largely expressed a general expectation of what the codes would do, rather than the effects of actual code provisions, which came later. In a limited number of cases, specific effects can be traced. In these cases in general the effect in either raising or sustaining prices seems unmistakable but was stronger in the early stages of the experiment and later weakened, or in some cases

disappeared entirely, as a result either of lack of compliance or of the stimulus afforded to increased production or of other difficulties. In a few cases prices were actually lowered, as where price filing in some instances led to a more actively competitive market, or where a relatively low minimum price tended to become the general standard.

"Various trade practice measures taken under N.R.A. accomplished certain useful specific things, usually of limited scope. A few individual price wars were stopped. There was some reduction of style piracy, and some desirable standardization of products. The practice of 'loss leaders' was in some degree controlled. The new N.R.A. machinery was able to bring about some improvement in the way of more effective dealing with those admittedly unethical forms of competition which were already outlawed as unfair.

"Under N.R.A. business men came to think more in terms of the common interests of their industry, as expressed, for example, in the idea that only as the industry succeeds, can individual enterprises within that industry gain sound success. This awareness of common interests represents a step in advance, even though it needs to be broadened to include the idea that only as it contributes to a successful national economy can an industry as a whole permanently succeed.

"N.R.A. gave both to rivals in the same industry and to members of different industrial groups an experience of working together, of trying to adjust differences and to formulate a common policy for the general good. The effort itself had value, and because it was made, subsequent efforts may be one step nearer success, if only by avoiding previous mistakes. It is, however, clear that no real commonly agreed-on policy emerged; that the experiment yielded relatively small results in this direction, compared to the total effort.

"If industry should again be confronted with a similar program, it would not attempt to get quite so much in the way of protection against competition, if only because some industries learned on their own account that some of these things did not work. And we think the same may be said as to some of the auxiliary labor provisions of the codes.

"It is possible for critical historians to appraise N.R.A. as an attempt to cure depression by attacking symptoms rather than underlying causes; and to deal with conflicting interests and promote all-round prosperity by way of the general principles of giving everyone a chance to take something from someone else without making much progress toward finding standards of general good by which to determine a just division or one tending to increase the total national dividend. These criticisms might contain a measure of truth worth serious consideration, but as appraisals they would be utterly one-sided. They would fail to recognize the following facts: (1) In this case symptoms became causes of further disturbance; (2) the more fundamental causes of depression were largely beyond the reach of a rescue policy started after these causes had had their effect; (3) relief of symptoms was in itself legitimate and useful, so long as it did not actually hamper cure of the disease; (4) knowledge of causes was imperfect and to wait for deliberate assessment of them so far as known would have prevented prompt action; (5) the same is true of standards for resolving conflicts of interest between groups; (6) N.R.A. was in considerable part an experiment to see how far industry proposals would uncover policies usefully related to causes of depression and would develop means of resolving conflicts of group interests. So regarded, the experiment yielded some results, though not final solutions of the problems raised.

"A permanent policy for the future cannot be absolved on these same grounds from the duty of considering causes and standards. Such a policy should meet more exacting criteria than those proper for judging N.R.A."

47 ❨ Telegram to Admiral Cary T. Grayson, Chairman of the American Red Cross, on Flood Relief. April 7, 1936

I have been in close contact with the Red Cross, various relief administrations, emergency conservation officials and Army officers in Washington. They report that all Federal agencies are cooperating in prompt relief measures. I have allocated $2,500,000 to the Works Progress Administration for immediate emergency work in the affected areas.

48 ❨ "The Period of Social Pioneering Is Only at Its Beginning"—Address to the Young Democratic Club, Baltimore, Md. April 13, 1936

President Fenneman, President Wickham, and you, my friends, young and old, of Baltimore and Maryland and lots of other places:

You who fill this great armory tonight represent a cross-section of millions of young people who have come to maturity since 1929. You are the symbol of young men and women living in every State of the Union, affiliated with every political party and belonging to every so-called stratum of society.

The world in which the millions of you have come of age is not the set old world of your fathers. Some of yesterday's certainties have vanished; many of yesterday's certainties are questioned. Why have some vanished? Why have many been questioned? Because the facts and needs of civilization have changed more greatly in this generation than in the century that preceded us.

I need not press that point with you. You are measuring the present state of the world out of your own experiences. You have felt the rough hand of the depression. You have walked the streets looking for jobs that never turned up. Out of that have come physical hardship, and, more serious, the scars of disillusionment.

159

The temper of our youth has become more restless, more critical, more challenging. Flaming youth has become a flaming question. And youth comes to us wanting to know what we propose to do about a society that hurts so many of them.

There is much to justify the inquiring attitude of youth. You have a right to ask these questions — practical questions. No man who seeks to evade or to avoid deserves your confidence.

Many older people seem to take unmerited pride in the mere fact that they are adults. When youth comes crashing in on them with enthusiasms and ideals, they put on their most patronizing smiles, and pat the young man or the young woman on the shoulder, and in a worldly wise sort of way send them out with what they call their blessing. But — as every young person knows — that is not a blessing; it is a cold shower. What they have really said to you is this: "You're young. Enjoy your enthusiasms and your ideals while you can. For when you grow up and get out in the world you will know better." And the tragedy is that so many young people do just that: they do grow up and, growing up, they grow away from their enthusiasms and from their ideals. That is one reason why the world into which they go gets better so slowly.

Your objective, I take it, in the widest sense is this: an opportunity to make an honest living; a reasonable chance to improve your condition in life as you grow older; a practical assurance against want and suffering in your old age; and with it all the right to participate in the finer things of life — good health, clean amusement, and your share in the satisfactions of the arts, the sciences and religion.

Faced with that objective, it is clear that many of the old answers are not the right answers. No answer, new or old, is fit for your thought unless it is framed in terms of what you face and what you desire, unless it carries some definite prospect of a practical down-to-earth solution of your problems.

During the next few months you are going to read and hear and I think you are going to be thoroughly bored by many so-called answers. There are two or three or four new panaceas in every day's papers. Here is one that I picked out at random from three on the same page of one newspaper. The eminent author suggests a four-point cure for all our ills. I hope you will be as thrilled and excited by them as I was. Here they are:

1. Establish a monetary unit with a definite gold content, subject to change only by the Congress of the United States.
2. Restore convertibility of money into gold coin and restore private ownership of gold.
3. I hope you understand what this means, I do not: Accept responsibility as the world's greatest creditor Nation. Isn't that pretty?
4. And finally, put Federal finances in order.

I ask you what do panacea planks like these offer to you as a way out of the problems that you have been facing today and will get up to face tomorrow morning? Is there opportunity, is there work today, is there assurance for tomorrow, is this the practical, definite answer for which you are looking? Most important of all, in these panaceas, is there even a recognition in that type of panacea of the fact that the youth of America has any problems at all?

No, my friends, you have a right to expect something better than that. You have a right to expect that those in authority will do everything within their power to help restore conditions that make employment and opportunity possible; more than that, you have the right to expect that you will be protected, in so far as humanly possible, from the physical and mental and spiritual ravages of economic and social maladjustment.

Some counselors say, "Confidence and normal prosperity will restore everything—will give us all jobs." They generally mean by that the confidence and prosperity of seven and eight years ago. But, my friends, 1928 and the first seven or eight months of 1929 were no millennium. You and I know the simple fact that while production in our Nation was increasing and profits were increasing in 1928 and 1929, unemployment simultaneously was growing at an astounding rate. Return to the 1928 and 1929 kind of prosperity is no sufficient answer for us. The best that the captains of industry and the captains of the country could do for you before the depression was not good enough then and it is not good enough today.

And you and I know now, that while the total production of America is about back to the high point before the depression, only a little over 80 percent as many human beings are engaged in turning out that production. It does not matter very greatly what the cause of this is. It may be a greater efficiency; it may be the development of new machinery; it may be a variety of other causes as well. We cannot legislate against a greater efficiency nor can we legislate against the use of new tools. Nor would we if we could. But the fact remains. And that fact requires an answer.

Some people tell you that even with a completely restored prosperity there will be a vast permanent army of unemployed. I do not accept that. No man who is sensitive to human values dares to accept it. That is why we are not content merely to restore what is sometimes called prosperity. We propose to attack the problem from every conceivable angle.

We readily admit that a greater purchasing power, far more widely distributed, will mean the consumption of more goods — industrial products and farm products. We know that the production of more goods will mean more employment. Most business men, the great majority of them, believe with us that a greater purchasing power on the part of more people will help; they know that their own businesses will be helped thereby.

To work in unity toward that end constitutes one form of attack, an important one; but there are others which we must not overlook.

Our working population in almost every part of the country increases every year. It increases both because of population increase and because more and more women are working for wages. That is as it should be. But when we face your problems, these increases raise the question as to whether it is not possible and right to limit the active working ages at both ends.

We in your Government are seeking to extend the school age of America, to extend it in every State in the Union, and to make it easier for boys and girls to stay in school. Work out for your-

selves what would happen if all the boys and all the girls of fourteen and fifteen and sixteen and seventeen, who are now working
in industry, found it possible to stay in school until they were at
least eighteen years old. How many jobs would that give to the
young people of the Nation who have graduated from high school
and from college? And, by no means the less important, how much
better equipped would be these youngsters who are now at work
if they could stay in school to the completion of their education?

And, at the other end of life, in the same way, ask yourselves
how many jobs would be created if the great majority of people
who are now over 65 — to take a figure at random — if all of them
were in a position to retire in security for the balance of their
days on earth. And how much greater happiness would such security give to their old age?

There is another angle of reemployment which, from the point
of view of youth, is worth pursuing. I shall point it by an illustration. In a certain manufacturing industry, comparatively a small
industry, the average hours of weekly work were greatly curtailed
under the operation of the National Industrial Recovery Act, and
curtailed, incidentally, with the complete support of the great majority of employers within the industry. When this Act came to
an end — I shall not describe its decease — when it came to an end,
the average hours of work in that industry were a little over 36.4
per week. Since that time the great majority of employers in this
particular industry continued the old N.R.A. scale of hours. But,
gradually, first a few and then a larger number of employers
began lengthening the work week. The result today is that the
average of employment in this industry is nearly 40 hours per
week. Not a serious difference you say. And yet if you figure it
out on the assumption that there were 166,000 men and women
in this industry, 10 percent or 16,000 people have either lost their
jobs or, by working longer hours, are actually preventing 16,000
other people from getting employment. Actually the records show
that 1,400 people lost their jobs and 15,250 other people were
kept from getting work.

It seems reasonable, therefore, that industry can contribute in great measure to the increase of employment, if industry as a whole will undertake reasonable reductions of hours of work per week, while, at the same time, it keeps the average individual's pay envelope at least as large as it is today.

It has always seemed to me that because the practices of employment definitely affect the problems of unemployment, the Government must give, and the Government will give consideration to such subjects as the length of the working week, the stability of employment on an annual basis, and the payment of at least adequate minimum wages. A Government doing that is a Government that is working actively at the answers to your problem.

We do not yet know enough in a changing economic order to guarantee any Nation permanently or completely against times of depression. We believe, however, that steps like these which we have taken and are taking will at least greatly cushion depressions — will prevent the up-curve from rushing to a violent, mad peak of false prosperity and prevent another violent, mad descent into another slough of suffering and disillusionment like the one from which for the last three and a half years we have been surely emerging.

And there is another aspect to the answer which you have a right to expect from us. What are we doing — that is your question — what are we doing about the casualties of depression? Since 1929 those casualties, in America, have run into the millions. They are a charge upon us as a people. I have recognized that fact. And, by every reasonable means, we have sought to care for those casualties — to keep them from the physical suffering of hunger; to keep them from the mental suffering of a loss of American morale.

In regard to all these problems, in regard to every problem that arises, there are counselors these days who say: "Do nothing"; other counselors who say: "Do everything." Common sense dictates an avoidance of both extremes. I say to you: "Do something"; and when you have done that something, if it works, do it some more; and if it does not work, then do something else.

Yes, you young people want action. You believe, as I believe, that the something which needs to be done, can be done. How significantly American it is to believe that.

The vigor of our history comes, largely, from the fact that, as a comparatively young Nation we have gone fearlessly ahead doing things that were never done before. We subdued a wilderness that men said could never be conquered. We established a civilization where others insisted a civilization could not survive. Between 1776 and 1789 we built a Republic, a Government for which, in the extent of its democracy, there had been no precedent — a Government which Royalists declared could not endure.

We did all these things with zest. The very air was exhilarating. We were young; we were getting things done — worthwhile things. And it is part of the spirit of America to believe that now, in our day, we can do equally well in getting things done. Once again, the very air of America is exhilarating.

I, for one, do not believe that the era of the pioneer is at an end; I only believe that the area for pioneering has changed. The period of geographical pioneering is largely finished. But, my friends, the period of social pioneering is only at its beginning. And make no mistake about it — the same qualities of heroism and faith and vision that were required to bring the forces of Nature into subjection will be required — in even greater measure — to bring under proper control the forces of modern society. There is a task which, for importance and for magnitude, calls for the best that you and I have to offer.

There cannot be too many Americans thinking about the future of America. Our country richly endowed today in body, mind and spirit, still has need of many things. But I am certain that one of its chief needs today is the releasing and the enlistment of the spirit of youth.

Do not underestimate the significance of that spirit. Yesterday Christendom celebrated Easter — the anniversary of the Resurrection of Our Lord who, at the beginning of His ministry was thirty years of age and at His death was only thirty-three. Christianity began with youth and, through the last two thousand years, the spirit of youth repeatedly has revitalized it.

Our war for independence was a young man's crusade. Age was on the side of the Tories and the Tories were on the side of the old order. At the Revolution's outbreak George Washington was forty-three, Patrick Henry thirty-eight, Thomas Jefferson whose birthday we are celebrating today was thirty-two and Alexander Hamilton was eighteen.

Our Constitution, likewise, was the creation of young minds. The average age of the men who wrote the Constitution was about forty-four. The qualities of youth are not of a sort that self-satisfied people welcome in 1936 any more than self-satisfied people welcomed them in 1776.

I have used the words "the qualities of youth." Be wise enough, be tolerant enough, you who are young in years, to remember that millions of older people have kept and propose to keep these qualities of youth. You ought to thank God tonight if, regardless of your years, you are young enough in spirit to dream dreams and see visions — dreams and visions about a greater and finer America that is to be; if you are young enough in spirit to believe that poverty can be greatly lessened; that the disgrace of involuntary unemployment can be wiped out; that class hatreds can be done away with; that peace at home and peace abroad can be maintained; and that one day a generation may possesses this land, blessed beyond anything we now know, blessed with those things — material and spiritual — that make man's life abundant. If that is the fashion of your dreaming then I say: "Hold fast to your dream. America needs it."

49 ❨ Address at the Dedication of the New Department of Interior Building, Washington, D. C. April 16, 1936

Mr. Chairman, Mr. Secretary and all of you who are gathered here today at this dedication of the first large, monumental building that was started in Washington in this Administration and is being completed in this Administration:

ON BEHALF of the Government I want to extend my thanks and my appreciation to those who have taken part in the actual construction of the new Interior Department Building: to my old friend, Waddy Wood, the architect, to my old friend, Admiral Peoples, the head of the Procurement Division, and also to those who have been in charge of procuring the materials, of undertaking the contract and especially to the workmen who have done the job.

Every American who loves his country should take to heart the earnest and sensible plea of the Secretary of the Interior for a vigorous, continuing national policy of conservation. As for myself, I am dedicated to this cause. And the Department of Interior, as now constituted, is fully alive to the imperative necessity of protecting and preserving all of our natural resources.

Without a national policy of conservation, a Nation less bountifully endowed than ours would have ceased to exist long ago. The remarkable thing was that the people of the United States were so complacent for so long in the face of exploitation, waste and mismanagement, yes, and even larceny of the natural wealth that belongs to all the people.

But not everybody remained insensible to what was happening. On occasion there came as cries from the wilderness warnings against the ravaging of our forests, the waste of our topsoil and our water supplies, and the dissipation of our oil reserves and mineral deposits. Theodore Roosevelt, for one, when I was a very young man, rose up and battled against this squandering of our patrimony. He, for the first time, made the people as a whole conscious that the vast national domain and the natural resources of the country were the property of the Nation itself and not the property of any class, regardless of its privileged status.

Supported by an awakened country, which by now is beginning to realize the truth of the old warnings, we in these later days have devoted our thoughts and energies to the conservation of that God-given wealth. Employing every agency of Government to protect our birthright we have in the past several years made advances far beyond the hopes of earlier-day conservationists. But the battle goes on and must be carried forward with renewed vigor if future generations are to receive the full benefits that are their due.

This Department, the Department of the Interior, was first known as the Home Department, and it was a pretty good name. It was established four score and seven years ago, and since that time its activities have been intertwined with the internal development of the Nation itself. I found a few days ago the report of the Committee of the House of Representatives which favored creation of this Department over a century ago, and it gives us an interesting picture of the times. This report said:

"The general fact remains unaffected that war and preparations for war have been practically regarded as the chief duty and end of this Government, while the arts of peace and production, whereby Nations have subsisted, civilization advanced, and happiness secured, have been esteemed unworthy of the attention, or foreign to the objects of this Government. It seems to us that this should not always continue, but that we should, as a wise people, reorganize the Government so far as to fulfill these duties also, which are suggested by the nature, aspirations and wants of our race as physical, moral and intellectual beings; that it should do something toward protecting the people against those internal enemies — ignorance, destitution and vice — as well as against those foreign foes who may invade or who it is apprehended may assail us."

Think of the time when that was written, nearly a hundred years ago, and think of the progress that has occurred since those days.

And so, the Department of the Interior came into being with

a Secretary in the President's Cabinet, a Secretary who had juris-
diction over four people, the Commissioner of the General Land
Office, the Commissioner of Patents, the Commissioner of Indian
Affairs and the Commissioner of Pensions.

I am wrong, he had jurisdiction over one more person, the only
employee, a chief clerk at $2,000 a year.

Mr. Secretary, we have grown up since 1849; you have more
than five people under you today.

As the country expanded and the needs of the people grew, the
activities of the Interior Department broadened to new fields of
endeavor. I like to think that this building speaks for the progress
we are making every year.

In the design for the building, architects have been guided by
sound principles of utility and economy. Without sacrificing any
of the dignity deserving of a great department of the Federal
Government, they have conceived a useful building, a building
of practical simplicity. They have been sparing in the application
of rich ornament, but convenience, comfort, and sunlight have
not been sacrificed.

I think that we have acted wisely in erecting this new building at this time. We have incorporated it in our public works
program, which was established as a means of providing sorely
needed employment in the building trades and the industries
supplying them, and which has already been successful in aiding
the return of the Nation to better times. This building rising
above us is but a unit of our great public works program which
is erecting thousands of schoolhouses, hospitals and other public
buildings in every State of the Union.

Other factors in addition to the problem of relieving unemployment influenced our decision to erect this building without further delay. The great Federal family in Washington, like other
large families, has its own serious housing problem. We have
grown over a long period of years until governmental buildings
have been taxed to capacity, and every available square foot of
space put to necessary use.

Government departments have been forced to seek space in

buildings other than those owned by the Federal Government. We are now leasing several million square feet of office space in over a hundred privately owned office buildings and have been obliged, in a few cases, even to find quarters in residences and apartment houses. We are eager to complete this building for the practical purpose of reducing the rent bill of the family. When this building is in use, many Government workers will be gathered back under a roof owned by the Government of the United States.

As I view this serviceable new structure I like to think of it as symbolical of the Nation's vast resources that we are sworn to protect; and this stone that I am about to lay, as the cornerstone of a conservation policy that will guarantee to future Americans the richness of their heritage.

> (The President, in laying the cornerstone, said, "I think it will be interesting to you to know that the trowel which I am about to use is the same trowel that was used by the first President of the United States, in 1793, in laying the capitol cornerstone itself. I think it is a good augury.")

50 ⟪ A Radio Address on the Third Anniversary of C.C.C. April 17, 1936

To THE million and a half young men and war veterans who have been or are today enrolled in the Civilian Conservation Corps camps, I extend greetings on this third anniversary of the establishment of the first C.C.C. camp. Idle through no fault of your own, you were enrolled from city and rural homes and offered an opportunity to engage in healthful, outdoor work on forest, park and soil-conservation projects of definite practical value to all the people of the Nation. The promptness with which you seized the opportunity to engage in honest work, the willingness with which you have performed your daily tasks, and the fine spirit you have shown in winning the respect of the communities in which your camps have been located merit the admiration of the entire country. You and the men who have guided and supervised your efforts have cause to be proud of the record the C.C.C. has made in the development of sturdy manhood and in the initiation and prosecution of a conservation program of unprecedented proportions.

I recall that on July 17, 1933, at a time when the corps was just getting into stride, I predicted that through the C.C.C. we would graduate a fine group of strong young men, trained to self-discipline and willing and proud to work. I did not misjudge the loyalty, the spirit, the industry, or the temper of American youth. Although many of you entered the camps undernourished and discouraged through inability to obtain employment as you came of working age, the hard work, regular hours, the plain, wholesome food, and the outdoor life of the C.C.C. camps brought a quick response in improved morale. As muscles hardened and you became accustomed to outdoor work you grasped the opportunity to learn by practical training on the job and through camp educational facilities. Many of you rose to responsible positions in the camps. Since the corps began, some 1,150,000 of you have been graduated, improved in health, self-disciplined, alert, and eager for the opportunity to make good in any kind of honest employment.

Our records show that the results achieved in the protection and improvement of our timbered domain, in the arrest of soil wastage, in the development of needed recreational areas, in wildlife conservation, and in flood control have been as impressive as the results achieved in the rehabilitation of youth. Through your spirit and industry it has been demonstrated that young men can be put to work in our forests, parks, and fields on projects which benefit both the Nation's youth and conservation generally.

NOTE: The foregoing speech was made on the third anniversary of C.C.C. At the time of this writing the C.C.C. has passed the fourth year of its activities.

The benefits of this new venture in unemployment relief and con-servation work have been apparent on every hand.

At the end of the fourth year it had supplied direct work to almost 2,000,000 people. It had enabled enrollees to contribute $350,000,000 by allotment from their pay toward the support of their dependents. It had supplied purchasing power by buying more than $800,000,000 worth of food-stuffs, wearing apparel, machinery and other supplies. It had improved the morale and physical health of more than 1,500,000 young men at an age when they might have been forming habits of idleness, which would have affected their entire lives.

The C.C.C. has provided a long-range conservation program, which has enhanced the present and future values of the country's natural resources. It has saved and improved vast areas of forest land; it has helped to control soil erosion, reduce flood damage and increase the recreation facilities of the Nation.

Its benefits were felt in every State in the Union. Using C.C.C. funds, 7,436,321 acres of forest land were added to our national forests, 65,511 acres for wild-life protection, 199,214 acres were added to the national parks.

The work in forests, parks and fields included forest protection, forest culture, prevention of erosion, reforestation of denuded and burnt-over acres, preservation of the woods from fires, pests and diseases, the construction of trails, lookout houses, outside telephone systems, water facilities, and training for fire fighting.

The work of the C.C.C. has increased recreational opportunities in national parks, Government forests, State forests and in State, county and metropolitan parks.

Lodges, cabins, trails, museums, lakes, water and sewage systems, picnic and camp-ground developments, and better fishing facilities have all been added for the public's use.

Many thousands of acres of unused public range lands have been reclaimed and improved for grazing by the construction of tanks and reservoirs, the digging of wells, construction of dams, revegetation, erosion control and the construction of trails and driveways.

The C.C.C. men have worked on the game refuges in revegetation, construction of fire guards, fences, trails, dams and the development of springs and water holes. It has played an important part in the development of the migratory water-fowl refuges. It has directly assisted in the expansion and development of a nationwide system of wild-life refuges without parallel in any other country. It has cooperated with the United States Bureau of Fisheries, National Park Service and United States Forest Service, in the improvement of streams and ponds and the restocking of waters with fish.

It has helped in flood control indirectly by controlling erosion and fire, and by planting forests. It has helped directly by building dams and other flood-control projects. It has reclaimed and saved millions of acres of land by its work on drainage.

In the early days of C.C.C. I authorized work on Indian Reservations, and the enrollment of Indians, by Executive Order No. 6131, May 12, 1933, and Executive Order No. 6147, May 26, 1933. Drought conditions had brought the Indians to extreme destitution. As a result, however, of the steady employment and adequate food their condition has improved. It is estimated that about 50,000 Indians have been employed by the C.C.C. since 1933.

The greatest and most worthwhile achievement of the Corps, however, was the help given to the young men themselves. There were 1,500,000 of them, and more than 135,000 veterans. They were given employment, shelter, clothing, food, self-discipline, practical training, a good chance at a camp education, and a chance to help support their families. No one will ever be able to estimate in dollars and cents the value to the men themselves in morale, in health and in adaptability to later competitive life.

For further discussion of C.C.C. see Items 21, 31, 90 and 113 of Vol. II; Item 165, Vol. III; Item 45, this volume.

51 ❪ A Letter to the Daughters of the American Revolution on National Defense. April 20, 1936

My dear Mrs. Becker:

I HAD looked forward with pleasure to the opportunity to appear this year before the 45th annual Continental Congress of the Daughters of the American Revolution. You will understand, I am sure, why that is not now possible. I shall be grateful, however, if you will extend my cordial greetings to the officers and delegates assembled.

This Administration, as you know, stands for adequate national defense. It stands, also, for the policy of the good neighbor. These are not contradictory principles. As they are followed by this Administration they represent an expression of the purpose of peace.

There is much confusion of thought and some unnecessary apprehension on this matter of national defense. There are sincere and patriotic people who have been led to believe that our military and naval establishments are inferior and inadequate. That, so stated, is a totally wrong conclusion. It has been the aim of this Administration to make our national defense efficient and to keep it adequate. Today our defense forces are on a stronger peace-time basis than before. It is our purpose to keep them that way.

There are other equally sincere and patriotic people who look upon our system of national defense as much too large for our needs; an unnecessary expense, a threat, perhaps, to peace. That, too, is a totally wrong conclusion. When we say adequate defense we mean just that. The prospect of a war of aggression has no place in our American policy. It has no place in our military or naval program. We are maintaining a system that will meet our defensive needs. We have no plans for any other kind of system.

Americans generally will agree that some measure of preparedness for defense is necessary. They disagree as to how much is necessary. The policy of the Government on that point is determined by several factors. First of all, it is determined by a very common-sense fact. If we take on any of the obligations of self-protection, it follows that we must take on all the obligations of self-protection. We have, for example, two extensive and widely separated coasts to guard. There would be no sense in a preparedness policy adequate for the defense of only one coast. Defense must be adequate, not sectionally adequate, but nationally adequate.

Now our answer to the question as to what is nationally adequate is not always the same. It changes — is bound to change — with changing international situations. If this were a disarming world it is obvious that our needs would be proportionately decreasing. I regret that today this is not that kind of world. I regret it deeply.

But here we confront the question of disarmament. On that issue our policy is clear. That policy has two elements in it. First, we propose to press, continually, for a limitation of armaments by international agreement. Second, failing to get that, we will make no increase of our own armaments unless other powers by increasing their armaments make increase by us necessary to our national safety.

If progress in armament limitation has been slow, progress in other areas has been rapid. We have stated the principle of the good neighbor as the standard for the conduct of our foreign policy. We have begun the practice of that principle. Already that practice has ushered in a new era of good-will between ourselves and the great Nations of the Americas. One after another we are liquidating the causes of friction and misunderstanding between us. A new confidence has been established. This summer's Pan-American Conference will meet in an atmosphere of unprecedented friendliness. What we have achieved in that one area is a measure of what we desire to achieve through the whole range of our international relationships.

That achievement is wholly consistent with our program of national defense. It is an expression of the very objectives on which our national defense is based.

We have a disinterested, consistent and successful foreign policy. In it we give no thought to a war of aggression on the part of the United States. We stand firmly by our solemn treaty obligations renouncing war as an instrument of national policy.

Very sincerely yours,

Mrs. William A. Becker,
Daughters of the American Revolution,
Washington, D. C.

(This letter was read at the 45th Continental Congress of the Society in Washington, D. C., April 20, 1936.)

52 ❡ A Greeting on the Centennial of the Ancient Order of Hibernians. April 21, 1936

My dear Mr. McCullen:

THE observance of the centennial of the founding of the Ancient Order of Hibernians turns our thoughts backward into American history, in every phase of which the Irish have borne so notable a part. To all who are taking part in the centennial celebration I send hearty felicitations.

The year 1836 seems far away to us; and yet the Irish began their migration to America long before that. They made their special contributions to the upbuilding of this country in the Colonial and Revolutionary periods and from the beginning of our life as a Nation down to this centennial year of the A.O.H. their activities have been manifold.

We must not forget that it was an Irish Colonial Governor, Thomas Dongan, afterwards Earl of Limerick, who gave the City of New York its first charter in 1686. There is not time to enlarge upon the constructive contributions which the Irish have made in the upbuilding of New York and of the United States from Dongan's day down to our own.

In peace and in war they have been in the forefront of all activity. New York has not forgotten and can never forget the old Sixty-ninth Regiment of Infantry — the "fighting Irish" of song and story.

With deep appreciation do we recall the services of the successor of the old Sixty-ninth, the One Hundred Sixty-fifth Infantry Regiment in the Rainbow Division. And that brings to mind a gallant figure whose name is forever associated with the One Hundred Sixty-fifth Regiment. I counted him among my dearest friends. He was in our midst but a few short years ago; his passing brought sorrow to all hearts; his memory is in benediction. Father Duffy was characteristically Irish in the apostolic zeal of his ministry, in the fervor of his patriotism and in his love and good-will toward all men. I know he will have a place in the hearts of all who take part in this celebration. I like to think of Father Duffy as typical of the great race which has given so much to America.

Very sincerely yours,

Edward J. McCullen, Esq.,
Ancient Order of Hibernians,
New York City.

(This letter was read at the centennial celebration of the Order in New York City, May 2, 1936.)

53 ❨ "Nationwide Thinking, Nationwide Planning and Nationwide Action Are the Three Great Essentials to Prevent Nationwide Crises"—Address at the Thomas Jefferson Dinner, New York City. April 25, 1936

Governor and Mrs. Lehman, President McMahon, Judge Collins, and you who celebrate once more the birthday of Thomas Jefferson:

IT IS a very deep pleasure to be welcomed this way, to be welcomed back to my home State of New York.

Our State has loyally supported those progressive policies of government, in the making of which so many of you who are here tonight have taken an honorable and successful part. New York State has a long record of almost a generation of liberal government, each succeeding Administration of State affairs building for the future upon the best which the past has given us.

I want to take this occasion, this auspicious occasion, to compliment the State on its great good fortune in the loyal, competent and unselfish service of its present Governor, Herbert Lehman.

He has continued to extend and strengthen the humane laws for which this State has been noted. History repeats itself. He has met the same type of opposition today which some of us as youngsters—and Bob Wagner was one of them—met in the State Legislature twenty-five years ago. The people of this State and the people of every State meet with obstacles. For example, it has come to me all the way to Washington that the present Assembly of this State declines to meet the obvious requirements of the State Constitution to provide the sum necessary to meet the debt requirements of the State during the coming fiscal year, and that this same Assembly is opposed to providing relief for those in need. But, my friends, twenty-five years ago and ten years ago and five years ago we won, and Herbert Lehman is going to win again.

As a New Yorker, I am confident, and I think you are too, that

177

a vast majority of our citizens, this autumn as in the past, will invite Governor Lehman to serve at least two years more as our Chief.

A century ago this country was regarded as an economic unity. But as time went on, things happened. The country, bit by bit, was cut up into segments. We heard, more and more, about the problems of particular localities, the problems of particular groups. More and more people put on blinders; they could see only their own individual interests or the single community in which their business happened to be located.

It is only in these comparatively recent days that we have been turning back to the broader vision of the Founding Fathers.

The cities of the Nation, and the countrysides near them, have come to realize each other's existence. The same idea now is spreading on a truly national scale.

That is why, while I may be breaking another precedent—and they say in Washington that my day is not complete without smashing at least one precedent—I can come here to the City of New York and talk with you about the cotton problem of Georgia, the corn and hog problem of Iowa, the wheat problem of the Dakotas, the dust storms of the West, the destructive tornadoes in the South, and the floods in the Northeast. In the same way I would not hesitate to discuss the slum clearance problems or any other problems of the big cities of the East with any farmer audience in Georgia or Iowa or the Dakotas or anywhere else, because we are becoming nation-minded.

The strong arm of the Nation is needed not in immediate relief alone. We all grant that. It is needed also in taking measures of prevention before natural disasters occur. It is needed equally in taking measures to prevent economic disasters which are not natural, but are made by man.

During these past three years I am quite convinced that the Hester Street and Park Avenue of this city have both come to understand that they belong in the same economic pattern and indeed to the same Nation as the cotton, corn and hog belts, and the flood areas and the dust bowls. Not so long ago it was the farm against the city and the city against the farm. But from now on, if both are to prosper, it must be and shall be the farm with the city and the city with the farm.

Some economists are still trying to find out what it was that hit us back in 1929. I am not a professional economist but I think I know. What hit us was a decade of debauch, of group selfishness — the sole objective expressed in the thought — "every man for himself and the devil take the hindmost." And the result was that about 98 percent of the American population turned out to be "the hindmost."

Let me illustrate what happened by taking the case of the garment workers in the City of New York. They make about 40 percent of all the clothes of the Nation worn outside of New York City. Their work and wages in this city were dependent on the sales they made all over the country. The garment workers' depression here did not begin in 1929. It began back in 1921, when the depression began on the farms of the Nation. But back in the twenties, people in power still thought of prosperity chiefly in industrial or financial terms. They overlooked the farm depression; and because it went unrelieved, the troubles that started among the farmers in 1921 finally and inevitably reached the garment workers on Eighth Avenue.

Nebraska's corn and Eighth Avenue's clothing are not different problems; they are the same national problem. Before the war a Nebraska farmer could take a two-hundred-pound hog to market and buy a suit of clothes made in the City of New York. But in 1932, in order to get that same suit of clothes, he had to take two and a half hogs to market. Back in the twenties a cotton farmer had to raise seven pounds of cotton to buy one pair of New York-made overalls. By 1932, however, he had to raise fourteen pounds of cotton to get those New York overalls.

Let us get the common sense of it.

Obviously, the farmers stopped buying as many clothes and when the farm districts stopped buying, New York's garment districts soon started breadlines. That, however, was only half of the vicious circle. When the garment district's breadlines grew longer, buying power in the cities as a whole grew less. Other breadlines formed. Every man on a new breadline meant one person who ate less and wore less. Because the garment worker ate less the farmer sold less and his income went down. And so the vicious strangling circle was complete. Today we have broken that throttlehold. The American electorate proposes that it shall not be renewed.

And while I am talking of food consumption at the end of this grand dinner, here is a fact of equal interest to the city dweller and the farmer population. If all of the seven million people living in the City of New York could afford to buy the bread and meat and vegetables and milk and fish and cotton and wool that their health and decent living call for, then we in this country would need crop production from three million more acres of good crop land than we are using today to feed and clothe the City of New York. I propose to continue the fight for more food and better homes. I propose that the man who was forgotten in those olden days shall not be forgotten again.

This tie-up between cities and farms is one of the chief reasons why in 1933 we sought a national solution for a national problem. We sought simultaneously to raise the farmer's cash income and to add to the working man's pay envelope. What our success has been you can prove by the simple process of putting the financial pages of any newspaper published in 1936 alongside the financial pages of the same newspaper published in 1932. By financial pages, I do not mean, as some of you might think, merely the stock market quotation pages, although you will agree that they, too, have at least passed panic prices. By financial pages I mean the published prices of farm products and raw materials and the many reports of industrial earnings. And, by the way, speaking of activity, speaking of progress and a greater prosperity, every time that I come back to the City of New York I keep looking, looking for that grass that was to grow in our city streets!

Some individuals are never satisfied. People complain to me about the current costs of rebuilding America, about the burden on future generations. I tell them that whereas the deficit of the

Federal Government this year is about three billion dollars, the national income of the people of the United States has risen from thirty-five billion dollars in the year 1932 to sixty-five billion dollars in the year 1936. And I tell them further that the only burden we need to fear is the burden that our children would have to bear if we failed to take these measures today.

Building national income and distributing it more widely, mean not only the bettering of conditions of life, but the end of, and insurance against, individual and national deficits in the days to come.

Nationwide thinking, nationwide planning and nationwide action are the three great essentials to prevent nationwide crises for future generations to struggle through.

Other individuals are never satisfied; one of them, for example, that I read about the other day, belongs to a newly organized Brain Trust—not mine. He says that the only way to get complete recovery—and I wonder if he really admits we have had any recovery at all—is to lower prices by cheapening the costs of production.

Let us reduce that to plain English. You can cheapen the costs of industrial production by two methods. One is by the development of new machinery and new technique and by increasing employee efficiency. We do not forbid that. But do not dodge the fact that this means fewer men employed and more men unemployed. The other way to reduce the costs of industrial production is to establish longer hours for the same pay or to reduce the pay for the same number of hours. If you lengthen hours you will need fewer workers for the same output. More men out of work! If you choose lower wages for the same number of hours you cut the dollars in the pay envelope and automatically cut down the purchasing power of the worker himself.

Reduction of costs of manufacture by cutting wages or lengthening hours does not mean more purchasing power and more goods consumed. It means the exact opposite.

The history of that period from 1929 to 1933 shows that consumption of goods actually declines with a declining price level.

And the reason is obvious. The reason is that in such periods the buying power of the Nation goes down faster than the prices go down.

On the other hand, if you increase buying power prices will go up, but more goods will be bought. Wages ought to, and must, go up with prices. It does not mean unsound inflation or sky-rocketing prices; those should be avoided, just as we seek to avoid deflation and bankruptcy sale values. What we do seek is a greater purchasing power and a reasonably stable and constant price level, and we are attaining that end. It is my belief, and I think it is yours as well, that the industry and agriculture of America sub-scribe to that objective. Toward that end, representative Govern-ment of every form is working. The objective cannot be obtained in a month or a year — we know that. But, my friends, results, proven by facts and figures, show that we are on our way — very definitely on our way. Higher wages for workers, more income for farmers, mean more goods produced, more and better food eaten, fewer unemployed and lower taxes.

That is my economic and social philosophy, and, incidentally, that is my political philosophy as well.

I believe from the bottom of my heart that it is the philosophy of the America of 1936.

54 ❬A Résumé of the Participation of Federal Groups in Rescue Work in Flood Areas. May 7, 1936

My dear Admiral Grayson:

This is to acknowledge and thank you for your letter of April 27th, concerning the participation of organized Federal groups for rescue work in areas devastated by flood.

A study of the situation, pertaining to circumstances of gov-ernmental participation in emergency relief work, discloses the fact that such groups have been organized and have cooperated extensively and effectively with the American Red Cross, and with the civil authorities, on every occasion of major disaster of any nature.

The specific steps thus far taken by the Navy and Coast Guard may be summed up as follows:

(1) Navy Relief Force — organized at the direction of the Commander-in-Chief, U. S. Fleet, aboard vessels of the Battle Force and Scouting Fleet, for the purpose of furnishing immediate relief and assistance to centers of population in the event of major disasters temporarily beyond the control of the local civil authorities.

(2) Rescue groups composed of the personnel of the various Navy Recruiting Stations throughout the country organized as required.

(3) Rescue groups of the U. S. Coast Guard which have participated in flood relief and rescue work, in many cases transporting its surf-boats over long distances by land to the scene of operations. In addition, Coast Guard vessels especially constructed for the purpose are in active commission in the performance of flood relief duty.

(4) Rescue and relief groups organized as required from the units of the U. S. Fleet Reserve and the U. S. Volunteer Communication Reserve.

Due to conditions under which the U. S. Naval Reserve operates, as specified by law, no specific steps have been taken to organize special rescue groups within its various units, but these organizations of the Fleet and Volunteer Communication Reserve, located in the various Naval Districts throughout the country, together with their boats and other equipment, have been immediately available on all occasions requiring their services. As Naval Reservists, they cannot, under the present law, be ordered to perform active duty in peacetime without their own consent, but they have voluntarily responded to the many appeals of the civil authorities and have rendered an extensive amount of outstanding service in the rescue and safeguarding of life and property, and on a non-pay basis. As regards the particular matter of boats, Naval Reserve units on navigable waters have, in general, been provided with boats, but the amount of equipment issued to the Reserve is dependent entirely upon the appropriations made available by Congress.

The files of the Navy Department contain reports of the activities of the Naval Reserve in practically every Naval District of the country, including disaster by earthquake, tornado, hurricane, fire and flood. Prominent on the list are the California earthquake of March, 1933, centering in and about Long Beach; the Florida hurricanes of 1933 and 1935, and the various floods of the Mississippi, Missouri, Ohio, Allegheny, Susquehanna, Monongahela, Delaware, Connecticut, Merrimack, Mohawk and Potomac River Valleys, including the many extremely serious conditions of the present year.

In these situations, the personnel of the Naval Reserve has evacuated the populace, rationed marooned groups of workers, supplied electric light and current, distributed food and clothing, provided temporary shelter for the homeless, policed the several affected areas and protected life and property. Naval Reserve Medical Officers have treated the sick and injured, without compensation of any sort. Members of the Volunteer Communication Reserve have operated N.C.R. Emergency Circuits at the request of the American Red Cross, in assisting to carry out the Red Cross Emergency Communication Plan, published to the Service in June, 1930, which provides for making emergency contacts by master and alternate control Reserve Radio Stations with Naval District Shore Radio Stations.

In many cases the Naval Reserve maintained the only communication between the stricken areas and the rest of the country. Naval, Naval Reserve, and Coast Guard aircraft have surveyed conditions from the air, directed and coordinated relief efforts and transported food, clothing and medical supplies to the suffering communities.

I am sure that the Navy and Coast Guard will be pleased to consider any suggestions which will increase the effectiveness of their cooperation with the Red Cross in rescue work and that they will be pleased to discuss such suggestions with you or any representative you may designate.

Very sincerely yours,

Admiral Cary T. Grayson,
Chairman, American Red Cross,
Washington, D. C.

NOTE: For other discussions of flood relief work during this year, see Items 37, 38, 41 and 42 of this volume.

55 ❨ A Greeting on the Centenary of the Death of James Madison. May 8, 1936

Dear Mr. Morris:

I DEEPLY regret that I cannot be present to join with the members of the New York County Lawyers Association in their observance of the centenary of the death of James Madison. This is indeed an occasion in which I should like to have a part.

No one can examine the life of James Madison without being conscious of the great services which he rendered to his country. Nor is it possible to read his writings, and particularly the papers which he contributed to the *Federalist,* without being impressed by the acuteness of his mind and his constant habit of interpreting political theory in terms of economic and political realities. Without referring in detail to his services as Secretary of State and President or discussing his rank as a political thinker, we should not overlook, on an occasion like this, certain of Madison's characteristics which are peculiarly American, and particularly his lifelong interest in the education of youth, his consistent defense of civil liberty, and his advocacy of religious tolerance and freedom. But above all, we should think of the gifts of enterprise and vision which he demonstrated in his work in assisting in the framing and adoption of the Constitution.

It seems to me particularly fitting that one hundred years after his death we should recall the following words, which show his at-

185

tachment to the Union and his fervent belief that the people of the United States constitute a Nation with common interests and a common purpose:

"May it not be regarded as among the providential blessings to these States, that their geographical relations, multiplied as they will be by artificial channels of intercourse, give such additional force to the many obligations to cherish that union which alone secures their peace, their safety, and their prosperity?"

These words should be an incentive to all of us to do our part to promote the safety, the welfare, and the prosperity of our country which James Madison served with so much intelligence, integrity, and courage.

Very sincerely yours,

Mr. Robert C. Morris,
President, New York County Lawyers Association,
New York, N. Y.

(This letter was read at the ceremonies at the New York County Lawyers Association, New York City, May 13, 1936.)

56 ⟨The Two Hundred and Ninety-fifth Press Conference (Excerpts). May 15, 1936

(United States Housing Bill—Resettlement Administration.)

THE PRESIDENT: I am going down the river over to Annapolis and into the Bay and I shall get back Sunday afternoon, late.

Q. Do you expect to sign any important bills before you leave over the week-end?

THE PRESIDENT: I shall sign a few I have in the basket and I shall act on the others over the week-end. . . .

Q. Mr. President, have you worked out the details of the Wagner Housing Bill yet?

THE PRESIDENT: No, I think they are making very good progress. I think there ought to be something over the week-end on it. . . .

Q. What about the future of the Resettlement Administration?

THE PRESIDENT: What part of it?

Q. There is a story in the morning papers that it is going to be washed out.

THE PRESIDENT: No, there is a great deal of confusion of thought about the Resettlement Administration. For example, there are perfectly practical reasons for handling — I have forgotten the exact numbers — 550,000 relief families who are being kept off the work relief rolls, by both small grants to try to rehabilitate them on their own farms, and small loans keeping them on their own farms. That form of relief is, of course, a great deal cheaper than if we were to take them off the farms and put on work relief. I think there are 550,000 or 600,000 families in that category. That work is going on.

Another phase of it is moving certain families from farms where they cannot possibly make a living, where they have proved that a living cannot be made, and trying to put them on better land. That is the second phase of the work. That is bound to go on because, on any analysis, it is cheaper than work relief.

Then, a third phase that really goes in with both of those — I have forgotten the term used — is helping those families either on their original farms, or on new farms with advice, because in a great many cases they have neither the experience nor, I am sorry to say, in some cases, the education to make good. Therefore, we think in the long run it will be much cheaper if we can constantly visit those people, and see that the lady of the house puts up vegetables and fruits, etc., and that the men of the family kill their own hogs for winter use, cultivate the land in the right way and try to put something back into the land to avoid erosion and to alternate crops.

In other words, the idea is to keep an educational system going with the expectation that after a year or two of that they will be better able to run things themselves. The figures show that that work is extraordinarily effective. Just offhand, I think that between 100,000 and 200,000 families have been educated in the past two years to run their own show and are now capable of doing it without any further Government aid. That is quite a lot of human beings.

Then the fourth phase of the work relates to rural settlements and semi-rural settlements. Of course a fairly large program has been undertaken on that, and it is bound to be carried through to completion. Whether we shall start any more new ones that we have not undertaken, I doubt. They might be called "samples" dotted here and there around the country.

Q. Those are the four Greenbelt projects?

THE PRESIDENT: No, those are the four out of a great many. They happened to be a certain type near cities. For example, the one between here and Baltimore is very nearly halfway finished, and that will not be a farm proposition. It is primarily for people who live in Washington and Baltimore. That is suburban. There are a great many others which are primarily rural.

Q. Mr. President, how about the purchase of submarginal land? Isn't that another feature of their work?

THE PRESIDENT: Well, that of course has been going ahead; and I do not believe there will be very much more money spent on submarginal land because we are cleaning up existing funds. It does not mean the program is over. It means that in the coming fiscal year we shall not spend as much money on that as we have in the past fiscal year. . . .

(See Item 50, Vol. IV, for discussion of Resettlement Administration.)

57 ❪ A Greeting to the National Conference of Social Work. May 23, 1936

My dear Monsignor Keegan:

IT IS with sincere regret that I find myself unable to be at the 1936 meeting of the National Conference of Social Work. I have great concern for the work of social welfare agencies and the efforts of social workers to make this country a more neighborly place in which to live. Cognizant, therefore, of the value of your deliberations and proceedings, I assure you of my deep interest in the high purposes for which you are convened.

The National Conference of Social Work is indeed an expression of the social conscience of America. Its members have consecrated their lives to the bringing about of a better social order wherein men and women shall have greater opportunity to enjoy the blessings of life. Many of us are accustomed to appealing for the cause of humanity. Let us remember that humanity is not society; humanity is just plain folks. Some of our so-called leaders have made the mistake of looking upon men and women as economic and social units. Logically, therefore, they speak of men and women as individuals, just as they would of other things — of animals or plants or atoms.

In matters of social welfare we should keep sight of the fact that we are not dealing with "units," "individuals" or with "economic men." We are dealing with persons. Human personality is something sacred. It enjoys the light of reason and liberty. It grows by rising above material things and wedding itself to spiritual ideals. Our social order is worthy of human beings only in so far as it recognizes the inherent value of human personality. Our cities, our States and our Nations exist not for themselves but for men and women. We cannot be satisfied with any form of society in which human personality is submerged.

To you as President of the Conference and to all who participate I send my deepest and most heartfelt congratulations.

Very sincerely yours,

Right Reverend Monsignor Robert Fulton Keegan,
President, National Conference of Social Work,
Atlantic City, New Jersey.

(This letter was read at the 63rd annual meeting in Atlantic City, N. J., May 26, 1936.)

58 ❨ Informal Extemporaneous Remarks to the Triennial Conference of the Associated Country Women of the World. June 1, 1936

UNTIL comparatively recent years people in almost every Nation believed a current saying that farmers would never be able to agree among themselves. If this saying applied to the farmers, I, as a mere man, suppose it applied to the farmers' wives and daughters as well.

Recent history has exposed the fallacy; we have changed it to read—farmers and farmers' wives and farmers' sons and farmers' daughters can cooperate and do cooperate.

The very fact of this cooperation has made possible here and abroad the great progress that has been made in improving the conditions of life in rural communities.

People are prone to forget that by far the greater part of the world's population is actively engaged in agriculture or is directly dependent on the results of agriculture. This means that you ladies have a great responsibility for today and for the future; it means that you can raise not only the standards of agricultural life but the standards of all life as well.

For we are coming more and more to realize that the city dwellers cannot be prosperous, cannot work in their factories and their stores unless the agricultural population and those dependent on them have a greater purchasing power throughout the years.

Your task and mine concerns itself not only with new problems: we are confronted with the necessity of undoing past mistakes, of restoring the former gifts of Nature to their former value, and of seeing to it that harmful practices of the olden days shall not be repeated.

We are trying many new things. Most of them we believe will succeed; some of them may not succeed, and in such cases we shall seek better substitutes.

I congratulate you on this fine gathering which has exceeded our hopes both in numbers and in the scope of territory represented. We, citizens of the United States, are proud to present to you, the representatives of so many other Nations, a cross-section of the farm women of our country. We are glad to have you visit the United States and, as a result of this friendly meeting, the farm life of every Nation is bound to march forward with increasing efficiency and increasingly high standards.

59 ⟨ The Three Hundredth Press Conference (Excerpts). June 2, 1936

(Passamaquoddy Project — Supreme Court decision on New York minimum-wage law.)

Q. Mr. President, do you see any way in which the Passamaquoddy Project can be continued?

THE PRESIDENT: You will have to ask them on the Hill.

Q. In view of the Supreme Court's series of opinions about the New Deal objectives, do you see any way in which those objectives can be reached within the existing framework of the Constitution?

THE PRESIDENT: I think I shall have to reframe your question: Have you any comment on the Supreme Court decision?

Q. Comment on this decision or on the series of them?

THE PRESIDENT: On this particular decision the only thing I can say is that it will be and is of very great interest to practically everybody in the United States. They should read all three opinions, the opinion of Justice Butler, the opinion of the Chief Justice, and the opinion of Justice Stone, because it is the combination of the three that indicates that for the present a majority of the Court have made one fact fairly clear. I am, of course, interested in that fact because when I was Governor of New York we did discuss and, just after I left, the Legislature passed this minimum-wage law.

It seems to be fairly clear, as a result of this decision and former decisions, using this question of minimum wage as

191

an example, that the "no-man's-land" where no Government — State or Federal — can function is being more clearly defined. A State cannot do it, and the Federal Government cannot do it. I think, from the layman's point of view, that is the easiest way of putting it and about all we can say on it.

Q. How can you meet that situation?

THE PRESIDENT: I think that is about all there is to say on it. (*Laughter*)

Q. I think there are dangers in the existence of that "no-man's-land."

THE PRESIDENT: I think that is all there is to say about it. . . .

(See Introduction to Vol. IV for discussion of this case, *Morehead vs. Tipaldo,* 298 U.S. 587.)

60 ❢ A Tribute to Speaker Joseph W. Byrns on the Occasion of His Death. June 4, 1936

SPEAKER BYRNS belonged to that school of statesmen which is the hope and justification of our democracy. By a happy coincidence he represented for more than a quarter of a century the Hermitage District of Tennessee, a district of sentimental significance because it holds the sacred dust of Andrew Jackson; and there was about Speaker Byrns a simplicity and rugged honesty which we have come to associate with the name of Jackson. Fearless, incorruptible, unselfish, with a high sense of justice, wise in counsel, broad of vision, calm in adversity and modest in victory, he served his State and the Nation with fidelity, honor and great usefulness.

I personally mourn the passing of a steadfast friend of many years.

61 ⟨The President Requests All Bankers to Cooperate in Cashing Bonus Checks. June 8, 1936

DISBURSEMENT of bonds and checks to veterans in payment of adjusted service certificates, as provided by the Adjusted Compensation Payment Act, 1936, will begin on June 15. Payments will involve the issuance of a large number of checks drawn on the Treasurer of the United States. The first group of checks will be for amounts less than $50 drawn on the Treasurer by Federal disbursing officers and mailed directly to veterans at their designated addresses. The second group of checks, to be issued in connection with the redemption of adjusted service bonds of 1945, will be in amounts of $50 or multiples thereof, and will be in the form of Treasurer's checks or checks drawn on the Treasurer by postmasters designated fiscal agents of the United States.

In order that the veterans may receive the fullest benefit contemplated by the Congress, and that the funds to be disbursed may begin to flow through the channels of trade without unnecessary delay, it is essential that our banks throughout the country extend all possible assistance by cashing these checks at par upon proper identification.

I urge all bankers to extend the fullest cooperation to the Government in the encashment of these checks promptly and in full.

62 ⟨A Presidential Statement on Approving Bill for Vocational Education. June 8, 1936

I HAVE approved H. R. 12120, a bill "to provide for the further development of vocational education in the several States and Territories," because of my deep interest in providing our young people with adequate opportunities for vocational training. So many criticisms have been directed at the bill in its present state, however, that it seems to me advisable, before the Act goes into effect on July 1, 1937, that a disinterested group review its provisions in relation to the experience of the Government under the existing program of Federal aid for vocational education, and the relation of such training to general education and to prevailing economic and social conditions.

Accordingly, I shall take steps in the immediate future for an appointment of such a group with instructions to make studies and recommendations which will be available to the Congress and the Executive at the beginning of the next session.

63 ⟨ Informal Extemporaneous Remarks at a Religious Service in Rockport, Arkansas. June 10, 1936

My friends:

I AM very happy to have come here to take part in this religious service. It means a great deal to me.

This particular spot has seen much history. It has seen many famous men pass through here on their way west. It has seen Americans through many generations, but remember that in all those days, and in this one, religion has taken part in everything that has occurred.

I always remember that in the earliest days of the white settlement of North America, in the days of the landing at Plymouth, the colonization of Jamestown and the founding of New Amsterdam, the first thing that the earliest colonists did when they set foot on shore was to hold a religious service. It seemed to be in our American blood. And so, as the Nation developed and as men moved across the Alleghenies and across the Mississippi, religion went hand in hand with them.

I am glad to think that in these more recent days the spiritual qualities of the American people are keeping pace with the progress of the more material civilization. And that is why, you good people who live in this section of Arkansas, I ask you always to keep that spiritual faith and to remember the early days when your ancestors brought religion across the Mississippi.

NOTE: These remarks and the following speeches printed as Items 64 to 72 inclusive, of this volume, were delivered during my trip to and from the centennial celebrations in Arkansas and Texas, June 8 to June 15, 1936. On this trip, I also delivered short informal talks, not included in these volumes, at: Knoxville, Tenn., June 9; Fort Worth Fair Grounds, Tex., June 12; Dennison, Tex., June 13; Muskogee, Okla., June 13; Louisville, Ky., June 14; Martinsburg, W. Va., June 15.

64 ("Self-Government We Must and Shall Maintain"—Address at Little Rock, Arkansas. June 10, 1936

Governor Futrell, my friends of Arkansas:

FOR me this has been a glorious day and this is a splendid climax. While, as some of you know, I have been in the State of Arkansas before this, my visits hitherto have been too much like those of a bird of passage; and this is the first chance that I have had to see the State at closer range, and especially to enjoy the generosity, the kindness and the courtesy of true Arkansas hospitality.

I have seen your parks; I have seen the beauties of your mountains and rivers. Arkansas can claim every warrant for the name "wonder State." It is doubly a privilege to meet you face to face and to join with you in the celebration of the one hundredth anniversary of the admission of this great State into the Union.

It is possible that some of our citizens who live in the original thirteen States along the Atlantic seaboard may have the natural idea that white men first became acquainted with their part of the country, and that the territory lying west of the Mississippi is all very new. I am certain that it is not generally realized back there in the East that Hernando De Soto, the tireless Spanish explorer, set foot in what is now Arkansas, as early as the year 1541, more than half a century before the founding of Jamestown and New Amsterdam and Plymouth; or that the French explorers,

Marquette and Joliet, coming southward from Canada, saw this country when the civilization of the Atlantic seaboard was still in its infancy. Nor have they sufficiently been told that the first settlement under the flag of France was made under the direction of De Tonti at Arkansas Post as far back as 1686.

First under the flag of France, the young settlement, as we know, passed to the flag of Spain, to be recovered by Napoleon for France in 1800, and finally brought under our own American flag by the Louisiana Purchase three years later.

That Louisiana Purchase has always had a special significance for me. I am interested in it for family reasons because Robert R. Livingston, our Minister to France, negotiated the purchase by direction of President Thomas Jefferson — and I must admit that Livingston, who was of Scotch descent, drove a very shrewd bargain.

I am also interested because President Jefferson, seeing the complexities which the Emperor Napoleon faced in a coalition of hostile European powers, had the courage, the backbone, to act for the benefit of the United States without the full and unanimous approval of every member of the legal profession. Indeed, he was told by some of his closest advisers and friends that the Constitution of the United States contained no clause specifically authorizing him to purchase or acquire additional territory; and he was told that because specific authority did not exist under that great Charter of Government, none could be exercised. Jefferson replied that there were certain inherent qualities of sovereignty which could not be separated from the Federal Government, if such a Federal Government was permanently to endure; and furthermore, he told them that if he delayed, the Emperor of the French might change his mind and the great territory west of the Mississippi River would be lost forever to American expansion. He and Robert R. Livingston and James Madison put the treaty through; and the next Congress appropriated the money to pay for it; and, my friends, nobody carried the case to the Supreme Court. As a result, Louisiana and Arkansas and Missouri and Iowa and Minnesota and Kansas and

Montana and North Dakota and South Dakota and the larger portions of Wyoming and Colorado and Nebraska and Oklahoma fly the Stars and Stripes today.

The hardy pioneers whom we commemorate, who peopled Arkansas and laid the foundations for statehood here and throughout the vast new domain west of the Alleghenies, brought about a veritable renaissance of the principle of free government upon which this Republic was founded.

I have not the time nor is it necessary to follow the fascinating story in detail down to the admission of Arkansas into the Union only a few days less than one hundred years ago. That year of attainment of statehood by Arkansas is an important one in American history, not so much because it was marked by a Presidential election, but because 1836 was the last full year of the Presidency of Andrew Jackson.

It is not without the greatest historical significance that Arkansas was received into the Union in 1836. Jackson's great work for the country was approaching completion. He was in the full tide of his remarkable powers and in the exercise of an extraordinary influence upon the minds and opinions of the mass of his countrymen.

When Arkansas became a State we must remember that our national Government was not quite fifty years old. Charles Carroll of Carrollton, the last surviving signer of the Declaration of Independence, had been dead only four years. Only six years had passed since Webster had delivered his reply to Hayne. Men who had followed Washington through the Revolution were to be found in every community, and the manners and mode of the pioneer period were the order of American life. Andrew Jackson, the contemporary and counselor of the Arkansas pioneers of 1836, made his home across the Mississippi in the neighboring State of Tennessee, and was known to the Arkansans of that day as a fellow frontiersman who had carried into the Presidency those neighborly instincts of the frontier which made possible the first truly democratic Administration in our history.

The older I grow and the more I read history, the more I reflect upon the influence of the men and events of one generation upon the life and thought of the generations that follow. A hundred years have passed since Arkansas attained statehood in that last year of Jackson's Presidency, but throughout this century our American political life has flowed with the vigor of a living stream because the sturdy hand of Andrew Jackson deflected its course from the stagnant marshes of a seaboard oligarchy into the channels of pure American democracy.

Prior to Jackson's day it may be said, without danger of exaggeration, that the leadership of the Nation was, with rare exceptions, in the hands of men who, by birth or education, belonged to a comparatively small group — and the reason is not far to seek. Universal education was not yet fully established in those days; communication difficulties prevented the dissemination of news except in the larger communities and along the main avenues of transportation; the very ballot was, in many States, limited to those who had special property qualifications.

The wave of popular acclaim that swept Andrew Jackson into his high office was the result of the recognition by the people of the United States that the era of a truer democracy in their national life was at hand. I need not describe the dismay that the election of Jackson excited — and honestly excited — in the hearts of the hitherto elect, or the widespread apprehension that it aroused among the so-called guardian groups of the Republic.

Groups such as those have never fully disappeared from American political life, but it will never be possible for any length of time for any group of the American people, either by reason of wealth or learning or inheritance or economic power, to retain any mandate, any permanent authority to arrogate to itself the political control of American public life.

This heritage, my friends, we owe to Jacksonian democracy — the American doctrine that entrusts the general welfare to no one group or class, but dedicates itself to the end that the American people shall not be thwarted in their high purpose to remain the custodians of their own destiny.

The frontier spirit that brought men into the Arkansas wilderness, and later was to carry them even further in their conquest of the West, inspired in the hearts and minds and souls of those men a new ideal of our national democracy. Perhaps it would be more exact to say that the frontier spirit caused a rebirth of the earlier ideal of free government. To that changed ideal the neighborly contacts of the frontier contributed in liberal measure. The rugged pioneers helped to fashion the new national spirit. The men who tamed the wilderness hereabouts were part of a new movement in our American life.

It was indeed a critical moment in American history when, in our early national period, the dauntless and intrepid pioneers strode across the Alleghenies to establish new commonwealths like Arkansas. In that hard life of the frontier, where the personal qualities of the men and not the inheritance of caste or of property were the measure of worth, true democratic government was given its greatest impetus.

In the early days of the Republic — those days when Arkansas became a State — our life was simple. There was little need of formal arrangements, or of Government interest, or action, to insure the social and economic well-being of the American people. In the life of the pioneer, sympathy and kindly help, ready cooperation in the accidents and emergencies of the frontier life were the spontaneous manifestation of the American spirit. Without them the conquest of a continent could never have been made.

Today that life is gone. Its simplicity has vanished and we are each and all of us, whether we like it or not, parts of a social civilization which ever tends to greater complexity. And in these later days, the imperiled well-being, the very existence of large numbers of our people, have called for measures of organized Government assistance which the more spontaneous and personal promptings of a pioneer generosity could never alone have obtained. Our country is indeed passing through a period which is urgently in need of ardent protectors of the rights of the common man. Mechanization of industry and mass production have put unparalleled power in the hands of the few. No small part of our problem today is to bring the fruits of this mechanization and mass production to the people as a whole.

The measure of the need has been the measure of the organization necessary to meet it. The human sympathy of our people would have tolerated nothing less. Common sense will tolerate nothing more.

Self-government we must and shall maintain. Let me put it thus, in a way which every man and woman can understand: Local government must continue to act with full freedom in matters which are primarily of local concern; county government must retain the functions which logically belong to the county unit; State Governments must and shall retain State sovereignty over all those activities of government which effectively and efficiently can be met by the States.

Let us analyze a little further: Why was a State Government set up here in Arkansas? The answer is that the colonization of this area had reached the point where individual settlements needed a uniformity of ordinances and laws. They needed a central body to govern in respect to those things which had grown beyond the scope of town government or county government.

In the same way the Federal Government itself was organized under a Constitution because in the days following the Revolution it was discovered that a mere Federation of independent States was such a loose organization, with constant conflicts among the thirteen States themselves, that a Constitution and a national organization were needed to take care of government beyond and across State lines.

The Constitution provided the best instrument ever devised for the continuation of these fundamental principles. Under its broad purposes we intend to and we can march forward, believing, as the overwhelming majority of Americans believe, that the Constitution is intended to meet and to fit the amazing physical, economic and social requirements that confront us in this modern generation.

If you have been in Washington recently, you will have seen beneath one of the symbolical figures which guard the entrance to our great new Archives Building this quotation from Shakespeare's "Tempest" — "What is past is prologue." Times change but man's basic problems remain the same. He must seek a new approach to their solution when the old approaches fail him. The roar of the airplane has replaced the rumble of the covered wagon; and the frontiers of the American continent are spanned in less time today than it took to cross a single county of Arkansas a century ago. It is idle for us now, as it was for the flatterers of King Canute, to ignore the facts of physics or the economic and social consequences of applied science.

These problems, with growing intensity, now flow past all sectional limitations. They extend over the vast breadth of our whole domain. Prices, wages, hours of labor, fair competition, conditions of employment, social security, in short the enjoyment by all men and women of their constitutional guaranties of life, liberty and the pursuit of happiness — these questions, reflected with the speed of light from the Atlantic to the Pacific, from the Canadian Border to the Gulf of Mexico — these problems we are today commencing to solve. It is true that the new approach to these problems may not be immediately discernible; but organization to meet human suffering can never be predicated on the relaxation of human effort.

Whether it be in the crowded tenements of the great cities or on many of the farm lands of the Nation, you and I know that there dwell millions of our fellow human beings who suffer from the kind of poverty that spells undernourishment and underprivilege. If local government, if State Government, after exerting every reasonable effort, are unable to better their conditions, to raise or restore their purchasing power, then surely it would take a foolish and short-sighted man to say that it is no concern of the national Government itself.

We know that equality of individual ability has never existed and never will, but we do insist that equality of opportunity still

201

must be sought. We know that equality of local justice is, alas, not yet an established fact; this also is a goal we must and do seek.

If we seek to know what human effort can do in the face of adversity, we shall ever find inspiration and guidance in the achievements of the American pioneers, not merely those who founded the Nation, but those who extended its boundaries from ocean to ocean, of whom the first Arkansans were the prototypes.

Arkansas has given many distinguished men to the Nation; but, my friends, I want to tell you very simply and from the heart, that in the meeting of our difficult problems of today, no man deserves greater credit for loyal devotion to a great cause of humanity than my old friend and associate, Senator Joseph T. Robinson.

May I, in closing, repeat that historical maxim: "What is past is prologue." Its meaning is not obscure. Out of the story of mankind's long struggle to govern itself, we should learn lessons which will guide us in solving the problems which beset us today.

The frontier, as we have been recalling it in this rapid survey of the planting of new States, has forever passed; but it has left a permanent imprint upon our political life and upon our social outlook. The Western Frontier from Jackson's time and the admission of Arkansas a hundred years ago, down to the admission of the last States within recent memory, produced a constant renaissance of the principles of free government. The liberal tendencies of those, whom for nearly a century we have called our Western statesmen, have been sometimes too little understood in the older, more conservative East. It was the frontier and its spirit of self-reliance which ever kept alive the principles of democracy and countered the opposing tendency to set up a social caste, based upon wealth, or education, or family, or financial power.

We still find inspiration for the work before us, in the old spirit which meant achievement through self-reliance; a willingness to lend a hand to the fellow down in his luck through no fault of his own. Upon those principles our democracy was reborn a century ago; upon those principles alone will it endure today and in the days to come.

65 ❲ "To Maintain Principles by Means of Peace Rather Than by Means of War" —Address at San Jacinto Battleground, Texas. June 11, 1936

Governor Allred, Mr. Mayor, Mr. Jones and you good people of Texas who have come here today:

I AM grateful to you for the sympathy and sincerity in your welcome to me in coming back to Texas.

There are very few spots in the United States which have witnessed events equal in significance to that which took place at San Jacinto.

Here a century ago was a great frontier of the civilization of America. On the twenty-first day of April, 1836, General Houston and the small body of fewer than eight hundred men under his command held in large measure in their keeping the future of our country as it is constituted today.

The patriots whose memories we are honoring today were victorious in just the same spirit that fired the Colonists of 1776. I like to think of General Houston sending Deaf Smith back to destroy Vince's bridge, over which he had brought his army, so that neither reinforcements nor retreat were a possibility.

Most of these men who fought in this battle had come across the Alleghenies or from the settlements of Kentucky and Tennessee and Missouri into that vast virgin territory over which our now friendly neighbors, south of the Rio Grande, then held sway. And I think it is worthy of note that in front of me are six flags that flew over this ground on which we stand, the fleur-de-lis of France, the flag of Spain, the flag of Mexico, the flag of the Republic of Texas, the Stars and Bars and at last the Stars and Stripes. The spirit of independence lived in this air. Veterans of Concord and Lexington, of Saratoga and of Yorktown were still alive a century ago; the acquisition of the Louisiana territory and the second war for independence were events of very recent history; and, be it not forgotten, the people of Mexico themselves had won their independence from Spain but fifteen years before.

Venturous spirits were willing to meet the difficulties and the dangers that came with carrying the civilization of the East into the further West—the land of unlimited promise. They were willing to comply with all the conditions required by the Mexican Government, when it gave to Stephen F. Austin permission to settle colonies in Texas and to grant to each settler a tract of land.

The settlers rebelled, however, when their civil liberties were restricted, when trial by jury and public education for their children were taken away; but they did this, I am glad to say, only after a prolonged effort on their part to have Mexico modify this decision had failed. Those efforts included two conventions, one in 1832 and one in 1833, and another trip by Stephen Austin to the Mexican capital to plead the cause of the Texas colonists.

And so, when all else failed, the Texas Declaration of Independence, signed at Washington-on-the-Brazos, March 2, 1836, was as natural and inevitable a consequence as the earlier Declaration at Philadelphia on July 4, 1776.

Such action could mean nothing short of a resort to arms, and the fall of the Alamo and the massacre at Goliad soon followed. Those were discouraging days for the Texans. The Army of Independence under General Houston could not immediately engage General Santa Anna, with his superiority of numbers and equipment. Delay and retreat were necessary, but Houston's sagacity in biding his time, notwithstanding criticism and opposition in his own camp, was rewarded at last here at San Jacinto. The story of the conflict on this field has often been told. When the day was ended, victory was overwhelming. Texas had won.

The vast territory first set up as the Lone Star Republic, and later admitted to the Union as the Lone Star State, has contributed generously in its sons and in its resources to the development of the Nation all through these hundred years. San Jacinto opened another gateway for the westward sweep of the American people across the plains and the mountains to the shores of the Pacific.

It is easy, therefore, to share with you the pride which you take in San Jacinto—to share with you the fine thought of dedicating this field as one of the historic shrines of America.

You will agree with me that we as a Nation desire no further expansion. The establishment of Texas, made possible at this spot by Sam Houston's men, seems to have been justified by the natural colonization of the succeeding years. But those heroes gave us more than territory; they set an example which in itself is a glorious heritage, a just cause for State and national commemoration.

It has been a great personal satisfaction to me to come here, and it is a special pleasure to me to meet Colonel Andrew Jackson Houston.

What a magnificent combination of names that is! Although, Colonel Houston, you are many, many years my senior, yet I am proud to know that my father knew your father. I shall always remember, when I was a small boy, how my father used often to tell me that, when he was a very young man, he was sent to Washington by his law office to carry papers to Senator Houston of Texas. And my father told me how, on arriving in Washington, he was ushered into a huge, high-ceilinged room in one of those old balconied hotels on Pennsylvania Avenue. There, in this great room, propped up in a great bed, nightgown and nightcap, even though it was past the noon hour, lay that splendid old man, that gentleman who had been Governor of Tennessee, liberator of Texas, President of the Republic, Governor of his State of Texas and Senator from his State. There he was, holding a levee, transacting public and private business, and preparing for the session of the Senate, which, in those days, did not begin until late in the afternoon. His office and his home were in his hotel room. It would seem that the manners and customs of the Senators of the United States, like other manners and customs, have undergone a great change. And my good friend, Morris Sheppard, agrees to that.

This and the eastern part of your great State, through which I came this morning, can truly be called the cradle of Texas liberty. I have been glad to revisit your beautiful city of Houston. Typical of American enterprise, you have brought the commerce of the world to your door by the ship canal through which I have recently passed.

And, too, I have seen a glimpse of the future, for I have in my office at the White House a model that Jesse Jones gave me, a model of the beautiful memorial that you are to erect here as an everlasting reminder of the bravery of Sam Houston and his men.

Men fought here for principles they loved more dearly than their own lives. Liberty-loving people will always do battle for principles that they believe to be right. Civilization, alas, has not yet made it unnecessary for men to die in battle to sustain principle. It is, however, my hope that in this generation the United States, by its own example, can maintain and help to maintain principles by means of peace rather than by means of war.

The pioneers of Texas and the liberators of Texas, looking down on us today, I am certain would say Amen to the thought that we can win by peace and eliminate the necessity of war.

66 ("We Can Carry on a National War for the Cause of Humanity without Shedding Blood" — Address at the Alamo, San Antonio, Texas. June 11, 1936

Governor Allred, Mr. Mayor, my friends of San Antonio:

FATE has been kind to me today. In my many travels, a visit to the Alamo has hitherto been impossible. I, therefore, welcome this opportunity of visiting this shrine to pay my small tribute to the heroes who laid down their lives a hundred years ago, in order that Texas might become, first, an independent Nation, and later a mighty State of the Union.

We are not lacking in many monuments of noble deeds, but

the Alamo stands out in high relief as our noblest exemplification of sacrifice, heroic and pure.

Travis and Bowie and Crockett and Bonham, and the hundred and seventy-eight who were their comrades, by their supreme sacrifice, made Texas live.

Without the inspiration of the cry, "Remember the Alamo," this great Southwest might never have become a part of the Nation.

Without the tradition of the Alamo, every community throughout the land, every young man and every young woman about to enter upon the duties of citizenship, would have lacked one of our noblest symbols of the American spirit.

I cannot help feeling that the brave men who died here saw on the distant horizon some forecast of the century that lay ahead. I hope they know that we have not discarded or lost the virility and ideals of the pioneer. I hope they know that the overwhelming majority of the Americans of 1936 are once more meeting new problems with new courage—that we, too, are ready and willing to stand up and fight for truth against falsehood, for freedom of the individual against license by the few.

Unlike them, we do not need to take up arms; we are not called upon to die; we can carry on a national war for the cause of humanity without shedding blood. The heroes of the Alamo fought not solely for their individual homes or their individual communities. They knew their families and their immediate neighbors could not survive if the great Southwest fell. United action alone could win. So we, in this latter day, are thinking and acting in terms of the whole Nation, understanding deeply that our firesides, our villages, our cities and our States cannot long endure if the Nation fails.

Travis' message, "I shall never surrender," is a good watchword for each and every one of us today.

It is with a feeling of deep reverence and humble veneration that I have placed a wreath on this shrine where the blood of a hundred and eighty-two Americans was shed—but not shed in vain.

67 ❲A Rear-Platform Speech at Austin, Texas. June 11, 1936

Governor Allred, my friends of Austin:

IT IS a great regret to me that I cannot make a longer stop here tonight, in order to receive more of this perfectly magnificent hospitality not only from you but from Governor Allred and his official family.

As San Jacinto and the Alamo represent to me the struggle for independence and the earlier days of the Republic, so this capital city represents the later days of the Republic and these long years of statehood since Texas became the twenty-eighth star in the national flag.

I have recalled on this trip through Texas the amazing lives of General Houston, of Stephen F. Austin, of those who founded the German colony of Baron Von Bastrop, and of that far-seeing son of one of my States, that Georgian, Mirabeau B. Lamar.

Texas has always had men who had a zest for life, for peace, for progress—men who have won honors at home and abroad. They have sat in this your capital city. They have served in the halls of the national Legislature in Washington and in the Cabinets of Presidents.

That fine tradition continues today. You know, I am sure, that I lean very heavily on men and women from the Lone Star State, who are rendering such fine and unselfish service to the Government of the United States.

This is a fitting place for me to say to all Texas that to one Texan not only I but the whole Nation owes a special debt, one who began his long and distinguished public service, his long career as a member of your Legislature here in Austin, a Texan whom I proudly and very affectionately call my helpmate, John N. Garner, Vice President of the United States.

I am glad to be here with your distinguished Governor and with your distinguished senior Senator from Texas. I am sorry indeed that it is only because of very important official business in

Washington that Jack Garner and Tom Connally cannot be here at my side tonight.

I am glad to see the President of your great university. I understand that somewhere in his pocket he has a button for me to press.

(The President received the button with which he was to explode the first dynamite charge commencing work on the new museum of the State University.)

I am particularly interested, as you know, in history. I am greatly interested in the history of Texas and I am very happy that the Nation has had some part in starting this museum in your capital city. Now I am going to hold it up and press the button and you will hear the noise of the explosion in a moment. There she goes!

68 ⟨ "We Are in the Process of Restoring Democracy in Opportunity" — Address at the Texas Centennial Exposition, Dallas, Texas. June 12, 1936

Governor Allred, my friends of Texas:

I HAVE come here today to bear the tribute of the Nation to you on your hundredth birthday, for you are one hundred years young!

I am here also because I conceive it to be one of the duties and the privileges of the Presidency of the United States to visit, from time to time, every part of the Union.

Many years ago when I was appointed Assistant Secretary of the Navy by President Woodrow Wilson in 1913, I had visited, as I recall, only about twenty States, but during the next few years I had the fortunate opportunity of going into all the others.

Seeing things at first hand is a mighty good habit. I have been fortunate indeed, for as a result of personal contacts with every part of the United States during many years past, I have tried honestly to visualize the problems of every part of the land in their relationships to the problems of every other part, and in their relationships to the unity of the whole.

This great Centennial Exposition is not for Texas alone; it is for the people of all the other forty-seven States as well. I hope and I believe that they will take full advantage of it.

During these past three years, with the return of confidence and the great increase in prosperity, the excellent custom of getting acquainted with the United States has asserted itself. We see a great tide of travel by rail, by plane, by ship and by automobile. We Americans are indeed seeing things at first hand. May the habit spread.

Coincident with this return of better days, we have witnessed three great Expositions — the Century of Progress in Chicago, so popular that it was kept open for a second year; the California International Exposition in San Diego, which is open again this summer in its second successful year; and now the third is this fine Exposition commemorating the Centenary of the Independence of Texas. May you good people have all the fine luck that you so well deserve!

You down here live in the biggest State in the Union. But it is not mere acres that count in this world; it is, rather, the character of the people who dwell upon them. You, the people of Texas, have been tried by fire in these hundred years. You have come through. You have commenced a war for independence. You have apparently been defeated; and then you have won out. You have gone through the difficult days of the War between the States and the trials of Reconstruction. You have had to fight against oppressors from within and oppressors from without.

More than a generation ago your farmers were among the first to rebel against exploitation. In those years it was exploitation by the railroads. In that period of monopoly, of combinations, of overcapitalization, of high rates and poor service and discrimination against the small shipper, you in Texas established a landmark in the regulation of public utilities for the good of their users.

Later, when industrial development came to Texas, you were confronted, as other people have been before and since, by corporations that got out of hand. Here again you called into play the old Texas spirit of freedom for the individual, and out of it came your anti-trust laws, preceded by only one other State in all the Union.

It is, as I recall my history, a fact that during that period there were many prophets of evil who foretold the ruin of Texas by the enactment of legislation to curb these abuses. Yet it is a matter of record that several years later an authoritative survey had this to say of your State: "No part of the Union is more prosperous, no other State has so systematically pursued a policy of corporation regulation, and no other State is so free from the domination of special interests."

Why did the people of Texas do this more than a generation ago? They believed in democracy in government, but they discovered that democracy in government could not exist unless, at the same time, there was democracy in opportunity.

You found that certain forms of monopoly — the combinations of public utilities and other businesses which sought their own ends — were undemocratic because they were bearing down heavily on their smaller competitors, and on the people they served. Because of this they were taking away opportunity.

Today we have restored democracy in government.

We are in the process of restoring democracy in opportunity.

In our national life, public and private, the very nature of free government demands that there must be a line of defense held by the yeomanry of business and industry and agriculture. I do not mean the generalissimos, but the small men, the average men in business and industry and agriculture — those who have an ownership in their business and a responsibility which give them stability. Any elemental policy, economic or political, which tends to eliminate these dependable defenders of democratic institutions, and to concentrate control in the hands of a few small, powerful groups, is directly opposed to the stability of government and to democratic government itself.

Most of us believe, furthermore, if the tendency in the dozen years following the World War had been permitted to continue, that the inevitable consequence would have been the destruction of the base of our form of government. For its splendid structure there would have been substituted as a natural result, an autocratic form of government.

I have spoken of the prophets of evil who plagued your great reforms in Texas. They were blood brothers of some who seek to operate on a national scale. After you in Texas had done so much to restore democracy in opportunity, you found as we in other States found, that the evils we had sought to eradicate had merely jumped over the boundary into some other State. The old abuses of the railroads were finally curbed only after teeth were put into the Interstate Commerce Law and nationwide regulation was made effective. Banking reforms were tried in many States, but here again reform became effective only when the Federal Government was enabled to operate throughout the Union, first by the Federal Reserve Act, and finally by means of the splendid legislation of the past three years. Individual States attempted courageously to regulate the sale of fly-by-night securities and attempted courageously to regulate the exchanges, but you and I know that from the point of view of the Nation as a whole, the effective curbing of abuses was made possible only when the Congress of the United States took a hand by passing the Securities Act and the Stock Exchange Act.

So it goes with the constructive reform of many other abuses which, in the past, have limited or prevented democracy in opportunity. The more progressive of the States may do their share, but unless the action of the States is substantially uniform and simultaneous, the effectiveness of reform is nullified, crippled by the chiselers, who, like many other evil-doers, are, alas, still with us.

The net result of monopoly, the net result of economic and financial control in the hands of the few, has in the past meant and means today, in large measure, the ownership of labor as a commodity. If labor is to be a commodity in the United States, in the final analysis it means that we shall become a Nation of boarding-houses, instead of a Nation of homes. If our people ever submit to that, they will have said "good-bye" to their historic freedom. Men do not fight for boarding-houses. Men do fight and will fight for homes.

I have spoken of the interest which all the country should take in this great Exposition. I mean this as a symbol for the concern which every locality should have in every other locality in every other State. The prosperity which has come to Texas through the products of its farms and ranches, the products of its mines, the products of its oil fields, and the products of its factories, has been made possible chiefly because other parts of the Nation were in possession of the buying power, the consuming power, to use what you have produced. On the other side of the picture, thousands of factories and thousands of farms in the North and in the East and in other parts of the land have been enabled more greatly and more widely to sell their wares, because of the prosperity of you, the people of Texas. I have spoken not once but a dozen times of the necessity of interdependence of each State on every other State. It is a lesson which cannot be driven home or preached too often.

I have taken great happiness in these past three years in the lessening of sectionalism which is apparent on every hand. More and more we have been thinking nationally. That in itself is good, but it would not have been good if at the same time we had not come to understand more deeply that that national good-neighbor policy must extend also to those neighbors who lie outside of our national borders. You in this great State of Texas, whose boundaries extend for hundreds of miles along those of our sister Republic of Mexico, can well understand what the good-neighbor policy means throughout the Americas. We—all Americans, North Americans, Central Americans and South Americans—seek to banish war in this hemisphere; we seek to extend those practices of good-will and closer friendship upon which peace itself is based.

And so, my friends, I wish you once more every happiness and all the good luck in the world.

I salute the Empire of Texas.

69 ⟮At the Unveiling of the Robert E. Lee Memorial Statue, Dallas, Texas. June 12, 1936

I AM very happy to take part in this unveiling of the statue of General Robert E. Lee.

All over the United States we recognize him as a great leader of men, as a great general. But, also, all over the United States I believe that we recognize him as something much more important than that. We recognize Robert E. Lee as one of our greatest American Christians and one of our greatest American gentlemen.

70 ⟮Informal Extemporaneous Remarks at a Luncheon in Dallas, Texas. June 12, 1936

It HAS been a wonderful day. I always regret the fact that I seem to be getting off a train and getting on a train, not having time to stay and visit, as we used to say back home. The little, short glimpse that I got today of the Exposition thrilled me, and I wish I could have seen all of the buildings and, incidentally, the Midway as well.

I spoke this morning about getting to know the people. I got that idea from another President of the United States away back about the year 1905. A young lady that I was engaged to, also a member of the family, and I were stopping in the White House, and the then President Roosevelt—this was after supper—was visibly perturbed and was stamping up and down in front of the fireplace in the Oval Room upstairs. The various members of the family did not know what was the matter with T. R., and finally somebody said, "What is the trouble tonight?" "Oh," he said, "you know that bill for the creation of a large number of national parks? I am not going to be able to get it through this session because there are a lot of people up there that cannot think beyond the borders of their own States." And then he clenched his fist and said, "Sometimes I wish I could be President and Congress too."

Well, I suppose if the truth were told, he is not the only President that has had that idea.

And somebody said, "What would you do if you could be President and Congress too for just a few minutes?" He said, "I would pass a law or a Constitutional Amendment"—and T. R. was always a little bit vague about the difference between laws and constitutional revisions—"I would pass something making it obligatory for every member of the House, candidate for the House, candidate for the Senate" (Hatton [Sumners] and Morris [Sheppard], you remember this), "to file a certificate before they can be elected, certifying that they had visited in every State of the Union." And he said, "That same thing should apply to every high public official in Washington."

Well, the more I study Government, State Government for a good many years and national Government also for a good many years, the sounder I think that general theory is—perhaps not just that kind of practice of it.

When I think back, even to the days when I was a boy, one of the first things that I can remember was the weeklies of the period, the headlines of the papers, telling about the opening of the Cherokee Strip in Oklahoma. I can remember the first time that I crossed the continent. And when I see today the enormous changes that have taken place in my lifetime—and I am not an octogenarian yet—I am amazed by the fact that this country, in its expansion, has acquired a greater unity with every passing year. When people from the Southwest came East thirty or forty years ago they were regarded as strange people. They did not talk the same language. Their problems were different. And yet today, as you and I well know, you can go into any city, North, East, South or West, and you will find the same kind of people with largely the same kind of problems in their lives and in their businesses.

For a country of this size, three thousand miles one way and nearly two thousand the other, the fact of our unity is one of the things that amazes foreigners more than any other thing. Of course, in Washington, I see a great many people who come there from Europe. They are men in public life, newspaper editors, economists, business men, and so forth, and the first question that I always put to them is, "How long have you been here?" And they will say, perhaps, "A week."

"Where have you been?"

"New York City."

"Where are you going?"

"Back home again."

And then I say, "I suppose you are going to write a book about America when you get back."

Lack of information about the United States on the part of our European friends is one of the most amazing things in the history of the present world. I do not suppose it is any exaggeration to say that in the small towns in the United States, especially since the World War and since the papers have fallen into the custom of printing a great deal of foreign news, the average American citizen knows more about world affairs and is more interested in world affairs than the people in the big towns and small towns of any other Nation in the world.

We have become not only Nation-minded, but we have become world-minded. That is one reason why we are trying to work so hard in the cause of peace.

I am, of course, and a great many other people are, worried about the dangers that beset the world. Things are not going so well on the European Continent and on the Asiatic Continent as they are going in the American Hemisphere. That has been the reason why I have tried to keep the feet of this country on the ground, hoping that by our example — our example of unity, our example of world unselfishness, our example of trying to build up trade between all the Nations — we might have some effect on the rest of the world that is thinking too much of armaments and war. And the response in this country has been magnificent.

As I have said, we seem to understand very well what the problems of the world are. We have, perhaps, a kind of sympathy for their problems. We want to help them all that we can; but they have understood very well in these latter years that that help is going to be confined to moral help, and that we are not going to get tangled up with their troubles in the days to come.

You gentlemen who are running this wonderful Exposition here in Dallas are performing a real service for the whole country in helping the people to know their country. I congratulate you on a real accomplishment.

71 ❧ "We Do Not Change Free Government When We Arm Ourselves with New Weapons against New Devices of Crime and Cupidity"— Address at George Rogers Clark Memorial, Vincennes, Ind. June 14, 1936

Governor McNutt, Governor Horner, my friends of Indiana:

EVENTS of history take on their due proportions only when viewed in the light of time. With every passing year the capture of Vincennes, more than a century and a half ago when the Thirteen Colonies were seeking their independence, assumes greater and more permanent significance.

I come, as you know, from the Valley of the Hudson; and the first grave danger, as the War of the Revolution progressed, lay in the effort of the British, with their Indian allies, to drive a wedge from Canada through the Valley of Lake Champlain and the Valley of the Mohawk, to meet the British frigates from the City of New York at the head of navigation on the Hudson River. If this important offensive in the year 1777 had been successful, New England would have been cut off from the States lying south of New York, and by holding the line of the Hudson River the British, without much doubt, could have conquered first one half and then the other half of the divided Colonies. That was our first great crisis.

The defeat and surrender of General Burgoyne at Saratoga became recognized as the definite turning point of the military operations of the Revolution.

But there was another great danger. Danger lay thereafter not in the immediate defeat of the Colonies, but rather in their inability to maintain themselves and grow after their independence had been won. The records of history show that the British planned a definite hemming-in process, whereby the new Nation would be strictly limited in area and in activity to the territory lying south of Canada and east of the Allegheny Mountains. Toward this end they conducted military operations on an important scale west of the Alleghenies, with the purpose, which was at first successful, of driving back eastward across the mountains all those Americans who, before the Revolution, had crossed into what is now Ohio and Michigan and Indiana and Illinois and Kentucky and Tennessee.

In that year, 1778, the picture of this Western country was dark indeed. The English held all the region northwest of the Ohio, and their Indian allies were burning cabins and driving fleeing families back across the mountains south of the river. Indeed there were only three forts that remained in all of Kentucky, and their fall seemed inevitable.

In that moment, against the dark background, rose the young Virginian, George Rogers Clark. Out of despair and destruction he brought concerted action. With a flash of genius, the twenty-six-year-old leader conceived a campaign—a brilliant masterpiece of military strategy. Working with the good-will of the French settlers through these States, and overawing the Indians by what perhaps we can call sheer bravado, he swept through to Kaskaskia and other towns of the Illinois country.

But the menace of the regular British forces remained. Colonel Henry Hamilton, the British Commander of the Northwest, had come down from Detroit. He seized and fortified Vincennes. Fort Sackville, where we stand today, as long as it remained uncaptured, made Clark's position untenable. His desperate resolution to save his men and the Northwest by a mid-winter march and an attack by riflemen on a fort manned by the King's own regiment and equipped with cannon marked the heroic measure of the man.

It is worth repeating the story that the famous winter march began at Kaskaskia with a religious service. To Father Pierre Gibault, and to Colonel Francis Vigo, a patriot of Italian birth, next to Clark himself, the United States is indebted for the saving of the Northwest Territory. And it was in the little log church, predecessor of yonder Church of Saint Francis Xavier, that Colonel Hamilton surrendered Vincennes to George Rogers Clark.

It is not a coincidence that this service in dedication of a noble monument takes place on a Sunday morning. Governor McNutt and I, aware of the historic relationship of religion to this campaign of the Revolution, and to the later Ordinance of 1787, have understood and felt the appropriateness of today.

Clark had declared at Kaskaskia before he began his famous march, that all religions would be tolerated in America. Eight years later the Ordinance of 1787, which established the territory northwest of the Ohio River, provided that "no person demeaning himself in a peaceable and orderly manner shall ever be molested on account of his mode of worship or for religious sentiments in the said territory."

And the Ordinance went on to declare further that "religion, morality and knowledge being necessary to good government and the happiness of mankind, schools and the means of education shall forever be encouraged." It seems to me that one hundred and forty-nine years later the people of the United States, in every part thereof, could reiterate and continue to strive for the principle that religion, morality and knowledge are necessary to good government and the happiness of mankind.

Today religion is still free within our borders; it must ever remain so.

Today morality means the same thing as it meant in the days of George Rogers Clark, though we must needs apply it to many, many situations of which George Rogers Clark never dreamt. In his day among the pioneers there were jumpers of land claims; there were those who sought to swindle their neighbors, even though they were all poor in this world's goods and lived in sparsely settled communities. Today among our teeming millions there are still those who by dishonorable means seek to obtain the possessions of their unwary neighbors. Our modern civilization must constantly protect itself against moral defectives whose objectives are the same, but whose methods are more subtle than those of their prototypes of a century and a half ago. We do not change our form of free government when we arm ourselves with new weapons against new devices of crime and cupidity.

Today, as in 1787, we have knowledge; but it is a vastly wider knowledge.

During the past week I have traveled through many States; and as I have looked out in the daylight hours upon the countryside of Tennessee and Alabama and Arkansas and Texas and Oklahoma, I have tried to visualize what that countryside looked like a short century and a half ago. All of it was primeval forest or untilled prairie, inhabited by an exceedingly small population of nomadic Indian tribes. It was untouched by the civilization of the white man.

In most of this vast territory, as here a little farther north in the Middle West, Nature gave her bounteous gifts to the new settlers, and for many long years these gifts were received by them without thought of the future. Here was an instance where the knowledge of the day was as yet insufficient to see the dangers that lay ahead.

Who, for example, even among the second and third generations of the settlers of this virgin land, gave heed to the future results that attended the cutting of the timber which denuded the greater part of the watersheds?

Who, among them, gave thought to the tragic extermination of the wild life which formed the principal article of food of the pioneers?

Who among them had ever heard the term "submarginal land" or worried about what would happen when the original soil played out or ran off to the ocean?

Who among them were concerned if the market price for livestock for the moment justified the overgrazing of pastures, or a temporary boom in the price of cotton or corn tempted men to forget that rotation of crops was a farming maxim as far back as the days of ancient Babylon?

Who among them regarded floods as preventable?

Who among them thought of the use of coal, or oil, or gas, or falling water as the means of turning their wheels and lighting their homes?

Who among them visualized the day when the sun would be darkened as far east as the waters of the Atlantic by great clouds of topsoil borne by the wind from what used to be grassy and apparently imperishable prairies?

Because man did not have our knowledge in those older days, he wounded Nature and Nature has taken offense. It is the task of us, the living, to restore to Nature many of the riches we have taken from her in order that she may smile once more upon those who come after us.

George Rogers Clark did battle against the tomahawk and the rifle. He saved for us the fair land that lay between the mountains and the Father of Waters. His task is not done. Though we fight with weapons unknown to him, it is still our duty to continue the saving of this fair land. May the Americans who, a century and a half from now, celebrate at this spot the three hundredth anniversary of the heroism of Clark and his men, think kindly of us for the part we are taking today in preserving the Nation of the United States.

72 ❨ On Visiting the Birthplace of Abraham Lincoln. June 14, 1936

I HAVE visited the cabin in which Abraham Lincoln was born. I have come here individually, as one of many millions of Americans whose lives have been influenced for the good by Abraham Lincoln.

I live, temporarily, in the same house and the same rooms once occupied by him. The very window from which he gazed in the dark days is the same.

But this cabin is even more personal than the scenes of his official life, for here was born and lived the child. Here was the promise, later to be so splendidly fulfilled.

I have taken from this cabin a renewed confidence that the spirit of America is not dead, that men and means will be found to explore and conquer the problems of a new time with no less humanity and no less fortitude than his.

Here we can renew our pledge of fidelity to the faith which Lincoln held in the common man — the faith so simply expressed when he said:

"As I would not be a slave, so I would not be a master. This expresses my idea of democracy. Whatever differs from this, to the extent of the difference, is no democracy."

(See note to Item 63, this volume.)

73 ❨ The First Step against Collusive Bidding on Government Supplies. June 15, 1936

My dear Mr. Attorney General:

I AM sending you herewith the report to the President by the Federal Trade Commission in relation to collusive bidding on steel sheet piling.

You will note that the Federal Trade Commission definitely finds the existence of collusion. In accordance with their recommendation, I am referring the whole matter to you for appropriate action.

Please also note the further recommendations of the Commission:

(a) That the President request all purchasing officials of the Federal Government to collect and furnish evidence regarding instances where there has been collusive or identical bidding.

(b) That the President give consideration to recommending legislation to the Congress to make existing unfair practices unlawful.

Will you be good enough to prepare for me the necessary letters to purchasing agents to be sent out by me at once, and also to prepare a draft of recommendations to the Congress at its next session?

Very sincerely yours,

The Attorney General,
Department of Justice,
Washington, D. C.

74 ❬ The President Submits to the Congress Recommendations of the International Labor Organization Held at Geneva. June 18, 1936

To the Congress:

THE Congress, by a Joint Resolution approved June 19, 1934, authorized me to accept membership for the Government of the United States in the International Labor Organization. Pursuant to that authorization I accepted such membership on behalf of the Government of the United States.

Representatives of this Government and of American employers and American labor attended the Nineteenth Session of the Conference of the International Labor Organization, held at Geneva June 4-25, 1935.

That Conference adopted, the American representatives voting favorably, five Draft Conventions and one Recommendation, to wit:

The Draft Convention concerning the employment of women on underground work in mines of all kinds.

The Draft Convention limiting hours of work in coal mines (revised 1935).

The Draft Convention concerning the reduction of hours of work to forty a week.

The Draft Convention concerning the establishment of an international scheme for the maintenance of rights under invalidity, old-age and widows' and orphans' insurance.

The Draft Convention concerning the reduction of hours of work in glass-bottle works.

The Recommendation concerning unemployment among young persons.

In becoming a member of the Organization and subscribing to its constitution, this Government accepted the following undertaking in regard to such draft conventions and recommendations:

"Each of the Members undertakes that it will, within the period of one year at most from the closing of the session of the Conference, or if it is impossible owing to exceptional circumstances to do so within the period of one year, then at the earliest practicable moment and in no case later than eighteen months from the closing of the session of the Conference, bring the Recommendation or draft Convention before the authority or authorities within whose competence the matter lies, for the enactment of legislation or other action." (Article 19 [405], Paragraph 5, Constitution of the International Labor Organization.)

"In the case of a Federal State, the power of which to enter into conventions on labor matters is subject to limitations, it shall be in the discretion of that Government to treat a draft convention to which such limitations apply as a recommendation only, and the provisions of this Article with respect to recommendations shall apply in such case." (Article 19 [405], Paragraph 9, Constitution of the International Labor Organization.)

In accordance with the foregoing undertaking the above-named five Conventions and one Recommendation are herewith submitted to the Congress with the accompanying report of the Secretary of State, to which the attention of the Congress is invited.

75 ❡ Presidential Statement on Revocation of Neutrality Proclamations in War between Italy and Ethiopia. June 20, 1936

WHEN it was ascertained that a state of war existed between Italy and Ethiopia, I performed the duty imposed upon me by legislation, by issuing proclamations making effective an embargo on arms, ammunition and implements of war from the United States to the belligerent countries and admonishing American citizens to abstain from traveling on belligerent vessels.

In doing so, I was standing upon a question of fact. Having now ascertained that, in fact, the conditions which led to the issuing of the proclamations have ceased to exist, I have, in conformity with the duty imposed upon me, issued proclamations revoking my earlier proclamations.

Therefore, the statements which I issued in respect to commercial transactions with the belligerents are no longer applicable.

NOTE: It had become apparent that a state of war no longer in fact existed in Ethiopia. Accordingly with the foregoing statement I issued Proclamations Nos. 2179 and 2180, revoking my previous Proclamations of October 5, 1935, Nos. 2141 and 2142 with respect to the export of arms to these belligerents and with reference to the travel by American citzens on belligerent vessels. (See Items 143 and 144 of Vol. IV.)

During all the period between my proclamations of October 5, 1935, and the date of these proclamations, the embargo on the export of arms had functioned effectively. Although there were a number of attempts to violate the embargo, the combined efforts of the Departments of State, Treasury and Justice prevented the success of any attempt so far as any knowledge has come to the attention of the authorities.

76 ❲ The Three Hundred and Third Press Conference (Excerpts). June 23, 1936

(Committee to study cooperatives in some European countries.)

Q. We have a slim crowd for you today, Mr. President.

Q. Just the second-string men. *(Laughter)*

THE PRESIDENT: I would not stand for it for a minute.

MR. EARLY: I pointed out this morning that any news out of here might compete with Philadelphia *(where the Democratic National Convention was in progress)*.

Q. We might get some local stuff here today.

THE PRESIDENT: For the benefit of all of you, there is no general news and, for the benefit of Russ *(Young)*, there is no local news. . . .

Q. Harry Hopkins had a group in the other day. On their way out they did not talk very much. They said something about studying cooperative enterprises in Europe.

THE PRESIDENT: I was going to release that next week, but I might as well tell you that now. There are three men going abroad: Jacob Baker, Assistant Works Progress Administrator; Leland Olds, who is the Secretary of the New York State Power Authority, and Charles E. Stuart, of the engineering firm of Stuart, James and Cooke, of New York.

They are going abroad on the first of July to make a report on cooperative enterprises in certain parts of Europe. They are going to the British Isles, Sweden, Denmark and Finland and, I think, Norway, although it is not down here, Czechoslovakia, Switzerland and France. Also, possibly, Hungary.

They are to study the cooperative developments in Europe in relation to cooperative stores, housing, credit, insurance, banking, electrical distribution, cooperative producers, cooperative marketing and, in general, the coordinating of these different kinds of cooperatives with each other and with other forms of conducting the same services, also the relationship of these different Governments to these cooperative agencies.

This is a thing you will not want to use, but I think it is tremendously interesting; and you might perhaps use it as background without attributing it to me. I became a good deal interested in the cooperative development in countries abroad, especially Sweden. A very interesting book came out a couple of months ago — *The Middle Way*. I was tremendously interested in what they had done in Scandinavia along those lines. In Sweden, for example, you have a royal family and a Socialist Government and a capitalistic system, all working happily side by side. Of course, to be sure, it is a smaller country than ours; but they have conducted some very interesting and, so far, very successful experiments. They have these cooperative movements existing happily and successfully alongside of private industry and distribution of various kinds, both of them making money. I thought it was at least worthy of study from our point of view.

I think this Committee of three will be gone only about two months or two months and a half and it will necessarily be just a hasty survey — a bird's-eye view of what has been accomplished over there. It is especially important because in this country, as you may know, there has been a substantial growth of the cooperative movement in various parts of the country among producers, such as farmers, and among middlemen and among consumers.

It is something that has nothing political in it, from a partisan point of view.

Q. To whom do they report, to you?

THE PRESIDENT: Yes.

Q. Do you see a way of putting unemployed to work? Is it a move toward putting unemployed to work through cooperatives?

THE PRESIDENT: Only indirectly. In Scandinavia the unemployment situation is not a serious one. They still have their unemployed but, since going on these general methods, the number of unemployed has decreased quite sharply.

Q. Isn't the cooperative movement an answer to monopoly rather than unemployment, viewed in that light?

THE PRESIDENT: Yes. . . .

77 ⟨ Informal Extemporaneous Remarks to the Members of Kiwanis. The White House, Washington, D. C. June 24, 1936

As A fellow member, I am very happy to greet you here.

I think you know of my fairly long association with the Kiwanis; and I think you know also of my very special interest in one of the many fine things the Kiwanis is doing, and that relates to looking after crippled children. I know of the practical results of this work in a great many communities. I think we all recognize that there are a good many fields, a good many problems in our modern life, where it is in every way best for the country that the primary and preliminary responsibilities should rest upon civilian organizations and not wholly on the Government.

That is as it should be. It applies, that principle, to a great many things that we have to cope with in these days. As we all know, there have been an advance in science, and an advance in public understanding of a great many things that, in the old days, were taken for granted. A couple of generations ago there were a great many evils about which nobody bothered their heads.

In this work the more that can be done by the citizens of each community, the better it is. That is why I am very proud of what Kiwanis International has accomplished in these years.

It is through organizations like Kiwanis that we are able to spread through the communities — not merely through our own membership, but to all of our friends and neighbors — what might be called a better education among the masses of the people, a better understanding of the problem. It is the old idea of sitting around a table and talking it over.

One of my jobs in Washington is to sit around a table and talk it over. I do it every day that I am here. They are talks that touch practically every phase of our national life.

One of the other things that we seem to have accomplished in these more recent years is the spread of understanding that the country is one big country and that the handling of problems in one locality affects the handling of problems in all other localities and communities. In other words, the force of example is of tremendous importance and effect in a great continent such as ours.

You probably have heard the term, "good neighbor." We seem to have established the principle fairly well in our relations with all of the Governments of North, Central and South America. What I hope is that we will extend the doctrine of the good neighbor to all of the communities within our own borders. In that work Kiwanis has accomplished much.

I wish I could have attended the various meetings of this convention. Some day, when I get through with my job here, I hope you will let me come just as a delegate.

78 ❦ A Letter of Congratulation to the National Youth Administration. June 26, 1936

My dear Mr. Williams:

O NE year ago today when I signed the Executive Order creating the National Youth Administration and placing its affairs in your hands, I predicted that the return on the investment would be high.

I am happy to see that this prediction, twelve months later, has been fulfilled. I am still more gratified that Congress, sharing in this belief, has seen fit to include a substantial allotment for the National Youth Administration in the Deficiency Bill for 1937.

No greater obligation faces the Government than to justify the faith of its young people in the fundamental rightness of our democratic institutions and to preserve their strength, loyalty and idealism against the time when they must assume the responsibilities of citizenship. The splendid record of the National Youth Administration in helping some 600,000 young men and women against the despair of idleness seems to me excellent testimony that our means of meeting that obligation are sound.

It is my sincere hope that the influence and usefulness of the National Youth Administration will continue to widen during the coming year.

Very sincerely yours,

Honorable Aubrey Williams,
National Youth Administration,
Washington, D. C.

(See Item 86A, Vol. IV, for a discussion of the National Youth Administration.)

79 ⟨ "We Are Fighting to Save a Great and Precious Form of Government for Ourselves and the World"—Acceptance of the Renomination for the Presidency, Philadelphia, Pa. June 27, 1936

Senator Robinson, Members of the Democratic Convention, my friends:

H ERE, and in every community throughout the land, we are met at a time of great moment to the future of the Nation. It is an occasion to be dedicated to the simple and sincere expression of an attitude toward problems, the determination of which will profoundly affect America.

I come not only as a leader of a party, not only as a candidate for high office, but as one upon whom many critical hours have imposed and still impose a grave responsibility.

For the sympathy, help and confidence with which Americans have sustained me in my task I am grateful. For their loyalty I salute the members of our great party, in and out of political life

in every part of the Union. I salute those of other parties, especially those in the Congress of the United States who on so many
occasions have put partisanship aside. I thank the Governors of
the several States, their Legislatures, their State and local officials
who participated unselfishly and regardless of party in our efforts
to achieve recovery and destroy abuses. Above all I thank the
millions of Americans who have borne disaster bravely and have
dared to smile through the storm.

America will not forget these recent years, will not forget that
the rescue was not a mere party task. It was the concern of all of
us. In our strength we rose together, rallied our energies together,
applied the old rules of common sense, and together survived.

In those days we feared fear. That was why we fought fear.
And today, my friends, we have won against the most dangerous
of our foes. We have conquered fear.

But I cannot, with candor, tell you that all is well with the
world. Clouds of suspicion, tides of ill-will and intolerance gather
darkly in many places. In our own land we enjoy indeed a full-
ness of life greater than that of most Nations. But the rush of
modern civilization itself has raised for us new difficulties, new
problems which must be solved if we are to preserve to the United
States the political and economic freedom for which Washington
and Jefferson planned and fought.

Philadelphia is a good city in which to write American history.
This is fitting ground on which to reaffirm the faith of our fathers;
to pledge ourselves to restore to the people a wider freedom; to
give to 1936 as the founders gave to 1776—an American way of
life.

That very word freedom, in itself and of necessity, suggests
freedom from some restraining power. In 1776 we sought freedom from the tyranny of a political autocracy—from the eight-
eenth century royalists who held special privileges from the
crown. It was to perpetuate their privilege that they governed
without the consent of the governed; that they denied the right
of free assembly and free speech; that they restricted the worship

of God; that they put the average man's property and the average man's life in pawn to the mercenaries of dynastic power; that they regimented the people.

And so it was to win freedom from the tyranny of political autocracy that the American Revolution was fought. That victory gave the business of governing into the hands of the average man, who won the right with his neighbors to make and order his own destiny through his own Government. Political tyranny was wiped out at Philadelphia on July 4, 1776.

Since that struggle, however, man's inventive genius released new forces in our land which reordered the lives of our people. The age of machinery, of railroads; of steam and electricity; the telegraph and the radio; mass production, mass distribution — all of these combined to bring forward a new civilization and with it a new problem for those who sought to remain free.

For out of this modern civilization economic royalists carved new dynasties. New kingdoms were built upon concentration of control over material things. Through new uses of corporations, banks and securities, new machinery of industry and agriculture, of labor and capital — all undreamed of by the fathers — the whole structure of modern life was impressed into this royal service.

There was no place among this royalty for our many thousands of small business men and merchants who sought to make a worthy use of the American system of initiative and profit. They were no more free than the worker or the farmer. Even honest and progressive-minded men of wealth, aware of their obligation to their generation, could never know just where they fitted into this dynastic scheme of things.

It was natural and perhaps human that the privileged princes of these new economic dynasties, thirsting for power, reached out for control over Government itself. They created a new despotism and wrapped it in the robes of legal sanction. In its service new mercenaries sought to regiment the people, their labor, and their property. And as a result the average man once more confronts the problem that faced the Minute Man.

The hours men and women worked, the wages they received, the conditions of their labor—these had passed beyond the control of the people, and were imposed by this new industrial dictatorship. The savings of the average family, the capital of the small business man, the investments set aside for old age—other people's money—these were tools which the new economic royalty used to dig itself in.

Those who tilled the soil no longer reaped the rewards which were their right. The small measure of their gains was decreed by men in distant cities.

Throughout the Nation, opportunity was limited by monopoly. Individual initiative was crushed in the cogs of a great machine. The field open for free business was more and more restricted. Private enterprise, indeed, became too private. It became privileged enterprise, not free enterprise.

An old English judge once said: "Necessitous men are not free men." Liberty requires opportunity to make a living—a living decent according to the standard of the time, a living which gives man not only enough to live by, but something to live for.

For too many of us the political equality we once had won was meaningless in the face of economic inequality. A small group had concentrated into their own hands an almost complete control over other people's property, other people's money, other people's labor—other people's lives. For too many of us life was no longer free; liberty no longer real; men could no longer follow the pursuit of happiness.

Against economic tyranny such as this, the American citizen could appeal only to the organized power of Government. The collapse of 1929 showed up the despotism for what it was. The election of 1932 was the people's mandate to end it. Under that mandate it is being ended.

The royalists of the economic order have conceded that political freedom was the business of the Government, but they have maintained that economic slavery was nobody's business. They granted that the Government could protect the citizen in his right to vote, but they denied that the Government could do anything to protect the citizen in his right to work and his right to live.

Today we stand committed to the proposition that freedom is no half-and-half affair. If the average citizen is guaranteed equal opportunity in the polling place, he must have equal opportunity in the market place.

These economic royalists complain that we seek to overthrow the institutions of America. What they really complain of is that we seek to take away their power. Our allegiance to American institutions requires the overthrow of this kind of power. In vain they seek to hide behind the Flag and the Constitution. In their blindness they forget what the Flag and the Constitution stand for. Now, as always, they stand for democracy, not tyranny; for freedom, not subjection; and against a dictatorship by mob rule and the overprivileged alike.

The brave and clear platform adopted by this Convention, to which I heartily subscribe, sets forth that Government in a modern civilization has certain inescapable obligations to its citizens, among which are protection of the family and the home, the establishment of a democracy of opportunity, and aid to those overtaken by disaster.

But the resolute enemy within our gates is ever ready to beat down our words unless in greater courage we will fight for them.

For more than three years we have fought for them. This Convention, in every word and deed, has pledged that that fight will go on.

The defeats and victories of these years have given to us as a people a new understanding of our Government and of ourselves. Never since the early days of the New England town meeting have the affairs of Government been so widely discussed and so clearly appreciated. It has been brought home to us that the only effective guide for the safety of this most worldly of worlds, the greatest guide of all, is moral principle.

We do not see faith, hope and charity as unattainable ideals,

234

but we use them as stout supports of a Nation fighting the fight for freedom in a modern civilization.

Faith—in the soundness of democracy in the midst of dictatorships.

Hope—renewed because we know so well the progress we have made.

Charity—in the true spirit of that grand old word. For charity literally translated from the original means love, the love that understands, that does not merely share the wealth of the giver, but in true sympathy and wisdom helps men to help themselves.

We seek not merely to make Government a mechanical implement, but to give it the vibrant personal character that is the very embodiment of human charity.

We are poor indeed if this Nation cannot afford to lift from every recess of American life the dread fear of the unemployed that they are not needed in the world. We cannot afford to accumulate a deficit in the books of human fortitude.

In the place of the palace of privilege we seek to build a temple out of faith and hope and charity.

It is a sobering thing, my friends, to be a servant of this great cause. We try in our daily work to remember that the cause belongs not to us, but to the people. The standard is not in the hands of you and me alone. It is carried by America. We seek daily to profit from experience, to learn to do better as our task proceeds.

Governments can err, Presidents do make mistakes, but the immortal Dante tells us that divine justice weighs the sins of the cold-blooded and the sins of the warm-hearted in different scales.

Better the occasional faults of a Government that lives in a spirit of charity than the consistent omissions of a Government frozen in the ice of its own indifference.

There is a mysterious cycle in human events. To some generations much is given. Of other generations much is expected. This generation of Americans has a rendezvous with destiny.

In this world of ours in other lands, there are some people, who, in times past, have lived and fought for freedom, and seem to have grown too weary to carry on the fight. They have sold their heritage of freedom for the illusion of a living. They have yielded their democracy.

I believe in my heart that only our success can stir their ancient hope. They begin to know that here in America we are waging a great and successful war. It is not alone a war against want and destitution and economic demoralization. It is more than that; it is a war for the survival of democracy. We are fighting to save a great and precious form of government for ourselves and for the world.

I accept the commission you have tendered me. I join with you. I am enlisted for the duration of the war.

80 ❲ A Letter Urging Governor Herbert H. Lehman, of New York, to Become a Candidate for Reelection. June 29, 1936

Dear Herbert:

FOR some weeks, and particularly since the close of the New York State legislative session, I have been giving careful thought to some matters of grave importance to the country, and especially their relationship to the State of New York. May I repeat to you what I have already told you — that I was deeply disappointed when you stated that you would not again be a candidate for Governor; though at the same time, as you know, I fully appreciate the valid personal reasons which impelled you to make the statement and sympathized with you in those reasons.

Nevertheless I am writing frankly and with deepest sincerity to tell you what I conceive to be the other side of the picture.

For many years you and I have worked for many kinds of social legislation; much legislation of this type has been enacted, but at the same time much remains unfulfilled.

Our State was and still is among the pioneers, and today the

Federal Government is making it possible for all the States to join in this great work.

The next two years, I think, will be very critical ones, and what takes place in New York will have an outstanding effect all over the Nation.

If the next State administration should be in the hands of any individual whose heart is not in the right place in respect to these great ideals or is even in part controlled by those who are unsympathetic to objectives which you and I have, we would fail. More than that, I fear that many of the excellent laws put on the statute books during your four years as Governor would be repealed, weakened, or enforced by people who had their tongues in their cheeks.

The State of New York would be hurt thereby; even more important to the Nation, the Nation would be hurt thereby, for that kind of example is imitated and spreads.

I have referred to social legislation, such as fair wage laws, unemployment insurance, old-age pensions, care of the destitute, but I should include the equally wide range of legislation affecting public utilities and conservation and, in general, the lives of the average citizen.

I am convinced that your return to Albany for another two years would have a splendid effect on all the rest of the country. That magnificent and richly deserved tribute which was given to you in Philadelphia last week shows what the other States think of your fine and successful leadership.

I hope, therefore, that not only for the State but for the national good, you will be willing to reconsider your statement that you would not run again. Such reconsideration would make me very happy. More than that, it would make millions of people all over the United States very happy.

With my affectionate regards,

Very sincerely yours,

Governor Herbert H. Lehman,
Albany, New York.

81 ❮ "We Seek to Pass on to Our Children a Richer Land—a Stronger Nation"—Address at Dedication of Shenandoah National Park.

July 3, 1936

Governor Peery, Secretary Ickes, ladies and gentlemen:

I AM very glad to come back to Virginia.

The creation of this Park is one part of our great program of husbandry—the joint husbandry of human resources and natural resources. In every part of the country, local and State and Federal authorities are engaged in preserving and developing our heritage of natural resources; and in this work they are also conserving our priceless heritage of human values by giving to hundreds of thousands of men the opportunity of making an honest living.

I saw this work in progress when I was here two years ago. I have seen it in progress in many other parts of the land; and so I can say, from first-hand evidence, that the product of the labor of the men of the Civilian Conservation Corps, who have opened the Shenandoah National Park and other parks to the use and enjoyment of our citizens, is as significant as though instead of working for the Government they had been working in a mill or in a factory. They have a right to be as proud of their labor here as if they had been engaged in private employment.

In bygone years we have seen, and even we of this generation have seen, the terrible tragedy of our age, the tragedy of waste—waste of our people, waste of our land. It was neither the will nor the destiny of our Nation that this waste of human and material resources should continue any longer. That was the compelling reason that led us to put our idle people to the task of ending the waste of our land.

The involuntary idleness of thousands of young men ended three years ago when they came here to the camps on the Blue

Ridge. Since then they have not been idle. Today they have ended more than their own idleness, they have ended the idleness of the Shenandoah National Park. It will be a busy and useful place in the years to come, just as the work of these young men will, I am confident, lead them to busy and useful lives in the years to come.

Our country is going to need many other young men as they come to manhood, need them for work like this — for other Shenandoahs.

Is it a dream? Shall I perhaps be accused of an exaggerated passion for planning if I paint for you a picture? You who are here know of the great usefulness to humanity which this Skyline Drive achieves from now on, of the greater usefulness which its extension, south through Virginia and North Carolina and Tennessee to the Great Smoky Mountains National Park, will achieve.

In almost every other part of the country there is a similar need for recreational areas, for parkways which will give to men and women of moderate means the opportunity, the invigoration and the luxury of touring and camping amid scenes of great natural beauty like this.

All across the Nation — and it is three thousand miles — at this time of the year, and in many parts of the Nation at all times of the year, people are starting out for their vacations in national and State parks. Those people will put up at roadside camps or pitch their tents under the stars, with an open fire to cook by, with the smell of the woods, and the wind in the trees. They will forget the rush and the strain of all the other long weeks of the year, and for a short time at least, the days will be good for their bodies and good for their souls. Once more they will lay hold of the perspective that comes to men and women who every morning and every night can lift up their eyes to Mother Nature.

There is merit for all of us in the ancient tale of the giant Antæus, who, every time he touched his Mother Earth, arose with strength renewed a hundredfold.

This Park, therefore, together with its many sisters which are

239

coming to completion in every part of our land, is in the largest sense a work of conservation. Through all of them we are preserving the beauty and the wealth of the hills and the mountains and the plains and the trees and the streams. Through all of them we are maintaining useful work for our young men. Through all of them we are enriching the character and the happiness of our people.

We seek to pass on to our children a richer land — a stronger Nation.

And so, my friends, I now take great pleasure in dedicating Shenandoah National Park, dedicating it to this and succeeding generations of Americans for the recreation and for the re-creation which they shall find here.

82 ⟨ "America Has Lived and Grown under the System of Government Established by Jefferson and His Generation" — Address at the Home of Thomas Jefferson, Monticello, Virginia. July 4, 1936

Senator Glass, Governor Peery, Mr. Gibboney, ladies and gentlemen:

As my old friend, Carter Glass, has so well suggested, I have come here today to renew my homage to the sage of Monticello.

It was symbolic that Thomas Jefferson should live on this mountain-top of Monticello. On a mountain-top all paths unite. And Jefferson was the meeting point of all the vital forces of his day.

There are periods in history when one man seems great because those who stand beside him are small. Jefferson was great in the presence of many great and free men. When we read of the patriots of 1776 and the fathers of the Constitution, we are taken into the presence of men who caught the fire of greatness from one another, and who all became elevated above the common run of mankind.

The source of their greatness was the stirring of a new sense of freedom. They were tasting the first fruits of self-government and freedom of conscience. They had broken away from a system of peasantry, away from indentured servitude. They could build for themselves a new economic independence. Theirs were not the gods of things as they were, but the gods of things as they ought to be. And so, as Monticello itself so well proves, they used new means and new models to build new structures.

Of all the builders of those days it is perhaps generally conceded that Benjamin Franklin and Thomas Jefferson possessed what may be roughly described as the most fertile minds. Franklin was stranger to no science, to no theory of philosophy, to no avenue of invention. Jefferson had those qualities in equal part; and with greater opportunity in the days of peace which followed the Revolution, Jefferson was enabled more fully to carry theory into practice.

Farmer, lawyer, mechanic, scientist, architect, philosopher, statesman, he encompassed the full scope of the knowledge of his time; and his life was one of the richest diversity. To him knowledge and ideal were fuel to be used to feed the fires of his own mind, not just wood to be left neatly piled in the woodbox.

More than any historic home in America, Monticello appeals to me as an expression of the personality of its builder. In the design, not of the whole alone, but of every room, of every part of every room, in the very furnishings which Jefferson devised on his own drawing board and made in his own workshop, there speaks ready capacity for detail and, above all, creative genius.

He was a great gentleman. He was a great commoner. The two are not incompatible.

He applied the culture of the past to the needs and the life of the America of his day. His knowledge of history spurred him to inquire into the reason and justice of laws, habits and institutions. His passion for liberty led him to interpret and adapt them in order to better the lot of mankind.

Shortly before taking the office of President he wrote to a friend, "I have sworn on the Altar of God eternal hostility against every form of tyranny over the mind of man." His life served that consecration. Constantly he labored to enlarge the freedom of the human mind and to destroy the bondage imposed on it by ignorance, poverty and political and religious intolerance.

On one day of his long life he gave to the world a Declaration of Independence on behalf of political freedom for himself and his fellow Americans. But his Declaration of Independence for the human mind was a continuing achievement, renewed and reiterated every day of his whole life.

One hundred and sixty years have passed since the Fourth of July, 1776. On that day, Thomas Jefferson was thirty-three years old. His imagination, his enthusiasm and his energy, the qualities that youth offers in every generation, were symbolic of that generation of men, who not only made a Nation in the wealth of their imagination and energy, but, because their youthful wings had not been clipped, were able to grow with the Nation and guide it in wisdom throughout their lives.

Through all the intervening years, America has lived and grown under the system of government established by Jefferson and his generation. As Nations go, we live under one of the oldest continuous forms of democratic government in the whole world. In that sense we are old.

But the world has never had as much human ability as it needs; and a modern democracy in particular needs, above all things, the continuance of the spirit of youth. Our problems of 1936 call as greatly for the continuation of imagination and energy and capacity for responsibility as did the age of Thomas Jefferson and his fellows.

Democracy needs now, as it found then, men developed, through education, to the limit of their capacity for ultimate responsibility. Emergencies and decisions in our individual and community and national lives are the stuff out of which national character is made. Preparation of the mind, preparation of the

242

spirit of our people for such emergencies, for such decisions, is the best available insurance for the security and development of our democratic institutions.

Was the spirit of such men as Jefferson the spirit of a Golden Age gonè now, and never to be repeated in our history? Was the feeling of fundamental freedom which lighted the fire of their ability a miracle we shall never see again?

That is not my belief. It is not beyond our power to re-light that sacred fire. There are no limitations upon the Nation's capacity to obtain and maintain true freedom, no limitations except the strength of our Nation's desire and determination.

On the hillside below where we stand is the tomb of Thomas Jefferson. He was given many high offices in State and Nation. But the words recorded above his grave, chosen by himself, are only these:

> "HERE WAS BURIED THOMAS JEFFERSON, AUTHOR OF THE DECLARATION OF AMERICAN INDEPENDENCE, OF THE STATUTE OF VIRGINIA FOR RELIGIOUS FREEDOM, AND FATHER OF THE UNIVERSITY OF VIRGINIA."

The honors which other men had given him were unimportant; the opportunities he had given to other men to become free were all that really counted.

83 ❪The Three Hundred and Sixth Press Conference (Excerpts). July 7, 1936

(Drought of 1936 — Resettlement — Passamaquoddy and Florida Ship Canal — Proposed drought inspection trip.)

THE PRESIDENT: Let us talk agriculture. I have here some pretty up-to-date charts which I think Steve (*Early*) can take out to the Press Room and pin up so that you can see them.

They show pasture conditions on June 1 — the black belt is the extreme drought — and the conditions on July 1. See what a difference there is. This here (*indicating*) is the statement of rains from July 1 to 6, so that the three of them give you a pretty good idea.

The general situation is that while there are still drought conditions in the Southeast, that is to say Southern Kentucky, Northern Tennessee and Georgia, North Carolina and South Carolina, they are not our principal problem. There are also drought conditions, as I said before, in Eastern Oklahoma and Western Arkansas which have been slightly relieved in the last two or three days.

The principal problem is, of course, in the Northwest, especially in the Dakotas, Eastern Montana, Northeastern Wyoming and extending now into Northeastern Minnesota.

There are, all told, in all of these drought areas, including the Southeast and Southwest, about 204,000 families who need some form of immediate cash relief. The bulk of them are, of course, in the Northwest.

We have worked out a fairly comprehensive plan by which we are putting 50,000 to work at the present time, on W.P.A. jobs. These 50,000 are doing useful work, chiefly in the following forms: first, digging wells, in other words getting down to water; and, second, building earth dams, so that when rains do come they will not all run off all of a sudden; third, building farm-to-market roads. Those are the three principal forms of actual relief work. Those workers are being paid weekly wages, and will continue until snow flies. In other words, they will be taken care of with actual work until it is impossible to work outdoors in that area.

Q. May I interrupt to ask you what the weekly wage is?

MR. AUBREY WILLIAMS: About $15 a week.

THE PRESIDENT: About $15 a week. That will keep them going and, in a good many cases, will take care of some of their needs into the winter. I shall not say through the winter, but into the winter.

Q. Has that payment started?

THE PRESIDENT: In Minnesota they are going to work at the present rate of 800 new workers a day. In North Dakota it is 2,000 new workers a day; in South Dakota 2,800 new workers a day; and in Montana, Eastern Montana, 400 new workers a day.

Q. Does your chart show a breakdown for the Southeast as against the Northwest in the number of sufferers?

THE PRESIDENT: No, I don't think so. The great bulk is of course in the Northwest.

Q. Mr. President, those are chiefly wheat States, are they not?

THE PRESIDENT: Mostly wheat, yes.

Q. Isn't the wheat ready for harvest?

THE PRESIDENT: No, there isn't any to harvest. It just isn't there to harvest.

MR. WILLIAMS: The spring wheat crop has been hit so hard that very little of it will be harvested in this area.

THE PRESIDENT: The wheat crop will be about 15 percent of normal.

   Then, number two, we are taking care of 50,000 families with subsistence loans and subsistence grants. That is part of the regular Resettlement work, but this work is in addition — in other words, these are new people. Then of the 200,000 that are already on subsistence loans and grants, there are 70,000 there; so that gives you a total of 150,000 who are either being taken care of or are going to be taken care of in the course of the next few days at this rate of putting them

245

on. The program will be actually under way probably in a couple of weeks.

That leaves a gap, which still has to be filled, of about 34,000 families, and we are working toward that end.

Now, the cattle problem. I shall take that up first. Cattle are going out of that area, as a private enterprise, in fairly large volume; but the price is holding up. Individual cattle raisers who have fair-sized herds are able to move their cattle out quite satisfactorily at the present time, to move them out to market or to feeding, one or the other.

The people who find it difficult to handle the situation are chiefly the small cattlemen, the individual fellow who has only eight or ten or fifteen or twenty head, and with him it is principally a problem not only of getting them out, but of keeping some title in them. In other words, we don't want him to lose all of his breeding cattle for next year or lose his immediate title. That is why we are going to use every effort not to buy cattle ourselves and process them for food. We prefer to loan the money to those individuals and let them ship the cattle out as feeders. They would retain the title to them.

You know the process: You send the cows out to somebody else who has grass, for instance in Western Montana and Idaho, and you pay that man so much a month a head. I think the usual price is a dollar a head a month or something along that line. You retain the title to the cattle you ship out. They are not immediately processed. That also gives you an opportunity of retaining breeder stock for next year.

The wheat acreage this year, mind you, is nearly 10 percent higher than the average wheat acreage from 1928 to 1932. Now, that explodes a great many stories, doesn't it? It explodes lots and lots of stories, especially the ones written for political effect. Ten percent more wheat acreage in the country this year than for the average of 1928 to 1932. Of course the yield is going to be way below the average. That is caused by the drought, but the actual acreage planted to wheat is nearly 10 percent higher than the average of those years.

Q. What were those years?

THE PRESIDENT: 1928 to 1932. The same thing is true of corn acreage. It is up over last year; and so is the wheat acreage. In other words, the shortage is not due to any decrease in acreage. Write that down. It is due to drought.

Q. What are the payments for crop curtailment?

THE PRESIDENT: Soil conservation, in other words, putting in a rotation of crops.

Q. I meant how much will go to those States in these payments?

THE PRESIDENT: Turning it into pasture land and vice versa. I cannot tell you the actual figure.

MR. TUGWELL: We would have to look it up.

Q. These farmers will get money?

THE PRESIDENT: Oh, yes. . . .

Now, as part of the program, we also have to encourage the harvesting of forage crops in order to take care of those cattle which have not enough feed in the drought area. We do that without any decrease in benefits for the people who did not plow their land but turned it into a feed crop.

Q. Is that a monetary encouragement?

THE PRESIDENT: No, they have their contract — they have their benefit contract. It is not a contract — you know if they go in for diversified farming, they get so much of a bonus. They get the same bonus if they cut their forage crop and ship it into the drought area, no more.

Q. Will that be enough feed for the cattle?

THE PRESIDENT: We hope so.

Q. Tell us about Mr. Farley. (*Laughter*)

THE PRESIDENT: Then, there is another thing we might as well explode. I'm afraid somebody back there is not interested in farming. I shall come to the other feature; it is all right.

Q. Before we get into this, can you tell me in dollars what this is going to amount to?

THE PRESIDENT: No, not yet. That is too much spot news. Let us look at this thing from the immediate angle.

Q. Does this fund come from W.P.A. money?

THE PRESIDENT: It comes from all kinds, W.P.A., Resettlement, Surplus Commodity Corporation, etc. Now, what I do want to point out is this: Up there in the Northwestern area there have been stories, as usual, that we are going to take everybody away and depopulate the country.

Q. You would not take them away, would you?

THE PRESIDENT: We are not going to take them away at all. Nobody ever had any idea, in his sane moments, of depopulating the country. What we are going to change is what might be called the economy of the country. The country is going to support a population. As wheat land, no; it is not working because the water table drops down 8 inches a year. The result is the water runs off and the surface blows away.

We figure that a proper use of this country will support, perhaps not quite as many people, but very nearly. There are lots of human beings today who can remain there if they will do the right thing. For instance, if we can get grass back there, it means that the acreage will be used more and more for cattle. People have to look after cattle. There are certain places out there, certain valleys, where the water table has not disappeared, where you can grow vegetables, truck and small crops that take human beings to look after them. There are certain areas which can be and should be forested. It will take human beings to look after that.

What we are working on is a plan to avoid a continuation of what we have been through now for the last three or four years. The Federal Government has spent somewhere around $300,000,000, and, just so long as we do not change the economy, we are going to have to spend money year after year, unless the cycles change. We are going to have to take care of people on relief if they keep on with their present economy.

248

What we are trying to do is to work out a program that will keep the great bulk of the population out in the same area and at the same time make it unnecessary to spend each year millions of dollars to keep them from starving.

Q. For how long a period did you say that $300,000,000 has been spent?

THE PRESIDENT: In the last three or four years, 1933, '34, '35 and '36, four years. . . .

I considered going out there this week but what I wanted to do was to get this program actually under way. It will take another three or four weeks before it is under way.

The chief need will come, of course, in the winter and what we are working at now is to give these people work and provide for fall planting and for taking care of their cattle. It is a program that will take a month or six weeks to get under way.

That is why I am planning some time in August to go out to this Northwest dust bowl to look over the situation and see how these plans now adopted are working out, to take a look-see trip to see how it is going, because it is a very important national question.

If this drought area spreads or is allowed to spread, it will necessarily move around. It will move east and south into Nebraska, Kansas, Iowa, Minnesota and Wisconsin, and we have to stop it from coming east and south and west.

Q. Mr. President, what States do we understand you will visit, personally visit?

THE PRESIDENT: Oh, probably the Dakotas and possibly Minnesota.

Q. Any political speeches on this trip?

THE PRESIDENT: No, certainly not. . . .

Q. Do you have any plans for Quoddy after the present money has run out?

THE PRESIDENT: Only that I am working very hard in the case of Quoddy and the Florida Ship Canal to use the existing plant so that it won't lie idle.

249

Q. The existing plant?

THE PRESIDENT: Yes, the existing plant. In the case of the Florida Ship Canal we are negotiating with the University of Florida for the use of the buildings down there for — I think they call it an Extension Service Course.

Q. That would be a short-term lease?

THE PRESIDENT: Yes.

Q. Does that mean that you are abandoning the Ship Canal?

THE PRESIDENT: Have to. The same with Quoddy.

Q. How about Quoddy? Do you think you can use the buildings up there?

THE PRESIDENT: I cannot tell you yet, but I am working very hard to find a useful occupation for the buildings.

Q. We will probably have to rent them.

THE PRESIDENT: There is a very good hotel in Eastport.

Q. I did not see one.

Q. Do you mean the Quoddy power project is abandoned?

THE PRESIDENT: I cannot devote any money to it. How can I? I don't know. . . .

NOTE: With respect to the drought of 1936 discussed in this Press Conference, see Items 90, 99, 101, 131A of this volume. For speeches made during the drought inspection trip which I spoke of during the conference, see Items 101, 103, 105-113, 116-118, and 120 of this volume. With respect to "Quoddy," see Item 92, this volume.

84 ⟨ Informal Extemporaneous Remarks to Stock Cattlemen on Grazing Policy. July 8, 1936

IT IS good to see you all, and I wish I could attend the conferences you are having because I have been tremendously interested in the problem of public lands, not only on the forestry end but, especially in the State of New York itself, on the grazing end. I run into it on my other farm down in Georgia where we have a good deal of that problem.

I am glad that this cooperative movement is going so well because, under this Taylor Act, one of the essentials is to have cooperation from the people who use the public land.

During the past two or three years we have made great progress along that line; and we have certainly learned a great deal about the use and care of land. During our lifetime we have had some pretty horrible examples of the misuse of land. People who live on the land are becoming more and more conscious of the misuse to which the land has been put.

We are learning each year about the better use of land. Twenty-five or thirty years ago very few people understood, for instance, what over-grazing really meant. We have come to understand it better. We do not know about it fully. Nor do we know what the final solution of the problem of drought is going to be. We do know that in a great many parts of the country the water table, as we call it, is dropping down pretty seriously and that in a good many areas the top surface of the land is blowing away.

We also know that a good many areas, that used to be in trees, are no longer in trees. We have not the final answer; and it is up to all of you good people to help us to find the final answer. A lot of the work is still experimental; and that is why the interest of the local people is of such great importance.

We are buying under this new Act, I think, sixty million acres more to be added to the original acreage under the Taylor Act, and we are getting a national policy in regard to it which seems to be working out pretty well.

I am keen about the work you are doing. As I said, I wish I could go to your own conferences and sit in with you because, like everybody else, I have a good deal to learn.

(For a discussion of grazing and the Taylor Act, see Items 112 and 187 of Vol. III.)

85 ❡ A Letter on the Extension of Civil Service to New Government Employees. July 9, 1936

My dear Mr. Gordon:

THANK you for your letter of June 27th, which I have read with much interest.

As to the classified service, I find that in the past two or three years the positions brought within the competitive classified service by Executive Orders outnumber by more than 9,000 the comparatively few which have been taken out of the classified service. During the fiscal year ended June 30, 1935, there was an increase of about 4,600 in the number of classified employees in the regular branches of the service; and when the annual tabulation is prepared as of June 30, 1936 (which it is hoped will be early in August), it is certain that there will be a further marked increase because of the fact that either by Act of Congress or by Executive Order the following agencies have been added to those which operate under the Civil Service Law:

Alien Property Custodian
Bituminous Coal Commission
Farm Credit Administration
Federal Communications Commission
Labor Relations Board
Securities and Exchange Commission
Railroad Retirement Board
Motor Carrier Bureau of the Interstate Commerce Commission

Social Security Board
Public Utility Regulation
Soil Conservation Service
U. S. Railroad Administration
National Training School for Boys
Certain positions in the C.C.C. Camps
Rural Electrification Board.

As to the exemption from the classified service of positions of attorney by Congress, you will, of course, appreciate the fact that when Congress takes such action there is no power resting in the President to bring such positions within the competitive classified service. I have recommended to Congress approval of bills which have been introduced in both the House and the Senate which would give to the President authority to issue Executive Orders which would bring within the classified service groups of positions and Federal Agencies which are now exempt by statute. As to the Social Security Board, Congress has stated that appointments to positions of attorney and expert in that Board may be made without regard to the Civil Service Act and rules, and the President is without power to direct the Board in the matter of making appointments to these positions.

Very sincerely yours,

Charles Gordon, Esq.,
Chairman of Civil Service Committee,
Lawyers' Security League,
New York, N. Y.

86 ⟨ Presidential Statement on the Arbitration of the Boundary Dispute between Ecuador and Peru. July 9, 1936

ON FEBRUARY 6, 1934, I consented to serve as arbitrator in the boundary dispute between the Republic of Ecuador and the Republic of Peru in accordance with the terms of the Ponce-Castro Oyanguren Protocol concluded between those two countries in 1924, which provided that if the two Governments were unable to fix a definitive line through direct negotiation, the zone upon which they could not agree should be submitted to the arbitral decision of the President of the United States. I have been particularly glad to receive, today, the visit of the Ambassador of Peru and of the Minister of Ecuador, who have officially advised me that the nature of the arbitration has now been agreed upon by the two Governments through a further protocol signed on July 6th, last, which also provides that the Delegations of the respective countries will commence their final negotiations in Washington on September 30th, next.

253

This decision of these two great Republics to hasten the peaceful adjudication of this long-continuing controversy will be regarded as a cause for encouragement and gratitude by all lovers of peace on the American Continent. It will do much to insure the success of the deliberations of the twenty-one American Republics at the approaching Inter-American Peace Conference.

(On this subject, see also Item 20, Vol. III; and Item 140, this volume.)

87 ❨ The First United States High Commissioner to the Philippines Resigns. July 9, 1936

THE President received the following letter from the Honorable Frank Murphy, United States High Commissioner to the Philippine Islands:

Dear Mr. President:

Believing that continuance of your leadership and the success of the Democratic Party in the coming State and national elections are of first importance to the people of Michigan and the country at large, I have decided to make myself available to the Democratic Party as a candidate for the office of Governor of Michigan in the event I should be chosen at the party primary in September.

This decision has been reached after careful consideration and numerous conferences with party leaders in my own State who have assured me that my candidacy would meet with the general approval of members and friends of the Democratic Party in Michigan and would materially promote the success of our cause.

Subject to your approval, therefore, I tender herewith my resignation from the Office of United States High Commissioner to the Philippine Islands, effective at your pleasure. In taking this step I desire to express my gratitude for the privilege of representing our Government in the Philippines, first as Governor-General and later as High Commissioner, at a time when high ideals of public service and sound practices in governmental finance were being established for a young Nation. We have been privileged to help a people toward their freedom. Under your sympathetic direction the affairs of fourteen million people in a large and important possession on the other side of the world have been administered with due regard for their national ideals and aspirations and with a high sense of trusteeship for their economic and political welfare. It has been our constant aim to accord them fair treatment and equal consideration with our own people and all others owing allegiance to the American flag and authority.

Important problems are still pending for solution, one of which is the satisfactory settlement of future economic relations and conditions of trade between the two countries. It is to be hoped that these and other matters affecting the future welfare and security of the Philippine people will be settled on a basis of permanent interest and friendship, creditably to ourselves and our posterity. The Philippine people may be assured of my faith in them, my continuing deep interest in their welfare and the success of their Government, and my confidence in the happy consummation of our present enlightened policy of mutual respect and good-will.

With firm belief in our cause, and assurance of high personal regard and esteem, I remain

.

Very respectfully,
FRANK MURPHY
United States High Commissioner

The President replied as follows:

My dear Frank:

I HAVE received with mixed feelings your letter of resignation. While I regret that circumstances prompt you to relinquish the great office of High Commissioner to the Philippine Islands, the sense of regret is tempered by the thought that your action may pave the way for utilization in other fields of the varied and diverse talents which you have so successfully exercised in the discharge of your duties in the Pacific Archipelago.

For the way in which you have performed your duties I have only the highest praise. Great events have taken place during your tenure, first, as Governor-General and latterly as High Commissioner.

255

You have guided with integrity, sympathy, understanding, tact and discretion the aspirations of a people numbering more than 14,000,000 souls in their struggle to achieve nationhood. You have by wise exercise of the powers conferred upon you not only justified my own highest expectations; you have done a service for your country and for the cause of humanity.

As a result of your efforts there has grown up between the United States and the Philippines a feeling of cordiality and mutual trust without a parallel in the history of relations between a sovereign and a dependent people. This mutual cordiality and good-will have been achieved without sacrificing other considerations. On the practical side of affairs you have balanced the budget while, at the same time, you have set high ideals of social justice and social responsibility.

These are some of the considerations that come to mind now that you have signified your desire to be relieved of your duties. In all the circumstances, therefore, I feel that I cannot do otherwise than to hold your resignation in abeyance with the understanding that, effective September 5th, next, you will be given leave of absence for two months without pay. Meanwhile, if developments should compel, at a later date, a reluctant acceptance of your resignation, I shall find reassurance in the fact that your superb knowledge of Philippine affairs, as well as the rich experience which you have gained, will be available always through the wise counsel you can give us in time to come.

With renewed assurance of my personal regard, I am

Very sincerely yours,

88 ❡ "People Require and Demand Up-to-date Government in Place of Antiquated Government"—Address at the Dedication of the Triborough Bridge, New York City. July 11, 1936

Governor Lehman, Mayor LaGuardia, Secretary Ickes, Commissioner Moses, ladies and gentlemen:

MANY of you who are here today, old people like myself, can remember that, when we were boys and girls, the greater part of what is now the Boroughs of the Bronx and Queens was cultivated as farm land. A little further back, but not much more than a hundred years ago, my own great-grandfather owned a farm in Harlem, right across there [indicating], close to the Manhattan approach of this bridge. But I am quite sure, Bob Moses, that he never dreamed of the bridge.

In the older days there was no need for a structure like this connecting Long Island and Manhattan and the mainland; and even if a vast population in those days had needed it, human ingenuity and engineering skill could not have built it.

Some of us who are charged with the responsibilities of Government pause from time to time to ask ourselves whether human needs and human inventions are going to change as rapidly in the generations to come as they have in the generation that has passed. It is not alone that, as time goes by, we are confronted with new needs created by hitherto undreamed of conditions; it is also because growth in human knowledge labels as needs today things which in the olden days we did not think of as needs.

For example, it was not so long ago that no one used to protest against the dumping of sewage and garbage into our rivers and harbors. No one used to protest that our schoolhouses were badly ventilated and badly lighted. No one used to protest because there were no playgrounds for children in crowded tenement areas. No one used to protest against firetraps and factory smoke.

257

In those days Government was not interested in helping to provide bathing beaches, swimming pools and recreational areas; nor had those who toiled in those days conceived the thought that they were entitled to at least one day of rest in seven or entitled to an annual vacation.

There are a few among us, luckily only a few, who still, consciously or unconsciously, live in a state of constant protest against the daily processes of meeting modern needs. Most of us, I am glad to say, are willing to recognize change and to give it reasonable and constant help.

Government itself, whether it be that of a city or that of a sovereign State or that of the union of States, must, if it is to survive, recognize change and give to new needs reasonable and constant help. Government itself cannot close its eyes to the pollution of waters, to the erosion of soil, to the slashing of forests, any more than it can close its eyes to the need for slum clearance and schools and bridges. Government itself is, of necessity, more complex because all life is more complex. The machinery of government and the cost of government under Mayor Seth Low in 1901, for example, would not serve the essential needs of the people of the City of New York in the days of Mayor LaGuardia in 1936. People require and people are demanding up-to-date government in place of antiquated government, just as they are requiring and demanding Triborough Bridges in the place of ancient ferries.

This Triborough Bridge was neither in its conception nor in its building a matter of purely local concern. Nation, State and city, each in its own way, have contributed to the gigantic undertaking. And it will serve the people not only in all the boroughs of this largest of cities; it will serve also the people of Long Island, of up-state New York and our neighbors of Connecticut and New Jersey; and it will serve the hundreds of thousands of those living in all the other States and in foreign countries, who visit New York on matters of business and of pleasure. And so you see that the United States has an interest and a stake in this bridge.

At a time of great human suffering the construction of this bridge was undertaken among the very first of the tens of thousands of projects launched by States and counties and municipalities and financed in part with Federal funds.

You, Governor Lehman, and you, Mayor LaGuardia, are personally familiar with this great array of public improvements. You know of the other tunnels and bridges, of the sewage disposal programs, of the schoolhouse and hospital construction, of the additions and repairs to public buildings and public enterprises of every kind. Because of your deep personal interest in all of this work, you have visualized its progress in every part of the Nation. I am grateful to both of you for the cooperation you have given me as President of the United States.

And I am grateful to you, the workers, from the members of the Commission itself and the engineers, all the way down the ladder — I am grateful to you workers, skilled and unskilled, here at the site and those workers in the mills and shops many miles distant, without whose strong arms, willing hands and clear heads there would be no celebration here today.

May the Triborough Bridge, in the years to come, justify our efforts and our hopes by serving truly the city, the State and the Nation!

89 (Informal Extemporaneous Remarks at the Roosevelt Home Club Celebration, Hyde Park, N. Y. July 11, 1936

Friends and neighbors:

VERILY, my holiday has begun. It has begun with this nice homecoming meeting here in Hyde Park and with another nice family party which is to take place at five o'clock.

I can look forward now to two or three weeks of freedom from official cares except, possibly, for the reading and acting on some forty or fifty dispatches a day, the signing of a bag full of mail once every four or five days unless, of course, I get caught in a fog down the coast of Maine, and I am rather praying for fog.

I have been hearing some wonderful things this afternoon. You know, I have been hearing Judge Mack on the air. I have heard his speeches in conventions and I have always wondered what he looked like when he was making a speech. Now I know.

And I have also discovered something else. When Mrs. Moses Smith gave the flowers to my wife, somebody said, "Speech, speech," and my wife said, "I never make a speech."

Live and learn!

But I suppose that today, up to the time my holiday began at three o'clock, was a fairly typical one of my life in the last three or three and a half years. I started off this morning when I got off the train in New York, and the first person I conferred with was the Mayor of the City of New York. We talked about new projects, useful projects on which to put unemployed people to work, such as new schoolhouses and bridges, waterworks, and so forth. And then I talked with the Governor of the State of New York in regard to floods, for a large portion of our State, as you know — the Southern Tier — has been visited twice in the last two years with very serious floods on a number of rivers. After that I conferred with the Administrator of Relief, Harry Hopkins, and his assistant in New York, in regard to the very serious situation that has occurred for the second time in the Northwest. I can only give you a picture of it by telling you that two hundred and seventy-five counties are seriously affected by this drought. We have in this State, as you know, sixty-two counties, and out there the average size of a county is about twice the size of one of our counties. So you can get an idea of the land area that is affected.

There are some two hundred and four thousand families, as I remember it — and that is a lot of families — and there are a great many more people when you come down to the individuals, probably over a million, possibly a million and a half, who probably have no idea, no clear idea, as to what the future holds in store for them.

They are brave people, just as the people of this whole country have been brave during the serious days of the depression. They have kept up their heads, and they have kept up their hopes, and they have a right to expect that they will have every reasonable help not only in remaining alive, but in having some future, some worth-while future, made possible for them.

And so all the agencies, not only of the Federal Government but of the State Governments and the local county Governments, are joining in the great task of relieving the burdens and solving the problems which the drought has brought upon them. Their crops are burning up; their cattle have nothing to eat; and they themselves have very little to eat or drink, because most of their wells have dried up.

The next thing I had to do today was the opening of the Triborough Bridge. We are very apt to think in terms of the spectacular and the obvious—things like the Triborough Bridge which costs sixty million dollars, which unites three great boroughs, each with a population of more than a million souls. That is the spectacular side of what we have been doing. Of course, that bridge put a great many people to work who needed work, not only on the bridge itself, but back in the factories and in the forests and in the mines. I suppose, first and last, there were fifteen or twenty thousand people who were engaged at work in constructing that bridge, either at the site or away from the site.

We are apt to think of the help that each of our three forms of government, local, State and Federal, has given—we are apt to think of all that just in terms of this enormous structure. Yet, if we analyze it, we find that the help depends very much on the size of the community.

I shall give you an example: A little while ago I received in Washington a letter from a small town in the Middle West. There were four hundred voters in the town. The letter was signed by three hundred and ninety of them. I do not know what party the other ten belonged to. But the three hundred and ninety signatures expressed the idea to me that the finest thing that has happened to their town was the building of a new schoolhouse. To them that schoolhouse had been the great need of that town, and it was the one thing that they and their wives and children wanted. They had not been able to raise the money to build it out there. Nobody would take their bond; no bank would lend it to them except, perhaps, at a very high rate of interest. It was an honest, God-fearing community. They believed that over a period of ten or twelve or fifteen years they could pay back the loan, if they could get it on reasonable terms. The result was that the Federal Government made them the loan, and gave them a portion of the cost of the building in what we call "work relief." The building was built and the town feels just as proud of that little schoolhouse as the seven million people who live in New York City feel about their Triborough Bridge.

All over the country, in the thirty-one hundred counties, some useful work has been done. Speaking of schools, there have been built in the last three years over thirty thousand new schools in the United States. They have been built with Federal aid. There are more than a million desks—additional desks—for pupils. In other words, we can educate a million more children than we could three years ago.

We have built, I cannot tell you off-hand how many, but we have built not hundreds, but thousands of bridges. We have built I do not know how many thousands of miles, not only of fine hard concrete roads, but also of farm-to-market roads that have been needed so much in every State.

It is an interesting thing to me that the usefulness of all of these thousands and tens of thousands of projects has depended, in large part, on the interest of the individual community. Of course, as you know, the origin of these projects is, in almost every case, in the community. The community knows that it has a certain number of people to take care of; and they have been told that those people should, if possible, be given useful work. Therefore, it has been the community itself which has suggested what that work should be.

Where the community takes the greatest interest the work itself is the most valuable, the most permanent, and the most satisfactory. On the other side of the picture, in those communities where there is very little interest in the needs of the community, we have the occasional projects that do not seem to anybody to be especially useful from a permanent point of view. So, the ultimate responsibility comes back to just where it was in the days of the New England town meetings in the year 1650, in other words, to local interest in government and local understanding of government problems.

We have very little to fear in this country, if we can increase in the next few years understanding of, and interest in, government such as we have seen in this country in the past three years. That has been the greatest contribution of the four years of the depression followed by the three years of the revival.

And so, as Mr. Wilson has so well put it in the prayer, I cannot help feeling that the undertaking heart goes with equal strength and equal importance with the understanding of the problem itself. I think we have increased the functioning of our understanding heart in this country. There are more and more people who are looking at the social needs of our land. There are more and more people who are coming to realize that in many other Nations they have already gone farther toward meeting social needs than we have, and that we have to go a good long way to catch up with them, to bring ourselves up to the modern conception or ideal of personal security for the men, women and children who make up the great mass of our population.

That has been our ideal during these years; and I believe that it is going to be the ideal of the country during the next few years. I believe that the country is going to insist on the maintenance of that ideal and insist on action looking toward its accomplishment.

90 ❡ White House Statement on the Appointment of the Great Plains Drought Area Committee. July 22, 1936

The President has appointed the following as members of the Great Plains Drought Area Committee:

Morris L. Cooke, Chairman,
Rural Electrification Administration, Washington, D. C.

Frederick H. Fowler,
National Resources Committee,
Washington, D. C.

John C. Page,
Bureau of Reclamation,
Washington, D. C.

Hon. Rexford Tugwell,
Resettlement Administration,
Washington, D. C.

Col. Richard C. Moore,
Corps of Engineers, U. S. Army,
Kansas City, Missouri.

Hon. Harry L. Hopkins,
Works Progress Administration,
Washington, D. C.

In letters addressed to the members of this Committee, the President said:

I am writing to ask you to serve as a member of a Great Plains Drought Area Committee to carry on a study looking toward the most efficient utilization of the natural resources of the Great Plains area, and especially toward practicable measures for remedying the conditions which have brought widespread losses and distress to so many inhabitants of the Missouri, Platte and Arkansas valleys, the Panhandles of Oklahoma and Texas, and contiguous areas.

We have supposed that the modes of settlement and of development which have been prevalent represented the ordinary course of civilization. But perhaps in this area of relatively little rain, practices brought from the more humid part of the country are not most suitable under the prevailing natural conditions. At any rate, circumstances make it obvious that relief activities are not sufficient and that a competent study and recommendations are desirable.

I should like to have the committee make an early study of the conditions there, so that I may have the benefit of its views with respect to them, at a meeting which I shall arrange to hold with the Committee at some point within this area some time in August.

Chairman Cooke has advised the President of the receipt of a letter signed by W. R. Ronald, Chairman of the Central Northwest Regional Planning Commission, which convened in St. Paul, Minnesota, on July 8th. This Commission decided, at the St. Paul meeting, to hold a conference at Aberdeen, South Dakota, on August 7th for the purpose of formulating a program for the States of North and South Dakota, Montana and Wyoming. Chairman Cooke has called a meeting of the Great Plains Drought Area Committee for tomorrow, when this letter will be acknowledged. Mr. Ronald will be requested to postpone the meeting of State officials scheduled for August 7th in order that members of the Great Plains Drought Area Committee can meet with them in the drought area about August 20th.

NOTE: The bad effects of the 1934 drought had not entirely disappeared when the Mid-West and some portions of the Southeast were struck in 1936 by another drought. The experience gained in 1934 was helpful, however, in meeting the problems of 1936.

In June, as soon as the situation became obviously serious and dangerous, I appointed an Inter-departmental Drought Committee to co-ordinate and accelerate the drought relief activities of the various Government and State agencies. The Chairman of this Committee was the Secretary of Agriculture; and the Committee included the Acting Budget Director, the Administrator of the Resettlement Administration and the Administrator of W.P.A.

This Committee immediately undertook a survey of the drought situation and of the actions appropriate to meet the emergency. So far as possible, existing agencies of Government were used.

The first designations of emergency drought areas were made July 7th, and included 268 counties. A month later 890 emergency drought counties in twenty-one States had been included; and by the end of 1936, the officially designated drought area covered 1,194 counties in twenty-five States. These counties were certified as drought areas on the basis of reports received from directors of the extension service and from representatives of the Bureau of Agricultural Economics. The extension of the various drought relief measures depended upon this official designation of the drought areas to be included.

During the first week in July the operation of the soil conservation program (see Item 28, this volume) was modified so as to encourage an increase in the production of needed food and feed crops which had been stricken by the drought.

About the same time, a cattle-purchase program was authorized and developed as a precautionary measure to prevent demoralization of prices in the event that the drought began to force a dumping of livestock upon the market. In carrying out this program, as in the one of 1934, meat products which were purchased were turned over to the Federal Surplus Commodities Corporation, formerly the Federal Surplus Relief Corporation, and were given by it to various State relief agencies for distribution among the hungry unemployed.

The cattle-purchase program was coordinated with such other measures as distribution of feed supplies in the drought area, and loans and grants designed to relieve the pressure on farmers within the area to sell their cattle at a sacrifice. A sheep-purchase program along the same lines as the cattle-purchase program was approved in August, 1936.

In the late summer of 1936, a seed-purchase program to preserve small grains adapted for seed pur-

poses and to keep them from milling and other commercial uses was inaugurated. Corn loans on selected seed and on regular corn were extended; and they made possible the orderly selection, storage, distribution and farm marketing of 1936 seed corn.

The purchase of food, feed and other farm products in 1936 became particularly important because hunger and need developed in the various areas where there had been natural catastrophes — in the Northeast, where there had been floods, in the South, where there had been tornadoes, and in the areas of the Great Plains and other regions struck by drought. Approximately 55,000,000 pounds of food and 15,000,000 pounds of feed were shipped by A.A.A. into the drought area alone for relief distribution in nineteen States.

As a clearing house for information, the Federal Livestock Feed Agency was opened at Kansas City in July. Its activities were designed to assist in stabilizing feed practices, facilitate distribution of feedstuffs and livestock, and prevent speculation. It located surplus supplies of feed, and advised farmers and cattlemen where to purchase them at moderate cost. To facilitate the sale and transfer of cattle from drought-affected regions, freight rates were reduced as in 1934 for livestock and feed out of and into the drought area.

Cooperating in the whole drought program were the Resettlement Administration, Works Progress Administration, Soil Conservation Service, the Bureau of Biological Survey, and the Farm Credit Administration. (For a statement of crop and feed loans by the Farm Credit Administration within and without drought areas see Item 29, Vol. III; Item 22, Vol. IV.)

The drought aid program of the Resettlement Administration was announced and put into effect on July 14, 1936, in twenty-five States as follows: Minnesota, Wisconsin, Illinois, Indiana, Ohio, Iowa, Missouri, Kentucky, North Carolina, Tennessee, Virginia, West Virginia, Georgia, South Dakota, South Carolina, Arkansas, Kansas, Nebraska, Montana, North Dakota, Oklahoma, Texas, Colorado, Wyoming, New Mexico.

The activities of the Resettlement Administration in the drought area involved both emergency and long-range phases.

Under the emergency phase its immediate activities were directed toward: (1) providing destitute families with subsistence; (2) providing help for livestock feed maintenance; and (3) financing farm operations in the fall of 1936 and spring of 1937.

The long-time program looked forward to retiring submarginal land by Government purchase or otherwise, and to relocating or resettling the farm families formerly residing on such land in other localities where there were better prospects for successful farming. This

was in line with the general program of the Resettlement Administration (see Item 50, Vol. IV).

The actual providing of work relief for destitute families in drought areas, other than the regular work of rural rehabilitation of the Resettlement Administration was assumed by the W.P.A. This procedure was consistent with the general policy of relieving destitution wherever possible by work rather than by dole. The money earned in work relief would enable farm families to engage in soil improvement and water conservation, which in turn would contribute to the solution of the drought problem in the years to come. The Resettlement Administration, in this way, was permitted to concentrate on its emergency program of direct relief to drought victims, and its customary program of rehabilitation through small, carefully supervised loans to farm families which could obtain credit from no other source. W.P.A. programs of work relief improved the morale of farmers in the drought area by employing them on projects which were recognized as having economic value.

As soon as the emergency drought counties were certified, W.P.A. assistance was extended to aid those in the greatest need. When the certifications were first made, the State Administrators in the five States which had been hardest hit by the drought (North Dakota, South Dakota, Minnesota, Montana and Wyoming) were authorized to provide

267

employment for 55,000 persons. As the situation became more serious, and as many other hundreds of counties were added, the employment quotas were increased. By the end of October, 1936, almost 325,000 persons were working on W.P.A. projects in twenty-one States. It is estimated that approximately $100,-000,000 was spent by W.P.A. to employ needy drought sufferers, who otherwise might have suffered great privation, if not actual starvation, in these areas.

Victims of the drought who were employed were assigned either to projects already in operation or to new projects. New projects were begun with the double purpose, first, of providing employment, and second, of alleviating, as far as possible, the physical effects of the drought. Most of the work was done on such projects as farm-to-market roads, water-conservation work, building dams on streams, constructing reservoirs and digging wells. Most of these projects of conservation were adopted as a part of a long-range program to provide small lakes and reservoirs in States in the drought area in order to prevent excessive water run-off leading to flood conditions and in order to stabilize the water supply in dry seasons of the year. Although there were a few large projects, most of them involved small reservoirs, pasture ponds and dams at strategic points along streams or at the outlet of lakes, to provide water for livestock during dry seasons. These smaller projects were more easily accessible to workers and could therefore provide a more widespread employment. Other jobs done by W.P.A. workers during the drought consisted in fighting pests and forest fires.

However, there were a great many farm families in need of assistance whose employable members could not be engaged by W.P.A. either because of distance from available works projects, or because of conflict with duties on their own farms. These cases received subsistence grants from the Resettlement Administration on the basis of need. The total number of such families reached the sum of 100,000, as of December 7, 1936.

In line with its regular rural rehabilitation program, aid was extended by the Resettlement Administration to many farmers in the drought area who could not qualify for financing from other agencies, such as the emergency crop and feed loans from the Farm Credit Administration. The Resettlement Administration undertook to make loans to these farmers wherever there was a reasonable expectation of a crop sufficient to warrant the loan. The total amount of such loans to farmers in the drought area for emergency feed and crop purposes exceeded $12,180,000.

A very valuable information service was maintained by the Resettlement Administration, designed to prevent aimless migration of families from the drought areas. It furnished information on the kind of farming in other areas, on the availability of land and employment in other areas and in which regions resettlement was not desirable.

The land-use planning work of Resettlement Administration in the drought areas consisted of the study of land conditions, the analysis of problems which have come from unwise use of land, and the development of methods for correcting existing maladjustments. These methods included the purchase of submarginal land, the improvement of landlord-tenant relationships, range protection, guidance of public credit facilities, and development of intensive programs, involving several of these activities, for certain particular areas where maladjustments in land had become most severe.

As in 1934, the drought of 1936 dug deeply into the food and feed supply of the Nation. The area which had been planted to corn, small grains and flaxseed, but which was abandoned because of crop failure in the drought, totaled about 32,000,000 acres. In addition, about 12,000,000 acres of winter wheat were lost. Because of losses in various crops, it is estimated that the total acreage of crops (excluding fruits) harvested in 1936 was only about 315,000,000 acres, which was 21,000,000 acres less than was harvested in 1935 and at least 10 percent less than the harvested acreage in any of the dozen years preceding the droughts of 1933 and 1934. The number of animal units on January 1, 1937, as a result of two years of drought-curtailed crops, was the smallest since 1929.

The material and its arrangement in this note and in the discussion of the 1934 drought were in part taken from the 1936 Report of A.A.A. (Agricultural Conservation, 1936).

See also Items 83, 99, 101, and 131A of this volume.

91 ⟨ The President Places Postmasters under Civil Service Regulation. Executive Order No. 7421. July 22, 1936

BY VIRTUE of and pursuant to the authority vested in me by Section 1755 of the Revised Statutes (U. S. C., Title 5, Sec. 631), by the Act of July 12, 1876 (U. S. C., Title 39, Sec. 31), and as President of the United States, it is hereby ordered that whenever a vacancy occurs in the position of postmaster in any office of the first, second, or third class as the result of (1) death, (2) resignation, (3) removal, or (4) expiration of term, the following procedure shall be observed, in accordance with the provisions of the Civil Service Act of January 16, 1883 (22 Stat. 403), and the rules and regulations made pursuant to the said Act, in so far as such provisions may be applicable:

SECTION 1. (a) The Postmaster General may recommend to the President the appointment of the incumbent, or the appointment by promotion of a classified employee in the postal service in the vacancy office, provided either such incumbent or such classified employee is found eligible by the Civil Service Commission by noncompetitive examination; or

(b) Upon request of the Postmaster General, the Civil Service Commission shall forthwith hold an open competitive examination to test the fitness of applicants to fill such vacancy and shall certify the results thereof to the Postmaster General, who shall thereupon submit to the President for appointment to fill the vacancy the name of the highest eligible unless it is established to the satisfaction of the Civil Service Commission that the character or residence of such eligible disqualifies him for appointment. This procedure shall be followed in all examinations announced by the Civil Service Commission subsequent to the date of this order.

SECTION 2. No person may be admitted to the examinations provided for in Section 1 hereof unless he has been a bona fide patron of the office for which a postmaster is to be appointed, for at least one year immediately preceding the time fixed for the close of receipt of applications.

SECTION 3. No person who has passed his sixty-seventh birthday shall be appointed acting postmaster in any office of the first, second, or third class unless he is already in the postal service, nor shall any such person, except as provided in Section 4 hereof, be admitted to any examination which may be held for any such office under the provisions of Section 1.

SECTION 4. In all examinations held under the provisions of Section 1 hereof, the age limit prescribed in Section 3 shall be waived as to candidates who are entitled to military preference as a result of service in the World War, the Spanish-American War, or the Philippine Insurrection, and in rating the examination papers of such candidates the Civil Service Commission shall add five points to their earned ratings and make certification to the Postmaster General in accordance with their relative positions thus acquired. The time such candidates were in the service during such wars may be reckoned by the Commission in making up the required length of business experience.

SECTION 5. This order supersedes all prior Executive Orders affecting or relating to the appointment of postmasters to post offices of the first, second, and third classes.

NOTE: The foregoing Executive Order extended the action I took in Executive Order No. 6203, July 12, 1933 (see Vol. II, Item 96), by limiting the appointment to the highest eligible person on the list. In the First Session of the 75th Congress, a bill carrying out in part the suggestions made in my letter of July 12, 1933, accompanying Executive Order No. 6203 passed the House; but no action was taken on it in the Senate.

I therefore determined to accomplish the same results by the foregoing Executive Order extending the safeguards of the merit system to the appointment of postmasters of the first, second and third classes.

92 (The Three Hundred and Ninth Press Conference (Excerpts). July 29, 1936

Held at Herring Beach, Campobello Island, N. B.

(Proposed Eastern flood area inspection trip — Proposed Western drought area inspection trip — Passamaquoddy.)

Q. What are your plans after you leave Quebec? Are you going to the Connecticut Valley?

THE PRESIDENT: Cannot answer that without Mac. I am going to detrain somewhere up in Vermont near Winooskie Dam that the C.C.C. Vermont camps have built, and from there motor to Montpelier, have a talk with the Governor and all State officials and Federal officials who are in any way connected with Federal projects, and get Vermont problems in my mind. We shall motor from there, stop one or two places either at sites of dams or work in progress. In Hanover I hope the Governor of New Hampshire and people will come for the same kind of conference; then I shall get on the train and go down to Springfield for conference with all Massachusetts officials in relation to the Massachusetts end of it.

Q. Will that include Governor Curley?

THE PRESIDENT: Include all State officials.

Get to Hyde Park late Saturday night. Shall not get off train in Springfield—get there about 5:30 for conference, no work to see in Springfield in way of flood control. Get to Hyde Park 10:30 or 11.

Q. How long do you plant to stay at Hyde Park?

THE PRESIDENT: Something less than a week, then go back to Washington. Beyond that nothing definite. . . .

Q. Have you given any consideration to a campaign swing to Coast in early September?

THE PRESIDENT: Have nothing planned except what I talked about before. Later in August I shall go to Southern New York and Northern Pennsylvania flood areas, also Western Pennsylvania and Ohio flood areas. I do not know whether it will be the same trip or two different trips.

Q. What plans have been submitted to you of work already done on Quoddy Village?

THE PRESIDENT: I cannot tell you now—bound to be vague, cannot give anything concrete. If any of you haven't seen it, go and see it.

The whole conception of it in the beginning was based on the simple fact that the use of power both in Canada and in the United States is increasing at the rate, let us say roughly, of 10 to 15 percent every year, and we think that it is going to continue to increase. Therefore, there can be more power developed of all kinds, coal, hydroelectric, and if we can find a new method, so much the better. This Passamaquoddy thought was originated in 1921 when the Severn

272

River in England was being considered for tidal power development, and on the coast of France, where they have forty-foot tides. In 1921 I talked with Owen Young of the General Electric about the possibilities of the Bay of Fundy. He was much interested and they made a preliminary rough survey. They found it was of interest and well worth while studying, but that the demand for power at that time did not justify anything further.

In 1926 or '27 Cooper came along with his survey, which was financed by General Electric, Aluminum Company of America and the Westinghouse. They found his plans were practical, but again there was the matter of demand. So, in '33 we had our first study made, and they assured us that it was a good proposition. Government engineers held it entirely feasible. At that time it did not seem feasible to talk to Canada in regard to joining. We went ahead with plans of developing on our side of the line, experimentally on a smaller scale, according to the development of power that we could sell.

Ever since that date the science of transmission of electricity has grown by leaps and bounds; private companies, like G. E. and Westinghouse, are working on direct current instead of alternating, which means much lower cost of production and much lower loss of power. If it succeeds as they think it will, that tidal power from the Bay of Fundy, both American and Canadian side, could be transmitted down to New York areas. In other words, there would be free power both ways across the boundary. We shall come to it.

Q. Will you talk about this in Quebec?

THE PRESIDENT: Yes, without doubt, if Friday is a long enough day.

As to the next step, the first thing, when it is thoroughly understood that this is a useful experiment, is to put it through on a small preliminary scale, using relief money which would have to be used in any case. We have got to take care of these people. We have had them on road build-

273

ing and schoolhouses. Money has got to be spent, as approximately 5,000 people are on relief in Eastern Maine.

You can make it clear that whether something is done by the next Congress or not, these people who have been on the Quoddy project from relief rolls are going to remain on relief rolls doing something else. Obviously they have to.

As to what is going to be done with those buildings, that will be decided in the course of the next week. They will be usefully employed.

Q. Did Harry Hopkins have any ideas?

THE PRESIDENT: Yes, we have been talking and trying to get the best possible ideas.

Q. Can you allocate any of the $1,425,000,000 to carry further this work?

THE PRESIDENT: No, I made that clear dozens of times.

Q. Where are you to get the money?

THE PRESIDENT: I shall use the buildings for something. I cannot carry on the project without an Act of Congress.

Q. Do you plan to make any inspection through the Quoddy Village?

THE PRESIDENT: I may go over on the *Potomac*; I can see almost everything there is from the water.

Q. Where does the Dust Bowl trip fit in?

THE PRESIDENT: Somewhere around the end of August.

Q. Anything in the line of politics, for this is a campaign year, you know?

THE PRESIDENT: Is this the year, Fred? I had forgotten that.

Q. Are you going to listen to Colonel Knox Saturday night?

THE PRESIDENT: I shall be on the train.

Q. Is there anything to the story around here that you might discuss with Lord Tweedsmuir about making Eastport a free port of entry?

THE PRESIDENT: New one on me.

Q. Have you talked with the Prime Minister of New Brunswick about that?

THE PRESIDENT: Passamaquoddy is Passamaquoddy, and includes

both sides of the line. Off the record, wouldn't it be nice to have free ports on both sides? Quoddy is just one of those dreams of the future. Either country having extra power could send it without any duty. It seems to be one of the last things in the world to put duty on.

Q. In your talk with the Prime Minister, will that embrace a proposition of Canada going into the proposal?

THE PRESIDENT: I think the first thing that should be done is experimenting in first tidal power in the world. It seems to be worth while trying, and it will be the largest in the world. It was a very good project in view of the fact that people were on relief. There is one other factor which we must consider. When I was a little boy we used to have three steamers a week to Lubec, Eastport and St. John. Now you don't see any— showing the economic condition of Eastern Maine. Anything that can be done to raise economic status is pretty good; otherwise we shall have to look forward to relief for many years to come. . . .

NOTE: The Passamaquoddy project for the development of electric power through the operation of tides was authorized May 28, 1935, by an initial allotment of ten million dollars under Emergency Relief Appropriation Act of 1935. This allotment was subsequently reduced to seven million dollars of which about six and one-half million dollars have been spent.

Work was commenced in July, 1935, and during the height of the operations a maximum of 5122 persons was employed. The work was stopped on June 30, 1936, due to the failure of the Congress to authorize further work and to appropriate funds for the continuation of the original project.

The buildings and equipment were turned over by the War Department, which was in charge of the original work, to the National Youth Administration for use in connection with a vocational training school to be established and operated by that administration.

See also Item 83, this volume.

93 ❨ Address on the Occasion of a Visit to Quebec, Canada. July 31, 1936

Your Excellency, Mr. Prime Minister, my friends and neighbors of Canada:

FROM the very moment I received the hospitable invitation of your Governor-General, I have been filled with the most happy anticipation of this all too brief visit. Canada and its people have ever had a real hold on my affection; and I am happy again to be able to assure you of this fact in person and to express my grateful appreciation of the warmth of your welcome.

That I am not a stranger may be illustrated by the fact that since the age of two I have spent the majority of my summers in the Province of New Brunswick, and it may be proved also by my recent most refreshing cruise along the beautiful shores of the Maritime Provinces where once more I have found friendship, relaxation and deep contentment.

Nor am I ignorant or unmindful of the charms of other sections of this great Dominion—Ontario and that great empire which extends west of it to the Pacific.

But to many of my countrymen, and I am no exception to this rule, Quebec has a fascination all its own. The Plains of Abraham and the cliffs which lead to them are eternal memorials to brave French, to brave British and to brave American colonials who fell in battle, be it in victory or in defeat.

Yet there is a nobler monument. For on these fields of battle was born the living miracle which we are privileged to see today —two great racial stocks residing side by side in peace and friendship, each contributing its particular genius in the molding of a Nation. That is a monument worthy of those who gave their lives; this is an example from which all thinking men draw deep satisfaction and inspiration.

While I was on my cruise last week, I read in a newspaper that I was to be received with all the honors customarily rendered to a foreign ruler. Your Excellency, I am grateful for the honors;

but something within me rebelled at that word "foreign." I say this because, when I have been in Canada, I have never heard a Canadian refer to an American as a "foreigner." He is just an "American." And, in the same way, across the border in the United States, Canadians are not "foreigners," they are "Canadians."

I think that that simple little distinction illustrates to me better than anything else the relationship between our two countries.

On both sides of the line we are so accustomed to an undefended boundary three thousand miles long that we are inclined perhaps to minimize its vast importance, not only to our own continuing relations, but also to the example which it sets to the other Nations of the world.

Canadians and Americans visit one another each year by the hundreds of thousands — but, more important, they visit one another without the necessity of a passport. And, within recent months, another significant action speaks louder than words, for the trade agreement which I had the privilege of signing with your Prime Minister last autumn is tangible evidence of the desire of the people of both countries to practice what they preach when they speak of the good neighbor.

In the solution of the grave problems that face the world today, frank dealing, cooperation and a spirit of give and take between Nations are more important than ever before. The United States and Canada, and, indeed, all parts of the British Empire share a democratic form of government which comes to us from common sources. We have adapted our institutions on both sides of the border to our own needs and our own special conditions, but fundamentally they are the same.

The natural sympathy and understanding that exist between us were, I feel, demonstrated in the universal feeling of grief when the news of the death of the late King George was received in the United States. We felt not only that the head of a friendly Nation had been removed, but that a friend whose voice had penetrated into almost every home in the United States had been taken from us — a great king and a great gentleman.

It has also been my privilege in bygone years to know his Majesty, King Edward, and we look forward to the day when, finding it possible to come again to the Dominion, he may also visit with his neighbors in the United States.

Monsieur le Premier Ministre de Québec, Monsieur le Maire:

Cᴇs *aimables paroles que vous venez de m'adresser au nom de votre grande province et de votre belle ville, et que vous adressez, par moi, au peuple des Etats-Unis, me touchent profondément, et je vous prie de croire que je suis très sensible à la chaleur de votre accueil.*

Que de scènes de valeur et d'héroïsme ce nom de Québec évoque en nous, et que de noms illustres s'associent à ce noble roc!

C'est pour rendre hommage à ces héros que viennent tous les ans à Québec des milliers de mes compatriotes. Ils y prolongent leur séjour, séduits par la beauté merveilleuse de ce site, le doux charme de ses campagnes et l'accueil hospitalier de ses habitants. Cette hospitalité canadienne, si douce et si franche, est devenue une tradition dans mon pays. C'est par ces échanges de visite, par ces contacts répétés entre Canadiens et Américains que nous parviendrons à resserrer encore les liens déjà étroits qui unissent nos deux peuples.

(Translation):

Mr. Prime Minister of Quebec, Mr. Mayor:

The words of kindness which you have addressed to me in the name of your great Province and of your beautiful City and which you address through me to the people of the United States touch me deeply; and I beg you to believe that I am deeply sensible of the warmth of your welcome.

What scenes of valor and heroism this name of Quebec stirs

in us; what illustrious names are associated with this noble rock!

It is to pay homage to those heroes that thousands of my compatriots come every year to Quebec. Here they prolong their stay, lured by the great beauty of this site, by the soft charm of your countryside and by the hospitable greeting of your inhabitants. This Canadian hospitality, so simple and so open, has become a tradition in my country.

It is by these exchanges of visits, by these continuous contacts between Canadians and Americans that we shall come to tighten the close bonds which already unite our two peoples.

And Mr. Mackenzie King, you already know the path to Washington. I hope that you will come and visit me and revisit me again.

And Your Excellency, we are looking forward, as you know, to a visit from you and her Excellency to Mrs. Roosevelt and myself at the White House as soon as it may be convenient for you. May we speed the day when the heads of the Canadian and American Nations will see more of each other, not as foreigners, but as neighbors and friends.

NOTE: In July I took a vacation with my sons in the schooner yacht *Sewanna*, starting from Rockland, Maine, proceeding by easy stages to Shelburne, Nova Scotia, and thence to Campobello Island, N. B., near Eastport, Maine. From there I visited Quebec as the guest of the Governor General of Canada, H. E. Lord Tweedsmuir.

After this address at Quebec I made a short inspection of the New England districts which had been damaged by floods, in order to see the extent of the damage and the measures taken to repair it, and to discuss remedial measures for the future.

On August 1, I visited the Waterbury Dam, the Wrightsville Dam and arrived at Montpelier for a conference with the Governor of Vermont, various officials of Vermont and various Federal officials. I then drove over to New Hampshire and held a similar conference with the Governor of New Hampshire, various State officials of New Hampshire and various Federal officials.

That same day I arrived at Springfield, Mass., for a similar conference with the Governor of Massachusetts, various State officials of Massachusetts and Federal officials.

94 ❮ A Greeting to Labor's Non-Partisan League. August 3, 1936

My dear Major Berry:

I⊤ GIVES me very real pleasure to extend a word of greeting through you to Labor's Non-Partisan League upon the occasion of the meeting of its State chairmen in Washington.

I am certain that you and your associates are coming to Washington to join in a thorough consideration of the vital issues of the time and to consider how best to cooperate in the great task of promoting national progress and of enlarging the sphere of human rights through democracy of opportunity. It is fully realized by all of us that you are gathering to support a political cause, but that merely makes it the more certain that you are determined to enlarge the scope of human welfare in our Nation.

I should like to have you know that I am sincerely proud that you are gathering in support of my candidacy. This could not be the case if you did not know, out of the experience of the past three years, that the present Administration has endeavored to promote the ideal of justice for the great masses of America's wage earners and to make that ideal a reality.

We all know that our country has been going through profound changes and that these changes have necessitated special reconsideration of the problems of the wage earners and the farmers. Automatic machinery, the device of corporate ownership and management, the monumental accumulations of capital—these are some of the factors that have made it necessary for our country and its Government to look at men and measures from a new point of view, seeking new means for the restoration of equality of opportunity.

During the past three years we have endeavored to correct through legislation certain of the evils in our economic system. We have sought to put a stop to certain economic practices which did not promote the general welfare. Some of the laws which were enacted were declared invalid by the Supreme Court. It is a notable fact that it was not the wage earners who cheered when those laws were declared invalid. I greet you in the faith that future history will show, as past history has so repeatedly and so effectively shown, that a return to reactionary practices is ever short lived. Having tasted the benefits of liberation, men and women do not for long forego those benefits. I have implicit faith that we shall find our way to progress through law. Your support is a priceless contribution toward continued faith in that outcome.

What is of vast importance at this critical time is the fact that we have a common heritage of principle and that we are bound, with millions of our fellow Americans, in a common determination to preserve human freedom and enlarge its sphere and to prevent forever a return to that despotism which comes from unlicensed power to control and manipulate the resources of our Nation, and the destiny of human lives.

In extending to all who attend your meeting my hearty felicitations I am heartened by the conviction that we are all working for the same ideal — the restoration and preservation of human liberty and human rights.

Very sincerely yours,

Major George L. Berry,
President, Labor's Non-Partisan League,
Washington, D. C.

(This letter was read at the first national convention of the League in Washington, D. C., August 10, 1936.)

95 ❮ Informal Extemporaneous Remarks at the C.C.C. Camp near Johnstown, Pa. August 13, 1936

MY FIRST thought in coming to Johnstown and to this section of the great State of Pennsylvania is to bear to you a simple word of thanks and of gratitude to you good people who showed such heroic courage last March when you found yourselves in dire peril. You have shown the finest qualities of good American citizenship and the whole country is grateful to you for the way you faced danger at that time.

We want to keep you, as far as we can, from having to face that situation again in the days to come. I need not assure you that the Federal Government, so long as I have anything to do with it, is going to cooperate with your communities and with your State in taking every possible measure to prevent floods in the future.

I came here especially to see with my own eyes what I had read about and seen in photographs. I am going through various sections of the country on that same mission because I believe I can render better service if I see things at first hand than if I just sit in Washington.

Again I want to express my gratitude to you for your courage at the time of the flood and the way you are facing this situation today. Many thanks.

NOTE: The foregoing remarks at Johnstown, Pa., and some remarks earlier in the same day at Altoona, Pa., were made at the beginning of an inspection trip which I made between August 13th and August 15th through the flood-damaged districts of Pennsylvania and Ohio. (See also Item 96, this volume.) Other extemporaneous speeches were made during this trip at Altoona, Pa., August 13; Erie, Pa., August 14; Wilkes-Barre, Pa., August 15; Mauch Chunk, Pa., August 15, which are not printed in these volumes.

During the course of this trip I had several conferences with Governor Earle of Pennsylvania, various State officials of Pennsylvania and Federal officials with respect to the repair of flood damage and the proper steps for the future.

After my speech at Chautauqua (Item 97, this volume), I continued the inspection trip and reached the flooded New York area in the neighborhood of Binghamton. There I held similar conferences with the Governor of New York State and various State and Federal officials.

From Binghamton the flood inspection trip was continued and included the area in and around Wilkes-Barre, Pa.

96 ⟨ Informal Extemporaneous Remarks at a Luncheon at the Great Lakes Exposition, Cleveland, Ohio. August 14, 1936

President Crawford, Senator Bulkley, ladies and gentlemen:

I AM on a real holiday and having an exceedingly good time. I was very glad in fact when the radio announcer said that this was not going to be a political speech. I took occasion to wiggle my finger with joy at my old college friend, Chester Bolton.

I said I had learned a lot after that drive this morning. After we had gone about three-quarters of the way, the Mayor of Cleveland called attention to the large number of people and I said, "How many people do you think I have seen?" He said, "Oh, about three million." I congratulate Cleveland on its growth.

There was only one thing I was worried about. We have been trying to put people to work, but I am afraid that the number of work-hours accomplished today in this charming city will be away below what they ought to be.

This is the third exposition that I have gone to in 1936. The fact of three great expositions in the country—and there is a fourth way out on the Coast—all running simultaneously in one year, means something. It means that things are a lot better in the country than they have been for some years past. I learned something else. I had always supposed that an exposition took anywhere from three to five years of planning before it was held. Now we know that we can stage one in six months if the community is behind it.

I think you have rendered a real service, not merely to the city and the State, not merely to all of those States which border on the Great Lakes, but also to the whole of the country. I wish I could have spent a good many days, not only looking at the more serious exhibits, but also playing on the Midway.

As you know, at this time of the year I am trying to see at first hand, some of the work which is being carried on by government

283

of all kinds. I have been especially desirous of seeing the work that was caused, not by a depression, not by man, but by what we used to call in the old days "an act of God." That is why I have been visiting some of the flood areas in the East and shall visit more. That is why I am going out to the great drought area of the West. I believe that by seeing things at first hand, I can get a better picture and I can have a more useful impression in Washington than if I merely sat at my desk there and read a great many pages of reports and looked at photographs.

What I have seen leads me to believe more and more that the country as a whole recognizes some of these great national problems, such as the prevention of floods and the curtailment of the consequences of drought, not merely from a local point of view but from a national point of view. The destruction of property, the loss of lives in a place like Johnstown, or on the Connecticut River in New England, the serious impairment of health, the destruction of crops and livestock in the Far West—all of these catastrophes affect those of us who are fortunate to live in places that have not been afflicted by flood or drought. It is a very encouraging thing, I think, to all of us, to realize that the Nation as a whole is looking at the Nation as a whole from a national point of view more and more with every passing year.

These expositions further strengthen that purpose of national understanding and national solidarity. I should like to see some exposition started somewhere that would have as its principal objective the drawing of a record number of people from the farthest points of the country as well as from points nearer home. The facts that people all over the East are visiting this exposition in Cleveland, that they are coming here from the South, that the State of Florida has put up a fine building here and that people from the Coast are stopping off on their way to and from the East, mean that Cleveland is rendering a national service.

Incidentally, it is not just a question of education and instruction; it is also a question of having a good time. A good many people in this country today are entitled to a good time after the things they have been through and especially after the courage

284

with which they have faced difficult conditions during these past few years.

I am proud of the American people. I was proud, for instance, yesterday, to see the expressions on the faces of the people of Johnstown, Pennsylvania, who, working together as a unit, came through a very serious disaster to their town. That spirit has not failed us in the past, and it is not going to fail us in the future.

That is why I think I am entitled to say to you, on behalf of the Nation, that you are doing a fine job here in Cleveland — a fine job for the Nation.

I only wish I could stay for a whole week and see it all.

97 ⟨ "I Have Seen War. . . . I Hate War" — Address at Chautauqua, N. Y. August 14, 1936

A S MANY of you who are here tonight know, I formed the excellent habit of coming to Chautauqua more than twenty years ago. After my Inauguration in 1933, I promised Mr. Bestor that during the next four years I would come to Chautauqua again. It is in fulfillment of this that I am with you tonight.

A few days ago I was asked what the subject of this talk would be; and I replied that for two good reasons I wanted to discuss the subject of peace: First, because it is eminently appropriate in Chautauqua and, second, because in the hurly-burly of domestic politics it is important that our people should not overlook problems and issues which, though they lie beyond our borders, may, and probably will, have a vital influence on the United States of the future.

Many who have visited me in Washington in the past few months may have been surprised when I have told them that personally and because of my own daily contacts with all manner of difficult situations I am more concerned and less cheerful about international world conditions than about our immediate domestic prospects.

I say this to you not as a confirmed pessimist but as one who still hopes that envy, hatred and malice among Nations have reached their peak and will be succeeded by a new tide of peace and good-will. I say this as one who has participated in many of the decisions of peace and war before, during and after the World War; one who has traveled much; and one who has spent a goodly portion of every twenty-four hours in the study of foreign relations.

Long before I returned to Washington as President of the United States, I had made up my mind that pending what might be called a more opportune moment on other continents, the United States could best serve the cause of a peaceful humanity by setting an example. That was why on the 4th of March, 1933, I made the following declaration:

> "In the field of world policy I would dedicate this Nation to the policy of the good neighbor — the neighbor who resolutely respects himself and, because he does so, respects the rights of others — the neighbor who respects his obligations and respects the sanctity of his agreements in and with a world of neighbors."

This declaration represents my purpose; but it represents more than a purpose, for it stands for a practice. To a measurable degree it has succeeded; the whole world now knows that the United States cherishes no predatory ambitions. We are strong; but less powerful Nations know that they need not fear our strength. We seek no conquest; we stand for peace.

In the whole of the Western Hemisphere our good-neighbor policy has produced results that are especially heartening.

The noblest monument to peace and to neighborly economic and social friendship in all the world is not a monument in bronze or stone, but the boundary which unites the United States and Canada — 3,000 miles of friendship with no barbed wire, no gun or soldier, and no passport on the whole frontier.

Mutual trust made that frontier. To extend the same sort of mutual trust throughout the Americas was our aim.

The American Republics to the south of us have been ready always to cooperate with the United States on a basis of equality and mutual respect, but before we inaugurated the good-neighbor policy there were among them resentment and fear, because certain Administrations in Washington had slighted their national pride and their sovereign rights.

In pursuance of the good-neighbor policy, and because in my younger days I had learned many lessons in the hard school of experience, I stated that the United States was opposed definitely to armed intervention.

We have negotiated a Pan-American convention embodying the principle of non-intervention. We have abandoned the Platt Amendment which gave us the right to intervene in the internal affairs of the Republic of Cuba. We have withdrawn American marines from Haiti. We have signed a new treaty which places our relations with Panama on a mutually satisfactory basis. We have undertaken a series of trade agreements with other American countries to our mutual commercial profit. At the request of two neighboring Republics, I hope to give assistance in the final settlement of the last serious boundary dispute between any of the American Nations.

Throughout the Americas the spirit of the good neighbor is a practical and living fact. The twenty-one American Republics are not only living together in friendship and in peace; they are united in the determination so to remain.

To give substance to this determination a conference will meet on December 1, 1936, at the capital of our great Southern neighbor, Argentina, and it is, I know, the hope of all Chiefs of State of the Americas that this will result in measures which will banish wars forever from this vast portion of the earth.

Peace, like charity, begins at home; that is why we have begun at home. But peace in the Western world is not all that we seek.

It is our hope that knowledge of the practical application of the good-neighbor policy in this hemisphere will be borne home to our neighbors across the seas.

For ourselves we are on good terms with them — terms in most cases of straightforward friendship, of peaceful understanding.

But, of necessity, we are deeply concerned about tendencies of recent years among many of the Nations of other continents. It is a bitter experience to us when the spirit of agreements to which we are a party is not lived up to. It is an even more bitter experience for the whole company of Nations to witness not only the spirit but the letter of international agreements violated with impunity and without regard to the simple principles of honor. Permanent friendships between Nations as between men can be sustained only by scrupulous respect for the pledged word.

In spite of all this we have sought steadfastly to assist international movements to prevent war. We cooperated to the bitter end — and it was a bitter end — in the work of the General Disarmament Conference. When it failed we sought a separate treaty to deal with the manufacture of arms and the international traffic in arms. That proposal also came to nothing. We participated — again to the bitter end — in a conference to continue naval limitations, and when it became evident that no general treaty could be signed because of the objections of other Nations, we concluded with Great Britain and France a conditional treaty of qualitative limitation which, much to my regret, already shows signs of ineffectiveness.

We shun political commitments which might entangle us in foreign wars; we avoid connection with the political activities of the League of Nations; but I am glad to say that we have cooperated whole-heartedly in the social and humanitarian work at Geneva. Thus we are a part of the world effort to control traffic in narcotics, to improve international health, to help child welfare, to eliminate double taxation and to better working conditions and laboring hours throughout the world.

We are not isolationists except in so far as we seek to isolate ourselves completely from war. Yet we must remember that so long as war exists on earth there will be some danger that even the Nation which most ardently desires peace may be drawn into war.

288

I have seen war. I have seen war on land and sea. I have seen blood running from the wounded. I have seen men coughing out their gassed lungs. I have seen the dead in the mud. I have seen cities destroyed. I have seen two hundred limping, exhausted men come out of line — the survivors of a regiment of one thousand that went forward forty-eight hours before. I have seen children starving. I have seen the agony of mothers and wives. I hate war.

I have passed unnumbered hours, I shall pass unnumbered hours, thinking and planning how war may be kept from this Nation.

I wish I could keep war from all Nations; but that is beyond my power. I can at least make certain that no act of the United States helps to produce or to promote war. I can at least make clear that the conscience of America revolts against war and that any Nation which provokes war forfeits the sympathy of the people of the United States.

Many causes produce war. There are ancient hatreds, turbulent frontiers, the "legacy of old forgotten, far-off things, and battles long ago." There are new-born fanaticisms, convictions on the part of certain peoples that they have become the unique depositories of ultimate truth and right.

A dark old world was devastated by wars between conflicting religions. A dark modern world faces wars between conflicting economic and political fanaticisms in which are intertwined race hatreds. To bring it home, it is as if within the territorial limits of the United States, forty-eight Nations with forty-eight forms of government, forty-eight customs barriers, forty-eight languages, and forty-eight eternal and different verities, were spending their time and their substance in a frenzy of effort to make themselves strong enough to conquer their neighbors or strong enough to defend themselves against their neighbors.

In one field, that of economic barriers, the American policy may be, I hope, of some assistance in discouraging the economic source of war and therefore a contribution toward the peace of the world. The trade agreements which we are making are not only finding outlets for the products of American fields and American factories but are also pointing the way to the elimination of embargoes, quotas and other devices which place such pressure on Nations not possessing great natural resources that to them the price of peace seems less terrible than the price of war.

We do not maintain that a more liberal international trade will stop war; but we fear that without a more liberal international trade, war is a natural sequence.

The Congress of the United States has given me certain authority to provide safeguards of American neutrality in case of war.

The President of the United States, who, under our Constitution, is vested with primary authority to conduct our international relations, thus has been given new weapons with which to maintain our neutrality.

Nevertheless — and I speak from a long experience — the effective maintenance of American neutrality depends today, as in the past, on the wisdom and determination of whoever at the moment occupy the offices of President and Secretary of State.

It is clear that our present policy and the measures passed by the Congress would, in the event of a war on some other continent, reduce war profits which would otherwise accrue to American citizens. Industrial and agricultural production for a war market may give immense fortunes to a few men; for the Nation as a whole it produces disaster. It was the prospect of war profits that made our farmers in the West plow up prairie land that should never have been plowed, but should have been left for grazing cattle. Today we are reaping the harvest of those war profits in the dust storms which have devastated those war-plowed areas.

It was the prospect of war profits that caused the extension of monopoly and unjustified expansion of industry and a price level so high that the normal relationship between debtor and creditor was destroyed.

Nevertheless, if war should break out again in another continent, let us not blink the fact that we would find in this country thousands of Americans who, seeking immediate riches — fools' gold — would attempt to break down or evade our neutrality.

They would tell you — and, unfortunately, their views would get wide publicity — that if they could produce and ship this and that and the other article to belligerent Nations, the unemployed of America would all find work. They would tell you that if they could extend credit to warring Nations that credit would be used in the United States to build homes and factories and pay our debts. They would tell you that America once more would capture the trade of the world.

It would be hard to resist that clamor; it would be hard for many Americans, I fear, to look beyond — to realize the inevitable penalties, the inevitable day of reckoning, that come from a false prosperity. To resist the clamor of that greed, if war should come, would require the unswerving support of all Americans who love peace.

If we face the choice of profits or peace, the Nation will answer — must answer — "We choose peace." It is the duty of all of us to encourage such a body of public opinion in this country that the answer will be clear and for all practical purposes unanimous.

With that wise and experienced man who is our Secretary of State, whose statesmanship has met with such wide approval, I have thought and worked long and hard on the problem of keeping the United States at peace. But all the wisdom of America is not to be found in the White House or in the Department of State; we need the meditation, the prayer, and the positive support of the people of America who go along with us in seeking peace.

No matter how well we are supported by neutrality legislation, we must remember that no laws can be provided to cover every contingency, for it is impossible to imagine how every future event may shape itself. In spite of every possible forethought, international relations involve of necessity a vast uncharted area. In that area safe sailing will depend on the knowledge and the experience and the wisdom of those who direct our foreign policy. Peace will depend on their day-to-day decisions.

At this late date, with the wisdom which is so easy after the event and so difficult before the event, we find it possible to trace the tragic series of small decisions which led Europe into the Great War in 1914 and eventually engulfed us and many other Nations.

We can keep out of war if those who watch and decide have a sufficiently detailed understanding of international affairs to make certain that the small decisions of each day do not lead toward war and if, at the same time, they possess the courage to say "no" to those who selfishly or unwisely would let us go to war.

Of all the Nations of the world today we are in many ways most singularly blessed. Our closest neighbors are good neighbors. If there are remoter Nations that wish us not good but ill, they know that we are strong; they know that we can and will defend ourselves and defend our neighborhood.

We seek to dominate no other Nation. We ask no territorial expansion. We oppose imperialism. We desire reduction in world armaments.

We believe in democracy; we believe in freedom; we believe in peace. We offer to every Nation of the world the handclasp of the good neighbor. Let those who wish our friendship look us in the eye and take our hand.

98 ⟨ A Greeting to the Y.M.C.A. August 19, 1936

My dear Mr. Mease:

As an expression of man's highest aspirations, religion has been universal among people throughout all history. Worship has played a fundamental role in all social evolution.

Growing out of the work of the churches and enlarging the field of church activity, the Young Men's Christian Association developed as an institution where emphasis was placed essentially upon Christianity in action rather than upon Christian beliefs and Christian modes of thought. Young men found in it a place where they could carry out their Christian impulses.

It is difficult to imagine what a difference it would have made if no organization such as the Y.M.C.A. had been developed in this country. Down through the decades the Y.M.C.A. has grown strong. It has adjusted itself to the changing needs of the times. During this recent depression it has done valiant service in providing programs of guidance, education, and recreation for the millions of unemployed young men who have stood in great need of such programs.

I am glad to join with the many friends of the Y.M.C.A. in paying tribute to Sir George Williams, the founder of this great organization. His life should be an inspiration to the boys and young men who find in the Y.M.C.A. the preparation for the social leadership which they are to assume in the future.

Very sincerely yours,

Mr. C. R. Mease,
Chairman, Founder's Day Committee,
Newark, New Jersey.

99 ❲ Invitation to the Governors of the Drought States for a Drought Conference with the President. August 21, 1936

As you probably know, I am coming West next week to get at first hand all the information I can with respect to the situation in the drought area. We plan to arrive in Des Moines early morning, Tuesday, September 1st, and I would appreciate it very much if you could find it convenient to meet us there for a general discussion of the situation. To this conference I am also inviting Governors Herring, Cochran, Park and Marland.

I am asking Governor Herring, as our host, to advise you as to the detailed plans for the conference.

NOTE: I had decided to make a personal inspection of that part of the United States which had been visited by the drought of 1936, in order to see at first hand the effects of the drought and in order to discuss with local officials and farmers on the spot the best means of continuing relief to the distressed area as well as a long-range program for the alleviation of future droughts.

The foregoing telegram was typical of the telegrams which I sent to the various Governors and United States Senators and other officials of the States covered by the drought, asking them to meet with me at specific times and places on the inspection trip for the purposes of such discussions.

During this inspection trip I made many speeches, some of which are included as Items 101, 103, 105, 106, 107, 108, 109, 110, 111, 112, 113, 116, 117, 118 of this volume.

In addition to those I also made extemporaneous speeches at Garrette, Ind., August 26; Pierre, S. D., August 29; Atlantic, Iowa, September 3; Barry, Mo., September 4; State Fair Grounds, Indianapolis, Ind., September 5; Connersville, Ind., September 5, which have not been included in these volumes for lack of space. My drought survey trip covered the period from August 26, 1936, to September 5, 1936.

I held major conferences at Bismarck, North Dakota, Pierre, South Dakota, Des Moines, Iowa, Springfield, Illinois, and Indianapolis, Indiana, and several smaller conferences including one at Sidney, Nebraska, and one at Rapid City, South Dakota. The largest and most important of these conferences was the one at Des Moines, Iowa.

At several stops in the drought area, I motored into the country to have personal talks on the ground with farmers in the area and to inspect at first hand various water conservation projects, which were being used to supply employment locally to men who were out of work because of the drought, and which were intended to help protect farms and communities in the Great Plains area against water shortage in the event of future drought.

In these talks with farmers I obtained detailed information about their production and price problems on the farm, about the raising of self-sustaining amounts of vegetables, poultry and milk for home use; about the effects of the Federal soil conservation programs and of the various State and Federal pond and reservoir construction projects; about the value of summer fallow for storing moisture in the soil and increasing the dependability of wheat and corn production.

I also discussed the possibilities of better safeguards against dust storms, of protection against floods by storing flood water for use during dry periods in the Great Plains area, and possibilities of a return to the raising of grass in the low arid and wind regions.

I also discussed the matter of overgrazing in some of the range areas and plans for protecting livestock by emergency measures to provide feed. In my conversations with these farmers I inquired as to the condition of their crops and livestock, feed and water supplies, their drought losses, their credit requirements and the need for work relief and other forms of rehabilitation necessary to carry them through the winter months and to get them started at producing again.

I made such trips into the country at Bismarck, Mandan and Jamestown, North Dakota; Aberdeen, Pierre and Rapid City, South Dakota; and Sidney, Nebraska.

At the formal conferences which I held with the Governors of the States, they were at liberty to bring in such of their staff as they desired, including economists, advisers on special topics, State extension leaders, State engineering authorities, and State conservation, forestry, game and fisheries officials. The W.P.A. Director for the respective States, and the Federal, regional or State Director of Resettlement were also present.

In general, the various State delegations presented material and opinions relating to drought damage, feed and water shortage, and unemployment. They also presented plans or views on an efficient program for feed and water conservation. Discussions were had with respect to large reservoirs for the storage of water and also with respect to the building of small ponds for water storage on individual farms.

The conference at Bismarck, North Dakota, was held on August 27 (see Item 103, this volume), on which date a preliminary report of the Great Plains Drought Area Committee was presented (see Item 104, this volume).

The conference at Pierre, S. D., was on August 29, as was the conference at Rapid City, S. D.

On August 31st, a conference was held at Sidney, Nebraska (see Item 109, this volume). From Sidney, Nebraska, the train went to Salt Lake City to attend the funeral of Secretary of War Dern (see Item 102, this volume), and returned through Nebraska to Des Moines, Iowa, where the most important conference of the trip was held on September 3rd. The conferences were informal, without any set program. At Des Moines, conferences were held separately with each of the seven State delegations of Missouri, Iowa, Kansas, Nebraska, Oklahoma, Wisconsin and Minnesota.

After this conference the train proceeded to Springfield, Ill. (see Item 117, this volume), where another similar drought conference was held. The following day another drought conference was held at Indianapolis, Ind. (see Item 118, this volume), which included not only officials from Indiana but also officials from Michigan, Kentucky and Ohio.

On my return to Washington I made a radio speech in which I discussed the entire drought-inspection trip (see Item 120, this volume).

100 (Letters Suggesting the Application of Civil Service Rules to Employees of the Home Owners Loan Corporation. August 25, 1936

Dear Mr. Mitchell:

THE Home Owners Loan Corporation was created as an emergency agency to meet the mortgage crisis in the urban home field, and the Act provided that its employees should be selected without regard to the provisions of the Civil Service Act. This was necessary in order to organize the service quickly and to render immediate assistance not only to home owners, but to the savings and commercial banks, building and loan associations, insurance companies and other mortgage-lending institutions which were foreclosing mortgages.

The Corporation has been in existence for more than three years, and it has progressively sought to test and select its employees on the basis of merit. Now, at the conclusion of its lending activities, the Corporation is engaged in reducing its force. It is at this point, and also with respect to the future work of the Corporation and of the Federal Home Loan Bank Board and its subsidiaries, that I am confident the Civil Service Commission, with its accepted standards, can render most effective service. I am aware that further legislation is necessary to place the positions in the Federal Home Loan Bank Board and its subsidiaries within the competitive classified service; but now that much of the emergency is past and the work of the Board has been stabilized, I feel that so far as practicable the principles and methods of the merit system established by the Civil Service Act should be further extended in its personnel relationships.

The Federal Home Loan Bank Board and its agencies have for more than two years received the assistance of the Civil Service Commission in the development of standards and policies for the selection and payment of its employees. I have addressed a letter to Chairman Fahey of the Federal Home Loan Bank Board, suggesting that he arrange with your Commission to extend as far as possible the application of civil service qualifications with respect to prerequisite experience, education, and other necessary conditions for employment.

I know that your Commission will be very glad to cooperate with the Federal Home Loan Bank Board in applying to every possible position within its organization the principles of the civil service system. I request, therefore, that you take the necessary steps to bring this about in cooperation with the representatives of the Board.

Very sincerely yours,

Hon. Harry B. Mitchell, President,
Civil Service Commission,
Washington, D. C.

My dear Mr. Fahey:

I HAVE given much consideration to the questions we have discussed with respect to the future employment program of the Federal Home Loan Bank Board and its subsidiaries. One of these, the Home Owners Loan Corporation, was organized to meet a financial crisis in the urban home field, and now that the emergency is largely past, it faces the problems incident to gradual reduction of force and a program of gradual liquidation over a period of years.

The Act of 1933 creating this Corporation, as well as the Act of 1932 establishing your Board, placed employment outside the provisions of the Civil Service Act. It will, of course, require action by Congress to bring the positions of your organizations within the competitive classified service.

Now that much of the work of the Board and its subsidiaries has been stabilized, I believe that so far as possible every advantage should be taken of the standards and practices developed under the Civil Service Act of 1883 and the Classification Act of 1923. Pending legislative authority it is appropriate and entirely possible to apply the principles involved in these two statutes to the work of your organization.

I have accordingly addressed a letter to Chairman Mitchell of the Civil Service Commission, expressing my desire that the Commission cooperate fully in rendering all possible assistance to your organization in applying its standards to the work of your Board. It is gratifying that your Board has gone such a long way already in grading and classifying employees and in building an efficient staff, but I am certain that the Civil Service Commission can be helpful in further application of the standards that are common to the regular established organizations of the Federal Government.

Very sincerely yours,

Hon. John H. Fahey, Chairman,
Federal Home Loan Bank Board,
Washington, D. C.

101 ❡ Rear-Platform Extemporaneous Remarks at Gary, Ind., during Drought Inspection Trip. August 26, 1936

WHEN we came into the station just now, Paul McNutt said, "So this is Indiana." May I say that it is a lot happier-looking Indiana than the last time I was here?

Of course I am very glad to know that things are going so much better, that there is so much more prosperity in Gary and in the other great industrial centers of the Middle West.

I am on this trip because I want to see at first hand some of the problems and some of the difficulties of our neighbors further west, who have not had a chance to make any crops at all this year. And I am doing it not only to help them, but also because I believe, and I think you believe, that their prosperity out there in the Western farming area has a very direct influence on our prosperity further east in the industrial centers.

My friends, I am glad to stop here this time. The last time we went through Gary, we hurried through at about forty miles an hour trying to make up time. I hope the next time I shall not only be able to make a stop, but be able to get off and see more of you in your own home town.

102 ❨A Tribute to Secretary of War George Dern on the Occasion of His Death.

August 27, 1936

AN UPRIGHT, able and honest public servant is lost to our national life in the death of Secretary Dern. Quiet and unassuming, he mastered with singular thoroughness all of the varied problems which fall within the jurisdiction of the War Department and administered his office with tact, discretion and good judgment. The Army of the United States has lost a devoted leader.

For many years George Dern and I have been close associates, first as Governors of our respective States, and lately, for nearly four years, in Washington. I am deeply grieved that he has left us.

103 ❨Informal Extemporaneous Remarks at Bismarck, N. D., during Drought Inspection Trip.

August 27, 1936

As YOU know, I came out here to see things with my own eyes. I felt that I could learn a lot more by coming out than by just reading blueprints and reports back in Washington.

What I have seen confirms me in the belief that I have had for a long time — the belief that we are going to win out in this problem.

It really comes down to three problems: The first is the immediate one of keeping people going who have lost their crops and their livestock. The second is to keep them going over the winter until next year, when we hope we shall have more rain. The third problem relates to the future — not only the future of North Dakota, but the future of a good many other States. It relates to working out a plan of cooperation with Nature instead of continuing what we have been doing in the past — trying to buck Nature.

That means cooperation between all the agencies involved. There are a lot of Federal agencies, there are State agencies and there are local agencies, and our chief problem now is to work out a plan that all of these different agencies can carry out, working intelligently with each other and not crossing wires.

It means we have got to have the cooperation of the people in the cities as well as of the people on the farms. It is just as much their problem as it is the problem of the farmers themselves. Indeed, in an agricultural country, there would not be any cities if there were no farms.

There was another reason for my coming out here, and that was to look at you people. Back East there have been all kinds of reports that out in the drought area there was a widespread despondency, a lack of hope for the future, and a general atmosphere of gloom. But I had a hunch — and it was right — that when I got out here I would find that you people had your chins up, that you were not looking forward in despair to the day when this country would be depopulated, but that you and your children fully expected to remain here.

And that is what we all want to see — the people in every part of the country. We want to see this country remain fully populated; we want to see it attain a greater prosperity than ever.

A few days ago I was passing through one of the greatest industrial centers in the United States, Gary, Indiana, where you pass through mile after mile of steel factories. I told them there what is perfectly true, that your problem out here is their problem back there, because of the perfectly obvious fact that steel factories would not run at full capacity unless the agricultural States were in a position to buy farm implements and other products of the steel mills.

I have learned a great deal today, and I am going to learn more in the next few days. I get a picture which reassures me as to the future of the so-called Great Plains drought area. You are en- titled to reassurance of the fact that the Government — not only the Federal Government, but the State Government and the local government — can and must and will go ahead with win- ning out through a system of careful long-range planning.

I ask for your cooperation through many, many years to come in putting that kind of program into effect. And again I say that I know you are not licked.

104 ⟨ Summary of the Great Plains Drought Area Committee's Preliminary Report and Conclu- sions Submitted during Drought Inspection Trip. August 27, 1936

Since January 1, 1933, Federal agencies alone have spent in the Great Plains region on works related to conservation of physical as- sets, about $140,000,000, not including grants, loans and relief dis- bursements amounting to approximately $335,000,000.

We offer a basic program at this time because we believe there is general agreement as to the main facts among those most familiar with the situation, and because we are convinced that activities for permanent rehabilitation and reconstruction already undertaken must be speeded up and expanded if the Great Plains area is to avoid a worse disaster than has yet befallen it.

A trip through the drought area, supplementing data already on record, makes it evident that we are not confronted with merely a short-term problem of relief, already being dealt with by several agencies of the Federal Government, but with a long-term problem of readjustment and reorganization.

The agricultural economy of the Great Plains will become increas- ingly unstable and unsafe, in view of the impossibility of permanent increase in the amount of rainfall, unless over-cropping and over- grazing and improper farm methods are prevented. The future of the region must depend on the degree to which farming practices conform to natural conditions. Because the situation has now passed out of the individual farmer's control, the reorganization of farming practices demands the cooperation of many agencies, including the local, State and Federal Governments.

Our proposals will look toward the greatest possible degree of stabilization of the region's economy, a higher and more secure income for each family, the spreading of the shock of inevitable droughts so that they will not be crushing in their effects, the conservation of land and water, a steadily diminishing dependence on public grants and subsidies, the restoration of credit of individuals and of local and State Governments, and a thoroughgoing consideration of how great a population, and in what areas, the Great Plains can support.

These objectives are not now attainable by individual action, but we believe they will restore an individual independence which has been lost.

The problem of the Great Plains is not the product of a single act of Nature, or of a single year or even a series of exceptionally bad years; it has come into being over a considerable period of time, and time will be required to deal with it.

The basic cause of the present Great Plains situation is an attempt to impose upon the region a system of agriculture to which the Plains are not adapted — to bring into a semi-arid region methods which are suitable, on the whole, only for a humid region.

Extreme instances can be found in which more than 90 percent of the entire net cash income of a wheat farm over twenty years was concentrated in a single year. Yet each year some or all of the wheat land was plowed and the soil exposed to the destructive forces of sun and wind.

Nature and the wheat market combined to make wheat farming highly speculative.

Although the dust storms of 1934 and 1935 have been visible evidence to nearly every American living east of the Rocky Mountains that something is seriously wrong, the extent of erosion on the Great Plains has not yet been accurately determined. It is safe to say that 80 percent is now in some stage of erosion and as much as 15 percent may already have been injured seriously and permanently.

The Federal Government must do its full share in remedying the damage caused by a mistaken homesteading policy, by the stimulation of war-time demands which led to over-cropping and over-grazing, and by encouragement of a system of agriculture which could not be both permanent and prosperous.

Arrest of the wastage of soil by erosion and efficient use of the water resources of the region are basic in any long-range program for the Great Plains Drought Area.

Accomplishment of these two objectives involves engineering, proper agricultural practices, financing and a revision of policies by all public agencies concerned.

The region should be divided into sub-areas and studies should be made to determine the kinds of agricultural practice and engineering treatment required to fit each portion to its indicated use.

Certain sub-marginal lands should be taken permanently out of commercial production.

Soil conserving practices should be followed on arable lands, such as re-grassing, contour plowing, listing, terracing, strip-cropping and the planting of trees. Grazing can often be benefited by contour furrowing and water spreading. Grazing and cropping should be carefully integrated.

Water should never be allowed needlessly to go to waste. In addition to the water conservation which is inherent in soil conserving practices, thousands of small but substantial dams should be constructed. These serve to hold back run-off for use in dry periods, provide a more adequate water supply for stock and help to insure a feed supply by making possible small irrigation systems for groups of families. In many places, flood irrigation by water-spreading is feasible. Some readjustment of water rights appears essential, since it is contrary to the principles of conservation to allow water to be diverted to poor lands when there is not enough to supply neighboring lands of better quality.

The work relief program, the program of major public works and action by farmers themselves, working in cooperating groups, can contribute to the carrying out of this program. Long-term credit must be made available to farmers attempting to help themselves. In addition, public acquisition of lands too seriously injured to warrant restoration by private enterprise should be continued if the change which is urgently needed in the land-use patterns of the region is to be accomplished. Federal, State and county governments should cooperate in this activity.

Land not too far depleted for restoration should be leased or optioned by the Government with the stipulation that the owners carry on an approved program of restoration to grass or forest.

City zoning ordinances should be studied for precedents for public action to protect land against uses held to be harmful to the public interest.

Wherever possible the cooperative principle should be invoked and encouraged. The Taylor Grazing Act and the grazing regulations in the National Forests and on State lands should be administered with the definite aim of stimulating cooperative grazing associations. Assistance should be offered such grazing associations to prevent overgrazing of their lands.

Local committees should be encouraged, to insure that the wishes and interests of local people receive adequate expression. All governmental agencies should consult and cooperate with these local committees.

All of the proposed activities should be coordinated parts of a well-devised program envisaging the entire region. The emergency is a test of the democratic system which can be met without any exercise of arbitrary power by any agency.

We need to know approximately how many people the region should be expected to support under conditions of scientific agriculture. We need to know to what extent population could voluntarily be relocated with advantage to itself. Aimless intra-regional migrations should not be encouraged; yet in many cases a different grouping might produce happier and more prosperous communities. At present it cannot finally be said whether or not the region can support adequately the population now residing within its limits. In the long run a change from cropping to grazing would undeniably reduce the population of some areas. Nevertheless, it is possible that a sounder agricultural economy, with more opportunities for assured family incomes and higher living standards, might increase subsidiary opportunities for employment. The fundamental purpose of any worth-while program must be not to depopulate the region but to make it permanently habitable. The drift away from the Great

Plains has already begun and is likely to continue unless remedial measures are taken without delay.

The regional agriculture must rest on the development of holdings which will actually support a family in independence and comfort. Undoubtedly these holdings must be larger than those now prevailing in many parts of the Plains, while in other parts farmers are attempting cultivation of too much land.

Since tenancy, imposing upon the tenant the necessity of "mining the land," is peculiarly unfitted to conditions now existing on the Great Plains, there would seem to be justification for the use of the public credit to enable competent tenants to purchase and operate their own farms.

We recommend thorough exploration of the possibilities of covering the unavoidable risks resulting from the irregular alternation of good years and bad by some form of insurance. A proposed solution, which studies by the Department of Agriculture indicate may be actuarially sound, calls for the collection of a portion of the surplus in bumper years with repayment in kind during years when crops fall below normal.

We are convinced that in many vital respects the initiative must be taken by the Federal Government. We suggest a study to determine what new Federal legislation, if any, may be necessary in order to permit the central Government to promote the transfer from crop to grass farming where necessary.

We recommend the establishment of a Board, representative of pertinent Federal and State agencies, to integrate and implement the lines of action suggested. The Board should suggest ways in which current relief activities may in considerable measure be made the first steps in the consummation of a long-range program. The various agencies at work in the field should have coterminous areas and the unit should be the county or district composed of several counties.

We endanger our Democracy if we allow the Great Plains or any other section of the country to become an economic desert.

105 ❡ Rear-Platform Extemporaneous Remarks at Jamestown, N. D., during Drought Inspection Trip. August 28, 1936

I AM very glad that I have had the chance to come into North Dakota. It is a big State and I have seen only a very small section of it; but I have learned something at first hand which confirms me in my thought that our problems not only here but in a great many other parts of the country can be described in three words — better land use.

This morning, when we came into that rain storm, I felt that my luck has held, because two years ago, in 1934, when I was coming back from the Coast and I got into the drought area, the rain followed me the whole way.

In fact, this morning one of the Eastern newspapermen on the train, when he woke up, got one eye open, looked out of the window, and said, "What is this, a flood-control trip?" He had been with us up in New England and in Pennsylvania where they have had literally millions of dollars' worth of damage from floods. There it is a good deal different from what we see out here.

I am perfectly sure that with cooperation between the three different kinds of government — local government, State Government and Federal Government — we are going to find a solution for our problem, not only of taking care of the immediate necessities now and through this winter, but, beyond that, of working out a long-range system of planning that will use the land for the best purposes.

I am very appreciative of the greeting that you have given me here, also of that of the good people back in Bismarck and Mandan. I know that we can count on your cooperation. We are all pulling together, the Nation as a whole for the Nation's good — and that includes you.

106 ❡ Rear-Platform Extemporaneous Remarks at Aberdeen, S. D., during Drought Inspection Trip. August 28, 1936

I AM mighty glad to come back into South Dakota and to be here with my old friend, Tom Berry. I have had a very interesting day. I have been out this way a good many times before, as you know. I was saying on the train before we came in that right here on the platform were three Governors, Governor Berry, Governor Bulow and Governor Roosevelt. And Tom Berry said, "No, in South Dakota there is just one Governor and that is I."

You have a great problem before you — not just taking care of the immediate needs caused by the drought this year and of the needs of this coming winter, for we are going to take care of that. I have been thinking more about the future, for I want to see South Dakota continue to grow and prosper.

I understand there are some people that are not in favor of planning ahead. I believe there are some people that say it is not worth spending money to save money. Somebody said yesterday, up in North Dakota, that he believed if you could save ten million dollars by spending one million dollars it was worth while.

Because this is an agricultural section of the country, it is absolutely necessary for you who live in the cities to realize that too, because there would not be any cities if there were not any farms.

While we are still young at this game, we are learning something more about it every year that goes by. We are getting excellent cooperation between the local government, the State Government and the Federal Government. Things are beginning to click pretty well; and that is so because we believe we can win out in this fight.

In one way, I do not like to call it a fight because one of our troubles in the past has been that we have been fighting Nature. Now it is time for us to cooperate with Nature.

I have come out here to learn more about the conditions at first hand. I shall take back to Washington with me the picture of a whole lot of people with courage, with their chins up, who are telling me that they are going to see it through. And I am going to help.

107 ❨ Rear-Platform Extemporaneous Remarks at Huron, S. D., during Drought Inspection Trip. August 28, 1936

My friends:

I AM sorry I cannot be here by daylight, but it is better to come at night and have you greet me this way than not come at all.

I have had a very interesting two days, first in North Dakota and today in parts of South Dakota. I have had my old friend, Governor Berry, with me, and also Senator Bulow, and I have seen a lot of things I came out here to see at first hand.

What I have seen in these last two days convinces me that we are on the right track. We are trying to restore this country out through here to a position where we can go ahead in South Dakota to better times, not only in the cities, but on the farms.

I told the good people this morning that of course no city in an agricultural country can exist unless the farms are prosperous. We have to cooperate with one another instead of trying to buck one another.

That is why we have been trying to do what they call "planning." I hear the word "planning" is not popular with some people, but one reason why the water table has sunk as low as it has is that we did not think about the future twenty years ago. When we think of that, we know that planning makes good sense; and that is why this cooperative work is going to go forward pretty well.

Not only the Federal Government, but the State Government and the local governments, the people on the farms and the people in the cities are cooperating to make good on what we are trying to do.

It is a fine thing to know that you people out here are not despondent the way some people back East have told us. I have come out here to find you with your chins up, looking toward the future with confidence and courage. I am grateful to you for the attitude you are taking.

As I said, it is a question of working together and I am very, very certain that we shall have your cooperation in making the days to come more happy and prosperous than in the past.

Incidentally, I notice a good deal of change up here from the days when wheat was selling at twenty-five cents and corn at ten cents, even if we have not got so much wheat and corn. And next year we hope that we shall have them and that the prices for them will be better than they were in the old days.

I am glad to be here, although I wish I could have been here by daylight. I hope some day in the future to come back by daylight and see more of you. Many thanks.

Now I hope you will excuse me. I have to go back into the car and do some work. Good night.

108 ⟨Informal Extemporaneous Remarks at Mount Rushmore National Memorial. August 30, 1936

I THINK, my friends, that there are two people who told me about this in the early days. One of them was Mr. Borglum and the other was Senator Norbeck.

On many occasions, when a new project is presented to you on paper, and, later on you see the accomplishment, you are disappointed; but just the opposite is the fact in what we are looking at now. I had seen photographs, I had seen the drawings, and I had talked with those who are responsible for this great work. Yet I had had no conception until about ten minutes ago, not only of its magnitude, but of its permanent beauty and of its permanent importance.

Mr. Borglum has well said that this can be a monument and an inspiration for the continuance of the Democratic-Republican form of government, not only in our own beloved country, but, we hope, throughout the world.

This is the second dedication. There will be others by other Presidents in other years. When we get through, there will be something for the American people that will last not merely through generations but for thousands and thousands of years.

I think that we can perhaps meditate a little on those Americans ten thousand years from now, when the weathering on the faces of Washington and Jefferson and Lincoln shall have proceeded to perhaps the depth of a tenth of an inch, and wonder what our descendants — and I think they will still be here — will think about us.

Let us hope that at least they will give us the benefit of the doubt, that they will believe we have honestly striven every day and generation to preserve for our descendants a decent land to live in and a decent form of government to operate under.

I am very glad to have come here today informally. It is right and proper that I should have come informally, because we do not want formalities where Nature is concerned.

What we have done so far exemplifies what I have been talking about in the last few days — cooperation with Nature and not fighting against Nature.

I am happy to congratulate all of you not only on what we see today, but on what is going to happen in the future at Mount Rushmore.

109 ⟨ Informal Extemporaneous Remarks at Sidney, Nebr. August 31, 1936

As you know, I am here on a sad mission — on my way to attend the funeral of a very distinguished American, the Secretary of War, George Dern. As you will all remember, Secretary Dern was a native of the State of Nebraska. Because of this mission I cannot, with propriety, make a long speech to you. I want simply to tell you that I am taking this opportunity to look into some of the problems of this part of Nebraska.

I am sorry that the Governor is not here because of illness, but I expect to see him in Des Moines next Thursday. I am glad that the State is so well represented by my old friend, Congressman Coffee, who is with us today.

I want particularly to learn something at first hand about what you have done in this part of the State in relation to summer fallowing. As I understand it, you have taken the lead in this, and that is at least partly responsible for your making as much as a 20 percent crop. There are a great many sections of the country that have not made any crop.

I want also to hear about the progress of the cattle-purchasing program here on the part of the Federal Government.

All of these things are tying in together. I am confident that we shall have in this State the same fine cooperation on the part of local government and its citizens with the State and Federal Governments that I have found everywhere I have gone on my travels.

110 ❨ Rear-Platform Extemporaneous Remarks at Cheyenne, Wyo., during Drought Inspection Trip. September 2, 1936

As you know, I have already had a very successful conference with Governor Miller in regard to the drought situation in Wyoming. That is in line with the conferences that I am having with the Governors of all those States which are affected by the present drought problem.

I was very glad to see, coming through this State on the U. P., that farther west the conditions are not so bad. I am sorry that I have not the time to inspect that part of the State, the northeast, where the drought problem has been very serious.

We are trying to tie in all of the various agencies that have to do with drought, the local authorities, the State Government and then the Federal Departments. That is why, on this train, we have the Secretary of Agriculture, the Administrator of Resettlement and the Administrator of Relief, all working together toward a program which we hope is going to make things better in the years to come.

As a matter of fact, of course, the problem in this State is not so serious as it was in 1934 and I am glad to see on this trip that we are much more prosperous, taking things by and large, than we were then.

One of the best indications of our increasing prosperity is the very large number of tourists that are moving around this part of the country this summer. In the national parks and in the national forests the actual number of people who are seeking recreation during the summer is greater than it was in 1929, and that is saying a lot.

The train is about to pull out. It has been good to see you. Good-bye.

111 ⟪ Rear-Platform Extemporaneous Remarks at Laramie, Wyo., during Drought Inspection Trip. September 2, 1936

As you know, I went to Salt Lake City on a very sad mission. Secretary Dern knew all this Western country very well; he was born in Nebraska and moved on through to Utah. I felt, through these years in Washington, that he was one of those people who always keep their feet on the ground, which is a very great asset. He was a wonderful man and a fine public servant and we are going to miss him, not only in his own State and in Washington but throughout the Nation.

I have been reading this morning one of Secretary Wallace's charts — he is standing right here beside me — and I am very glad to see from that chart that you people from around Laramie and this part of the country got pretty good pasture this year — a great deal better than during the 1934 conditions. This chart shows one of the advantages of having a national Government; you can get information right away from all parts of the country. It shows, for example, that you were able to furnish some additional pasturage here for cattle brought in from the outside.

The point which I think we all ought to realize is that this is necessarily a national picture. What happens to cattle in Texas and in North Dakota affects your prosperity here in Wyoming; and that is true not only of cattle in other parts of the country but of other crops. You are affected by what happens to corn and hogs in the Middle West. It is a queer thought, but it is actually true, and if you will think it out you will see that I am right. In the same way, your prosperity is affected by what happens to the cotton farmer down South. If the cotton farmer gets pretty good prices and has good crops it means that he and his family will buy more beef. That is a simple illustration.

That is why we are trying to look at the whole agricultural problem, not just from the question of drought, but from the point of view of the general economic system. And in spite of drought and other things, we do know that the purchasing power of the country as a whole has gone up a good deal and, therefore, we have a better chance in the agricultural communities today than we had a few years ago.

The train is moving out, so I am not going to give you any more economics. I am just going to say good-bye.

112 ⟨ Rear-Platform Extemporaneous Remarks at Julesburg, Colo., during Drought Inspection Trip. September 2, 1936

My friends:

WHEN my plans were changed I found that I was going through a corner of Colorado and I sent a telegram to Governor Johnson, asking him to join the train in order that I could have with him the same kind of conference that I have had with the Governors of a number of other States that have been affected by the drought. So, for the past couple of hours, we have been talking on the train.

We have Secretary Wallace of the Department of Agriculture with us, Administrator Tugwell of the Resettlement Administration and Mr. Hopkins of the Relief Administration. We have been going over the situation as it affects this particular State.

I wish I had more time to study at first hand the situation in Colorado. Apparently the State as a whole is pretty fortunate, although this eastern section, both the northeastern section and the southeastern section, have been affected a good deal.

As you know, we are all working together. We have three problems before us: The first is the immediate problem of taking care of the feeding of people during the summer. The second is the problem of taking care of people during the next winter until next spring, when we hope we shall have more rain. The third problem relates to long-range planning, so that we can beat this problem once and for all by the proper use of land.

As you know, we are all interested in this. It is something that is fairly new because twenty-five years ago, when we had all the land in the world still open to settlement, that problem did not exist. Today the unlimited land of the old days of the frontier is gone; and we find that we have to use land in a different and better way than we used it during the past generation.

I believe that by cooperation between the people, the local governments, the State Government and the Federal Government we are going to work out something that will mean greater prosperity for all of the people, not only in the drought section, but in every part of the country as well.

I have been preaching back East that if one section of this country, like the Great Plains area, has a bad year or is seriously affected, it affects the people back East, the people down South and the people on the Coast very nearly as much as it does you

314

people who are in the drought area. That is why I am here on a "look-see" trip.

I am glad to see you and I hope to come back again to see you one of these days soon.

113 ⦅ Rear-Platform Extemporaneous Remarks at North Platte, Nebr., during Drought Inspection Trip. September 2, 1936

I wish very much that I could have arranged a schedule so that I could have driven out to see the second largest dirt dam in the United States.

I am very familiar with the blueprints of the Sutherland project and I saw some of the dirt farther up the line, where they are carrying the water under the waters of the South Platte. I am delighted to know that this project is 95 percent complete.

This project and the other two large projects in this State splendidly illustrate what can be accomplished by cooperation between different governmental agencies. As you know, most of its cost is being raised by you people who are interested in the project itself. I think I am right in saying that the contribution of the Federal Government is only 30 percent of the entire cost of the project. That 30 percent has meant giving work to somewhere around 3,000 people; it has served two good purposes.

When I was up in one of the New England States, where they have the somewhat different problem of flood control, I saw another great earth dam which was constructed to hold back the waters of one of the rivers in Vermont which, only a few years ago in one cloudburst, did six million dollars' worth of damage. The total cost of that dam was only about a million and a half dollars. This spring there was another cloudburst there, with just as much rain as they had had in 1927; but that dam was enough to hold back all the waters resulting from that cloudburst, and there was not one dollar's worth of damage.

Our problem here is just the opposite; but I can say to you what I said to the Governor of Vermont when he was sitting beside me in the automobile on the top of that dam. I said, "Governor, it seems to me that this is a pretty good example of cooperative boondoggling between your State and the Federal Government."

This is another example of fine cooperative boondoggling, which is going to make its influence felt not only upon you who are here today but also upon the coming generations who will inhabit this part of the United States.

You are doing a splendid piece of work. In this drought area trip I have been impressed, as some of you know, by the splendid attitude of the people in all of these States. And we do not want to depopulate these States; we want to make them a better and safer place in which to live.

114 (Presidential Statement on the Summation of the 1937 Budget. September 2, 1936

CONTINUING the practice inaugurated last year, the attached summation revises the Budget for the fiscal year 1937 by reflecting the changes affecting the estimates of revenues and expenditures which have occurred since the 1937 Budget was transmitted to Congress in January, 1936. Two outstanding events have taken place since that time which have materially affected the receipts and expenditures of the Government. The first of these was the decision of the Supreme Court declaring the Agricultural Adjustment Act unconstitutional, as a result of which the Government lost substantial revenue from processing taxes. The second was the passage by the Congress of the Adjusted Compensation Payment Act providing for the immediate payment at their face value of the veterans' adjusted service certificates, which by their terms were not due until 1945.

As a result of the Supreme Court decision the estimated revenue from processing taxes for the fiscal year 1936 was reduced by

$452,000,000. Up to the time of that decision the Agricultural Adjustment Administration had expended in accordance with law the sum of $325,000,000 and had made substantial commitments for additional expenditures in anticipation of revenue from this source. To provide for carrying out the moral obligation of the Government with respect to the commitments already entered into with farmers and which on their part had been at least partially performed, Congress appropriated $296,000,000.

By the enactment of the Soil Conservation and Domestic Allotment Act, which included authority for an annual appropriation of not to exceed $500,000,000, Congress provided a new farm program to preserve to the farmers the benefits of fair and adequate prices for the product of their labors.

The passage of the Adjusted Compensation Payment Act caused an increase in payments to veterans for the past year of $1,674,000,000 and will result in further payments estimated at $560,000,000 on this account during the present fiscal year.

To meet the additional requirements of the Treasury on account of these expenditures the Congress was requested to provide sufficient additional revenue, (1) to make good the loss of processing taxes in the fiscal year 1936, (2) to defray the annual cost of operation of the new farm program, and (3) to amortize over a period of nine years the cost of payment of the adjusted service certificates.

The Revenue Act of 1936, enacted by the Congress in response to this request, will produce, on the basis of estimated business conditions for the calendar year 1936, annual revenue in the amount of $652,000,000. For the fiscal year 1937 the amount of this revenue will be only $328,000,000, since only the first and second of the quarterly payments of income taxes under this Act will be made to the Treasury within that year. For the same year, however, there will be a non-recurring revenue of $82,-000,000 from the so-called windfall taxes.

REVIEW OF THE FISCAL YEAR 1936

The total receipts amounted to $4,115,956,615 against the estimate in the 1937 Budget of $4,410,793,946, a net decrease of $294,837,331. After taking into consideration the loss in processing taxes of $452,000,000, receipts from other sources amounted to $157,000,000 more than was estimated. Total receipts showed a net increase of $316,000,000 over those for 1935, and receipts from sources other than processing taxes showed an increase over 1935 of $760,000,000.

The total expenditures of the Government for the fiscal year ended June 30, 1936, amounted to $8,879,798,258. The estimated expenditure shown in the Budget of last January of $7,645,301,338 did not, of course, include $1,674,000,000 for adjusted compensation payments. Except for these payments the expenditures would have been about $439,000,000 less than the January estimate.

The deficit for the year amounted to $4,763,841,642, which included $403,240,150 for statutory debt retirement. Deducting this amount leaves a net deficit of $4,360,601,492. The estimated net deficit as shown in the Budget of last January was $2,682,482,392. Had it not been for the invalidation of processing taxes and the passage of the Adjusted Compensation Payment Act, the net deficit would have been less than the January estimate by more than $400,000,000.

The public debt increased during the year $5,077,650,869, but in that time the balance of cash in the general fund of the Treasury likewise showed an increase of $840,164,664.

FORECAST FOR THE FISCAL YEAR 1937

Total receipts in the fiscal year 1937 are now estimated at $5,665,839,000, a net increase of $12,000,000 over the amount of the 1937 Budget estimate. The estimated increases in general revenue more than offset the revenue losses, due in part to the invalidation of the special taxes levied under the provisions of the Agricultural Adjustment and Bituminous Coal Conservation Acts, and in part to the method finally adopted for collecting taxes under the Social Security Act which will defer to the fiscal year 1938 the collection of a portion of these taxes. The losses from these causes amount to $668,000,000, which are slightly more than offset by the following estimated increases in revenue: $410,000,000 (including $82,000,000 from the windfall taxes) resulting from the Revenue Act of 1936; $33,000,000 from delayed collections of taxes on carriers and their employees; and $237,000,000 constituting an upward revision of revenue estimates due chiefly to improvement in business conditions.

The expenditure requirements for the fiscal year 1937 are now estimated at $7,762,835,300, which includes $560,000,000 to complete the payments of adjusted compensations to veterans and $580,000,000 for statutory debt retirement.

Some of the principal items included in the expenditure requirements are as follows: The Agricultural Adjustment Administration will require $585,000,000 and the Civilian Conservation Corps $300,000,000. The requirements of the Agricultural Adjustment Administration will be greater for 1937 than for 1936, due to the interruption of that program in the past year by the Supreme Court decision and the consequent postponement of expenditures. The expenditures for the Civilian Conservation Corps for 1937 will be less than those for 1936 due to the reduction made in the number of enrollees as compared with the number for 1936.

The operations of the Social Security Board and the establishment of the Old-Age Reserve Account will require an additional $405,000,000. The Board commenced operations late in the fiscal year 1936 and its expenditures, therefore, were not large during that year. The Old-Age Reserve Account will require an initial contribution in 1937 of $265,000,000.

For interest on the public debt $825,000,000 will be required. In view of the general improvement in business conditions, it is estimated that there will be required a net amount of $1,835,-000,000 for recovery and relief, an amount materially less than that for the fiscal year 1936.

The estimated expenditures for the other establishments are $448,986,000 greater than the expenditures for 1936, due principally to the development of the regular annual public works program and to increased expenditures for national defense.

The estimated deficit for 1937 is $2,096,996,300, which includes $580,000,000 for statutory debt retirement and $560,-000,000 for further payments under the Adjusted Compensation Payment Act. Deducting the amount of the statutory debt retirement leaves a net deficit of $1,516,996,300. This does not mean that there will be an increase in the public debt of this amount for the reason that it is contemplated during the year to reduce the working balance of the general fund by approximately $1,-100,000,000. The following statements show the contemplated changes during the year in the working balance of the general fund and in the gross public debt.

GENERAL FUND

Working balance June 30, 1936	$2,225,112,350
Receipts from taxes and miscellaneous sources	5,665,839,000
Receipts from sale of new public debt obligations (net after deduction of refunding issues and of statutory debt retirements)	750,000,000
Funds available fiscal year 1937	$8,640,951,350
Expenditures $7,762,835,300	
Less:	
Statutory debt re- tirements $580,000,000	
Veterans' bonds to be issued 560,000,000 1,140,000,000	
Cash required to meet ordinary expenditures $6,622,835,300	
Cash required to meet redemp- tion of veterans' bonds 800,000,000	
Cash required to meet redemp- tion of national bank notes .. 100,000,000	
Total cash required during fiscal year 1937..	7,522,835,300
Estimated working balance June 30, 1937	$1,118,116,050

PUBLIC DEBT

Gross public debt June 30, 1936 .... $33,778,543,494
New public debt obligations:
  (a) To be sold to the public (net
       as above) $750,000,000
  (b) To be issued to veterans 560,000,000

      Total new public debt obli-
        gations $1,310,000,000
Less redemptions:
  Veterans' bonds ... $800,000,000
  National bank notes 100,000,000   900,000,000

     Net increase in debt 410,000,000

    Estimated gross public debt June 30, 1937 .. $34,188,543,494

The following table shows total receipts and expenditures for each of the fiscal years 1934, 1935, 1936 and revised estimates for 1937. It will be noted that there is a substantial reduction in the deficit (excluding debt retirement and veterans' bonds) for each of the years following the peak of 1934.

(In millions of dollars)

	1934	1935	1936	1937 (est.)
Receipts	3116	3800	4116	5666
Expenditures	7105	7375	8880	7763
Gross deficit	3989	3575	4764	2097
Deduct:				
Debt retirement	360	573	403	580
Veterans' bonds	—	—	1674	560
Deficit (excluding debt retirement and veterans' bonds)	3629	3002	2687	957

In my message to Congress on March 18, 1936, requesting an appropriation of $1,500,000,000 for relief of unemployment, I stated that that request, together with those previously submitted to the Congress to provide for the Civilian Conservation Corps and certain public works, would, if acted upon favorably by the Congress, give security during the next fiscal year to those most in need, on condition, however, that private employers hire many of those now on relief rolls. I further stated that should industry cooperatively achieve the goal of reemployment, the appropriation of $1,500,000,000, together with the unexpended balances of previous appropriations, would suffice to carry the Federal works program through the fiscal year 1937, and that only if industry failed to reduce substantially the number of those now out of work would another appropriation and further plans and policies be necessary. The unemployed are continuing to be absorbed in industry, and I believe that there will be a further substantial increase of such employment during the coming months. Whether it will be sufficient to permit such a reduction in work relief rolls as will bring them within the amount appropriated by Congress is a matter that cannot be determined for several months.

In estimating, moreover, the amount that would be necessary to care for a reduced number of unemployed during the current fiscal year, no account could be taken of the serious drought which has affected large sections of our country. To relieve this serious situation in the drought areas will require the expenditure of substantial amounts from the emergency relief appropriation, although the total amount that will be needed for this purpose cannot be determined at this time.

Another survey of the unemployment problem and the amount required for drought relief will be made early in the coming calendar year, and if additional appropriations for these purposes are found necessary, the amounts expended therefrom will, of course, increase the estimated expenditures shown in this summation. It is confidently expected that any such requests for additional funds will amount to less than $500,000,000.

115 ❲Address at the Dedication of the Mark Twain Memorial Bridge, Hannibal, Mo. September 4, 1936

I⟋ is with earnest American pride and with a glory in American tradition that I enjoy this happy privilege today — joining in this tribute to one who impressed himself upon the lives of youth everywhere all through the last fourscore years and ten.

To look out across this pleasant vista where the life of Mississippi River boyhood was captured and recorded for posterity and to have a part in its commemoration is a privilege that I am happy to experience.

No American youth has knowingly or willingly escaped the lessons, the philosophy and the spirit which beloved Mark Twain wove out of the true life of which he was a part. Abroad, too, this peaceful valley is known around the world as the cradle of the chronicles of buoyant boyhood — and we are all boys.

Mark Twain and his tales still live, though the years have passed and time has wrought its changes on the Mississippi. The little white town drowsing in the sunshine of the days of Huckleberry Finn and Tom Sawyer has become the metropolis of Northeastern Missouri. The tiny handful of complacent population has grown to twenty-five thousand souls — the seventh largest city in your State and the fourth in bustling industry. The old steamboat landing is still there; the railroads and the buses and the trucks have not ended water transportation on the river — and for that I am very glad.

It was my privilege last year to have a part in the opening of the centennial commemoration of Mark Twain's birthplace. On that occasion from the White House I pressed a key which caused a light to shine from the tall tower on Cardiff Hill — the Mark Twain Memorial Lighthouse. The perpetuation of Mark Twain's name, birthplace, and the haunts of his youth is very dear to me, especially because I, myself, as a boy — a younger boy than I am now — had the happy privilege of shaking hands with him.

That was a day I shall never forget. With every American boy and every American who has ever been a boy I thrill today at this great structure joining two great States in the commemoration of youth's immortal.

When old Moses D. Balis and his associates found their way to the junction of the Hannibal and the Mississippi back in 1818, they little thought of the great stage of happy youth on which they were lifting the curtain. Likewise they and the older folk of the tiny river settlement in Hannibal had little thought that Sam Clemens, playing about the steamboat landing, would live through the ages.

Likewise, they had little thought that the cabins and the frame houses and the white-washed fences would give way to thriving industrial plants, modern buildings, a splendid city hall and other impressive public structures.

In place of the schoolhouse from which Huck Finn lured Tom Sawyer to truancy and the old swimming hole, you have eighteen modern grade schools, a high school, parochial schools and a fine library.

The old candles and the oil lamps which Tom Sawyer had to fill are gone. In their places you have one of the most successful municipal electric-light and power plants in the country.

And today we mark one more step of progress — one more imprint of a changing order — a necessarily changing order — this great structure spanning the Mississippi. The river ferry started to go when the old railroad bridge joined Missouri and Illinois back in 1870. As the years went by, this structure carried the rail, the horse-drawn and the motorized commerce in and out of Hannibal across the river. Time has now taken another step, and today we eliminate the hazards of railroad crossings, of high waters and of mixed rail and vehicular traffic.

This bridge, with its three-quarters of a million dollars' outlay, stands symbolic of what can be accomplished by the cooperation of local governments and the Federal Government. Here, in this act of progress, we find the Federal Government, the City of Hannibal, the State of Missouri and the State of Illinois all joined together in coordinated action. Together they have given you this new bridge.

And, my friends, working together in the days to come, they will greatly further the prosperity and convenience of the people of the United States in every part of the Nation.

116 ❡ Rear-Platform Extemporaneous Remarks at Jacksonville, Ill., during Drought Inspection Trip. September 4, 1936

My friends, I am a little bit rusty on local history but I hope that Jacksonville was named after Andrew Jackson.

We have been having a marvelously interesting trip, a trip on which I have learned a great deal about many sections of the country that have been going through this drought. I am more and more convinced that the country is beginning to understand that if one part of the Nation suffers, every other part suffers also.

When I was passing through Gary, Indiana, I said from the back of the train that the prosperity of the steel workers in Gary was very much influenced by the ability of people out on the prairies to buy automobiles and harvesters. And when I was out in the cattle country I told them that the prosperity of the cotton growers of the South had a very direct effect on the prices that they were getting for their cattle. I don't think they saw it for a minute; but then I pointed out that if the people down in the cotton country had a good crop and got good prices for their cotton they would buy more Western beef.

That is the spirit with which we are seeking our objective in our national Government — to bring all parts of the country in together so that every part will be prosperous.

It is going to take planning; and I am not the least bit afraid of that. If we had started planning a generation ago, we would not have had so much trouble today. Prosperity is coming back, and when it comes back we want to be quite sure that it does not disappear again overnight.

I am glad to have had the chance to stop here. I always wish that instead of going through at thirty or forty miles an hour on the train I could go through a little more slowly by automobile and get to see more of the country and more of the people living in it. It is a great experience, going through the United States. It is one of the great privileges of being President.

Now we are going on to Springfield to have a conference with Governor Horner, my old friend, and with officials of the State Government of Illinois. I am quite certain that I am going to get the same cooperation from them that I have found in the other States I have visited. I am looking forward to an interesting afternoon and I hope to come back to this State again — what shall I say? — before the third of November.

117 ⟨ Informal Extemporaneous Remarks at the Executive Mansion, Springfield, Ill. September 4, 1936

GOVERNOR HORNER is not only a very delightful host, but serves an awfully good meal. And, incidentally, after that meal he put on a show for me that was as good as any Governor has put on in this whole Western trip of mine. In other words, he called in all of the real experts in this State who know about drought conditions and the problems of water conservation and soil erosion. I suppose some people would call them a brain trust, but the fact remains that they "know their stuff" or else they would not keep their positions in the universities and colleges having to do with scientific research and practical farm problems.

As a result of this meeting, I have come away with a much better picture of the problem all along the line than when I came. In a nutshell, I can only repeat what I said before — that there are today and there will be all through this winter a good many thousands of farmers who, through no fault of their own, will have to have some kind of help. For these people the Government proposes — the State Government and the Federal Government and the local government — to see them through.

We are not only glad to see them through for the present time and this coming winter. We are trying to make it possible in the days to come for them not to be in need — in other words, to plan the use of land better than we have ever done it before.

We cannot prevent droughts — they come from on high — but at least we can order our farm economy in such a way that we shall have less shortage of water in the future after it comes out of the heavens and, also, that we shall have better soil. We should not let the soil run off into the rivers as we do today.

All of these things call for planning. The interesting thing to me is that the people in the very large cities, in the manufacturing centers, are beginning to understand that the problem of the farmer directly affects them in their manufacturing employment. After all, the purchasing power of this country is lodged, at least half, in the agricultural population. If that purchasing power is lessened, it means that there is less work for the men and women in the cities who are manufacturing the goods used on the farm. In the same way, if the people in the cities can be kept busy with plenty of work at better wages — not good wages but better wages — it means that they will have more money to buy beef and pork and lots of other things.

So you see that we have what has been called integrated economy — an economy that ties in every part of the Nation. It ties in the East with the Middle West and the Middle West with the Far West. It ties in the North with the South because, for example, if the Southern cotton farmer gets a good crop and gets a decent price for his crop, he will be able to buy a whole lot of things that are manufactured in the State of Illinois.

The country is becoming conscious of this. The country is becoming nationalistic in the best sense of the word and not in the exclusive sense of the word. We do not want to build a wall around ourselves and have no trade with any other Nation in the world. What we are getting is a national point of view in that we are appreciating in each section the problems of all the other sections. That is why it has been of such interest to me in the past ten days to go through the Middle West and the Northwest and the Great Plains area.

I am going back to Washington tomorrow afternoon, after I shall have had another conference in Indiana. I am going there with a great deal more knowledge than I had before I started. I hope to make use of that knowledge through better coordination of the activities of the Federal Government and the coordination of those activities with the fine work that your State Government and your local governments are doing.

In other words, we are all a part of one big whole, and we have to pull together.

118 ⟨Informal Extemporaneous Remarks at Luncheon at Indianapolis, Ind.

September 5, 1936

I TOLD my old friend, Governor McNutt, that I would say a few words of greeting and thanks for this most delightful day. I shall always remember these visits to Indianapolis. In the 1932 campaign, I think the thing that stands out most clearly in my memory was that wonderful meeting in the Circle with that sea of faces—they seemed millions—in front of me. On this visit I have been glad to see more of the city and more of the fine work that has been carried on in the recent past.

And thank you for a most delightful luncheon. I was saying to Fred Van Nuys that your orchestra knows when to play the right State tune, which is somewhat different from what happened back in 1924 in Madison Square Garden, at the Democratic Convention. We had a magnificent band. The bandmaster came to me before the Convention opened, and said, "Would it be all right when the roll of States is called for me to play the proper tune?" I said, "That is a splendid idea." Things went all right through the A, C and D's and we got down to G, and they called Georgia. This New York City band played, "Marching through Georgia."

There is only one piece of bad news: We have been trying at the head table to get Senator Barkley of Kentucky to sing *Wagon Wheels*.

I am not talking politics on this trip, and I shall not talk drought to you. I have been doing that for nearly two weeks. I do want to say this, and I think I can say it with perfectly good faith and without bringing politics into it. This trip, at the end of August and beginning of September, 1936, is a tremendous contrast to the trips that I made and lots of other people made in the autumn of 1932. I shall always remember, in going almost every day through the country districts and the manufacturing districts, not only the garb, the clothing of people, but the faces of people. It was a harrowing experience as I campaigned in that year, because there was such obvious want in almost every part of the country. As Alben Barkley and I were going across the State of Kentucky, he would say, jokingly perhaps, to the people who thronged around the end of the train, "You have the same clothes that you had in 1928 when I was through here." And it was all too true; there was not enough clothing to go round, and there was not enough food to go round.

Those were difficult years that we went through. I am thankful, as an American, that today the faces of the people and the clothing they wear show that their mental condition and their physical condition are a whole lot better than they were at that time. I think everybody who goes through the country at the present time feels that we have come through a very dangerous and a very sad experience.

It is not a question, in my judgment, that ought to be brought into politics, into the partisan give and take of a campaign—it is a fact. Today the people of the country, of all parties and in every section, are looking forward to the future with a great deal more hope than they could possibly have looked forward to in 1932. For that reason this trip of mine has been a happy trip. Even people who have been hard hit by the drought have a new courage to go through the year without losing hope. That is true not only in the drought areas, but here in the State of Indiana, where, I am happy to say, conditions are much better with regard to crops.

So, at the end of this trip of nearly two weeks, I am going back to Washington in a happy frame of mind. I am glad to be here in Indiana, among so many old friends of both parties. I told Arthur Vandenberg that if he had been nominated against me we might have teamed up and run a joint campaign, and we would both have saved money.

It has been fine to see you. Many thanks for a delightful day.

119 ❨ Labor Day Greetings to the Workers of America. September 6, 1936

To the Workers of the United States:

I SEND hearty Labor Day greetings to America's workers everywhere. I feel that there is cause for rejoicing among wage earners as Labor's annual day approaches. Labor Day is a day on which it is natural for us to take account of stock to see where we stand with respect to those vital problems which affect so profoundly the lives and destinies of the Nation's workers. We have made progress. We must continue to move forward.

Employment and weekly pay envelopes have increased steadily during the past three years, stimulated by the spending of the Federal Government in useful ways. This increased buying power of wage earners and farmers has resulted in increased sales by merchants, more orders for factories, and rising profits for investors.

We have witnessed significant changes during the past few years, changes which necessitate special reconsideration of basic problems with a view to finding a new approach to their solution. Our aim must be to achieve and maintain a national economy whose factors are so finely balanced that the worker is always sure of a job which will guarantee a living wage. By a living wage

I mean a wage which will insure the worker and the worker's dependents a living in accordance with American standards of decency, happiness and self-respect. The wage earners of America do not ask for more. They will not be satisfied with less.

120 ❨ The First "Fireside Chat" of 1936, Following the Drought Inspection Trip — "We Are Going to Conserve Soil, Conserve Water, Conserve Life." September 6, 1936

I HAVE been on a journey of husbandry. I went primarily to see at first hand conditions in the drought States, to see how effectively Federal and local authorities are taking care of pressing problems of relief and also how they are to work together to defend the people of this country against the effects of future droughts.

I saw drought devastation in nine States.

I talked with families who had lost their wheat crop, lost their corn crop, lost their livestock, lost the water in their well, lost their garden and come through to the end of the summer without one dollar of cash resources, facing a winter without feed or food — facing a planting season without seed to put in the ground.

That was the extreme case, but there are thousands and thousands of families on Western farms who share the same difficulties.

I saw cattlemen who because of lack of grass or lack of winter feed have been compelled to sell all but their breeding stock and will need help to carry even these through the coming winter. I saw livestock kept alive only because water had been brought to them long distances in tank cars. I saw other farm families who have not lost everything but who because they have made only partial crops must have some form of help if they are to continue farming next spring.

I shall never forget the fields of wheat so blasted by heat that they cannot be harvested. I shall never forget field after field of corn stunted, earless and stripped of leaves, for what the sun left the grasshoppers took. I saw brown pastures which would not keep a cow on fifty acres.

Yet I would not have you think for a single minute that there is permanent disaster in these drought regions, or that the picture I saw meant depopulating these areas. No cracked earth, no blistering sun, no burning wind, no grasshoppers are a permanent match for the indomitable American farmers and stockmen and their wives and children who have carried on through desperate days, and inspire us with their self-reliance, their tenacity and their courage. It was their fathers' task to make homes; it is their task to keep those homes; it is our task to help them win their fight.

First, let me talk for a minute about this autumn and the coming winter. We have the option, in the case of families who need actual subsistence, of putting them on the dole or putting them to work. They do not want to go on the dole and they are one thousand percent right. We agree, therefore, that we must put them to work for a decent wage; and when we reach that decision we kill two birds with one stone, because these families will earn enough by working, not only to subsist themselves, but to buy food for their stock, and seed for next year's planting. Into this scheme of things there fit of course the Government lending agencies which next year, as in the past, will help with production loans.

Every Governor with whom I have talked is in full accord with this program of providing work for these farm families, just as every Governor agrees that the individual States will take care of their unemployables, but that the cost of employing those who are entirely able and willing to work must be borne by the Federal Government.

If then we know, as we do today, the approximate number of farm families who will require some form of work relief from now on through the winter, we face the question of what kind of work they should do. Let me make it clear that this is not a new question because it has already been answered to a greater or less extent in every one of the drought communities. Beginning in 1934, when we also had serious drought conditions, the State and Federal Governments cooperated in planning a large number of projects, many of them directly aimed at the alleviation of future drought conditions. In accordance with that program literally thousands of ponds or small reservoirs have been built in order to supply water for stock and to lift the level of the underground water to prevent wells from going dry. Thousands of wells have been drilled or deepened; community lakes have been created and irrigation projects are being pushed.

Water conservation by means such as these is being expanded as a result of this new drought all through the Great Plains area, the Western corn belt and in the States that lie further south. In the Middle West water conservation is not so pressing a problem. Here the work projects run more to soil erosion control and the building of farm-to-market roads.

Spending like this is not waste. It would spell future waste if we did not spend for such things now. These emergency work projects provide money to buy food and clothing for the winter; they keep the livestock on the farm; they provide seed for a new crop, and, best of all, they will conserve soil and water in the future in those areas most frequently hit by drought.

If, for example, in some local area the water table continues to drop and the topsoil to blow away, the land values will disappear with the water and the soil. People on the farms will drift into the nearby cities; the cities will have no farm trade and the workers in the city factories and stores will have no jobs. Property values in the cities will decline. If, on the other hand, the farms within that area remain as farms with better water supply and no erosion, the farm population will stay on the land and prosper and the nearby cities will prosper too. Property values will increase instead of disappearing. That is why it is worth our while as a Nation to spend money in order to save money.

I have used the argument in relation only to a small area. It holds good, however, in its effect on the Nation as a whole. Every State in the drought area is now doing and always will do business with every State outside it. The very existence of the men and women working in the clothing factories of New York, making clothes worn by farmers and their families; of the workers in the steel mills in Pittsburgh, in the automobile factories of Detroit, and in the harvester factories of Illinois, depends upon the farmers' ability to purchase the commodities they produce. In the same way it is the purchasing power of the workers in these factories in the cities that enables them and their wives and children to eat more beef, more pork, more wheat, more corn, more fruit and more dairy products, and to buy more clothing made from cotton, wool and leather. In a physical and a property sense, as well as in a spiritual sense, we are members one of another.

I want to make it clear that no simple panacea can be applied to the drought problem in the whole of the drought area. Plans must depend on local conditions, for these vary with annual rainfall, soil characteristics, altitude and topography. Water and soil conservation methods may differ in one county from those in an adjoining county. Work to be done in the cattle and sheep country differs in type from work in the wheat country or work in the corn belt.

The Great Plains Drought Area Committee has given me its preliminary recommendations for a long-time program for that region. Using that report as a basis we are cooperating successfully and in entire accord with the Governors and State planning boards. As we get this program into operation the people more and more will be able to maintain themselves securely on the land. That will mean a steady decline in the relief burdens which the Federal Government and States have had to assume in time of drought; but, more important, it will mean a greater contribution to general national prosperity by these regions which have been hit by drought. It will conserve and improve not only property values, but human values. The people in the drought area do not want to be dependent on Federal, State or any other kind of charity. They want for themselves and their families an opportunity to share fairly by their own efforts in the progress of America.

The farmers of America want a sound national agricultural policy in which a permanent land-use program will have an important place. They want assurance against another year like 1932 when they made good crops but had to sell them for prices that meant ruin just as surely as did the drought. Sound policy must maintain farm prices in good crop years as well as in bad crop years. It must function when we have drought; it must also function when we have bumper crops.

The maintenance of a fair equilibrium between farm prices and the prices of industrial products is an aim which we must keep ever before us, just as we must give constant thought to the sufficiency of the food supply of the Nation even in bad years. Our modern civilization can and should devise a more successful means by which the excess supplies of bumper years can be conserved for use in lean years.

On my trip I have been deeply impressed with the general efficiency of those agencies of the Federal, State and local Governments which have moved in on the immediate task created by the drought. In 1934 none of us had preparation; we worked without blueprints and made the mistakes of inexperience. Hindsight shows us this. But as time has gone on we have been making fewer and fewer mistakes. Remember that the Federal and State Governments have done only broad planning. Actual work on a given project originates in the local community. Local needs are listed from local information. Local projects are decided on only after obtaining the recommendations and help of those in the local community who are best able to give it. And it is worthy of note that on my entire trip, though I asked the question dozens of times, I heard no complaint against the character of a single work relief project.

The elected heads of the States concerned, together with their State officials and their experts from agricultural colleges and State planning boards, have shown cooperation with and approval of the work which the Federal Government has headed. I am grateful also to the men and women in all these States who have accepted leadership in the work in their locality.

In the drought area people are not afraid to use new methods to meet changes in Nature, and to correct mistakes of the past. If over-grazing has injured range lands they are willing to reduce the grazing. If certain wheat lands should be returned to pasture they are willing to cooperate. If trees should be planted as wind-breaks or to stop erosion they will work with us. If terracing or summer fallowing or crop rotation is called for they will carry it out. They stand ready to fit, and not to fight, the ways of Nature.

We are helping, and shall continue to help the farmer, to do those things, through local soil conservation committees and other cooperative local, State and Federal agencies of Government.

I have not the time tonight to deal with other and more comprehensive agricultural policies.

With this fine help we are tiding over the present emergency. We are going to conserve soil, conserve water and conserve life. We are going to have long-time defenses against both low prices and drought. We are going to have a farm policy that will serve the national welfare. That is our hope for the future.

There are two reasons why I want to end by talking about reemployment. Tomorrow is Labor Day. The brave spirit with which so many millions of working people are winning their way out of depression deserves respect and admiration. It is like the courage of the farmers in the drought areas.

That is my first reason. The second is that healthy employment conditions stand equally with healthy agricultural conditions as a buttress of national prosperity. Dependable employment at fair wages is just as important to the people in the towns and cities as good farm income is to agriculture. Our people must have the ability to buy the goods they manufacture and the crops they produce. Thus city wages and farm buying power are the two strong legs that carry the Nation forward.

Reemployment in industry is proceeding rapidly. Government spending was in large part responsible for keeping industry going and putting it in a position to make this reemployment possible. Government orders were the backlog of heavy industry; Government wages turned over and over again to make consumer purchasing power and to sustain every merchant in the community. Businessmen with their businesses, small and large, had to be saved. Private enterprise is necessary to any Nation which seeks to maintain the democratic form of government. In their case, just as certainly as in the case of drought-stricken farmers, Government spending has saved.

Government having spent wisely to save it, private industry begins to take workers off the rolls of the Government relief program. Until this Administration we had no free employment service, except in a few States and cities. Because there was no unified employment service, the worker, forced to move as industry moved, often traveled over the country, wandering after jobs which seemed always to travel just a little faster than he did. He was often victimized by fraudulent practices of employment clearing houses, and the facts of employment opportunities were at the disposal neither of himself nor of the employer.

In 1933 the United States Employment Service was created — a cooperative State and Federal enterprise, through which the Federal Government matches dollar for dollar the funds provided by the States for registering the occupations and skills of workers and for actually finding jobs for these registered workers in private industry. The Federal-State cooperation has been splendid. Already employment services are operating in thirty-two States, and the areas not covered by them are served by the Federal Government.

We have developed a nationwide service with seven hundred district offices, and one thousand branch offices, thus providing facilities through which labor can learn of jobs available and employers can find workers.

Last spring I expressed the hope that employers would realize their deep responsibility to take men off the relief rolls and give them jobs in private enterprise. Subsequently I was told by many employers that they were not satisfied with the information available concerning the skill and experience of the workers on the relief rolls. On August 25th I allocated a relatively small sum to the employment service for the purpose of getting better and more recent information in regard to those now actively at work on W.P.A. projects — information as to their skills and previous occupations — and to keep the records of such men and women up-to-date for maximum service in making them available to industry. Tonight I am announcing the allocation of two and a half million dollars more to enable the Employment Service to make an even more intensive search than it has yet been equipped to make, to find opportunities in private employment for workers registered with it.

Tonight I urge the workers to cooperate with and take full advantage of this intensification of the work of the Employment Service. This does not mean that there will be any lessening of our efforts under our W.P.A. and P.W.A. and other work relief programs until all workers have decent jobs in private employment at decent wages. We do not surrender our responsibility to the unemployed. We have had ample proof that it is the will of the American people that those who represent them in national, State and local Government should continue as long as necessary to discharge that responsibility. But it does mean that the Government wants to use resources to get private work for those now employed on Government work, and thus to curtail to a minimum the Government expenditures for direct employment.

Tonight I ask employers, large and small, throughout the Nation, to use the help of the State and Federal Employment Service whenever in the general pick-up of business they require more workers.

Tomorrow is Labor Day. Labor Day in this country has never been a class holiday. It has always been a national holiday. It has never had more significance as a national holiday than it has now. In other countries the relationship of employer and employee has been more or less accepted as a class relationship not readily to be broken through. In this country we insist, as an essential of the American way of life, that the employer-employee relationship should be one between free men and equals. We refuse to regard those who work with hand or brain as different from or inferior to those who live from their property. We insist that labor is entitled to as much respect as property. But our workers with hand and brain deserve more than respect for their labor. They deserve practical protection in the opportunity to use their labor at a return adequate to support them at a decent and constantly rising standard of living, and to accumulate a margin of security against the inevitable vicissitudes of life.

The average man must have that twofold opportunity if we are to avoid the growth of a class-conscious society in this country.

There are those who fail to read both the signs of the times and American history. They would try to refuse the worker any effective power to bargain collectively, to earn a decent livelihood and to acquire security. It is those shortsighted ones, not labor, who threaten this country with that class dissension which in other countries has led to dictatorship and the establishment of fear and hatred as the dominant emotions in human life.

All American workers, brain workers and manual workers alike, and all the rest of us whose well-being depends on theirs, know that our needs are one in building an orderly economic democracy in which all can profit and in which all can be secure from the kind of faulty economic direction which brought us to the brink of common ruin seven years ago.

There is no cleavage between white-collar workers and manual workers, between artists and artisans, musicians and mechanics, lawyers and accountants and architects and miners.

Tomorrow, Labor Day, belongs to all of us. Tomorrow, Labor Day, symbolizes the hope of all Americans. Anyone who calls it a class holiday challenges the whole concept of American democracy.

The Fourth of July commemorates our political freedom — a freedom which without economic freedom is meaningless indeed. Labor Day symbolizes our determination to achieve an economic freedom for the average man which will give his political freedom reality.

121 ❨Informal Extemporaneous Remarks at Asheville, N. C. September 10, 1936

YESTERDAY and today I am carrying out a promise to myself made nearly thirty years ago, because it was nearly thirty years ago that I was last in Asheville. In those days I said to myself that I wanted to come back. I wanted to see all this marvelous country and go up into these Great Smoky Mountains. I suppose in those days I could not have gotten there in an automobile or even in a horse and buggy.

So I came on this pleasure trip, and it has been a pleasure every single minute. I have been tremendously impressed with what we are doing in opening up the Smokies through this great national park. I am not the only one impressed, because the number of visitors up there in the park has so far outstripped road building and facilities that it is a problem as to how to handle the people.

As some of you perhaps know, there is nothing in Nature I am as fond of as a tree. Here in North Carolina and across the line in Tennessee we have without question the most wonderful tree growth in all the United States — trees that perhaps are not quite so big as some of the trees of the Pacific Coast, but I am told by all the experts and scientists — you might call them brain trusters — that there are more varieties of trees and shrubbery and flowers down here than anywhere else.

I hope to come back in the years to come, either as a Government servant or as a private citizen — it makes very little difference which. I want to come back and spend some time seeing the new roads that are going to be opened, seeing more of this wonderful part of the United States. And I am quite sure that millions of other Americans are going to come down here, as I want to come, and spend more time. So you might just as well get ready now to receive them.

122 ❲ "Your Life and Mine, Though We Work in the Mill, the Office or the Store, Can Still Be a Life in Green Pastures and beside Still Waters" —Address at the Green Pastures Rally, Charlotte, N. C. September 10, 1936

(Just before this speech was begun a thunderstorm subsided, the sun came out and there was a rainbow in the sky. This was the reason for the first sentence of this speech.)

Governor Ehringhaus, Mr. Mayor, my friends of Charlotte:

I NOTICE that the rainbow shines in the sky; and it is a fitting climax to two of the most delightful days that I have ever spent in my life.

I am grateful, Governor Ehringhaus, for your hospitality; and may I, through you, thank the people of the Old North State for the welcome that they have given me?

I am told that this meeting is a Green Pastures Meeting. And the showers that we have passed through today prove that the pastures of North Carolina are green.

Green pastures! What a memory those words call forth! In all our schooling, in every part of the land, no matter to what church we happen to belong, the old Twenty-third Psalm is in all probability better known to men, women and children than any other poem in the English language.

And in this great lyric, what do we best remember? Two lines:

"He maketh me to lie down in green pastures;
He leadeth me beside the still waters."

It does not greatly matter whether that symbol of an ideal of human physical and spiritual happiness was written in its original three thousand or five thousand or ten thousand years ago. It might have been written as well in the twentieth century of the Christian era.

Have you ever stopped to think that happiness is most often

341

described in terms of the simple ways of Nature rather than in the complex ways of man's fabrications? Perhaps it is because peace is necessary to ultimate happiness. Perhaps, therefore, when we seek a symbol of happiness, we do not go to the rush of crowded city streets or to the hum of machinery to find the simile.

The ancient psalmist did not use the parable of the merchants' camel train or the royal palace or the crowded bazaar of the East. He had, in his day, as we have today, the problems of competing trade and social crowding; and I venture to suggest that long before the Christian era, the ancient civilizations of the East were confronted with problems of social economics which, though small in point of human numbers and small in point of worldly goods, were still, by comparison, as potent in their effect and as difficult in their solution as the extraordinarily similar problems of social economics that face us in this country today.

Be it remembered then, that those kings and prophets reverted, just as we do today, to the good earth and the still waters when they idealized security of the body and mind.

A recent writer has suggested that the present President of the United States, perhaps because of where he was born and where he was trained and perhaps because of his natural proclivity, inevitably reverts to terms of land and water in his approach to any great public problem. I fear that I must plead guilty to this charge, though I do so with the reservation that this is in spite of the fact that during the greater part of my life I have been in far closer contact with the more exciting and more highly competitive give and take of the profession of the law, the practice of business and the exactions of public service.

Green pastures! Millions of our fellow Americans, with whom I have been associating in the past two weeks, out on the Great Plains of America, live with prayers and hopes for the fulfillment of what those words imply. Still waters! Millions of other Americans, with whom I also have been associated of late, live with prayers and hopes either that the floods may be stilled—floods that bring with them destruction and disaster to fields and flocks, to homesteads and cities—or else they look for the Heaven-sent rains that will fill their wells, their ponds and their peaceful streams.

Many years ago, I talked with a learned man about this continent—about what North America was like when the white man came. I asked him if the Great Plains, which extend hundreds and hundreds of miles from the Mississippi to the Rockies, were always bare of trees, always the pasturage of buffalo and antelope.

"Yes," he replied. "For many hundreds of years before the white man came, but it is my belief that trees could have grown and still could grow on those plains, but that they have been prevented from growing by the constant succession of prairie fires, set either by the lightning or the red men."

I asked him whether the streams of the Southland were always brown and full of silt before our white ancestors moved in. "No," he said, "in those earlier days, during the greater part of the year, the Southern rivers were clear streams, except perhaps for a week or so in the springtime, when they had moderate freshets, small floods. When they occurred, some soil but very little soil was washed from the uplands, from the mountains of the South into the Atlantic Ocean and the Gulf; but because these were seasonal only in their effect and small in volume, the natural accretion of new topsoil took the place of that which had run off to the sea."

If history gives a name to the day and age in which we are living, I hope it will call this the era of rebuilding, for it is my firm conviction that unless we, in our generation, start to rebuild, the Americans of a century hence will have lost the greater part of their natural and national heritage.

My friends, it is because I have spent so much of these latter years in this Southland, and because I have come to know its fine people, its brave history, its many problems, that I speak not as a stranger to you who are gathered here from seven States.

I have seen the denuding of your forests; I have seen the washing away of your topsoil; I have slid into the ditch from your red clay highways. I have taken part in your splendid efforts to save your forests, to terrace your lands, to harness your streams and to push hard-surfaced roads into every county in every State. I have

343

even assumed the amazing role of a columnist for a Georgia newspaper in order that I might write powerful pieces against burning over the farm woodlot and in favor of the cow, hog and hen program.

May I add that it is because of practical experience on my own farm, that many years before I was inaugurated President I came to the conclusion that cotton, as it stood then, was essentially a speculative crop and that the planter of cotton, because he had nothing to say about the price he would receive, could never tell when he put the seed in the ground whether he would make a big profit by selling his crop for twenty-five cents a pound or go broke by selling his crop for five cents a pound.

It is perhaps a bit of history hitherto unrecorded that in the month of March, 1933, I said this to the Secretary of Agriculture, Mr. Wallace. I said, "In respect to cotton"—and I talked to him about lots of crops—"I have a definite objective. The cotton farmer has been cursed for a generation by the fact of insecurity. The price for his crop has run up the scale and down the scale and up the scale and down the scale again. In recent years"— mind you, I was speaking in 1933—"in recent years his total aggregate production has been so great that thirteen million bales overhang the market. He will starve on five-cent cotton—the South will starve on five-cent cotton—and just as long as this appalling carryover hangs over the market, he will never get a price that will even bring him out whole. My objective, Mr. Secretary, is to control and reduce that unwieldy surplus; to get for the cotton planter ten-cent cotton the first year we are in office, and twelve-cent cotton or more for the next three years. You and I must keep that goal ever before us."

And, my friends, I ask you in simple fairness, have we attained that goal?

You know the story of cotton. You know the story of tobacco, too. There again your national Government had a goal. I do not believe that the great tobacco-growing States of the Nation would wish to go back to the days of "every man for himself and let the devil take the hindmost."

344

Again, long before I went to Washington, I was convinced that the long road that leads to green pastures and still waters had to begin with reasonable prosperity. It seemed axiomatic to me that a cotton farmer who could get only five cents a pound for his crop could not be in a position properly to fertilize his land, or to terrace it, or to rotate his crops, or to keep a cow or a few head of cattle, or to plant a little orchard, or to cultivate a garden — in other words, to work out for himself and his family a well-rounded, reasonably secure life that would tide him and them over a lean year of drought.

The same thing held true, I thought, in the case of the farmer whose principal crop was tobacco or whose principal crop was peaches or whose principal crop was corn or wheat or cattle or hogs.

In other words, we could not go ahead to the next step of prevention of soil erosion throughout the South and indeed throughout the Nation, to the transfer of thin pastures into forests and the transfer of submarginal plowed land into pastures and trees; we could not go ahead to the use of many modern methods to stop soil erosion and to prevent floods until and unless the farmers of the Southland were able to make a reasonably decent living out of their farms.

And what is the answer? Today, because of better prices for farm commodities, we are actually and actively engaged in taking these second steps. Not only have we aroused a public understanding and approval of the need of ending soil erosion and water run-off, but we have enabled the public, through a practical prosperity, to begin to pay their debts, to paint their homes, to buy farm tools and automobiles, to send more boys and girls through school and college, to put some money in the bank and, incidentally, to know for the first time that the money in the bank is safe.

So much for the green pastures and the still waters in their more literal physical terms. Those ancient words apply, however, with equal force to men and women and children. Your life and

345

mine, though we work in the mill or in the office or in the store, can still be a life in green pastures and beside still waters.

No man, no woman, no family can hope in any part of the country to attain security in a city on starvation wages any more than they can hope on a farm to attain security on starvation crop prices. I do not have to tell you, who live in any of these Southern States, all of which have factories in them, that a family that tries to subsist on a total wage income of three or four hundred dollars a year is just as much a drag on the prosperity of America as the farm family that seeks to subsist on a yearly cash income of a hundred or two hundred dollars a year.

That is why a good many thinking people in finance and in business and in every other walk of life believe that the National Recovery Act, during its short term of life, accomplished as much for the restoration of prosperity, through the establishment of the minimum wage, the shortening of hours and the elimination of child labor, as any law put on the statute books of the Federal Government in the past century and a half.

In the summer of 1934, the head of one of the great mail-order houses said to me, "Do you remember my telling you a year ago that the purchasing power of the South had dropped to almost zero? Look at this report of our sales in all the Southern States. All of our sales have increased, but those in the South have come back faster than any, and the reason is that the South at last has begun to acquire purchasing power."

Finally, in this fourth year of definite upturn, you and I have come to appreciate another significant and inevitable result. You and I live under three kinds of government—and to all three we, as citizens, pay taxes. Our local real estate taxes, mainly on real estate, go to the support of local and state functions of government such as schools and highways, city and county administrations, water supply, sewer systems, street lighting, peace officers and State institutions. Our Federal taxes, none of which by the way is on real estate, come in the form of tobacco and similar excises, and income, inheritance, and corporation taxes and are spent in the running of the Federal Government for national defense, for pensions, for forests, for parks, for highways, for public works of all kinds and for relief of the unemployed.

Four years ago all of us, in every part of the United States, found that without any change in the local or State tax schedules, the tax receipts had fallen off to an alarming degree. The result was that counties and municipalities and States were failing to balance their budgets, or else were unable to carry out the ordinary and orderly functions and obligations of State and local government. Schools were being closed or curtailed; teachers were unpaid; roads lacked repairs; the borrowing of money for permanent improvements had become impossible. With the Federal Government, despite additional new forms of taxes in those days, receipts of revenue in 1932 had been cut in half.

The value of those tangible private assets on which taxes were based had fallen so low that even if the income had been there to pay taxes with, the sums received would have put all forms of government increasingly in the red. And even when some remnant of value remained on which to levy a tax, the taxpayer did not have the wherewithal to make the payment and was beginning to lose the very property which was taxed.

That is why I go back to the original thesis that any commonsense, logical governmental policy had to begin with the building up of farm and other property values, and crop values, and the increase of workers' wages if that now historic corner was ever to be turned.

History records that only a few years ago farmers were not making both ends meet; workers in factories were not making both ends meet; the small business man was not making both ends meet; and the corporation was not making both ends meet. As a logical result, local governments were not making both ends meet, and neither were State Governments, and neither was the National Government.

Incidentally, as another result in those days, the individual who had to borrow, the corporation which had to borrow and the Government which had to borrow—all of them were compelled to pay unconscionable and ruinous interest rates.

347

History will also record that by the year 1936 a very much larger number of individuals are back in the black; so are most of our small business men; so are most of our corporations and so are almost all of our municipal and county and State Governments.

History will also record that individuals and corporations and Governments are paying today a far more reasonable rate of interest than at any previous time in the history of the American Republic.

In the process of attaining these successful ends, my friends, individual liberties have not been removed, and I believe that the Governor of North Carolina and almost every other Governor in every one of the forty-eight States will agree that the inherent rights of the sovereign States have not been invaded. It was obvious, of course, because of the economic unity of the entire Nation in these modern days that no group of individuals and no individual States acting all alone could, by themselves, take the action necessary to restore the purchasing power of the United States as a whole. Only the Federal Government could ask and receive the cooperation of all the States in heading a nationwide plan.

I speak to you today as common-sense American men and women. You will agree that from the material aspect, based on the sound concept of restoring purchasing power and prosperity to the great mass of our citizens, this Nation's consuming power has been and is being rapidly restored. I trust, therefore, that you will likewise agree that better conditions on the farms, better conditions in the factories, better conditions in the homes of America are leading us to that beautiful spiritual figure of the old psalmist — green pastures and still waters.

NOTE: On this short trip from September 8th to September 10th I also made brief informal talks at Salisbury, N. C., September 10th, and Greensboro, N. C., September 10th.

123 ❲ "Are You and I Paying Enough Attention to 'Human Engineering'?"—Address to the Third World Power Conference, Washington, D. C. September 11, 1936

Ladies and gentlemen of the World Power Conference:

I DESIRE to add my personal greeting to the official greeting which it has been the pleasure of the Government of the United States of America to extend to you. The United States considers it an honor and a privilege to be the host of the Third World Power Conference and of the Second Congress of the International Commission on Large Dams.

The World Power Conference and its associated International Commission are very notable institutions.

It is one of the achievements of our generation that business men, engineers, lawyers, social workers and other people of affairs should meet in international assemblies not merely for promotion of the abstract sciences and techniques in which they may respectively be engaged, but for exploration of the application of these to national welfare and betterment of the conditions of human life.

There are very special reasons why we in the United States prize the opportunity to provide the forum for discussion of the problems which are being presented to your Conference.

We are relatively a young Nation, facing now the problems of matured national life. Many among you represent Nations of far longer experience.

We have a strong conviction that any success we may have in organizing the household of this Nation, now come of age, will depend in large measure on the degree to which and the manner in which we make available the natural energies which have been given us in great abundance. We shall therefore study the records of your proceedings with painstaking care.

For a century, for longer than that, population in the United

States has increased, both naturally and by immigration, at an exceptional rate; but recently there has set in a decline in the rate of increase. Experts in vital statistics now calculate that we shall have reached a point of stationary population within approximately the next twenty-five years.

For two centuries the dramatic aspect of national growth was territorial expansion—successive waves of human beings from the Atlantic to the Allegheny Mountains, to the Mississippi Valley, to the prairies, to the Rocky Mountains and at last to the Pacific Coast. The addition of improved lands has come to a stop; in fact, in many parts we have overdone it and must restore some of them to more natural conditions.

With these have appeared other evidences of maturity. For a period following the establishment of the Union about 85 percent of our people lived on farms; today, however, nearly 75 percent live in cities and villages. During our earlier years the proportion of young people in the population increased much more rapidly than the proportion of old people. Today, for various reasons, the proportion of old is increasing more rapidly than the proportion of young people.

With such changes have come also changes in social habits and in points of view.

Under conditions of maturity of a Nation there is, justifiably, an increasing concern on the part of nearly every citizen for his economic security. In the earlier days of our Nation's youth there was no such dominating concern. As a people we could then be happy-go-lucky—a characteristic of youth.

National maturity requires that we have new points of view, and that we do some things at least in different ways.

This matter of economic security, I take it, is not to be achieved by aiming for restriction of national income—real national income—but by aiming for more abundant and more widely distributed national income. A satisfying standard of living and security for a national household of nearly one hundred thirty million people are to be realized only by high productivity, broadly and equitably distributed, and wisely proportioned with respect to its drain on national natural resources and to the variety of human wants that it is destined to satisfy.

It is for such reasons that your deliberations are of significance to me, and will be followed with minute attention. Your scientific and engineering genius is destroying one world—the world of relative scarcity—but has it yet undertaken to create the new world of abundance which is potential in your command over natural energies? Is creation of greater abundance dependent on further scientific and engineering achievements so much as on suitably organizing and utilizing the engineering already incorporated into your technique?

These two questions, more simply stated, resolve themselves into this: Are you and I paying enough attention to "human engineering"?

Granted, there are many aspects of the problem. For example, it is possible to conceive—for us to conceive at least—that the conversion and application of energy, in the coming generation, will be so directed that half of the population can provide the basic machine-made products necessary for the welfare of the whole of the population. We can conceive that this would mean that the people between twenty and fifty years of age may be able to produce the basic commodities for themselves and also for all others below and above those ages.

If that condition should arise, it is the duty of you who would be so greatly responsible for it to think what would be the effect on our leisure, our culture and our way of life. May I respectfully suggest that the answer should not be left wholly in the hands of bankers, Government officials or demagogues?

In anticipation of all manner of possibilities and simultaneously with the study of their far-reaching results, we can and must take every preparatory step now within our power.

Fundamental among these is conservation of resources, their evaluation in terms of the services they may render, including the conditions under which these may be rendered, and their utilization in the light of such evaluation. Although it is a principle of physics that energy cannot be destroyed, it has been revealed by experience that man can destroy those particular forms of energy in which energy is usable by him. In such an evaluation the physical and mental energies of human beings must be included with coal, petroleum, gas, electricity and many other forms.

To make such an evaluation, a higher form of accounting than any yet developed by commerce and industry appears to be essential. It must be a form of accounting that takes social values, now left to mere assumption, into its calculations and measures them. If a Nation were to establish in its social balance sheet a capital account for its energy assets, and were to charge against that account the water that it permits to go unused, as well as the coal and the oil that are used; or if the petroleum industry were charged with the gas that it permits to go to waste — a quantity, by the way, that is enormous in these United States; then perhaps all citizens would perceive that public policy and private conduct in respect of our natural resources should be quite different from what they now are.

It seems to me, as a layman, that the outstanding gift of modern science and engineering to society is greater knowledge of the characteristics of electric energy, together with a very substantial degree of command over it. Its flexibility is what makes electrical energy impressive; its transportability; its divisibility. The invention and adaptation to use of the steam engine was a great event in human history. It caused an industrial revolution. In a very large sense it remade the world. It created new social-industrial problems, many of which are still far from solution. It is not irrational to believe that in our command over electric energy a corresponding industrial and social revolution is potential, that it may already be under way without our perceiving it.

One of the social changes brought on by the invention and use of the steam engine was the concentration of workers into large factories and of people into large cities. We have not known what to do about it. Workers had to go to the steam engine, whose energy could not be divided into parts and sent out to them.

Now we have electric energy which can be and often is produced in places away from where fabrication of usable goods is carried on. But by habit we continue to carry this flexible energy in great blocks into the same great factories, and continue to carry on our production there. Sheer inertia has caused us to neglect formulating a public policy that would promote opportunity for people to take advantage of the flexibility of electric energy; a policy that would send it out wherever and whenever wanted at the lowest possible cost. We are continuing the forms of over-centralization of industry caused by the characteristics of the steam engine, long after we have had technically available a form of energy which should promote decentralization of industry. What is economically sound is to be determined by social accounting more than by our present methods.

I had occasion recently to visit the Great Plains area of the United States where the greatest drought in history has thrown an oppressive burden upon the people of those States. In planning for the better use of those millions of acres, power is a factor of vital importance—power to be used primarily for the conserving of the water supply—power, the application of which is essential not only to the cities, but to the farms and ranches of that whole area.

I speak of power in its many forms. It may be true, as I understand some of the authorities among you prophesy, that the world's oil reserves, because of their limited supply, some day may have to be apportioned to specific uses. It may be true that new applications of alcohol, processed from the products of the soil, may increase the usefulness of the internal combustion engine; but in any event it seems most probable that a greater use of electrical energy is absolutely essential in every sector, rural as well as urban, in the United States, and, indeed, in the whole world.

A sound and courageous public policy will lead toward its consummation.

One who considers the matter with forthright vision cannot convince himself that public policy for promotion of availability of electric energy can really harm the electric industry that exists today. It would give opportunity for that industry to add to achievements already great. The more integrated its sources of energy, the less it would require of excess capacity and the lower would be its costs. The broader the base of consumers of a product that is now classed as a necessity, the lower would be its costs and the greater its stability. A great many years ago Dr. Steinmetz observed that electricity is expensive because it is not widely used, and at the same time it is not widely used because it is expensive. Notwithstanding reductions in rates and increase of consumption since his day—which, by the way, have demonstrated the truth of his words—his observation still holds true. There is a vicious circle which must be broken, and a wise public policy will help to break it.

I still hold to the belief of two years ago, when I spoke as follows:

> "We are going to see, I believe, with our own eyes electricity and power made so cheap that they will become a standard article of use, not only for agriculture and manufacturing, but also for every home within reach of an electric-light line.
>
> "The experience of those sections of the world that have cheap power proves very conclusively that the cheaper the power the more of it is used."

These words were spoken at Grand Coulee. The Government of the United States has promoted the construction of several great reservoirs, which I trust that you will inspect on your grand tour, primarily for navigation or reclamation, but with incidental values for flood control and the regulation of stream flow. Among other incidentals is the generation of electric power. This may prove to be the force that breaks the vicious circle to which I have referred. If these are not sufficient, the influence of additional meritorious projects awaiting development can be added.

Two great dams of the Tennessee Valley Authority have been completed and are making their contribution to the public weal. Grand Coulee is far enough along to enlist your interest, as also is Bonneville of the Columbia River. At Boulder Dam on the mighty Colorado the gates were closed months ago; a great lake has come into being behind the dam; generating equipment has been installed in the power plant; and at this moment the powerful turbines are awaiting the relatively tiny impulse of electric current which will flow from the touch of my hand on the button which you see beside me on the desk, to stir them to life, to stir them into creative activity — to generate power.

Boulder Dam, in the name of the people of the United States, to whom you, Boulder Dam, are a symbol of greater things in the future, and in the honored presence of guests from many Nations, I call you to life!

NOTE: The Third World Power Conference met in Washington, September 7-12, 1936, at the invitation of the United States. Previous conferences had confined themselves in the main to the technical side of power development. The Third World Power Conference, however, devoted its discussions to the problems of power development primarily in relation to social and economic needs.

The subject of the Conference was "The National Power Economy" considered in its broadest sense as including energy sources, development and utilization. The discussion concerned: its physical and statistical basis; its technical, economic, and social trends; the relation thereto of the fuel-producing, processing and distribution industries, and of electric and gas utilities; practices and policies respecting organization, control and public regulation; national and regional planning of power development and use; conservation of fuel and water resources; rationalization of the distribution of gas and electricity; and a national power and resources policy.

Fifty-two countries participated in the Conference. Approximately 700 persons from abroad attended, as well as some 2,000 Americans. The Conference was organized by the Government in cooperation with the utility and manufacturing industries and the engineering societies of the country.

Concurrently with and as a part of this conference, the Second Congress on Large Dams was held. Its program dealt with a limited number of technical questions. The following specific problems were considered: special cement; design and waterproofing of shrinkage, contraction and expansion joints; study of the facing of masonry and concrete dams; geotechnical studies of foundation materials; calculation of the stability of earth dams.

The Conference brought together leading figures of the world to discuss the implications of the power era; afforded an opportunity for an exchange of views; and made available the latest compilation of authoritative data from the major countries of the world on this subject.

The Conference and the Congress adopted no resolutions, conventions or treaties. The transactions of the Conference will comprise probably ten volumes and those of the Congress five volumes. These transactions will contain not only the papers presented at the Conference by representatives of the different countries, but also summary statements of the discussions at the sessions and at the round-table conferences arranged in connection with seven study tours participated in by various of the delegates before and after the main meetings in Washington.

124 ❡ A Letter of Solicitude to a Policeman Injured while Safeguarding the President. September 14, 1936

My dear Mr. Mangum:

I have learned with very great regret that you were injured Sunday evening while safeguarding my return to the White House.

I cannot resist the impulse to assure you of my sincere appreciation of your effort in my behalf. I do hope that your injuries are not serious and that you will have a speedy recovery.

Very sincerely yours,

Mr. Percy G. Mangum,
Washington, D. C.

125 ⟨A Letter of Appreciation to the American Labor Party for Its Support. September 16, 1936

My dear friends:

I HAVE learned with a sense of deep appreciation through your letter of August 29th that the American Labor Party, New York State, will throw its full support to me this year. It gives me much pleasure to become your candidate.

The assurance that your organization recognizes me as the leader of progressive forces in favor of humanity in government quickens the sense of responsibility on my part. The issues are clear-cut and sharply defined this year. Opposed to us are all of the forces of reaction and special privilege.

But the fight for democracy in our industrial economy and for the maintenance of our American democratic institutions against the attacks of predatory interests must go on without abatement. The loyal support which you pledge on behalf of the American Labor Party gives me new strength and new courage to continue the struggle and renewed faith that we shall not know defeat.

Very sincerely yours,

American Labor Party,
New York, N. Y.

126 ⟨A Greeting on the Seventy-fourth Anniversary of the Proclamation of Emancipation. September 16, 1936

My dear Bishop Wright:

I APPRECIATE the opportunity of extending greetings to all those who are planning to participate in the celebration of the Seventy-fourth Anniversary of the issuance of the Preliminary Proclamation of Emancipation by President Lincoln.

It is an occasion for recalling the great progress which Negroes

357

have made as citizens of our Republic. It also is an occasion for remembering that in the truest sense freedom cannot be bestowed, it must be achieved; and that there must be constant vigilance if it is to be maintained. The record which our Negro citizens have made in their own personal and racial development and their contribution to the material advancement of our country and to the promotion of its ideals are well known.

I heartily congratulate them on their record, and hope that in the future, as in the past, they will continue to show intelligence, industry and fortitude in striving for the best our Democracy offers.

Very sincerely yours,

Right Reverend R. R. Wright, Jr.,
Bishop, African Methodist Episcopal Church,
New York, N. Y.

127 ⟨ Address to the Conference on the Mobilization for Human Needs, the White House, Washington, D. C. September 16, 1936

Chairman Swope, ladies and gentlemen:

I AM glad once more — what is it, the third time, Mr. Swope, or the fourth time? — to greet the representatives of this great annual Mobilization for Human Needs.

We are all heartened by clear evidences of returning prosperity. You are here in spite of that fact and because of that fact. Returning prosperity means that you have a right to expect greater assistance for the splendid work that you are doing in every community. Returning prosperity means, however, that a vast amount of important work in every field, work which we all had to defer during the depression years, can and must be taken up anew.

As I told you in former years, when human distress reaches the point that Government assistance is absolutely necessary, Gov-

ernment up to the limit of its local, its State and its Federal resources must and does act. Happily, private organizations are now
in a better position to accomplish greater things than for many
years past. This increase in prosperity heightens the obligation of
every individual to aid in the relief of distress in his or her own
community.

Through you I appeal to every man, woman and child in the
United States for a revival throughout the length and breadth of
the land of the spirit of charity. But that word "revival" is not the
right word, because in the difficult years which have passed that
spirit of charity showed itself unselfishly and generously. Increase
of the spirit of charity would be a better way of putting it, for I
am very proud of the support of the country's welfare services of
all kinds during the past seven years.

I resent and you resent, I am very certain, those supercilious
and uncharitable sneers which from a small element among us
have been directed against those in need and against those who
have been honestly seeking to help those in need.

The cooperation that the Federal Government has given in social welfare activities seems to me to extend rather than contract
the responsibility of the private activities for local relief.

Since the low point of the depression, great and substantial
progress has been made. The national income, for example, will
soon be double what it was at the low point. Nearly six million
more men and women are now at work in private industry. Three
million others are engaged in useful work provided or assisted by
various forms of government. Factory payrolls for the first quarter of the year were more than $70,000,000 greater per week,
greater than they were in the first quarter of 1933. Systematic
and successful efforts to raise the buying power of wage earners
and farmers have increased the business of merchants and brought
orders to manufacturers. Confidence has returned to the great
mass of our people — confidence on the part of all except a small
minority who seek to profit from the preaching of fear.

Personal and family insecurity — that difficult problem of past
years — the Federal Government and the State Governments have

undertaken to dissipate at least in part by the enactment of the Social Security Act providing for cooperative Federal and State public welfare, public assistance, unemployment compensation and old-age benefits.

To the extent that local and State and Federal Governments help in these fields, to that extent private welfare activities are freed from these appropriate public responsibilities and, therefore, are enabled more effectively and extensively to do those things which private activities are best fitted to carry on.

Efforts of private agencies to encourage private reemployment of those on the relief rolls, efforts of private agencies to continue and extend medical care of all kinds, efforts of private agencies to minister to the hundreds of thousands of cases which present special problems, efforts of private agencies to build up recreational opportunities — all of these and a dozen more are tasks that are more fitted to private than to Government administration.

The generosity of our American people has been and is a fine tradition; we have never failed to heed the call of distress. I have confidence that the appeal about to be launched for this Fifth Mobilization for Human Needs will strike a responsive chord throughout the country. I know that the men and women of the Nation will accept their local responsibilities even more readily than they have ever done before. And so I say to you: May you have all the success that you deserve.

NOTE: For speeches on the same subject in other years, see Item 123, Vol. II; Item 162, Vol. III; Item 150, Vol. IV.

128 ⟨ From a Letter to Senator James Couzens, Urging Him to Head the Maritime Commission. September 17, 1936

Dear Jim:

WHAT I want to convey to you in very simple terms is that you and your ideals and ability must not, because of a political system, be lost to the country. As you are aware, one of the most difficult problems before us is that of American shipping. Ever since the mail subsidies of the eighteen forties, when the merchant marine legislation was first passed, shipping has gone through ups and downs, but always more or less the victim of party politics or of shipping lobbies.

Today I am confronted with constituting a Maritime Commission under the new bill, which, although not perfect, is very definitely a step in the right direction, giving powers to this independent commission which are far greater than any previously granted. In fact, this new commission can put our sea-borne trade back on its feet in an honest way.

What I need and what the country needs is a fearless chairman of this Maritime Commission, who will take the responsibility in setting up and putting through a new and permanent mercantile marine policy. Experts on engineering, ship design, ship management, etc., can be hired, but a chairman with the capacity and the courage I seek cannot be hired; he must be drafted. That is why I want you on the first of January to undertake the task of heading the Maritime Commission. I would ask you to serve at once, but I cannot do this under the Constitution until your term of office as Senator has expired. . . .

Hon. James Couzens,
Washington, D. C.

129 ⟨ A Greeting to the Annual Convention of the American Philatelic Society. September 17, 1936

My dear Mr. Klein:

As one stamp collector to a fellowship which knows so well the compensations of the hobby, I send hearty felicitations to all who attend the annual convention of the American Philatelic Society. The best thing about stamp collecting as a pursuit is that the enthusiasm which it arouses in youth increases as the years pass. It dispels boredom, enlarges our vision, broadens our knowledge of geography and in innumerable ways enriches life and adds to its joys.

Very sincerely yours,

Mr. Eugene Klein,
American Philatelic Society,
Philadelphia, Pennsylvania.

(This letter was read to the convention of the Society in Omaha, Nebr., September 24, 1936.)

130 ⟨ Address Delivered at the Harvard University Tercentenary Celebration. September 18, 1936

President Conant, distinguished guests, my fellow alumni:

I AM here today in a joint and several capacity: first, as the President of the United States; second, as Chairman of the United States Harvard Tercentenary Commission, which is composed of five members of the Senate, five members of the House of Representatives, a representative of the United States Army and one of the Navy, and two representatives of the Universities of the United States, the distinguished Presidents of the University of California and the University of North Carolina; finally, I am here as a son of Harvard who gladly returns to this spot where men have sought truth for three hundred years.

The roots of Harvard are deep in the past. It is pleasant to remember today that this meeting is being held in pursuance of an adjournment expressly taken one hundred years ago on motion of Josiah Quincy.

At that time many of the alumni of Harvard were sorely troubled concerning the state of the Nation. Andrew Jackson was President. On the two hundred fiftieth anniversary of the founding of Harvard College, alumni again were sorely troubled.

Grover Cleveland was President. Now, on the three hundredth anniversary, I am President.

To go back a little further, in the words of Euripides:

> "There be many shapes of mystery.
> And many things God makes to be,
> Past hope or fear.
> And the end men looked for cometh not,
> And a path is there where no man sought.
> So hath it fallen here."

In spite of fears, Harvard and the Nation of which it is a part have marched steadily to new and successful achievements, changing their formations and their strategy to meet new conditions, but marching always under the old banner of freedom.

In the olden days of New England, it was Increase Mather who told the students of Harvard that they were "pledged to the word of no particular master," that they should "above all find a friend in truth."

That became the creed of Harvard. Behind the tumult and the shouting, it is still the creed of Harvard.

In this day of modern witch-burning, when freedom of thought has been exiled from many lands which were once its home, it is the part of Harvard and America to stand for the freedom of the human mind and to carry the torch of truth.

For centuries, the grand old saying, "The truth is great and will prevail," has been a rock of support for persecuted men.

But it depends on men's tolerance, self-restraint, and devotion to freedom, not only for themselves but also for others, whether the truth will prevail through free research, free discussion and the free intercourse of civilized men, or will prevail only after suppression and suffering — when none cares whether it prevails or not.

Love of liberty and of freedom of thought is a most admirable attribute of Harvard. But it is not an exclusive possession of Harvard or of any other university in America or anywhere else. Love of liberty and freedom of thought is as profound in the homes, on the farms and in the factories of this country as in any university. Liberty is the air Americans breathe. Our Government is based on the belief that a people can be both strong and free, that civilized men need no restraint but that imposed by themselves against abuse of freedom. Nevertheless, it is the peculiar task of Harvard and of every other university and college in this country to foster and maintain not only freedom within its own walls, but also tolerance, self-restraint, fair dealing and devotion to the truth throughout America.

Many students who have come to Harvard in the past have left it with inquiring and open minds, ready to render service to the Nation. They have been given much and from them much has been expected. They have rendered great service.

It is, I am confident, of the inner essence of Harvard that its sons have fully participated in each great drama of our Nation's history. They have met the challenge of the event; they have seen in the challenge opportunity to fulfill the end the University exists to serve.

As the Chief Executive of the Nation I bring to you the solicitation of our people. In the name of the American Nation I venture to ask you to cherish its traditions and to fulfill its highest opportunities.

We need in the days to come as we needed in the past from Harvard men like Charles William Eliot, William James, and Justice Holmes, who made their minds swords in the service of American freedom.

They served America with courage, wisdom and human understanding. They were without hatred, malice or selfishness. They were civilized gentlemen.

The past of Harvard has been deeply distinguished. This University will never fail to produce its due proportion of those judged successful by the common standard of success. Of such the world has need. But to produce that type is not the ultimate justification that you would make for Harvard. Rather do we here search for the atmosphere in which men are produced who have either the rare quality of vision or the ability to appreciate the significance of vision when it appears. Where there is vision, there is tolerance; and where there is tolerance, there is peace. And I beg you to think of tolerance and peace not as indifferent and neutral virtues, but as active and positive principles.

I am not, you will observe, conceiving of the University as a mere spectator of the great national and international drama in which all of us, despite ourselves, are involved. Here are to be trained not lawyers and doctors merely, not teachers and business men and scientists merely; here is to be trained in the fullest sense — man.

Harvard should train men to be citizens in that high Athenian sense which compels a man to live his life unceasingly aware that its civic significance is its most abiding, and that the rich individual diversity of the truly civilized State is born only of the wisdom to choose ways to achieve which do not hurt one's neighbors.

I am asking the sons of Harvard to dedicate themselves not only to the perpetuation, but also to the enlargement of that spirit. To pay ardent reverence to the past, but to recognize no less the direction of the future, to understand philosophies we do not accept and hopes we find it difficult to share, to account the service of mankind the highest ambition a man can follow, and to know that there is no calling so humble that it cannot be instinct with that ambition; never to be indifferent to what may affect our neighbors; always, as Coleridge said, to put truth in the first place and not in the second; these I would affirm are the qualities by which the "real" is distinguished from the "nominal" scholar.

It is only when we have attained this philosophy that we can "above all find a friend in truth." When America is dedicated to that end by the common will of all her citizens, then America can accomplish her highest ideals. To the measure that Harvard participates in that dedication, Harvard will be justified by her effort, her purpose, and her success in the fourth century of her life.

131 ⟨ The President Creates a Crop Insurance Committee for Protection against Farm Surpluses and Farm Scarcity. September 19, 1936

Dear Mr. Secretary:

THE Government's long-time drought and land-use program should be completed and put into operation at the earliest possible moment, and immediate steps are to be taken with this objective.

I am appointing two committees of representatives of Federal agencies to head this work, to confer with farm organization leaders and others on the problems and to develop specific programs.

One committee, on which I want you to serve as chairman, and in your absence Dr. A. G. Black, Chief of the Bureau of Agricultural Economics, is to work out a plan of crop insurance. The other, which is to succeed the temporary Great Plains Drought Area Committee, is to work out plans for a land-use program for better permanent protection against drought.

The Crop Insurance Committee will consist of yourself and Dr. Black; H. R. Tolley, Administrator of the Agricultural Adjustment Administration; Wayne C. Taylor, Assistant Secretary of the Treasury; and Ernest G. Draper, Assistant Secretary of Commerce.

The Crop Insurance Committee is directed to prepare a report and recommendations for legislation providing a plan of "all risk" crop insurance. In preparing its report, the Committee should utilize the extensive crop insurance studies now being made in the Department of Agriculture. Final recommendations for legislation should be formulated with the advice and assistance of national farm organization leaders so that the plans can be submitted to Congress with the approval and support of the representatives of the farmers. I suggest that it may be found wise for the first year to limit the application of the plan to one or two major crops as a start. My general suggestions to your Committee follow.

In the past three and one-half years, the Government has helped farmers to meet emergencies of two kinds. The first was a collapse of prices resulting from huge surpluses for which the foreign markets disappeared. The second was a failure of crops in wide areas resulting from drought. Each of these emergencies, except for Government action to assist farmers, would have had devastating consequences to consumers and business as well as to farmers.

The time has come to work out permanent measures guarding farmers and consumers against disasters of both kinds. Crop insurance and a system of storage reserves should operate so that the surpluses of fat years could be carried over for use in the lean years.

Measures of this kind should make three important contributions to the general welfare of the country as a whole: First, protection of the individual farmer's income against the hazards of crop failure or price collapse; second, protection of consumers against shortages of food supplies and against extremes of prices; and third, assistance to both business and employment through providing an even flow of farm supplies and the establishing of stability in farm-buying power. Since 1933, the A.A.A. payments have proved their usefulness to agriculture as well as business in assuring farmers some income both in time of price collapse and in time of crop failure.

I have been impressed by the work of the Department of Agriculture in developing actuarially sound methods for affording farmers the use of the insurance principle in protecting them against hazards which for centuries have handicapped their occupation. I am especially interested in its studies of a plan providing for the payment of premiums and insurance in commodities. This should make it possible to base the premium rates on the productivity of the individual farms as shown by records of past production, a large number of which the A.A.A. county committees already have on file. This method should avoid making farmers of one region pay for the risks of another region. By making this insurance available only to farmers cooperating in farm and soil conservation programs, the plan would be safeguarded from the price dangers which the Federal Farm Board operations invited in the years from 1929 to 1932. By using existing records of cooperating farmers and farm committeemen it would appear that premiums based on risk experience could be as fairly assessed as with existing forms of private insurance.

The expense in the past to Federal, State and local Governments of burdens caused by drought shows it is time to begin using the economical principle of insurance to lessen the financial and human costs of drought in the future.

There should be no question that the welfare of the entire Nation would be served by including, as keystones of our agricultural policy, crop insurance and storage of reserves along with conservation of soil and water, better land use, and increased farm income.

Crop insurance properly worked out should give adequate abundance to consumers even though there are several years of severe drought, while at the same time farmers would be protected from the low prices like those of 1932 which might result from several years of good weather.

I am sending similar letters to Administrator Tolley, Assistant Secretary Taylor, Assistant Secretary Draper, and Dr. Black.

Very sincerely yours,

Honorable Henry A. Wallace,
Secretary of Agriculture,
Washington, D. C.

(See note to the following Item.)

131A ❰ The President Creates a Committee to Recommend a Long-Term Program for the Utilization of the Resources of the Great Plains Area. September 19, 1936

My dear Mr. Cooke:

I AM writing to ask you to serve as chairman of a special committee whose duty it will be to make a report to me not later than January 1st on a long-term program for the efficient utilization of the resources of the Great Plains area. I am anxious that we leave no stone unturned in exploring and reporting on all the possibilities of this region, as one in which reasonable standards of living can be maintained by the largest possible population. We should face the fact that the climatic conditions make special safeguards absolutely necessary. I would like your report to include such recommendations for legislation as you may deem necessary. The report now called for is an amplification of the recommendations presented to me at Bismarck.

In the letter appointing the earlier committee I said:

> "We have supposed that the modes of settlement and of development which have been prevalent represented the ordinary course of civilization. But perhaps in this area of relatively little rain, practices brought from the more humid part of the country are not most suitable under the prevailing natural conditions. At any rate, circumstances make it obvious that relief activities are not sufficient and that a competent study and recommendations are desirable."

You are advised that I am appointing another committee to report on the crop insurance feature of this general problem. After consulting with the heads of their several Departments I have designated the following to serve with you on this committee: Prof. Harlan H. Barrows, member Water Resources Committee, National Resources Committee, Chicago, Illinois; Dr. H.

H. Bennett, Chief, Soil Conservation Service, Department of Agriculture, Washington, D. C.; Dr. L. C. Gray, Chief, Division of Land Economics, Bureau of Agricultural Economics, Department of Agriculture, Washington, D. C.; Col. F. C. Harrington, Assistant Administrator, Works Progress Administration, Washington, D. C.; Col. Richard C. Moore, Division Engineer, Missouri River Division, Corps of Engineers, United States Army, Kansas City, Missouri; Mr. John C. Page, Acting Director, Bureau of Reclamation, Washington, D. C.; and Dr. Harlow S. Person of the Rural Electrification Administration, Washington, D. C.

Sincerely yours,

Hon. Morris L. Cooke,
Administrator,
Rural Electrification Administration,
Washington, D. C.

Similar letters were sent to the officials appointed by the President to serve on the Committee to report on the long-term program "for the utilization of the resources of the Great Plains area."

NOTE: As a result of the various studies carried on by the Great Plains Drought Committee and other agencies, and from my own experience on the recent trip which I had made through the drought areas, I was convinced that the time had come for the initiation of a long-range program which would have as its objectives: (1) a proper use of land for better and more permanent protection against drought, and (2) a system of producing and storing crops which would provide a steady food supply over the years of fluctuating plenty and scarcity, which would be large enough to insure sufficient food for the Nation at fair prices, but not so large as to result in price-depressing surpluses which would spell ruin for the farmers.

132 ⟨ White House Statement on a Conference to Establish a Southeastern Power Pool. September 19, 1936

President Roosevelt today called a conference of representatives of public and private interests to meet at the White House on September 30th, for the purpose of discussing the possible establishment of a Southeastern Power Pool through the cooperation of the Tennessee Valley Authority and the private utility interests in that region.

The conference is being called at this time because the existing contracts between Commonwealth & Southern and the Tennessee Valley Authority for interchange of power and common use of transmission facilities — a rudimentary form of power pooling — are due to expire soon.

If a satisfactory understanding regarding the pooling of power and transmission facilities in the Southeastern States can be reached at this conference, a basis will perhaps be laid for working out similar arrangements in other regions affected by major Federal power projects.

In explanation of the scope and purposes of the conference, the President said:

THE public interest demands that the power that is being or soon will be generated by the Tennessee Valley Authority and at the Bonneville Dam and other Public Works projects should be made to serve the greatest number of our people at the lowest cost and, as far as possible, without injury to existing actual investment. To this end, I have for several months been conferring informally with representatives of the Federal Power Commission, the National Resources Committee, the Tennessee Valley Authority, and the Rural Electrification Administration, as well as with utility executives, engineers and economists.

These discussions indicate agreement to a remarkable degree that this objective can best be attained by cooperative pooling of power facilities within each region, including those of the Federal projects, the privately owned utilities, and the municipal plants, through the joint use of the existing transmission line networks under the control of the members of the pool. Such a pool, it appears, will smooth out the peaks and valleys of separate system operations, reduce the amount of necessary reserve capacity and postpone the need for investment in new generating facilities.

I am advised that by this means investment in transmission lines and generating facilities could be kept to a minimum, service strengthened, and large economies in operation effected. If so, these great savings, based on fair contractual relations between the public and private agencies participating, should make it possible to bring cheap and abundant power to the gate of every community in the region at uniformly low rates.

Engineers and rate experts tell me that by such pools power could be made available throughout great regions at wholesale rates as low as, if not lower than, the wholesale rate at which the T.V.A. is now supplying power to communities, private utilities, and industries. The regional network would also promote rapid expansion of the Government's rural electrification program.

There is every reason why we should thoroughly explore the possibilities of working out a sound plan for such regional power pools. I am, therefore, calling a conference to consider this subject and attempt to devise a plan that will promote the public and private interests involved.

We are not without actual experience in the advantages, as well as the difficulties, of such a plan. For two and one-half years, a group of private utilities in the Southeast and the T.V.A. have been jointly using transmission lines and exchanging power on a contractual basis. This experience is relevant in weighing the possibilities of a more comprehensive regional power pool. The impending expiration of this arrangement makes early consideration of future plans appropriate.

I hope and believe that, with the cooperation of those interested, we shall be able to work out a constructive plan that will extend to the Southeast and other great regions of our country the benefits and comforts that can be secured through proper development of our unparalleled natural resources.

NOTE: The Conference which was called in accordance with the foregoing statement met on October 20, 1936. There were present representatives of the Commonwealth and Southern Corporation, T.V.A. and the Federal Power Commission, for the purposes set forth in the foregoing statement.

While the negotiations were in progress, a sweeping preliminary injunction was issued by a lower court against the Tennessee Valley Authority, upon the application of nineteen utility companies, including certain companies which were parties to the conference. The securing of the injunction made it advisable to discontinue these conferences; and although the injunction was dissolved on January 26, 1937, no further negotiations with reference to the proposed power pool have been undertaken.

133 ⟨ The Beginnings of a Plan to Improve the Farm Tenancy Situation. September 21, 1936

Dear Sir:

THOUGHTFUL people everywhere have been gravely concerned with the steady increase in farm tenancy from 1880 to 1935. Since the earliest days of their history, it has been an ideal of the American people that every American should have an ownership interest in land or in some other means of production. Despite this fundamental objective, we have seen farm tenancy increase relative the farm ownership decade by decade. An enduring agricultural civilization must be built on the firm foundation of home and farm ownership. Any long-time improvement of the welfare of the Nation and of farm people involves improvement of the tenancy situation.

The tenancy problem in the United States cannot be solved overnight. But through Government financing of land purchased by tenants, other countries, notably Ireland and Denmark, have substantially increased farmer ownership of farm land. I think we need some such approach. It should give tenants who have demonstrated their ability to manage land an opportunity to buy farms on long-time terms at moderate interest rates.

I am asking you, therefore, to meet with Congressman Marvin Jones, Chairman of the Agricultural Committee of the House of Representatives, and cooperate in preparing plans for meeting the tenancy problem that might be undertaken by the Federal Government.

I realize your long interest and that of Congressman Jones in this important problem and wish that you and he would arrange to meet with me early in December when we can complete our recommendations to Congress for legislation designed to bring about improvements in the tenancy situation.

Very sincerely yours,

Senator John H. Bankhead,
U. S. Senate,
Washington, D. C.

(A similar letter was sent to Congressman Marvin Jones, Chairman of the Corresponding House Committee.)

NOTE: For a further discussion of the subject of farm tenancy, see Item 218, this volume.

134 ⟨A Telephoned Address to the New York Herald Tribune Forum. September 23, 1936

ANYTHING that makes for tolerance of opinion and contributes to the general education of our people in the issues of governmental policy is of vast value. Therefore I like the Forum idea. May we have more of them and cover the country with them.

It is not likely that such a brief expression of a point of view as is possible on such an occasion as this will persuade the convinced political partisan to change his or her position, but it may start such people to thinking and convey the idea that prejudice is a rather weak substitute for logic in determining the questions that are of such vital consequence to our country as a whole and to each individual citizen thereof.

It is natural, I suppose, in a campaign year, for advocates and adversaries of any policy or process of government to relapse into exaggeration and invective, and so becloud the controversy as to make it possible for the future of the country to be determined in rancor and temper instead of by calm deliberation and clear thinking.

I do not know that there is any actual remedy for this state of affairs, but I believe that it is within the power and the province of the press to make whatever improvement is possible. I do not think that anybody objects to a statement of opinion or an argument, either pro or con, being put forth in the editorial pages provided the editorials do not contain misstatements of fact. That, unless I entirely misunderstand newspaper psychology, is what the newspaper editorial columns are for. I do not believe — and I do not think any disagreement is possible on this subject — that a journal's news columns ought to be tampered with, either by coloring news or by leaving out news. The news is the commodity that is marketed to the whole people. I may be accused of idealism when I suggest that a Republican reader of a Democratic newspaper is entitled to all the news that appertains to his segment of the political landscape and that a Democratic reader of a Republican newspaper should not be fed exclusively on a Republican diet. And I would apply the same idealism to the headlines.

The Forum idea, conducted impartially, is an indication of the objective which most fair-minded people seek. I cannot help contrasting a Nation which more and more is encouraging any friendly discussion on all manner of public problems with those countries which unfortunately have made public discussion difficult if not impossible.

In the welter of passion which is apparently still inseparable from our political campaigns, you and I hear about the liberty of the press — regimentation of the press against the Government and regimentation of the press by the Government. It is doubtful if the United States ever had an Administration since the days when Washington was accused of despotism and aspirations to kingship that had the slightest desire to muzzle anybody. The unchecked virulence of assaults on almost every Administration since the beginning of our history in itself is best proof of that statement.

An old friend of mine who, although a successful man of affairs in New York, has led a somewhat narrow existence, asked me the other day if it was true, as many of his friends had told him, that three-quarters of all the money spent for relief of the needy unemployed in these past few years had gone for overhead and only one-quarter to the needy unemployed themselves. He asked me further if it was true, as he had been told by his friends, that all our bank deposits were insecure and our insurance policies worthless. I wrote him that it would be best for him to look up the answers himself. I suggested that he attend your Forum yesterday and today. I hope he has been with you.

The time may come when the policies of the Nation will be determined with the serenity and logic with which any serious business problem is decided among the directors of the business, but I must reluctantly confess that we have not reached that day.

I wish I might have attended the Forum in person. If I had been with you, I might have been moved to take part in the discussion. My part, in that case, would at least have been tempered by good humor, an effort to develop the facts, and a desire to present constructive remedies for current ills. I send to you my compliments and good wishes.

135 ❮A Treasury Statement on International Monetary Arrangements among Great Britain, France and the United States. September 25, 1936

By authority of the President, the Secretary of the Treasury makes the following statement:

1. The Government of the United States, after consultation

with the British Government and the French Government, joins with them in affirming a common desire to foster those conditions which safeguard peace and will best contribute to the restoration of order in international economic relations and to pursue a policy which will tend to promote prosperity in the world and to improve the standard of living of peoples.

2. The Government of the United States must, of course, in its policy toward international monetary relations take into full account the requirements of internal prosperity, as corresponding considerations will be taken into account by the Governments of France and Great Britain; it welcomes this opportunity to reaffirm its purpose to continue the policy which it has pursued in the course of recent years, one constant object of which is to maintain the greatest possible equilibrium in the system of international exchange and to avoid to the utmost extent the creation of any disturbance of that system by American monetary action. The Government of the United States shares with the Governments of France and Great Britain the conviction that the continuation of this twofold policy will serve the general purpose which all the Governments should pursue.

3. The French Government informs the United States Government that, judging that the desired stability of the principal currencies cannot be insured on a solid basis except after the reestablishment of a lasting equilibrium between the various economic systems, it has decided with this object to propose to its Parliament the readjustment of its currency. The Government of the United States, as also the British Government, has welcomed this decision in the hope that it will establish more solid foundations for the stability of international economic relations. The United States Government, as also the British and French Governments, declares its intention to continue to use appropriate available resources so as to avoid as far as possible any disturbance of the basis of international exchange resulting from the proposed readjustment. It will arrange for such consultation for this purpose as may prove necessary with the other two Governments and their authorized agencies.

4. The Government of the United States is moreover convinced, as are also the Governments of France and Great Britain, that the success of the policy set forth above is linked with the development of international trade. In particular it attaches the greatest importance to action being taken without delay to relax progressively the present system of quotas and exchange controls with a view to their abolition.

5. The Government of the United States, in common with the Governments of France and Great Britain, desires and invites the cooperation of the other Nations to realize the policy laid down in the present declaration. It trusts that no country will attempt to obtain an unreasonable competitive exchange advantage and thereby hamper the effort to restore more stable economic relations which it is the aim of the three Governments to promote.

NOTE: In September, 1936, an acute European monetary situation threatened to develop into disastrous competitive currency depreciation, and even to result in serious political consequences. In order to meet this situation, on September 25, 1936, after consultation with the Governments of Great Britain and France, the Secretary of the Treasury, by my authority, issued the foregoing statement announcing certain common principles with respect to international monetary relations. Similar statements were issued by Great Britain and France. These three Governments declared, among other things, that they proposed to take "into full account the requirements of internal prosperity . . . to maintain the greatest possible equilibrium in the system of international exchange and to avoid to the utmost extent the creation of any disturbance of that system" by internal monetary action. The three Governments invited the cooperation of other Nations in the effectuation of this policy.

To implement this "tripartite declaration," the Secretary of the Treasury announced on October 13, 1936, that the United States was offering to sell gold to the stabilization funds of those countries whose funds likewise were offering to sell gold to the United States on satisfactory terms. France and Great Britain were named as complying with these conditions for the purchase of gold from the United States.

On November 24, 1936, Belgium, The Netherlands and Switzerland, having declared their adherence to the principles of the tripartite declaration, were added to the list of countries to which the United States was offering to sell gold. It will be recalled that immediately after the passage of the Gold Reserve Act and upon the issuance of the devaluation Proclamation, the Secretary of the Treasury had announced (see Item 16, Vol. III) that he would sell gold for export whenever our exchange rates with gold standard currencies reached the gold export point. Included in the statement of November 24, 1936, was the provision that this statement "of January 31, 1934, relating to the sale of gold for export, is accordingly withdrawn."

These steps were taken in furtherance of our purposes in the international sphere, particularly those relating to the elimination of broad fluctuations in exchange rates and the avoidance of competitive depreciation of currencies.

The measures referred to, while perhaps the most important, were not the first of our attempts to deal with monetary problems by international action. Reference has already been made to the international silver agreement of 1933. Again, on January 6, 1936, announcement was made by the Secretary of the Treasury that a financial arrangement had been entered into with Mexico. This involved the purchase by the United States, on a month-to-month basis, of certain silver produced in Mexico. On March 4, 1936, announcement was made of an understanding with the Dominion of Canada for the pur-

chase of silver newly mined therein. On May 18, 1936, the Secretary announced that, after conferences with representatives of the Chinese Ministry of Finance, the United States had indicated its willingness, under certain conditions mutually acceptable, to make purchases from the Central Bank of China of substantial amounts of silver and also to make available, to the Central Bank of China, dollar exchange for currency stabilization purposes under conditions which safeguarded the interests of both countries.

It may also be appropriate at this time to refer briefly to two other announcements made by the Secretary of the Treasury. On July 9, 1937, he stated that the monetary cooperation which resulted from conferences with representatives of the Chinese Ministry in May, 1936, had contributed to the successful functioning of the new Chinese monetary system, with benefits to the internal economy of China as well as to American trade; and that arrangements had been made through which the Government of China would purchase from the United States Treasury a substantial amount of gold, the Chinese Government being aided in thus augmenting its gold reserves by the purchase by the United States Treasury of an additional amount of silver from the Chinese Government.

On July 17, 1937, the Secretary of the Treasury announced an agreement with the United States of

Brazil under which gold was to be sold at the request of the Brazilian Government up to a total of 60 million dollars, and dollar exchange was to be made available to the Government of Brazil for the purpose of promoting exchange equilibrium, under conditions safeguarding the interests of both countries.

136 ❪ Informal Extemporaneous Remarks at the Dedication of the Medical College, Syracuse University, Syracuse, N. Y. September 29, 1936

CHANCELLOR GRAHAM, my first duty is to report to you that the cornerstone is well and truly laid.

I have a great satisfaction. I have laid many cornerstones and, so far as I know, none of the buildings has tumbled down yet.

I am renewing an old association in coming back to Syracuse and Syracuse University. And, incidentally, I am very proud of being an honorary alumnus of the University.

I had many associations with the University long before I became Governor. As a grower of trees, I was very familiar with and received the cooperation of the State College of Forestry.

I have been to the Medical Center before, at the time of the opening — I think — of the Psychopathic Hospital. I am tremendously interested in the splendid work that is being carried on at this great Medical Center, not only here but outside of the limits of the University and the institutions which form it. Also, I am somewhat familiar with the other problems of the City of Syracuse, such as how to make the State Fair pay, and how to get rid of the tracks in the middle of the city. At last that dream has come true and when I came in a few minutes ago to the new station, I said to myself, "I shall never be bothered by Mayor Marvin again."

All of these projects — those which have been carried out solely by private enterprise and those which have been carried out by city enterprise, those that have been carried out by State or Federal enterprise and those, incidentally, that have been carried out through a combination of all of these forces — they have done much, especially in these last few years, to solve some of our nationwide problems.

I am very glad that the Secretary of the Interior has spoken to you about the objective of the work that we have helped to do, about the number of men and women who have been given work through the erection of these buildings, about the tremendous stimulus to education which has been made possible through keeping up, patching and erecting much-needed buildings — school buildings and medical buildings — throughout all of the more than 3,000 counties of the United States.

We think of the hundreds of men who have worked and who are working on these buildings here. Think also of the hundreds of men who have worked and are working in other places, creating the materials, getting them out of the mines and quarries and the factories in order to make buildings of this type possible.

And then there is another phase I believe we should remember. You and I know that in these days of stress, many of the municipalities and many of the institutions of learning throughout the country have found it difficult to make both ends meet. In that crisis, in order to keep up the work of municipalities and of private institutions, the Federal Government has been able to give the kind of assistance which has prevented the imposition of taxes which, in many cases, otherwise would have become unnecessarily high. The State has also helped during all of these years. Without Federal and State help we can well assume that the home owner and the small business man would have been far more thoroughly swamped with local taxes than he actually has been.

I am particularly happy to take part in the dedication of this medical building. As I remember it, this Medical College is a direct descendant of old Genesee College, or, as we used to call it in the olden days, Genesee. And I remember, too, that it was Genesee College which gave the first doctor's degree in America to a woman, Dr. Elizabeth Blackwell. May that fine tradition be preserved in the days to come!

The country needs a large number of well-trained doctors and nurses, and, in the field of education, we need a large number of well-trained teachers. We have not reached the limit.

We all know the reasons that are usually given for the need of turning out trained persons—persons trained in social sciences. But there is another reason that is worth suggesting. During a period like this in which machinery reduces the use of human labor in the production of things, society needs to extend the use of human labor both mentally and physically. The kind of labor that doctors and teachers furnish is a splendid example. The country needs to extend that kind of labor in providing better care and better education for all of our people in every community, because we have been so late in taking up the slack that other forms of modern invention have created for us. There is a big field there. Medical care in the United States is not adequate. There are thousands of communities throughout the length and breadth of the land which need more doctors, more nurses, better doctors and better nurses, in the same way that there are thousands of communities throughout the land that need better trained and better equipped teachers.

That is why I say that these medical centers, of which Syracuse Medical College is furnishing such a fine example, need the interest and the support of every citizen.

I am very certain that the University and the citizens of the City of Syracuse and the citizens of the State of New York are proud of the work that is being carried on here.

I congratulate you not only on what you have done in the past, but, with the added assurance of the facilities which this building will provide, I congratulate you on the usefulness to humanity that you will afford to future generations of America.

137 ❬ The Opening of the 1936 Presidential Campaign—"Never Has a Nation Made Greater Strides in the Safeguarding of Democracy." Address Delivered at Democratic State Convention, Syracuse, N. Y. September 29, 1936

(False campaign issues — Growth of communism prevented by this Administration — Rejection of all communist support in campaign — Comparison of Republican and Democratic leadership and philosophy — Liberalism the best protection of far-sighted conservative — "I am that kind of conservative because I am that kind of liberal.")

Ladies and gentlemen:

FROM force of long habit I almost said, "My fellow delegates."

Tonight you and I join forces for the 1936 campaign. We enter it with confidence. Never was there greater need for fidelity to the underlying conception of Americanism than there is today. And once again it is given to our party to carry the message of that Americanism to the people.

The task on our part is twofold: First, as simple patriotism requires, to separate the false from the real issues; and, secondly, with facts and without rancor, to clarify the real problems for the American public.

There will be—there are—many false issues. In that respect, this will be no different from other campaigns. Partisans, not willing to face realities, will drag out red herrings—as they have always done—to divert attention from the trail of their own weaknesses.

This practice is as old as our democracy. Avoiding the facts— fearful of the truth—a malicious opposition charged that George Washington planned to make himself king under a British form of government; that Thomas Jefferson planned to set up a guillotine under a French Revolutionary form of government; that

383

Andrew Jackson soaked the rich of the Eastern seaboard and planned to surrender American democracy to the dictatorship of a frontier mob. They called Abraham Lincoln a Roman Emperor; Theodore Roosevelt a Destroyer; Woodrow Wilson a self-constituted Messiah.

In this campaign another herring turns up. In former years it has been British and French — and a variety of other things. This year it is Russian. Desperate in mood, angry at failure, cunning in purpose, individuals and groups are seeking to make Communism an issue in an election where Communism is not a controversy between the two major parties.

Here and now, once and for all, let us bury that red herring, and destroy that false issue. You are familiar with my background; you know my heritage; and you are familiar, especially in the State of New York, with my public service extending back over a quarter of a century. For nearly four years I have been President of the United States. A long record has been written. In that record, both in this State and in the national capital, you will find a simple, clear and consistent adherence not only to the letter, but to the spirit of the American form of government.

To that record, my future and the future of my Administration will conform. I have not sought, I do not seek, I repudiate the support of any advocate of Communism or of any other alien "ism" which would by fair means or foul change our American democracy.

That is my position. It always has been my position. It always will be my position.

There is no difference between the major parties as to what they think about Communism. But there is a very great difference between the two parties in what they do about Communism.

I must tell you why. Communism is a manifestation of the social unrest which always comes with widespread economic maladjustment. We in the Democratic party have not been content merely to denounce this menace. We have been realistic enough to face it. We have been intelligent enough to do something about it. And the world has seen the results of what we have done.

In the spring of 1933 we faced a crisis which was the ugly fruit of twelve years of neglect of the causes of economic and social unrest. It was a crisis made to order for all those who would overthrow our form of government. Do I need to recall to you the fear of those days — the reports of those who piled supplies in their basements, who laid plans to get their fortunes across the border, who got themselves hideaways in the country against the impending upheaval? Do I need to recall the law-abiding heads of peaceful families, who began to wonder, as they saw their children starve, how they would get the bread they saw in the bakery window? Do I need to recall the homeless boys who were traveling in bands through the countryside seeking work, seeking food — desperate because they could find neither? Do I need to recall the farmers who banded together with pitchforks to keep the sheriff from selling the farm home under foreclosure? Do I need to recall the powerful leaders of industry and banking who came to me in Washington in those early days of 1933 pleading to be saved?

Most people in the United States remember today the fact that starvation was averted, that homes and farms were saved, that banks were reopened, that crop prices rose, that industry revived, and that the dangerous forces subversive of our form of government were turned aside.

A few people — a few only — unwilling to remember, seem to have forgotten those days.

In the summer of 1933, a nice old gentleman wearing a silk hat fell off the end of a pier. He was unable to swim. A friend ran down the pier, dived overboard and pulled him out; but the silk hat floated off with the tide. After the old gentleman had been revived, he was effusive in his thanks. He praised his friend for saving his life. Today, three years later, the old gentleman is berating his friend because the silk hat was lost.

Why did that crisis of 1929 to 1933 pass without disaster?

The answer is found in the record of what we did. Early in the campaign of 1932 I said: "To meet by reaction that danger of radicalism is to invite disaster. Reaction is no barrier to the radical, it is a challenge, a provocation. The way to meet that danger is to offer a workable program of reconstruction, and the party to offer it is the party with clean hands." We met the emergency with emergency action. But far more important than that, we went to the roots of the problem, and attacked the cause of the crisis. We were against revolution. Therefore, we waged war against those conditions which make revolutions — against the inequalities and resentments which breed them. In America in 1933 the people did not attempt to remedy wrongs by overthrowing their institutions. Americans were made to realize that wrongs could and would be set right within their institutions. We proved that democracy can work.

I have said to you that there is a very great difference between the two parties in what they do about Communism. Conditions congenial to Communism were being bred and fostered throughout this Nation up to the very day of March 4, 1933. Hunger was breeding it, loss of homes and farms was breeding it, closing banks were breeding it, a ruinous price level was breeding it. Discontent and fear were spreading through the land. The previous national Administration, bewildered, did nothing.

In their speeches they deplored it, but by their actions they encouraged it. The injustices, the inequalities, the downright suffering out of which revolutions come — what did they do about these things? Lacking courage, they evaded. Being selfish, they neglected. Being short-sighted, they ignored. When the crisis came — as these wrongs made it sure to come — America was unprepared.

Our lack of preparation for it was best proved by the cringing and the fear of the very people whose indifference helped to make the crisis. They came to us pleading that we should do, overnight, what they should have been doing through the years.

And the simple causes of our unpreparedness were two: First, a weak leadership, and, secondly, an inability to see causes, to understand the reasons for social unrest — the tragic plight of 90 percent of the men, women and children who made up the population of the United States.

It has been well said that "The most dreadful failure of which any form of government can be guilty is simply to lose touch with reality, because out of this failure all imaginable forms of evil grow. Every empire that has crashed has come down primarily because its rulers did not know what was going on in the world and were incapable of learning."

It is for that reason that our American form of government will continue to be safest in Democratic hands. The real, actual, undercover Republican leadership is the same as it was four years ago. That leadership will never comprehend the need for a program of social justice and of regard for the well-being of the masses of our people.

I have been comparing leadership in Washington. This contrast between Democratic and Republican leadership holds true throughout the length and breadth of the State of New York. As far back as the year 1910, the old Black Horse Cavalry in Albany, which we old people will remember, was failing to meet changing social conditions by appropriate social legislation. Here was a State noted for its industry and noted for its agriculture — a State with the greatest mixture of population — where the poorest and the richest lived, literally, within a stone's throw of each other — in short a situation made to order for potential unrest. And yet in this situation the best that the Republican leaders of those days could say was: "Let them eat cake." What would have happened if that reactionary domination had continued through all these hard years?

Starting in 1911, a Democratic leadership came into power, and with it a new philosophy of government. I had the good fortune to come into public office at that time. I found other young men in the Legislature — men who held the same philosophy; one of them was Bob Wagner; another was Al Smith. We were all joined in a common cause. We did not look on government as something apart from the people. We thought of it as something to be used by the people for their own good.

New factory legislation setting up decent standards of safety and sanitation; limitation of the working hours of women in in-

387

dustry; a workmen's compensation law; a one-day-rest-in-seven law; a full train-crew law; a direct-primary law — these laws and many more were passed which were then called radical and alien to our form of government. Would you or any other Americans call them radical or alien today?

In later years, first under Governor Smith, then during my Governorship, this program of practical intelligence was carried forward over the typical and unswerving opposition of Republican leaders throughout our State.

And today the great tradition of a liberal, progressive Democratic Party has been carried still further by your present Governor, Herbert H. Lehman. He has begun a program of insurance to remove the spectre of unemployment from the working people of the State. He has broadened our labor legislation. He has extended the supervision of public utility companies. He has proved himself an untiring seeker for the public good; a doer of social justice; a wise, conscientious, clear-headed and businesslike administrator of the executive branch of our Government. And be it noted that his opponents are led and backed by the same forces and, in many cases, by the same individuals who, for a quarter of a century, have tried to hamstring progress within our State. The overwhelming majority of our citizens, up-state and down-state, regardless of party, propose to return him and his Administration to Albany for another two years.

His task in Albany, like my task in Washington, has been to maintain contact between statecraft and reality. In New York and in Washington, Government which has rendered more than lip service to our Constitutional Democracy has done a work for the protection and preservation of our institutions that could not have been accomplished by repression and force.

Let me warn you and let me warn the Nation against the smooth evasion which says, "Of course we believe all these things; we believe in social security; we believe in work for the unemployed; we believe in saving homes. Cross our hearts and hope to die, we believe in all these things; but we do not like the way the present Administration is doing them. Just turn them

over to us. We will do all of them — we will do more of them —
we will do them better; and, most important of all, the doing of
them will not cost anybody anything."

But, my friends, these evaders are banking too heavily on the
shortness of our memories. No one will forget that they had their
golden opportunity — twelve long years of it.

Remember, too, that the first essential of doing a job well is to
want to see the job done. Make no mistake about this: the Republican leadership today is not against the way we have done
the job. The Republican leadership is against the job's being
done.

Look to the source of the promises of the past. Governor Lehman knows and I know how little legislation in the interests of
the average citizen would be on the statute books of the State of
New York, and of the Federal Government, if we had waited for
Republican leaders to pass it.

The same lack of purpose of fulfillment lies behind the promises of today. You cannot be an Old Guard Republican in the
East, and a New Deal Republican in the West. You cannot promise to repeal taxes before one audience and promise to spend
more of the taxpayers' money before another audience. You cannot promise tax relief for those who can afford to pay, and, at the
same time, promise more of the taxpayers' money for those who
are in need. You simply cannot make good on both promises at
the same time.

Who is there in America who believes that we can run the risk
of turning back our Government to the old leadership which
brought it to the brink of 1933? Out of the strains and stresses of
these years we have come to see that the true conservative is the
man who has a real concern for injustices and takes thought
against the day of reckoning. The true conservative seeks to protect the system of private property and free enterprise by correcting such injustices and inequalities as arise from it. The most
serious threat to our institutions comes from those who refuse
to face the need for change. Liberalism becomes the protection
for the far-sighted conservative.

Never has a Nation made greater strides in the safeguarding of democracy than we have made during the past three years. Wise and prudent men — intelligent conservatives — have long known that in a changing world worthy institutions can be conserved only by adjusting them to the changing time. In the words of the great essayist, "The voice of great events is proclaiming to us. Reform if you would preserve."

I am that kind of conservative because I am that kind of liberal.

NOTE: The foregoing speech marked the beginning of the 1936 campaign for the Presidency.

A great many of the campaign speeches, prepared and extemporaneous, are printed in these volumes as Items 137, 141-144, 147-191, 194, 195, 199-208.

In addition to those which have been included, I made other extemporaneous or rear-platform speeches which have been omitted here for lack of space.

The campaign trips of this year consisted of a short trip through West Virginia and Pennsylvania on October 1st, covering Items 141 to 144 incl., including speeches, not here printed, delivered at Morgantown, West Va., October 1, and Connellsville, Pa., October 1; a Western trip from October 8th to October 17th, covering Items 147 to 188 incl., including speeches, not here printed, made at Cumberland, Md., October 8th; Plattsmouth, Nebr., October 10th; Denver, Colo. (Fitzsimmons Hospital), October 12th; Kansas City, Kansas, October 13th; East St. Louis, Ill., October 14th; Alton, Ill., October 14th; Pontiac, Ill., October 14th; Lansing, Mich., October 15th; Pontiac, Mich., October 15th; Dayton, Ohio, October 16th; Springfield, Ohio, October 16th; Columbus, Ohio, October 16th; a trip through New England from October 21st to October 22nd, covering Items 189 to 191 incl., and also Item 194, including speeches, not here printed, made at Fall River, Mass., October 21st; Taunton, Mass., October 21st; Brockton, Mass., October 21st; Waltham, Mass., October 21st; Marlboro, Mass., October 21st; Meriden, Conn., October 22nd; Waterbury, Conn., October 22nd; New Haven, Conn., October 22nd; Bridgeport, Conn., October 22nd; Westport, Conn., October 22nd; Norwalk, Conn., October 22nd; Stamford, Conn., October 22nd; a trip from New York City through New Jersey, Pennsylvania and Delaware, on October 28th and October 29th, covering Items 199 to 203 incl., including also speeches, not here printed, made at Bayonne, N. J., October 28th; Sunbury, Pa., October 29th; and speeches in New York City on October 30th and 31st, covering Items 204, 205, 206, including a speech in the Bronx, New

York City, on October 31st, not here printed.

The campaign was wound up by speeches at Poughkeepsie on the day before election (Items 207 and 208) and also speeches on the same day at Beacon, Newburgh, Kingston and Rhinebeck, all in New York State, not here printed.

In the preparation of campaign speeches as well as speeches on other occasions I have called on many different people for advice and assistance. This was also my custom during my term as Governor of New York. On various subjects I have received drafts and memoranda from different people, varying from short suggestions as to a sentence here and there, to long memoranda of factual material and, in some cases, complete addresses.

In addition to such suggestions, I make it a practice to keep a "speech material file." This file is kept by Miss Marguerite A. LeHand, who has been my personal secretary for eighteen years, and who is my personal secretary in the White House. She has rendered invaluable, loyal service to me during my terms as Governor and as President, in relieving me of innumerable details and in giving sound, common-sense suggestions. Whenever anything catches my eye, either in the mail or in the press or in the course of reading articles, memoranda, or books, which I think will be of value in the preparation of a speech, I ask her to put it away in the speech material file.

A large part of this material passes through her hands regularly because there is brought to her every day my personal mail as well as mail which the Executive Office staff believes I should see personally. Much of it she handles herself, bringing the rest to my personal attention. I go over this mail with her; and many of the replies she dictates herself. For those that require personal dictation by me, replies are dictated to Miss Grace Tully, who acts as my personal stenographer and also as general assistant to Miss LeHand.

In preparing a speech I usually take the various drafts and suggestions which have been submitted to me and also the material which has been accumulated in the speech file on various subjects, read them carefully, lay them aside, and then dictate my own draft, usually to Miss Tully. Naturally, the final speech will contain some of the thoughts and even some of the sentences which appeared in some of the drafts or suggestions submitted.

I suppose it is human that two or three of the many persons with whom I have consulted in the preparation of speeches should seek to give the impression that they have been responsible for the writing of the speeches, and that one or two of them should claim authorship or should state that some other individual was the author. Such assertions, however, are not accurate.

On some of my speeches I have prepared as many as five or six successive drafts myself after reading drafts and suggestions submitted by other people; and I have changed drafts from time to time after consulting with other people either personally or by telephone.

138 ❧ The Chairman of the Social Security Board Resigns in Order to Defend the Act from the Current Campaign of Misrepresentations. The President Accepts the Resignation. September 29, 1936

Dear Governor Winant:

YOUR letter tendering your resignation as a member of the Social Security Board greatly distresses me. You are, of course, right in regarding the Social Security Act as "America's answer" to the "great human need" of "effective social machinery for meeting the problems of dependency and unemployment."

Like you, also, "I have never assumed that the Social Security Act was without fault. I had assumed and even hoped that time and experience might dictate many and important changes."

The Act was conceived and passed by the Congress as a humanitarian measure. Its passage transcended party lines. The opposition in both houses was, practically speaking, negligible. I share your regret that the evanescent passions of a political campaign have fanned the flames of partisan hostility to this non-partisan legislation.

Equally right are you in recognizing the "intention of Congress to create a non-partisan board, with personnel protected under civil service, and to insure non-partisan administration of the Act." Your appointment was intended to insure that it would be so administered. And, as you state, "it has been so administered."

Under such conditions I should have thought that you might have felt free to correct any misconception of the purpose of the legislation or any misinterpretation of its details. Appropriate education of the public mind regarding public measures is one of the inherent duties of an administrator.

For that reason I have hesitated to accept your resignation. I did not wish to lose the benefit of your devoted and disinterested service in the administration of the social security program. Yet, upon reflection and after talking with you, I have come to appreciate your position and the sense of public duty which impelled your resignation and your wish to be free as a citizen, not simply to clear up misconceptions and misinterpretations of the Act, but actively to defend the "constructive provisions" of the Act and to oppose spurious substitutes.

It is, therefore, with the deepest regret that I yield to your wish and accept your resignation. My regret is tempered by the knowledge that you have resigned only in order the better to defend the great work which you have so well begun.

Very sincerely yours,

Hon. John G. Winant,
Washington, D. C.

139 ❡ A Greeting to the Atlantic Deeper Waterways Association. September 30, 1936

My dear Mr. Moore:

In my letter to your association last year it was my pleasure to point out to the members of the Atlantic Deeper Waterways Association the progress which had been made in harbor and waterway improvements along the Atlantic Coast with funds of the Emergency Relief Appropriation Act. These meritorious public works have been continued and during the past fiscal year funds totalling more than $24,300,000 have been expended in the improvement of rivers and harbors on the eastern seaboard. This year has been noteworthy in witnessing the completion of the 1,435 mile inside route of the Intracoastal Waterway from

Trenton, New Jersey, to Miami, Florida. Much credit for this accomplishment belongs to your association and it is to be congratulated therefor. Other waterway projects of permanent value to the nation sponsored by your organization have been completed or are progressing in a satisfactory manner.

It is a pleasure for me again to extend my greetings to the members of your association on the occasion of its twenty-ninth annual convention. Your organization, since its inception at Trenton in 1907, has been most active in sponsoring waterway improvements along the Atlantic Coast. I may say to you that these improvements are being prosecuted vigorously and that funds for the fiscal year 1937 amounting to $24,000,000 have been allotted to this purpose. Permit me to congratulate you on the success which has attended your efforts and express my appreciation of your continued interest in national waterway improvements which serve to increase business and industry, improve employment, and provide lasting benefits to the Nation's welfare.

Very sincerely yours,

Hon. J. Hampton Moore,
President, Atlantic Deeper Waterways Association,
Philadelphia, Pennsylvania.

140 ⟨ The President Welcomes the Delegates to the Conference on the Peru-Ecuador Boundary Dispute. September 30, 1936

IN THE agreement signed at Lima on July 6, 1936, by the Minister for Foreign Affairs of Peru and the Minister of Ecuador to Peru for the purpose of making operative the provision of the protocol of June 21, 1924, it is stated that these two great Republics, throughout the course of the long discussion of their boundary controversy, have never faltered in their determination to settle this boundary question by pacific means and have ever been confident of their ability to arrive at a complete and permanent solution of the controversy.

It is in that spirit that the delegations of Ecuador and Peru meet in Washington today. I welcome you to the capital of my country, which shares with your countries the conviction that disputes between Nations, when the will for agreement exists, can always be resolved by the peaceful methods of negotiation, conciliation or arbitration.

Within the past few years several boundary disputes in this hemisphere have been settled by peaceful means. Two other American Republics at the present time are giving clear evidence of their faith in and adherence to this procedure. These are matters for legitimate pride on the part of the Nations of the New World. It is my sincere hope, which I am confident will be fulfilled, that another important chapter in this inspiring record may be written by the delegations of Peru and Ecuador as a result of the friendly negotiations which are being initiated today.

The protocol of June 21, 1924, provides for a further protocol to embody the terms of the common agreement reached through these discussions. After the ratification of this agreement by the Congresses of your two countries, if there is a territorial zone upon which agreement has not been possible, that zone is to be submitted to the arbitral determination of the President of the United States. If that duty falls to me, I pledge to you my best endeavors to conclude successfully the work of peace which you are about to begin.

The maintenance of peace in this Western Hemisphere must be the first concern of all of our peoples and of their Governments. I am confident that your deliberations here will furnish further encouragement and support for the practical application of the principle of the pacific settlement of disputes among Nations.

So you are doubly welcome to the United States and to this capital. You are very welcome because of your high purposes and you are equally welcome as distinguished representatives of our two sister Republics. I wish you Godspeed in your mission of peace.

NOTE: The foregoing statement delivered at the inauguration of this conference is indicative of the continuation of the efforts by the United States to help in settling the boundary dispute between these two Nations (see Item 20, Vol. III, and Item 86, this volume).

141 ⟮ Campaign Address at the Mountain States Forest Festival, Elkins, W. Va. October 1, 1936

(Accomplishment of the Administration in wild-life conservation.)

THE setting in which we are gathered today for this Forest Festival turns our thoughts toward conservation.

This wonderland of natural beauty is at one and the same time a challenge and a justification. It demonstrates what can be done in the way of conservation of our resources. It shows us how prodigal Nature is in her gifts, while at the same time it emphasizes the necessity for men to supplement Nature's work in order that the rich gifts which are ours may be brought to their fullest usefulness in the service of all mankind.

The State of West Virginia is rightly proud of its glorious natural scenery, but the State also shows to us what happens when man flies in the face of Nature. Today I have seen many square miles of splendid mountains which have been denuded of timber. I have seen yellow streams carrying eroded silt and soil from the steep slopes.

In this State, as in many others, we are proud of the growing consciousness of the people themselves that man's errors in the past must be corrected by man in the future. In this worth-while effort the State and the Federal Government are working hand in hand.

Here and hereabouts you see what can be done through the National Forest Service in cooperation with the work of the State Conservation Preserves; you have an opportunity to see at first hand the practical contribution to enlightened conservation that is being made by our C.C.C. camps and all of the other agencies whose activities are directed to the preservation of our matchless resources here at the gateway to the Monongahela National Forest.

No part of our conservation work is more important than the protection of our wild life. It is a work into which we can all enter, heart and soul, because there is no political partisanship in an activity whose object is to preserve and restore the life of our great out-of-doors.

I am sure that those in this audience who are devotees of outdoor life, whether fishermen, hunters, naturalists, campers or hikers, will rejoice to know what has been done during the last three and one-half years to protect and perpetuate our wild life. In the past it had been shamefully neglected and exploited. One of the earliest concerns of my Administration on assuming office was to provide a national wild-life restoration program and a policy that would make certain that the conservation of our wild animals, birds and fishes would thereafter take rank with the conservation of the other great renewable resources of the Nation. Plans to accomplish this had been available for years but, I am sorry to say, they had been in great part ignored.

We have evolved a national wild-life conservation program which proposed, largely in conjunction with giving work to the unemployed, to provide abundantly for the needs of wild life by purchase and retirement of agricultural lands that were submarginal in character, by the purchase of other suitable lands, and by making generous allocations of public lands, all to be set aside as sanctuaries.

Allotments totaling nearly $15,000,000 have been made from current emergency funds to support this great wild-life program —an amount greater than the total of all funds previously appropriated for that specific purpose in all our American history. In addition, I approved an Act of Congress continuing an appropriation of $6,000,000 of emergency funds for the same kind of purposes, making altogether nearly $21,000,000 for the conservation of water fowl, birds and other valuable forms of American wild life.

We have outlined and enacted a legislative program to give effect to our policy:

(1) The Duck Stamp Bill, which has raised about $700,000 a year for the protection of migratory birds.

(2) The Coordination Bill, requiring active cooperation of each department of the Administration and Cabinet officers in the enforcement of game laws.

(3) The Robinson Bill, creating game sanctuaries on all public properties — a big step forward.

Besides that, we went further. We completed the Migratory Bird Treaty with Mexico, a treaty which had hung fire for nearly twenty years. That treaty supplements a similar treaty with our neighbor, Canada, which gives protection to birds on their Southern flight. By the terms of the treaty with Mexico, protection is given migratory birds on their Northern flight.

I cite these facts because critics of this Administration have lately been engaged in expressing dissatisfaction with the progress of wild-life restoration by the Federal Government during the past three years. Apparently, while some people want us to save money, these critics do not think we spent enough money. Yet, in pursuance of this program, the Nation has acquired and set aside in these past three years some 4,800,000 acres of land and dedicated them to the restoration and perpetuation of valuable wild life. Many of the refuges have been located on the principal resting and breeding grounds of wild fowl of all kinds; others are placed along the main migratory flight lanes, while still others afford rest and food and safety to the birds in their winter quarters.

Out in the Western country great ranges have been established to perpetuate the big-game species — the elk, antelope, mountain sheep and the deer. All these sanctuaries afford shelter and security to hosts of song and insectivorous birds and to a great variety of other wild creatures.

The total area of Federal wild-life sanctuaries that had been acquired in the United States in all previous years before 1933 amounted to only 1,800,000 acres. And so since June 30, 1934, more than two and one-half times as much wild-life sanctuary area has been acquired or is now being acquired than in all the preceding years in the history of our Government. This work is now going on; and I believe that for the next four years it will be continued with the same vigor and singleness of purpose.

It is pertinent to remind you here that this touches the lives and the homes of an enormous number of Americans. Seven million of our citizens take out fishing licenses each year, and six million more take out annual hunting licenses, a veritable army of thirteen million citizens to uphold the banner of conservation.

Drainage and drought and over-shooting have greatly decreased the numbers of our waterfowl and other types of our wild life. For three consecutive years, at the cost of much bitter criticism, I have approved regulations drastically reducing the open shooting seasons and bag limits and prohibiting the use of certain devices known to be unduly destructive. As a consequence we are informed that there is evidence that these species have shown some increase in numbers, and it is believed that through our action they may now survive the disasters and the killings of former years.

Such, my friends, is a brief and very incomplete statement of the ways and means by which this Administration has made effective its recognition of the fact that the wild life in our fields and woods and waters constitutes a resource of vital importance to all Americans, and that it is the responsibility of the Federal Government in cooperation with the States to safeguard it for future generations. At last we are making definite progress.

The State of West Virginia understands this program. You have not only vast natural resources but you have vast human resources. And I am thinking not only of the birds and the beasts and the fishes; I am thinking also of the necessity of keeping them from becoming extinct in order that the human resources, our children and our grandchildren, may have them here in their generation.

142 ❡ Rear-Platform Extemporaneous Remarks at Grafton, W. Va. October 1, 1936

I AM glad to come back here. The last time I came through, there was no such thing as the Tygarts Valley Dam, and I am glad to see it now. I am not talking politics, but I am calling your attention to the fact that this dam up here is a pretty good boondoggling idea.

I am told by the engineer in charge that here in Grafton there are no people who want work who cannot get work. And so, as has been well said on a number of occasions this morning on the train, we are not here to defend the New Deal, we are here to proclaim it.

This is a very different sight from what I saw in West Virginia in 1932. I believe the country is well on the way not only toward recovery, but toward the kind of recovery that is going to stay.

143 ❡ Rear-Platform Extemporaneous Remarks at Fairmont, W. Va. October 1, 1936

(The first year free from national bank failures in fifty-five years.)

I AM glad to come back to Fairmont and to note that it is a much more prosperous-looking community than the last time I was here.

I am glad to be here with Senator Neely and Governor Kump and your Congressman and also your next Governor.

I received a telegram a few moments ago on the train and through you good people I am going to make an announcement about it. The telegram reports that for the first time in fifty-five years we have completed one full year without a single national bank failure in the United States. From that, I am inclined to think that the banks of the United States are safer than they have been in fifty-five years.

I have been much interested in seeing that great dam that is under construction farther up-stream. The engineer in charge told me that in July and in August of this year there has been a greater tonnage of water-borne freight on the Monongahela River than on any other stream in the United States.

I am glad that the Federal Government is thus cooperating with the communities of this part of the country. I call it pretty successful cooperative boondoggling.

It is good to be with you and I hope to come back one of these days soon. Many thanks.

144 ⟨ Campaign Address at Forbes Field, Pittsburgh, Pa. "The Only Way to Keep the Government Out of the Red Is to Keep the People Out of the Red." October 1, 1936

(Government finances — Administration's battle against the depression — Checking of deflationary spiral — Balanced budget vs. human misery — Restoration of purchasing power — Cost of program and increase of national debt — Sound investment in the future of America — Payment of debt out of increased national income.)

Mr. Chairman, Governor Earle, my friends of Pennsylvania:

A BASEBALL park is a good place to talk about box scores. To-night I am going to talk to you about the box score of the Government of the United States. I am going to tell you the story of our fight to beat down the depression and win recovery. From where I stand it looks as though the game is pretty well "in the bag."

I am convinced that when Government finance or any other kind of finance is honest, and when all the cards are on the table, there is no higher mathematics about it. It is just plain, score-board arithmetic.

When the present management of your team took charge in 1933, the national scoreboard looked pretty bad. In fact, it looked so much like a shut-out for the team that you voted a change of management in order to give the country a chance to win the game. And today we are winning it.

When the new management came to Washington, we began to make our plans — plans to meet the immediate crisis and plans that would carry the people of the country back to decent prosperity.

You and I and everybody else saw the millions out of work, saw the business concerns running in the red, saw the banks closing. Our national income had declined over 50 percent — and, what was worse, it showed no prospect of recuperating by itself. By national income I mean the total of all income of all the 125,-000,000 people in this country — the total of all the pay envelopes, all the farm sales, all the profits of all the businesses and all the individuals and corporations in America.

During the four lean years before this Administration took office, that national income had declined from eighty-one billions a year to thirty-eight billions a year. In short, you and I, all of us together, were making forty-three billions — spelled with a "b," not an "m" — forty-three billion dollars less in 1932 than we made in 1929.

Now, the rise and fall of national income — since they tell the story of how much you and I and everybody else are making — are an index of the rise and fall of national prosperity. They are also an index of the prosperity of your Government. The money to run the Government comes from taxes; and the tax revenue in turn depends for its size on the size of the national income. When the incomes and the values and transactions of the country are on the down-grade, then tax receipts go on the down-grade too. If the national income continues to decline, then the Government cannot run without going into the red. The only way to keep the Government out of the red is to keep the people out of the red.

And so we had to balance the budget of the American people before we could balance the budget of the national Government.

That makes common sense, doesn't it?

The box score when the Democratic Administration came to bat in 1933 showed a net deficit in our national accounts of about $3,000,000,000, accumulated in the three previous years under my predecessor.

National income was in a downward spiral. Federal Government revenues were in a downward spiral. To pile on vast new taxes would get us nowhere because values were going down — and that makes sense too.

On top of having to meet the ordinary expenses of Government, I recognized the obligation of the Federal Government to feed and take care of the growing army of homeless and destitute unemployed.

Something had to be done. A national choice had to be made. We could do one of two things. Some people who sat across my desk in those days urged me to let Nature take its course and to continue a policy of doing nothing. I rejected that advice because Nature was in an angry mood.

To have accepted that advice would have meant the continued wiping out of people of small means — the continued loss of their homes and farms and small businesses into the hands of people who still had enough capital left to pick up those homes and farms and businesses at bankruptcy prices. It would have meant, in a very short time, the loss of all the resources of a multitude of individuals and families and small corporations. You would have seen, throughout the Nation, a concentration of property ownership in the hands of one or two percent of the population, a concentration unequaled in any great Nation since the days of the later Roman Empire.

And so the program of this Administration set out to protect the small business, the small corporation, the small shop, and the small individual from the wave of deflation that threatened them. We realized then, as we do now, that the vast army of small business men and factory owners and shop owners — together with

403

our farmers and workers—form the backbone of the industrial life of America. In our long-range plan we recognized that the prosperity of America depended upon, and would continue to depend upon, the prosperity of them all.

I rejected the advice that was given to me to do nothing for an additional reason. I had promised, and my Administration was determined, to keep the people of the United States from starvation.

I refused to leave human needs solely in the hands of local communities—local communities which themselves were almost bankrupt.

To have accepted that advice would have been to offer bread-lines again to the American people, knowing this time, however, that in many places the lines would last far longer than the bread. In those dark days, between us and a balanced budget stood millions of needy Americans, denied the promise of a decent American life.

To balance our budget in 1933 or 1934 or 1935 would have been a crime against the American people. To do so we should either have had to make a capital levy that would have been confiscatory, or we should have had to set our face against human suffering with callous indifference. When Americans suffered, we refused to pass by on the other side. Humanity came first.

No one lightly lays a burden on the income of a Nation. But this vicious tightening circle of our declining national income simply had to be broken. The bankers and the industrialists of the Nation cried aloud that private business was powerless to break it. They turned, as they had a right to turn, to the Government. We accepted the final responsibility of Government, after all else had failed, to spend money when no one else had money left to spend.

I adopted, therefore, the other alternative. I cast aside a do-nothing or a wait-and-see policy.

As a first step in our program we had to stop the quick spiral of deflation and decline in the national income. Having stopped them, we went on to restore purchasing power, to raise values,

404

to put people back to work, and to start the national income going up again.

In 1933 we reversed the policy of the previous Administration. For the first time since the depression you had a Congress and an Administration in Washington which had the courage to provide the necessary resources which private interests no longer had or no longer dared to risk.

This cost money. We knew, and you knew, in March, 1933, that it would cost money. We knew, and you knew, that it would cost money for several years to come.

The people understood that in 1933. They understood it in 1934, when they gave the Administration a full endorsement of its policy. They knew in 1935, and they know in 1936, that the plan is working.

All right, my friends, let us look at the cost. Since we could not get the money by taxes we borrowed it, and increased the public debt.

President Hoover's Administration increased the national debt in the net amount of over three billion dollars in three depression years, and there was little to show for it. My Administration has increased the national debt in the net amount of about eight billion dollars and there is much to show for it.

Put that figure of eight billions out here on the scoreboard, and let me tell you where the dollars went.

Over a billion and a half went for payment of the World War Veterans' Bonus this year instead of in 1945. That payment is now out of the way, and is no longer a future obligation of the Government.

As for the other six and a half billions of the deficit we did not just spend money; we spent it for something. America got something for what we spent — conservation of human resources through C.C.C. camps and through work relief; conservation of natural resources of water, soil and forest; billions for security and a better life. While many who criticize today were selling America short, we were investing in the future of America.

Contrast those expenditures and what we got for them with

405

certain other expenditures of the American people in the years between 1920 and 1930. During that period not merely eight billions but many more billions came out of American pockets and were sent abroad — to foreign countries where the money was used for increasing foreign armaments, for building foreign factories to compete with us, for building foreign dwellings, swimming pools, and slaughter houses, for giving employment to the foreign unemployed — foreign boondoggling, if you will.

Those dollars, billions of them, were just as good American money — just as hard-earned — just as much the reward of our thrift — as the dollars we have spent during these three years at home giving work to the unemployed. Most of those dollars sent abroad are gone for good. Those billions, lost to us under previous Administrations, do not, by the way, include the other billions loaned by the United States to foreign Governments during and immediately after the War.

I ask you the simple question: Has it not been a sounder investment for us during these past three years to spend eight billion dollars for American industry, American farms, American homes and the care of American citizens?

I have used the figure of eight billion dollars as representing the net increase in our national debt. Immediately people will rush into print or run to the microphone to tell you that my arithmetic is all wrong. They will tell you that the increase in the national debt is thirteen billions instead of eight. That is technically and morally just as correct as if someone were to try to scare you about the condition of your bank by telling you all about its liabilities and not telling you about its assets.

That is technically and morally just as correct as telling you good people here in Pennsylvania that none of your bank deposits or insurance policies is sound.

When you are told that the United States Treasury has thirteen billions more of liabilities than it had in 1933, you should also be told that it has six billion dollars of increased assets to set off against these liabilities.

In three years our net national debt has increased eight billions of dollars. But in two years of the recent war it increased as much as twenty-five billion dollars. National defense and the future of America were involved in 1917. National defense and the future of America were also involved in 1933. Don't you believe that the saving of America has been cheap at that price? It was more than defense — it was more than rescue. It was an investment in the future of America.

And, incidentally, tonight is an anniversary in the affairs of our Government which I wish to celebrate with you and the American people. It is October first, and it marks the end of a whole year in which there has been not a single national bank failure in all the United States. It has been fifty-five years since that kind of record has been established. You and I can take this occasion to rejoice in that record. It is proof that the program has worked.

Compare the scoreboard which you have in Pittsburgh now with the scoreboard which you had when I stood here at second base in this field four years ago. At that time, as I drove through these great valleys, I could see mile after mile of this greatest mill and factory area in the world, a dead panorama of silent black structures and smokeless stacks. I saw idleness and hunger instead of the whirl of machinery. Today as I came north from West Virginia, I saw mines operating, I found bustle and life, the hiss of steam, the ring of steel on steel — the roaring song of industry.

And now a word as to this foolish fear about the crushing load the debt will impose upon your children and mine. This debt is not going to be paid by oppressive taxation on future generations. It is not going to be paid by taking away the hard-won savings of the present generation.

It is going to be paid out of an increased national income and increased individual incomes produced by increasing national prosperity.

The deficit of the national Government has been steadily declining for three years running, although technically this year it did not decline, because we paid the Bonus this year instead of 1945. Without the Bonus the deficit would have declined this year also.

The truth is that we are doing better than we anticipated in 1933. The national income has gone up faster than we dared then to hope. Deficits have been less than we expected. Treasury receipts are increasing. The national debt today in relation to the national income is much less than it was in 1933, when this Administration took office.

The national income was thirty-eight billions in 1932. In 1935 it was fifty-three billions and this year it will be well over sixty billions. If it keeps on rising at the present rate, as I am confident that it will, the receipts of the Government, without imposing any additional taxes, will, within a year or two, be sufficient to care for all ordinary and relief expenses of the Government — in other words, to balance the budget.

The Government of this great Nation, solvent, sound in credit, is coming through a crisis as grave as war without having sacrificed American democracy or the ideals of American life.

145 ⟨Address at the Dedication of the Medical Center, Jersey City, N. J. October 2, 1936

Senator Moore, Mayor Hague, my friends and neighbors of Jersey City:

I DO not think there is any person with red blood in his veins who would not be thrilled by this wonderful sight. I am very happy to come here to take part in the dedication of this, the third largest medical institutional group in the whole of the United States.

The Mayor has been kind enough to say that this Medical Center would not have been possible without financial help from the Federal Government. But, my friends, remember that it was not just financial help that created this Medical Center. It was something more important than dollars and cents. It was a dream of your Mayor dating back many years. That is what built the Medical Center.

In the great work of taking care of sick people, the Federal Government and the local governments have been glad to play their part. It is true that the Public Works Administration in Washington has helped various communities to increase the capacity of American hospitals in the past two years by 50,000 beds.

During the depression the difficulty of obtaining funds through municipal or private sources would have meant a serious shortage in taking care of sick people and in giving them adequate facilities, had it not been for Federal assistance through loans and grants.

But there is another reason for increasing the bed capacity of the hospitals of the country. The medical and nursing professions are right in telling us that we must do more, much more, to help the small-income families in times of sickness.

Let me with great sincerity give the praise which is due to the doctors and the nurses of the Nation for all that they have done during those difficult years that lie behind us, often at great sacrifice, in maintaining the standards of care for the sick and in devoting themselves without reservation to the high ideals of their profession.

These professions can rest assured that the Federal Administration contemplates no action detrimental to their interests. The action taken in the field of health, as shown by the provisions of the splendid Social Security Act recently enacted, is clear.

For that Act does not only provide unemployment insurance for people who, through no fault of their own, get out of work. That Act contains four provisions dealing with health that are very often forgotten, especially in the heat of a political campaign. Those provisions received the support of outstanding doctors during the hearings before the Congress. The American Medical Association, the American Public Health Association and the State and Territorial Health Officers Conference, and I think the nurses' associations as well, came out in full support of the public health provisions. The American Child Health Association and the Child Welfare League endorsed the maternal and child health provisions.

This in itself assures the Nation that the health plans will be carried out in a manner compatible with our traditional social and political institutions. Let me make that point very clear. All States and Territories are now cooperating with the Public Health Service. And nearly all of them are cooperating in maternal and child health service, and in service to the crippled children of the Nation.

Public support is behind this program. Let me add that the Act contains every precaution for insuring the continued support and cooperation of the medical and nursing profession.

In the actual administration of the Social Security Act we count on the cooperation in the future, as hitherto, of the whole of the medical profession throughout the country. The overwhelming majority of the doctors of the Nation want medicine kept out of politics. On occasions in the past attempts have been made to put medicine into politics. Such attempts have always failed and always will fail.

Government, State and national, will call upon the doctors of the Nation for their advice in the days to come.

A great many years ago I discovered something, and so did Mayor Hague. We discovered a common bond, a common interest in the cause of the crippled child. That common bond has persisted through the years. I have tried to help in my limited way. Frank Hague has done a great service not only to you good people who are alive today in Jersey City and Hudson County, but a service that is going to last for many, many generations to come. It is a service than which there is none higher within the range or the bounds of human endeavor. Mayor Hague, his associates, and the people of this city have pointed the way for many other communities in the Nation. May they see and emulate the fruition of this splendid dream.

146 ⟨ Informal Extemporaneous Remarks at the Ground-Breaking Ceremonies of the Queens Midtown Tunnel, New York City.

October 2, 1936

(Federal public works program in cooperation with New York City.)

Mr. Mayor, Mr. Chairman, ladies and gentlemen:

THIS card is a very essential part of this ceremony *(referring to membership card in Operating Engineers Union presented to him before the ceremony)*. Without it, they would not start that shovel working.

I think the Mayor is right, and I hope he is right, about the capacity in which I am to come back here in 1939. But even if I am then a private citizen, I do want somebody to ask me to ride through the tunnel in the first procession that goes through.

I go back a long way—I go back four years more than half a century—and that is why I am qualified to talk about the epic of Queens. It is one of the most amazing stories in all of modern civilization, the story not only of Queens, but of all these Boroughs of the City of New York. Half a century ago they were separate cities; and out here they were villages. Within our own lifetime, we have seen a great Borough in the greatest city in the world grow until it has more than a million human beings living within its borders. Those human beings deserve good transportation.

When I was a small boy there were only the old Brooklyn Bridge and a lot of ferries. Sometimes in the winter time, the ferries did not run because of the ice. If you wanted to get out into the country and see green fields and cows and chickens, all you had to do was to take a ferry across to Queens. I believe there are still half a dozen farms in this Borough, but their days, too, are numbered. So, in this half century of one generation, we have seen one of the greatest transitions that have ever occurred in our history.

I go back a few years to when I came back from Washington, after the World War, to practice law in New York. At that time I attended a conference, I think in 1921 or 1922, to talk about a tunnel from Manhattan to Queens. It is true that it has taken fifteen years to get action; but, on the other hand, as the Mayor said, it has taken only six or seven months since we put our shoulders to the wheel and got the bill through the Legislature at Albany. Now, here is the steam shovel.

I am very proud of what has been done. I am proud of the privilege that we have had in Washington in helping the City of New York to start and complete a large number of very important public works, public works that will be useful, public works that are giving employment to thousands of men and women. I also want to say that these public works which have been initiated would not have been possible had it not been for an intelligent and aggressive Administration in the City of New York.

Every once in a while your Mayor would slip down to Washington; and when I heard he was coming in I would say to myself, "There go another five or ten millions." But we have not minded. We have been proud to help because the things that have been initiated have been useful projects, things that have been badly needed. As you know, there were four or five years when interest rates were so high and the lack of teamwork so glaring, that we fell behind in this great city and in all the other communities, in carrying forward public works that were of the utmost importance. In these last three years, we have been trying to catch up; and I believe we are catching up.

I congratulate the people of Queens, the people of Manhattan, and the people of the whole city, on what is going to happen in about a minute and a half when, as a member of the Union, I press the button which will put the shovel in operation.

Are you ready? Let her go!

147 ❰ Rear-Platform Extemporaneous Remarks at Dubuque, Iowa. October 9, 1936

MY FRIENDS, I am glad to come to Dubuque. I had planned this visit way back last spring. I planned it with a very great citizen of this State and of this city, and I am only sorry he cannot be with us today.

Louis Murphy was a great and kind man, a close friend of mine. Instead of talking politics, I want to read to you a few sentences from a very wonderful tribute which was paid to Louis Murphy at the time of his funeral here. I want to read them to you because these words are not political, and yet they are concerned with better government all over the United States.

In this tribute Father Sheehy said this about the late Senator:

"When Senator Murphy was vested with the responsibilities of his high office, millions were subject to varying degrees of privation and want. Drastic measures were necessary, and perhaps some of them, as the late Senator himself admitted, may have been unwise. But he could not stand idly by and do nothing.

"The people of Iowa in electing Senator Murphy to the Senate vested him with the responsibility of championing a new social order in which class and privilege would be abolished. Four years of devastating want had all but extinguished the sacred fire of hope in their hearts. Senator Murphy was determined that the young people of this generation might be allowed to live normal, self-respecting lives. He voted for every relief measure, but he knew that the bread of charity was bitter bread and he was concerned that the problem of unemployment should be solved. He had no sympathy for those who would destroy private property. He knew that all rights are human rights. He did not wish to destroy the savings of the industrious and the more fortunate; yet he rejected both in theory and in practice irresponsible individualism.

"To him social justice meant primarily that the common good must, particularly in such times as these, take precedence over personal gain. He was determined that no one should starve in this land of plenty. He fought with all his powers to keep a balance between the prices of farm produce and those of products of city workers.

"In his struggle for what he thought right, Senator Murphy kept a cool, detached mind, ignoring the swarming tribe of rabble-rousers who today make both our hearts and our ears ache."

And so, the spirit of Louis Murphy will long hover over the City of Dubuque and the State of Iowa.

It seems to me, my friends, that there is a great moral lesson in what I have read; there is a great lesson which points the direction toward which our country must go.

I am out here on what I suppose some people will consider a political trip. Nevertheless, I am primarily concerned about the future of the country; we all are. I am trying to gain better first-hand information as to the needs of the country in the days to come. It will be useful to me, whether I am reelected or not. I am merely one comparatively small unit among those concerned in the future of the country. Its future lies, today and in the days to come, in the hands of you good men and women, especially young people; and I am not worried so long as its conduct remains in your hands.

Now, I am going to look at some projects.

148 ❧ Rear-Platform Extemporaneous Remarks at Oelwein, Iowa. October 9, 1936

MY FRIENDS, I am very glad to come through here today. I have never been in this part of the State before, and it was about time for me to come here.

You know, I find it terribly hard after four years to start in making political speeches again. One reason is that for the last four years I have been so engrossed in trying to bring things back, and that goes far beyond the mere lines of party politics.

There is one mighty nice thing about these trips, and that is that, so far as I can tell in going along the railroad, the expressions on the faces of the railroad men make me know that they are now all right. After all, we are all tied in together economically, and that is the lesson I am preaching. We shall not have successful railroads, we shall not have more employment on the railroads, unless the farmers are prosperous; and the farmers cannot be prosperous unless the city dwellers have enough money and enough work to buy what the farmers produce.

And so it goes all the way through the whole scale of human endeavor. The small merchants cannot sell their goods either to the farm population or to the city population unless there is buying power. What we have been trying to do in the past four years, from the point of view of economics, has had a comparatively simple objective — getting people work and producing buying power for them.

As I go through the country this year, in comparison with 1932, I see an enormous difference — an enormous difference in the prosperity of the country as a whole and in every part of it that I have visited.

I am not making one kind of speech in the East and another kind of speech in the West. I am not making one kind of speech to farm people and another kind of speech to industrial workers. In the last four years we have gained a great knowledge of the interdependence of every part of the Nation with every other part. If the men and women who work in clothing factories in the City of New York are out of a job, they do not buy so much pork. That kind of example goes for every known product of the land.

I am especially glad that the railroads are getting back on their feet again. Of course the Government has had some share in getting them back on their feet again. We loaned them a lot of money, and they are repaying it. It was a good investment. In just the same way, the Government has helped to get the banks back on their feet; we loaned them some money, and it was a good investment.

And so my friends — this is not a prepared speech — I just want to talk to you as one neighbor to another. I don't pretend to be a farmer; I happen to be by profession a lawyer. But I have farmed the best part of my life, up on the Hudson River and down in the State of Georgia, so I do know about some of the problems of agriculture in the United States. Every day that I go through this country I try to learn more about it; and that is going to stand me in good stead whether or not I go back to the White House for the next four years. And, incidentally, I get a tremendous kick out of it.

It is good to see you all.

149 ❪ Rear-Platform Extemporaneous Remarks at Hayfield, Minn. October 9, 1936

I AM glad to come to this section of Minnesota. I have never been on this railroad before. I hope in the next three or four years to come through by automobile and get a better idea of this country.

One of the things we ought to think a lot about in this campaign is what has happened to our national point of view in the last four years. In every section of the United States we have gained the understanding that prosperity in one section of the country is absolutely tied in with prosperity in all the other sections. Even back in the Eastern States and cities, they are beginning to realize that the purchasing power of the farmers of the Northwest will have a big effect on the prosperity of the industry and of the industrial workers of the East. In just the same way, I know you realize that if the factories in the big industrial cities are running full speed, people will have more money to buy the foodstuffs you raise.

I am told by the experts — and it is an interesting fact — that if every family in the United States lived on what might be called a class-A diet, that is the kind of diet that the doctors and dietitians would like us all to have for our own good and our own health, we would have to put 40,000,000 acres more land into production of foodstuffs.

In the last analysis, it comes down to the question of purchasing power. And we have raised the purchasing power in this country from about thirty-eight billion dollars in 1932 to over sixty billion dollars this year. And we have not stopped yet.

It is good to see you all. *(A telephone wire was being strung into the train at that moment.)* You know, one of the interesting things about trying to campaign and be President at the same time is that in almost every station we come to, there is a telephone message from Washington, and they string a wire through a car window and somebody talks directly from the train with one of the Government Departments, perhaps with the Treasury Department in relation to the stabilization of foreign exchange, or with the State Department in relation to what is going on, perhaps, in far distant lands. Here I am, pretty nearly in the center of the country, and yet I can keep in touch with the Government in Washington almost every hour of the day or night.

(Audience: Are we going to fight?)

I hope we will never fight again as long as you and I are alive. The interesting thing is that while affairs are in pretty dangerous condition in Europe and in other parts of the world, this good-neighbor policy that we have established pretty satisfactorily in this hemisphere, not only with Canada on the north but with all the Republics on the south, seems to be catching hold among the people themselves in other parts of the world. If in the long run the people themselves get it, then those who rule those countries must get it too. So I believe that our foreign policy is really making for peace throughout the world.

Good-bye and good luck.

150 ⟨ Informal Extemporaneous Remarks at Dowling School for Crippled Children, Minneapolis, Minn. October 9, 1936

THIS welcome that you children have given me reminds me very much of the welcome that the children give me down in Warm Springs, Georgia. Down there, as up here, there are a lot of them in wheel-chairs and a lot of them with crutches and a lot of them with arm-rests, but they have the same kind of cheerful faces you have.

I am glad the Federal Government has been able to help the School of Minneapolis, especially in building the swimming pool. I hope that all of you will be able to learn to swim, because that is about the only exercise I can take, and I know how much you will enjoy it if you learn.

It is fine to come here today. I am glad to see all of you. I wish I could go through the School and see the work you are doing. Some day I know that I shall be able to come and have the time to see all that you are doing.

151 ⟨ Campaign Address at St. Paul, Minn. "This Administration Is Determined to Continue in Active Support of the Ever-Growing Farm Cooperative Movement." October 9, 1936

(Tribute to the late Gov. Floyd Olson — Interdependence of all sections and groups in the Nation — Prosperity of agriculture and industry dependent on each other — Administration's support of farm cooperatives — Reciprocal foreign trade agreements — The effect on world trade and world peace.)

Senator Shipstead, Chief Justice Devaney, my friends of Minnesota:

MAY I first of all tell you of the great thrill that I have had during the past two hours in driving through St. Paul and Minneapolis at the wonderful reception that you have given me?

As most of you know, I had planned to visit Minnesota on my trip of inspection to the drought areas the end of August. The untimely death of the Secretary of War kept me away. It was at that time also that this State suffered a very great loss in the passing of a virile, magnetic and liberal American leader, Floyd Olson. He had been my friend for many years. I miss him greatly today.

Much water has run over the dam since those days in 1932 when, as Governor of New York, I was the guest of Governor Olson in this very building, the day that he presided at a great gathering in this city. During these more than four years, one of our most important national achievements has been the strides that we have made everywhere in thinking in national terms. And if I remember it, sitting in Governor Olson's office with him, occupying at his insistence his Governor's chair, that was what we were talking about in those days—making America safe in national terms. As a result of those four years America has never been so united as it is today.

In Iowa and in southern Minnesota on one or two occasions I have used the example that the great industrial centers of the East have come to realize that their prosperity is dependent on the prosperity of the farmers of the West. We have come to understand that the agricultural prosperity of the Northwest is directly affected also by the agricultural prosperity and the city prosperity of all the rest of the country. I have farms—two of them—one in New York and the other in Georgia. Georgia will buy Minnesota flour if Georgia gets a decent price for its cotton. Minnesota will buy overalls made of Georgia cotton if Minnesota gets a decent price for its wheat.

People in the manufacturing cities will find more employment at better wages if the farm families of the Nation have the wherewithal to purchase manufactured goods. And the farmers of the Nation will sell larger crops at better prices if the industrial workers in the cities have more money to buy dairy products, vegetables, fruit, pork and beef.

These are lessons, national lessons, that seem very obvious to us today, and yet it is not so very long ago that we had no policy at all about them.

In our local and sectional relationships also—relationships between the different farm regions and between city and country—we have in these four years come to recognize the closeness of the interdependence and the usefulness of the cooperative ideal.

Minnesota is a good place to talk about farm cooperatives. Here dairy and live-stock farmers have pioneered and pointed the way. Here and in Wisconsin have been built the greatest cooperative organizations in the Nation for processing and marketing dairy products.

When three and a half years ago the Administration undertook to meet the desperate and long-neglected needs of agriculture, we turned to the cooperative idea, and called to Washington representatives of the great cooperatives and other farm organizations to work out a program with us.

The Triple A itself had as its foundation and its essence the cooperative idea. Administered locally by community committees selected by the farmers themselves, it was a picture of economic democracy in action. I pay my tribute — with the rest of the Nation — to the patriotic zeal of the committees of farmers who did so much through their earnest cooperation for our adjustment and conservation program. The farmers of America will not forget what they have done, and what they are doing.

This Administration, from the very start, came to the support of the cooperative ideal by vigorous action. That support has continued. That support will continue.

It established a central bank for cooperatives with twelve regional banks to aid in marketing and purchasing.

It held out the helping hand of credit to production credit associations to enable farmers to finance production through their own banks.

The Triple A worked directly with the cooperatives in their marketing agreement program. By loans to cooperatives we helped to bring the comforts of electricity to many farms of the Nation.

We did not stop at merely lending money. When farm prices were threatened, the Administration held them up by purchasing surplus products through farm cooperatives for distribution to hundreds of thousands of families faced with hunger in our great cities.

Nevertheless, while the Federal Government can help through its resources — and you know the many ways in which we have used national resources to help localities — we in Washington have recognized that cooperation and cooperatives must come from the people themselves. Government can see to it that the rules of the game are fair as between cooperative enterprise and other enterprise. But the initiative, the management itself, must spring and carry on from the bottom up, rather than from the top down.

This Administration is determined to continue in active support of the ever-growing farm cooperative movement.

I am happy in the strengthening of this movement at home. But, my friends, let us remember that the same spirit of cooperation is an essential part of our relations with the other Nations of the world. It is this realistic factual appreciation of the benefits of cooperation that lies behind our consistent and successful efforts to reestablish foreign markets for our farm products.

You will remember back three and a half years ago, in the spring of 1933, our American foreign trade had fallen off to about a third of its former value. That was what I inherited.

Let us go back to fundamentals once more. The very word "trade" means articles of commerce flowing in two directions. It is not a one-way street. At last we have come to understand this in our domestic trade within our own borders. For instance, no single State can produce either crops or merchandise and continue indefinitely to sell them to other States for money alone. Eventually, they have to be paid for in other products as well.

Foreign trade is just like that. There cannot be a revival of foreign exports without a revival of foreign imports — unless, of course, we do as we did between 1920 and 1930 — lend our money to foreign Nations to enable them to buy our own farm and industrial products.

But I have a suspicion that America has learned her lesson once and for all about that kind of frenzied finance.

The Secretary of State of the United States has spoken in Minnesota clearly and unequivocally in regard to the trade agreements that have been made with fourteen foreign countries for mutual trade advantage. He pointed out to you the chapter and verse of the statistical record which shows what these argreements have accomplished to increase the trade and income not only of the industrial workers, but of the farmers of the Nation. It was not a question of winning or losing any treaty. Mutual advantage has been the successful objective; and our exports during the first half of this year, as compared with last year, have increased by one hundred and thirty-two million dollars.

To Canada, our neighbor on the north, the twenty-four million dollars of our increased exports during the first six months have included exports not only of manufactured articles but also of agricultural products. American industry and American agriculture are both benefiting by increased general trade. The figures prove it; and our growing consumption and better farm prices prove it.

I wish every American — city dweller and farmer alike — could fasten this home truth in his memory: When the Nations of the world, including America, had jacked their tariffs to the highest point and enacted embargoes and imposed quotas, farm prices throughout the world were at their lowest, and world trade had almost ceased to exist.

Today, under the leadership of the United States, other Nations of the world are coming to recognize that home truth. Back in 1932, although there was a tariff on wheat of forty-two cents a bushel, you all know that the wheat which you produced up here in the Northwest was selling as low as thirty cents a bushel. There were no farm imports then to worry about; but low prices were plenty to worry about.

Within the past two weeks splendid progress has been made in giving a greater stability to foreign exchange. Within that same time there have been lifted many quotas and embargoes including those on important American agricultural export products.

But, my friends, the increasing restoration of trade, the increase in industry, the increase in employment — they all serve more than a mere economic end. For three years we have had faith that it would turn us and other Nations away from the paths of economic strife which lead to war and toward economic cooperation which leads to international peace.

Peace cannot be attained in this old world of ours just by getting sentimental about it. Peace depends upon the acceptance of the principle and practice of the good neighbor. That practice is

founded on the Golden Rule, and must be fortified by cooperation of every kind between Nations.

Peace makes money; peace saves money for everybody. A prosperous world has no permanent room in it for dictatorship or for
war. In striving for peace, I am confident that the American people seek it with their hearts and with their heads as well. Enlightened self-interest is justification for what we do.

Confident in the practical wisdom of the ends we seek, with full
faith that it will serve in a practical way for peace on earth and
good-will between men and Nations, we shall continue on our
way.

152 ⟪ Rear-Platform Extemporaneous Remarks at Creston, Iowa. October 10, 1936

I AM glad to get into this section of the State. I understand that
you good people were pretty hard hit by the drought this year. As
you know, I have been going around the United States trying to
get first-hand information in regard to drought conditions and a
lot of other conditions.

I am glad to come here for another reason. I understand that
Henry Wallace was born about fourteen miles from here.

Down in Washington we have never had a Secretary of Agriculture, certainly not in our generation, who has understood farm
problems as well as Henry Wallace, and who has tied them into
the national economy as well as he has.

Creston is a pretty good example of what I mean when I speak
about national economy. There are a lot of railroad men in this
town; and there are more jobs on the railroads. The railroads of
the country are picking up. We have helped them with Federal
loans, which, by the way, they are paying back, but their prosperity is caused more by the fact that a greater volume of goods is
moving over the tracks. That involves national economy in the
best sense. It means more food products, more manufactured
products, and, most important of all and behind it all, more pur-

chasing power. Looking at you people, I should say that, in spite of the drought, you have more purchasing power than you had in 1932.

At the very beginning of my Administration the Federal Government undertook to help in raising purchasing power. Yes, we incurred a deficit in doing it, but I shall put it to you this way: Suppose I were to say to anybody in this crowd, "If you, by borrowing $800, could increase your annual income $2,200 every year, would you do it?" Well, that, in effect, is what happened in this country. We increased the national debt a net of a little less than eight billion dollars but we increased the annual national income over twenty-two billion dollars.

Of course, in a campaign, all kinds of figures are presented, but most of them are presented by people who have never read the budget of the United States Government. And you can take my word for it — as one who has read it a great many times — and it is bigger than a Sears Roebuck catalogue — that what I am telling you is strictly according to the figures.

I am glad to have been here. I wish I could get out and drive around and see conditions. As you know, we are using every means at the disposal of the Federal Government to prevent droughts as serious in the future. We cannot regulate the weather altogether, but we are cooperating with the different States and the local governments in trying to prevent future droughts from being as disastrous as they are today.

153 ❧ Rear-Platform Extemporaneous Remarks at Red Oak, Iowa. October 10, 1936

I AM glad to have a chance to come into this section. I have been hearing a lot about it from Congressman Wearin in Washington for a good many years.

It is a big problem that we are facing. It is a problem which is going to be solved for one very good reason, and that is that the people of the United States know more about government today than they did four years ago.

I realize, of course, that you have had a drought in this part of Iowa, a pretty severe drought. You know the steps we are taking in cooperation with the local and State Governments to remedy these drought conditions, and so to order things that, while we shall have droughts again, their effects, in the future, will not be so serious as they have been this year.

Yet, at the same time, we know that there can be conditions which are the exact opposite of drought — the possibility of piling up surpluses of agricultural products such as we were faced with when I first went to Washington. We all know the results of those surpluses as well as we know the results of droughts. What we are trying to do is to bring about a balanced system of economy in the United States, and I believe that the people all over realize that no one section of the country can be prosperous unless the other sections of the country are also prosperous.

The city dwellers have to have money to buy food and more food. Last year, somebody in the Department of Agriculture, in cooperation with a lot of expert doctors and dietitians, made a survey of what the people of the United States eat. Then they classified as Class A, the diet that we all ought to have. Diet B was graded as a pretty good diet but not the best. And they found that, as a Nation, we are living today in the United States, on the average, on Diet C. That is the actual fact.

Why is it? It is because people have not the purchasing power for either a B-diet or an A-diet. Incidentally, if all of us had the proper kind of diet in the United States, we would have to put 40,000,000 acres more land into the production of foodstuffs.

In these past three and a half years it has been a tremendously interesting experience to go around the United States and survey agricultural problems. We have made some real strides, but we have not gone far enough yet. We are going further along the lines we have laid down already, and, at the same time, we are going to work on new things.

Somebody in this campaign said something about a farm policy

425

that changes its model every year. Well, isn't the automobile better than it was twenty years ago? It is the same principle. Every year they get out a model that is a little better than it was twenty years ago. And so, while Model-T farming may have been all right ten years ago, we have got away from it and we now have a model 1936 farming.

It is mighty good to see you. I wish I could go through the country in an automobile instead of on a train; but I am going to come back during the next four years.

154 ⟨ Rear-Platform Extemporaneous Remarks at Pacific Junction, Iowa. October 10, 1936

Good morning.

We have had an awfully interesting couple of days. I can see by looking at your corn that you people out here in this corner of the State have been through a drought. As you know, we are doing all we can by the principle of cooperation between local government and State Government and Washington to improve drought conditions all through this area from here west. I think we are getting somewhere.

Of course there are all kinds of campaign stories going around to which the average citizen with a little common sense does not pay much attention. Just for example, we got a telegram on the train this morning from a certain section of the country that there are a lot of people going around to people's homes saying that, if I get reelected, the debt of the United States is going to be liquidated by levying a tax on everybody's home and farm in the United States. That is a pretty good idea of what some people are reduced to. And yet, you know it is an interesting fact that there are still some people in this country who do not know that taxes on real estate are levied only for local and State purposes. In fact, in most States they are levied for local purposes only.

We have been learning a lot in the last four years about government. Just so long as we keep on taking an interest in government, I am not much worried about the future of the democratic form of government under our Constitution.

You hear a lot about debts. Well, a little farther up the road I put a question to a big crowd. We have borrowed eight billion dollars more than we owed four years ago and here is the question: Suppose somebody came to you and said: "If you will borrow eight hundred dollars, it will increase your income every year by more than twenty-two hundred dollars," would you do it or not?

Well, all you have to do to get a picture of American national finance is just to add a whole lot of zeros to those figures. In other words, we have gone into debt a little less than eight billion dollars net, but our annual income today is over twenty-two billion dollars more than it was in 1932. I call that a pretty good investment.

I am looking forward to coming out here again during the next four years. Things here are a lot better than they were in 1932 and things are going to be a lot better by 1940 than they are now.

155 ❨ Informal Extemporaneous Remarks at State Capitol, Lincoln, Nebr. October 10, 1936

(Increase of national debt outweighed by increase of national income — Model-T farming out of date — Work relief as opposed to dole.)

Governor Cochran, Mayor Bryan, my friends of Nebraska:

I AM glad to come here, to be here in the presence of so many old friends. It is so long since I have been in this capital city of the State, that this wonderful structure that I face had not then even been started.

I have seen — in fact all the people of America have seen — photographs of this wonderful capitol building. Every one of them ought to come here and see it — a great structure, worthy of a great State.

I am not here to deliver a formal, carefully prepared address to you. I want to talk to you for a few minutes just as one of your fellow Americans who has great privileges. One of the privileges which I have in abundance is that of getting to know the United States. I suppose that I have been not once but a good many times in every State in the Union. One of the great lessons of the last three and a half or four years is the need of our thinking in national terms, because we have come to realize that anything that harms one State harms all the States. And back in the East, back in the great industrial centers, they have at last come to realize that they cannot be prosperous there unless you people are prosperous out here.

That has been one of the cardinal impulses that has directed all of our program during these past three years in Washington — the thought that we had to help everybody and not just a few people here and there. And as I have come west over the railroads, I no longer see the long trains of empty cars on the sidings. I see engines, that had been laid aside in 1929 for lack of use, being brought out of the shops, put on the tracks, and started down the rails with a string of freight cars behind them.

Why is that? It is because the freight cars have something to haul. And the reason the freight cars have something to haul is because people have money to buy things with — that is pretty obvious. The national income of the United States this year will have risen from about thirty-eight billion dollars in 1932 to well over sixty billions in 1936. In other words, it seems to me like a fairly simple mathematical question to put to you. If somebody that you trusted were to come to you and say, "Look here, will you borrow $800 so as to get an increase in your annual income of $2,200?" would you do it or not?

That is what has happened to our national finances. All you have to do is to add a lot of zeros to those figures. We have borrowed a net of eight billion dollars more in these three and a half years, and we have increased the national income over twenty-two billion dollars — and that is a pretty good investment.

You know, during a campaign I always like to have a few days in between trips, so that I can sit quietly for an hour or two or perhaps go to bed and, before I turn out the light, read some of the things that the other fellows are saying.

I got a telegram this morning on the train from a woman in Nebraska who was complaining that people are going up and down through this State, going to farms and going to homes, and saying to the families in those farms and homes: "If this man Roosevelt should go back into the White House, what will he do? Why, he will slap some kind of tax on your home and your farm and take it away from you to pay the national debt."

Now, my friends, I believe in this motto right in front of me on the capitol — "The Salvation of the State is Watchfulness in the Citizens." For the last three and a half years the citizens of this country have developed a watchfulness and an understanding greater than they have ever had before; and because of that they are going to be able to distinguish the true from the false in this election.

Of course most people — I will not say everybody, but give us a few more years and it will be everybody — most people understand that taxes on real estate are levied in great part for the benefit of local government, and in some States in small part for the maintenance of State Government. There never has been, and there never will be, a Federal tax on farms or homes, as long as I have anything to do about it.

Yes, I get a lot of amusement — I was going to say a big kick — out of this campaign.

Somebody, talking about the national farm program of the last three and a half years — which, by the way, is operated in conjunction with the State Governments, the State colleges and the local county committees right down to the individual farmer — said that it was just like an automobile: its model was changed every year.

Well, I accept that simile; it is good. In other words, the automobile, like farming, improves through the years, and the policy relating to the automobile and the policy relating to farming ought to have a new model every year. I want to express to you

429

my belief that the Model-T type of farming may have been all right between 1920 and 1930, but it is out of date today.

Of course, as you know, the Federal Government, working with the local governments, has made possible the saving of homes, and the saving of farms. You know also that the great bulk of all that money that was loaned is going to come back to the Treasury. In the same way because it is all part of the same picture, the money we have loaned to keep the railroads going until the production and consuming power of the country could catch up is also being repaid. The money we loaned to keep the banks open — and, by the way, for the first time in fifty-five years, there has not been for this whole year a national bank failure in all the United States — that money, that saved the banks, is coming back to the Treasury.

Some money was not merely loaned. That is true. Some money was spent to keep a good many million families from starving in these three and a half years — to give people work instead of a dole. I believe in work and not in a dole. That money was spent in a good cause, and, as one of my high-class business friends from New York remarked to me the other day, "If there were as little waste by corporations in spending a sum like that as there has been in the Federal expenditure of that money, there would be fewer bankrupt corporations in the United States today."

It comes back to your motto: "The Salvation of the State is Watchfulness in the Citizens." Read, learn, mark, and inwardly digest — and "inwardly digest" means separating the wheat from the chaff of a national campaign.

I believe — I know — that the American people know how to separate the wheat from the chaff, and that is why I am confident of their verdict on the third day of November.

156 ❨ Campaign Address at Omaha, Nebr. "The American Farmer Living on His Own Land Remains Our Ideal of Self-Reliance and of Spiritual Balance." October 10, 1936

(Indorsement of candidacy of Senator George W. Norris — The Administration's accomplishments in behalf of agriculture, farmers, and land conservation — Future farm program — Farm tenancy — Crop insurance.)

Mrs. Hitchcock, Governor Cochran, Mr. Mayor, you my friends of Nebraska and neighboring States:

I AM glad to come back to Nebraska after an absence of only a few weeks; and I am especially glad to come for the first time to this marvelous Aksarben Coliseum, and to receive your greetings.

First of all, a word to you as Nebraskans. I hope that this word will be heard by the citizens of the other forty-seven States, because I know that what I am going to say represents the conviction of the great majority of those who are devoted to good government, clean government, representative government.

On this platform sits a man whose reputation for many years has been known in every community — a man old in years but young in heart — a man who through all these years has had no boss but his own conscience — the Senior Senator from the State of Nebraska, given to the Nation by the people of Nebraska — George W. Norris.

Outside of my own State of New York, I have consistently refrained from taking part in elections in any other State.

But Senator Norris' name has been entered as a candidate for Senator from Nebraska. And to my rule of non-participation in State elections I have made — and so long as he lives I always will make — one magnificently justified exception.

George Norris' candidacy transcends State and party lines. In our national history we have had few elder statesmen who like him have preserved the aspirations of youth as they accumulated the wisdom of years.

He is one of the major prophets of America.

Help this great American to continue an historic career of service.

Nebraska will be doing a great service not only to itself, but to every other State in the Union and to the Nation as a whole, if it places this great American above partisanship, and keeps George Norris in the Senate of the United States.

I want to take you back four years, to 1932. In that year, when I was a candidate for the Presidency, I pledged my Administration to a farm policy that would help the farmer. Tonight every man and woman on an American farm, east or west, who has read today's market reports knows that we have done what we said we would do.

What needed to be done?

You remember that in March, 1933, after twelve lean years, farm income was disappearing and farm prices had sunk to a bankruptcy level.

In 1932 America's farm population was the greatest in our history, and yet the farmers' income was the lowest for the quarter century for which we have records. Farmers represented 25 percent of the Nation's population—but they got only 7 ½ percent of the national income.

The spectre of foreclosure stalked the farmer's plow.

American agriculture was on the road to pauperism.

When the World War ended, the Nations of Europe whom we had been feeding went back to farming for themselves. Our farmers were left holding the bag—a bag that bulged with vast quantities of wheat and corn and cotton for which the market had disappeared.

That was the farmer's plight. What did Republican leadership do about it?

The best that it could offer was the Farm Board, a contraption that set an all-time high for extravagant futility. It met the problem of unsalable and unexplorable surpluses by piling up bigger surpluses.

To finish the job, the Republican Smoot-Hawley tariff robbed the farmer of his last chance for a foreign market.

We found that this conspicuous failure of Government to help the farmer had created — by March 4, 1933 — a state of mind in the Nation which, itself, seemed to bar the way out for the farmer's difficulties. There was a defeatist attitude — a conviction that the farmer could not be helped, that all efforts were foredoomed to failure, that any party which dared to substitute action for talk would get its political fingers burned.

Along with this defeatism there was the belief that money spent on the farm problem was money wasted — that the only excuse for spending it was to keep the farmer in line — to buy political peace.

That was what had happened to American agriculture when this Administration came into office.

That was the débris of twelve years of failure which we had to clear away before we could begin to lay the basis for a permanent agricultural prosperity.

Tonight you know that the ground has been cleared of that débris. After twelve years in which he has been harassed and weighed down by the burdens of each succeeding day, the farmer at last has begun to get into the clear, so that he can begin again to take thought for tomorrow.

Back of what we did was the conviction that the agricultural problem is not a problem for the farmer alone — that it is a problem for the Nation as a whole. That is the way we attacked it.

And the Nation is now going along with the farmer. Now for the first time in this industrial period of our history, the American people understand that there is a definite bond between agriculture and industry, that the money we have used for the restoration of American agriculture has been an investment in the restoration of American industry, an underwriting for the wages of American labor, a stimulus for profits in American business.

The defeatist attitude has at last itself been defeated.

Back of what we did was a second conviction — that a sound

farm policy must be a policy run by farmers. Ours is that kind of policy. The farmers of America moved into the Department of Agriculture on the day that Henry Wallace set up shop there. For the very first time, a national farm program was made in conference with, and with the agreement of, the farm leaders of all our farm organizations — a program which came out of the free and open councils of farmers rather than out of the vote-catching schemes of politicians.

With these convictions, this Administration put its hand to the plow. It has not turned, it will not turn, back.

I am going to tell you in just seven sentences what we have done. Every man and woman on an American farm can expand these seven sentences in terms of the recovery that has come to each of them in the last three and a half years.

First, by our Agricultural Adjustment Act, our monetary policy, our soil conservation program, and our assistance to farm co-operatives, we have raised the farmers' net annual income by three and a half billion dollars to a sum three times what it was in 1932.

Second, through the Farm Credit Administration we have saved thousands of homes and farms from foreclosure and have reduced the staggering burden of the farmers' debts.

Third, through reciprocal trade treaties and international currency stabilization, we have begun to recover the farmers' foreign markets in the only way in which they can be recovered and held — by a policy of mutual international advantage which today is bearing fruit in the reopening of markets for American farm products in all of the fourteen countries making these agreements — by a policy which, for example, within the last ten days has brought about lower tariffs in France, Italy and Switzerland for the benefit of our farmers. And, my friends, a growing trade is making for international peace.

Fourth, by our program to revive business, to increase employment, to raise business and professional incomes and the wages of labor, and to increase the purchasing power and consumption of the average American family, we have restored national income, and prepared the way for the steady and long-time expansion of the farmers' home market.

Fifth, by our program of land use and conservation we have ended the policy of immediate glut and eventual waste, and have laid the basis for a permanent plenty.

Sixth, by our program of rural electrification, by our farm-to-market roads, by our aid to rural schools, we have begun to get for the farmer his fair share in the comforts, the advantages, the wider interests and the deeper satisfactions which go to make the good life for himself and for his children.

And seventh, when disastrous drought struck the land in many parts of our country, we rushed immediate and direct relief to the farmers and stockmen to save them from want—a policy that some people call waste, but that you and I call wise.

There is the record. In those seven sentences, the farmer and the farmer's family can measure for themselves the vast difference between the desperation which was theirs in the spring of 1933 and the recovery which is theirs in 1936. From what that record has done and is doing for you, judge for yourselves our determination and our capacity to carry this program through.

After having neglected a twelve-year opportunity for help to the American farmer, as his condition got worse and worse, what does Republican leadership now offer?

First of all, it would scrap the present program, which it has condemned as a "subterfuge" and a "stop-gap." It would junk the farmers' organization to carry it out. It would end the farmers' program of cooperation, and send them back to the "free competition"—or "rugged individualism" if you will—that wrecked them in 1932.

Next, it would substitute a system of tariff equivalent payments, not for any permanent contribution to farm wealth or national income, but merely as a cash hand-out—in other words, a dole. These payments, under their plan, would be made only to the producers of exportable farm crops—specifically hogs, wheat, cotton and tobacco. Dairymen, cattlemen, sugar growers and pro-

435

ducers of other varieties of crops of which there normally is no exportable surplus would be left out.

What about the effect of such a scheme? Would it serve to protect farmers from price collapse under a burden of surpluses? Would it guard them in the future against a disaster like 1932?

No plan could lead the Nation back faster to such a crisis.

The proposed plan of the Republican leaders is a straight subsidy of unlimited farm production. In a year or two of normal weather, it would pile surplus on top of surplus, driving prices down and down and down. It is the Federal Farm Board all over again, and it means nine cents for corn again as it did in 1932.

Finally, to make the parallel with 1932 letter perfect, the Republican leaders now propose to repeal the Reciprocal Tariff Act, and go back to the old Smoot-Hawley tariff policy. Once again, as in 1932, the farmers would have price-crushing surpluses at home, and no place abroad to sell them.

What about the cost? It would run to one and a half and possibly even two billion dollars every year. This vast sum would be spent not to save agriculture, but to wreck it and with it to wreck the Nation.

Either this plan which they advocate in the West, or the curtailment of expenditures which they talk about in the East, would have to be discarded. Both promises cannot possibly be carried out at the same time.

For the first time in many cruel years, we are getting the problem of the business of farming well in hand. Do you now want to turn that problem over to the care of those who did nothing about it in the past? Do you want to turn it over to those who now make inconsistent, campaign-devised, half-baked promises which you and they know they cannot keep?

It has been said that the Administration's farm program changes each year like new models of automobiles. I accept that simile. The automobile of today is the same kind of vehicle, in principle, as it was twenty years ago. But because the automobile manufacturer did not hesitate to pioneer, because he was willing to make yearly changes in his model, the Nation now drives a car that is vastly improved. Farming, too, is the same in principle now as it has always been. But because the farmer has been willing to pioneer, because, with the aid of scientists, economists and engineers he has been willing, year after year, to change, because of these things both the product of the farms and the business of farming have been vastly improved. It is the aim of our policy not only to prevent the return of yesterday's model, but to make tomorrow's model better than today's. Good as it was in the old days, we have passed beyond Model-T farming.

Our long-time policy of prudence and farm progress includes a program of conservation against land wastage and soil impoverishment. From the beginning, such a program has been basic in our plans. On October 25, 1935, months before the action of the Supreme Court on the Triple A, I said publicly that it was the intention of the framers of that Act as it was my intention "to pass from the purely emergency phases necessitated by a grave national crisis to a long-time more permanent plan for American agriculture."

We knew that our soil had been recklessly impoverished by crops which did not pay. Because we stand committed to a philosophy of continuous plenty, we have set ourselves resolutely against waste—waste that comes from unneeded production, waste that imperils the Nation's future by draining away the abundance with which God has enriched our soil.

Increasing production alone in an unlimited way appeals to no person who thinks the problem through. Increasing consumption must go hand in hand with it. Here is a simple figure to mull over. If every family in the United States had enough earning capacity to live on what the doctors and dietitians call a Class-A Diet, we would need foodstuffs from forty million acres more than we are using today. America's diet is better than that of most other Nations, but from the point of view of better national health, it is still inadequate. I seek to increase purchasing power so that people can pay for more food and better food, and in turn provide a larger and larger domestic market for the farmer.

437

It is a further part of our long-time farm policy to attack the evil of farm tenancy. In this we have already made a good beginning with lower interest rates and better prices. We are preparing legislation, in cooperation with farm leaders, to submit to the Congress in January to help solve this problem. We cannot, as a Nation, be content until we have reached the ultimate objective of every farm family owning its own farm.

Further, we propose to give to the farmer and to the consumer, a sound plan of crop insurance in kind against extreme fluctuations of supply and of price. No one wins from such fluctuations except the speculator. The farmer and the consumer lose together. That is why crop insurance is a protection for both. At one and the same time it banishes the consumer's fear of a food shortage and the farmer's fear of a food surplus. Until both are protected, neither is safe. The ultimate interests of the farmer and the consumer of America are the same.

That, my friends, is why I am not making one kind of speech to the farmers out here and another kind of speech to consumers in the big cities of the East. The same speech and the same policy must go for both.

It has taken a lot of education in these last few years, but the city dweller has now come to know that unless the farmer receives fair prices for what he produces, he cannot buy the things that are turned out in the shops and factories of the cities.

And so we plan for the future of agriculture — security for those who have spent their lives in farming; opportunity for real careers for young men and women on the farms; a share for farmers in the good things of life abundant enough to justify and preserve our instinctive faith in the land.

In all our plans we are guided, and will continue to be guided, by the fundamental belief that the American farmer, living on his own land, remains our ideal of self-reliance and of spiritual balance — the source from which the reservoirs of the Nation's strength are constantly renewed. It is from the men and women of our farms, living close to the soil that this Nation, like the

Greek giant Antæus, touches Mother Earth and rises with strength renewed a hundredfold.

We want to perpetuate that ideal, we want to perpetuate it under modern conditions, so that man may be strong in the ancient virtues and yet lay hold of the advantages which science and new knowledge offer to a well-rounded life.

157 ❨Informal Extemporaneous Remarks at Fort Warren, Cheyenne, Wyo. October 11, 1936

(Benefits of travel — Inter-American highway — American example for peace.)

General Humphreys, ladies and gentlemen:

I AM glad to come back here. As you know, I am not a stranger. I think it was in 1920 that I first came to Fort D. A. Russell. I was here four years ago after the name had been changed in honor of a very old friend of mine, Senator Warren. I am glad to come back here today, not only because it is Sunday, and a day off, but also because it is an anniversary. This happens to be Mrs. Roosevelt's birthday. So I am having a very nice home party.

I was telling the General when we were out a little west of here and saw the rifle ranges, that my only worry was that these boys who learned to shoot in this clear atmosphere would not be able to see the targets when they get back to the effete east.

It's a grand country. In traveling through this part of the West I always feel that Cheyenne is a sort of crossroads of all this part of America. It corresponds, as I said to Senator O'Mahoney this morning, to the same position in our country as the Panama Canal occupies between North and South America — one of the crossroads of travel from the north to the south and the east to the west, and it is a pretty fine crossroads to come back to.

As a matter of fact, one of the great things that has happened is the pick-up in travel. I am very, very happy back in the State of New York, when I hear of people who are going to get in their automobiles and get to know their own country. There are more and more of them doing it every year. There are more and more people from the coast and the plains who are coming East each year and seeing some of our scenery. In up-state New York, you know, we are quite proud of that scenery, even though our highest point is only about five thousand feet, about a mile lower than you are here. But a mile up in the air in New York State seems very, very high.

Every year that goes by we in this country are getting to know each other better. It seems to me that sectional lines are getting narrower and narrower. We are beginning to appreciate more deeply that we talk the same language and have the same point of view about life.

It is fine that this Nation is setting an example for peace in the world. And that is a good thing to say on a Sunday; it is also a good thing to say at an Army fort; and I know that the Army agrees with me in that statement just as much as you men and women civilians do.

And that is one reason why we have a very fine though a very small Army—because we are keeping our Army in training in the interest of peace. I think we are making strides in the sense that we are setting an example for other Nations in the way of peace. Certainly on this continent our neighbors to the north in Canada, and to the south, all the way down to Cape Horn, have begun to realize the point and the objective of the ideal of the good neighbor. In this entire hemisphere, all the way from the North Pole down to the South Pole, there isn't any war going on anywhere at the present time, and we are very proud of that.

I have talked about travel, about getting to know our own country. In December there is going to be held in the capital of the Argentine Republic a great conference of the twenty-one American Republics in the interest of more firmly cemented peace in this hemisphere. I think probably one of the topics down there is going to be the building of a great highway all the way from North America down through Central America and into South America. By such a highway, we people up here can get to know our neighbors on the south — can take a holiday, put the family into an automobile and drive down through Central America and across the Panama Canal and all the way through to Chile or the Argentine.

It will give us, a Nation of one hundred and twenty-five million people, a chance to get to know those other Americans who are pretty fine human beings and should get to be better known. It will give them a chance to meet us up here and see more of us. That is the kind of thing which is going to help keep peace in the world — a better knowledge of the peoples of the world.

I always reflect about this when I come to a place like Cheyenne, where there are hundreds of people passing through every hour. I am glad they are able to come here to get some of the fine spirit of Wyoming. I know a good deal about it, not just because Senators and Representatives from Wyoming tell me about it, but because I have seen it first hand. I am very glad to have been able to have this holiday with you today, and I hope to come back and see you again very soon.

158 ⟪ Rear-Platform Extemporaneous Remarks at Greeley, Colo. October 12, 1936

Good morning. I have just got through breakfast; and I am glad to come back here to be introduced by Fred Cummings, who is an old friend of mine.

The last time I stood here, I think, was with Mrs. Roosevelt in 1920 when I was running for Vice President. A lot of things have happened since that time.

For example, I know of a lot of things that have happened to the beet-sugar industry. I want to tell you a story about that. It relates to beets, and it relates to a lot of other products. Way back in the campaign of 1932, a man brought on the train a chart showing the fluctuations of prices of various raw materials and agricultural commodities — cattle, sheep, corn, cotton, wheat, sugar, minerals such as gold, silver and copper, and so forth and

441

so on. I found from that chart that some of these commodities had fluctuated an average of 400 percent up or down between 1920 and 1932. Well, I do not believe there is any permanent prosperity in a commodity that fluctuates 400 percent up or down, any more than there is in a mortgage or a home that fluctuates 400 percent up or down.

Therefore, back in 1932, we laid plans to try to iron out these up-and-down fluctuations and get commodities to more stable year-in and year-out price levels.

I think we have accomplished a good deal along that line. Sugar beets form one pretty good example. The average grower of sugar beets has recognized the fact that he is better off, if, when he puts his seed in the ground, he knows approximately what the price is going to be when he harvests his crop, than he would be in a highly fluctuating, speculative market. Whenever there are great fluctuations in prices, the only seller who really ever makes money is the speculator. That is why we have tried to stabilize the prices of various farm commodities and other commodities as well.

I say this merely to give you one little slant on the general policy that the Government has been following during the last four years. I think that in the long run it is a sound policy for the country as a whole, whether it applies to the raw products of the soil or to the raw products of the mines.

If you are interested in following it further, go and get a chart of the prices of any of these raw materials from the nearest library and see what I mean. If you will follow the line showing the prices as they have advanced or declined, you will see a zigzag that will horrify you even if you check it back for only fifteen years.

I am going on from here down to Denver, and then farther down to Pueblo. It is the first time that I have been down in the middle part of the State since I took office in 1933. I have, however, been what they call "a traveling President." I have been trying to keep in personal touch with the Nation. I have been pretty well all around Colorado and I have touched a corner of Colorado several times. I am glad now to be able to get into the middle of the State and see at first hand some of the conditions. It is going to help me during the next four years.

159 ⟨ Campaign Address at Denver, Colo. "We Have Sought and Found Practical Answers to the Problems of Industry, Agriculture, and Mining." October 12, 1936

(Administration's accomplishments in behalf of miners, stockmen, and sugar-beet producers — Conservation of water — Soundness of our monetary system.)

AMERICA pauses today to honor Christopher Columbus—a great Italian whose vision and leadership and courage pointed the way to this new world of ours. Once launched upon this great voyage, he did not turn back. There were those who offered him the counsel of despair. There were those who thought that the price they were paying was too great. But the valiant admiral, firm to his purpose, sailed on. And all America pays him tribute today.

The spirit that animated those voyagers four centuries ago is not alien to these Western plains and mountains. You are scarcely removed one generation from men and women who, cast in the same mold, sought to conquer nature for the benefit of the Nation.

It is from the rich diversity of climate, soil and people that this country has always derived its strength. The lives of you men and women in the mountains and plains are tied up with those on the farms and in the cities.

In our unified national economic life, we have come to realize that industry is not immune if agriculture or mining languishes.

The great but uneven prosperity of the nineteen-twenties

443

made us neglect for too long the growing signs that things were not going right with the farmer and miner.

Surely by now we have learned that lesson. Surely you remember the idleness of your gold and silver mines, and your copper, coal, lead, and zinc mines, your oil fields, your railroads, your farms, your ranches; all of them had suffered together in the collapse of prices and income.

And when that stream of business had dried on the farms and plains and in the hills, the stream of business throughout the Nation also dried.

In the complete stagnation of business, of mines and of farms, there was only one agency capable of starting things going again — the Government — not local government, not forty-eight State Governments, because they, strive as they would, had reached the limit of their resources, but the Federal Government itself. And yet, up to March 4, 1933, the Federal Government held back, doing nothing except to lend dollars to people at the top with the vain hope that some of it would trickle down, and except to fold its arms, stand still and wait for a certain famous corner to come to it.

When this Administration came in, its first act was to discover where the corner was and then to turn it. The turning of it involved action, and the action was based on two obvious and simple methods of locomotion: first, by spending money to put people to work, and, second, by lending money to stop people from going broke.

It meant doing these two things in the industrial East, and in the South, and in the Middle West, on the Plains, in the Rockies and out on the Coast. We knew that the only practical way to turn the corner was to start the whole country turning the corner at the same time.

One of the first jobs we undertook was assistance to the miners and farmers in the West.

Those of you who now see business moving again in your local shops and stores and factories know that your merchant's goods began to move off his shelves for the first time and that the wheels of your factories and mills began to turn for the first time, only after the Government had begun to spend money and had provided employment for millions of people on all kinds of projects.

Of course, we spent money. It went to put needy men and women without jobs to work, and to buy materials the processing of which put other men and women to work. You on the plains and throughout the great mountain area can judge for yourselves whether the work was worth doing.

Washington did not originate the projects. You did. You told us where reclamation projects were needed. You told us where water should be conserved. You told us where floods should be controlled. You told us where new homesteads should be located. You told us how Denver wanted to get its new water supply. You told us where roads needed to be improved. You told us, in short, in every State and city and county throughout this great region and, indeed, throughout these United States, the most practical way of giving work and at the same time creating public improvements of a permanent, useful character. And in the overwhelming majority of cases your advice was good.

Today in the late autumn of 1936 it is a pitiful spectacle to see Republican leaders call this great program waste and extravagance, for they are the same leaders who, when their own State or city or county was involved, were the first to run to Washington pleading for Federal aid. Consistency is still a virtue in life, but when it comes to a campaign year "consistency" is a word that cannot be found in the Republican campaign vocabulary. And, at that, inconsistency is a mild term to apply to it.

Take the effective example of livestock. If we had had more irrigation, more reservoirs, in the past, fewer cattle and sheep would have been threatened with starvation on the range during the drought years.

Lack of foresight on the part of former Administrations compelled us to buy up sheep and cattle which otherwise would have died in their tracks from lack of food and water.

This Administration is proud that it spent money to buy cattle and sheep in those days.

Republican leaders tell us that this, too, was a policy of waste.

Who benefited? The stockman who found a market and was literally saved from bankruptcy; the banker who held the mortgage on the stock; the merchant with whom both the stockman and the banker dealt; the packer who processed the meat. But, above all, those who benefited most were the unfortunate men and women and children on the relief rolls — hundreds of thousands of families all over the country — to whom the meat was distributed. Even the hides of these animals were saved.

I call that work program and cattle-buying program an investment to preserve America — the whole of American national life. Do you call it waste?

Much talk is heard about imports hurting the cattle industry. But the simple truth is that cattle imports have always been small, and always will be small as long as we have good range in the West and maintain our soil fertility in the Corn Belt. Cattle imports were largest when prices were best, as in 1929. Cattle imports were smallest when prices were lowest, as in 1932 and early 1933. The income to cattlemen in the first six months of 1933, when Canadian imports were less than 500 head, was less than one half of what it was in the first six months of 1936, when Canadian imports were larger, but still were only a trickle compared to domestic production. I believe it is better to prosper with small imports from Canada than it is to sink into depression and stay there with no imports at all.

Our cattle programs were carried out in cooperation with the stockmen themselves. And now also in the protection and development of the range we are acting in cooperation with them. Stock raising is a major industry in America. Its successful future shall be preserved.

Twenty years ago I was in the Mississippi Valley at the time of a great flood. I saw the waters of the Arkansas surge into the waters of the Mississippi. I asked where those waters came from. They told me that a part of them had come hundreds and hundreds of miles—all the way from Colorado. Farther up the river I saw the Missouri discharging its waters into the waters of the Mississippi. I asked where these waters had come from. They told me that a part of them had come from the Dakotas, from Montana, from Wyoming and from Colorado.

In later years I saw the bed of the Arkansas River bone dry; I saw many of the tributaries of the Missouri River bone dry.

It has been a part of our program from the very beginning to conserve the water resources of the country so that the beds of the rivers of all the important watersheds of America will work for the people of all the States through which they run.

There is nothing new in this. Way back in the summer of 1934, when I was dedicating the Fort Peck Dam in Montana, I said:

"People talk about the Fort Peck Dam as the fulfillment of a dream. Why, it is only a small portion of a dream. The dream itself covers all the important watersheds of the States, and one of these watersheds is what we call the watershed of the Missouri, not only the main stem of the Missouri, but countless tributaries that run into it, and countless of the tributaries that run into these tributaries.

"Before man—before American men and women get through with the job, we are going to make every ounce and every gallon of water that flows from the heavens and the hills count before it makes its way down to the Gulf of Mexico."

I want to see that day come soon. It will help each and every State which lies between here and the Mississippi River. The work which we have already put under way to realize that dream is only a forerunner of what we hope to do in the days to come.

There were other resources of this great Western country, the development of which we undertook as an important and necessary part of the rounded objective. Take beet sugar for instance. I do not have to recite the record of steadily declining income in that industry before March, 1933. World production of sugar had expanded at such a rate that there was more sugar in the world than could possibly be consumed. What we tried to do, and what we succeeded in doing, was to adjust the supply of sugar so that a farmer who raises it gets a more adequate return. And you, the raisers of sugar beets, I congratulate not alone on better and steadier prices; I congratulate you also on the substantial reduction you have made in the employment of hired children in the fields. In this word of thanks I know I am joined by the fathers and mothers of America.

Take a final example. In these great mountain chains which extend from our northern to our southern border exists a storehouse of enormous wealth, its ultimate yield as yet unguessed.

The revival of industry, of farming and of transportation has provided a revival of mining—coal and iron and oil and copper and lead and zinc and many other metals.

But the Government has contributed by direct action as well. When we laid the ghost of the old gold parity of the dollar, when we purchased gold and purchased silver too, you in the mountains felt the old thrill of the search for precious metal. Old developments again became profitable. New developments sprang up. Mining became again an industry where men could find jobs.

The great bullion reserves now in the United States Treasury—and you in Denver know something about them—are sufficient to redeem every dollar of our currency far more than 100 percent; and yet people for partisan purposes are willing to spread the gospel of fear that our currency is not on a sound foundation. I tell you, and you know, that our monetary system is the soundest in the world today.

I tell you, and you will agree, that we are around the corner. Private employment is picking up. That means that Government expenditures for work for the unemployed are coming down. That means that the total of Government expenditures will decline. Turning the corner also means that Government income from existing taxes, without new taxes, is going up.

I repeat to you what I said in Pittsburgh two weeks ago, that decrease in expenditures and increase in income mean within a year or two a balanced budget and the beginning of reduction in the national debt.

When Republican leaders speak out here, they proclaim their sympathy with all these Western projects and promise you more and more of them. They cost money — they cost a lot of money. But when these same gentlemen speak to audiences in the East they proclaim that they are going to cut Government expenditures to the bone. If you will look in your history books you will find that about two thousand years ago there was an old Roman god named Janus. Janus had two faces. He faced both ways. He had two mouths. I need not explain that parable any further.

Are you willing to turn America, are you going to turn America over to those who in past years shut their eyes to the problems of this Nation?

This Administration has shown the way because it had the will to do.

We have sought and found practical answers to the problems of industry and agriculture and mining. We have clung to no outworn method as an excuse for failure to act. We have had faith not in panaceas, but in the courage and resourcefulness of men and women to meet their problems themselves if given a chance, an opportunity that is the right of every American. We have used the resources of Government to give that chance, not to a favored few, but to all the people of this great Nation with all of their richly diversified interests.

We are made firm by the same spirit that made Columbus surge on — by the same spirit that made the ancestors of you who dwell in these mountains and on these plains win through the untrailed wilderness, across turbulent rivers and unknown plains and deserts, over unscaled heights, to claim, develop and hold a new and great empire for America.

We have shown our determination in the past by action. You can trust us to prove that determination in the future by more action, sound action, action that is saving and will continue to save the Constitutional representative form of government in which all America rejoices.

160 ❲ Rear-Platform Extemporaneous Remarks at Colorado Springs, Colo. October 12, 1936

MY FRIENDS, four years ago we had a big crowd in Colorado Springs, and today it is just twice as big.

(Voice in Audience: Twice as many votes, too.)

That is a good idea; and I hope that you are also twice as happy as you were in 1932.

I am glad to see all these signs you display telling me to look at things. That is just what I am doing in coming out here, just what I have been doing on a good many trips in the last four years — trying to get to know this country better. I have seen the Garden of the Gods in Colorado Springs on several occasions before, and some day I want to come up here and spend a week or two.

You know, there has been a good deal of difference in tourists. In 1932, when I came out through here, there were a lot of tourists — but they were riding in box cars. This year there are more of them — and they are riding in Pullmans.

That is one thing I am very happy about. People all over the country have more wherewithal with which to travel and see their own country. I tell people back East that their duty is to come out West rather than go over across to Europe.

It is fine to see you all. There are a number of very distinguished gentlemen up here on the platform. Here is my old friend, your Congressman, the Senator and the Governor. And may I also present — I think you have seen this person before — may I present to you Mrs. Roosevelt?

161 ❲ Rear-Platform Extemporaneous Remarks at Pueblo, Colo. October 12, 1936

I GO back a good many years, to the campaign of 1920, when I spent most of a day and evening in Pueblo; and I remember that I spent a good part of the evening trying to beat Alva Adams in bowling at the "Y." But I think he was a better bowler than I was.

In going through this country this year I find that things certainly are a whole lot better than they were in 1932. In this particular section of the State I know that you are interested in a lot of things that I, too, am interested in — soil conservation, getting water on the land, irrigation, and the prevention of floods.

We have been trying to accomplish a great many of these things that are badly needed by people in various communities of the Nation. Up at the Capitol of the State this morning, I told the people of Denver, that in carrying out these public works of various kinds we were trying principally to construct those things that were recommended by the localities themselves, by the Governor and the people back home. The result has been that through this expenditure of money, we have done much to help prosperity back to its feet right at home.

You will notice, if you travel as much as I do, that there are very few empty freight cars standing these days on the sidings of the railroads of the country. A great many old engines have been brought out of the roundhouses and reconditioned. More engines are being built, more steel is being used in all kinds of construction — and you people in Pueblo ought to know about the use of steel.

As a matter of fact, the whole process ties in together. With the return of prosperity we are getting more tourists; we are getting more freight to haul on the railroads; we are getting better prices for our crops. I am looking forward confidently to a continuation of that renewed prosperity.

I hope to be able to come back here from Washington during the next four years and see how it has grown.

It is good to see you all. Next time I hope I can spend a little longer time, and perhaps Alva Adams will give me another chance to beat him bowling.

162 ⟨ Rear-Platform Extemporaneous Remarks at La Junta, Colo. October 12, 1936

I AM glad to come back to La Junta. I have been here many times before. It looks to me as if things are a little bit better than they were in this section four years ago, the last time I went through.

I do not have to talk to you people about the Arkansas Valley. You know this end of it a lot better than I do. I can tell you, however, that I have had a tremendous interest in all of the plans for the whole watershed of the Arkansas, from away back in the Rockies to the point where it hits the Mississippi River.

This morning I described in Denver what we are doing. We have a perfectly definite and sound objective. We want to make every drop, every gallon of water that runs down the river serve some useful purpose to mankind on its way to the sea. That is what we are trying to do in developing these irrigation and flood control projects. In about an hour, incidentally, I am going to pass through the site of what will eventually be the Caddoa Dam.

I am sorry to be a little bit late for the melon season. But I believe they found a few late comers which are on board the train; and we are going to have them for supper tonight.

I am glad to come into a railroad town, because you people know of the splendid progress that railroad transportation has made in the last year. The reason that freight and passenger traffic is picking up all the time is that people on the whole have more money to spend.

Four years ago there were some tourists, but they were riding on the box cars and the roofs of trains. This year they are riding in Pullmans, and there are more of them, and there are going to be still more to come.

In connection with our railroad problem, we have been trying to tie it into the broad policy of social security; and that is one reason why the Railroad Retirement Act, that splendid piece of legislation, was passed by the Congress. I feel very certain that that statute, together with the Social Security Act, is going to do much good for the people of this country in the years to come.

If we can keep this new and sounder prosperity going at the same speed it is picking up at the present time, we need not worry much about paying back the comparatively small sum of money we borrowed to get recovery in the past four years.

163 ❦ Rear-Platform Extemporaneous Remarks at Syracuse, Kansas. October 12, 1936

My friends, I have been trying to persuade some of the Eastern people on this train that this is not Syracuse, New York. A good many of them I think have never been west of the Mississippi before, but I have been through here a good many times in my life. I am glad to come back.

As you know, I have been watching some of the difficult problems that you have had to face during this past summer. I realize what the drought has done all through this part of the country, and I want to tell you that I am very, very much interested in the work that the Federal Government is trying to do to alleviate drought conditions so that they will not be as bad in the future as they have been this year. We have an enormous number of national problems which we are trying to solve in a national way.

Things certainly are better. At least, people who raised only five or ten bushels of wheat to the acre got more than twenty-five or thirty cents a bushel, which was the price in 1932.

Because we know we always have to look ahead with respect to farming or business or anything else, the Federal Government has planned a program for the agricultural part of the Nation which is going to maintain prices. That is a long step. If, in addition to that, we can bring more water to the land where needed by keeping the water table up, and if we insist on using land only for its best purposes, then farming in the days to come will be a much more secure career for anybody than it ever before has been in our country.

The first thing we are trying to do is to stabilize prices. After all, you are not the only people who have been farming. I have done it myself both in the North and the South. One of the things we have suffered from most is the fluctuation of prices in the last ten or fifteen years, prices running up and down the scale as much as 400 or 500 percent. I want to be able to know, when I plant a crop, approximately what it is going to bring when I harvest it.

That is one of the results for which we are working. When you have these fluctuations, there is only one group which benefits from them — speculators. We want an agricultural system in which the growers of crops make the profits rather than the speculators in crops.

I am glad to get into Kansas again. I wish the train were not pulling out because I would like to say a lot more to you. Good night.

164 ⟨ Rear-Platform Extemporaneous Remarks at Garden City, Kansas. October 12, 1936

My FRIENDS, I am glad that we are able to stop here for a while but I do wish it were daylight. I am not going to make a campaign speech at this hour of the night. Some day I hope to get in through this section by daylight and see some of your problems at first hand. Of course, I have read about them and have read all the reports about the drought and about the subject of water conservation. I can say that your Government is extremely interested in the whole problem of water.

As I travel all the way down the Arkansas River, I am confirmed in the opinion I formed years ago — that in the watersheds out here in the West we have to aim ultimately at making use of every single drop of water that comes out of the heavens, as it comes down through all the States between the Rocky Mountains and the Mississippi River.

We have not only the problem of soil conservation; we also have the problem of floods. As you know, I am a great believer in trying to think and plan ahead. If we had thought and planned ahead twenty-five or fifty years ago we would be a good deal further along in the solution of both these problems than we are today.

Those problems and others which we face cannot be solved in the course of five years or ten years, but we have learned a great deal about scientific law. When I was a small boy, people did not appreciate nearly as much as we do today the dangers of flying in the face of Nature. I am convinced that by the cooperation of the Federal Government and the State Government and the local government, and by taking the advice of people who live on the land itself, we are going to make this whole country out through here a much safer place in which to live in the course of the next generation. We are aiming at security, security not just for one year or two years but security which comes from attaining the objective of making farming and cattle-raising real careers, by which a man and his wife and family can earn a decent living.

And that, in turn, is all part and parcel of what we are trying to do to provide security against unemployment and old-age distress throughout the United States. We do not pretend to be infallible in our efforts — but we are at least trying.

Well, the train is pulling out. Good night.

165 ❧ Rear-Platform Extemporaneous Remarks at Dodge City, Kansas. October 12, 1936

MY FRIENDS, I have been through here many, many times before. I wish that this time I could have been in this part of the State by daylight, because I have wanted to see as much of conditions here as I could with my own eyes.

I know some of the problems that you have had, especially in this drought year. But I am not going to talk to you about your own local affairs or about your State affairs because you know more about them than I do.

I do want to say a few words about what we have been trying to do all through this drought area during the past few months, and what we are going to try to do this winter and next spring.

The problem we are up against is almost nationwide. For while the drought area does not cover the whole Nation, the results of the drought affect people in the East and all the way out on the Pacific Coast. That is well borne out by the brighter side of the picture we have seen during these past three years—a renewed and growing prosperity which affects all parts of this interdependent Nation.

The fact of an increasing purchasing power means that the merchants in all of these towns are selling more goods. When they sell more goods, it means that the people in the industrial areas have more work, and if they have more work, they can eat more beef and more wheat. When they buy more beef and more wheat, the farmers are more prosperous. That is what makes it a rounded picture. While I recognize the fact, for instance, that you have had a mighty short wheat crop this year, it is just so much better that wheat is bringing a dollar a bushel or more instead of the thirty cents of four years ago. I think we are coming to recognize the interdependence of all groups all over the country.

I was saying this morning that three years ago, when I came through, there were a lot of tourists going through the West but that they were going through on box cars and on the tops of trains. Now there are more tourists, but they are going through in Pullmans.

And the cost of it? Yes, there has been cost in keeping people from starvation, in keeping people from losing their farms and their homes. But it is money not only well spent; it is money which is coming back a thousand times over.

What we have to do is to bring some of these figures with nine or twelve zeros after them down to a point where you and I can understand them. I shall put it to you this way. I shall put it in the form of a question: If somebody came to you and said, "If you will borrow $800 and by borrowing that $800 increase your annual income by $2,200," would you borrow it or not?

Well, that is about what has happened in the past three years. The Federal Government has gone into debt a net amount of eight billion dollars, but the annual national income has increased over twenty-two billion dollars.

I am fairly confident that if we keep things going the way they are now headed, if we tackle problems like the drought with the idea that you people and your children and your children's children are going to remain here and keep on being farmers or raising cattle in this section — I am confident that when I come back here again during the next four years I shall find things much better than they are today.

Incidentally, let me remind you that I am making the same kind of talk out here in Western Kansas that I am making back East.

This is, as you know, a very informal talk. I wish I could visit with you a little longer. I am going to ask you to excuse me, however, for a very simple reason. I have a sort of double duty to perform these days. I am a candidate for reelection, and this is, therefore, I suppose, a political trip. Nevertheless, at almost every station that we have come to, I have been receiving documents and papers to be signed and telegrams or telephone messages on which I have to take action. This afternoon there have been an unusually great number of things sent to me to pass upon. I have to remember the fact, therefore, that in addition to being a candidate I am still the President of the United States.

So, my friends, I am going to ask you to excuse me because I simply have to go back to work on mail and telegrams, if I am to get to bed before midnight. I wish you all sorts of luck. Good night.

457

166 ❧ Campaign Address at Wichita, Kansas. "We Are Coming Through a Great National Crisis with Flying Colors." October 13, 1936

(Increase of security, in its broader sense, at home and abroad.)

Senator McGill, my friends of Kansas:

I AM ESPECIALLY happy to come here at the time of this, your celebration of the seventy-fifth anniversary of the admission of Kansas to the Union.

In my boyhood days, one of my earliest recollections was going about fifteen miles back into Dutchess County, trying to shoot a woodcock. The place I went through was known locally as Kansas, and I often wondered why it was called Kansas. Long years later, in trying to find out the origin of the name, I ran across an old file of a local newspaper and found that in 1857 an enterprising railroad man had come into Dutchess County and had offered a free trip to Kansas to anybody who wanted to go there. That was one of the ways in which Kansas was settled, as you all know. Back there in Dutchess we feel that we have a special link with this State because a great many families, I think three or four dozen, came out here in those early days.

I come back here after four years to find that things have changed a good deal. I have noticed in traveling on the railroad that there is a different type even of tourists. Four years ago there were a lot of tourists who were riding in box cars and on top of trains. Today they are riding in their own automobiles and in Pullmans.

You know, on a day like this it seems a pity to have to mention an election. But we people have a habit once every four years of having a grand fight, and getting over it the day after election. November 3d is exactly three weeks from today and I expect to survive those three weeks.

If later on I shall have to write another book I am going to have a chapter in it about bedtime stories—political bedtime stories. It will be a very amusing chapter. I am going to fill it with whispering ghosts and stalking bogey-men, and I am going to end the chapter by telling how the American men and women on the third of November, 1936, refused to be frightened by fairy tales. You people do not look to me the least bit frightened.

And yet some people have been trying to tell you all kinds of things about what this Administration is seeking to do. They have tried, I am sorry to say, to spread the gospel of fear not only in the factories, which is an old outworn trick, but this year they are even trying to bring fear into the homes and firesides of America.

But I know that the people of this country have not such short memories. They remember only too well the real fear — the justified fear — felt all over the Nation in 1932, to be frightened by this silly false fear which is now being preached. The Republican leaders who are trying to do it, incidentally, happen to be the very ones whose blindness to facts and refusal to act caused the real fear and the real danger of national disaster in 1932.

What this Administration has done since 1933 to clear up the debris which had been left over by twelve years of neglect need not be repeated; you all know it. You know what the "devil-take-the-hindmost" policy of the nineteen-twenties brought down upon our heads. You know that the vast speculative gains of a few were made without any regard to the deep injuries which they were causing to the great masses of our people.

In the spring of 1933, these same speculators pleaded with me for help — help of any kind — just so long as it would save them from bankruptcy. Most people thought that they had learned their lesson. We hoped that they would join with our average citizens in working for some kind of security against a recurrence of those panic years.

Yet here they are — three years later — giving vague lip service to that word "security" and, at the same time, seeking to block, to thwart, and to annul every measure that we have taken to restrain the kind of individualism which hurts the community itself, individualism run amuck.

I use this word "security" not in the narrower sense of old-age pensions and of unemployment insurance, fine as these objectives are. I use it in the broader sense — confidence on the part of men and women willing to carry on normal work, and willing to think of their neighbors as well as themselves, confidence that they will not have to worry about losing their homes, about not having enough to eat, about becoming objects of charity. Add to that one more objective: that all Americans may have full opportunity for education, for reasonable leisure and recreation, for the right to carry on representative Government and for freedom to worship God in their own way.

That philosophy has been the philosophy and the practical objective of your national Administration at Washington. I do not seek to discuss with you the pros and cons of your local government or of your State Government in Kansas. You know more about that than I do. Let me say only, and in very simple terms, that I do not believe that Kansas would have pulled through the difficult problems of the past four years as splendidly as it has, had it not been for Federal cooperation and Federal assistance in many fields of your endeavor.

If you think we were wrong to give this assistance, then, to be logical, you must ask that in the days to come every State in the Union shall set itself up as an individual entity for the solution of all of the problems of all of its inhabitants, save possibly the maintenance of the Army, the Navy and the handling of our foreign affairs.

Our broader interpretation of security and of the methods of procuring it is well illustrated by what you have seen us do. Our endeavors have fallen into three broad classifications.

First, immediate and direct assistance — including work for the unemployed; help for drought areas; buying of drought-stricken cattle; building of ponds and irrigation projects; seed loans; assistance to the youth of the Nation, and dozens of other instances of that kind.

Second, protection against recognized abuses of many kinds — including the battle of the Federal Government against kidnapping, blackmail, bank robberies and other menaces to life and liberty; safeguarding innocent investors against fake securities; the regulation of stock exchanges; regulation of overreaching practices of some utility companies and the establishment of power yard-sticks to force reasonable electric rates; elimination of unsafe banking practices.

Third, the reduction of interest rates; the saving of farms and homes from mortgage foreclosures; the insurance of bank deposits; the loans that have been made to keep railroads going; the assistance given to States, counties and cities, enabling them to build much-needed, useful public works; old-age pensions; unemployment insurance; assistance to rural schools; the C.C.C. camps; farm-to-market roads. These, and many more like them, give you a broad picture of the more permanent and long-range measures, many of which will improve not only your lives, but those of your children as well.

There was at one time a school of thought in this country that would have us believe that those vast numbers of average citizens who do not get to the top of the economic ladder do not deserve the security which Government alone can give them. And in the past, unfortunately, that philosophy has had too large a hand in making our national economic policies. That school of thought left Washington on March 4, 1933.

The farmers of the Nation furnish a very good example of what Government can do, not only in direct help, but also in providing security for the future. From a state of collapse in 1932, agriculture has not only been brought back to life, but has also received the encouragement of Government which enables it to face the future with confidence.

Is there among the many farmers in this audience, a single one who would want to go back to the uncooperative formula — the rugged individualism, the economic freedom of 1932?

Don't you and your wife and your children look forward to a

461

safer, better future today than you did three and a half short years ago?

I have used farming as an illustration of greater security because Kansas is a great farming State. You know, however, that the mining areas and the livestock areas and the industrial areas of the country are likewise receiving their share of a greater security. Every part of the Nation is sharing it together.

Last April in the City of New York I dared to talk farming to a New York City audience. I told them that one of the best things that had come out of these three years was the realization by city dwellers that they could not be prosperous until the farmer was also prosperous. In the same way I have dared to talk to people in great agricultural States about the needs of the industrial workers in the big cities, and how closely their welfare is tied up with the lot of the farmer.

People who are spreading the gospel of fear talk about setting one class against another. They have intimated that farmers belong to one class, industrial workers to another, and business to still another. I deny it. They all belong to the same class, for the very simple reason that none of these occupations can survive without the survival of the others.

The people who talk about these class distinctions are the very ones who are encouraging class antagonism. For they tell one story in the East and another story in the West; they tell one story in the city and another story on the farm. That is not my way, and never will be my way.

Taking it by and large, we are coming through a great national crisis with flying colors. We have not lost our self-respect. We have not changed our form of government. We have a net national debt which, though greater in dollars, is actually less in proportion to the income of the Nation and in proportion to the wealth of the Nation than the national debt was on March 4, 1933.

From the point of view of national income and national wealth, we are better able to bear our debt now than we were then. And, within a year or two, with income increasing and expenditures declining, we shall be able to balance the budget, and start paying down on the debt.

There is one final form of security on which I have not yet touched. In addition to security at home and in the home, we have sought for security from war with other Nations. We have not been content merely to talk about peace. We have done something about it. We are trying to break down the economic barriers, to soften the economic rivalries, to end the economic strife between Nations; for these have been the causes and fore-runners of war. We have taken the lead among the Nations of the world in restoring economic peace which is so essential to military peace.

In the whole of the Western Hemisphere, all the way from the North Pole to the South Pole, we have preached, and we have gained recognition of, the doctrine of the good neighbor. We have extended the right hand of fellowship. Many Nations of the earth have taken that outstretched hand. We propose, of course, no interference with the affairs of other Nations. We seek only by force of our own example to spread the gospel of peace throughout the world.

We are gaining peace and security at home. I am confident that I have the support of the American people in seeking peace and security abroad.

167 ❲ Rear-Platform Extemporaneous Remarks at Florence, Kansas. October 13, 1936

(A better balance of price levels.)

MY FRIENDS, I have been out through these parts many times before, as you know. In every State I have been in, which in-cludes not only the agricultural States but the industrial States as well, things seem to be coming back. People, on the whole, are a lot better off than they were four years ago.

There is no panacea either of mind or medicine that the Nation can take that will cure it of all its ills overnight. But, as you know, we in Washington have been trying to build up a great many things all through the country that needed to be built up, realizing that the industrial workers in the cities cannot be prosperous unless the farmers are prosperous too. You can see the results by watching the railroads. The old strings of empty cars on the sidings that we used to see from 1929 to 1933 are almost all out at work, going up and down the line, full of various kinds of products.

At the same time, we have worked for a greater security for the people. One of our basic troubles in the past was found in the fluctuation of prices. Some time ago, I got a chart showing the prices which raw materials of all kinds brought between 1920 and 1933. That was a period of about thirteen years, and the line indicating prices was a zigzag line that went up and down and up and down. The farmer, the miner, the producer of industrial goods could never know what he was going to get because of this fluctuation. And so we have been trying to work out what might be called a more ordered economy, a more stable price level.

To use a simple example: if you borrowed or loaned a thousand dollars this year, we have tried to see to it that by 1940 when you pay the money back or get the money back, you will pay or receive the same kind of a thousand dollars that you handled originally instead of dealing in debts which had to be paid, for instance, as occurred not so long ago, with dollars worth three times as many bushels of wheat as when they were incurred. There were many hundreds of thousands of debts that were incurred when wheat was selling at a dollar a bushel but fell due when wheat was selling at 33 cents, so that it took just three times as many bushels of wheat to pay them off. That just is not right; and so we are trying to work for a better balance of price levels in order to prevent its recurrence. It is going to take a number of years to do; but I think the people of this country want stability and security in their economy, so that they will know from day to day, from year to year, that the future is not going to leave them objects of charity.

It is a big task that we have before us. I do not pretend to be the final word as to whether we are going to accomplish it or not; but I do know that in these past four years we have been getting somewhere, and I am determined that we will continue to get somewhere farther in the next four years.

168 ⟨ Rear-Platform Extemporaneous Remarks at Emporia, Kansas. October 13, 1936

MY FRIENDS, I am very glad to come to Emporia. But I do not see Bill White. *(Laughter, applause.)*

I wish he were here because I have known him for a great many years, and he is a very old friend of mine. He is a very good friend of mine for three and a half years out of every four years.

(Somebody in the audience said that Mr. White was in the audience and coming up. The President said, "Where is he?" Mr. White then came toward the rear platform.)

Hello, Bill, glad to see you. Come on over here. How are you?

Now that I see him, I shall not say anything about the other six months. *(Laughter, applause.)*

You get so much politics in Emporia both ways that you do not need any political speech, but I do want to say this: I have been tremendously impressed all through this summer and autumn with the great interest that is being taken by the voters of the United States in national problems. It has been demonstrated in the last week or two by an increased registration and by increased enrollments. I am quite confident that we shall have several million more voters go to the polls this election day. That is entirely as it should be. I believe also that the people, more and more, are making up their own minds. They are not believing everything that is said to them; and I am quite certain that they are not believing everything they read.

(Audience: "No.")

In other words, they are winnowing out the chaff from the grain; and it is a fine thing that the public in this country is taking such an interest in its own Government.

Yes, the people are not being swayed this year by some of the things that have swayed them in the past because, taking them by and large, our economic problems are in far better shape than they were four years ago. I think they are sounder than they have been for a great many years.

Certainly everything I have seen on this trip makes me know down in the bottom of my heart that the people appreciate that things are better and are sounder. We have a little more time than we had in those days to make up our minds about things. Thank the Lord, we are going into this election with a smile on our faces.

The bitterness that comes up every four years in our American system of government does not last and that is good too.

And so, my friends, I am very glad to have had the chance to stop here. I always wish on these trips that I could go through by motor instead of by train; that I could talk to more people; that I could see more of the problems of industry and agriculture at first hand.

I think I must have been preordained for the career of the commercial traveler because I like to travel so much. It is one of the great privileges of the Presidency that I have the opportunity to go around this country so that I may get a first-hand picture of conditions.

Some day I hope I shall be able to come back to Emporia and spend a little more time with you and, when I get back, it may be in one of those three-and-a-half-year periods when Bill White is with me.

(The President then turned to Mr. White and said, "How are you? All right?" to which Mr. White replied, "Fine." There was a great deal of applause when the President shook hands with Mr. White.)

169 ⟪ Rear-Platform Extemporaneous Remarks at Olathe, Kansas. October 13, 1936

I AM glad to come here, but I wish that I could spend a little bit more time than I am allowed on this trip. I am glad to come to this home town of former Governor Hodges.

I have been tremendously interested in coming through Kansas today to see with my own eyes a lot of things I have been reading in reports back in Washington. I could not get here on the trip to the drought areas. You have had some pretty hard times with your crops in this State; but I take it that conditions here this year are not quite as bad as they were in the western part of the State.

I think you all realize that what we have been trying to do for agriculture in the past three years has been aimed at greater security for the men, women and children on the farms. I think we have got somewhere.

Somebody remarked that our agricultural policy was like that of the automobile makers—a new model for every year. I accept that simile; I think it is a pretty good one. Each year we are making great progress in our national policy toward agriculture.

Of course, it has to be a national policy. It cannot be forty-eight different kinds of policies. And each year, in working toward the ultimate goal of security for agriculture, we not only have changed the laws, but we plan to continue to change them. We are not changing the fundamental objectives; but we are saying, just like the automobile manufacturer, that while the principle of the car is the same as it was twenty years ago, we have got past Model T. While Model-T agriculture may have been all right ten years ago, we do not want it any more. We have got beyond it.

There is no question, also, that our objective of a greater stability of prices for crops is something that the whole Nation not only needs, but wants. Certainly it is important for us not to go back to nine-cent corn and thirty-cent wheat and two-cent hogs. Having put the price level back to a more reasonable figure, we believe that we shall be able to keep it there.

Yes, this year we are planning; and why not? After all, that is one of the things that Government is intended to do, to think not in terms of just this year and the next, but, for the good of the people, to think for many long years ahead.

When you build a schoolhouse—and I know you have built some new schoolhouses in Kansas, some of them with the help of the Federal Government—you are building it, not just for the number of children who will attend school this year, but you are thinking ten and twenty years ahead. You know from experience that the improvements which go on in education have not stopped going on. You know that the improvements have to continue in the future in every single thing we do, just as they have in the past. That is the simplest way of expressing the philosophy that lies behind the kind of government we have been trying to give in the past four years.

One of the important factors in trying to work out a Government program in these past four years has been the fact that we tried to give to the communities every assistance based on what they themselves decided were their needs. Through these years, our whole farm program has been built up with the co-operation of the farmers themselves. We are trying to get the best cross-section of expert opinion we can find.

That has been the basis of what we have been trying to do, and I think in another four years we shall be able to carry the country a good many steps farther toward a greater security and prosperity.

Good-bye and good luck.

170 ❧ Campaign Address at Kansas City, Mo. "America Will Have to Be Led in the Days to Come by the Youth of Today." October 13, 1936

(The Administration's efforts in behalf of the youth of the nation.)

Governor Park, Mr. Mayor, my friends of Missouri:

IT IS good to see once again smiling faces, and to hear happy cheers from young America.

I have just come through Eastern Colorado and Western Kansas — parts of our national dust bowl — where deep holes in the ground and swirling clouds of dust show the erosion which years of man's neglect have wrought in the soil. And in your own States you have all seen other examples of waste in the physical resources of our country — water, trees, birds and other wild life.

But through the years of this depression we have had destruction even more tragic than that — waste in men and women, in human skill, character and life. Of all of the appalling waste of the days of false prosperity and recent disaster, human erosion has been the most calamitous.

There was, unfortunately, for a long time in the high places of Government in Washington a school of thought that human waste was the concern only of private charity and local communities. We have learned a lot since those days. We no longer believe that human beings hit by flood, drought, unemployment or any other national disaster should be left to themselves with the sole help of such charity as may be locally available to them. We know from sad experience that there may not be enough to go round.

Government since March 4, 1933, has begun to take stock of the human resources of the Nation and it is determined to preserve them.

As we take stock, we recognize that the most priceless of our human assets are the young men and women of America — the raw material out of which the United States must shape its future.

Nature's deepest instinct is the concern in every parent's heart for the welfare of the children. It is a law of nature which equals even the instinct for the preservation of life itself. Indeed it is part of that law, for without the preservation of youth, the race itself would perish. And so, the highest duty of any Government is to order public affairs so that opportunities for youth shall be made ever broader and firmer.

We Americans have never lost our sense of this obligation. To a greater degree than any other peoples we have sought to give each rising generation a little better chance in life than the one that preceded it. The little red schoolhouse for the education of the young, and the church for the training of their spiritual qualities, have always been the first structures to rise in every new settlement, as our ancestors pushed new frontiers through the wilderness. The school is the last expenditure upon which America should be willing to economize.

Those of us who helped build up the fantastic jazz era of the nineteen-twenties, which crashed down over our heads, must feel a peculiarly deep sense of responsibility to our boys and girls who were sunk with us in the ruins.

I need not remind the young people of this country of the black future which lay ahead of them in those days. That was the era of the wanderers — boys and girls who had grown tired of living on the vanishing savings of their parents, and who had set out on the highways in all directions to look for work which they could not find.

Those in school and those out of school could not look forward to a place in the community. The door of opportunity had been slammed in their faces.

Hanging around on street corners, roaming about the country in bands vainly looking for work — there was the real danger which America faced.

When the history of the dark days out of which we are now coming is written, it will be said that the great marvel of this period was that those young people have come through, with a full faith in democracy and with a high resolve to preserve it at all costs.

Cities couldn't help, counties couldn't help, States couldn't help. Even big business couldn't help. They had all come to the end of their resources. The youth of America had apparently come pretty close to the end of the road.

That was the condition that confronted your Federal Government on March 4, 1933. Your Federal Government acted.

Before it laid its hands to any other problem — and there were many of them — it set up the C.C.C. camps to put an immediate end to that hopeless condition. It cost money to do that, just as it cost our pioneer fathers and mothers money to build the schools in which we have all been trained.

We have done much in the way of a beginning to remove the things in America which have made for waste in human beings. On the farms and in the cities — throughout the Nation — we are starting to remove those glaring inequalities, those deep-rooted maladjustments which did so much to bring about disaster.

The American people joined with us in 1933 to start this job. A vast majority of the American people in 1936 are with us to see it through. We have made the start in these days, confident that you — the youth of the country — will carry on to finish the job.

That is why we have a national youth program. That is why through our C.C.C. camps and the National Youth Administration we are trying to keep young people at useful work or in useful education. In high schools and in colleges the Federal Government has lent a helping hand in keeping youth at the job of learning. Out in the woods, out in the open, the Federal Government has kept the self-respect and the health of hundreds of thousands of young people.

The Federal Government for many years has spent a good many millions of dollars — well-spent dollars too — to conserve our forests, our crops and our livestock. We believe in that kind of conservation. You all know how much we have done in that kind of conservation. But now we have begun to spend money on much more important conservation — to save the energy, the ability and the spirit of youth. No money was ever better spent.

Nothing has made me happier on this trip than seeing at first hand that the youthful hitch-hiker has disappeared from our highways and from the box cars and freight trains. The youth of the land can once more look forward with confidence and courage just as we of the older generation did in our day.

No greater satisfaction can come to me than the realization that the youth of America understand what we have tried to do — and approve. They know that the price we have paid to save our country has been worth while.

America has lost a good many things during the depression. Some of them needed to go; I am glad that they have gone. We have lost, for example, that false sense of values that puts financial success above every other kind of achievement. We have lost a little of our cocksureness, a little of the bumptiousness which the Pharisee had when he thanked God that he was not as other people. We have lost something of that feeling that ours is an "every-man-for-himself" kind of society, in which the law of the jungle is law enough.

But many things we have saved — things worth saving. We have saved our morale. We have preserved our belief in American institutions. In this world of ours where some Nations have taken perilous detours, we have faced our problems and have met them with a democracy. Within that democracy we are determined to keep on solving them.

We have saved above all our faith in the future — a faith under which America has only begun to march.

In that march America will have to be led in the days to come by the youth of today.

It has been our job to clear the ground of what in too many places was a social and economic wilderness. That pioneering has only begun. It will be for you to continue it.

You will discover that in pushing forward this great program of social betterment and social security, you will be met by the same opposition, the same relentless resistance which faced the frontiersmen of the early West. You will find that your fight against selfishness and injustice, against oppression, and, above all, against war, will take you into a man-sized struggle.

I am telling you this not to discourage you, but to stimulate you. Our fight — yours and mine — is to keep our democracy safe by keeping it moving forward. In such a fight it is an unhappy place to be on the side lines. To the young people of America I say: Join with us; ours is the real struggle to continue and preserve democracy in America.

171 ⟨ Rear-Platform Extemporaneous Remarks at Carrollton, Mo. October 13, 1936

MY FRIENDS, I am very glad, after an absence of only a little over a month, to come back into Missouri as the guest of my old friend the Governor, and of you good people.

There is one great advantage that this State has. In order to get from the East to about twenty other States, you have to go through Missouri. And your geographical location is such that you get in this State a pretty good bird's-eye view of people from the East and from the West and from the North and the South. That is one reason why Missouri is a good barometer of political conditions. At the present moment the barometer says, "fair and warmer."

(Audience: "Pretty hot.")

We have had a perfectly grand day coming through another famous State, Kansas. And then this evening, before supper, I attended what I think was the most amazing meeting that I have ever witnessed in my whole career. That new Auditorium in Kansas City is something that everybody in the United States ought to see. And, as for the people in it, that is something that the people in this country ought to hear.

It has been a wonderful outpouring, a very wonderful reception, that I have had all through today; and let me tell you that I am very, very grateful for it. It leads me to believe that my conclusion is right: that the people of this country today are taking a greater and a more intelligent interest in national affairs and the problems of the country than ever before in our history — and that is a grand thing.

The registration figures in every part of the country show that there are going to be more votes cast three weeks from today than we have ever had before in the past; and I am not the least bit afraid of the results as long as everybody gets out and votes.

There is another thing that has appealed to me, on this trip and on the other trips I have made all through this year, even on that trip when I went out to look at the drought areas of the country, and that is that we have more security and a greater degree of prosperity and, incidentally, a sounder prosperity than we have had for a good many years.

I believe that if we can only keep on going, not stopping just where we are, there are lots of things still to be done. There are any number of improvements still to be made; and we do not want to turn the Government back to a point of view which will cause that progress to stop.

I am confident that we are going forward for four years to come.

172 ⟨ Address at the Dedication of a World War Memorial, St. Louis, Mo. "Our Goal Is a Sounder and More Permanent Well-Being in America." October 14, 1936

You and I join here with the rest of the Nation in dedicating this site as a memorial to the valiant dead of the World War. Here will rise a fitting structure — a symbol of devoted patriotism and unselfish service.

We in America do not build monuments to war. We do not build monuments to conquest. We build monuments to commemorate the spirit of sacrifice in war — reminders of our desire for peace.

The memory of those whom the War called to the beyond urges us to consecrate the best that is in us to the service of country in times of peace. We best honor the memory of those dead by striving for peace, that the terror of the days of war will be with us no more. In what we have done during the last three years to promote national recovery at home, to extend the hand of the good neighbor to the Nations of the world, to break down the barriers to commerce which divide Nation from Nation, we are promoting the course of peace throughout the world.

Here at home is the call to service too.

Inequalities in our social order call for correction. A true patriotism urges us to build an even more substantial America where the good things of life may be shared by more of us, where the social injustices will not be encouraged to flourish. The many different occupations in our economic and social order can and must be tied more closely together for their mutual advantage and for the advantage of America.

It is significant that the site of this memorial to the veterans of the World War is also the site of the beginning of the old Oregon trail. Here those pioneers of old left to begin that long trek across an unknown country. They faced the dangers ahead of them with stout heart and determined mind. They carried the civilization of their day to new outposts. They carried the spirit of America to a broader destiny.

We seek to follow their example along another trail. They turned not back. Let us not turn back in what we seek in these years, for our goal is a sounder and more permanent well-being in America.

We honor them and we will carry on.

May the beauty of the monument which is rising on this site cast a beneficent light on the memories of our comrades, may its substantial structure typify the strength of their purpose, and may it inspire future generations with the desire to be of service to their fellows and their country.

All major wars have brought about major disturbances in our social and economic machinery. The late War has been no exception. New problems arise to take the places of the old. We rejoice here that these problems are being met and solved without im-

475

pairing our faith and confidence in the people's ability to do it themselves by the peaceful processes of democratic representative Government.

No place could be more fitting to reaffirm that faith and confidence than a monument to those who have died in a gallant effort to save democracy for the world. No place could be more fitting to renew our resolve that that faith will guide us and direct these our efforts of today. May we keep the faith.

173 ⟨ Rear-Platform Extemporaneous Remarks at Springfield, Ill. October 14, 1936

MY FRIENDS, it is always an inspiration to come back to the home of Lincoln.

Here I am again, after an absence of only about a month. I am glad to be here standing by the side of my old friend, Governor Horner. And I am glad he has said a word about courage; but the real courage I want to talk about is the courage of the American people. After those years that we went through, we can feel very proud of the way we have come back, with smiling faces and with the determination never to go through that kind of period again.

There are so many things I should like to talk about that I could keep on campaigning for a couple of months. You are here in the heart of a great agricultural community, a great agricultural State. I am telling the people in the East as well as in the West, that the prosperity of the farmers of the Nation makes for the prosperity of the industrial workers in the greater cities. The industrial workers cannot have prosperity unless the farmers do. I think we recognize that in these past three years we have gone a long way toward reestablishing a parity, of reestablishing the purchasing power of the farmers, a purchasing power which started to slip in 1920 and kept on slipping right down to 1933.

We are determined that we will keep on going — working for a balanced economy. We want you people here in Illinois to be prosperous, but we want the people in the South to be prosperous too, also the people out on the Plains and on the Pacific Coast. After all, when you come down to it, down in the South where I have a farm myself — incidentally, I do not make much money on it — if they get a good price for their cotton it means that they can up here. In the same way, if you have more money up here to buy more corn and more hogs and more things produced by you spend you can buy more overalls made out of the cotton of the South. In other words, it is a rounded whole.

We do not want to accept this theory that some economists have that we have to have a continual fluctuation between prosperity and depression. We want to bring prosperity back and make it stay.

All through the country I find evidence of a real understanding of what your Government is trying to do. I find real evidence of their determination to keep on. That is why, on November 3rd, I am looking forward to receiving the news of the vote of the State of Illinois.

174 ⟪ Rear-Platform Extemporaneous Remarks at Bloomington, Ill. October 14, 1936

MY FRIENDS, I am glad to come to Bloomingburgh and I am glad to be on this platform with my old friends, Senator Lewis and Governor Horner.

I think I am right in saying that you people live in a country which is the second in all the United States in the value of its agricultural production.

On this trip I have been finding some ghosts. When I was farther out West I found that people were going around telling about the ghosts of taxes. They were telling people that if I were reelected, I was going to impose a Federal tax, in some perfectly weird, ghost-like manner, on every farm and home in the United States.

But, luckily, my friends, there are not many actual believers in ghosts these days. Today, when I came into Illinois I found that a new ghost has been raised up before your faces. I am not worried. It is a new one, though. They tell you in this State, I understand, that I propose that no loans shall be made on any farm land for more than twenty-five dollars an acre.

Well, let us look at that picture for a minute. If I were lending money on farm land, the first question I would ask is, "How much can that land produce?" I own some farm land myself. Down in the State of Georgia I have a lot of land that I would not lend five dollars an acre on. But, up on the Hudson River, I have some pretty good land on which I would gladly lend a hundred dollars an acre. That kind of ghost in a political campaign always comes back on the fellow who raised it, for the simple reason that the people in this country have a lot more sense than some give them credit for.

During the last three years and a half, I believe that one of the greatest gains made by the United States has been the fact that more men and women of voting age — and I include in that statement some of them below voting age — are taking a more intelligent interest in their Government than ever before in our history.

There are some people in the United States who would like to turn the conduct of Government over to a selected, self-chosen few. I would rather leave it in the hands of what we call the democracy of the United States.

In the past three and a half years, we have gone a long way and in the next four years we are going even further. That is why, my friends, on the night of November 3rd next, I have not the least worry about what the telephone and telegraph are going to carry to me as the message of the people of the State of Illinois.

Mrs. Roosevelt wants me to thank you very much for these perfectly grand flowers and also for the box of candy.

Good-bye and good luck.

NOTE: It will be noticed that in my foregoing remarks at Bloomington, Ill., I referred to the city as *Bloomingburgh.* The mistake caused much amusement among the members of the press and of my party on the campaign train.

The reason for the error was that I had received a telegram that very morning stating that my old friend, former Assemblyman John K. Evans of *Bloomingburgh, N. Y.*, was very ill. In fact, he died in 1937. He was a former close associate of mine during the Senatorial contest in the 1911 Legislature in Albany; and I was thinking of him and our past association, as I proceeded to the rear platform of the train to speak. The "slip" was caused by the tenor of my thoughts at the time; and I did not realize the mistake until the train was again under way and it was laughingly brought to my attention.

175 ❧ Rear-Platform Extemporaneous Remarks at Joliet, Ill. October 14, 1936

MY FRIENDS, I am glad to be here and I am glad also to be going through the State with Governor Horner.

As I have traveled through a great many States I have been thinking of a simile. Four years ago or, to be more accurate, on the fourth of March, 1933, the Government and the people of the United States, so far as their prosperity went, were a good deal like a freight train that had a broken axle and had gone off the track. Well, the first job was to put the freight train back on the track and we did it. The next job was to get it moving again and we did it. Today, all over the United States, people have got more buying power and people are living better than they were four years ago. And I believe that that is going to continue for the next four years.

We are coming to understand that the prosperity of the country is not just dependent on factories running, because factories cannot run unless people buy the things that are made in them. We need prosperity among the farmers as well; and if the farmers are prosperous, the industrial workers of the Nation will be prosperous. Then, too, we have tried to provide more security for the average family. We have tried to make your bank deposits safe. It is only about a week ago that we established a record for the first time in fifty-five years when we went through one full year without the failure of a single national bank in any part of the United States.

I am having a mighty interesting trip; and, so far as I am concerned, I am having such a good time that I wish this campaign could go on until December 3d instead of November 3d. But, my friends, two weeks from next Tuesday when I get reports from the State of Illinois, I feel confident that the State of Illinois is going to help to keep the present Government going for another four years.

Mrs. Roosevelt wants me to thank you very much for this very beautiful bunch of roses.

176 ❲ Campaign Address at Chicago, Ill. "It Was This Administration Which Saved the System of Private Profit and Free Enterprise." October 14, 1936

(The Administration's accomplishments on behalf of business — Dangers of monopolies.)

Mr. Chairman, Governor Horner, Mayor Kelly, my friends of the great State of Illinois:

I SEEM to have been here before. Four years ago I dropped into this city from the airways — an old friend come in a new way — to accept in this hall the nomination for the Presidency of the United States. I came to a Chicago fighting with its back to the wall — factories closed, markets silent, banks shaky, ships and trains empty. Today those factories sing the song of industry; markets hum with bustling movement; banks are secure; ships and trains are running full. Once again it is Chicago as Carl Sandburg saw it — "The City of the big shoulders" — the city that smiles. And with Chicago a whole Nation that had not been cheerful for years is full of cheer once more.

On this trip through the Nation I have talked to farmers, I have talked to miners, I have talked to industrial workers; and in all that I have seen and heard one fact has been clear as crystal —

that they are part and parcel of a rounded whole, and that none of them can succeed in his chosen occupation if those in the other occupations fail in their prosperity. I have driven home that point.

Tonight, in this center of business, I give the same message to the business men of America — to those who make and sell the processed goods the Nation uses and to the men and women who work for them.

To them I say:

Do you have a deposit in the bank? It is safer today than it has ever been in our history. It is guaranteed. Last October 1st marked the end of the first full year in fifty-five years without a single failure of a national bank in the United States. Is that not on the credit side of the Government's account with you?

Are you an investor? Your stocks and bonds are up to five- and six-year high levels.

Are you a merchant? Your markets have the precious life-blood of purchasing power. Your customers on the farms have better incomes and smaller debts. Your customers in the cities have more jobs, surer jobs, better jobs. Did not your Government have something to do with that?

Are you in industry? Industrial earnings, industrial profits are the highest in four, six, or even seven years! Bankruptcies are at a new low. Your Government takes some credit for that.

Are you in railroads? Freight loadings are steadily going up. Passenger receipts are steadily going up — have in some cases doubled — because your Government made the railroads cut rates and make money.

Are you a middleman in the great stream of farm products? The meat and grain that move through your yards and elevators have a steadier supply, a steadier demand and steadier prices than you have known for years. And your Government is trying to keep it that way.

Some people say that all this recovery has just happened. But in a complicated modern world recoveries from depressions do not just happen. The years from 1929 to 1933, when we waited for recovery just to happen, prove the point.

But in 1933 we did not wait. We acted. Behind the growing recovery of today is a story of deliberate Government acceptance of responsibility to save business, to save the American system of private enterprise and economic democracy—a record unequaled by any modern Government in history.

What had the previous Administration in Washington done for four years? Nothing. Why? For a very fundamental reason. That Administration was not industrially-minded or agriculturally-minded or business-minded. It was high-finance-minded—manned and controlled by a handful of men who in turn controlled and by one financial device or another took their toll from the greater part of all other business and industry.

Let me make one simple statement. When I refer to high finance I am not talking about all great bankers, or all great corporation executives, or all multimillionaires—any more than Theodore Roosevelt, in using the term "malefactors of great wealth," implied that all men of great wealth were "malefactors." I do not even imply that the majority of them are bad citizens. The opposite is true.

Just in the same way, the overwhelming majority of business men in this country are good citizens and the proportion of those who are not is probably about the same proportion as in the other occupations and professions of life.

When I speak of high finance as a harmful factor in recent years, I am speaking about a minority which includes the type of individual who speculates with other people's money—and you in Chicago know the kind I refer to—and also the type of individual who says that popular government cannot be trusted and, therefore, that the control of business of all kinds and, indeed, of Government itself should be vested in the hands of one hundred or two hundred all-wise individuals controlling the purse-strings of the Nation.

High finance of this type refused to permit Government credit to go directly to the industrialist, to the business man, to the homeowner, to the farmer. They wanted it to trickle down from the top, through the intricate arrangements which they controlled and by which they were able to levy tribute on every business in the land.

They did not want interest rates to be reduced by the use of Government funds, for that would affect the rate of interest which they themselves wanted to charge. They did not want Government supervision over financial markets through which they manipulated their monopolies with other people's money.

And in the face of their demands that Government do nothing that they called "unsound," the Government, hypnotized by its indebtedness to them, stood by and let the depression drive industry and business toward bankruptcy.

America is an economic unit. New means and methods of transportation and communications have made us economically as well as politically a single Nation.

Because kidnappers and bank robbers could in high-powered cars speed across state lines it became necessary, in order to protect our people, to invoke the power of the Federal Government. In the same way speculators and manipulators from across State lines, and regardless of State laws, have lured the unsuspecting and the unwary to financial destruction. In the same way across State lines, there have been built up intricate corporate structures, piling bond upon stock and stock upon bond — huge monopolies which were stifling independent business and private enterprise.

There was no power under Heaven that could protect the people against that sort of thing except a people's Government at Washington. All that this Administration has done, all that it proposes to do — and this it does propose to do — is to use every power and authority of the Federal Government to protect the commerce of America from the selfish forces which ruined it.

Always, month in and month out, during these three and a half years, your Government has had but one sign on its desk — "Seek only the greater good of the greater number of Americans." And in appraising the record, remember two things. First, this Administration was called upon to act after a previous Administration and all the combined forces of private enterprise had failed. Secondly, in spite of all the demand for speed, the complexity of the problem and all the vast sums of money involved, we have had no Teapot Dome.

We found when we came to Washington in 1933, that the business and industry of the Nation were like a train which had gone off the rails into a ditch. Our first job was to get it out of the ditch and start it up the track again as far as the repair shops. Our next job was to make repairs — on the broken axles which had gotten it off the road, on the engine which had been worn down by gross misuse.

What was it that the average business man wanted Government to do for him — to do immediately in 1933?

1. Stop deflation and falling prices — and we did it.

2. Increase the purchasing power of his customers who were industrial workers in the cities — and we did it.

3. Increase the purchasing power of his customers on the farms — and we did it.

4. Decrease interest rates, power rates and transportation rates — and we did it.

5. Protect him from the losses due to crime, bank robbers, kidnappers, blackmailers — and we did it.

How did we do it? By a sound monetary policy which raised prices. By reorganizing the banks of the Nation and insuring their deposits. By bringing the business men of the Nation together and encouraging them to pay higher wages, to shorten working hours, and to discourage that minority among their own members who were engaging in unfair competition and unethical business practices.

Through the A.A.A., through our cattle-buying program, through our program of drought relief and flood relief, through the Farm Credit Administration, we raised the income of the customers of business who lived on the farms. By our program to provide work for the unemployed, by our C.C.C. camps, and other measures, greater purchasing power was given to those who lived in our cities.

484

Money began going round again. The dollars paid out by Government were spent in the stores and shops of the Nation; and spent again to the wholesaler; and spent again to the factory; and spent again to the wage earner; and then spent again in another store and shop. The wheels of business began to turn again; the train was back on the rails.

Mind you, it did not get out of the ditch itself, it was hauled out by your Government.

And we hauled it along the road. P.W.A., W.P.A., both provided normal and useful employment for hundreds of thousands of workers. Hundreds of millions of dollars got into circulation when we liquidated the assets of closed banks through the Reconstruction Finance Corporation; millions more when we loaned money for home building and home financing through the Federal Housing program; hundreds of millions more in loans and grants to enable municipalities to build needed improvements; hundreds of millions more through the C.C.C. camps.

I am not going to talk tonight about how much our program to provide work for the unemployed meant to the Nation as a whole. That cannot be measured in dollars and cents. It can be measured only in terms of the preservation of the families of America.

But so far as business goes, it can be measured in terms of sales made and goods moving.

The train of American business is moving ahead.

But you people know what I mean when I say it is clear that if the train is to run smoothly again the cars will have to be loaded more evenly. We have made a definite start in getting the train loaded more evenly, in order that axles may not break again.

For example, we have provided a sounder and cheaper money market and a sound banking and securities system. You business men know how much legitimate business you lost in the old days because your customers were robbed by fake securities or impoverished by shaky banks.

By our monetary policy we have kept prices up and lightened the burden of debt. It is easier to get credit. It is easier to repay.

We have encouraged cheaper power for the small factory owner to lower his cost of production.

We have given the business man cheaper transportation rates.

But above all, we have fought to break the deadly grip which monopoly has in the past been able to fasten on the business of the Nation.

Because we cherished our system of private property and free enterprise and were determined to preserve it as the foundation of our traditional American system, we recalled the warning of Thomas Jefferson that "widespread poverty and concentrated wealth cannot long endure side by side in a democracy."

Our job was to preserve the American ideal of economic as well as political democracy, against the abuse of concentration of economic power that had been insidiously growing up among us in the past fifty years, particularly during the twelve years of preceding Administrations. Free economic enterprise was being weeded out at an alarming pace.

During those years of false prosperity and during the more recent years of exhausting depression, one business after another, one small corporation after another, their resources depleted, had failed or had fallen into the lap of a bigger competitor.

A dangerous thing was happening. Half of the industrial corporate wealth of the country had come under the control of less than two hundred huge corporations. That is not all. These huge corporations in some cases did not even try to compete with each other. They themselves were tied together by interlocking directors, interlocking bankers, interlocking lawyers.

This concentration of wealth and power has been built upon other people's money, other people's business, other people's labor. Under this concentration independent business was allowed to exist only by sufferance. It has been a menace to the social system as well as to the economic system which we call American democracy.

There is no excuse for it in the cold terms of industrial efficiency.

486

There is no excuse for it from the point of view of the average investor.

There is no excuse for it from the point of view of the independent business man.

I believe, I have always believed, and I will always believe in private enterprise as the backbone of economic well-being in the United States.

But I know, and you know, and every independent business man who has had to struggle against the competition of monopolies knows, that this concentration of economic power in all-embracing corporations does not represent private enterprise as we Americans cherish it and propose to foster it. On the contrary, it represents private enterprise which has become a kind of private government, a power unto itself — a regimentation of other people's money and other people's lives.

Back in Kansas I spoke about bogey-men and fairy tales which the real Republican leaders, many of whom are part of this concentrated power, are using to spread fear among the American people.

You good people have heard about these fairy tales and bogey-men too. You have heard about how antagonistic to business this Administration is supposed to be. You have heard all about the dangers which the business of America is supposed to be facing if this Administration continues.

The answer to that is the record of what we have done. It was this Administration which saved the system of private profit and free enterprise after it had been dragged to the brink of ruin by these same leaders who now try to scare you.

Look at the advance in private business in the last three and a half years; and read there what we think about private business.

Today for the first time in seven years the banker, the store-keeper, the small factory owner, the industrialist, can all sit back and enjoy the company of their own ledgers. They are in the black. That is where we want them to be; that is where our policies aim them to be; that is where we intend them to be in the future.

Some of these people really forget how sick they were. But I know how sick they were. I have their fever charts. I know how the knees of all of our rugged individualists were trembling four years ago and how their hearts fluttered. They came to Washington in great numbers. Washington did not look like a dangerous bureaucracy to them then. Oh, no! It looked like an emergency hospital. All of the distinguished patients wanted two things—a quick hypodermic to end the pain and a course of treatment to cure the disease. They wanted them in a hurry; we gave them both. And now most of the patients seem to be doing very nicely. Some of them are even well enough to throw their crutches at the doctor.

The struggle against private monopoly is a struggle for, and not against, American business. It is a struggle to preserve individual enterprise and economic freedom.

I believe in individualism. I believe in it in the arts, the sciences and professions. I believe in it in business. I believe in individualism in all of these things—up to the point where the individualist starts to operate at the expense of society. The overwhelming majority of American business men do not believe in it beyond that point. We have all suffered in the past from individualism run wild. Society has suffered and business has suffered.

Believing in the solvency of business, the solvency of farmers and the solvency of workers, I believe also in the solvency of Government. Your Government is solvent.

The net Federal debt today is lower in proportion to the income of the Nation and in proportion to the wealth of the Nation than it was on March 4, 1933.

In the future it will become lower still because with the rising tide of national income and national wealth, the very causes of our emergency spending are starting to disappear. Government expenditures are coming down and Government income is going up. The opportunities for private enterprise will continue to expand.

The people of America have no quarrel with business. They

insist only that the power of concentrated wealth shall not be abused.

We have come through a hard struggle to preserve democracy in America. Where other Nations in other parts of the world have lost that fight, we have won.

The business men of America and all other citizens have joined in a firm resolve to hold the fruits of that victory, to cling to the old ideals and old fundamentals upon which America has grown great.

177 ⁅ Rear-Platform Extemporaneous Remarks at Grand Rapids, Mich. October 15, 1936

(Building and repair of homes — Revival of furniture industry.)

Mr. Mayor, Governor Murphy, my friends:

I AM very glad to come to Grand Rapids. I have always had a soft spot in my heart for Grand Rapids and this part of the State of Michigan, because so many of the good people here are descended from the same old Holland stock as I.

When we are making up the budget down in Washington, every department of the Government wants to have a little bit more money, as you can well imagine. When the President of the United States starts in to pare the budget and cut it down, the favorite expression is that it is my old Dutch blood which cuts it down.

Last night in Chicago, I was talking about conditions as they were four years ago and comparing them with conditions of today. Grand Rapids is a very good example of what has happened in four years. One of the points I made was that the return of prosperity did not just happen. Something had to be done — action had to be taken — to bring prosperity back.

In Grand Rapids you have an example of how we thought things through. The first thing necessary in 1933 was to stop people from starving, to give relief, to provide immediate work, to lend money to municipalities for furnishing work — in other words, to stop the deflation from going on.

After we had done that, there came the next step — the taking of measures to enable people to improve their living conditions. Through the establishment of many agencies, after we had saved many homes, we encouraged people to build new homes and to repair old homes. The Federal Housing Administration, in the last two years, has been responsible for the building or improvement of over five hundred million dollars' worth of homes. Let it be made perfectly clear that this money was not Government money. It was all private money from private lending agencies and all the Government did was to insure a portion of the loan. And, incidentally, it was a pretty good business proposition, because the loans are now being paid back, for the simple reason that people now have work.

Then came a third step — and this is where Grand Rapids comes in. After the homes were built and modernized, they had to have something to put into them, and Grand Rapids is providing the furniture that goes into those new and modernized homes.

It is, of course, a matter of record that the furniture industry, just to take one example of many industries today, is working at a much higher peak than at any time since 1929. I believe that the people of this country appreciate the fact that intelligent interest on the part of their Federal Government has resulted in very great strides in the last three and a half years toward bringing the country back to normal prosperity.

My friends, I hope in the next four years I shall be able to come to Grand Rapids as President of the United States and see you again.

178 ⦅ Informal Extemporaneous Remarks at At-wood Stadium, Flint, Mich. October 15, 1936

(Work relief vs. a dole.)

My friends of Flint:

I READ in the papers that this economic recovery we see about us is not real. I have read lots of things in the papers and so have you. For example, I read the other day that some of our friends on the other side of the fence are telling us that other Nations are better off than we are. Well, I do not believe it; and I do not think you do either.

All we need to do is to take a look across the ocean to discover whether we are doing better on this side than some other Nations are. Believe me, there are a lot of people on the other side, who wish they lived here. We are not boasting about it; we are not moved by any braggadocio about it. Our policies in the last few years, including, incidentally, our recent policy of establishing reciprocal trade agreements with other Nations, have paved the way for a greater lasting security and good-will among Nations. I truly believe, in spite of the dark spectacle in some lands, that this generation and this Government have the best opportunity in a long time to take the lead in outlawing war as a relic of cave-man days.

When some Republican spokesmen say that others are better off than we are, you and I know that they are only taking the counsel of desperation. They know that our policies are breaking a rift in the clouds of international doubt and anxiety. I call it true Americanism to set the world on its way to tranquillity.

My friends, the Republican leaders profess to be the custodians of the American system; and yet they find fault with everything that you and I know makes America the envy of the world in this good year of 1936.

I am thinking of Flint as it was in January, or February, or March of 1933, and Flint was not the only city that faced conditions of desperation. Faced with that widespread suffering from unemployment, this Administration, as you know, has followed a fixed policy — a policy that does not believe in the dole, on the ground that temporary charity without work results in a breakdown of self-respect. We did not believe in the dole then, and we do not believe in it today.

We do believe in work and, so far as it is necessary in this land, we will continue to provide work. So long as men and women need to be saved from starvation, we will continue to provide work, because these men and women need to be saved also from disintegration of morale. The millions of unemployed Americans lost many things in the depression, but there is one thing which we tried to see to it that they did not lose — they did not lose their self-respect.

And so we have come through the worst economic crisis in our history, and we have kept our morale. Money spent to do that was money soundly invested. We faced that choice in 1933; and it was a test of what I call straight economic thinking and good economic statesmanship, even if some professors did not agree with us.

We could have gone into the relief problem by spending, let us say, a dollar for a dole. That dollar for a dole would have kept unemployed men just alive — just in a state of suspended animation. Or we could think beyond our noses and spend, say, a dollar and a half on work instead of a dollar on a dole. That extra half dollar would maintain the normal relationships of the unemployed with their families and their grocers, and their merchants, and so on down the line. They could later slip back into normal industry in a normal way.

Yes, we chose to spend money in order to save men. But who can measure in dollars and cents what the self-respect and the morale of a people mean to their Nation? They must be measured, rather, in terms of the preservation of the families and the normal life of America.

But work relief has done more than that. In these many communities throughout the land, it has helped the unemployed to make a contribution of social value to the life of the Nation. Across the entire country a far-reaching series of structures has been built by the working unemployed — and I see a W.P.A. sign right out there by the gate — structures which for generations to come will contribute to the well-being and permanent happiness of the Nation.

Remember that no project has been adopted by the Federal Government except on recommendation of the local community itself. You people of Michigan initiated the projects in Michigan. And the people of the other States also told us which projects they wanted in their States. In the vast majority of cases your advice was good. This year you and I have noticed that the projects which are being criticized are never the projects in the community in which the critic lives. They are generally a thousand miles away.

You can look in your own towns, your own counties all through America, to see for yourselves what this work relief program has done — in schools and roads and pavements and reforestation and flood prevention and sanitation and in fifty or a hundred different types of undertakings that have no peacetime parallel in all of our history.

I am sorry not to meet an old friend of mine here — that there has passed on to the great Beyond General Guy Wilson whom I met in 1918 up on the Marne.

I am glad to have had this chance to come to Flint today. I am glad that things are so much better than they were a short four years ago.

My friends, all I can tell you very simply but very much from the heart, is that I am striving and shall continue to strive to bring a better balanced economy to the United States of America.

179 ❨Informal Extemporaneous Remarks at Hamtramck Stadium, Detroit, Mich.

October 15, 1936

("Boondoggling.")

My FRIENDS, I am glad for many reasons to be with you tonight at this great gathering. I am happy to be here by the side of my old friends, Senator Couzens, Governor Murphy, Prentiss Brown and many others; and I am glad, also, to come to this dedication of one of the projects in which the Federal Government has been able to help your city.

As I came through those streets tonight, lined by thousands of men, women and children, I was thinking mostly about the children. I was thinking mostly about the days to come when they would be the citizens of the United States and would take our places in the conduct of the affairs of the State and of the Nation.

During these past three and a half years we have tried to do much to save the United States for these children. We have tried to keep people from starving; we have tried to save the homes of the Nation; we have tried to restore employment to the people of the Nation. I think that in these three years we have come a long way.

But it has not been only the immediate emergency that we have had to cope with. We have been thinking about some of the things that the country needs in addition to bare food and lodging. That is why a great stadium of this kind has been built. This stadium is one of the things that will last for many years and contribute toward the enjoyment and recreation, not only of us older people but of the younger generation as well.

Yes, I am thinking of a future America, where we may all have a little bit more of the better things of life than we have today, a little bit more in the way of money compensation for our work, a little bit more in the way of holidays—shorter hours and Saturdays off and Sundays off as well.

Some people in this country have called it "boondoggling" for us to build stadiums and parks and forests and to improve the recreational facilities of the Nation. My friends, if this stadium can be called boondoggling, then I am for boondoggling, and so are you.

I am looking forward to a continuation in the next few years of the policy that will work for the good of the average citizen in the United States, that will not forget the forgotten man. It has been a privilege to be with you tonight; and I hope that some time in the next four years I shall be able to leave Washington, and visit with you again.

180 ❲ Campaign Address at Detroit, Mich. "Shall the Social and Economic Security and Betterment of the Masses of the American People Be Maintained and Strengthened?" October 15, 1936

(Effect on industry of Federal spending — Prevention of future major depressions — The yearly pay envelope.)

Governor Murphy, Senator Couzens, my friends:

I AM standing at the spot in front of the City Hall to which during the four terrible years, from 1929 to 1933, thousands of unemployed men and women of Detroit came to present problems of human existence to a great Mayor, Frank Murphy.

I am glad that he is standing beside me today. His splendid record, first as Governor General of the Philippines and later as High Commissioner of the United States to the Commonwealth of the Philippines, stands out as one of the most successful administrations in our history. The whole country is proud of Frank Murphy and proud of what he has done.

I knew something of the problems of Detroit in the depression years, not only from Frank Murphy, but also from my brother-in-law who was his City Controller.

We all knew that during those years the Government of this city pared its operating expenses to the bone, using every penny it could scrape together for the relief of thousands of men and women who were literally on the verge of starvation. When money had to be raised, the Mayor and Controller would go to private bankers in New York where they were compelled to pay very high interest rates for further loans.

By the spring of 1933 the city of Detroit could borrow no more from private sources and the government of the State of Michigan was unable to render any substantial help.

I recite these facts because while the problem of human relief in Detroit was one of the most difficult in the Nation, yet there were thousands of other municipalities faced with the same kind of crisis.

There they were on the fourth of March, 1933! And what was called for?

Action — immediate action — by the new Federal Government in Washington; and it is now admitted by all but the most blind partisans, that that was what saved the day. It was the only thing left which could save the day.

Relief and work relief through the use of Federal funds saved American humanity, and as the months went by it saved also the solvency of cities and States in every part of the Nation.

After we had stopped the immediate crisis, our next step was to restore the purchasing power of the people themselves. I need not recite to you the many steps we took. You are as familiar with them as I am. In great part you are glad today, I am sure, that we took these steps.

The problem involved building up purchasing power of every kind. In restoring it there is one element often overlooked by those who dwell in great industrial cities — the building up of the prices which farmers obtain for their farm products.

Let me give you a simple example. A South compelled to sell its cotton for five cents a pound, a Middle West compelled to sell its corn for ten or fifteen cents a bushel, its hogs for two or three cents a pound, its wheat for thirty cents a bushel, could buy no automobiles made in Detroit. But a South with ten- or twelve-cent cotton, a Middle West with seventy-five-cent corn, seven-cent hogs and dollar wheat, can start and has started buying passenger cars, trucks and tractors.

In all other fields of production prices and values also rose. Miners went back to work. Eastern factories opened their closed doors.

The dollars that we spent in relief, in work relief, in C.C.C. camps, in drought relief, in cattle and hog buying and processing, each of those dollars went to work. They were spent in the shops of the city and in the stores of the small towns and villages. They were spent again by the retailers who bought from wholesalers. They were spent again by wholesalers who bought from manu-facturers and processors. They were spent again in wages to those who worked and in purchases from those who produced the raw materials back in the mines and on the farms. And once again they were spent in the stores of the cities and the shops of the small towns and villages. You know how many of these dollars have finally come to the City of Detroit in the purchase of auto-mobiles.

I am reminded of a popular song. Literally the music went round and round and round and a lot of it came out right here in Detroit.

All I need to repeat is the statement known to most of you here, that 1936 promises to be the second largest year of auto-mobile production in our history—three and a half times the value it was in 1932.

Detroit today is a very different city from what it was three years ago, and while the wheels of industry turn fast and while unem-ployment is very greatly decreased, yet there are many problems not yet solved. I do not accept the conclusion of many Repub-lican leaders that major depressions are inevitable in modern life. It is not enough that we have ended the days in 1932 when work-ers in this city received for their labor as low as five or six dollars for two weeks' work. It is not enough that we have saved many homes and put thousands of people to work. I believe that it is the duty of Government to bend every effort to prevent another major catastrophe such as that which hit this country as a result of the Republican leadership which ran Government from 1921 to 1933.

There are a thousand and one things still to be done. It has been suggested that the Government's agricultural program is a "hit or miss" affair not worthy of support because, like an automobile, a new model is brought out every year. I have been glad to accept that comparison. I have told the farmers of this country that farming and farm policies, like automobile making, ought to improve each year, that Model-T farming may have been all right ten years ago but that we do not want Model-T farming or Model-T anything else in the year 1936.

I have suggested that the automobile industry and every other industry still need great improvements in their relationship to their employees. And I will illustrate the point by a story from my own personal experience. In the spring of 1934 there came to Washington representatives of the automobile workers, most of them young men without much experience in organized labor. One of them, a former Marine who had served through battle after battle in France, told me he was a machinist and that his pay was $1.25 an hour or $10.00 a day. I told him I thought that was a pretty good wage scale, and his reply was this: "Yes, Mr. President, it is a good hourly rate and a good daily rate but last year I worked only sixty-eight days." In other words, the total income of himself, his wife and his children was $680 for a year. On this yearly pay total he had lost the home on which he had paid down hundreds of dollars. He and his family were seeking to exist on $680 a year.

As a result of that meeting and of subsequent meetings with company officials, I stressed the need of spreading the work more evenly through the year and of working toward raising the yearly pay envelope of Detroit and other automobile cities from six or seven hundred a year to over a thousand or twelve hundred a year. Certain steps looking toward that end have been taken but they are not sufficient. It is my belief that the manufacturers of automobiles and the manufacturers of many other necessary commodities must, by planning, do far more than they have done to date to increase the yearly earnings of those who work for them.

Your Administration has that kind of objective in mind. It is my belief that the people of Detroit, like the people of the rest of the country, are going to ask on November 3d that the present type of Government continue rather than the type of Government which in its heart still believes in the policy of laissez faire and the kind of individualism which up to only three and a half years ago, frankly, put dollars above human rights.

When the smoke and dust of this political campaign clear away on the night of November 3d, history will record that the outstanding issue of the campaign was this: Shall the social and economic security and betterment of the masses of the American people be maintained and strengthened or not? You and I are not afraid of that verdict. It is going to be yes.

181 ❨Informal Extemporaneous Remarks at Cincinnati, Ohio. October 16, 1936

(Greater human security.)

WHAT is a little rain between friends? I am very glad to come to Cincinnati. I am very glad this morning to have seen some of the work with which the Federal Government has been able to help, first that slum clearance project, and then the bridge, and now this stadium.

I think all of you understand why the Federal Government has helped in work of this kind. In the first place, as we all know, we had an unemployment situation three years ago which was so imperative to remedy that we simply had to put people to work. Then came the question of finding the best kind of work for them, and that was put up to the localities. The communities—the cities and counties—throughout the United States told us what they most needed. And so the great bulk of the money that has been spent to give people jobs has been usefully spent, and spent at the request and upon the suggestion of the different States and municipalities of the Nation.

You know, I am sure, that this has aided very much in the national recovery which we have had during the past three years. There is not a merchant, or manufacturer, or professional man, or industrial worker, or wage earner in this whole city, I am sure, who does not say that things are better than they were.

And most of them know, too, that the recovery did not just happen of its own accord. It had to have the active help of Government.

And so today, my friends, in going around the country, I see tremendous improvement on every side.

We are also attempting to give a greater security to the Nation in the days to come. We are thinking about our children, we are thinking about fathers and mothers in their old age, we are thinking of greater permanency of jobs; all of these are objectives which modern civilization has delayed too long in taking up. But we have made a good start in taking them up.

By security, I do not mean just a living, just having enough to eat and a place to sleep. I mean a living according to the American standard—a standard which provides a decent diet, a decent education and a reasonable amount of leisure and recreation. That is why projects like this stadium that serve the enjoyment of people—just for sheer good times—are just as worth while as building bridges and stopping floods.

That kind of security, as we see it, applies not only to people with respect to their own individual family lives, but ought to apply to their occupations and ought to apply to the businesses which employ them.

That is why we are trying to make it a rounded picture—something that will affect not merely one part of the country but something that will affect every kind of occupation and business.

And so, my friends, on November 3d, which is not so very far off, we are going to have the issue presented to us: Shall we continue in the future, as we have been doing, to try to attain greater human security?

I am not the least bit worried about the result.

182 ⟨ Rear-Platform Extemporaneous Remarks at Galion, Ohio. October 16, 1936

(Thinking in national terms — Diversification in farming.)

MY FRIENDS, I am glad to come back through Galion. I have been here many times before. I am particularly glad to see, by the expression on your faces, that you are much more cheerful than you were in 1932.

You know, while I am theoretically a lawyer, I am also a bit of a farmer. I farm in two places, one on the Hudson River and the other down in Georgia. That is why I know something about farm prices. One reason why I think you here are more cheerful is because corn is selling at better than ten or fifteen cents a bushel and because hogs and cattle are selling at better than three or four cents a pound.

Of course, improvement in agricultural prices was one of the vital parts of the program that we started three years ago. And I am not going through the country making one kind of speech to farm people and another to city people. Nor am I making one kind of speech in the West and another kind in the East.

I believe that in the past few years the people of this country have begun to think in national terms. You, I know, understand that unless farm prices are good, the great farming population of this country cannot buy the things that are made in the cities. That means that the railroads do not make money because there are no goods to be hauled; and, in the same way, the people in the cities, unless they have work, cannot buy the produce of the farms in the country. In other words, we are all in the same boat, no matter what our occupation, no matter whether we live on the farm or in the city, no matter whether we live in the North or the South.

I know from personal experience that people in the cotton belt in this country cannot buy the foodstuffs produced in the North if they have to sell their cotton for four or five cents a pound. In the same way, you people cannot buy overalls made of southern cotton when you get only ten or fifteen cents a bushel for your corn.

I have always been particularly interested in the fact that this part of Ohio has gone in for diversification in farming. The more that we can diversify our farming all through the country and not have to depend entirely on one crop, the better it will be for the Nation as a whole. In that respect, you are setting a perfectly fine example for the farmers in the State of New York and for the farmers out West and for the farmers down South.

I am mighty glad to see you and I want to thank you on behalf of Mrs. Roosevelt for the flowers. They are perfectly beautiful, and there has not been a sunflower aboard the train yet. (*The sunflower was the campaign flower of the Republican candidate for President, Gov. Alfred M. Landon.*)

My friends, on the third of November I am expecting a telegram from the State of Ohio saying that all is well.

183 ❡ Campaign Address at Cleveland, Ohio. "The Interest of Every Business Man Is Bound to the Interest of Every Wage Earner." October 16, 1936

(*Figures of recovery — Fair wages and hours for workers not only simple justice but also good business — Waste of stockholders' money in false propaganda.*)

I AM glad, indeed, to come back to Cleveland; although once more I find that I am denied the privilege of seeing more of your Exposition.

I have had a wonderful time today, coming across Ohio with

your Governor and your Senators. Indeed, it has been a very exciting and a very instructive trip all through the last ten days.

It has been cheering after these hard years to see on all sides smiling faces and happy crowds again. Four years ago there were crowds too, but they had the anxious faces of uncertainty and doubt, faces shadowed by trouble and fear of the future. During the past week the hundreds of thousands of men and women and children I have seen have cheerful faces and voices of courage and hope.

I am sure that you people in Cleveland and other parts of Ohio need no proof that your factories, your shops, your stores, your farms, are all doing bigger business, that those who work in them are getting more and fatter pay envelopes. If anyone needs recovery figures for Ohio, listen to these: Compare the first half of 1936 with the first half of 1933. What do you find? Employment in all industries is up 36 percent. Payrolls in all industries are up 83 percent. Electric power production is up 44 percent. Farm income, excluding benefit payments, is up 53 percent. Department store sales in the Cleveland Federal Reserve District are up 44 percent. Retail furniture sales in the same district are up 86 percent. And, one of the finest things of all, building permits in 47 Ohio cities have increased by 367 percent, from seven and one-half million to thirty-five million dollars. Residential construction in the same cities has increased 741 percent, from about two million dollars to about eighteen and one-half million dollars.

These figures show an increase in business for every group in Ohio. The fact that recovery has come to all of these groups is a refutation of the old theory which had guided the previous Administration, the old theory which I call the "trickle down" theory. That theory is that if you lend some money to the few financial interests at the top of the economic pyramid, it will trickle down and some of it will find its way into the pay envelopes of the workers, into the ledgers of the millions of independent business men throughout the Nation, and into the pocketbooks of the farmers. But the trouble with that theory was that there was always too little left to trickle down more than half way.

Our theory for the last three and a half years has been just the opposite. We have acted on the conviction that the way to bring about recovery was to tackle the problems of those who were at the bottom of the economic pyramid, to increase earnings and income, and through them the purchasing power of everybody. We knew that sales could not be made to people who had lost the power to buy.

And so we tackled the problem from the point of view of all groups. What is happening today shows the soundness of that program.

Particularly was that true of the wage earners of the Nation. For the first time in many years the industrial workers and wage earners of America have had an Administration in Washington which was determined to give them an opportunity for a fairer wage and a more decent standard of working hours. We were determined to do this not only because that was simple justice, simple Americanism, but also because it was good business. And the business men of America now know that it was good business. They know that a great portion of their regained sales comes from the increasing purchasing power of those who work in the cities and on the farms.

The interest of every business man is bound to the interest of every wage earner. Whether he is running a store on the corner or is a stockholder in a corporation, big or little, he is financially better off when wages and working conditions are good than when wages and working conditions are poor. Surely the last panic proved that!

Remember that when men and women are idle, they are not in the market for the products of industry. When wages are low and the working week is long, their purchasing power is limited.

It is to the real advantage of every producer, every manufacturer and every merchant to cooperate in the improvement of working conditions, because the best customer of American industry is the well-paid worker. And the best guarantee of corporate dividends is a rising standard of living.

If the workers in a particular industry are poorly paid they become poor customers of every other industry and of every other merchant. And the corporation directors and lawyers who use the money of their stockholders to persuade their stockholders that they ought to chastise the Administration that is trying to broaden home and foreign markets for their own goods are, to put it mildly, a little foggy in their thinking processes.

In this era, when many families hold stocks in many diversified industries, it does them no good to depress the condition of labor in any industry. They profit best when labor profits best.

I said in Chicago, and I repeat here that the business men of America, the investors in business enterprises, are going to show on November 3d that they have not been frightened or fooled by the expensive propaganda of those who would seek to spread the gospel of fear—fear that this Administration is antagonistic to business.

Read the record of what we have done for business and you will find the answer to that charge. I repeat here that the record shows that no Administration in the history of the United States has done so much to encourage the business of the Nation.

Back in the spring of 1933 the whole system of free enterprise and private profit was on the edge of ruin. It had been dragged there by the same leaders who are now trying to scare you. It was because of our determination to keep the American system that we succeeded in doing what we did at a time when the system was almost buried under the ruins.

Few of the public are being fooled this year.

Every now and then stockholders and bondholders in the United States are flooded with literature warning them against returning this Administration to office. They probably will be appealed to again. That literature is being sent out from the center of the great financial district of New York. The money of the stockholders is being used to finance this literature. This waste of stockholders' money is being perpetrated by the same group which had brought business as a whole to its knees during the dark days of the depression. We fight only against that kind of concentrated wealth and economic power which in the old days used to dictate not only to the business of the Nation but to Government itself—against that small minority of financial interests whose concern was not the welfare of the Nation, not the welfare of business in America, but solely the extension of their own power. It is the glory of America that the standard of living is higher here than in any country or at any other time in the history of the world. The underlying issue in every political crisis in our history has been between those who, laying emphasis on human rights, have sought to exercise the power of the Government for the many and those, on the other hand, who have sought to exercise the power of Government for the few. We are now coming to learn that the interests of the few are best served when the interests of the many are best safeguarded.

That is our fight now. It will be won now as it has always been won in America since the day on which the members of the Continental Congress declared inalienable the rights to life, liberty and the pursuit of happiness.

And so, on the third of November, which I take it is two weeks from next Tuesday, I am expecting a telegram from Cleveland and from Ohio; and I am confident of what that telegram will say.

Before we pull out, may I thank you all for staying here? We were very late getting in, but it was because of the very large crowds all the way from Cincinnati. I am grateful to you.

184 ❰ Informal Extemporaneous Remarks at the New Athletic Field, Niagara Falls, N. Y. October 17, 1936

(Public works project—"Boondoggling"—Friendship with Canada.)

I AM very glad to come back to Niagara Falls after an absence, I think, of four years. Many things have happened in those four years. I believe, from what I saw on the streets a few minutes ago, that it is a happier Niagara Falls today than it was then.

I take great pleasure in coming to this dedication of this stadium today. There are many reasons why we ought to be proud of what we have been doing. This stadium, like many others in the country, represents a twofold effort. The first is to give work to people who need work, and the other is to build physical improvements for the future.

As you people know, all of these projects on which the Federal Government is helping local governments have been conceived by the particular localities assisted. The projects have been thought of in the first instance by the local government, by citizens' associations and civic organizations. For that reason the Federal Government has been very glad to go along with projects that the localities themselves have wanted.

I suppose that this particular stadium might be called "boondoggling"; but it is pretty good boondoggling. In creating these new monuments — for they are really monuments — we are thinking not only about very practical things like waterworks and sewage disposal plants and projects of that kind which every community needs. We are also thinking about the kind of projects that will be useful as recreation to us and to our children. More and more, we are getting shorter working hours in this country; and we have to do more things which will give people a chance to enjoy themselves when they are not working.

With the advent of the automobile, we are building great parks in almost all of the States — State parks of which you have a very good example here in Niagara Falls, and Federal parks. We are building improved highways and farm-to-market roads, and we are going in for reforestation. And we are also building things like this stadium, places where we can come to watch baseball and football games. My one regret is that you have not a football game scheduled this morning.

May I say, in closing, just one further thing to you people who live close to the Border? I believe that in these past two or three years the relations between the United States and our great neighbor, the Dominion of Canada, have come to a point of friendship and understanding which we have never had in bygone years. It is a splendid thing, and I am very happy that this undefended border of ours has become internationally famous. People in other continents talk about this border between us and Canada. They cite it as an example of what they wish they had between themselves and their neighbors.

You who live along the border are in large part responsible for this friendly feeling on both sides of the border. We can thank you people here in Niagara Falls and I think I can even go so far as to thank our Canadian neighbors on the other side of the river for the splendid understanding between this country and Canada, for the example that you are all giving to the rest of the world on behalf of a better understanding and peace between Nations.

Thank you and good-bye.

185 ⟨ Address at the Dedication of the Federal Building, Buffalo, N. Y. October 17, 1936

(Public works project — Responsibility of Federal Government toward the unemployed.)

Mr. Chairman, Mr. Mayor, Congressman Mead, my friends of Buffalo:

THIS occasion brings back memories, because it is not so very long ago that I took part in the laying of the cornerstone of this building over here on the left — the State Office Building. And now I am proud to take part in the dedication of this very beautiful Federal Building on the right.

That building is a part of a very great program throughout the Nation. It was a program designed first and foremost to give work to the unemployed. It was what we Americans had decided was an American substitute for the dole. All through the Nation there have been projects like these, most of them smaller, of course, but all designed with that primary objective.

But that was only the primary objective. Of course, there were others. A second purpose which was part of this program was to provide useful public works, each of which would serve a need in every community. All the way from Coast to Coast you will find a series of projects devoted to recreation, or transportation, or sanitation, or Government service, all of which, incidentally, were initiated on the recommendation of the local communities themselves.

All of the money that the Government placed into these structures has already started the wheels of trade and commerce turning again in sections where they had been stagnant for so many years. The money which the workers received in the erection of this building and on all the other projects throughout the United States undoubtedly was a major factor in restoring purchasing power in the hands of the worker, the shopkeeper, the manufacturer and the farmer.

A structure like this is particularly economical, even so far as dollars go. This building will house the Federal Departments which cover Buffalo and the surrounding territory. We must remember that up to now in this case and similar cases the Government was obliged to pay rent for that space, owning nothing and, at the end of the rental period, having nothing. So it seemed just ordinary good business to build our own building and keep the rent in our own treasury, a policy that was adopted in this State many years ago. The State Office Building in Albany, the State Office Building in New York City and now the State Office Building here in Buffalo are testimonials to the foresight and good business sense of the State of New York.

The amount of money which was placed in circulation by what went into this building and similar buildings is hard to estimate. Every dollar that was put in did its work many times over. When the worker spent the dollar in the local shop it resulted in a profit. When the retailer spent it with the wholesaler, it resulted in a profit. When the wholesaler spent it with the manufacturer it resulted in a profit. And when the manufacturer bought his raw materials from the farmer or other producer of raw materials, again there was a profit. And so each dollar as it started in the stream of trade and commerce made new business, new profits, new income, new work and new purchasing power in the community. If you multiply the dollars which went into this building by the thousands of projects all over the United States, you will see what we mean when we say that this great program of the United States served as the first shock troops in the battle against depression, starting anew the processes of business.

I have just returned to my native State from a trip which has taken me into many parts of the United States — into areas devoted to agriculture, to mining, to cattle and sheep raising, to great manufacturing industries. And everywhere I went I saw the cheerful faces and happy voices which told me that we had come back a long way to a real prosperity.

I need not compare the Buffalo of today with the Buffalo as I saw it the first time I was here. You will recall, I am sure, those years that I had the privilege of being the Chief Executive of this State. Already in 1930 the problem of depression and unemployment had become severe. And you will recall that it was in 1931 that I, as Governor, called the Legislature of the State of New York into Special Session to provide relief for the distressed unemployed of the State. New York was the first State in the Union definitely to accept the responsibility of seeing to it that so far as the State's resources could prevent it, none of its citizens who wished to work should starve.

You will remember in those days, not so long ago, the depression had made it impossible for private agencies and local communities to carry the burden, and so the duty fell upon the State, and New York State was the first to accept the responsibility of carrying on with the task. But again, as the years went on, it was found impossible not only for the great and rich States, like ours, but for every other State to carry the whole of the burden of the depression, and thereafter from the fourth of March, 1933, the Federal Government in Washington undertook to carry that part of the burden which the communities themselves and the States were unable to bear. And, my friends, so long as I am President of the United States, we will continue to carry out that responsibility.

Just one word in closing. I am always glad to get back to my State. I wish for the City of Buffalo and for those communities in the western end of our State every possible success. May we grow not only in material wealth but also in the good citizenship for which we all strive.

186 ⟨ Campaign Address at Rochester, N. Y. "That Government Which Thinks in Terms of Humanity Will Continue." October 17, 1936

(The opposition to social and progressive economic legislation.)

It was a very nice thought on the part of you good people of Rochester to give me this testimonial in this place. It is not only the spot where I was nominated for the Governorship of this great State in 1928, but it is also the spot where I attended my first political convention in 1910.

I remember that meeting of twenty-six years ago chiefly because of the fact that the City of Rochester was so crowded that twelve of us from the Hudson River counties had to sleep in one room, and ten of us fought all night against the other two who wanted the single window kept closed. Those in favor of fresh air won the day. Perhaps there is a parable in this, because I have been fighting ever since in behalf of fresh air and fresh opportunity for the people of this country.

Since the Rochester convention of 1928 much has happened. That year we were in the midst of the great jazz era, socially, politically, economically, and financially. We were even then a sick Nation though we had not yet begun to feel the pain—the headaches and the heartaches.

It was a lop-sided economy we were living in. The wealth of

the Nation was being concentrated quickly and steadily into the hands of a few individuals who were not only running the major part of our commerce and industry, but were actually running the processes of the national Government itself. It is an unfortunate fact that they were interested in their own welfare instead of in the welfare of the great majority of the people who were engaged in business, industry and agriculture.

The process of gobbling up more and more independent businesses by merger, by purchase or by reorganization was going on apace.

It was not long after I became Governor that the skies fell, and the crash came; and it is perhaps worth noting that when that happened your State Government undertook many policies which were ultimately the basis of the national legislation of the past three and a half years. We in New York started the ball rolling.

From 1929 to the spring of 1933, your State Government had to fight the depression alone. Yet it is a fact that this State was the first to undertake in a major way the care of its needy unemployed. It was, I think, the first State to tie in the success of its farming population with the prosperity of its industrial population, for it was in those years that we undertook to remove sub-marginal land from cultivation, to extend our forestry and our parks, our farm-to-market roads, and our cooperation with the farm organizations and the farmers themselves.

In those years also we started the splendid system of relief for the aged; we worked for the development of water power and for the reduction of rates for electricity, and we greatly strengthened the laws for the protection of labor.

It is also true that in the same period the opposition to social and economic legislation of this kind came from the same sources in this State which have opposed, and are opposing, the same type of forward-looking legislation and administration in the national capital.

I am happy indeed that during these past three and a half years the State of New York has continued and strengthened liberal

Government under the wise and conscientious leadership of our great Governor, Herbert H. Lehman. His has been a task of great magnitude, but he has met each problem with successful action. He and I are happy today that the worst of the crisis is over. He and I are fighting today against the return of former conditions and former schools of thought.

Thank you, my friends, for this welcome. Thank you for coming out in this rain. I am glad to stand here without a hat, for they tell me that rain is good for thin hair.

I am happy to be back in my own home State, for I am proud of it. Deep down in my heart I am confident that Government which thinks in terms of humanity will continue in Albany and Washington in the days to come.

187 ⟨Informal Extemporaneous Remarks at Utica, N. Y. October 17, 1936

MY FRIENDS, I am glad to be back in Utica and Oneida County again. Most of you good people have seen me and I have seen you many times before.

A little while ago, although it was raining in Buffalo this morning and in Rochester a little later on, I looked out of the side window of the car and I saw a rainbow. I think that is a mighty happy omen.

We have had a very wonderful trip through a great many States. Everywhere that we went there was one thing that was different from the year 1932 — there are now smiles on the faces of the men and women of America.

There is no question but that things are better in every part of the country. As you know, we have tried to work during these past three and a half years for a well-rounded economy. It has not been just a question of bringing one section of the country back or one State back at the expense of the others. We tried to bring back an economy, a prosperity, that would work all the way down the line, so that we could have a wider distribution of wealth and, with it, a few more good things for the average citizen of the country.

And in addition, we have been thinking not merely in terms of greater prosperity for the moment; we have been trying to look ahead, trying to look ahead toward obtaining a greater security for the men, and the women, and the children who are going to live in this country after us. That has been a very important objective which we have kept constantly before our eyes. I am convinced by personal observation that the people have come to realize more and more, especially in these past three and a half years, the importance of taking an active interest in Government itself and in the problems of Government.

As you know, it was only a few months after I first went to Albany as Governor in 1929 that this country was hit by the worst crash it had ever had in all its history. In those days in Albany, without any help from Washington, we started some of the things that we have transferred to Washington since I went there. We started old-age pensions in this State. We took care of needy unemployed in this State. With the help of the farmers and the farm leaders themselves we began, for the first time, a farm program in this State.

We still have to go a long way in all of these programs. In other words, we cannot keep just the same old Model T that we used to have ten years ago.

And since I have been down in Washington you have had in Albany a Government which has had to face great problems; but, under the leadership of Governor Lehman, you have had the same kind of forward-looking liberal Government, trying to take care of the great majority of the people, that we have been trying to maintain in Washington.

My friends, I am mighty glad to come back into my own home State. It is a pretty fine State to live in.

I am quite confident, from all that I have seen and from the great crowds that have come down to meet us, as to what the people of the State of New York are going to say about their two Governments in Albany and in Washington on Tuesday, November third.

188 ❧ Informal Extemporaneous Remarks at Albany, N. Y. October 17, 1936

Governor Lehman, Mayor Thatcher, and my old friends and neighbors:

I THINK I said on another occasion, four years ago, that I just could not make a formal speech to you people; and I feel that way now again, because this has been the best homecoming that I have ever had.

You know, Albany must mean something to a man and to his wife who started living here when they were a very young married couple. In those early days, beginning in 1911, we occupied two different houses at different times in Albany. I was then what might be called a kid Senator. Many years afterwards, after having been in Washington for a while, we came back to this old house; and those four years that we spent here were very happy years for all of our family.

We got to know all the people who lived across the street and on each of the side streets, so that we were able to recognize them every time we went in and out of the Executive Mansion. We almost felt as if they had been brought up with us.

And now, after four years, there is nothing strange about coming back here to Albany; it is a place that has meant so much in the lives of Mrs. Roosevelt and myself, especially when there are in the Executive Mansion two people of whom we are very, very fond, Governor and Mrs. Lehman.

I am inclined to think that Albany agrees with the rest of the State of New York that we cannot afford to have any change in the occupants of the Executive Mansion for the next two years. And I quite frankly am looking forward in the next two years at least, perhaps four years, to coming up to Albany with my wife to spend the day and visit with Herbert Lehman and his wife.

We have had a very wonderful trip through the United States these past days. I seem to thrive on ten nights in a sleeping car. And it has been a great lesson to compare the faces of the people today with the faces of the people as they were four years ago.

I think we have a happier America; I think we have a better America than we had then; and I believe also that, under the leadership of Governor Lehman, we have a much happier and a much better State of New York.

My friends, let me tell you again how happy both Mrs. Roosevelt and I are to come back here tonight and to have this wonderful reception, this truly wonderful homecoming you have given us. It is delightful to come here as the guests of Governor and Mrs. Lehman and of my old friend, Mayor Thatcher.

189 (Campaign Address at Providence, R. I. "We Believe That the Material Resources of America Should Serve the Human Resources of America." October 21, 1936

MY FRIENDS, here I am back in Rhode Island and glad to be here. I am glad that Governor Greene spoke of Rhode Island and Providence Plantations as the cradle of religious liberty.

I remember also that this State was so independent that it did not ratify the Constitution of the United States until two years after it was in effect. And I remember also that Rhode Island is a very important part of the United States, for around me lies the most highly industrial and densely populated State in the Union.

I could speak to no people who better understand the interdependence of modern economic life.

I have said that what the present national Administration has tried to do was to adjust statecraft to reality — the reality of forty-eight States which have agreed to live together in a machine age.

When this Administration came to Washington on the fourth of March, 1933, the machine of our national economy had completely broken down. For twelve long years it had been neglected by those who believed that machines did not need tending. We tried to rebuild that machine, to modernize it and to turn on the purchasing power.

It was the biggest peacetime job ever attempted. It called for energy in a hundred directions at once, it called for imagination and for willingness to face facts.

Because it was a modern machine it needed money in circulation to get it going and keep it going. Therefore, we had to obtain purchasing power for the farmer, work for the unemployed, loans to industry, safety and courage for banks.

How much did we spend? Enough to get results — enough to be sure not to fail. There would have been no second chance if we had failed once.

You and I are used to venturing capital to gain profits. And in these three and a half years our venture has succeeded.

Prosperity measured in dollars is coming back. There is none among you to deny it. But there is a higher measure for prosperity: the measure of permanency, the measure of security.

We seek not the prosperity of 1929 but the kind which will mean to every American family an assurance of safety of the home, safety of old age, safety of savings, safety of employment.

You have been talked to about regimentation. I am opposed to the kind of regimentation under which you labored and suffered in the days of the false prosperity and in the days of the great depression.

We believe that people are even more important than machines. We believe that the material resources of America should serve the human resources of America.

We will not again allow people to be regimented by selfish minorities into bankruptcies and breadlines.

I wish that on this visit I might stay longer. But I know Rhode Island, its cities, its farms, its waters and its valleys. I carry to you the same message I have given in the West and in the South: you are a vital and necessary part of a united whole. Your Federal Government seeks your well-being for your own sake and for the sake of your sister States.

190 ⟨ Campaign Address at Boston, Mass. "In a World Which in Many Places Has Gone Undemocratic We Have Gone More Democratic." October 21, 1936

(Interdependence — Figures of recovery — This Administration and business in New England — Monopolies.)

Governor Curley, Mr. Mayor, my friends of Boston:

I RETURN to the New England from which came most of my ancestors. I come from visiting many other States. Hardly one among them has not received men and treasure, brawn and brains, from New England's inexhaustible reserves.

The average American as I have met him on these voyages is no longer indifferent to the problems of Government. And it is my opinion that there is more downright political intelligence than ever before in our entire history.

In a world which in many places has gone undemocratic, we have gone more democratic. It is a bad sign for those who believe that the American people can be swept off their feet by rabble-rousers this year. The American mind today is above the rabble level. Two weeks from today, the day after election, the American air will be cleaner and American democracy will be safer.

I want to speak to you briefly and simply about the prosperity of all the Nation, for in that prosperity all New England has an immediate and a direct interest. The golden State House dome symbolizes in itself the preservation of the political unity of the Nation. But New England is heir to the lasting fruits of another great New England tradition — the tradition of being a part in the economic development of the entire Union, and of sharing in all of its prosperity.

In the most immediate sense, the problems of the great population of the West and South are your problems too. Their welfare and prosperity are your welfare and prosperity.

The sale of New England's shoes depends in part on the price of Kansas' wheat and Georgia's cotton. Prosperity for the California fruit grower depends in part on the prosperity of the New England textile mill. New England savings have prospered in developing Western mines and railroads and stockyards and farms.

I have thought much of this interdependence as I have traveled through the great Western country.

And I am confident that level-headed New England knows how true that is, knows it in spite of a cantankerous minority that in every difficult time has found spokesmen to try to persuade New England that its interest is not the interest of the rest of the Union. They tell New England today as they have told it before that it has been ruined by Government policies designed to benefit only the rest of the Union.

We all know that New England has had its troubles. We all know that New England is coming out of its troubles.

If you need figures to prove that, here they are for the State of Massachusetts: Payrolls for the first half of 1936 are up 32 percent over the first half of 1933. Retail sales are up 20 percent. Farm income, excluding benefit payments, is up 37½ percent. Building construction in sixty-two Massachusetts cities is up 100 percent. Does that look to you like the end of private enterprise?

For many years under Republican Administrations, New England was handicapped. What were the causes?

Every realistic business man of New England knows. First: That New England had established standards of wages and of living which put some of its industries at a competitive disadvantage with sections of the country which had not reached those standards.

Second: That those lower standards were exploited by an absentee landlordism which exported from New England too much of its capital—capital that was used elsewhere to compete with industries at home.

Third: Concentrated wealth and economic power gobbled up or wiped out or moved away hundreds of small independent New England businesses—the kinds of businesses with which at one time New England had conquered the markets of the world.

What did Republican leadership do to meet those difficulties? A high protective tariff alone could not help New England meet the unfair competition from domestic competitors on the one hand, and the unfair competition of monopoly on the other. To make matters worse, that tariff shut off the foreign commerce on which the sea coast population and industrial population of New England had lived.

The full fruit of these Republican policies of twelve years is found in the record of what happened to New England's industries under those policies. New England was engulfed by the depression five years before the rest of the country. That is New England's debt to the Republican leadership of the boom era.

What has this Administration done?

We have raised wages and living standards in other sections of the country. They are being brought up toward the standards of New England. That kind of unfair competition is being destroyed. Most of us are in favor of that.

We have begun the first real offensive in our history against that concentrated wealth and monopolistic power which almost destroyed the small businesses and diversified industries of New England. Most of us are in favor of that.

By reciprocal trade agreements, we have begun to reopen foreign markets for New England products and New England shipping and trade. Most of us are in favor of that.

We have increased the purchasing power of New England's customers out on the farms and in the cities of the Nation. And most of us are in favor of that.

New England has traditionally been a land of moderate-sized independent business, a land of economic democracy. Its far-seeing statesmen have always understood that democracy was impossible under the relentless pressure of concentration and monopoly wielded by the new power of high finance. The New England Puritan spirit of simplicity, the New England passion for democracy, the New England genius for democratic statescraft, are the very sources of that program of this Administration which set itself to end such concentration of wealth and economic power.

Daniel Webster spoke for all that was wisest in New England when he said at Plymouth Rock: "The freest Government, if it could exist, would not be long acceptable, if the tendency of the laws were to create a rapid accumulation of property in few hands, and to render the great mass of the population dependent and penniless. Universal suffrage could not long exist in a community where there was great inequality of property."

What have we done in our fight against monopolies?

We have taxed the intercorporate dividends of holding companies. We have graduated taxes on corporations according to income, just as taxes on individuals were graduated long ago. We have made it harder for big corporations to retain the huge undistributed profits with which they gobble up small business. We have raised the surtaxes on big incomes and the estate taxes on big fortunes. We have regulated the financial markets through which mergers and consolidations and monopolies are created with other people's money.

Way back in 1776 John Adams wrote to his friend Patrick Henry:

"The decree is gone forth, and it cannot be recalled, that a more equal liberty than has prevailed in other parts of the earth, must be established in America. The exuberance of pride which has produced an insolent domination in a few, a very few, opulent monopolizing families, will be brought down nearer to the confines of reason and moderation, than they have been used to."

I am glad to travel in the company of John Adams and Daniel Webster. Boston and Massachusetts and New England have not lost the spirit that has made the Nation great.

191 ⟨ Campaign Address at Worcester, Mass. "In 1776 the Fight Was for Democracy in Taxation. In 1936 That Is Still the Fight." October 21, 1936

(Recovery — Taxation — Taxes graded to ability to pay — Hidden taxes — False pay-envelope propaganda on Social Security Act.)

Senator Walsh, Governor Curley, Mayor Sullivan, and my friends of New England:

I AM glad to be in New England — New England from which have come most of my forebears. In recent weeks I have traveled through a great part of the United States. I have spoken about farming and mining and livestock, about business big and little, about the wage earner, about the national debt, about drought and flood, about work for the needy unemployed and about security — security for our people and for their homes.

I have found a Nation more greatly prosperous, more definitely on the highway to complete recovery than at any time in the past seven years. I have seen the record of what we have done in the faces of the people I have met. We have banished Old Man Gloom.

It has taken only one day of driving through Rhode Island and Massachusetts to prove to me that New England is in step and on the march with the rest of the Nation.

I have seen things today even more welcome to me than your lovely autumn foliage. I have seen the smoke from factories which three and a half years ago were smokeless. I have heard the sound of mills which three and a half years ago were silent. I have seen men at work who three and a half years ago were jobless. I have seen women and children who, after long years of fear, have begun to live and hope again.

Three and a half years ago we declared war on the depression. You and I know today that that war is being won.

But now comes that familiar figure — the well-upholstered hindsight critic. He tells us that our strategy was wrong, that the cost was too great, that something else won the war. That is an argument as old as the remorse of those who had their chance and muffed it. It is as recent as the claims of those who say that they could have done better.

You may remember the First Battle of the Marne in the World War. Almost everybody thought that it was Marshal Joffre who had won it. But some refused to agree. One day, a newspaperman appealed to Marshal Joffre: "Will you tell me who did win the Battle of the Marne?" "I can't answer that," said the Marshal. "But I can tell you that if the Battle of the Marne had been lost the blame would have been on me."

Our war, too — this war we are now finishing — had to be won. No price, we were told then, was too high to pay to win it. We did count the cost. But in the barrage that we laid down against the depression we could not stop firing to haggle about the price of every shell. We kept on firing and fighting. The important thing is that the war is being won.

Without that victory we cannot have the kind of America we know and love and want our children to live in.

New England, as one of the senior partners in the company of the States, has always stood for two of the fundamentals of American liberty: the Town Meeting, with its essential insistence on local control over local affairs, and the doctrine for which Sam Adams and his friends were willing to fight — the doctrine of democracy in taxation. While I do not happen to be a cousin of the distinguished Adams family, I consider myself, politically, a lineal descendant of old Sam.

In 1776 the fight was for democracy in taxation. In 1936 that is still the fight. Mr. Justice Oliver Wendell Holmes once said: "Taxes are the price we pay for civilized society." One sure way to determine the social conscience of a Government is to examine the way taxes are collected and how they are spent. And one sure way to determine the social conscience of an individual is to get his tax-reaction.

Taxes, after all, are the dues that we pay for the privileges of membership in an organized society.

As society becomes more civilized, Government—national, State and local government—is called on to assume more obligations to its citizens. The privileges of membership in a civilized society have vastly increased in modern times. But I am afraid we have many who still do not recognize their advantages and want to avoid paying their dues.

It is only in the past two generations that most local communities have paved and lighted their streets, put in town sewers, provided town water supplies, organized fire departments, established high schools and public libraries, created parks and playgrounds—undertaken, in short, all kinds of necessary new activities which, perforce, had to be paid for out of local taxes.

And let me at this point note that in this most amazing of campaigns, I have found sections of the Nation where Republican leaders were actually whispering the word to the owners of homes and farms that the present Federal Administration proposed to make a cash levy on local real estate to pay off the national debt. They know that the Federal Government does not tax real estate, that it cannot tax real estate. If they do not know that, I suggest they read the Constitution of the United States to find out.

New obligations to their citizens have also been assumed by the several States and by the Federal Government, obligations unknown a century and a half ago, but made necessary by new inventions and by a constantly growing social conscience.

The easiest way to summarize the reason for this extension of Government functions, local, State and national, is to use the words of Abraham Lincoln: "The legitimate object of Government is to do for the people what needs to be done but which they cannot by individual effort do at all, or do so well, for themselves."

Taxes are the price we all pay collectively to get those things done.

To divide fairly among the people the obligation to pay for these benefits has been a major part of our struggle to maintain democracy in America.

Ever since 1776 that struggle has been between two forces. On the one hand, there has been the vast majority of our citizens who believed that the benefits of democracy should be extended and who were willing to pay their fair share to extend them. On the other hand, there has been a small, but powerful group which has fought the extension of those benefits, because it did not want to pay a fair share of their cost.

That was the line-up in 1776. That is the line-up in this campaign. And I am confident that once more — in 1936 — democracy in taxation will win.

Here is my principle: Taxes shall be levied according to ability to pay. That is the only American principle.

Before this great war against the depression we fought the World War; and it cost us twenty-five billion dollars in three years to win it. We borrowed to fight that war. Then, as now, a Democratic Administration provided sufficient taxes to pay off the entire war debt within ten or fifteen years.

Those taxes had been levied according to ability to pay. But the succeeding Republican Administration did not believe in that principle. There was a reason. They had political debts to those who sat at their elbows. To pay those political debts, they reduced the taxes of their friends in the higher brackets and left the national debt to be paid by later generations. Because they evaded their obligation, because they regarded the political debt as more important than the national debt, the depression in 1929 started with a sixteen-billion-dollar handicap on us and our children.

Now let's keep this little drama straight. The actors are the same. But the act is different. Today their role calls for stage tears about the next generation. But in the days after the World War they played a different part.

The moral of the play is clear. They got out from under then, they would get out from under now — *if* their friends could get back into power and they could get back to the driver's seat. But neither you nor I think that they are going to get back.

As in the World War, we have again created a tax structure

to yield revenues adequate to pay the cost of this war against depression in this generation and not in the next.

New or increased taxes are not needed to enable us to balance the Federal Budget and to begin very soon a rapid reduction in the national debt. Recovery is with us. Federal revenues are increasing; emergency expenditures are decreasing. A balanced budget is on the way. Does that sound like bankruptcy to you?

Why this increase in Government revenues? Because the taxpayer earns more money and spends more money. Though he pays more money in taxes, he has more money left for himself and for his family.

For the average American we have reduced the individual income tax. Any family head who earns an income of less than $26,000 a year pays a smaller income tax in 1936 than he paid for 1932. That means that less than one percent of the heads of American families pay more than they did; and more than 99 percent pay less than they did, for more than 99 percent earn less than $26,000 per year. If you want the answer to this talk about high taxes under this Administration — there it is. Taxes are higher for those who can afford to pay high taxes. They are lower for those who can afford to pay less. That is getting back again to the American principle — taxation according to ability to pay.

You would think, to hear some people talk, that those good people who live at the top of our economic pyramid are being taxed into rags and tatters. What is the fact? The fact is that they are much farther away from the poorhouse than they were in 1932. You and I know that as a matter of personal observation.

A number of my friends who belong in these very high upper brackets have suggested to me, more in sorrow than in anger, that if I am reelected they will have to move to some other Nation because of high taxes here. I shall miss them very much but if they go they will soon come back. For a year or two of paying taxes in almost any other country in the world will make them yearn once more for the good old taxes of the U. S. A.

One more word on recent history. I inherited from the previous Administration a tax structure which not only imposed an unfair income tax burden on the low-income groups of this country, but also imposed an unfair burden upon the average American by a long list of taxes on purchases and consumption — hidden taxes.

In 1933 when we came into office, fifty-eight cents out of every dollar of Federal revenue came from hidden taxes. Leaving out of account the liquor tax — for liquor was illegal in 1933 — we have reduced these indirect taxes to thirty-eight cents out of every dollar.

How else have we improved and Americanized the tax structure?

First, we gave a credit to earned income — that is, income from personal work or service — thus substantially reducing taxes paid by the working citizen. Wasn't that the American thing to do?

Second, we decreased the tax rates on small corporations. Wasn't that the American thing to do?

Third, we increased the taxes paid by individuals in the higher brackets — those of incomes over $50,000 a year. Wasn't that the American thing to do?

Fourth, we increased still further the taxes paid by individuals in the highest brackets — those with incomes over one million dollars a year. Wasn't that the American thing to do?

Fifth, we increased the tax on very large estates. Wasn't that the American thing to do?

Finally, this year we had to find new revenues to meet the immediate bonus payments and to take the place of the processing taxes. This new tax, called the undistributed profits tax, is merely an extension of the individual income tax law and a plugging-up of the loopholes in it, loopholes which could be used only by men of very large incomes.

I want to say a word to you average investors and stockholders who are being flooded by propaganda about this tax — propaganda, incidentally, paid for by your money. It is being disseminated by those who have used corporations in the past to build up their own economic power, who seek, by holding back your dividends, to keep down their taxes.

It is a fact that 98.5 percent of all American corporations will pay a smaller normal corporation tax under the new law.

It is a fact that the law permits corporations to expand and build up adequate reserves.

But for the first time it gives the stockholder a practical chance to determine for himself whether to keep his earnings in the corporation for expansion purposes or to take them out. He is now the one — not the board of directors — to choose between using his dividends for something else and reinvesting them in the stock of the corporation.

What we are concerned with primarily is principle, and the principle of this law is sound. If in its application imperfections are discovered, they must be corrected for the good of American business.

I am certain that the average of our citizenship is not taken in by the amazing amount of other tax misinformation which has been turned loose in this political campaign.

People tell you there are fifty-eight taxes on a loaf of bread, or sixty-three taxes on a lady's coat. But stop, look and listen. You will find what the propagandists do not tell you: only two or three of all of them are Federal taxes imposed by the national Government. All the rest are imposed by local, town, county, city, district and State Governments. Two-thirds of all the taxes paid in America are State and local taxes, not Federal taxes.

This Administration has had something to do with these local taxes. It has made them easier to bear. At the request of local and State Governments for whom the local burden had become too heavy, we in Washington assumed the cost of paying in greater part for work for the needy unemployed. And, by a national fiscal policy aimed at reducing interest rates throughout the Nation we have greatly lightened the burden of carrying local government debts, helping those of you who own homes and farms or who pay rent.

I want to say a word also to the wage earners who are finding propaganda about the security tax in their pay envelopes. I want to remind them that the new social security law was designed for them, for the greater safety of their homes and their families. The fund necessary to provide that security is not collected solely from workers. The employer, too, pays an equal share. And both shares — yours and the employer's — are being held for the sole benefit of the worker himself.

I have spoken in Chicago and elsewhere of the simple fact that the overwhelming majority of business men are like the rest of us. Most of us whether we earn wages, run farms or run businesses are in one sense business men. All they seek and all we seek is fair play based on the greater good of the greater number — fair play on the part of the Government in levying taxes on us and fair play on the part of Government in protecting us against abuses.

Once more this year we must choose between democracy in taxation and special privilege in taxation. Are you willing to turn the control of the Nation's taxes back to special privilege? I know the American answer to that question. Your pay envelope may be loaded with suggestions of fear, and your dividend letter may be filled with propaganda. But the American people will be neither bluffed nor bludgeoned.

The seeds of fear cannot bear fruit in the polling booth.

Inside the polling booth every American man and woman stands as the equal of every other American man and woman. There they have no superiors. There they have no masters save their own minds and consciences. There they are sovereign American citizens. There on November 3d they will not fear to exercise that sovereignty.

192 ❨ A Letter to the Engineering Schools of the Nation on the Social Responsibility and Problems of Engineering. October 22, 1936

EVENTS of recent years have brought into clearer perspective the social responsibility of engineering.

In respect of wise use of natural resources such reports as those of the Mississippi Valley Committee, the National Resources Committee and the Great Plains Drought Area Committee have brought out the facts impressively. The enclosed report, "Little Waters," presents in miniature many of the social-engineering problems of soil and water conservation.

In respect of the impact of science and engineering upon human life — social and economic dislocations as well as advance in productive power — the facts are revealed with distressing clearness in public records of unemployment, bankruptcies and relief. The responsibility of scientists has been analyzed in noteworthy addresses such as, among the most recent, those presented at the Tercentenary Celebration of Harvard University and the meeting of the British Association for the Advancement of Science.

The design and construction of specific civil engineering works or of instruments for production represent only one part of the responsibility of engineering. It must also consider social processes and problems, and modes of more perfect adjustment to environment. Engineering must cooperate in designing accommodating mechanisms to absorb the shocks of the impact of science.

This raises the question whether the curricula of engineering schools are so balanced as to give coming generations of engineers the vision and flexible technical capacity necessary to meet the full range of engineering responsibility.

I am calling this matter to the attention of educators of high administrative authority in the hope that it may be thoroughly explored in faculty discussions and in meetings of engineering, educational and other pertinent professional associations.

Yours sincerely,

193 ❲A Tribute to Senator James Couzens on the Occasion of His Death. October 22, 1936

In the death of Senator Couzens the Senate of the United States and the people of Michigan and the Nation have lost a leader whose convictions were a part of the best that America aspires for and whose courage was a match for his idealism.

Senator Couzens did not enter public life because he sought either fame or power, but rather because of a service he believed he could render to the cause of progressive thought and political uprightness. He was a party member. But his prior obligation was to the well-being of the people whom he served. He never hesitated in that service.

The death of Senator Couzens to me is a great loss. But, more than that, it is a great loss to the multitudes of Americans whose needs and problems were always in the forefront of his thought and action.

194 ❲Informal Extemporaneous Remarks at Hartford, Conn. October 22, 1936

Governor Cross, Mayor Spellacy, my friends of Connecticut:

You are more than friends in Connecticut, for you are my neighbors. No one could fail to be inspired by this wonderful sight before me — tens of thousands of men, women and children. All of you are taking more of an interest in the problems of Government and the future of the country than at any time before in our American history.

I am here in a twofold capacity. I am here as President to talk with your Governor and your State officials, your Congressmen and your Senators, in regard to the problems of floods. And I am here also, I am told, as a candidate for a high public office.

My friend Tom Spellacy has told me that where I am standing today, at this moment, the water would have been up around my hips if I had been here at the time of the great flood.

I think that we can get a little lesson out of that flood — a lesson relating to Government, to the reason why your Government in Washington has to keep in close touch with the Governments of the States and of the cities of the Nation, and why, under certain circumstances, the Government at Washington has to step in to help.

This river of yours goes through four States — Vermont, New Hampshire, Massachusetts and Connecticut. A large part of the flood waters that came upon you recently had their origin in some other State. No matter what you do in Connecticut, no matter how many dikes you build, no matter how many precautions you take, unless the floods are controlled at the source of the river, your work will be in vain. That is why the problem of floods involves more than one State.

There are two approaches to the solution of that problem: The first is by the method of cooperation between States — the inter-state compact method — and I am glad to say that these States of New England are working together, planning for the control of floods. But, my friends, that method is insufficient in itself. You cannot ask the State of Vermont, for example, to pay the entire cost of controlling the flood waters that flow through Vermont. The chief benefit is going to be not to Vermont, but to Massachusetts and Connecticut. And so you come to the second approach to the problem — the duty of the Federal Government to control the waters of navigable rivers. You know that your Federal Government stands ready today to do its full share toward flood prevention in the future.

It is a happier Connecticut that I come back to than the Connecticut I saw in 1932.

At Hartford, Conn.

I do not particularly like figures and neither do you, but just listen for one minute.

In this State, employment in the City of Hartford alone is 45 percent greater this year than it was in 1932. Aggregate payrolls are 82 percent greater than they were in the spring of 1933. Twenty-three thousand workers have been reemployed by private industry and payrolls are running at the rate of forty-four million dollars a year more than before recovery began. Building construction is up four times what it was in those days, and the retail stores are selling 28 percent more merchandise than they sold then.

And because Connecticut, like the State of New York, is also an agricultural State, let me point out to you that the value of the farm products in your State — I mean the money actually received by the farmers of the State — has gone up somewhere between 30 and 40 percent.

And let me point out to you that, as we take stock, we are thinking not only of our own city, not only of our own State, not only of the region of States in which we live, but we are thinking about the Nation as a whole. For we realize that the prosperity of the West is reflected in the prosperity of the East, and that, unless the cotton farmer of the South can get a fair price for his cotton, he will be unable to buy the manufactured products of New England.

That is the lesson that we have learned these past three years, and that is why your Administration in Washington has been thinking about the return of prosperity in terms of the whole Nation and not just in terms of any one part of the Nation. And, my friends, I regard the State of Connecticut as a very integral part of the Nation.

I am glad that prosperity is back with us again and, believe me, it is going to stay.

And I know that on the third of November, some time in the evening, I am going to get a telegram from Wilbur Cross and a lot of my old friends here, telling me that the State of Connecticut is in the Democratic column.

195 ❬ Radio Campaign Address to Dinners of Business Men Held Throughout the Nation. "We Seek to Guarantee the Survival of Private Enterprise by Guaranteeing Conditions under Which It Can Work." October 23, 1936

(What this Administration did for American business and the competitive system — Monopolies — False pay-envelope propaganda on the Social Security Law.)

WHEN these dinners of business men throughout the country were first organized, I was asked to talk specifically for the business men of the Nation. But I said that it was impossible to make a speech for business men as members of a separate and distinct occupation from the rest of the people in America. There cannot be one type of speech for business men and another type of speech for industrial workers and for farmers.

We have no separate interests in America. There is nothing to say to one group that ought not to be said to all groups. What is good for one ought to be good for all. We can make our machinery of private enterprise work only so long as it does not benefit one group at the expense of another.

No one in the United States believes more firmly than I in the system of private business, private property and private profit. No Administration in the history of our country has done more for it. It was this Administration which dragged it back out of the pit into which it had fallen in 1933.

If the Administration had had the slightest inclination to change that system, all that it would have had to do was to fold its hands and wait — let the system continue to default to itself and to the public.

Instead we did what the previous Administration had declined to do through all the years of the depression — we acted quickly and drastically to save it. It was because of our belief in private enterprise that we acted, because of our faith in the essential and fundamental virtue of democracy and our conviction that individual initiative and private profit served it best.

You who read the business sections of the newspapers, the financial and commercial reports, know what we did and what its results have been.

But as your profits return and the values of your securities and investments come back, do not forget the lessons of the past. We must hold constantly to the resolve never again to become committed to the philosophy of the boom era, to individualism run wild, to the false promise that American business was great because it had built up financial control of industrial production and distribution in the hands of a few individuals and corporations by the use of other people's money; that Government should be ever ready to purr against the legs of high finance; that the benefits of the free competitive system should trickle down by gravity from the top to the bottom; and above all, that Government had no right, in any way, to interfere with those who were using the system of private profit to the damage of the rest of the American citizens.

Collapse of business was the price we paid for not facing intelligently the problems of private enterprise in a modern world.

There were those who advised extreme courses in the days of the crisis in 1933. Many said that deflation should take its course, wiping out in bankruptcy all but a handful of the strongest.

Some, including many business men, urged that the only solution was for Government to take everything over and run things itself.

We took the middle road. We used the facilities and resources available only to Government, to permit individual enterprise to resume its normal functions in a socially sound competitive order. We provided credit at one end of the business mechanism and purchasing power at the other. The broken pipes of the circulatory system of business have been welded together again.

An overwhelming majority of independent individual business men approve in their hearts what we did to save American business. I am equally sure that a handful of monopolistic business men hate what we did for American business. Business had become regimented. Free enterprise was being gobbled up piece by piece. Economic control of business in these few persons had developed into political control of Government itself. They did not want us to take American business out of their grip.

But we not only have freed Government from their domination; we are now freeing business also from their domination.

We have loosened the grip of monopoly by taking from monopolists their chief tools — the devices of high finance.

We are resolved to keep politics out of business. But at the same time we ask that business refrain from coercion in politics. Not only wage earners but nearly all business men resent the present attempts by a few employers to frighten their employees by misrepresentation. For example, a few employers are spreading half-truths about the Social Security Law, half-truths that tell the workers only of the workers' contribution, and fail to mention the employers' contribution. They conceal from the workers the fact that for every dollar which the employee contributes, the employer also contributes a dollar, and that both dollars are held in a Government trust fund solely for the social security of the workers.

Things like this bring certain types of employers into disrepute with other employers and with the great mass of our citizens. The real objective of this minority is the repeal of any form of social security to which they themselves have to contribute. For many years the record shows that this minority has been willing to take only a plan of unemployment insurance and old-age pensions to which the workers would be the sole contributors and which would cost the employers nothing at all.

All we ask of business and for business is the greater good of the greater number — fair treatment by it and fair treatment for it. We are reaching for the security which comes from an intelligent and honorable system of interdependent economics which every business man as well as everyone else can trust and into which he can venture with confidence.

We seek to guarantee the survival of private enterprise by guaranteeing conditions under which it can work.

We seek to insure the material well-being of America, and to make more firm the real foundations of a lasting democracy.

196 ❨ Address at the Dedication of the New Chemistry Building, Howard University, Washington, D. C. "Among American Citizens There Should Be No Forgotten Men and No Forgotten Races." October 26, 1936

Mr. Secretary, President Johnson, ladies and gentlemen:

I AM proud and happy on behalf of the United States of America to dedicate this building. And I have been greatly interested in learning a moment ago from the Chairman of the Executive Committee that the origin of Howard University was in a house of prayer.

I have a special interest in Howard University, because the Government of the United States has long had a special relationship to this institution.

Since 1879 Congress has made continuous and increasing appropriations, year by year, to help meet the general expenses of the University and its various departments and to provide new buildings. And in part at least the Department of the Interior shares in the responsibility for the administration of the University. In a very real sense, therefore, Howard is one of the Nation's institutions.

But I would be interested in this University even though the Government had no such relationship to it.

Its founding, many years ago, as an institution for the American Negro was a significant occasion. It typified America's faith in the ability of man to respond to opportunity regardless of race or creed or color.

The American Negro's response to this opportunity in the field of higher learning has been prompt and eager as in other fields. In 1867 at the first term of Howard University ninety-four students enrolled. Today there are nearly two thousand students on the lists.

Howard University has grown not only in numbers, but it has grown also in the range of its courses. To provide equal opportunities for Negro men and women, the University offers instruction in its colleges of liberal arts, medicine, dentistry, and pharmacy and in the schools of law, engineering, architecture and music. A graduate school, recently organized, attracts graduates of other colleges and universities and has helped to make Howard University a real center of Negro culture in America.

With justification Howard may take pride in its high standards of scholarship among other American universities. Its schools of law and medicine, for instance, are rated, I am told, among the Class-A schools in the Nation.

Despite the constant raising of the scholastic standards of the University, as the years went by, the demand for higher training and higher education among our Negro citizens has increased to an extent which has created a strain upon its facilities.

And so the Federal Government has provided three new structures for it at this time, and there are more to come. These structures, as a part of our building program, represent the happy conjunction of two important Federal Government programs to meet the difficulties of the depression. They are a part of our nationwide projects to reduce unemployment by building useful public works. They are also a part of our nationwide program to ensure the normal maintenance and necessary expansion of educational facilities for youth even in a time of depression.

Our purpose was not only to provide work in all sections for all parts of the population, but to enable them all to share in the benefits to be obtained from these works so long as bricks and mortar shall endure. As far as it was humanly possible, the Government has followed the policy that among American citizens there should be no forgotten men and no forgotten races. It is a wise and truly American policy. We shall continue faithfully to observe it.

Howard University has shared as of right in our public works program. These Government-financed improvements in the facilities of this great center of Negro education should enable it to continue to provide for its students cultural opportunities comparable to those offered by other first-class institutions of higher learning in the country.

At its last commencement Howard sent forth two hundred and forty-five graduates to join nearly ten thousand alumni in all parts of the world. Here is a record of which the Negro race may well be proud. It is a record of which America is proud. It is a further fulfillment of our dream of providing better and better educational facilities for all our people.

Today, we dedicate this new chemistry building, this temple of science, to industrious and ambitious youth. May they come here to learn the lessons of science and to carry the benefits of science to their fellow men.

197 ⟨Informal Extemporaneous Remarks at Dedication of Brooklyn College, Brooklyn, N. Y. October 28, 1936

Mr. Mayor, my friends:

I HAVE seen blueprints and I have seen photographs and now I see the real article with my own eyes.

Every time that the Mayor of the City of New York comes to Washington I tremble *(laughter)*, because it means he wants something and he nearly always gets it.

This project for Brooklyn College is killing two birds with one stone. We are not only putting to work, we not only have put to work, many thousands of good people who needed work; but we are also improving the educational facilities of this great Borough, not just for today but for generations to come.

Out of this depression, while there have been much misery and much suffering, there has also come much good; because, not only in this city, not only in every other city of the country, but in almost every county of the three thousand and more counties in the United States, there has been given to this country an opportunity to get better schools for the young people. That is why I am very keenly interested in all of these public works projects which have improved the schools of the Nation.

I am glad to come here today and to wish to Brooklyn College the fine and successful future that it deserves.

You, here, are doing a great work. May it live through the generations to come for the building up of a better American citizenship. I am glad to have been with you today. I have a somewhat hectic and hurried day, but I hope some time in the future to come back and see this building being used and occupied.

198 ❲ Address on the Occasion of the Fiftieth Anniversary of the Statue of Liberty. "Carry Forward American Freedom and American Peace by Making Them Living Facts in a Living Present." October 28, 1936

Mr. Ambassador, Secretary Ickes, Governor Lehman, Mr. Mayor, ladies and gentlemen:

FIFTY years ago our old neighbor and friend from across the sea gave us this monument to stand at the principal eastern gateway to the New World. Grover Cleveland, President of the United States, accepted this gift with the pledge that "We will not forget that liberty has here made her home; nor shall her chosen altar be neglected."

During those fifty years that covenant between ourselves and our most cherished convictions has not been broken.

Four hundred years ago, in Europe as well as in Asia, there was little hope of liberty for the average men of courage and good-will. The ambitions of a ruling class and the times alike conspired against liberty of conscience, liberty of speech, liberty of the person, liberty of economic opportunity. Wars, dynastic and religious, had exhausted both the substance and the tolerance of the Old World. There was neither economic nor political liberty — nor any hope for either.

Then came one of the great ironies of history. Rulers needed to find gold to pay their armies and increase their power over the common men. The seamen they sent to find that gold found instead the way of escape for the common man from those rulers. What they found over the Western horizon was not the silk and jewels of Cathay but mankind's second chance — a chance to create a new world after he had almost spoiled an old one.

And the Almighty seems purposefully to have withheld that second chance until the time when men would most need and appreciate liberty, the time when men would be enlightened enough to establish it on foundations sound enough to maintain it.

For over three centuries a steady stream of men, women and children followed the beacon of liberty which this light symbolizes. They brought to us strength and moral fibre developed in a civilization centuries old but fired anew by the dream of a better life in America. They brought to one new country the cultures of a hundred old ones.

It has not been sufficiently emphasized in the teaching of our history that the overwhelming majority of those who came from the Nations of the Old World to our American shores were not the laggards, not the timorous, not the failures. They were men and women who had the supreme courage to strike out for themselves, to abandon language and relatives, to start at the bottom without influence, without money and without knowledge of life in a very young civilization. We can say for all America what the Californians say of the Forty-Niners: "The cowards never started and the weak died by the way."

Perhaps Providence did prepare this American continent to be a place of the second chance. Certainly, millions of men and women have made it that. They adopted this homeland because in this land they found a home in which the things they most desired could be theirs—freedom of opportunity, freedom of thought, freedom to worship God. Here they found life because here there was freedom to live.

It is the memory of all these eager seeking millions that makes this one of America's places of great romance. Looking down this great harbor I like to think of the countless numbers of inbound vessels that have made this port. I like to think of the men and women who, with the break of dawn off Sandy Hook, have strained their eyes to the west for a first glimpse of the New World.

They came to us—most of them—in steerage. But they, in their humble quarters, saw things in these strange horizons which were denied to the eyes of those few who traveled in greater luxury.

They came to us speaking many tongues—but a single language, the universal language of human aspiration.

How well their hopes were justified is proved by the record of what they achieved. They not only found freedom in the New World, but by their effort and devotion they made the New World's freedom safer, richer, more far-reaching, more capable of growth.

Within this present generation, that stream from abroad has largely stopped. We have within our shores today the materials out of which we shall continue to build an even better home for liberty.

We take satisfaction in the thought that those who have left their native land to join us may still retain here their affection for some things left behind—old customs, old language, old friends. Looking to the future, they wisely choose that their children shall live in the new language and in the new customs of this new people. And those children more and more realize their common destiny in America. That is true whether their forebears came past this place eight generations ago or only one.

The realization that we are all bound together by hope of a common future rather than by reverence for a common past has helped us to build upon this continent a unity unapproached in any similar area or population in the whole world. For all our millions of square miles, for all our millions of people, there is a unity in language and speech, in law and in economics, in education and in general purpose, which nowhere finds its match.

It was the hope of those who gave us this Statue and the hope of the American people in receiving it that the Goddess of Liberty and the Goddess of Peace were the same.

The grandfather of my old friend the French Ambassador, and those who helped him make this gift possible, were citizens of a great sister Republic established on the principle of the democratic form of government. Citizens of all democracies unite in their desire for peace. Grover Cleveland recognized that unity of purpose on this spot fifty years ago.

He suggested that liberty enlightening the world would extend her rays from these shores to every other Nation.

Today that symbolism should be broadened. To the message of liberty which America sends to all the world must be added her message of peace.

Even in times as troubled and uncertain as these, I still hold to the faith that a better civilization than any we have known is in store for America and by our example, perhaps, for the world. Here destiny seems to have taken a long look. Into this continental reservoir there has been poured untold and untapped wealth of human resources. Out of that reservoir, out of the melting pot, the rich promise which the New World held out to those who came to it from many lands is finding fulfillment.

The richness of the promise has not run out. If we keep the faith for our day as those who came before us kept the faith for theirs, then you and I can smile with confidence into the future.

It is fitting, therefore, that this should be a service of rededication to the liberty and the peace which this Statue symbolizes.

Liberty and peace are living things. In each generation — if they are to be maintained — they must be guarded and vitalized anew.

We do only a small part of our duty to America when we glory in the great past. Patriotism that stops with that is a too-easy patriotism — a patriotism out of step with the patriots themselves. For each generation the more patriotic part is to carry forward American freedom and American peace by making them living facts in a living present.

To that we can, we do, rededicate ourselves.

199 ❨ Address at Roosevelt Park, New York City. October 28, 1936

(Foreign-born citizens — Housing for lower-income groups.)

Governor Lehman, Mr. Mayor, my friends of the East Side:

THERE are some experiences in this life which give one new strength, new purpose to carry on. Today, at the Statue of Liberty, and before this great gathering, I obtain inspiration to go on with the task that is mine. And I am very happy to see for the first time this park that was named after my dear mother, because I have not driven through here for two or three years. I can tell you very simply that I do not believe I have ever seen her made more happy in all her life than when this park was named after her. And it is something that I also shall always remember, and my children and my grandchildren in the years to come.

I have just come from the ceremonies at the Statue of Liberty. I suggested there that we should rededicate that Statue not to liberty alone but also to peace. I spoke there of the steady stream of human resources which the Old World poured on our shores and out of which our American civilization has been built.

Many of the people who came past the Statue of Liberty settled in this section of New York City. Here they wove into the pattern of American life some of the color, some of the richness of the cultures from which they came. Here they joined in that great process out of which we have welded our American citizenship.

We gave them freedom. I am proud — America is proud — of what they have given to us.

They have never been — they are not now — half-hearted Americans. In Americanization classes and at night schools they have burned the midnight oil in order to be worthy of their new allegiance.

They were not satisfied merely to find here the realization of the material hopes which had guided them from their native land. They were not satisfied merely to build a material home for themselves and their families.

They were intent also upon building a place for themselves in the ideals of America. They sought an assurance of permanency in the new land for themselves and their children based upon active participation in its civilization and culture.

Those who have come here of late understand and appreciate our free institutions and our free opportunity, as well as those who have been here for many generations. The great majority of the new and the old do not confuse the word "liberty" with the word "license." They appreciate that the American standard of freedom does not include the right to do things which hurt their neighbors. All of us, old-comers and new-comers, agree that for the speculator to gamble with and lose the savings of the clients of his bank is just as contrary to American ideals of liberty as it is for the poor man to upset the peddler's cart and steal his wares. To our newer Americans America is a great discovery. They who have never been so free before rejoice in our freedom. Our liberty is warmed by the fire of their devotion.

I am inclined to think that in some cases the newer citizens have discharged their obligations to us better than we have discharged our obligations to them. For example, their coming helped to intensify the housing problem in many of our great cities. We have not yet worked out an adequate answer to that problem.

As a matter of fact, we have, for too long, neglected the housing problem for all our lower-income groups. We have spent large sums of money on parks, on highways, on bridges, on museums, and on other projects of civic betterment. For the most part that was money well spent. But we have not yet begun adequately to spend money in order to help the families in the overcrowded sections of our cities to live as American citizens have a right to live.

You and I will not be content until City, State and Federal Governments join with private capital in helping every American family to live that way.

We need action to get better city housing. Senator Wagner and I had hoped for a new law at the last session of the Congress. We who believe in better housing have not been defeated. I am confident that the next Congress will start us on our way with a sound housing policy. We shall certainly get it if on November 3d you vote to send to Washington the kind of Government which I am confident you want—a Government which will continue to work for security of the home, for security of jobs, for security of savings, and for better homes in every part of the Nation.

My friends, let me thank you for this greeting that you have given me. It has been a wonderful day in my life, and I am going to end my speech now by cutting this cake.

200 ⟨ Campaign Address on John Mitchell Day at Wilkes-Barre, Pa. October 29, 1936

(John Mitchell—Gains of labor are the gains of all—Pay-envelope propaganda on Social Security Act—Purposes of the insurance provisions of the Act.)

My friends of Pennsylvania:

WHEN I found that I was to speak in Harrisburg today, and realized that it is John Mitchell Day, I determined to come by way of Wilkes-Barre. I wanted to pay my tribute to him, whom I was happy and proud to call my friend.

In 1913 I was Assistant Secretary of the Navy. I was asked at that time to examine charges of collusion in coal bids for the Navy. I needed help from someone whose integrity and knowledge I could trust. I recalled then how impressed Theodore Roosevelt had been with John Mitchell's handling of the great coal strike of 1902. I asked John Mitchell to help me. In three days he taught me a great deal about coal and mining. What he taught me saved the United States Navy many hundreds of thousands of dollars a year in its coal bill.

You in this anthracite region and miners in every other coal field in the United States have a fuller picture of this man who was one of the most significant figures in American labor history. For many years he went about the unspectacular but very necessary job of clearing the ground for the progress of a great labor movement. He taught a dispersed industry how to organize. He taught both management and labor that the only basis for stability is to be found in contracts that can and will be lived up to by both management and labor.

By victory in the first great battle of the mine workers he broke the tradition of defeat which had always hung over the aspirations of those he led. He convinced the public that the gains of labor were the gains of all, that the labor movement was something to be welcomed rather than feared. He made public opinion a judge to which labor could more confidently appeal. His work was necessary before other men could do theirs.

We now build upon the work of John Mitchell. He pioneered in his day for collective bargaining. Today we have put upon the Federal statute books the legal mechanism to make collective bargaining a reality.

He pioneered in his day for the education of the public. Today we aim to make the public conscious that the welfare of labor is the welfare of all.

Carrying forward his work and that of others like him, we have begun to build a system of old-age pensions and unemployment insurance to substitute for uncertainty a new security in the life of the wage earner and his family.

How far we have come is shown by the patriotic resentment with which labor and the public alike are meeting the latest attempts of a handful of employers, politicians, and newspapers to

547

mislead and coerce labor with regard to the Social Security Act. Here is repetition of the arrogance and the ruthlessness which the operators utilized to try to break the solid ranks of labor when the miners fought at Armageddon in 1902, more than thirty years ago.

No employer has a right to put his political preferences in the pay envelope. That is coercion even if he tells the whole truth.

But this propaganda misrepresents by telling only half the truth. Labor and a fair-minded public must place such tactics in a class with the coercion of the strong-arm squad and the whispering of the planted labor spy.

This pay-envelope propaganda has one clear objective — to sabotage the Social Security Act. To sabotage that Act is to sabotage labor. For that Act, as you know, was worked out with labor and enacted with the active support of labor — all kinds of labor.

Why do these employers seek to repeal the Social Security Act? Because under the Act they have to pay far more than half of the insurance given to the workers.

Get these facts straight.

The Act provides for two kinds of insurance for the worker.

For that insurance both the employer and the worker pay premiums, just as you pay premiums on any other insurance policy. Those premiums are collected in the form of the taxes you hear so much about.

The first kind of insurance covers old age. Here the employer contributes one dollar of premium for every dollar of premium contributed by the worker; but both dollars are held by the Government solely for the benefit of the worker in his old age.

In effect, we have set up a savings account for the old age of the worker. Because the employer is called upon to contribute on a fifty-fifty basis, that savings account gives exactly two dollars of security for every dollar put up by the worker.

The second kind of insurance is unemployment insurance to help the worker and his family over the difficult days when he loses his job. For the unemployment security of the worker, the employer under the Federal law puts up the entire premium —

two dollars. The benefits of this insurance go 100 percent to the worker, none to the employer. But the premiums for this unemployment insurance so far as the Federal Government is concerned are paid 100 percent by the employer.

Now let's add it all up. Beginning January first, for every one dollar which the worker is asked to put into an old-age account for himself, employers are required under the Federal Act to contribute three dollars to protect the worker from both unemployment and old age. That is, the worker contributes only one dollar to his old age security; he contributes nothing to his security against losing his job. But at the same time the employer has to put up two dollars for unemployment and one dollar for old age.

Three for one! There's the rub. That is what these propaganda-spreading employers object to. The record extending back several years shows that their purpose has always been to compel the workers alone to put up all the premiums both for their unemployment insurance and their old-age insurance. They are now trying to frighten the workers about the workers' one-dollar premium, so that they won't have to pay their three-dollar premium.

These propagandists — with allies whom I do not have to describe to you who know them — are driven in their desperation to the contemptible, unpatriotic suggestion that some future Congress will steal these insurance funds for other purposes. If they really believe what they say in the pay envelopes, they have no confidence in our form of government or its permanence. It might be well for them to move to some other Nation in which they have greater faith.

I know that American workers made wise as well as strong by the achievements of John Mitchell and his successors will not be fooled by this campaign any more than they were frightened by the strong-arm squads of the past.

John Mitchell taught labor that to win and to preserve the fruits of its victories, it must have a cool head as well as a warm heart. I know that labor will refuse to be robbed of its gains, that the progress begun by its friends will be safeguarded and carried forward, until the fuller security that is its right is won.

201 ❦ Campaign Address at Harrisburg, Pa. "Ours Has Been a Program of One for All and All for One." October 29, 1936

(Republican two-faced campaign — Administration's efforts in behalf of consumers.)

My friends of Pennsylvania:

PENNSYLVANIA is at once a great industrial State, a great commercial State, a great mining State and a great agricultural State.

The Pennsylvania farmer, unlike the farmer in the West, can see his own city market within a few hours' drive, just as my neighbor farmers in the Hudson River Valley. And the Pennsylvania industrial worker and merchant know how important to their prosperity is the prosperity of their neighbors, the farmers.

Pennsylvania rightly calls itself the Keystone State. Great tides of immigration have swept through it. Great routes of commerce have crossed it from the very beginning — famous wagon-roads and railroads and water routes from the East to the West and the North to the South and back again. Pennsylvania knows that American commerce transcends State lines and becomes interstate and international.

But because Pennsylvania has these great problems of commerce and of industry it has, also, great human problems — and those are the problems with which you and I are most deeply concerned.

The machine age has served well the men and women who use its excellent products. The new problem is to see to it that the machine age serves equally well the men and women who run its machines.

That is a problem not for Pennsylvania alone, not even for

industry alone. It is a problem for the Nation, and for all kinds of enterprise within the Nation. If modern Government is to justify itself, it must see to it that human values are not mangled and destroyed.

You and I know that that is sound morality and good religion. You and I know that it is also good business.

The simple fact of our dependence upon each other was either unknown or entirely ignored by the Republican leaders of the post-war period. Their doctrine was to give definite help at the top and to utter pious hopes for the bottom. Twelve years of that brought the inevitable crash.

When we came to Washington in 1933 it was our fundamental belief that faith without works is dead. We acted — not for a few of us but for all of us. That program worked.

But I am very much afraid that the Republican leadership is still the same. It still preaches the same heresy — class against class and region against region.

You do not need me to tell you this. They say it themselves, loudly. There are dozens of examples — but just take one. They are using it, for example, in what they call their market-basket campaign.

In the cities they make promises which they are careful to hide from the farmers. In the rural districts they make promises which they are careful to hide from the city dwellers. In the cities they promise to reduce food prices for the woman who carries the market-basket. In the country they promise to raise food prices for the man who grows the contents of that market-basket on the farm.

Now is that not a nice fairy story? You and I know that you cannot eat your cake in the city and have your cake on the farm. You and I know that after twelve years of that policy there was no cake, and there was very little bread. The American people are through with that kind of emptiness.

The prices of farm products have risen since 1932. It's a good thing for all of us that they have risen. We set out deliberately to raise them. It was their rise that helped to start all of us on the road to recovery again. Every home in America has benefited by that.

The prices the farmer was receiving in 1932 were so low that he had no cash income to buy industrial goods made in the cities. That threw people out of work in the cities. Today the farm's products bring more to the farmer. Here in Pennsylvania, for instance, cash income from farm production was 47 percent higher in 1935 than in 1932. That is typical of what has happened to farmers throughout the East and throughout the Nation. The farmer is able to buy more from the city. That means more people are at work in the cities, and that in turn means that the city dwellers buy more farm produce.

That is why the consumer's pocketbook has filled up faster than the price of food has gone up. The housewife pays more money for what she buys, but she has more money to buy it with, and she has more money left over after she has bought. Nationwide facts and figures prove this. Let us take a look at these figures.

From 1929 to 1932 food prices in the United States dropped 35 percent, but understand this: factory payrolls in the same period went down 58 percent. That made a large hole in the workers' market-basket.

The average city family paid less for what it bought in those years. But that family had still less with which to buy.

Some retail food prices have risen higher than others. Other food prices have advanced very little. To be fair you have to strike an average. The average advance of food costs since 1932 is 24 percent, a quarter more than they were four years ago.

But compare that — again using average figures for the country — with the factory payrolls. These have gone up since the spring of 1933, not 24 percent but 77 percent. And if you take the average of all city dwellers, their incomes have gone up faster and farther than food prices have gone up. To sum up: the Republican market-basket of 1932 cost less but the American consumer did not have the cash to fill it. Our market-basket in 1936 has much in it because people have money in their pockets to fill it with.

It is true that there is often too wide a spread between what the farmer gets and what the consumer pays. For that neither the farmer nor the consumer is responsible, and both the farmer and the consumer suffer.

We are engaged very definitely in seeking to solve that difficulty. First, we are vigilant and on guard against monopolies which are contrary to sound public policy even though they are not actually illegal. Second, we are seeking new means to eliminate waste and unnecessary duplication in distributing the food-supply of the Nation, to benefit both producer and consumer.

Through twelve years the Republicans proved that sectionalism will not work. We have proved in three and a half years that interdependence and unity will work.

Giving the farmer of Dauphin or Lancaster County a good break has given a good break to the steel worker of Pittsburgh, the coal miner of Scranton, the white-collar or factory worker of Philadelphia. And giving California, Minnesota and Texas a good break gives a good break to Pennsylvania, Ohio and New Jersey.

Ours has been a program of one for all and all for one. That doctrine has given us recovery. Continuing that practice will continue recovery.

You all remember that good old Republican slogan that was trotted out and polished up for every political campaign—the slogan of "the full dinner pail." And we know that the Republican leaders themselves were responsible for its sad end. Down to 1933, the full dinner pail turned out to be the empty market-basket.

I know that the American people will not return to power those leaders who emptied the national market-basket. I know that the American people will go forward with those who are succeeding in filling it once more.

202 ⟮ Campaign Address at Camden, N. J., on Human Security. October 29, 1936

Mr. Mayor, my friends of Camden:

I AM very, very grateful to you and to your City Government for naming this plaza in my honor. It is not very long ago that I read that some of the Federal funds intended for work relief were to be used to transform the plaza into a beautiful park; and it was suggested at that time that here is one case where grass has been made to grow in the city streets. *(Laughter) (Note: This was a reference to a statement made by President Hoover in the* 1932 *campaign that if Franklin D. Roosevelt were elected, grass would grow in the streets of hundreds of American cities.)*

I have come to Camden today for one perfectly valid reason: it is the principal city of Southern New Jersey, and, so far as I recollect in a somewhat varied experience, I have never made a speech here before.

Because Camden is a good cross-section of many different types of people who earn their living — commuters, white-collar workers, factory workers, and shipyard workers — I want to say a few words about a subject which affects every one of you — your own lives and the lives of your families — the subject of human security.

We have heard much about it during the last three and a half years for the very simple reason that the Nation has needed human security. We have needed it for the farmer and for the city dweller alike.

You who work in offices or factories or shipyards are hit when business slumps. Your future is tied up with the stability of the business in which you work.

Holding on to a job in these past few years was not the only problem you faced. You had to think of your families. You had to think of your homes. You had to think of the savings in the bank. You had to think about your modest investments and your insurance policies, and your mortgage payments. None of these things was safe in those days.

Today things are very different. Business of all kinds has begun to get in the clear. You know that your jobs are safer, that there are more jobs to go around and better pay for jobs. The threat to your savings, your investments, your insurance policies and your homes is being removed.

None of this came by chance. It came because your Government refused to leave it to chance. It came because your Administration thought things through — thought of things as a whole — planned a balanced national economy and acted in a score of ways to bring it to pass. Today I want to mention only two examples out of many.

First, your savings. We did not leave them to chance. Today for the first time your deposits in every national bank and in eight thousand State banks throughout the country are insured up to five thousand dollars — a total of forty-nine million accounts. In other words, 98½ percent of all bank accounts in these banks are insured. Never in all our history have we had as sound a banking structure as today. And I doubt very much if any of you will vote to go back to the unsafe banking conditions of 1932.

And once more, I remind the Nation that this month of October marks the end of one whole year in which there was not a single national bank failure — the first twelve-month period in fifty-five years that was free from such failures.

The other example I want to say a word about relates to the stability of what you and I call values. For twelve years before this Administration came into office, values of almost every kind of property were running up and down the scale like the mercury in a thermometer on a March day. Raw material prices were varying 400 and 500 and 600 percent. Real estate was alternately booming and collapsing.

As a result, the assets behind everything you and I owned were better one month and poorer the next. Bankers did not know what their portfolios would be worth from one month to the next. Commercial concerns had no assurance of the value of their bills receivable. Contractors could make only wild guesses in submitting their bids. Many stocks and bonds were worth crazy prices one month and very little the next.

After the crash, and after the long years of despair which followed it, one prayer went up from the American people—they wanted something to tie to—they sought stability because they knew that without stability they could not have security.

It has been our aim first of all to restore values to a normal and proper level. It is our aim to maintain them at a normal and proper level. In that way we believe there will be a greater security for the average American family no matter what may be the occupation of the members of that family.

My friends, today in Wilkes-Barre, Pennsylvania, I spoke very briefly in regard to the great Social Security Law which goes into effect next year. I spoke about those few business concerns and those few newspapers which are spreading false rumors in regard to this far-reaching Act. I told the people of Pennsylvania that for every dollar which the worker is asked to put into the fund under this law as a premium of insurance against old age, the employer is required to put in another dollar. And for the other form of insurance in the Act—unemployment insurance—the premium is paid solely by the employer and not by the worker. In other words, for the insurance which you get, you people are going to pay one dollar of premium and your employers are going to pay three dollars. Three to one, there is the rub! That is what the propaganda mongers really object to. Not satisfied with that, they are endeavoring to spread the unpatriotic suggestion that some future Congress may steal these insurance funds for other purposes.

And if these employers really believe what they are saying in their propaganda spread in pay envelopes, it proves that they have no confidence in our form of government. I suggest to them that it might be well for them to move to some other Nation in which they have a greater faith.

Your Administration has as its great objectives for all our citizens, in the cities and on the farms, in the West, in the South and in the East — greater permanence for employment, safety for earnings, protection for the home and a better security for the average man and his family. Those objectives can and will be attained. You and I are going to carry on until they are.

203 (Campaign Address at Wilmington, Del., on "Liberty." October 29, 1936

SAVE for my own home State of New York, this meeting in Wilmington marks the close of my campaign for the Presidency.

It seems appropriate that on this occasion I should make no political speech, because I can better describe the kind of liberty which our Administration has sought and continues to seek by reading to you the simple words of a great President who believed in the kind of liberty that we believe in — the great President who preserved the American Union.

These words are from the speech made by President Abraham Lincoln at the Sanitary Fair in Baltimore in 1864. And I ask that you good people give heed to these words for, although they are three-quarters of a century old, yet I think you will find that they apply to 1936. Abraham Lincoln said this:

"The world has never had a good definition of the word liberty, and the American people, just now, are much in want of one. We all declare for liberty; but in using the same word we do not all mean the same thing. With some the word liberty may mean for each man to do as he pleases with himself, and the product of his labor; while with others the same word may mean for some men to do as they please with other men, and the product of other men's labor. Here are two, not only different, but incompatible things, called by the same name, liberty. And it follows that each of the things is, by the respective parties, called by two different and incompatible names — liberty and tyranny."

And then Abraham Lincoln used this homely example. He said:

"The shepherd drives the wolf from the sheep's throat, for

which the sheep thanks the shepherd as his liberator, while the wolf denounces him for the same act, as the destroyer of liberty. . . . Plainly, the sheep and the wolf are not agreed upon a definition of the word liberty; and precisely the same difference prevails today among us human creatures . . . and all professing to love liberty. Hence we behold the process by which thousands are daily passing from under the yoke of bondage hailed by some as the advance of liberty, and bewailed by others as the destruction of all liberty."

And, in closing, Lincoln said this:

"Recently, as it seems, the people . . . have been doing something to define liberty, and thanks to them that, in what they have done, the wolf's dictionary has been repudiated."

My friends, today, in 1936, the people have again been doing something to define liberty. And the wolf's dictionary has again been repudiated.

What Abraham Lincoln said three-quarters of a century ago applies today as it did then. The people, men and women, of the City of Wilmington and the State of Delaware will, I think, appreciate their significance in the same measure as men and women in every other part of the Union.

And that is why, my friends, on Tuesday evening next I expect to get a message from the State of Delaware telling me that all is well.

NOTE: Wilmington is the home city and Delaware the home State of the Du Pont corporations and affiliate companies whose principal owners were instrumental in organizing and financing the "American Liberty League," composed chiefly of rich and powerful industrialists and financiers. The chief purpose of the organization was to oppose and defeat the New Deal. That is the reason for the selection of Wilmington, Del., as the place to read President Lincoln's discussion of the definition of "Liberty."

204 ⟨ Campaign Address at Brooklyn, N. Y., on the Administration's Record of Accomplishment. October 30, 1936

DURING the past month I have seen a great deal of our country and a great many of our people. Both the America and the Americans I have seen look very different from three and a half years ago.

Many important things have happened to them in those three and a half years. I could talk to you for hours about this better, happier America. What I am going to talk to you about for a few minutes, however, is some of the things that have brought about that better, happier America. I want to tell you in terms of actual achievement what we in Washington have done, what we have done to restore prosperity, what we have done to end abuses.

The first thing before us on that famous fourth of March, 1933, was to give aid to those overtaken by disaster. We did that, and we are not ashamed of giving help to those who needed help. We furnished food relief, drought relief, flood relief, work relief. We established the Federal Emergency Relief Administration; the Public Works Administration; the Civilian Conservation Corps; the Works Progress Administration. Some people ridicule them as alphabetical agencies. But you and I know that they are the agencies that have substituted food for starvation; work for idleness; hope instead of dull despair.

And on November 3d, America will say that that was a job well done!

The second thing we did was to help our stalled economic engine to get under way again. We knew enough about the mechanism of our economic order to know that we could not do that one wheel at a time. We had had enough of one-wheel economics. We proposed to get all four wheels started at once. We knew that it was no good to try to start only the wheel of finance. At the same time we had to start the wheels of agriculture, of workers of all classes, of business and industry.

559

By democratizing the work of the Reconstruction Finance Corporation and redirecting it into more practical and helpful channels we furnished fuel for the machine.

We primed the pump by spending Government money in direct relief, in work relief, in public works.

We established the Agricultural Adjustment Administration; the National Recovery Administration; the Farm Credit Administration; the Soil Conservation Program; the Home Owners Loan Corporation; the Federal Housing Administration; the Tennessee Valley Authority; the Resettlement Administration; the Rural Electrification Administration. We set up a sound monetary policy; a sound banking structure; reciprocal trade agreements; foreign exchange accords.

We created a National Labor Relations Board to improve working conditions and seek industrial peace. We brought the business men of the Nation together to encourage them to increase wages, to shorten working hours, to abolish child labor. With labor's aid and backing we took the first great step for workers' security by the Social Security Act — an act which is now being misrepresented to the workers in a pay-envelope propaganda by a few employers whom you will easily recognize as old time exploiters of labor who have always fought against contributing anything themselves to a sound security for the laboring man and his wife and children.

That Act is a new Magna Charta for those who work. In its preparation and in its enactment, it was supported not only by organized labor but by those other liberal groups — workers, employers, churches, private charities, educators who for many years have believed that modern Government can make provision against the hardship of unemployment and the terrors of old age.

On the passage of this law, in addition to overwhelming support on the part of Democrats in both the House and Senate, the country should note that seventy-seven Republican Representatives voted for it and only eighteen against it, and that in the Senate fifteen Republican Senators voted for it and only five against it.

-3-

Conservation Program; a sound ~~M~~ monetary policy; a sound ~~M~~ banking structure; reciprocal trade agreements; ~~international currency~~ *foreign exchange* *accords;* ~~stabilization;~~ Home Owners Loan Corporation; the Federal Housing Administration; the Tennessee Valley Authority.

We set up a National Labor Relations Board to improve working conditions and ~~M~~ stabilize industrial relations. We brought the business men of the Nation together to encourage them to increase wages, to shorten working hours, to abolish child labor. With labor's aid and backing we set up a new charter *for* workers security in the Social Security Act -- an act which is now being misrepresented to the workers in a pay-envelope propaganda by those old-time exploiters of labor who have always fought against ~~a real~~ *contributing* *anything themselves* ~~to~~ a sound security for the laboring man and his wife and children.

Some people call these things ~~which we did bureaucracy and~~ waste. ~~From what we know about America today,~~ You and I ~~call them~~ *know that* *they are* the means by which our stalled machine was started again.

And on November third America will say that that was a job well done.

FACSIMILE OF A PAGE OF THE FIRST DRAFT OF THE CAMPAIGN ADDRESS AT BROOKLYN, N. Y., OCTOBER 30, 1936. (ITEM 204)

We established the Agricultural Adjustment Administration;

the National Recovery Administration; the Farm Credit Administration;

the Soil Conservation Program; the Home Owners Loan Corporation; the

Federal Housing Administration; the Tennessee Valley Authority; a   *we set up*

sound monetary policy; a sound banking structure; reciprocal trade

agreements; foreign exchange accords.

We set up a National Labor Relations Board to improve
                                seek   *peace*
working conditions and ~~stabilize~~ industrial ~~relations~~. We brought

the business men of the Nation together to encourage them to increase

wages, to shorten working hours, to abolish child labor. With
                        took the first great step
labor's aid and backing we ~~set up a new machinery~~ for workers security
by
~~in~~ the Social Security Act -- an act which is now being misrepresented
                                                        a few employers whom you
to the workers in a pay-envelope propaganda by ~~these~~ old-time *will easily*
                                                                    recognize
exploiters of labor who have always fought against contributing   *as*

anything themselves to a sound security for the laboring man and his

wife and children.

A Some people call these things waste. You and I know that

they are the means by which our stalled machine was started again.

FACSIMILE OF THE SECOND DRAFT OF THE SAME PAGE

This fact is perhaps illustrative of the paradox that in the closing days of the campaign, a distraught Republican leadership, driven to desperation and urged on by the same sinister forces which generation after generation have opposed all social legislation, now repudiates its own Representatives and Senators in the halls of the Congress and leaves them looking positively silly.

The people of the State of New York recognize in this issue in a national campaign only another form of the struggle to which we have become accustomed in this State for many years past. Every man and woman here knows that we have been blessed with these great social reforms because we have had liberal Government in Albany. We know that we would not have had them if the Old Guard Republican leadership had been in power.

Governor Lehman has not merely exemplified in his splendid objectives this spirit of far-sighted progress, but he has practiced what he has preached, and thereby has continued to strengthen the civic conscience of the people of this State. There is none among you who believes that on Tuesday next there is one chance in a thousand that New York State will turn its Government back to the Old Guard.

To return to what the Federal Government has done in the past three and one-half years, some people call these things waste. You and I know that they are the means by which our stalled machine has been started on the road once more.

And on November 3d America will say that that was a job well done!

The third thing we did was to look to the future, to root out abuses, to establish every possible defense against a return of the evils which brought the crash. We established the Securities Exchange Commission; banking reforms; a sound monetary policy; deposit insurance for fifty million bank accounts—all aimed to safeguard the thrift of our citizens.

By our tax policy and by regulating financial markets, we loosened the grip which monopolies had fastened upon independent American business. We began also to free American business and American labor from the unfair competition of

561

a small unscrupulous minority. We established by statute a curb upon the overweening power and unholy practices of some utility holding companies.

By the Rural Electrification Act, by the Tennessee Valley Authority and similar projects we set up yardsticks to bring electricity at cheaper rates to the average American farm and the average American home. Through loans to private enterprise and in cooperation with cities, we promoted slum-clearance and established low-cost modern housing. We set up a National Youth Administration to help keep our youth in school and to hold open for them the door of opportunity. By a successful war on crime we have made America's homes and places of business safer against the gangster, the kidnapper and the racketeer.

Some people call these things meddling and interference. You and I know them to be new stones in a foundation on which we can, and are determined to, build a structure of economic security for all our people — a safer, happier, more American America.

On November 3d, the American people will say that that is a job well begun!

These are the things we have done. They are a record of three and a half years crowded with achievements significant of better life for all the people. Every group in our national life has benefited, because what we have done for each group has produced benefits for every other group. In our policies there are no distinctions between them. There will be none. If we are in trouble we are all of us in trouble together. If we are to be prosperous, if we are to be secure, we must all be prosperous and secure together.

Unfortunately, those who now raise the cry of class distinctions are the very leaders whose policies in the past have fostered such distinctions. When they were in power, they were content in the belief that the chief function of Government was to help only those at the top in the pious hope that the few at the top would in their benevolence or generosity pass that help on.

That theory of Government has been banished from Washington. It did not work. It was not and cannot be the answer to our problem. We have united all classes in the Nation in a program for the Nation. In doing that, we are bridging the gulf of antagonism which twelve years of neglect had opened up between them.

An equally important task remains to be done: to go forward, to consolidate and to strengthen these gains, to close the gaps by destroying the glaring inequalities of opportunity and of security which, in the recent past, have set group against group and region against region.

By our policies for the future we will carry forward this program of unity. We will not be content until all our people fairly share in the ever-increasing capacity of America to provide a high standard of living for all its citizens.

On November 3d, the American people will say that our policy for the future is their policy for the future.

205 ❡ Informal Extemporaneous Remarks at a Gathering of Workers at National Campaign Headquarters, New York City. October 31, 1936

I THINK I am entitled to say, "my fellow workers." Jim Farley has suggested that I am going to carry this District.

You know, I envy you because in previous years I have been at Headquarters during campaigns. I know how hard the work is, but it is fun; and I have missed being up here in New York City these past months helping you good people make the wheels go round.

But you, too, have missed something. I wish you could have been out on the road with me. It would have given you a perfectly tremendous thrill, just as it did me, going into a great many different parts of the country, seeing the faces of men, women and children, and especially seeing their interest in things American.

I think that the most important impression that I have carried with me through these past weeks has been that more than in any other campaign in all of our American history, people are taking an intelligent interest—reading, going and listening to people's talks, reading all the literature of both parties, and then making up their own minds. It is the greatest thing that has happened for our democratic form of Government in these later years.

I am glad that people have been reading the literature of both sides. I am glad that they have been going to meetings where people on both sides speak. It is an extension of the forum idea of getting both sides of the question presented. Of course, I may be, frankly, a little prejudiced, but I believe that the more people go to forums, the more people listen to both sides and read the literature of both sides, even the newspapers, the bigger our majority is going to be.

You at Headquarters, of course, prepare the material for this campaign, and see to it that every city and every county and every little hamlet is given the information; and I am very proud of the fact that our information has been kept at a pretty high level.

One reason for that is the fact that we have at the head of this campaign a man who has always been square. I have known Jim Farley for a great many years, and I have never known him yet to do or think a mean thing.

For a long time now—a good many years—he has been taking it on the chin with a smile and not batting an eyelid, because, I think, in the back of his head he has had the idea that in spite of all kinds of unfair attacks, the American people will read him for what he is, absolutely on the level.

And incidentally, of course, I get reports in Washington not only from Jim, but from lots of people, about what has been going on here in New York. After an experience with many headquarters dating back to 1912, I have come to the very definite conclusion that the National Headquarters this year has had perfect teamwork: no cross wires, everything clicking, and the result is going to bear that out next Tuesday.

And so I am very grateful, I am very grateful to all of you from Jim down to the office boy. And maybe the office boy will be National Chairman or President about thirty years from now.

I want to thank you for all that you have done, for the many hours that you have spent in overtime and regular time, not only working in the offices, but, as most of you have been doing, working in your own homes.

It has been an inspiration for me to know that I have had the support of all you good people not only the past few months, but also the past few years, and I think we are going to continue with that support in the next four years.

So once more let me thank you from the bottom of my heart. I wish I could meet each and every one of you in person. I want you to consider that I have shaken the hand of each and every one of you, and I hope that we will meet again some day soon.

I want to take this occasion, when you are all here, to send our thanks, yours and mine, to the many hundreds of men and women in all the States of the Union, in all the counties of the Union, in all the villages and cities of the Union, who in their way have been carrying on the same kind of task that we have been engaged in. I am going to ask Jim to send your regards, my regards, your thanks and my thanks to those in every part of the Nation who have been working toward this goal that we all believe we are going to reach next Tuesday.

206 ⟨ Campaign Address at Madison Square Garden, New York City. "We Have Only Just Begin to Fight." October 31, 1936

(American desire for peace and security at home and abroad — What we have done to fulfill that desire — We shall continue in our fight to attain our objectives.)

Senator Wagner, Governor Lehman, ladies and gentlemen:

ON THE eve of a national election, it is well for us to stop for a moment and analyze calmly and without prejudice the effect on our Nation of a victory by either of the major political parties.

The problem of the electorate is far deeper, far more vital than the continuance in the Presidency of any individual. For the greater issue goes beyond units of humanity — it goes to humanity itself.

In 1932 the issue was the restoration of American democracy; and the American people were in a mood to win. They did win. In 1936 the issue is the preservation of their victory. Again they are in a mood to win. Again they will win.

More than four years ago in accepting the Democratic nomination in Chicago, I said: "Give me your help not to win votes alone, but to win in this crusade to restore America to its own people."

The banners of that crusade still fly in the van of a Nation that is on the march.

It is needless to repeat the details of the program which this Administration has been hammering out on the anvils of experience. No amount of misrepresentation or statistical contortion can conceal or blur or smear that record. Neither the attacks of unscrupulous enemies nor the exaggerations of over-zealous friends will serve to mislead the American people.

What was our hope in 1932? Above all other things the American people wanted peace. They wanted peace of mind instead of gnawing fear.

First, they sought escape from the personal terror which had stalked them for three years. They wanted the peace that comes from security in their homes: safety for their savings, permanence in their jobs, a fair profit from their enterprise.

Next, they wanted peace in the community, the peace that springs from the ability to meet the needs of community life: schools, playgrounds, parks, sanitation, highways — those things which are expected of solvent local government. They sought escape from disintegration and bankruptcy in local and state affairs.

They also sought peace within the Nation: protection of their currency, fairer wages, the ending of long hours of toil, the abolition of child labor, the elimination of wild-cat speculation, the safety of their children from kidnappers.

And, finally, they sought peace with other Nations — peace in a world of unrest. The Nation knows that I hate war, and I know that the Nation hates war.

I submit to you a record of peace; and on that record a well-founded expectation for future peace — peace for the individual, peace for the community, peace for the Nation, and peace with the world.

Tonight I call the roll — the roll of honor of those who stood with us in 1932 and still stand with us today.

Written on it are the names of millions who never had a chance — men at starvation wages, women in sweatshops, children at looms.

Written on it are the names of those who despaired, young men and young women for whom opportunity had become a will-o'-the-wisp.

Written on it are the names of farmers whose acres yielded only bitterness, business men whose books were portents of disaster, home owners who were faced with eviction, frugal citizens whose savings were insecure.

Written there in large letters are the names of countless other

567

Americans of all parties and all faiths, Americans who had eyes to see and hearts to understand, whose consciences were burdened because too many of their fellows were burdened, who looked on these things four years ago and said, "This can be changed. We will change it."

We still lead that army in 1936. They stood with us then because in 1932 they believed. They stand with us today because in 1936 they know. And with them stand millions of new recruits who have come to know.

Their hopes have become our record.

We have not come this far without a struggle and I assure you we cannot go further without a struggle.

For twelve years this Nation was afflicted with hear-nothing, see-nothing, do-nothing Government. The Nation looked to Government but the Government looked away. Nine mocking years with the golden calf and three long years of the scourge! Nine crazy years at the ticker and three long years in the breadlines! Nine mad years of mirage and three long years of despair! Powerful influences strive today to restore that kind of government with its doctrine that that Government is best which is most indifferent.

For nearly four years you have had an Administration which instead of twirling its thumbs has rolled up its sleeves. We will keep our sleeves rolled up.

We had to struggle with the old enemies of peace — business and financial monopoly, speculation, reckless banking, class antagonism, sectionalism, war profiteering.

They had begun to consider the Government of the United States as a mere appendage to their own affairs. We know now that Government by organized money is just as dangerous as Government by organized mob.

Never before in all our history have these forces been so united against one candidate as they stand today. They are unanimous in their hate for me — and I welcome their hatred.

I should like to have it said of my first Administration that in it the forces of selfishness and of lust for power met their match. I should like to have it said of my second Administration that in it these forces met their master.

The American people know from a four-year record that today there is only one entrance to the White House—by the front door. Since March 4, 1933, there has been only one pass-key to the White House. I have carried that key in my pocket. It is there tonight. So long as I am President, it will remain in my pocket.

Those who used to have pass-keys are not happy. Some of them are desperate. Only desperate men with their backs to the wall would descend so far below the level of decent citizenship as to foster the current pay-envelope campaign against America's working people. Only reckless men, heedless of consequences, would risk the disruption of the hope for a new peace between worker and employer by returning to the tactics of the labor spy.

Here is an amazing paradox! The very employers and politicians and publishers who talk most loudly of class antagonism and the destruction of the American system now undermine that system by this attempt to coerce the votes of the wage earners of this country. It is the 1936 version of the old threat to close down the factory or the office if a particular candidate does not win. It is an old strategy of tyrants to delude their victims into fighting their battles for them.

Every message in a pay envelope, even if it is the truth, is a command to vote according to the will of the employer. But this propaganda is worse—it is deceit.

They tell the worker his wage will be reduced by a contribution to some vague form of old-age insurance. They carefully conceal from him the fact that for every dollar of premium he pays for that insurance, the employer pays another dollar. That omission is deceit.

They carefully conceal from him the fact that under the federal law, he receives another insurance policy to help him if he loses his job, and that the premium of that policy is paid 100 percent by the employer and not one cent by the worker. They do not tell him that the insurance policy that is bought for him is far more favorable to him than any policy that any private insurance company could afford to issue. That omission is deceit.

They imply to him that he pays all the cost of both forms of insurance. They carefully conceal from him the fact that for every dollar put up by him his employer puts up three dollars — three for one. And that omission is deceit.

But they are guilty of more than deceit. When they imply that the reserves thus created against both these policies will be stolen by some future Congress, diverted to some wholly foreign purpose, they attack the integrity and honor of American Government itself. Those who suggest that, are already aliens to the spirit of American democracy. Let them emigrate and try their lot under some foreign flag in which they have more confidence.

The fraudulent nature of this attempt is well shown by the record of votes on the passage of the Social Security Act. In addition to an overwhelming majority of Democrats in both Houses, seventy-seven Republican Representatives voted for it and only eighteen against it and fifteen Republican Senators voted for it and only five against it. Where does this last-minute drive of the Republican leadership leave these Republican Representatives and Senators who helped enact this law?

I am sure the vast majority of law-abiding businessmen who are not parties to this propaganda fully appreciate the extent of the threat to honest business contained in this coercion.

I have expressed indignation at this form of campaigning and I am confident that the overwhelming majority of employers, workers and the general public share that indignation and will show it at the polls on Tuesday next.

Aside from this phase of it, I prefer to remember this campaign not as bitter but only as hard-fought. There should be no bitterness or hate where the sole thought is the welfare of the United States of America. No man can occupy the office of President without realizing that he is President of all the people.

It is because I have sought to think in terms of the whole Nation that I am confident that today, just as four years ago, the people want more than promises.

Our vision for the future contains more than promises.

This is our answer to those who, silent about their own plans, ask us to state our objectives.

Of course we will continue to seek to improve working conditions for the workers of America — to reduce hours over-long, to increase wages that spell starvation, to end the labor of children, to wipe out sweatshops. Of course we will continue every effort to end monopoly in business, to support collective bargaining, to stop unfair competition, to abolish dishonorable trade practices. For all these we have only just begun to fight.

Of course we will continue to work for cheaper electricity in the homes and on the farms of America, for better and cheaper transportation, for low interest rates, for sounder home financing, for better banking, for the regulation of security issues, for reciprocal trade among nations, for the wiping out of slums. For all these we have only just begun to fight.

Of course we will continue our efforts in behalf of the farmers of America. With their continued cooperation we will do all in our power to end the piling up of huge surpluses which spelled ruinous prices for their crops. We will persist in successful action for better land use, for reforestation, for the conservation of water all the way from its source to the sea, for drought and flood control, for better marketing facilities for farm commodities, for a definite reduction of farm tenancy, for encouragement of farmer cooperatives, for crop insurance and a stable food supply. For all these we have only just begun to fight.

Of course we will provide useful work for the needy unemployed; we prefer useful work to the pauperism of a dole.

Here and now I want to make myself clear about those who disparage their fellow citizens on the relief rolls. They say that those on relief are not merely jobless — that they are worthless. Their solution for the relief problem is to end relief — to purge the rolls by starvation. To use the language of the stock broker, our needy unemployed would be cared for when, as, and if some fairy godmother should happen on the scene.

You and I will continue to refuse to accept that estimate of our unemployed fellow Americans. Your Government is still on the same side of the street with the Good Samaritan and not with those who pass by on the other side.

Again — what of our objectives?

Of course we will continue our efforts for young men and women so that they may obtain an education and an opportunity to put it to use. Of course we will continue our help for the crippled, for the blind, for the mothers, our insurance for the unemployed, our security for the aged. Of course we will continue to protect the consumer against unnecessary price spreads, against the costs that are added by monopoly and speculation. We will continue our successful efforts to increase his purchasing power and to keep it constant.

For these things, too, and for a multitude of others like them, we have only just begun to fight.

All this — all these objectives — spell peace at home. All our actions, all our ideals, spell also peace with other nations.

Today there is war and rumor of war. We want none of it. But while we guard our shores against threats of war, we will continue to remove the causes of unrest and antagonism at home which might make our people easier victims to those for whom foreign war is profitable. You know well that those who stand to profit by war are not on our side in this campaign.

"Peace on earth, good will toward men" — democracy must cling to that message. For it is my deep conviction that democracy cannot live without that true religion which gives a nation a sense of justice and of moral purpose. Above our political forums, above our market places stand the altars of our faith — altars on which burn the fires of devotion that maintain all that is best in us and all that is best in our Nation.

We have need of that devotion today. It is that which makes it possible for government to persuade those who are mentally prepared to fight each other to go on instead, to work for and to sacrifice for each other. That is why we need to say with the Prophet: "What doth the Lord require of thee — but to do justly, to love mercy and to walk humbly with thy God." That is why the recovery we seek, the recovery we are winning, is more than economic. In it are included justice and love and humility, not for ourselves as individuals alone, but for our Nation.

That is the road to peace.

207 ❧ Informal Extemporaneous Remarks at Poughkeepsie, N. Y. November 2, 1936

(My objective: a greater security within the framework of the American Government.)

My friends of Poughkeepsie:

I was thinking this afternoon about the first political speech that I made in this city way back in 1910. And it was a terrible speech.

I decided not long after 1910 that I would never make another political speech in the city of Poughkeepsie for the very good reason that everybody knows me. And so, in spite of newspaper headlines — and you and I have come to discriminate where they are concerned — in spite of all that, I am not going to make a political speech tonight. I am just going to tell you a few things that are on my chest and in my heart at the end of this campaign.

I have visited a great number of States. I have been in the South; I have been in the Middle West; I have been in the Far West; I have been in New England. And I have never seen a political campaign in twenty-five years — twenty-six years — where I could feel inside of me that people all over the country were taking as great and as intelligent an interest in the problems of Government.

One of the good things that came out of the depression was the fact that men and women, rich and poor, in every part of the country, have begun to study the future of America. They have been wondering whether we should do this, or that, or the other thing; and back of it all there has lain, as far as I can see, two very definite thoughts in people's minds. The first is to retain our American form of Government—the democratic system, spelled with a small "d"—the representative system of Government. The other thing that I have carried away with me in this campaign is the thought that people want progress, that they feel that there have been a great many things in the past that we did not do, but that with a great deal of modern knowledge and modern experience the time has come in the United States to accomplish more things for the average citizen.

People in the past have gone along with the idea that we could do without a great many things such, for instance, as security. Well, security means a kind of feeling within our individual selves that we have lacked all through the course of history. We have had to take our chance about our old age in days past. We have had to take our chances with depressions and boom times. We have had to take chances on our jobs. We have had to take chances on buying our homes.

I have believed for a great many years that the time has come in our civilization when a great many of these chances should be eliminated from our lives.

It has not been so much a question of party politics. Most of us would have followed any responsible leader who could have shown to the people of this country that he sought to eliminate at least some of those chances in life, some of the hardships that have come to a lot of people through no fault of their own.

I know conditions in this city and in this county pretty well. I have lived here for fifty-four years. And all through my life, ever since I have been of age to take any part in public affairs, which is at least a quarter of a century, I have been noticing a great many hardships that have affected the people of the city and the county. As I got older and was able to travel around the country, I found that the same kind of hardships affected people in every other community and county and state.

And that is why, as some of you who know me can perhaps realize, I have tried for a good many years to work for the elimination of these hardships.

We cannot reach a millennium or utopia in any four years, or eight years; but at least I have felt that people in responsible positions ought to start the ball rolling, that they ought to make an effort, through legislation and through public opinion, in a perfectly normal, sane, sensible way, to provide security — security for people so that they would not individually worry, security for their families, security for their homes, a greater security for their jobs, and, incidentally, a greater security for the people who employ them.

That has been an objective of mine for perhaps twenty-five years; and I believe that in these past few years we have taken steps that are going to help the American people toward a greater security within the framework of the American Government.

That is perhaps a simple expression of a simple philosophy. I think most of you agree with the philosophy at least. Everybody in public office makes mistakes. Every party in power makes mistakes. But, in the last analysis, the problem before the voters of the country, not only tomorrow but next year and the year after that, is whether they want to vote for those people who they believe will carry out that expression of a greater physical and mental and spiritual security for the people of this country.

Tonight at eleven o'clock I am speaking on a nationwide broadcast — and again the newspapers have said it is an appeal for votes. It is not. It is an appeal for people in this Nation to go to the polls — not an appeal to vote any ticket. It is an appeal to exercise their right as American citizens.

We have come a long way in 150 years. About a block from where I stand — up there on the corner of Main Street — there was a little old stone building, and in the year 1788 there was held there the Constitutional Convention of the State of New York. My great-great-grandfather was a member of that Convention. The question was: Should New York ratify the Federal Constitution? It was the year before the Federal Government was set up and George Washington was inaugurated our first

President. At that time the problem before this Convention in Poughkeepsie was whether the State of New York would ratify the Constitution as it was laid down, without a Bill of Rights.

Finally, the delegates from this State, up there in the little old stone building, ratified it only on this condition: "In full faith and confidence that a Bill of Rights would be added to the Constitution after the country was started under the new form of Government." And, largely because of the insistence of the State of New York in demanding a Bill of Rights, almost immediately the new Government submitted to the States the first Ten Amendments to the United States Constitution.

And in those days at the time of the first election, after the Constitution was ratified and the Government was set up, it is interesting for us to note that very few men — of course there were no women voting in those days — comparatively very few men voted. The reason for that was that in the early days of the United States, the franchise was limited to property holders. Most of this Dutchess County of ours in the early days of the Republic was inhabited by tenant farmers. A tenant farmer could not vote because he was not a freeholder and only freeholders could vote in this and the other counties of the State of New York and the other young States.

Today we have a very different proposition. The franchise is universal. You do not have to be the owner of real estate in order to vote.

The result is that in the early days of the Nation, with this limited franchise, the results of an election could not be called the rule of the majority, because so few people voted — only property holders. Today you have a different situation and by midnight tomorrow night, in all probability, whatever the result is, it will be definitely, clearly, and conclusively the will of the majority.

In the election of 1932, about forty million voters in the United States voted. This year there are about fifty-five million Americans who are eligible to vote tomorrow. I want to express the hope that as many as possible of those fifty-five millions will go to the polls, in order that we may have a clear-cut answer to the problems which will be voted on.

I go back a good many years in this city. I can remember when, in the spring, the streets were extremely muddy. I can remember when electric lights first came to Poughkeepsie. And I can remember the first telephone that was put in our house at Hyde Park, much to the horror of most of the family. I can remember that when a telegram came the entire household quaked, because telegrams were seldom sent in those days unless someone died. And, taking it by and large, in those forty or fifty years, I think we have made a good deal of progress not only in other parts of the country, but right here in this city and county; and that is one reason why I am terribly proud of good old Dutchess, whether they vote for me or not.

I am not asking any of you to vote for me, but I am expressing this thought: I hope very much that Dutchess County tomorrow will be found on the same side as the majority of the United States.

Good night and good luck.

208 ❮ Final Campaign Radio Speech of the 1936 Presidential Campaign. "Whoever Is Elected Tomorrow Will Become the President of *All* the People." November 2, 1936

(*Duty of every citizen to vote — Freedom and secrecy of the American ballot.*)

My friends:

I HAVE come home to my own county to vote with my fellow townsmen. My people have voted here in Dutchess County for more than a century. I cast my first vote here in 1903.

Tomorrow fifty-five million Americans are eligible to vote. I hope that all of those fifty-five millions will vote.

I like to think of these millions as individual citizens from Maine to the southern tip of California, from Key West to Puget Sound — farmers who stop their fall plowing long enough to drive into town with their wives — wage earners stopping on the way to work or the way home — business and professional men and women — town and city housewives — and that great company of youth for whom this year's first vote will be a great adventure.

Americans have had to put up with a good many things in the course of our history. But the only rule we have ever put up with is the rule of the majority. That is the only rule we ever will put up with. Spelled with a small "d" we are all democrats.

In some places in the world the tides are running against democracy. But our faith has not been unsettled. We believe in democracy because of our traditions. But we believe in it even more because of our experience.

Here in the United States we have been a long time at the business of self-government. The longer we are at it the more certain we become that we can continue to govern ourselves, that progress is on the side of majority rule, that if mistakes are to be made we prefer to make them ourselves and to do our own correcting.

When you and I stand in line tomorrow for our turn at the polls, we shall stand in a line which reaches back across the entire history of our Nation.

Washington stood in that line and Jefferson and Jackson and Lincoln. And in later days Cleveland stood there and Theodore Roosevelt and Woodrow Wilson. All these — in their day — waited their turn to vote. And rubbing elbows with them — their voting equals — is a long succession of American citizens whose names are not known to history but who, by their vote, helped to make history.

Every man and every woman who has voted in the past has had a hand in the making of the United States of the present. Every man and woman who votes tomorrow will have a hand in the making of the United States of the future. To refuse to vote is to say: "I am not interested in the United States of the future."

We who live in a free America know that our democracy is not perfect. But we are beginning to know also that, in self-government as in many other things, progress comes from experience. People do not become good citizens by mandate. They become good citizens by the exercise of their citizenship and by the discussions, the reading, the campaign give-and-take which help them make up their minds how to exercise that citizenship.

Not only are people voting in larger numbers this year. They also know more this year than ever before about the real issues. They are thinking for themselves. They listen to both sides. They no longer accept at face value opinions or even statements from newspapers, from political spokesmen and from so-called leaders of their communities. They insist on checking up.

I doubt if there was ever more downright political intelligence at the average American fireside than there is today.

For a century and a half we have had here free education and a free press, free public forums and a free pulpit. For more than a decade we have had a free radio. The American citizen of 1936, therefore, is a product of free institutions. His mind has been sharpened by the exercise of freedom. That is why I have no fear either of the threats of demagogues or the ambitions of dictators. Neither can get far nor long thrive among a people who have learned to think for themselves and who have the courage to act as they think.

This year they have thought things through to a point where the eternal simplicities mean more than the fuzz-buzz of technical talk. They know that the important thing is the spirit in which Government will face problems as they come up, and the values it will seek to preserve or to enhance. At bottom those are the things that count.

Still another thing heartens me. This year, not only are more people voting, not only have people thought things through more carefully; but more people in all parties have assumed the obligation of citizens to get out and work in the political process by which democracy maintains itself.

Nearly six months ago I said: "I make this specific recommendation — that each and every one who is interested in obtaining the facts and in spreading those facts abroad, each and every one of you interested in getting at the truth that lies somewhere behind the smoke-screen of charges and countercharges of a national campaign, constitute yourself a committee of one."

Hundreds of thousands have responded to that suggestion. Tonight I salute those committees of one, not only with personal gratitude but with the gratitude of a democracy that can only function if its people are willing to take honorable part in it.

And I also commend those who have worked in a similar honorable way in the opposition. They, too, have helped the public understand the issues before it, and that is a service to democracy.

I confidently look forward to their continued cooperation in the service of democracy. On Saturday night I said that "there should be no bitterness or hate where the sole thought is the welfare of the United States of America." That applies to men and women in all parties. It is true, tonight, on the eve of election. It will be true after the election.

Whoever is elected tomorrow will become the President of all the people. It will be his concern to meet the problems of all the people with an understanding mind and with no trace of partisan feeling.

Any President should welcome any American citizen or group of citizens who can offer constructive suggestions for the management of government or for the improvement of laws.

Society needs constant vigilance and the interest of individual men and women.

And when you go to the ballot box tomorrow, do not be afraid to vote as you think best for the kind of a world you want to have. There need be no strings on any of us in the polling place.

A man or woman in the polling booth is his or her own boss. There once was a time when the ballot was not secret. That is not so today. How a citizen votes is the citizen's own business. No one will fire you because you vote contrary to his wishes or instructions. No one will know how you vote. And do not let anyone intimidate you or coerce you by telling you otherwise.

In the polling booth we are all equals.

It is an experience in responsibility and humility to be permitted, as President, to know and share the hopes and the difficulties, the patience and the courage, the victories and the defeats of this great people.

Sometimes men wonder overmuch what they will receive for what they are giving in the service of a democracy — whether it is worth the cost to share in that struggle which is a part of the business of representative government. But the reward of that effort is to feel that they have been a part of great things, that they have helped to build, that they have had their share in the great battles of their generation.

However large or small our part, we can all feel with Theodore Roosevelt who said many years ago: "It is not the critic who counts; not the man who points out how the strong man stumbled, or where the doer of deeds could have done them better. The credit belongs to the man who is actually in the arena; whose face is marred by dust and sweat and blood; who strives valiantly; who errs and comes short again and again; who knows the great enthusiasms, the great devotions, and spends himself in a worthy cause; who at the best knows in the end the triumphs of high achievement; and who at the worst, if he fails, at least fails while daring greatly; so that his place shall never be with those cold and timid souls who know neither defeat nor victory."

209 ❡ A Telegram to the Republican Candidate. November 4, 1936

I am grateful to you for your generous telegram and I am confident that all of us Americans will now pull together for the common good. I send you every good wish.

Franklin D. Roosevelt

Governor Alfred M. Landon
Topeka, Kansas

NOTE: The results of the election were as follows: the popular vote for Roosevelt was 27,476,673; for Landon 16,679,583. The electoral vote for Roosevelt was 523 (46 States); for Landon 8 (2 States). The number of Democratic Senators was increased from 69 to 76; the number of Democratic Representatives from 322 to 333.

210 ❡ The President Greets His Neighbors on His Return to Washington. November 6, 1936

MY FRIENDS, I am very glad to come back among you, my old neighbors.

I formed a very good habit of coming to Washington when I was five years old; and I am glad that that habit will not be broken during the coming four years.

I have seen Washington grow during this half century and as an American I am very proud and happy in this wonderful Capital of ours. It is not only the most beautiful city in all the world but I think it is one of the grandest cities to live in in all the world.

This is a very wonderful greeting that you have given to me on this wonderful day. I am very thankful to you and hope to see much of you in the next four years.

211 ⟪A Radio Greeting to the Twenty-one American Republics. November 7, 1936

TODAY the Delegation of the United States to the Inter-American Conference for the Maintenance of Peace and the delegations of several other American Republics are sailing from New York for Buenos Aires, and I am taking this opportunity to wish them Godspeed and at the same time to send a word of greeting to the peoples of the twenty-one American Nations. It will be an auspicious moment, indeed, when our own representatives convene with those of the other Nations of this Hemisphere in the capital of our great Southern neighbor.

I say auspicious advisedly, for it is my thought that this will be no ordinary conference. No previous inter-American conference has assembled with the assurance which we possess today that every American Government and all of the American peoples now realize their joint responsibility for making sure that all of us on this Continent march forward in harmony and in understanding friendship along the paths of progress and of peace.

We in the New World are fortunate indeed. We must insure a continuance of our happy situation. A start has been made. Today, as never before, the Nations of the Western Hemisphere are joined together by an ever-increasing community of interests.

It is no exaggeration to say that in a world torn by conflicting demands, in a world in which democratic institutions are so seriously threatened, in a world in which freedom and human liberty itself are at stake, the Americans stand forth as a notable example of international solidarity, cooperation and mutual helpfulness.

Nevertheless, satisfactory as the international relationships on this Hemisphere may be, much is still to be done. The gains that have been made can be consolidated and constructive steps can be taken along lines heretofore untried. It seems to me that an unprecedented opportunity exists for the American Nations to cooperate in a friendly fashion to make the spirit of peace a practical and living fact.

I feel confident that on the solid foundation of inter-American friendship, equality, and unity the Conference at Buenos Aires will be able to take further steps for the maintenance of peace, thus insuring the continuance of conditions under which it will be possible, nay, inevitable, for the economic, social, cultural, and spiritual life of the Nations of this Hemisphere to reach full growth.

I hope with all my heart that the forthcoming Conference will give renewed hope and courage to the war-weary peoples of the world by demonstrating to them that the scourge of armed conflict can and will be eliminated from the Western Hemisphere.

(See Items 17, 222-227 of this volume.)

212 ❨ Address at the Dedication of the Jusserand Memorial in Rock Creek Park, Washington, D. C. November 7, 1936

THIS is far more than the formal dedication of a Memorial to a statesman of great accomplishment. It is an opportunity for many of M. Jusserand's old-time friends to gather here in a spot he loved and think back over the years when he was with us. This delightful place where we meet is hallowed by tender memories for his gentle companion whom we greet again in Washington. All of us are grateful that we may speak to each other in words of affectionate remembrance and appreciation of one whose valiant spirit hovers over this scene.

And there is opportunity also for his thousands of friends in every walk of life in France and in America to remember this afternoon the fine influence which M. Jusserand exerted in so many fields.

We know his splendid career as the representative of our sister Republic, the deep friendship between himself and Theodore Roosevelt, his wide knowledge and understanding of the American people.

But I would say one word of the man I knew so well during the years of the Great War. Few have been placed in a situation more difficult, more open every day and every hour to the possibility of a misunderstanding of grave issues by the American public.

I talked with him often. His poise, his determination to avoid all methods of propaganda, his insistence that the American people could best make up their own minds through the presentation of simple facts and principles had, in their ultimate effect, a telling influence on public opinion when this Nation through its President and its Congress made the great decision in April, 1917. Maintenance of the highest standard of diplomatic ethics brought its own reward.

All of us who knew him were amazed by his culture — a culture not superficial even though it embraced an interest in such a multitude of subjects. We can go far before we match the record of one of the greatest of diplomats, who, at the same time, in the field of letters saw his work crowned by the French Academy on one side of the Atlantic, won the Pulitzer Prize on the other, and in recognition of his learning was elected President of the American Historical Association.

We can almost say, "He was a great American as well as a great Frenchman." We link M. Jusserand's name forever with the names of Lafayette and Rochambeau and De Grasse and the other valiant Frenchmen whose services in this country entitle them for all time to the grateful remembrance of all Americans.

The people of the two great sister democracies will always regard him thus. We, his old personal friends, will often come to this Memorial with the added thought of the inspiring hours we spent with him and the deep affection we shall always feel.

213 ❨ A Greeting to the Third National Conference on Labor Legislation. November 7, 1936

My dear friends:

I WISH to send you my hearty greetings, and to welcome to Washington this large and representative gathering of State officials and representatives of organized labor. The sessions of the National Conference on Labor Legislation in 1934 and 1935 formulated a program for the raising of labor standards which commands my whole-hearted sympathy and approval, and that of my Administration. Furthermore, I believe the country has this last week given a mandate in unmistakable terms to its legislators and executives to proceed along these lines until working people throughout the Nation and in every State are assured decent working conditions, including safe and healthful places of work; adequate care and support when incapacitated by reason of accident, industrial disease, unemployment, or old age; reasonably short working hours; adequate annual incomes; proper housing; and elimination of child labor.

I hope that your Conference will give serious consideration as to how these objectives may be achieved and that when you return to your States you will assume the leadership in your communities for putting the necessary legislation on the statute books. I assure you that the Federal Government is willing to do its part in making these standards effective, and in supplementing the efforts of the States when problems assume an interstate or a national character. This coming year should be an outstanding one in the annals of labor legislation. I am indeed sorry that I cannot personally attend your sessions, but I assure you that I shall follow the outcome with a great deal of interest.

Sincerely yours,

NOTE: The Third National Conference on Labor Legislation met at Washington on November 9, 10 and 11, 1936. Similar conferences were also held in 1934 and 1935.

These conferences have provided

a medium for free exchange of experiences and objectives in the field of labor legislation. They have given a general uniform direction to labor legislation throughout the United States, and should provide the means for the gradual development of sound labor legislation.

Thirty-nine States were represented at this Third Conference. My letter mentioned some of the more important immediate goals of desirable State legislation. The annual conferences have had marked results in encouraging and bringing about progressive and sound labor legislation and in raising the general standards of labor legislation in the various States. Labor commissioners of the different States, State Federations of Labor, Governors of many States, have been able to call upon the conference for advice for drafting of legislation and for presentation of proposed legislation before legislative bodies.

214 ❲A Greeting to the National Reclamation Association. November 11, 1936

My dear Mr. Warden:

THE National Reclamation Association was organized to encourage the conservation of water, the greatest Western resource, and its use for irrigation. The program under the Federal reclamation policy has steadily gone forward and has relieved unemployment not only in the West, but in the industrial East where these Western developments create a market for the products of the factories. The prolonged drought has given added emphasis to the benefits of irrigation.

To the annual gathering of your Association in Spokane, November 23d and 24th, I send my greetings and best wishes for a successful meeting. Your achievements as a group are very gratifying, particularly in educating the public as to the place Federal reclamation takes in our economic existence and in helping administrative officers preserve a sound policy.

Very sincerely yours,

Mr. O. S. Warden, President,
National Reclamation Association,
Helena, Montana.

215 ⟨A Thanksgiving Day Proclamation.

November 12, 1936

I, FRANKLIN D. ROOSEVELT, President of the United States of America, hereby designate Thursday, the twenty-sixth day of November, 1936, as a day of national thanksgiving.

The observance of a day of general thanksgiving by all the people is a practice peculiarly our own, hallowed by usage in the days before we were a nation and sanctioned through succeeding years.

Having safely passed through troubled waters, it is our right to express our gratitude that Divine Providence has vouchsafed us wisdom and courage to overcome adversity. Our free institutions have been maintained with no abatement of our faith in them. In our relations with other peoples we stand not aloof but make resolute effort to promote international friendship and, by the avoidance of discord, to further world peace, prosperity, and happiness.

Coupled with our grateful acknowledgment of the blessings it has been our high privilege to enjoy, we have a deepening sense of our solemn responsibility to assure for ourselves and our descendants a future more abundant in faith and in security.

Let us, therefore, on the day appointed, each in his own way, but together as a whole people, make due expression of our thanksgiving and humbly endeavor to follow in the footsteps of Almighty God.

216 ⟨An Informal Talk at Greenbelt, Md.

November 13, 1936

ALTHOUGH I have seen the blueprints of Greenbelt, the sight of the project far exceeds anything I dreamed of.

I wish everyone in the country could see it. It's a splendid thing to have near both Baltimore and Washington. The project is an achievement that ought to be copied in every city in the Nation.

It's a good thing to get people out into the country, but more than that, it benefits the low-income groups.

217 ⟨ Suggestions for Study by the Business Advisory Council. November 16, 1936

My dear Mr. Secretary:

I REGRET that I shall be absent from Washington when the Business Advisory Council meets on November 19th and therefore wish you would extend my greetings.

I feel that the work of the Council in the study and solution of problems which confront the Government and business has been beneficial. I am deeply appreciative of the service the members have performed, necessitating many trips to Washington at their own expense, in addition to the sacrifice of time from their own personal affairs. This attitude symbolizes the type of cooperation essential to a continuity of the progress we are making.

We shall, I hope, pass into the next period of our Administration by looking to a wise and a more equitable balancing of the inter-related segments composing our economic and social life. To that end, the Business Advisory Council can render definite service.

Economic and social betterment hinges upon a continuous study of social trends, such as are reflected in human thought and action.

Study and analysis of these trends are a vital preliminary to the adoption of plans and procedures best suited to meet modern conditions. At this time I suggest a study on the part of the Council of the problem of further absorption of workers by private industry, the problem of improving living conditions of low income groups through low-cost housing and slum clearance, and the problem of improving wages and working conditions of employees in industry.

With renewed assurance of my appreciation of your endeavors, I am,

Very sincerely yours,

Honorable Daniel C. Roper,
Secretary of Commerce,
Washington, D. C.

218 ⟨ White House Statement and Letter on the Appointment of a Special Committee on Farm Tenancy. November 17, 1936

The President has appointed a special committee of farm leaders, editors, and persons prominent in public affairs to make a report on the most promising ways of alleviating the shortcomings of the farm tenancy system. Secretary of Agriculture Henry A. Wallace has been asked to serve as chairman of the committee, and L. C. Gray, Assistant Administrator of the Resettlement Administration, is designated Executive Secretary and Technical Director.

A continued increase in farm tenancy during the past half century was cited by the President in his letter to Secretary Wallace, as "significant evidence that we have fallen far short of achieving the traditional American ideal of owner-operated farms." The number of tenant farmers in the United States has grown steadily since the first count was taken in 1880, and this growth in tenancy has been "frequently associated with soil depletion and declining living standards."

Under the general auspices of the National Resources Committee, the special committee on farm tenancy is charged with the duty of reporting by February 1, 1937, on ways and means of developing a land tenure system "which will bring an increased measure of security, opportunity, and well-being" to farm tenants.

In his letter to Secretary Wallace, the President urged that the committee confer with other leaders in State and national affairs, and referred specifically to Senator John H. Bankhead of Alabama and Representative Marvin Jones of Texas who had worked actively for the enactment of farm tenancy legislation during the 74th Congress.

Herewith is a copy of the letter written by the President to Secretary Wallace, together with a list of those who have been asked to serve on the committee.

My dear Mr. Secretary:

I AM writing to ask you to serve as Chairman of a special committee which will make a report to me not later than February 1 on a long-term program of action to alleviate the shortcomings of our farm tenancy system.

I am anxious that we thoroughly examine and report on the most promising ways of developing a land tenure system which will bring an increased measure of security, opportunity, and well-being to the great group of present and prospective farm tenants. The rapid increase of tenant farmers during the past half century is significant evidence that we have fallen far short of achieving the traditional American ideal of owner-operated farms. The growing insecurity of many classes of farm tenants, frequently associated with soil depletion and declining living standards, presents a challenge to national action which I hope we can meet in a thoroughly constructive manner.

It is my thought that the first step in evolving a workable program is the preparation, under the general auspices of the National Resources Committee, of a comprehensive report by a special committee of persons who have both an extensive knowledge of the problem and a sympathetic interest in its solution. I am designating Dr. L. C. Gray, Assistant Administrator, Resettlement Administration, to serve as Executive Secretary and Technical Director for this special committee.

As you know, Senator John H. Bankhead and Representative Marvin Jones have manifested a keen interest in this problem and, during the 74th Congress, worked actively in behalf of proposed tenancy legislation. It is my desire that the committee consult with them. It will be helpful also to secure the views of other State and national leaders.

591

The list of persons whom I am asking to serve on this committee is enclosed.

Very sincerely yours,

Honorable Henry A. Wallace
Secretary of Agriculture
Washington, D. C.

NOTE: The decline in farm ownership in the United States during the past fifty-five years and the growth of a large group of farming tenants are an indication of the growing insecurity to which our farming population is becoming a victim. Farm tenancy increased from 25 percent of all farmers in 1880 to 42 percent in 1935. Even among those who still retain technical title to their land, hundreds of thousands of farm families have such diminished equities that they retain only a semblance of ownership.

Closely related to the farm tenants are the sharecroppers. There were 2,865,000 tenant farmers and share croppers in the United States in 1935, about two-thirds of whom are located in the South. Of the Southern tenants and croppers, two-thirds are whites and only one-third are Negroes. The cropper system is a form of tenancy which prevails principally in the Southern cotton and tobacco areas. Croppers operate 716,000 farms, or over 10 percent of all farms in the United States. They constitute 39 percent of all tenants in the South; and since they generally supply only their labor, they are normally the most insecure group of tenants.

In addition to these tenants and croppers there are a huge number of farm wage laborers. More than one quarter of all persons gainfully employed in agriculture in 1930 were farm wage laborers. The great majority of them are dependent upon irregular employment. A large number of them migrate long distances from home following the harvest seasons of the various crops from locality to locality.

The dangers and evils of farm tenancy are obvious. Although a small number of farm tenants, notably those related to their landlords, enjoy a rather satisfactory standard of living, the vast majority do not. The tenant's occupancy is uncertain at best, and ordinarily does not average more than two years. His sole object is to get as large a crop and as quick a crop as possible. He cannot afford to plant his rented farm to anything but cash crops. He does not expect to occupy the land permanently, and therefore he neither desires nor can afford to apply fertilizers except as they will give him the most immediate and abundant return. He

592

clearly cannot afford to plant soil-building crops. Expecting to remain temporarily only, the tenant farmer has little incentive to conserve or improve soil. He has no desire to maintain or improve the house, the barn, the shed or the woodlot. The natural result is that the soil is depleted and the farm gradually loses its fertility. This diminished fertility in turn contributes materially, in a vicious circle, to the growth of farm tenancy and the further impoverishment of the tenants and croppers.

While the results of farm tenancy by way of soil erosion are bad for our economic future, the erosion of rural society which results from it is even worse. The waste of human resources by reason of the instability and insecurity of tenant farm families has a more disastrous effect even than the waste of natural resources. Tenant families — men, women and children — move constantly from farm to farm almost every year. They can maintain no normal community participation. They cannot become a part of the local social order. Their children are frequently deprived of continued schooling. The extreme poverty of many tenants, particularly croppers, is reflected in a standard of living below levels of decency. Large families often live in two- or three-room houses, of poor construction, weather-beaten, unscreened, leaky. The physical surroundings are generally bleak and repulsive, with practically no sanitary arrangements. The result is chronic undernourishment of adults and children, making them ready subjects to pellagra, malaria, hookworm and rickets. Long-continued subjection to this type of poverty, insecurity and lack of normal community life dissipate any incentive for improving their lot. Our rural relief rolls indicate that over a million farm families have been beaten down into dependency in recent years. The money costs, as well as the social costs, can be avoided only if these farm families are placed in a better relationship to the land which will enable them to provide for themselves.

Legislation dealing with the problem of farm tenancy was passed in June, 1935, by the Senate, known as the Farmers' Home Bill. This Bill provided for a corporation with power to purchase land and resell it upon easy terms to tenant farmers and others. However, no action was taken upon the Bill in the House.

On February 16, 1937, I transmitted in a message to the Congress on the subject of farm tenancy a report of the Committee on Farm Tenancy which was set up by me in the foregoing document. The report created widespread public interest in farm tenancy and in related problems. As a result of my message of February 6, 1937, legislation was passed to aid tenant farmers.

219 ❨ Presidential Statement on the Reemployment Efforts of Private Industry. November 17, 1936

REEMPLOYMENT has been increasing rapidly during the last year, and reports from industry are to the effect that further gains in employment can be expected during the coming year.

Unemployment relief has reflected this improvement in employment. From the peak of 5,316,000 unemployed families and single persons in January, 1935, the number declined 28 percent by August, 1936.

Despite this decline a large number of unemployed remain on the W.P.A. and other governmental agencies.

These workers are to a large extent unskilled and a disproportionately large number are older workers — forty years and over. The sharpest revival in employment has been among skilled workers and relatively young workers. The unskilled and the older workers have shared in this revival to a much less extent.

In the relief message to Congress on March 18, 1936, I asked private business "to extend its operations so as to absorb an increasing number of unemployed." Many private businesses are responding — but much remains to be done.

Industry should continue to increase its reemployment efforts. To reduce substantially the unemployment relief rolls, industry must hire a larger number of the older workers and the unskilled workers. This problem will, I hope, be recognized by industry. It is widely known that many of the largest industries will not hire workers over forty years of age. To a large extent this policy is responsible for the relatively large number of older workers on relief. Leaders of business must recognize the consequences of this hiring-age policy; it condemns many in this group of workers to permanent unemployment.

It is scarcely necessary to point to the seriousness of this policy to the unemployed. Long continued unemployment for the older workers results sooner or later in unemployability. The non-em-

ployment of unskilled workers likewise leads eventually to unemployability, and this means a permanent problem of support.
And the burden of support is carried ultimately in large measure
by industry itself.

It is to the best interests of industry to recognize its responsibility, not only by substantially increasing employment but by
employing those in groups where many are now supported by
public funds. Industry can adjust its hiring policies so as to cause
the speediest reduction in the real social burden of unemployment. This means giving a fair share of the new jobs to the workers over forty and expanding opportunities for the hiring of unskilled workers.

In the relief message of March 18, 1936, I stated that "Only if
industry fails to reduce substantially the number of those now
out of work will another appropriation and further plans and
policies be necessary." Obviously industry has not yet increased
its employment sufficiently to permit the Government to withdraw its aid from the unemployed. Moreover, the severe drought
of this summer has required the use of a large sum of money
which would otherwise be available for general unemployment
relief. As a consequence, Congress will be asked to appropriate
enough funds to carry the program through the fiscal year 1937.

220 ⟨ The President Expresses His Thanks for the Congratulations Extended on His Reelection. November 18, 1936

I DESIRE once more to thank the American people for their messages of congratulation and good-will which I have received since
Election Day.

These messages have poured in literally by the thousands—
first at Hyde Park and latterly at Washington. They have long
since assumed a total which has made it impossible for me to undertake personal acknowledgment, and their mounting number
makes individual answer a physical impossibility.

However, I do want to assure one and all of my heartfelt appreciation of the generous impulse which moved so many of my fellow citizens to send these messages.

221 ⟨A Greeting to the Sponsors of the New York World's Fair. November 20, 1936

IT IS an inspiring thing for Nations and communities to have high objectives, to unite their energies in self-appraisal and boldly plan for the future.

The World's Fair to be held in New York beginning in 1939 is a challenge to all Americans who believe in the destiny of this Nation, and who welcome the knowledge that the exposition is to focus upon one central theme: building the world of tomorrow.

At this great fair all the world may review what the United States has achieved in the 150 years since George Washington was first inaugurated as President of the United States; here millions of citizens may visualize the national life which is to come.

That it will be a memorable and historic fair, that it will profoundly influence our national life for many years to come, and that success may attend every phase of its activities — these are the hopes of the people of the United States. All power to you sponsors.

Hon. Grover Whalen,
New York, N. Y.

222 ⁅ "All Instrumentalities for the Maintenance of Peace Must Be Consolidated and Reinforced." Address before a Joint Session of the National Congress and the Supreme Court of Brazil at Rio de Janeiro. November 27, 1936

Your Excellency and Gentlemen of the Congress and of the Supreme Court of Brazil:

NEARLY half a century ago a little boy was walking with his father and mother in a park of a city in Southern France. Toward them came a distinguished-looking elderly couple — Dom Pedro II and his Empress. That occasion was my first introduction to Brazil.

In the years that have passed since that day — years measured by the splendid history of the Republic of Brazil — I have had the pleasure of meeting many of your statesmen and of becoming increasingly familiar with the problems which mutually affect our two Nations.

My visit to Rio de Janeiro today is therefore the realization of a growing desire to see Brazil with my own eyes. Every student has been told of the majestic beauty in which your great city is cradled. But Rio is unique in that the reality far exceeds our expectations. A visit — even of a single day — is one of the outstanding experiences of my life.

The loveliness of nature would have been enough to bring me here — but my visit has another purpose. I was unwilling to come so far abroad without tendering my respects to the Government of Brazil, that sister Nation with which for more than a century we have maintained a tradition of good understanding, mutual regard, and cooperation, which is rare in history.

I have had the honor of greeting your great President; and this personal friendship between the Chief Executives of our two

Nations seems to me not only of practical benefit but also of profound significance.

You, gentlemen of the Congress, now afford me the courtesy of this agreeable opportunity of meeting in person the legislative branch of your Government and of exchanging thoughts directly with its members.

I could not but be deeply sensible of the unique honor offered by the presence in this chamber of your Supreme Court, a tribunal whose high traditions are known throughout the juridical world.

Thus, the executive, legislative, and judicial powers of the Government of Brazil have united in this demonstration of friendship toward the Nation which I have the honor to represent.

Let me now return thanks for this renewed proof of that brotherhood which has ever united Brazil and the United States —a fraternity not limited to the relations between our Governments but a fraternity which I have reason to know is made evident in every group in both countries whenever and wherever they meet. The fine record of our relations is the best answer to those pessimists who scoff at the idea of true friendship between Nations. In the present state of the world it is heartening that the two largest countries in this Hemisphere have been able, by the exercise of good-will, good temper, and good sense, to conduct the whole course of their relations without clash or conflict or ill feeling.

Not only that. The confidence in each other's aims and motives enables us to work together for the common good. We have a record of which we can be proud—a record of joint endeavor in the cause of peace in this New World. My country has derived strength and confidence from the farsighted, irreproachable attitude of Brazil in its devotion to arbitration, conciliation, and other methods for the peaceful settlement of international disputes.

Your first concern, like ours, is peace, for we know that war destroys not only human lives and human happiness but destroys as well the ideals of individual liberty and of the democratic form of representative government, which is the goal of all the American Republics.

I think I can say that if in the generations to come we can live without war, democratic government throughout the Americas will prove its complete ability to raise the standards of life for those millions who cry for opportunity today. The motto of war is: "Let the strong survive; let the weak die." The motto of peace is: "Let the strong help the weak to survive."

There is room for all of us, without treading on one another's toes. There are resources of nature adequate for our present and our future. We are happily free from ancient antagonisms which have brought so much misery to other parts of the world.

There are, it is true, conflicts of interest between the American States, but they cannot be called serious or difficult of solution when compared with the deeply rooted hates of other continents. There is no American conflict — and I weigh my words when I say this — there is no American conflict that cannot be settled by orderly and peaceful means. And it is in our common interest imperative that they be settled always by agreement and not by bloodshed.

We serve not ourselves alone. The friendly Nations of the Americas can render no greater service to civilization itself than by maintaining both domestic and international peace and by freeing themselves forever from conflict.

We are about to gather in a great American Conference called by President Justo in furtherance of the good-neighbor policy in which we all share. In this Conference we have the opportunity to banish war from the New World and dedicate it to peace. It is unthinkable to me that in this time of world-wide apprehension we should fail to seize the opportunity to meet what is a heavy responsibility. This is no time to hesitate. We must be guided by a serene and generous view of our common needs.

World horizons may be dark, but the time is auspicious for our task in America. The rest of the world presents a grim picture of armed camps and threats of conflict. But on our own continent armed clashes which in recent years have divided American countries have been happily brought to an end. It is gratifying to be able to pay well-deserved tribute to the very outstanding part played by your able and distinguished Foreign Minister Macedo Soares in the mediatory efforts of the representatives of six American Republics. And the Leticia question was settled here in Rio through the patient assistance and masterly diplomacy of Dr. Afranio Mello Franco.

The progress we have made must not be allowed to serve as a pretext for resting on our laurels; it should, on the contrary, stimulate us to new and increased effort. It is not enough that peace prevails from the Arctic to the Antarctic, from the Atlantic to the Pacific; it is essential that this condition be made permanent, that we provide effectively against the recurrence of the horrors of war, and assure peace to ourselves and our posterity.

All instrumentalities for the maintenance of peace must be consolidated and reinforced. We cannot countenance aggression, from wheresoever it may come. The people of each and every one of the American Republics—and, I am confident, the people of the Dominion of Canada as well—wish to lead their own lives free from desire for conquest and free from fear of conquest; free at the same time to expand their cultural and intellectual relationships and to take counsel together to encourage the peaceful progress of modern civilization.

Our aims will best be served by agreements which bring peace, security, and friendship among us and all our neighbors. Solidarity among the American States in the cause of peace constitutes no threat to other regions or races. The honorable adherence to solemn agreements among us will harm no other continent. On the contrary, the more firmly peace is established in this Hemisphere, the more closely we live up to the spirit as well as the letter of our agreements, the better it will be for all the rest of the world. Let us present a record which our Hemisphere may give to the world as convincing proof that peace lies always at hand when Nations, serene in their sovereign security, meet their current problems with understanding and good-will.

All of us have learned that no real, no lasting, prosperity can exist where it is secured at the expense of our neighbors; that among Nations, as in our domestic relations, the principle of interdependence is paramount. No Nation can live entirely to itself.

Each one of us has learned the glories of independence. Let each one of us learn the glories of interdependence. Economically we supply each other's needs; intellectually we maintain a constant, a growing exchange of culture, of science, and of thought; spiritually the life of each can well enrich the life of all.

We are showing in international relations what we have long known in private relations—that good neighbors make a good community.

In that knowledge we meet today as neighbors. We can discard the dangerous language of rivalry; we can put aside the empty phrases of "diplomatic triumphs" or "shrewd bargains." We can forget all thought of domination, of selfish coalitions, or of balances of power. Those false gods have no place among American neighbors.

Happily the relations between Brazil and the United States have transcended those lesser conceptions. Secure in unbroken respect and friendship, we meet with full respect, each for the other, with every hope that our mutual regard may prove useful to others as well.

There has never been a time when this confidence between Brazil and the United States was more precious or more needed.

I know from my enlightening conversation with President Vargas that we are entering the coming Conference deeply mindful of our responsibilities and the need to work in fullest understanding with all of the Republics of this Hemisphere. If we are guided by wisdom, such comprehension will banish conflict from this part of the world.

We are entitled to hope that we may thus contribute to the universal ideal that Nations throughout the entire world, laying weapons aside, may at last fulfill the greatest ambition which any Nation, large or small, can have—that of contributing steadily and, above all, generously to the advance of well-being, culture, and civilization throughout the changing years.

NOTE: Realizing the great importance of the Inter-American Conference for the Maintenance of Peace, which was being held at Buenos Aires commencing December 1, 1936 (see Item 17, this volume), I decided to visit the Conference in person.

I started on November 18, 1936, on the *U.S.S. Indianapolis*, visited Rio de Janeiro, Buenos Aires, and Montevideo, and made the various speeches which follow.

I was made to feel everywhere that the good-neighbor policy of the United States which had been consistently adhered to since March 4, 1933, had dissipated the last vestige of mistrust and suspicion on the part of the other American Republics toward the United States, and that there was a real bond of friendship and common interest between us.

On December 15th I returned to the United States from this Conference which had such far-reaching results for the future of the American Republics. (See Item 227, this volume.)

223 ❧ Informal Address at Banquet Given by President Getulio Vargas of Brazil at Rio de Janeiro. November 27, 1936

I CANNOT quite believe I am actually leaving Rio de Janeiro tonight because the wish is very much the father of the thought. Now that I have come to know your city and a little part of this great Republic, I should like very much to stay a week, indeed many weeks.

Your reception today, which is a reception not to me alone but to a sister Nation, has touched me very deeply. It has been a great privilege for me to make the acquaintance of your President. I have had the privilege of knowing some of his family before today and I hope that in the not too distant future we shall be able to welcome President Vargas at Washington as a visitor in the United States.

May I say a word about communications? I have always felt that the advent of the airplane and the advent of quicker steamship service are going to make a large difference in the future relationships of the Americas because science is going to make it easier for us to get to know each other better, and people who know each other well can be friends. So in the days to come I hope very much that we shall have more news of Brazil in the United States.

You have done much to help us in the United States in many ways in the past. We, I think, have done a little to help you, and may I suggest that you, with this great domain of many millions of square miles, of which such a large proportion is still open to human occupation, can learn much from the mistakes we have made in the United States.

So I invite you to come and benefit not only from the good things we have done but also from the errors we have committed in the past.

I am leaving you tonight with great regret. There is one thing, however, that I shall remember, and that is that it was two people who invented the New Deal — the President of Brazil and the President of the United States. So I am going to ask you to rise with me and drink to the health of my good friend President Vargas and to the great Republic of Brazil, our sister Nation.

224 ("Our Purpose, under Happy Auspices, Is to Assure the Continuance of the Blessings of Peace." Address before the Inter-American Conference for the Maintenance of Peace, Buenos Aires, Argentina. December 1, 1936

Members of the American Family of Nations:

O N THE happy occasion of the convening of this Conference I address you thus, because members of a family need no introduction or formalities when, in pursuance of excellent custom, they meet together for their common good.

As a family we appreciate the hospitality of our host, President Justo, and the Government and people of Argentina; and all of us are happy that to our friend Dr. Saavedra Lamas has come the well-deserved award of the Nobel Prize for great service in the cause of world peace.

Three years ago the American family met in nearby Montevideo, the great capital of the Republic of Uruguay. They were dark days. A shattering depression, unparalleled in its intensity, held us, with the rest of the world, in its grip. And in our own Hemisphere a tragic war was raging between two of our sister Republics.

Yet, at that conference there was born not only hope for our common future but a greater measure of mutual trust between the American democracies than had ever existed before. In this Western Hemisphere the night of fear has been dispelled. Many of the intolerable burdens of economic depression have been lightened and, due in no small part to our common efforts, every Nation of this Hemisphere is today at peace with its neighbors.

This is no conference to form alliances, to divide the spoils of war, to partition countries, to deal with human beings as though they were pawns in a game of chance. Our purpose, under happy auspices, is to assure the continuance of the blessings of peace.

Three years ago, recognizing that a crisis was being thrust upon the New World, with splendid unanimity our twenty-one Republics set an example to the whole world by proclaiming a new spirit, a new day, in the affairs of this Hemisphere.

While the succeeding period has justified in full measure all that was said and done at Montevideo, it has unfortunately emphasized the seriousness of threats to peace among other Nations. Events elsewhere have served only to strengthen our horror of war and all that war means. The men, women, and children of the Americas know that warfare in this day and age means more than the mere clash of armies: they see the destruction of cities and of farms; they foresee that children and grandchildren, if they survive, will stagger for long years not only under the burden of poverty but also amid the threat of broken society and the destruction of constitutional government.

I am profoundly convinced that the plain people everywhere in the civilized world today wish to live in peace one with another. And still leaders and Governments resort to war. Truly, if the genius of mankind that has invented the weapons of death cannot discover the means of preserving peace, civilization as we know it lives in an evil day.

But we cannot now, especially in view of our common purpose, accept any defeatist attitude. We have learned by hard experience that peace is not to be had for the mere asking; that peace, like other great privileges, can be obtained only by hard and painstaking effort. We are here to dedicate ourselves and our countries to that work.

You who assemble today carry with you in your deliberations the hopes of millions of human beings in other less fortunate lands. Beyond the ocean we see continents rent asunder by old hatreds and new fanaticisms. We hear the demand that injustice and inequality be corrected by resorting to the sword and not by resorting to reason and peaceful justice. We hear the cry that

605

new markets can be achieved only through conquest. We read that the sanctity of treaties between Nations is disregarded.

We know, too, that vast armaments are rising on every side and that the work of creating them employs men and women by the millions. It is natural, however, for us to conclude that such employment is false employment; that it builds no permanent structures and creates no consumers' goods for the maintenance of a lasting prosperity. We know that Nations guilty of these follies inevitably face the day when either their weapons of destruction must be used against their neighbors or when an unsound economy, like a house of cards, will fall apart.

In either case, even though the Americas become involved in no war, we must suffer too. The madness of a great war in other parts of the world would affect us and threaten our good in a hundred ways. And the economic collapse of any Nation or Nations must of necessity harm our own prosperity.

Can we, the Republics of the New World, help the Old World to avert the catastrophe which impends? Yes; I am confident that we can.

First, it is our duty by every honorable means to prevent any future war among ourselves. This can best be done through the strengthening of the processes of constitutional democratic government; by making these processes conform to the modern need for unity and efficiency and, at the same time, preserving the individual liberties of our citizens. By so doing, the people of our Nations, unlike the people of many Nations who live under other forms of government, can and will insist on their intention to live in peace. Thus will democratic government be justified throughout the world.

In this determination to live at peace among ourselves we in the Americas make it at the same time clear that we stand shoulder to shoulder in our final determination that others who, driven by war madness or land hunger, might seek to commit acts of aggression against us will find a Hemisphere wholly prepared to consult together for our mutual safety and our mutual good. I repeat what I said in speaking before the Congress and

606

the Supreme Court of Brazil: "Each one of us has learned the glories of independence. Let each one of us learn the glories of interdependence."

Secondly, and in addition to the perfecting of the mechanisms of peace, we can strive even more strongly than in the past to prevent the creation of those conditions which give rise to war. Lack of social or political justice within the borders of any Nation is always cause for concern. Through democratic processes we can strive to achieve for the Americas the highest possible standard of living conditions for all our people. Men and women blessed with political freedom, willing to work and able to find work, rich enough to maintain their families and to educate their children, contented with their lot in life and on terms of friendship with their neighbors, will defend themselves to the utmost, but will never consent to take up arms for a war of conquest.

Interwoven with these problems is the further self-evident fact that the welfare and prosperity of each of our Nations depend in large part on the benefits derived from commerce among ourselves and with other Nations, for our present civilization rests on the basis of an international exchange of commodities. Every Nation of the world has felt the evil effects of recent efforts to erect trade barriers of every known kind. Every individual citizen has suffered from them. It is no accident that the Nations which have carried this process farthest are those which proclaim most loudly that they require war as an instrument of their policy. It is no accident that attempts to be self-sufficient have led to falling standards for their people and to ever-increasing loss of the democratic ideals in a mad race to pile armament on armament. It is no accident that, because of these suicidal policies and the suffering attending them, many of their people have come to believe with despair that the price of war seems less than the price of peace.

This state of affairs we must refuse to accept with every instinct of defense, with every exhortation of enthusiastic hope, with every use of mind and skill.

I cannot refrain here from reiterating my gratification that in

607

this, as in so many other achievements, the American Republics have given a salutary example to the world. The resolution adopted at the Inter-American Conference at Montevideo endorsing the principles of liberal trade policies has shone forth like a beacon in the storm of economic madness which has been sweeping over the entire world during these later years. Truly, if the principles there embodied find still wider application in your deliberations, it will be a notable contribution to the cause of peace. For my own part I have done all in my power to sustain the consistent efforts of my Secretary of State in negotiating agreements for reciprocal trade, and even though the individual results may seem small, the total of them is significant. These policies in recent weeks have received the approval of the people of the United States, and they have, I am sure, the sympathy of the other Nations here assembled.

There are many other causes for war — among them, long-festering feuds, unsettled frontiers, territorial rivalries. But these sources of danger which still exist in the Americas, I am thankful to say, are not only few in number but already on the way to peaceful adjudication. While the settlement of such controversies may necessarily involve adjustments at home or in our relations with our neighbors which may appear to involve material sacrifice, let no man or woman forget that there is no profit in war. Sacrifices in the cause of peace are infinitesimal compared with the holocaust of war.

Peace comes from the spirit and must be grounded in faith. In seeking peace, perhaps we can best begin by proudly affirming the faith of the Americas: the faith in freedom and its fulfillment, which has proved a mighty fortress beyond reach of successful attack in half the world.

That faith arises from a common hope and a common design given us by our fathers in differing form but with a single aim: freedom and security of the individual, which has become the foundation of our peace.

If, then, by making war in our midst impossible, and if within ourselves and among ourselves we can give greater freedom and fulfillment to the individual lives of our citizens, the democratic form of representative government will have justified the high hopes of the liberating fathers. Democracy is still the hope of the world. If we in our generation can continue its successful application in the Americas, it will spread and supersede other methods by which men are governed and which seem to most of us to run counter to our ideals of human liberty and human progress.

Three centuries of history sowed the seeds which grew into our Nations; the fourth century saw those Nations become equal and free and brought us to a common system of constitutional government; the fifth century is giving to us a common meeting ground of mutual help and understanding. Our Hemisphere has at last come of age. We are here assembled to show its unity to the world. We took from our ancestors a great dream. We here offer it back as a great unified reality.

Finally, in expressing our faith of the Western World, let us affirm:

That we maintain and defend the democratic form of constitutional representative government.

That through such government we can more greatly provide a wider distribution of culture, of education, of thought, and of free expression.

That through it we can obtain a greater security of life for our citizens and a more equal opportunity for them to prosper.

That through it we can best foster commerce and the exchange of art and science between Nations.

That through it we can avoid the rivalry of armaments, avert hatreds, and encourage good-will and true justice.

That through it we offer hope for peace and a more abundant life to the peoples of the whole world.

But this faith of the Western World will not be complete if we fail to affirm our faith in God. In the whole history of mankind, far back into the dim past before man knew how to record thoughts or events, the human race has been distinguished from other forms of life by the existence, the fact, of religion. Periodic attempts to deny God have always come and will always come to naught.

In the constitution and in the practice of our Nations is the right of freedom of religion. But this ideal, these words, presuppose a belief and a trust in God.

The faith of the Americas, therefore, lies in the spirit. The system, the sisterhood, of the Americas is impregnable so long as her Nations maintain that spirit.

In that faith and spirit we will have peace over the Western World. In that faith and spirit we will all watch and guard our Hemisphere. In that faith and spirit may we also, with God's help, offer hope to our brethren overseas.

225 ❡ Informal Speech at Luncheon for President Agustin P. Justo, Buenos Aires, Argentina. December 2, 1936

AN OTHERWISE very delightful occasion makes me quite sad because within two hours I shall be going away and I am very, very sorry that I have to go away, because I cannot imagine a more delightful three days than I have had here. And yet, Mr. President, I do not feel as if I know Argentina yet, because to come only to Buenos Aires is to know only a part of this great Nation. One hundred and six years ago my grandfather came to Argentina. It has taken me more than a century to follow in his footsteps, and I am very certain that if I live it will not be another century before I come back. There is one matter which I should like to take this opportunity to say; and because it is a matter that affects both of our Nations — I might say an official matter — I shall read a very short statement.

Every Nation has the right and the duty to adopt such measures as may be necessary, in the interest of its own citizens, in order to prevent the entrance into its territory from abroad of contagious or infectious diseases prejudicial to human, animal or plant life.

But it is equally clear that quarantine or sanitary regulations should not be used as disguised tariff measures; nor should they ever be applied except in accordance with strict justice.

About a year ago the Argentine Government and the Government of the United States negotiated a sanitary convention which had for its purpose the removal of an inequitable situation which had arisen as a result of the all-embracing character of legislation adopted by the Congress of the United States. The ratification of this convention would make it possible for Patagonia, a sheep-raising area, where the hoof-and-mouth disease has not existed, and which territory is separated by natural barriers from the cattle-raising regions of the Republic, to be relieved from the sanitary embargoes now placed upon it.

This convention, which I had the honor of submitting to the Senate of the United States last year, affects in no wise existing tariff rates. It is intended solely to remove an obvious inequity resulting from an unnecessarily wide application of a sanitary embargo.

The ratification of this convention by the Senate of the United States would eliminate an injustice without detriment or prejudice of any kind to the legitimate interests of the cattle industry of the United States, and without relaxing in the least full sanitary protection of our own livestock. I intend to present these facts clearly to the attention of the members of the Senate of the United States, with the hope that our Senate may give its consent to the ratification of the simple instrument of justice.

May I further say that I trust that conversations may soon be undertaken between us in order to ascertain the bases which exist for the negotiation of a trade agreement between our two countries, which may prove to be mutually profitable to both the people of the Argentine Republic and the people of the United States.

So I may take this last opportunity — I wish there were many more — to thank you and the good people of Argentina for the very wonderful reception that you have given me, and on behalf of my son and the members of my party to extend to you our profound thanks for all that you have done for us. As I said last night, I am counting on a visit from you, Mr. President, and Señora de Justo in Washington just as soon as you can.

226 ❧ "We Are Seeking . . . to Use the Processes of Democratic Government in Solving the New Problems." Address at Montevideo, Uruguay. December 3, 1936

Your Excellency President Terra, and Señora de Terra:

I T IS a privilege today to be the guest of the Government of the Republic of Uruguay, and it is a great personal pleasure to which I have looked forward for many years.

Here three years ago, in this beautiful city of Montevideo, there was born a new era of friendship and confidence among the Americas. No one is entitled to more credit for this new day than Your Excellency, for you labored unceasingly and generously both as host and as statesman for the success of that conference.

I believe that when history comes to be written, the origin of the new American era will be placed here in the memorable year 1933. Truly, it is an inspiration for the average citizen of all our Republics that that conference is giving back its fruits in terms of achievement for the people of the world. During the past week I have become certain of this because I have seen in the faces of the men, women, and children in Rio de Janeiro, in Buenos Aires, and, today, in Montevideo a joyful expression of hope and faith which can and will inspire us, their chosen representatives, to even greater activity in the common cause.

You, Mr. President, have used a term in speaking of that great patriot, General Artigas, which can well be the inspiration of us all. You have spoken of his "serene and noble spirit of applied justice." It is because of this spirit which actuated the founding fathers of the American Republics that we their followers are inspired to maintain the democratic principles for which they fought.

I am particularly grateful for the kind words which you, Mr. President, have spoken concerning our policies in the United States of America. We fully join with you in the thought that the first battlefield of peace is that of securing well-being at home. It has been of special interest to me to know that you in the Republic of Uruguay have made such great advances in behalf of the well-being of your citizens.

In the days of General Artigas and of his friend President Monroe, human society had, of course, little conception of the economic and social problems which we face today. None of the fathers of any of our Republics had even heard of an eight-hour day, of minimum wages, of protection for women and children, of collective bargaining between employers and employees, of old-age security, of modern sanitation, of concrete highways, of railroads or steel buildings. The fathers had no thought of the telegraph, the radio, the automobile, or of travel by fast steamships and by air. They knew little of the problems of modern science, of modern finance.

And yet, you and I are very certain that if they were alive today the founders of our Governments would look with approval on what we are seeking to do to use the processes of democratic government in solving the new problems.

I recognize, as you do, that these new problems are common to all our Nations. I am glad that you have said that we have been compelled to abandon the comfortable attitude of statesmen of the old school. Every Nation in all the world has been compelled to recognize the fact of new conditions. It is of the utmost importance that the Nations of the New World have found it possible under vigorous leadership to find the answer within the spirit and the framework of constitutional government and democratic processes.

We have not completed our task. In accordance with the objectives and theory of democratic government, that task is a continuing one. We seek new remedies for new conditions; new conditions will continue to arise: sometimes the remedies succeed, and sometimes they must be altered or improved. But the net result is that we move forward. We learn, and ought to learn, much from each other — much that is good and some things which, from experience, we must avoid.

In the case of agriculture, for example, you are familiar with the fact that in the United States we did many things in the past which ran counter to the laws of nature and of sensible economics. In many parts of my country we have used land in such a way as to diminish its productiveness, we have harmed our supply of water, and we have lost our topsoil. Today our Government seeks to work with our farming population in correcting these mistakes and in bringing back a greater prosperity and a more permanent use of the land. I cite this as an example, which you undoubtedly know of, to show the need among all our Republics of keeping in close touch with each other, for many of our problems are similar.

On this delightful visit to Brazil, Argentina, and Uruguay I have been impressed with the immediate need for better and quicker services of travel and communication between North and South America. I look forward to the day when, instead of the journey being long and unusual, visits between the Nations of South America and those of Central America and of North America will be so usual and simple that tens of thousands of our citizens will meet each other in friendly intercourse every year.

And may I add that I hope that we shall have a much greater familiarity with each other's language. It is a great regret of my life that while with some difficulty I can read a little Spanish I cannot yet converse in it. These visits which I am making on this voyage are so enjoyable in every way that I look forward to an opportunity to return in the future. When that day comes I hope that I shall be able to speak with all of you in your native tongue.

And may I also express the hope that it will be possible for you, Mr. President and Señora de Terra, to be the guests of Mrs. Roosevelt and myself in Washington while we are still in the

White House. Nothing would give us and the people of the United States more pleasure.

It has touched me deeply that you have proposed a toast to Mrs. Roosevelt. She was deeply disappointed that she could not come with me, and she will be happy to know of your courtesy and of your thought of her.

I lift my glass to the good health and happiness of you and Señora de Terra, and to the continued prosperity, happiness, and progress of the people of the Republic of Uruguay.

227 (Statement by the President on His Return from the Inter-American Conference for the Maintenance of Peace. December 16, 1936

A VERY delightful trip has come to an end.

I am made especially happy by the continuing good news from the Inter-American Conference for the Maintenance of Peace. I have been in daily communication with Secretary of State Hull, and agree with him that the unceasing efforts on the part of the members of the Conference who represent the twenty-one American Republics justify the highest hopes of us all.

The Conference is still in session, and this is not the time to analyze its specific accomplishments. But we have every reason for gratitude for the far-reaching and historic accomplishments already in sight at Buenos Aires.

The Conference should be an inspiration to all the peoples of the Americas and an example to the rest of the world. Good neighbors we are; good neighbors we shall remain.

NOTE: The Inter-American Conference for the Maintenance of Peace, held at Buenos Aires (see Items 17 and 222, this volume), enabled the twenty-one American Republics to create among themselves new ties of friendship and peace.

From the very first it was evident that all of the American Republics were unanimous in their desire for peace among themselves as well as with the rest of the world.

Three main principles dominated the Conference: First, that no Nation in the Western Hemisphere professed any right to threaten the peace of its neighbors; second, that the integrity of every country, large or small, would be assured; third, that renunciation of war required some method of obtaining instantaneously the cooperative effort of the entire Hemisphere. The dominant idea was that any threat to the maintenance of peace on this continent must lead to immediate consultation to seek common policies and take common measures to prevent conflict. It was the basis of the major treaties and agreements negotiated at the Conference. The agreements provide a complete consultative system intended to meet the menace of conflict by the quick and active cooperation of the twenty-one Governments.

The three most important of the numerous accords reached at Buenos Aires were the following:

First, the convention to coordinate, extend and assure the fulfillment of the existing treaties between the American States. In this agreement the prior treaties requiring settlement of international controversies by pacific means are reaffirmed; and the Nations agree to consult with each other and to cooperate toward peace. They further pledge abstinence from hostilities for six months at least during such consultation. If any Nations should become involved in controversy, they agree to report to the other American Governments from time to time the progress made in the adjustment of their dispute. The agreement also provides that if war should take place between any American Republics, the other American Republics will consult to adopt in their character as neutrals a common attitude.

Second, the convention for the maintenance, preservation and reestablishment of peace. In this treaty the various American Governments pledge consultation with each other whenever the peace of the Americas is menaced and in the event of an international war outside America which might menace the peace of the American Republics.

Third, the additional protocol relative to non-intervention. This agreement reaffirms the Convention of Montevideo in 1933 (see Item 156, Vol. II), which contained the fundamental principle that "no State has the right to intervene in the internal or external affairs of others."

In addition to the foregoing three principal agreements, there were a number of other significant and far-reaching accords and resolutions designed to stimulate trade, cultural interchange and improve communication. During this session of three weeks the conference unanimously adopted a total of 11 treaties and conventions and 62 resolutions and declarations.

The Buenos Aires Conference is proof that in a world which is beset with rumors and threats of war,

616

Governments determined to keep alive the spirit of peace and willing to renew mutual trust and faith in treaties can move together in a co-operative search for the means of enduring peace.

228 ⟨ A Treasury Statement on the Sterilization of Gold. December 22, 1936

THE Secretary of the Treasury, after conferring with the Board of Governors of the Federal Reserve System, announces that he proposes, whenever it is deemed advisable and in the public interest to do so, to take appropriate action with respect to net additional acquisitions or releases of gold by the Treasury Department.

This will be accomplished by the sale of additional public debt obligations, the proceeds of which will be used for the purchase of gold, and by the purchase or redemption of outstanding obligations in the case of movements in the reverse direction.

NOTE: So successful had been the program for reestablishing the position of the dollar, that large amounts of capital, as has already been suggested, began flowing to the United States; the source appeared to be twofold: First, the return of American funds which had been sent abroad prior to 1933; and second, European capital coming to this country for safe and profitable investment. One indirect effect of this process, however, began, late in 1936, to cause concern. With the otherwise virtually equal balance of payments, importation of the funds in question largely took the form of imports of gold, and it was feared that the additions to our monetary and credit structure of the proceeds of this gold might subsequently re-sult in too great an internal expansion of credit, with a further and postponed result that, if and when such capital was again exported, the ensuing contraction of credit would also have an unfavorable effect on our economy. To minimize these dangers, the Secretary of the Treasury announced, on December 22, 1936, the initiation of a program that has since come to be known as "sterilization of gold."

These operations permit neutralizing the effect on member bank reserves of gold acquisitions or sales of such gold. Effects on reserves of additions to the gold supply, either from imports or from new production, can be offset by the sale to the public of an equivalent amount of United States Government obligations and by the setting aside of the purchased gold in an inactive account in the Treasury. In this way the gold so treated is kept out of the country's credit base.

Gold imported into this country and sold to the Treasury is paid for by Treasury checks. These checks are drawn upon the Treasury's balances at the Federal Reserve Banks and become available to member banks which deposit them at the reserve banks and, in exchange, receive credits to their reserve accounts. Reserve balances of member banks receiving Treasury checks are thereby increased. Prior to December, 1936, the Treasury did not offset this increase. It replenished its balances with the reserve banks by giving the reserve banks an equivalent credit in the gold certificate account. Under the "steri-lization" arrangement, the Treasury can segregate the gold and can replenish its balances at the Reserve Banks through the proceeds of Government obligations sold in the market. Purchases of such obligations out of funds on deposit with member banks result in a diminution of member-bank reserves, thus offsetting the previous increase.

The corresponding effects of an outward movement of gold held in this inactive fund can be similarly offset by the purchase or redemption of United States obligations in the market, thus restoring to it the funds lost through the export of gold. To this extent, therefore, the volume of the country's credit base would neither increase nor decrease as the result of changes in the supply of gold.

229 ❦ A Christmas Greeting to the Nation. December 24, 1936

I HAVE been reading the Christmas Carol to my family, in accordance with our old custom. On this eve of Christmas I want to quote to you the pledge of old Scrooge when, after many vicissitudes, he had come to understand in his heart the great lesson and the great opportunity of Christmastide.

"I will honor Christmas in my heart and try to keep it all the year. I will live in the Past, the Present and the Future. The Spirits of all Three shall strive within me. I will not shut out the lessons that they teach."

And at the end of the story is this glorious passage:

"Scrooge was better than his word. He did it all and infinitely more; and to Tiny Tim, who did NOT die, he was a second father. He became as good a friend, as good a master and as good a man as the good old city knew, or any other good old city, town or borough in the good old world. Some people laughed to see the alteration in him, but he let them laugh and little heeded them; for he was wise enough to know that nothing ever happened on this globe for good, at which some people did not have their fill of laughter in the outset. His own heart laughed; and that was good enough for him."

The teaching of the Sermon on the Mount is as adequate to the needs of men and of Nations today as when it was first proclaimed among the hills above the Sea of Galilee. In such measure as its spirit is accepted men and nations may lay claim to be seekers after peace on earth.

We of the Western Hemisphere have this year rendered special tribute to the spirit of Christmas, for we have pledged anew our faith in the arbitrament of reason and the practice of friendship. To that faith we bear witness tonight. May that faith make us happy today and tomorrow and through all the coming year.

230 ❰ A Letter to the National Conference on Venereal Disease Control. December 24, 1936

My dear Miss Roche:

I DEEPLY appreciate your invitation, and that of Surgeon General Parran, to address the opening session of the national conference on venereal disease control, and I wish it were possible for me to do so. Since I cannot attend in person, I am glad to convey to you, and through you to those in attendance at the meeting, this expression of my very deep interest in the success of your efforts.

The recent increase in public interest in the problem before the conference is extremely gratifying. With the assistance now being given by the Public Health Service through Social Security funds, it should be possible for State and local health authorities to develop needed facilities for the treatment and control of these diseases. It is my understanding that out of your deliberations there will come a statement of principles and methods which should be useful to every community in the country in applying most effectively the scientific knowledge which we have to minimize these serious hazards to the public health.

The Federal Government is deeply interested in conserving the resources of the country by all appropriate methods. The attainment of your objectives would do much to conserve our human resources and would reduce considerably the present large costs for the community care of the disastrous results of the venereal diseases. You have my best wishes for success.

Very sincerely yours,

Honorable Josephine Roche,
Assistant Secretary in Charge of Public Health,
Department of the Treasury,
Washington, D. C.

(This letter was read at the opening of the Conference in Washington, December 28, 1936.)

231 ⟨ The Three Hundred and Thirty-second Press Conference (Excerpts). December 29, 1936

(Neutrality legislation and the internal conflict in Spain — Shipment of war materials to Spain — Appointment of judges over sixty years of age — Breakdown of wages and hours standards.)

THE PRESIDENT: Hello, Fred *(Storm)*. Pretty good crowd today.

MR. STORM: Pretty good audience, yes.

THE PRESIDENT: I think Christmas cannot have been so very severe, there are so many.

MR. STORM: They are all on their feet. . . .

Q. Can you say whether you are giving any consideration to legislation that would strengthen the Arms Embargo Act, particularly in the case of civil war?

THE PRESIDENT: Obviously, there should be a further discretion vested in the President with the appropriate penalties to take care of internal strife. I leave out the words "civil war" for the perfectly obvious reason which is illustrative of why no Act can possibly take into consideration every future contingency.

In other words, ask yourself the question, Fred, what is a civil war and you see how impossible it is to define it.

The Confederate States, as I remember it, most of them seceded from the Union in the winter of 1861. Most of them had seceded some time before Sumter. Well, what was the status then? Was it a civil war?

Then, in the late April of 1861, Sumter was fired on. Hostilities were confined at that time to Charleston Harbor. Was there a civil war going on? I don't know. In the North, they called it a Rebellion; in the South, they called it a War between the States.

For a good many years we fought in this country a series of wars with the Redskins. They were recognized as wars because of the fact that special decorations were given to people who fought in them. They were the Indian Wars. Was that a civil war in the United States or not?

Further back, there was a Whiskey Rebellion, soon after the Revolution. Was that a civil war? I don't know.

In other words, civil war means anything or nothing; and the circumstances and the particular case must be decided on by somebody who has authority 365 days of the year. That is about the easiest answer.

Of course it seems obvious that today, in this particular case in Spain, there are two organized groups of armies and the normal person trying to define the Spanish situation would normally call that particular situation a civil war. There isn't much question about that.

In this particular case of the sale of these planes and engines, it is perhaps a rather good example of the need of some power in the Executive. It is, furthermore, an example of cooperation by business. As the State Department has told you, they have had a number of applications from American citizens and firms to sell munitions to the belligerents in

621

Spain, to one side or the other, and the State Department specifically and definitely requested them not to engage in the transaction on two grounds, the first that it was contrary to the Government policy, and the second that it was endangering, even if only to a slight degree, our desire to be neutral in this unfortunate happening in Spain.

Well, these companies went along with the request of the Government. There is the 90 percent of business that is honest, I mean ethically honest. There is the 90 percent we are always pointing at with pride. And then one man does what amounts to a perfectly legal but thoroughly unpatriotic act. He represents the 10 percent or less of business that does not live up to the best standards.

Excuse the homily, but I feel quite deeply about it.

Q. Supposing that the Government would not grant this license, or whatever you call it, for the exportation of those munitions?

THE PRESIDENT: We have to under the law. The law says we must issue them.

Q. There are some persons who say that you have discretion under the law and that it could be refused?

THE PRESIDENT: Couldn't do it. Absolutely not a chance. The law says that this Committee in the State Department shall grant the license.

Q. A mandamus could be obtained?

THE PRESIDENT: Of course, there is the other phase of the case. If legislation is passed extending even the present Neutrality Act to civil wars and I find, by an Executive finding, that a civil war exists in the same way that I would under the present Act that a war between two Nations exists, and that Act should become law within the next two weeks after Congress meets, we could then clamp down on this particular shipment under this particular contract or commission.

That immediately raises the question as to whether this particular individual could go to the Court of Claims and seek damages for the promise which he otherwise would claim he could have made.

The best way of answering that is to ask you to read the Supreme Court's decision in the Neutrality case the other day. There is an intimation in there, only an intimation — nobody can guess how the Supreme Court would rule in a case like that — but the intimation is there to the effect that, it being an act contrary to the request of the Government, and the conduct of foreign affairs being in the Executive, the Courts would not grant reimbursement to this individual for a loss of what he otherwise would have made as being contrary to public policy. But, as I say, you cannot tell until the case is decided.

Q. This manufacturer who obtained this license was quoted today as saying that his planes were not to be used for military purposes at all. He claims he had a perfectly valid right and that he would provide employment for 1,500 skilled workmen. He says they are not to be used for war purposes at all.

THE PRESIDENT: Of course that particular plea was made in 1914 and 1915 and 1916, in just the same way. They said that the export of machine guns would give work to Americans. That does not mean it is the right thing to do.

Q. Mr. President, did you see the story this morning that there was a recommendation forthcoming, asking that a Central Press Bureau be established under which all the press relations would be handled?

THE PRESIDENT: Oh, yes. Off the record, the *Times* Bureau had a brain storm. I never heard of it until I read it in the *Times*, and I don't want to hear any more about it. . . .

Q. Some of the Senators are complaining that they cannot make recommendations for Judges for the Judgeships that Congress created because of the 60-year age limit. My understanding was that the Department of Justice and yourself would not waive that 60-year age limit.

THE PRESIDENT: That has been an Executive prerogative for four years and I don't think I have sent to the Senate the name of any new judge over 60 years old and I think I shall stick to it. It is a pretty good rule.

623

Q. Can you tell us what Sidney Hillman dropped in this morning for?

THE PRESIDENT: We discussed a lot of things. Among others, we discussed the breakdown of both the maximum-hour and minimum-wage provisions that we enforced until a little over a year ago. There seems to be a general consensus of opinion and statistics — you might try to get a story out of the Department of Labor on that or out of the Central Statistical Board — showing the breakdown of the child labor provisions and also the minimum-wage, maximum-hour provisions.

There has been very little printed about it, but the fact remains that the breakdown has been constant and increasing.

I had one experience in the campaign — I don't think any of you who were with me saw it that particular day because it was half a mile back, I mean you were half a mile back. It was on that hectic ride from Providence to Boston.

We got into New Bedford and in that park there was the most awful jam. There must have been 20,000 people where there was room for only about a thousand and they were jammed around my car. There was a girl six or seven feet away who was trying to pass an envelope to me and she was just too far away to reach. One of the policemen threw her back into the crowd and I said to Gus *(Gennerich)*, "Get the note from that girl." He got it and handed it to me and the note said this: "Dear Mr. President: I wish you could do something to help us girls. You are the only recourse we have got left. We have been working in a sewing factory, a garment factory, and up to a few months ago we were getting our minimum pay of $11 a week (I think it was $11 a week) and even the learners were getting $7 or $8 a week. Today the 200 of us girls have been cut down to $4 and $5 and $6 a week. You are the only man that can do anything about it. Please send somebody from Washington up here to restore our minimum wages because we cannot live on $4 or $5 or $6 a week."

That is something that many of us found in the campaign — that many of these people actually think that I have the power to restore things like minimum wages and maximum hours and the elimination of child labor. That was just one example of a good many in the campaign. Of course letters keep coming in all the time which say that just by Executive Order or action I can take care of these individual cases. Of course, I haven't any power to do it. . . .

Q. Do you think something should be done to restore minimum pay and maximum hours by the Government?

THE PRESIDENT: Absolutely. But don't write any story saying that the President is going to restore N.R.A. That is the easy, sloppy method of writing a story. Anybody can do that. What I would like to have you do is to point out the fact that something has got to be done, and don't go beyond "something." Don't get out on a limb, because you know how often you have sawed off your own limb. Say that something has to be done about the elimination of child labor and long hours and starvation wages. That is as far as I could go. If I were writing the story, I would stick to that.

Q. What did you do with the letter you got in the crowd?

THE PRESIDENT: I sent it to the Department of Labor and I sent a copy to the Massachusetts Labor Commissioner. What happened, I do not know.

Q. Did you send a copy to the Supreme Court? *(Laughter)*

Q. Can we look for a specific recommendation from you some time early in the Session on this proposal?

THE PRESIDENT: I am not a prophet or the son of a prophet today. . . .

Q. Do you think the situation can be handled by State action without Federal help?

THE PRESIDENT: No.

Q. Did Sidney Hillman have a suggestion?

THE PRESIDENT: No. . . .

Q. Can a sweat shop, by offering to take men on for jobs paying $7 and $8 a week, force them off the W.P.A. rolls in order to do it?

THE PRESIDENT: That is a difficulty we face in a great many localities. People on the W.P.A. rolls have been offered jobs on such a low weekly or daily wage that we simply, in good conscience, could not throw them off W.P.A. rolls to take what we considered an inadequate daily wage. . . .

NOTE: The civil war in Spain broke out in July, 1936, at a time when the Congress was not in session. No provision had been made in the neutrality legislation of 1935 for civil warfare (see Item 117, Vol. IV). No legal means existed, therefore, by which the Government could prohibit the export of arms to Spain. However, the Government soon made its policy clear and definitely discouraged such exports.

On August 7th the Acting Secretary of State sent the following instructions to all our representatives in Spain:

"In conformity with its well-established policy of non-interference with internal affairs in other countries either in time of peace or in the event of civil strife, this Government will, of course, scrupulously refrain from any interference whatsoever in the unfortunate Spanish situation. We believe that American citizens, both at home and abroad, are patriotically observing this well-recognized American policy."

At home the Department of State sought to discourage exports of arms to Spain as a violation of the spirit of our neutrality policy, even though express legislation had not been enacted. For several months American munitions manufacturers respected this policy. In December, 1936, however, an application was made to export a quantity of airplanes and war materials. The license, unfortunately, had to be granted under the law; but the Government's disapproval of the conduct of the exporter was set forth in the foregoing statement.

The new Congress, which convened in 1937, almost immediately closed up this gap in our legislation by a Joint Resolution approved by me on January 8, 1937, prohibiting the export of arms and munitions to Spain (Public Resolution No. 1, 75th Congress).

232 ❡ An Exchange of Letters on the Establishment of a System of Retirement Pensions for Railroad Employees. December 26-30, 1936

December 26, 1936

Dear Sirs:

For several years the establishment and operation of a system of retirement annuities has been under consideration by the railroads and their employees. Because the legislation undertaken for the purpose of arranging for the payment of retirement annuities has been involved in litigation, efforts to resolve the issues through mutual discussion have been postponed.

The railroads and their employees have shown great aptitude in the cooperative solution of their problems. I sincerely hope that the retirement annuity problem can be resolved in the same manner. I therefore urge upon you the desirability of a conference between representatives of the railroads and of the railroad employees to consider the retirement problem and attempt to find a satisfactory solution.

The taxes under the carrier and carrier employee tax act expire on February 28th next and further consideration of this whole subject by Congress will be necessary early in the next session. In order that Congress might have the benefit of joint recommendations, I suggest a conference on these matters.

The Railroad Retirement Board has collected a wealth of information bearing on the problems which would be considered by such a conference and has in its possession all the relevant records compiled by the Federal Coordinator of Transportation. Its technical facilities can doubtless be of much value to such a conference and I am, therefore, requesting the Board to offer assistance in arranging for a conference, to make its information available and to render whatever possible aid it can to the conferees.

In view of the general desire that there may be an amicable

627

solution reached, I hope that you will take an interest in attempting to bring about that result.

Very sincerely yours,

Mr. J. J. Pelley,
President, Association of American Railroads,
Washington, D. C.
and
Mr. G. M. Harrison,
Railway Labor Executives' Association,
Cincinnati, Ohio.

December 29, 1936

My dear Mr. President:

This will acknowledge receipt of your letter of December 28th concerning the subject of retirement annuities for railroad employees, and suggesting the desirability of a conference between representatives of the railroads and their employees for the purpose of considering the retirement problem and attempting to find a satisfactory solution.

In accordance with your suggestion, arrangements are now actively under way for a meeting of representatives of management and employees for the purpose of considering this subject. We hope to hold this meeting about mid-January, and you may be assured that, when it is held, full and thorough consideration will be given the suggestions which you very kindly offer and outline in your letter.

In this connection, permit me to take occasion to express our appreciation for what you have to say as to the aptitude of railroad management and employees in considering and dealing with their problems of mutual interest in a cooperative way. At the same time, we wish also to thank you for your manifest interest and help at all times in doing everything that can consistently be done to assist in helping solve this and other problems of the industry.

Sincerely yours,

J. J. PELLEY

Honorable Franklin D. Roosevelt,
The White House,
Washington, D. C.

December 30, 1936

Dear Mr. President:

I acknowledge receipt of your letter of December 28th suggesting that representatives of the railroads and their employees undertake a conference for the purpose of endeavoring to reach a satisfactory solution of the existing controversy on the Railroad Retirement and Tax Acts.

We are now endeavoring to arrange for such conference and it appears that we will meet very shortly after the middle of January, 1937. It will be our purpose to exert every effort in the direction of reaching a satisfactory understanding with the representatives of the carriers.

I thank you for your interest in this matter and want you to know that your assistance, counsel and advice are greatly appreciated.

With kindest personal regards, I am

Very sincerely yours,

G. M. HARRISON

The President of the United States
The White House
Washington, D. C.

(See in this connection note to Item 120, Vol. III; and Item 69, Vol. IV.)

233 ⟨ Congratulations on the Inauguration of Governor Herbert H. Lehman, of New York.

January 1, 1937

ON THE occasion of the third inauguration of Herbert H. Lehman as Governor of the State of New York, I will be grateful if you will express to him and his associates in the Government of the State my warm congratulations and at the same time my personal regrets that I cannot be present in person.

Governor Lehman's leadership has won and maintained the confidence of the overwhelming majority of the citizens of our State. His leadership is an outstanding proof that the processes of democratic Government can serve current needs, maintain a sound credit and demonstrate unselfishness and honesty in the conduct of public affairs.

He and all of you who are associated with him have my very good wishes for the coming years.

234 ¶ Exchange of Letters with Andrew W. Mellon on the Gift of an Art Gallery to the United States (Excerpts).
December 22, 1936—January 1, 1937

December 22, 1936

My dear Mr. President:

Over a period of many years I have been acquiring important and rare paintings and sculpture with the idea that ultimately they would become the property of the people of the United States and be made available to them in a national art gallery to be maintained in the City of Washington for the purpose of encouraging and developing a study of the fine arts.

I have within the last few years transferred these paintings and sculpture to trustees with responsibility for carrying out this purpose and have given them full power and authority to deed these works of art to a national gallery if and when such an institution shall assume and be prepared to carry out the purposes intended. In addition, I have given to the trustees securities ample to erect a gallery building of sufficient size to house these works of art and to permit the indefinite growth of the collection under a conservative policy regulating acquisitions.

Such a gallery would be for the use and benefit of the general public; and it is my hope that it may attract gifts from other citizens who may in the future desire to contribute works of art of the highest quality to form a great national collection. In connection, therefore, with the intended gift, I shall stipulate that the proposed building shall not bear my name, but shall be known as "The National Art Gallery" or by such other name as may appropriately identify it as a gallery of art of the national Government.

In order to carry out this purpose, and with the approval of the other trustees, I wish to propose a plan to give the art collection which I have brought together, to the Smithsonian Institution or to the United States Government for the benefit of the people of this country, and also to erect or cause to be erected on public land a suitable building for such a National Gallery of Art, the design and materials of which shall be subject to the approval of the Fine Arts Commission. . . .

In addition to the gift of the art collection and a building in which it and similar collections may be housed and displayed, I plan also to establish an endowment fund for the proposed gallery, the income from which shall be used to pay the annual salaries of a director, assistant director, secretary, and curators of the gallery, and for possible future art acquisitions. The upkeep of the building and other administrative expenses and cost of operation would be provided in appropriations to be made by Congress, as for the other units of the Smithsonian Institution. . . .

By reason of the rarity and importance of these works of art, the general character of the collection is such that it will furnish the nucleus of a great National Collection and will give our country at once a National Gallery that will rank with the other great galleries of the world. . . .

If this plan meets with your approval, I will submit a formal offer of gift stating specifically the terms thereof, and the erection of the building may proceed immediately upon the acceptance of such offer and the passage of necessary legislation by Congress. Appropriate instruments of conveyance and gift will then be executed.

Sincerely yours,
A. W. Mellon

The President,
The White House,
Washington, D. C.

December 26, 1936

My dear Mr. Mellon:

When my uncle handed me your letter of December 22nd I was not only completely taken by surprise, but was delighted by your very wonderful offer to the people of the United States.

This was especially so because for many years I have felt the need for a national gallery of art in the capital. Your proposed gift does more than furnish what you call a "nucleus" because I am confident that the collections you have been making are of the first importance and will place the Nation well up in the first rank.

Furthermore, your offer of an adequate building and an endowment fund means permanence in this changing world.

Because the formal offer calls for specific statement of the terms and will have to be worked out before any request is made by me to the Congress for the necessary legislation, may I suggest that you, or whoever you may care to designate, should come to see me some afternoon this week?

Also, I think that we should discuss the formal announcement and the terms of it.

With my renewed appreciation of your letter, believe me,
Very sincerely yours,

Honorable A. W. Mellon,
Washington, D. C.

December 31, 1936
My dear Mr. President:

I wish to thank you for your kind letter of December 26th and greatly appreciate the interest you have shown in my plan for the establishment of a national gallery of art at Washington.

For the purpose of carrying this plan into effect, I hereby offer to give the art collection, which I have brought together, to the Smithsonian Institution or to the United States Government for the benefit of the people of the United States and to construct a suitable building in which to exhibit this collection and other works of art of like quality which other citizens may in the future contribute to the National Collection.

In connection with the offer which I have made on behalf of myself and the other Trustees, who have the responsibility of carrying out this purpose, and in accordance with the suggestion in your letter, I set forth below an outline of the definite terms and conditions under which the gallery is to be erected and, together with the art collection, is to be given to the Smithsonian Institution or to the

Government of the United States, all of which conditions are intended for the efficient management of the gallery and for safeguarding the high standard of quality which should be maintained in the art to be displayed therein. . . .

In addition to the gift of the art collection and a building in which it and similar collections may be housed and displayed, I further propose to establish an endowment fund for the gallery, the income from which shall be used to pay the annual salaries of a director, assistant director, a secretary and a curator of the gallery, and for future art acquisitions, but not for the upkeep of the building and other administrative expenses and salaries, which I have hereinbefore stipulated shall be provided in appropriations to be made by Congress. The amount of such endowment fund and the terms and conditions governing its operation will be subject to further consideration and will be stated in the instrument creating the fund.

The exact form of these gifts, and the details for carrying them into execution, are questions that can be agreed upon by counsel representing the Smithsonian Institution or the Government and myself.

Very sincerely yours,

A. W. Mellon

The President,
The White House.

January 1, 1937

My dear Mr. Mellon:

The outline of the terms and conditions under which the proposed "National Gallery of Art" is to be erected and maintained is admirably set forth in the letter you handed to me at our conference yesterday.

In accordance with our understanding, I am referring the correspondence to the Attorney General and the appropriate representatives of the Smithsonian Institution.

They will be able, I am sure, to work out, in conference with you, the details of this fine project and prepare the necessary papers, including a draft of enabling legislation.

I shall be happy to submit the matter, with a favorable recommendation, to the Congress at the first opportunity.

Very sincerely yours,

Honorable A. W. Mellon,
Washington, D. C.

235 ❨ The Annual Message to the Congress. January 6, 1937

Mr. President, Mr. Speaker, Members of the Congress of the United States:

FOR the first time in our national history a President delivers his Annual Message to a new Congress within a fortnight of the expiration of his term of office. While there is no change in the Presidency this year, change will occur in future years. It is my belief that under this new constitutional practice, the President should in every fourth year, in so far as seems reasonable, review the existing state of our national affairs and outline broad future problems, leaving specific recommendations for future legislation to be made by the President about to be inaugurated.

At this time, however, circumstances of the moment compel me to ask your immediate consideration of: First, measures extending the life of certain authorizations and powers which, under present statutes, expire within a few weeks; second, an addition to the existing Neutrality Act to cover specific points raised by the unfortunate civil strife in Spain; and, third, a deficiency appropriation bill for which I shall submit estimates this week.

In March, 1933, the problems which faced our Nation and which only our national Government had the resources to meet were more serious even than appeared on the surface.

It was not only that the visible mechanism of economic life had broken down. More disturbing was the fact that long neglect of the needs of the underprivileged had brought too many of our people to the verge of doubt as to the successful adaptation of our historic traditions to the complex modern world. In that lay a challenge to our democratic form of Government itself.

Ours was the task to prove that democracy could be made to function in the world of today as effectively as in the simpler world of a hundred years ago. Ours was the task to do more than to argue a theory. The times required the confident answer of performance to those whose instinctive faith in humanity made them want to believe that in the long run democracy would prove superior to more extreme forms of Government as a process of getting action when action was wisdom, without the spiritual sacrifices which those other forms of Government exact.

That challenge we met. To meet it required unprecedented activities under Federal leadership to end abuses, to restore a large measure of material prosperity, to give new faith to millions of our citizens who had been traditionally taught to expect that democracy would provide continuously wider opportunity and continuously greater security in a world where science was continuously making material riches more available to man.

In the many methods of attack with which we met these problems, you and I, by mutual understanding and by determination to cooperate, helped to make democracy succeed by refusing to permit unnecessary disagreement to arise between two of our branches of Government. That spirit of cooperation was able to solve difficulties of extraordinary magnitude and ramification with few important errors, and at a cost cheap when measured by the immediate necessities and the eventual results.

I look forward to a continuance of that cooperation in the next four years. I look forward also to a continuance of the basis of that cooperation — mutual respect for each other's proper sphere of functioning in a democracy which is working well, and a common-sense realization of the need for play in the joints of the machine.

On that basis, it is within the right of the Congress to determine which of the many new activities shall be continued or abandoned, increased or curtailed.

On that same basis, the President alone has the responsibility for their administration. I find that this task of Executive management has reached the point where our administrative machinery needs comprehensive overhauling. I shall, therefore, shortly address the Congress more fully in regard to modernizing and improving the Executive branch of the Government.

That cooperation of the past four years between the Congress and the President has aimed at the fulfillment of a twofold policy: first, economic recovery through many kinds of assistance to agriculture, industry and banking; and, second, deliberate improvement in the personal security and opportunity of the great mass of our people.

The recovery we sought was not to be merely temporary. It was to be a recovery protected from the causes of previous disasters. With that aim in view — to prevent a future similar crisis — you and I joined in a series of enactments — safe banking and sound currency, the guarantee of bank deposits, protection for the investor in securities, the removal of the threat of agricultural surpluses, insistence on collective bargaining, the outlawing of sweat shops, child labor and unfair trade practices, and the beginnings of security for the aged and the worker.

Nor was the recovery we sought merely a purposeless whirring of machinery. It is important, of course, that every man and woman in the country be able to find work, that every factory run, that business and farming as a whole earn profits. But Government in a democratic Nation does not exist solely, or even primarily, for that purpose.

It is not enough that the wheels turn. They must carry us in the direction of a greater satisfaction in life for the average man. The deeper purpose of democratic government is to assist as many of its citizens as possible, especially those who need it most, to improve their conditions of life, to retain all personal liberty which does not adversely affect their neighbors, and to pursue the happiness which comes with security and an opportunity for recreation and culture.

Even with our present recovery we are far from the goal of

that deeper purpose. There are far-reaching problems still with us for which democracy must find solutions if it is to consider itself successful.

For example, many millions of Americans still live in habitations which not only fail to provide the physical benefits of modern civilization but breed disease and impair the health of future generations. The menace exists not only in the slum areas of the very large cities, but in many smaller cities as well. It exists on tens of thousands of farms, in varying degrees, in every part of the country.

Another example is the prevalence of an un-American type of tenant farming. I do not suggest that every farm family has the capacity to earn a satisfactory living on its own farm. But many thousands of tenant farmers, indeed most of them, with some financial assistance and with some advice and training, can be made self-supporting on land which can eventually belong to them. The Nation would be wise to offer them that chance instead of permitting them to go along as they do now, year after year, with neither future security as tenants nor hope of ownership of their homes nor expectation of bettering the lot of their children.

Another national problem is the intelligent development of our social security system, the broadening of the services it renders, and practical improvement in its operation. In many Nations where such laws are in effect, success in meeting the expectations of the community has come through frequent amendment of the original statute.

And, of course, the most far-reaching and the most inclusive problem of all is that of unemployment and the lack of economic balance of which unemployment is at once the result and the symptom. The immediate question of adequate relief for the needy unemployed who are capable of performing useful work, I shall discuss with the Congress during the coming months. The broader task of preventing unemployment is a matter of long-range evolutionary policy. To that we must continue to give our best thought and effort. We cannot assume that immediate industrial and commercial activity which mitigates present pressures justifies the national Government at this time in placing the unemployment problem in a filing cabinet of finished business.

Fluctuations in employment are tied to all other wasteful fluctuations in our mechanism of production and distribution. One of these wastes is speculation. In securities or commodities, the larger the volume of speculation, the wider become the upward and downward swings and the more certain the result that in the long run there will be more losses than gains in the underlying wealth of the community.

And, as is now well known to all of us, the same net loss to society comes from reckless overproduction and monopolistic underproduction of natural and manufactured commodities.

Overproduction, underproduction and speculation are three evil sisters who distill the troubles of unsound inflation and disastrous deflation. It is to the interest of the Nation to have Government help private enterprise to gain sound general price levels and to protect those levels from wide perilous fluctuations. We know now that if early in 1931 Government had taken the steps which were taken two and three years later, the depression would never have reached the depths of the beginning of 1933.

Sober second thought confirms most of us in the belief that the broad objectives of the National Recovery Act were sound. We know now that its difficulties arose from the fact that it tried to do too much. For example, it was unwise to expect the same agency to regulate the length of working hours, minimum wages, child labor and collective bargaining on the one hand and the complicated questions of unfair trade practices and business controls on the other.

The statute of N.R.A. has been outlawed. The problems have not. They are still with us.

That decent conditions and adequate pay for labor, and just return for agriculture, can be secured through parallel and simultaneous action by forty-eight States is a proven impossibility. It is equally impossible to obtain curbs on monopoly, unfair trade practices and speculation by State action alone. There are those who, sincerely or insincerely, still cling to State action as a theoretical hope. But experience with actualities makes it clear that Federal laws supplementing State laws are needed to help solve the problems which result from modern invention applied in an industrialized Nation which conducts its business with scant regard to State lines.

During the past year there has been a growing belief that there is little fault to be found with the Constitution of the United States as it stands today. The vital need is not an alteration of our fundamental law, but an increasingly enlightened view with reference to it. Difficulties have grown out of its interpretation; but rightly considered, it can be used as an instrument of progress, and not as a device for prevention of action.

It is worth our while to read and reread the preamble of the Constitution, and Article I thereof which confers the legislative powers upon the Congress of the United States. It is also worth our while to read again the debates in the Constitutional Convention of one hundred and fifty years ago. From such reading, I obtain the very definite thought that the members of that Convention were fully aware that civilization would raise problems for the proposed new Federal Government, which they themselves could not even surmise; and that it was their definite intent and expectation that a liberal interpretation in the years to come would give to the Congress the same relative powers over new national problems as they themselves gave to the Congress over the national problems of their day.

In presenting to the Convention the first basic draft of the Constitution, Edmund Randolph explained that it was the purpose "to insert essential principles only, lest the operation of government should be clogged by rendering those provisions permanent and unalterable which ought to be accommodated to times and events."

With a better understanding of our purposes, and a more intelligent recognition of our needs as a Nation, it is not to be assumed that there will be prolonged failure to bring legislative and judicial action into closer harmony. Means must be found to adapt our legal forms and our judicial interpretation to the actual present national needs of the largest progressive democracy in the modern world.

That thought leads to a consideration of world problems. To go no further back than the beginning of this century, men and women everywhere were seeking conditions of life very different from those which were customary before modern invention and modern industry and modern communications had come into being. The World War, for all of its tragedy, encouraged these demands, and stimulated action to fulfill these new desires.

Many national Governments seemed unable adequately to respond; and, often with the improvident assent of the masses of the people themselves, new forms of government were set up with oligarchy taking the place of democracy. In oligarchies, militarism has leapt forward, while in those Nations which have retained democracy, militarism has waned.

I have recently visited three of our sister Republics in South America. The very cordial receptions with which I was greeted were in tribute to democracy. To me the outstanding observation of that visit was that the masses of the peoples of all the Americas are convinced that the democratic form of government can be made to succeed and do not wish to substitute for it any other form of government. They believe that democracies are best able to cope with the changing problems of modern civilization within themselves, and that democracies are best able to maintain peace among themselves.

The Inter-American Conference, operating on these fundamental principles of democracy, did much to assure peace in this Hemisphere. Existing peace machinery was improved. New instruments to maintain peace and eliminate causes of war were adopted. Wider protection of the interests of the American Republics in the event of war outside the Western Hemisphere was provided. Respect for, and observance of, international treaties and international law were strengthened. Principles of liberal trade policies, as effective aids to the maintenance of peace, were reaffirmed. The intellectual and cultural relationships among

640

American Republics were broadened as a part of the general peace program.

In a world unhappily thinking in terms of war, the representatives of twenty-one Nations sat around a table, in an atmosphere of complete confidence and understanding, sincerely discussing measures for maintaining peace. Here was a great and a permanent achievement directly affecting the lives and security of the two hundred and fifty million human beings who dwell in this Western Hemisphere. Here was an example which must have a wholesome effect upon the rest of the world.

In a very real sense, the Conference in Buenos Aires sent forth a message on behalf of all the democracies of the world to those Nations which live otherwise. Because such other Governments are perhaps more spectacular, it was high time for democracy to assert itself.

Because all of us believe that our democratic form of government can cope adequately with modern problems as they arise, it is patriotic as well as logical for us to prove that we can meet new national needs with new laws consistent with an historic constitutional framework clearly intended to receive liberal and not narrow interpretation.

The United States of America, within itself, must continue the task of making democracy succeed.

In that task the Legislative branch of our Government will, I am confident, continue to meet the demands of democracy whether they relate to the curbing of abuses, the extension of help to those who need help, or the better balancing of our interdependent economies.

So, too, the Executive branch of the Government must move forward in this task, and, at the same time, provide better management for administrative action of all kinds.

The Judicial branch also is asked by the people to do its part in making democracy successful. We do not ask the Courts to call non-existent powers into being, but we have a right to expect that conceded powers or those legitimately implied shall be made effective instruments for the common good.

The process of our democracy must not be imperiled by the denial of essential powers of free government.

Your task and mine is not ending with the end of the depression. The people of the United States have made it clear that they expect us to continue our active efforts in behalf of their peaceful advancement.

In that spirit of endeavor and service I greet the 75th Congress at the beginning of this auspicious New Year.

236 (The Annual Budget Message to the Congress. January 7, 1937

To the Congress of the United States:·

Pursuant to provisions of law I transmit herewith the Budget of the United States Government for the fiscal year ending June 30, 1938, together with this message, which is a part thereof. The estimates have been developed after careful analysis of the revenues, obligations, and reasonable needs of the Government, and I recommend appropriations for the purposes specifically detailed herein.

PART I

The programs inaugurated during the last four years to combat the depression and to initiate many needed reforms have cost large sums of money, but the benefits obtained from them are far outweighing all their costs. We shall soon be reaping the full benefits of those programs and shall have at the same time a balanced Budget that will also include provision for reduction of the public debt.

The fiscal plans of the Federal Government for these four years have been formulated with two objectives in mind. Our first was to restore a successful economic life to the country, by providing greater employment and purchasing power for the people, by stimulating a more balanced use of our productive capacity, and by increasing the national income and distributing it on a wider base of prosperity. Our second was to gain new advantages of permanent value for the American people. Both of these objectives can be accomplished under a sound financial policy.

Business conditions have shown each year since 1933 a marked improvement over the preceding year. Employment in private industry is increasing. Industrial production, factory payrolls, and farm prices have steadily risen.

These gains make it possible to reduce for the fiscal year 1938 many expenditures of the Federal Government which the general depression made necessary. Although we must continue to spend substantial sums to provide work for those whom industry has not yet absorbed, the 1938 Budget is in balance; and, except for debt reduction of $401,515,000, it will remain in balance even if later on there are included additional expenditures of as much as $1,537,123,000 for recovery and relief. We expect, moreover, if improvement in economic conditions continues at the present rate, to be able to attain in 1939 a completely balanced Budget, with full provision for meeting the statutory requirements for debt reduction.

In carrying out this policy the American people are obtaining lasting benefits. Economic protection of the aged and physically handicapped is being secured through the operations of the Social Security Act. Ability of the farmer to secure a more constant livelihood has been enhanced by the enactment of legislation especially designed for that purpose. The home owner has been benefited through the financing of mortgages at reasonable rates of interest. Investors in securities are being given a larger measure of protection by the Securities and Exchange Act. The market for corporate securities has been restored and industry has been able to finance its long-term requirements on a favorable basis. The rights of labor are being materially advanced through operation of the National Labor Relations Act.

I plan to submit at a later date an estimate of appropriation for additional relief for the fiscal year 1938, which I hope will not exceed the amount of $1,537,123,000, previously mentioned.

This hope is based on the assumption that industry will cooperate in employing men and women from the relief rolls in larger numbers than during the past year. Many of those in charge of industrial management, recognizing their obligation to the Nation, have furnished a large measure of employment to the jobless. Today, while it is true that in some sections of the country certain types of skilled workers are still seeking employment, it is nevertheless a fact that the great majority of those now receiving relief belong to the unskilled group. It is my conviction that if every employer or potential employer will undertake during the next six months to give employment to persons now receiving Government help, the national Budget can thereafter be kept definitely in balance. Without such cooperation on the part of employers, the question of a balanced Budget for 1938 must of necessity remain an open one, for the very good reason that this Government does not propose next year, any more than during the past four years, to allow American families to starve.

To continue the gains we are making and to accomplish in the 1939 Budget a complete balance between receipts and expenditures including debt reduction, we must now lay the groundwork of our future fiscal policy.

While relief expenditures should decline with greater reemployment, the normal growth of the country naturally reflects itself in increased costs of Government. Many of the old functions and duties of Government naturally cost more as the industrial and agricultural activities to which they are related expand in volume. The cost of new functions and duties can be substantially reduced only by curtailing the function or the duty. I propose shortly to submit to the Congress a broad plan for placing the Executive branch of the Government on a sounder and more responsible basis of management. The carrying out of such a plan will undoubtedly result in some saving in expenditures; but it must be remembered that what is generally known as overhead represents only a small fraction of total expenditures in any large business, Government or private.

Expenditures must be planned with a view to the national

needs; and no expansion of Government activities should be authorized unless the necessity for such expansion has been definitely determined and funds are available to defray the cost. In other words, if new legislation imposes any substantial increase in expenditures either in the expansion of existing or the creation of new activities, it becomes a matter of sound policy simultaneously to provide new revenue sufficient to meet the additional cost. The success of such a policy can be assured only through the full and friendly cooperation of the Congress and the Executive. Of this cooperation I am confident.

PART II

Recommendations

Temporary miscellaneous internal-revenue taxes. — I recommend that the Congress take steps by suitable legislation to extend the miscellaneous internal-revenue taxes which under existing law will expire next June and July, and also to maintain the current rates of those taxes which would otherwise be reduced next June. I consider that the revenue from such taxes or its equivalent is necessary for the financing of the Budget for 1938.

Postal receipts. — The estimates of appropriations for the Postal Service included in the 1938 Budget are predicated upon the continuance during that fiscal year of the 3-cent postage rate for first-class mail other than for local delivery. While the Government makes a profit on first-class mail, the Postal Service is not self-supporting because it carries other classes of mail at a considerable loss. It should be the definite policy of the Government to operate the Postal Service out of postal receipts, and a continuation of the 3-cent rate will be a necessary step toward the accomplishment of this purpose.

Civilian Conservation Corps. — The Civilian Conservation Corps has demonstrated its usefulness and has met with general public approval. It should be continued. I intend shortly to submit a supplemental estimate of appropriation to carry the Corps from March 31, 1937, to the end of the current fiscal year; and I

645

strongly recommend that Congress enact during its present session the necessary legislation to establish the Corps as a permanent agency of the Government.

Expenses of emergency agencies. — There are included in the 1938 Budget, pursuant to the direction of Congress at its last session, estimates of appropriations for the administrative expenses of certain emergency agencies and corporations. Such of the emergency agencies and corporations as may be continued by Congress should have all of their expenditure requirements made subject to the same scrutiny that is given by the Bureau of the Budget to the expenditure requirements of the regular departments and establishments; and I recommend that a provision to that effect be included in any future legislation for the continuance of any such agency or corporation.

PART III

Review of the fiscal years 1936 and 1937, and the fiscal program for 1938

This review concerns itself with the cash actually received and paid out by the Treasury in the fiscal year 1936, with the estimates of receipts and expenditures for the fiscal year 1937, and with the fiscal program for 1938.

Fiscal year 1936

Receipts. — Treasury receipts for the year ended June 30, 1936, amounted to $4,115,956,615, about $295,000,000 less than estimated a year ago. As a result of Supreme Court decisions, the Government lost about $457,000,000 in revenue from taxes levied under the Agricultural Adjustment Act and the Bituminous Coal Act. Had it not been for the invalidation of these taxes, the total revenues received during the fiscal year 1936 would have exceeded the revenue estimates of a year ago by $162,000,000.

The collection of taxes on carriers and their employees, estimated at $33,000,000, has been deferred to the fiscal year 1937 because of pending litigation. The receipts from income taxes were about $7,500,000 less than last year's estimate.

On the other hand, miscellaneous internal-revenue taxes produced $136,488,000 more than was anticipated; customs revenue, $33,621,000 more; miscellaneous receipts, $32,053,000 more; and realization upon assets, $1,483,000 more.

Expenditures.—The total expenditures for the fiscal year ended June 30, 1936 (exclusive of expenditures from postal revenues), amounted to $8,879,798,258, as compared with the estimate of $7,645,301,338 shown in the Budget submitted a year ago. This latter amount did not, however, include $1,673,493,000 for adjusted compensation payments to veterans. The expenditures for the year, excluding these payments, were, therefore, about $439,000,000 less than the estimate.

The total expenditures for recovery and relief were $2,776,-796,469 as against an estimate of $2,869,068,187. For the operation and maintenance of the regular departments and establishments of the Government the expenditures amounted to $3,276,872,306 as compared with estimates of $3,482,208,151. For statutory debt retirement there was expended $403,240,150, and for interest on the public debt $749,396,802, the amounts budgeted for these items being $552,025,000 and $742,000,000, respectively.

Deficit and public debt.—The gross deficit for the fiscal year 1936 amounted to $4,763,841,642. Excluding $403,240,150 for statutory debt retirement, there was a net deficit of $4,360,601,-492. The estimated net deficit as contained in the Budget submitted a year ago was $2,682,482,392, a difference of $1,678,119,-100. As previously indicated, the original estimate has been affected to the extent of $457,000,000 as a result of the invalidation of taxes levied under the Agricultural Adjustment and Bituminous Coal Acts and by the additional expenditure of $1,673,-493,000, under the Adjusted Compensation Act. If it had not been for the increase in the deficit due to these causes, the net deficit for the fiscal year 1936 would have been about $452,000,-000 less than that originally estimated.

The increase in the gross public debt during the year amounted to $5,077,650,869, but this sum included an increase of the balance in the general fund of the Treasury of $840,164,664. The gross public debt on June 30, 1936, was $33,778,543,494.

Fiscal year 1937

Receipts. — The income of the Federal Government during the fiscal year 1937 will increase sharply over that of 1936. It is expected that the total revenue from all sources (exclusive of postal revenues) will amount to $5,828,151,000. This represents an increase of $1,712,194,000 over the actual receipts for the fiscal year 1936 and an increase of $173,933,000 over the estimates contained in the 1937 Budget as submitted a year ago.

The general improvement in business conditions and the enactment of the Revenue Act of 1936 have resulted in additional revenues from taxes which will not only make up the loss in revenue due to the Supreme Court decisions invalidating the taxes levied under the Agricultural Adjustment and the Bituminous Coal Acts, but will produce additional income of approximately $174,000,000.

Since the Revenue Act of 1936 materially changes the tax structure, the individual items of revenue as contained in the original 1937 Budget will not be exactly comparable with the individual items in the 1937 Budget as revised in this message.

Income taxes are expected to yield $2,372,900,000, or $946,-325,000 more than was received from this source last year; miscellaneous internal revenue, $2,274,968,000, an increase of $265,-389,000; customs duties, $446,800,000, an increase of $59,988,000; and realization upon assets $31,830,000, an increase of $26,362,-000. In addition, it is expected that the new tax on unjust enrichment provided by the Revenue Act of 1936 will amount to $82,000,000 and that the tax on carriers and their employees will be $134,552,000, including $33,000,000 deferred from the previous fiscal year. The collection of taxes levied under the Social Security Act will begin in the last half of the fiscal year 1937, and it is expected that these taxes will produce additional revenue in the amount of $324,600,000.

The only item of revenue showing any decrease is that of miscellaneous receipts, in the amount of $50,325,000, which is due to reductions in interest payments made to the Treasury by the Reconstruction Finance Corporation.

Expenditures. — From present indications expenditures for the fiscal year 1937 (exclusive of expenditures from postal revenues) will amount to $8,480,804,000. Exclusive of statutory debt retirement and adjusted compensation payments, the total expenditures will amount to $7,512,779,000, an increase over comparable expenditures for 1936 of $709,714,000.

This amount is made up of increases of $371,192,000 on account of the Social Security Act, $85,603,000 on account of interest on the public debt, $194,161,000 for the general public works program, $123,442,000 for national defense, and $221,-914,000 for other purposes; and decreases of $93,321,000 for the Veterans' Administration, $74,996,000 for the agricultural adjustment program, and $118,281,000 for the Civilian Conservation Corps.

The amount of the recovery and relief expenditures has been estimated at $2,166,157,000, but there is included in the supplemental expenditure items $650,000,000 from an appropriation of $790,000,000 to be requested of Congress for the purpose of carrying the Works Progress Administration and related programs from February 1 to June 30, 1937. This will increase the estimated expenditures for recovery and relief to $2,816,157,000, an increase of $39,361,000 over 1936. The expenditures in the current fiscal year will include, however, the sum of about $165,000,000 for assistance given to individuals and communities directly or indirectly affected by the widespread drought conditions prevailing during the past summer. If this drought had not occurred, the net cost of recovery and relief for the current fiscal year would have been about $125,000,000 below the cost for the previous fiscal year.

Deficit and public debt. — The current estimates for the fiscal year 1937 show a gross deficit of $2,652,654,000. Deducting public debt retirement, the net deficit will be $2,248,129,000.

The increase in the public debt on account of the deficit, however, will be only $1,348,000,000 since it is anticipated that $900,-000,000 of the deficit will be financed from cash on hand. The working balance will be further reduced by net expenditures of about $42,000,000 for trust accounts and $100,000,000 for the retirement of national bank notes now a part of the public debt. This will reduce the working balance from $2,225,000,000 on June 30, 1936, to $1,183,000,000 on June 30, 1937. The gross public debt at the end of the current fiscal year is estimated at $35,026,000,000, an increase over 1936 of $1,248,000,000.

The estimated debt at the end of the fiscal year is based on contemplated expenditures set out in this Budget and does not take into account any change which may occur as a result of the Treasury policy in holding as "inactive" future acquisitions of gold.

Fiscal program for 1938

The expected increase in revenue and decrease in expenditures for relief both reflect the general improvement which has taken place in the economic conditions of the country. The Revenue Act of 1936, which was designed for the purpose of replacing revenue lost through the invalidation of processing taxes, of providing sufficient revenue to amortize the cost of the adjusted compensation payments, and of equalizing tax burdens, gives every indication of satisfactorily accomplishing those purposes. I should like, at this point, to emphasize the importance of maintaining the productiveness of the present tax structure, so that we may properly provide for the fulfillment of our fiscal program.

In legislation enacted during the last session of Congress, which created authorizations for future appropriations aggregating more than $1,500,000,000, there is included about $130,000,000 in the estimates of appropriations contained in this Budget. Such authorizations are contained in the new Federal Highway Act, the Rivers and Harbors and the Flood Control Acts, and the Rural Electrification Act.

There is also included $812,225,000 for social security grants and for the Government's contribution to the old-age reserve account, more than double the expenditures for these purposes in 1937, and there will be for several years still further increases in these requirements. It should be pointed out that these expenditures will be offset to a large extent by the increasing revenues under the Social Security Act.

No estimate of appropriation is presented for the needs of the Civilian Conservation Corps, since its extension beyond March 31 of this year is dependent on the action of Congress. In furtherance of my recommendation for the enactment of legislation to continue it as a permanent agency of the Government, there is included in the "Supplemental Items" an amount sufficient to meet the expenditure requirements for the fiscal year 1938.

The following table shows the distribution, on a functional basis, of the expenditure figures contained in this Budget and compares them with similar figures for previous years.

Actual and estimated expenditures of the Government for the fiscal years 1932–38
(Classifications include expenditures from both general and emergency funds)

[In millions of dollars]

	Estimated		Actual				
	1938	1937	1936	1935	1934	1933	1932
Regular operating expenditures:							
Legislative, judicial, and civil establishments...	771.8	859.0	781.1	597.7	572.5	697.5	978.8
National defense.........	991.6	964.9	911.6	709.9	540.3	667.8	707.6
Veterans' pensions and benefits..............	577.5	1,144.7	2,351.4	607.1	556.9	863.2	984.8
Interest on the public debt.	860.0	835.0	749.4	820.9	756.6	689.4	599.3
Total..............	3,200.9	3,803.6	4,793.5	2,735.6	2,426.3	2,917.9	3,270.5
Public works.............	908.3	1,146.7	868.7	704.3	551.9	427.7	439.5

The Annual Budget Message

Actual and estimated expenditures of the Government for the fiscal years 1932–38 (Continued)
(Classifications include expenditures from both general and emergency funds)

[In millions of dollars]

	Estimated		Actual				
	1938	1937	1936	1935	1934	1933	1932
Unemployment relief:							
Direct relief............	13.0	106.7	591.7	1,914.1	715.8	350.7	......
Work relief (W.P.A. and C.W.A.)	*a*.2	1,400.5	1,264.4	11.3	805.1	....	......
Civilian Conservation Corps	(*b*)	368.0	486.3	435.5	331.9	....	......
Total.................	13.2	1,875.2	2,342.4	2,360.9	1,852.8	350.7	......
Loans (net)..............	*c*153.3	*c*419.9	*c*175.2	80.5	788.6	874.4	404.0
Subscriptions to stock.......	17.2	51.5	69.3	156.8	826.5	110.7	627.0
Agricultural adjustment program..............	482.4	467.6	542.6	743.0	290.3	....	......
Less revenues...........	......	......	76.6	521.4	353.0	....	......
Net.................	482.4	467.6	466.0	221.6	*d*62.7	....	......
Social security............	836.0	399.6	28.4	....	....	......	......
Debt retirement..........	401.5	404.5	403.2	573.6	359.9	461.6	412.6
Miscellaneous.............	1.8	2.0	6.8	21.1	8.7	......	......
Supplemental items........	450.0	750.0	....	....	....	......	......
Grand total..........	*a*6,158.0	8,480.8	8,803.1	6,854.4	6,752.0	5,143.0	5,153.6

a To be increased by any amount appropriated by Congress for recovery and relief for the fiscal year 1938. As indicated in the message, it is hoped the amount will not exceed $1,537,123,000.

b Funds for continuation of the Civilian Conservation Corps are included under "Supplemental items."

c Excess of credits, deduct.

d Excess of revenues, deduct.

Receipts. — Treasury receipts in the fiscal year 1938 are expected to reach a total of $7,293,607,000, an increase of $1,465,456,000 over similar receipts for 1937 and $3,177,650,000 over 1936. This gain is largely due to an increase in income taxes as a result of improved business conditions and the operation of the Revenue Act of 1936.

The amount expected to be collected in 1938 from income taxes is $3,365,300,000, a gain of $992,400,000 over the fiscal year 1937. Miscellaneous internal revenue will produce $2,508,332,-000, or $233,364,000 more than is expected from this source for 1937. The tax on unjust enrichment and the taxes on carriers and their employees from which $82,000,000 and $134,552,000, respectively, will be derived in 1937, will produce no revenue in 1938, since under existing law these taxes expire during 1937. The first full year of tax collections under the Social Security Act will result in revenue of $774,800,000 in 1938, which sum is $450,200,000 greater than the anticipated revenue in 1937, when collections will be for only six months. It is believed that customs revenues will rise from $446,800,000 during the present fiscal year to $463,000,000 in 1938, a gain of $16,200,000. Miscellaneous receipts, however, will decrease $8,950,000, the 1938 collections being estimated at $151,550,000, as compared with $160,500,000 during 1937. From realization upon assets $30,625,000 will be received, while in 1937 receipts from this source will amount to $31,830,000.

Expenditures.—The expenditures for 1938 contemplated under this Budget (exclusive of those from postal revenues) will total $6,157,999,000, or approximately $2,323,000,000 less than is now estimated for 1937. General expenditures for regular activities amount to $5,841,968,000, as compared with $5,664,-647,000 in 1937, an increase of $177,321,000. The 1937 estimate, however, contains an amount of $563,500,000 for completion of adjusted compensation payments to veterans, so that the comparable increase over 1937 is $740,821,000. For recovery and relief there is included in the expenditures for 1938 the amount of $316,031,000, which, of course, is not the full amount that will be required for relief during that year. As previously indicated, it is our present hope that the additional amount to be requested for this purpose will not exceed $1,537,123,000. Thus the total expenditure for recovery and relief during 1938 would be $1,853,-154,000, or $963,003,000 less than the amount estimated for 1937.

Again I emphasize the contribution which employers can make to this attainment.

The general expenditures include $860,000,000 for interest on the public debt, an increase of $25,000,000 over the amount for the present fiscal year, and $401,515,000 for statutory debt retirements, a decrease of $3,010,000. Exclusive of the service on the public debt and the payment of adjusted compensation to veterans, there is a net increase of $718,831,000 in expenditures for regular activities as compared with 1937. This increase is accounted for as follows: For increased requirements under the Social Security Act, $436,337,000; for additional expenditures under the general public works program, $132,519,000; for national defense to provide for the increased strength of the Army as directed by Congress and to provide for replacement of naval vessels in accordance with existing authorizations, $92,882,000; for the necessary funds for the activities of the Railroad Retirement Board and for rural electrification, $39,566,000; and for increased needs of other activities, $17,527,000.

Surplus and public debt. — The surplus for the fiscal year 1938, as presented in this Budget, is $1,135,608,000, after providing for debt retirement. Excluding provision for debt retirement, the surplus will amount to $1,537,123,000. As I have previously stated, it is hoped the additional needs for relief during the fiscal year 1938 will not require expenditure of more than this latter amount. On this basis the estimated gross public debt, on June 30, 1938, will be about the same amount as at the close of the fiscal year 1937. This does not take into account any change which may occur as a result of the Treasury policy in holding as "inactive" future acquisitions of gold.

Appropriations. — The total appropriations recommended in this Budget aggregate $6,839,000,000, including those for the Postal Service, District of Columbia, and probable supplemental items, while the appropriations already made and prospective supplemental items for the fiscal year 1937, exclusive of requirements for recovery and relief, total $6,261,000,000, an increase of $578,000,000 for 1938. This increase is due to additional appropriations amounting to $309,000,000 on account of the Social Security Act; $80,000,000 required under the general public works program; and $189,000,000 on account of departmental requirements, including the national defense. The appropriations made and contemplated for recovery and relief for 1937 total $2,215,000,000, whereas it is hoped that corresponding appropriations for 1938 will not exceed $1,537,123,000.

PART IV

The District of Columbia

The first section of the 1937 District of Columbia Appropriation Act, approved June 23, 1936 (Public No. 762, 74th Congress), contains the following provision:

"Not to exceed $50,000 shall be available for expenditure, under the direction of the President, for making an independent study of the fiscal relations between the United States and the District of Columbia and enabling him to report to Congress at the beginning of the next regular session, what, in his judgment, is a fair and equitable amount to be paid by the United States as an annual contribution toward the expenses of the government of the District of Columbia; such sum shall be available for personal services without regard to the civil service laws and the Classification Act of 1923, as amended, and for such other expenditures as may be necessary in connection with such study."

Pursuant to the above, I appointed a director and an advisory committee of three members to conduct an independent study of the various elements and conditions affecting the fiscal relations between the United States and the District of Columbia.

The report contains detailed findings and recommendations with the supporting data and information collected from the Federal and District Governments in Washington and from 17 comparable American cities and the capital cities of 21 foreign countries.

The application of the basic principles and recommendations as outlined and detailed in the report is reflected in the following 3-point formula, which I recommend be carefully considered by the Congress with a view to enacting such legislation at this ses-

655

sion as may be necessary to establish equitable fiscal relationships between the two Governments.

I. *Intergovernmental contractual services.* — Contractual arrangements shall be established for the reimbursement of the cost of specific intergovernmental services supplied either Government by the other. Appropriations therefor shall be included in the respective annual departmental budgets.

II. *Capital outlays of joint interest.* — The National Capital Planning Commission (proposed in the report) shall determine the extent of the respective Federal and District interests in capital outlays and improvements to be included in the District budget.

III. *Per capita governmental costs.* — Pending the grant of broader powers of local control over purely local affairs, the excess of the District governmental costs per capita over the average of those in comparable cities shall be assumed by the Federal Government: *Provided, however,* That such excess District governmental costs shall be assumed only after allowance has been made for reimbursements due to unusual costs occasioned by Congressional enactments.

I also recommend that, concurrently with enactment of any legislation which carries into effect the provisions of this continuing formula, the substantive law providing for annual Federal contributions of a fixed percentage of District appropriations be repealed and that the system of annual Federal lump-sum contributions be abandoned.

The application of this formula to the 1938 Budget estimates would provide for a net reimbursement by the Federal Government to the District of Columbia of $2,533,357, made up as follows:

I. Intergovernmental contractual services	$1,996,407
II. Capital outlays	536,950
III. Excess per capita District of Columbia governmental costs	....
Total	$2,533,357

After the application of the formula there will still be a deficit in the general revenue account of the District of Columbia of about $9,800,000, which will make it necessary, of course, to provide additional revenue. Sources of additional revenue are indicated in the report.

237 ⟨ The President Urges Ratification of the Child Labor Amendment to the Constitution.

January 7, 1937

Dear Governor:

I AM sure you will agree with me that one of the most encouraging developments of the past few years is the general agreement that has been reached that child labor should be permanently abolished. Outstanding gains were made under the N.R.A. codes which have been maintained in many establishments through the voluntary cooperation of employers.

However, it is clearly indicated that child labor, especially in low-paid unstandardized types of work, is increasing. I am convinced that nationwide minimum standards are necessary and that a way should be found promptly to crystallize in legal safeguards public opinion in behalf of the elimination of child labor.

Do you not agree with me that ratification of the child labor amendment by the remaining twelve States whose action is necessary to place it in the Constitution is the obvious way to early achievement of our objective? I hope that you will feel that this can be made one of the major items in the legislative program of your State this year.

Very sincerely yours,

(The foregoing letter was sent by the President to the following Governors and Governors-elect: Governors Clyde Tingley, New Mexico; Richard Kirman, Nevada; Olin D. Johnston, S. C.; Herbert H. Lehman, New York; James V. Allred, Texas; R. L. Cochran, Nebraska; Harry W. Nice, Maryland; Wilbur L. Cross, Connecticut; Fred P. Cone, Florida; Charles F. Hurley, Massachusetts; Clyde R. Hoey, N. C.; Robert E. Quinn, Rhode Island; Leslie Jensen, S. D.; George D. Aiken, Vermont; and Governors-elect Gordon Browning, Tennessee;

Richard C. McMullen, Delaware; E. D. Rivers, Georgia; Walter A. Huxman, Kansas; Lloyd C. Stark, Missouri.)

238 ⟪ The President Transmits to the Congress a Report on Fiscal Relations between the United States and the District of Columbia. January 8, 1937

To the Congress:

PURSUANT to the provisions in the 1937 District of Columbia Appropriation Act approved June 23, 1936 (Public No. 762, 74th Cong.), I have the honor to transmit herewith for the consideration of Congress the following report on Fiscal Relations between the United States and the District of Columbia.

The major recommendations in this report are outlined in my 1938 Budget message as transmitted to you on this date. I have considered these findings and recommendations in collaboration with the Advisory Committee and the Director of the Study, and I earnestly commend these to your close consideration at this session of Congress. I urge early enactment of the necessary legislative measures to assure a continuing equitable determination of fiscal relations between the two governments.

Special attention is invited to Sections 10 and 13, which show that while the extent of local governmental service in the District of Columbia is substantially equal to that in seventeen comparable cities, both the property tax and the total tax load in the District of Columbia are lower than in any of these cities.

239 ⟪ Presidential Statement on Construction of Replacement Capital Ships. January 8, 1937

IN ACCORDANCE with the provisions of the Navy Appropriation Act of June 3, 1936, I have directed the Navy Department to proceed with the construction of two replacement capital ships. The keels of these ships may be laid in conformity with existing treaties at any time after January 1. Three of our battleships, the *Arkansas, Texas* and *New York*, will be more than twenty-six years old before these ships can be completed. If we are not to reduce our Navy by obsolescence, the replacement of capital ships can no longer be deferred.

The last Congress made an initial appropriation for "Two capital ships, as replacement of overage capital ships, to be undertaken only in event that the President determines as a fact that capital-ship-replacement construction is commenced by any of the other signatory powers to the Treaty for the Limitation and Reduction of Naval Armaments signed at London, April 22, 1930."

On July 29, 1936, Sir Samuel Hoare, First Lord of Admiralty announced that the orders for two battleships of the 1936 program had been let and stated:

"It is the intention that the keels should be laid at the earliest possible moment permitted by the Washington Naval Treaty; namely, in January, 1937. In order to achieve this object, it is essential to order the vessels now, and although complete specifications will not be available until October, there is sufficient information available to enable the contractors to prepare for laying down the keels in January next."

On December 12, 1936, France laid the keel of the capital ship *Jean Bart.*

In addition to these three capital ships whose construction has been undertaken since the passage of the Navy Appropriation Act, eight others are under construction in the following countries: three in France, two in Italy and three in Germany.

Some time will elapse before bids can be obtained and contracts awarded and additional time will be required for contractors to assemble material before the keels of our two ships can be laid.

240 ❨A Letter on Appropriations for W.P.A.

January 11, 1937

To the Speaker of the House of Representatives:

IN MY Budget message of January 5, 1937, I indicated my intention of requesting that Congress provide an appropriation of $790,000,000 for the purpose of carrying the Works Progress Administration and related programs from February 1 to June 30, 1937.

In general, the problem of relief has diminished with the extensive reemployment and recovery which have occurred in nearly all lines of business and industrial activity. At the beginning of the present winter at least 6,000,000 more workers were employed in non-agricultural jobs than in March, 1933, and of this number more than 1,000,000 have found jobs with private industry during the past year.

In my message of March 18, 1936, I stated:

"The ultimate cost of the Federal works program will thus be determined by private enterprise. Federal assistance which arose as a result of industrial disemployment can be terminated if industry itself removes the underlying conditions. Should industry cooperatively achieve the goal of reemployment, the appropriation of $1,500,000,000, together with the unexpended balances of previous appropriations, will suffice to carry the Federal works program through the Fiscal Year 1937. Only if industry fails to reduce substantially the number of those now out of work will another appropriation and further plans and policies be necessary."

Many private enterprises have cooperated and I hope that there will be further sustained efforts on the part of private employers. Great assistance can be given to the Government if all private employers in every part of the country will seek, in so far as they reasonably can, to obtain additional workers from the relief rolls.

In this connection it is worth noting that by far the larger part of those on the relief rolls fall into the category of unskilled workers.

As a result of the natural increase in our population, each year at least 400,000 new workers are seeking work, and this number of new jobs annually is necessary simply to prevent an increase in unemployment.

Certain other facts are worth noting. The tendency toward a longer work week has had an extremely important effect on re-employment. Hours of work in manufacturing industries, as shown by the Bureau of Labor Statistics index, averaged 33.3 hours per week in September, 1934. That average has increased by 20 percent, to more than 40 hours per week in October, 1936.

While among most industries and most employers the maximum hours established under the National Recovery Act have not been greatly increased, it is worth noting that in some industries and among some employers the former maximum hours have been unreasonably increased. Every action of an employer along these lines obviously tends toward the stepping up of production without an equivalent stepping up of employment. It is not unfair to say that these employers who are working their employees unreasonably long hours are failing to cooperate with the Government and their fellow citizens in putting people back to work.

In March, 1936, more than 3,400,000 employable persons were provided for by the Works Program, not including the Civilian Conservation Corps. At the present time, as a result of an exhaustive review of the needs of the families of workers on the works program, we have found that it will be necessary, during the winter months, to provide employment for at least 2,580,000 workers, of which number 250,000 will receive employment from funds appropriated in the Emergency Relief Appropriation Act of 1935. This represents a net reduction of more than 800,000 since last March. Further reductions will be made in the spring and summer, at the time of seasonal increases in private employment.

An unforeseen factor in Federal expenditures for the relief of destitution has been the drought, which laid waste a large area of

661

the country, and brought disaster to hundreds of thousands of farm families. During last summer and fall, an emergency program was developed to provide employment for the most destitute of the stricken families. With the advent of winter, about 250,000 of these families are being transferred from work projects to the Resettlement Administration, which will provide them with direct grants for subsistence through the winter, and make other provisions to get them started on an independent basis when the planting season arrives.

Since the balance of the present appropriation of $1,425,-000,000 for relief and work relief will be barely sufficient to finance this program through the month of January, I recommend that the Congress provide a supplemental appropriation of $790,000,000 for this purpose for the remainder of the fiscal year 1937.

We have promised that the men, women and children of America who are destitute through no fault of their own shall not be neglected. Before the end of this fiscal year I shall make specific recommendations to the Congress, defining in detail my views relative to the continuing problem of unemployment relief and its administration in 1938.

Respectfully,

NOTE: The programs of F.E.R.A., C.W.A. and W.P.A. (see Items 21, 55, 75, 155A and 161 of Vol. II; Item 31 of Vol. III; Item 54 of Vol. IV; and Item 36 of Vol. V), were a continuous effort to provide employment to persons who otherwise would have been unable to supply themselves with the necessities of life. In addition to the fact that these millions of people were kept from starvation, there is a record of physical accomplishments throughout the United States which will remain for years to come, and which have improved the physical as well as the mental and spiritual equipment of the Nation.

I am appending hereto an inventory of selected accomplishments of one of these agencies, W.P.A., through October 1, 1937:

PHYSICAL ACCOMPLISHMENT ON W.P.A. PROJECTS

Through October 1, 1937

UNITED STATES SUMMARY

CONSTRUCTION ACTIVITIES

		Number or Amount		
Type	Unit of Measurement	New Construction	Repairs and Improvements	Additions
Public Buildings—Total	Number	11,106	30,542	1,172
Schools and other educational buildings	Number	1,634	16,421	574
Gymnasiums, stadiums, park, and other recreational buildings	Number	3,722	2,033	203
Hospitals and other institutional buildings	Number	262	2,270	58
Courthouses, offices, and other administrative buildings	Number	537	2,263	106
Other public buildings (fire houses, hangars, storage structures, etc.)	Number	4,951	7,555	231
Demolition of Buildings	Number	xxxx	6,141	xxxx

		Number or Amount	
Type	Unit of Measurement	New Construction	Repairs and Improvements
Highways, Roads, Streets, and Related Facilities			
Highways, roads, and streets—Total	Miles	43,870	146,901
Rural primary roads	Miles	6,961	15,337
Rural secondary roads	Miles	29,742	115,703
Urban	Miles	6,319	14,848
Other (parks, cemeteries, etc.)	Miles	848	1,013
Bridges	Number	19,272	13,166
	Length in feet	612,521	520,665
Culverts	Number	183,084	30,061
	Length in feet	4,902,451	774,031
Sidewalks and paths	Miles	4,581	3,003
Curbs	Length in miles	3,938	917
Roadside landscaping	Miles	xxxx	38,685
Street signs	Linear ft. line painted	12,495,773	xxxx
	No. signs made	769,924	xxxx
	No. signs erected	320,352	xxxx
Airports and Airway Equipment (Excl. Buildings)			
Landing fields	Number	105	109
	Acres	14,348	15,070

663

Type	Unit of Measurement	Number or Amount	
		New Construction	Repairs and Improvements
Runways...................	Length in feet	852,834	244,676
Air markers...............	Number	8,357	xxxx
Recreational Facilities (Excl. Buildings)			
Athletic fields..............	Number	1,335	1,234
	Acres	7,213	9,702
Parks.....................	Number	770	2,866
	Acres	22,072	158,193
Playgrounds...............	Number	1,107	3,583
Swimming and wading pools..	Number	1,883	173
Golf courses...............	Number	103	167
Tennis courts..............	Number	3,076	1,094
Water Supply, Sanitation and Drainage Systems			
Water mains, aqueducts, or distribution lines.............	Miles	3,865	1,382
	No. of consumer connections	107,634	154,152
Storage tanks, reservoirs, and cisterns..................	Number	1,150	298
	Gals. capacity	1,788,052,000	2,402,878,100
Storage dams..............	Number	3,330	283
Wells.....................	Number	1,526	1,271
Treatment plants (excl. cesspools and septic tanks)			
Sewage..................	Number	228	131
Water..................	Number	51	55
Garbage incinerators.......	Number	24	22
Pumping stations...........	Number	229	86
Storm and sanitary sewers....	Miles	5,692	1,624
	No. of service connections	114,725	19,904
Mine sealing..............	No. of mines	7,523	xxxx
	No. of openings	66,750	xxxx
Sanitary toilets..............	Number	779,587	10,943
Mosquito control...........	Linear ft. of ditch	26,820,125	17,504,776
	Acres drained	835,950	455,038
	Gals. of spray used	1,184,819	xxxx
Drainage (other than roadside and mosquito eradication)..	Acres drained	807,452	5,335,587
Flood and Erosion Control—Navigation Aids—Irrigation			
Dredging (other than channels)	Cu. yds. of material dredged	9,656,574	xxxx
Dams (other than storage or power)..................	Number	15,855	145
Riprap (other than river bank)	Sq. yds. surfaced	3,376,950	361,505

664

Accomplishments of W.P.A.

Type	Unit of Measurement	New Construction	Repairs and Improvements
		Number or Amount	
Retaining walls and revetments	Number	9,347	1,029
	Linear feet	1,985,873	166,614
Levees and embankments.....	Linear feet	815,610	1,532,956
	Cu. yds. placed	9,164,621	6,903,296
Irrigation..................	Acres	193,918	1,283,314
	Miles of flume or canal	230	2,453
Miscellaneous			
Police and fire alarm signals ..	No. of boxes and signals	23,570	xxxx
	Linear ft. of line strung	3,063,702	xxxx
Lighting airports, parking lots, athletic fields, etc.	No. of places lighted	245	20
	Acres lighted	4,690	2,065
Fish hatcheries..............	Number	134	74
	Annual fingerling capacity	308,154,800	168,663,000

OTHER THAN CONSTRUCTION ACTIVITIES

Type	Unit of Measurement	Number or Amount
Conservation Activities (Not Elsewhere Classified)		
Reforestation.................	Acres.........................	21,131
	No. of trees planted............	9,789,184
Firebreaks....................	Miles.........................	1,196
Fire and forest trails...........	Miles.........................	2,481
Plant and tree nurseries........	No. of nurseries................	115
	No. of plants or trees planted.....	9,485,158
Bird and game sanctuaries.......	No. of sanctuaries established.....	825
Noxious plant eradication.......	Acres.........................	3,601,177
Spray treatments, disease, and insect pest eradication (except mosquito control).	Acres sprayed..................	639,159
	Gallons of spray used...........	11,256,776
	Tons of poisoned food used.......	6,097
Work in Libraries		
New branch libraries............	No. established.................	2,305
New traveling libraries..........	No. established.................	5,824
Cataloging for existing libraries...	No. of volumes cataloged........	18,272,529
Renovation of books............	Number.......................	29,855,417
Sewing Rooms..................	No. of articles made............	108,427,938
Canning and Preserving..........	Net pounds....................	24,026,581
School Lunches Served...........	Number.......................	128,057,654

Accomplishments of W.P.A.

Type	Unit of Measurement	Number or Amount
Medical, Dental and Nursing Assistance		
Medical and dental clinics conducted................	No. of clinics.................	1,654
	No. of persons examined........	1,355,373
	No. of persons treated..........	601,543
Nursing visits.................	No. of home visits made........	2,093,182
Nursing aid at immunizations....	No. of immunizations..........	550,749
Art		
Art classes....................	Average monthly attendance.....	55,231
Drawings, easel paintings, murals and sculptured works.........	Number.....................	54,244
Etchings, lithographs, woodblocks, etc.	No. of originals................	3,519
	No. of prints..................	21,341
Music		
Music classes.................	Average monthly attendance.....	140,321
Musical performances..........	Average number per month......	4,549
	Average monthly attendance.....	3,107,345
Theater		
Theatrical productions..........	Number.....................	1,501
Theatrical performances.........	Average number per month......	2,833
	Average monthly attendance.....	1,043,478
Writing.......................	No. of books and pamphlets written	116
	No. of copies distributed........	401,928
Local, State and National Planning and Research Surveys..........	Number.....................	1,620
Engineering Surveys.............	Square miles of mapping survey...	75,597
	Miles of line survey............	60,191
	No. of permanent markers set.....	57,883
Braille........................	No. of Braille pages transcribed...	1,146,913
	No. of Braille maps made........	40,635
Housekeeping Aides.............	No. of visits made..............	3,473,472
	No. of families aided...........	517,945
Museum Activities................	No. of articles constructed or renovated......................	3,269,496
Education (Month of October 1937)–Total	No. of classes.................	*100,145*
	No. of enrollees................	*1,144,689*
Literacy.....................	No. of classes.................	17,195
	No. of enrollees...............	192,481
Vocational...................	No. of classes.................	10,596
	No. of enrollees................	159,430
Nursery schools...............	No. of classes.................	1,481
	No. of enrollees................	40,243
Other.......................	No. of classes.................	70,873
	No. of enrollees................	852,680
Recreation		
Community centers operated.....	Number.....................	9,068
Community centers assisted......	Number.....................	6,220

When the work done by its predecessors, C.W.A. and F.E.R.A., is added to the W.P.A. figures above, the grand totals of accomplishment are, in many instances, multiplied. Examples: the three agencies combined, through October 1, 1937, built or improved 849,400 miles of highways, roads and streets; 51,700 bridges and grade crossings; 1,408,-864 sanitary toilets; 163,400 buildings; 13,900 miles of sewers and

8,120 miles of water mains; and 1230 airports.

In addition to all of the foregoing there were the physical accomplishments of the Public Works Administration (P.W.A.) described in Item 117 of Volume II. The following is a broad summary of the type and number of accomplishments within the P.W.A. program as of Nov. 30, 1937, taken from the P.W.A. Report as of that date.

NON-FEDERAL PROJECTS, FEDERAL PROJECTS, AND
FEDERAL LOW-COST HOUSING PROJECTS
ALL PUBLIC WORKS ADMINISTRATION PROJECTS

TABLE SHOWING ALLOTMENTS AND REPORTED PROJECT COSTS,
DISTRIBUTED BY TYPE OF PROJECT; AS OF NOVEMBER 30, 1937

Type of Project	No. of Projects	Total Estimated Cost	Allotment			Reported[1] Project Costs
			Total	Loan	Grant[2]	
Educational Buildings..	4,655	$ 693,122,728	$ 366,285,499	$ 85,007,363	$ 281,278,136	$ 561,056,772
Hospitals and Institutions for Medical Treatment..........	539	202,255,317	100,662,218	17,443,690	83,218,528	138,083,382
Public Buildings.......	3,012	343,490,061	245,913,315	12,930,202	232,983,113	281,298,284
Sewer Systems........	1,282	369,648,093	243,663,841	113,715,940	129,947,901	297,453,827
Water Systems........	1,907	197,018,378	117,767,391	50,884,891	66,882,500	183,122,341
Electric Power, Excluding Water Power....	210	92,627,593	65,551,361	28,401,200	37,150,161	17,846,132
Streets and Highways..	10,792	689,254,056	563,685,069	23,275,125	540,409,944	635,840,713
Engineering Structures.	390	347,859,903	246,928,410	159,199,596	87,728,814	235,333,237
Flood Control, Water Power and Reclamation...............	379	388,494,772	339,388,814	69,562,591	269,826,223	279,679,515
Limited Dividend Housing...............	7	11,760,399	10,403,391	10,403,391	—	11,760,399
Federal Low Cost Housing...............	51	136,669,759	136,669,759	—	136,669,759	109,607,950
Railroads............	32	200,974,500	200,974,500	200,974,500	—	200,974,500
Vessels..............	206	265,962,600	265,962,600	—	265,962,600	257,956,994
All Others...........	3,039	514,229,387	450,128,405	25,473,494	424,654,911	476,554,112
TOTALS...........	26,501	$4,453,367,546	$3,353,984,573	$797,271,983	$2,556,712,590	$3,686,568,158

[1] Subject to revision.

[2] Includes allotments to Federal Agencies.

NOTE: Reported project costs represent the cost of materials in place (including the cost of labor performed) and miscellaneous costs, for that portion of the work completed on each individual project.

Allotments made available under authority of the 4th Deficiency Act, fiscal year 1933 (Public 77–73d Congress), the Emergency Appropriation Act, fiscal year 1935 (Public 412–73d Congress), the Emergency Relief Appropriation Act of 1935 (Public Resolution No. 11–74th Congress), the First Deficiency Appropriation Act, fiscal year 1936, and the Public Works Administration Extension Act of 1937.

241 ⟮A Recommendation for Legislation to Reorganize the Executive Branch of the Government. January 12, 1937

To the Congress:

I ADDRESS this Message to the Congress as one who has had experience as a legislator, as a subordinate in an executive department, as the chief executive of a State and as one on whom, as President, the constitutional responsibility for the whole of the Executive Branch of the Government has lain for four years.

Now that we are out of the trough of the depression, the time has come to set our house in order. The administrative management of the Government needs overhauling. We are confronted not alone by new activities, some of them temporary in character, but also by the growth of the work of the Government watching the growth of the nation over more than a generation.

Except for the enactment of the Budget and Accounting Act of 1921, no extensive change in management has occurred since 1913, when the Department of Labor was established. The Executive structure of the Government is sadly out of date. I am not the first President to report to the Congress that antiquated machinery stands in the way of effective administration and of adequate control by the Congress. Theodore Roosevelt, William H. Taft, Woodrow Wilson and Herbert Hoover made repeated but not wholly successful efforts to deal with the problem. Committees of the Congress have also rendered distinguished service to the nation through their efforts from time to time to point the way to improvement of governmental management and organization.

The opportunity and the need for action now come to you and to me. If we have faith in our republican form of government, and in the ideals upon which it has rested for 150 years, we must devote ourselves energetically and courageously to the task of making that government efficient. The great stake in efficient democracy is the stake of the common man.

In these troubled years of world history, a self-government cannot long survive unless that government is an effective and efficient agency to serve mankind and carry out the will of the Nation. A government without good management is a house builded on sand.

In striving together to make our Government more efficient, you and I are taking up in our generation the battle to preserve that freedom of self-government which our forefathers fought to establish and hand down to us. They struggled against tyranny, against non-representative controls, against government by birth, wealth or class, against sectionalism. Our struggle now is against confusion, against ineffectiveness, against waste, against inefficiency. This battle, too, must be won, unless it is to be said that in our generation national self-government broke down and was frittered away in bad management.

Will it be said "Democracy was a great dream, but it could not do the job?" Or shall we here and now. without further delay, make it our business to see that our American democracy is made efficient so that it will do the job that is required of it by the events of our time?

I know your answer, and the answer of the Nation, because after all, we are a practical people. We know good management in the home, on the farm, and in business, big and little. If any nation can find the way to effective government it should be the American people through their own democratic institutions.

Over a year ago it seemed to me that this problem of administrative management of the Executive Branch of the Government should be a major order of business of this session of the Congress. Accordingly, after extended discussions and negotiations, I appointed a Committee on Administrative Management, to examine the whole problem broadly and to suggest for my guidance and your consideration a comprehensive and balanced program for dealing with the overhead organization and management of the Executive Branch as it is established under the Constitution.

The Committee has now completed its work, and I transmit to you its report, "Administrative Management in the Government of the United States." I have examined this report carefully and thoughtfully, and am convinced that it is a great document of permanent importance. I think that the general program presented by the Committee is adequate, reasonable and practical, and that it furnishes the basis for immediate action. The broad facts are known; the need is clear; what is now required is action.

The Committee on Administrative Management points out that no enterprise can operate effectively if set up as is the Government today. There are over 100 separate departments, boards, commissions, corporations, authorities, agencies, and activities through which the work of the Government is being carried on. Neither the President nor the Congress can exercise effective supervision and direction over such a chaos of establishments, nor can overlapping, duplication, and contradictory policies be avoided.

The Committee has not spared me; they say, what has been common knowledge for twenty years, that the President cannot adequately handle his responsibilities; that he is overworked; that it is humanly impossible, under the system which we have, for him fully to carry out his Constitutional duty as Chief Executive because he is overwhelmed with minor details and needless contacts arising directly from the bad organization and equipment of the Government. I can testify to this. With my predecessors who have said the same thing over and over again, I plead guilty.

The plain fact is that the present organization and equipment of the Executive Branch of the Government defeat the Constitutional intent that there be a single responsible Chief Executive to coordinate and manage the departments and activities in accordance with the laws enacted by the Congress. Under these conditions the Government cannot be thoroughly effective in working, under popular control, for the common good.

The Committee does not spare the Comptroller General for his failure to give the Congress a prompt and complete audit each year, totally independent of administration, as a means of holding the Executive truly to account; or for his unconstitutional assumption of Executive power; or for the failure to keep the accounting system of the Government up to date to serve as the basis of information, management and control.

The Committee criticizes the use of boards and commissions in administration, condemns the careless use of "corporations" as governmental instrumentalities, and points out that the practice of creating independent regulatory commissions, who perform administrative work in addition to judicial work, threatens to develop a "fourth branch" of the Government for which there is no sanction in the Constitution. Nor does the Committee spare the inadequacy of the Civil Service system.

To meet this situation and bring our administrative management up to date, the Committee presents an integrated five-point program which you will find set out in its Report. It includes these major recommendations:

1. Expand the White House staff so that the President may have a sufficient group of able assistants in his own office to keep him in closer and easier touch with the widespread affairs of administration, and to make speedier the clearance of the knowledge needed for Executive decision;

2. Strengthen and develop the managerial agencies of the Government, particularly those dealing with the budget and efficiency research, with personnel and with planning, as management-arms of the Chief Executive;

3. Extend the merit system upward, outward, and downward to cover practically all non-policy-determining posts; reorganize the civil service system as a part of management under a single, responsible Administration; create a citizen board to serve as the watchdog of the merit system; and increase the salaries of key posts throughout the service so that the Government may attract and hold in a career service men and women of ability and character;

4. Overhaul the 100 independent agencies, administrations, authorities, boards, and commissions, and place them by Executive Order within one or the other of the following twelve major

671

Executive departments: State, Treasury, War, Justice, Post Office, Navy, Conservation, Agriculture, Commerce, Labor, Social Welfare, and Public Works; and place upon the Executive continuing responsibility for the maintenance of effective organization;

5. Establish accountability of the Executive to the Congress by providing a genuine independent postaudit of all fiscal transactions by an Auditor General, and restore to the Executive complete responsibility for accounts and current transactions.

As you will see, this program rests solidly upon the Constitution and upon the American way of doing things. There is nothing in it which is revolutionary, as every element is drawn from our own experience either in government or large-scale business.

I endorse this program and feel confident that it will commend itself to you also with your knowledge of government, and to the vast majority of the citizens of the country who want and believe in efficient self-government.

No important advance can be made toward the major objectives of the program without the passage by the Congress of the necessary legislation.

It will be necessary to provide for the establishment of two new Departments, a Department of Social Welfare and a Department of Public Works, for the assignment by the President of all the miscellaneous activities to the 12 major departments thus provided, for reorganization of the civil service system, for modernizing and strengthening the managerial agencies of the Executive, and for making the Executive more strictly accountable to the Congress. By the creation of two new Departments nearly 100 agencies now not under regular Departments can be consolidated as to their administrative functions under a total of twelve regular Departments of the Government.

The remaining elements of the five-point program, though they must await your action on the basic legislation, may be initiated through appropriations and Executive Orders.

In placing this program before you I realize that it will be said that I am recommending the increase of the powers of the

Presidency. This is not true. The Presidency as established in the Constitution of the United States has all of the powers that are required. In spite of timid souls in 1787 who feared effective government the Presidency was established as a single, strong Chief Executive office in which was vested the entire Executive power of the national Government, even as the legislative power was placed in the Congress and the judicial in the Supreme Court and inferior courts. What I am placing before you is the request not for more power, but for the tools of management and the authority to distribute the work so that the President can effectively discharge those powers which the Constitution now places upon him. Unless we are prepared to abandon this important part of the Constitution, we must equip the President with authority commensurate with his responsibilities under the Constitution.

The Committee on Administrative Management, after a careful examination of recent attempts to reorganize the Government and of State reorganizations carried out so ably by Governor Frank O. Lowden in Illinois, Governor Alfred E. Smith in New York, Governor Harry F. Byrd in Virginia, Governor William Tudor Gardiner in Maine, and by other Governors, accepts the view held by my distinguished predecessors that the detailed work of reorganization is, as President Theodore Roosevelt said over 30 years ago, "essentially executive in its nature." The Committee accordingly recommends that reorganization should be a continuing duty and authority of the Chief Executive on the basis of standards set by the Congress. To make this safe, the Committee insists, however, that the Congress keep a watchful eye upon reorganization both through the annual budget and through the maintenance of strict executive accountability to the Congress under the independent audit of all financial transactions by an Auditor General. Under the proposed plan the Congress must by law establish the major departments and determine in advance the general principles which shall guide the President in distributing the work of the Government among these departments, and in this task the President is to act on the basis of careful research by the Bureau of the Budget and after conference with those primarily affected. Reorganization is not a mechanical task, but a human task, because Government is not a machine, but a living organism. With these clear safeguards, and in view of our past muddling with reorganization, one cannot but accept the logic and wisdom of the recommendations.

I would not have you adopt this five-point program, however, without realizing that this represents an important step in American history. If we do this, we reduce from over 100 down to a dozen the operating executive agencies of the Government, and we bring many little bureaucracies under broad coordinated democratic authority.

But in so doing, we shall know that we are going back to the Constitution, and giving to the Executive Branch modern tools of management and an up-to-date organization which will enable the Government to go forward efficiently. We can prove to the world that American Government is both democratic and effective.

In this program I invite your cooperation, and pledge myself to deal energetically and promptly with the executive responsibilities of reorganization and administrative management, when you shall have made this possible by the necessary legislation.

(See Items 43 and 43A and 241A of this volume.)

241A ❡ Summary of the Report of the Committee on Administrative Management Transmitted with the Preceding Message. January 12, 1937

MODERN management equipment for the Federal Government so that it may do promptly and efficiently what is expected of it by the American people is the keynote of the report made today to the President by his Committee on Administrative Management. The purpose of making Federal administrative management modern and businesslike is to make American democracy efficient. It is the view of the Committee that self-government cannot long survive even in this country unless it can do its work efficiently. "The forward march of American democracy at this point of our history," says the Committee, "depends more upon effective management than upon any other single factor." To this end a five-point program of reorganization of the Executive Branch of the Government is presented by the Committee including these major recommendations.

FIVE-POINT PROGRAM

Modernize the White House business and management organization by giving the President six high-grade executive assistants to aid him in dealing with the regular departments and agencies.

Strengthen the budget and efficiency research, the planning, and the personnel services of the Government, so that these may be effective managerial arms for the President, with which he may better coordinate, direct and manage all of the work of the Executive Branch for which he is responsible under the Constitution.

Place the whole governmental administrative service on a career basis and under the merit system by extending the civil service upward, outward and downward to include all non-policy-determining positions and jobs.

Overhaul the more than 100 separate departments, boards, commissions, administrations, authorities, corporations, committees, agencies and activities which are now parts of the Executive Branch, and theoretically under the President, and consolidate them within twelve regular departments, which would include the existing ten departments and two new departments, a Department of Social Welfare, and a Department of Public Works. Change the name of the Department of Interior to Department of Conservation.

Make the Executive Branch accountable to the Congress by creating a true postaudit of financial transactions by an inde-

675

pendent Auditor General who would report illegal and wasteful expenditures to Congress without himself becoming involved in the management of departmental policy, and transfer the duties of the present Comptroller in part to the Auditor, to the Treasury, and to the Attorney General.

These five points are woven together in a single comprehensive program.

EXECUTIVE TO ASSIGN BUREAUS

The report of the Committee does not deal with the abolition of emergency or established activities or jobs, which is stated to be a matter of policy for the President and the Congress to determine, but devotes itself entirely to setting up an efficient modern machinery of government. But in this process over eighty activities are abolished as separate and independent establishments and their work transferred either to the new Departments of Social Welfare and Public Works, or to one of the ten old departments. The exact placing of bureaus and activities is not set out in the report as this assignment of work is placed upon the Executive as a continuing responsibility, after research by the Bureau of the Budget, in accordance with efficiency and service standards to be fixed by Congress. Such assignment and division of work, once the standards have been set by law, is regarded by the Committee as an "Executive function."

No estimate of savings by reorganization is contained in the report, though these will follow, in the opinion of the Committee. Extensive economy beyond this point depends upon a change of policy, the abandonment of functions, and the demobilization of the staffs involved, and is outside of the terms of reference of the Committee on Administrative Management. The Committee points out, however, that the recommended plan of organization which ties all agencies into twelve departments is designed to permit the prompt and efficient demobilization of any activities which are later discontinued by act of Congress or Executive order.

ASSISTANTS FOR PRESIDENT

The proposed addition to the White House staff is not to be made up of "Assistant Presidents," says the Committee. It will be composed of half a dozen men, drawn from the very top of the existing career service or from outside, and will assist the President in organizing and maintaining contact with his departments. These executive assistants will not issue orders or make speeches, but will work directly and anonymously in the White House getting information when needed by the President in making decisions, and then seeing that decisions are promptly communicated to those who are involved. They would be like the private assistants of the president or general manager of a great private business. The Committee condemns the existing situation and says that the President of the United States, managing the biggest business in the world, now has less assistance of this sort than many State Governors, city managers and mayors, and executives of even small private concerns.

PERSONNEL REORGANIZATION

Extensive reorganization of the civil service system with increase of salaries for posts of great responsibilities is a part of the program. As the Committee says, "Government cannot be any better or more efficient than the men and women who work in it." It is pointed out that many of the people are now leaving the Government for industry because Government does not offer a satisfactory career. Top posts both in and out of the civil service are underpaid, and there is no systematic provision for transfer and advancement in the service. This is corrected by making personnel administration a part of every department, and a part of overhead management by establishing a Civil Service Administrator to work directly under the President, just as the Budget Director does now. This Administrator would devote his attention not only to giving civil service examinations, recruiting, classifying, etc., but even more to finding able people who can be brought into the Government especially on the lower rungs of career ladders, to discovering able persons in the service, and to seeing that they get training and opportunities for promotion, and generally to advancing the merit system and the career idea. Salaries in top posts should be increased, and the civil service extended upward to include all except the Secretaries, Under Secretaries, Assistant Secretaries, and similar positions.

Over 250,000 positions, some of which are now under merit principles, will be brought under civil service within one year. Unless designated as "temporary" or "policy-determining" by Executive Order, all Federal positions will be covered by the civil service. Those persons in these positions will not be given civil service status, however, without taking a qualifying examination given by the new Civil Service Administrator, and without being certified by their director as having "rendered satisfactory service" in their posts.

The Civil Service Commission, which has been the policeman of the civil service since 1883, will be abolished. The administrative duties will be transferred to the Civil Service Administrator, who though appointed by the President, is himself selected on the basis of competitive examination, while the protection of the system from politics is to be enforced by an unpaid citizen board, composed of seven members with seven-year overlapping terms and provided with funds for investigation. This Civil Service Board, says the Committee, for which the President can secure the ablest men and women of the country, drawn from business, administration, education, the professions, labor, and finance, will be "the watchdog of the merit system." Under the program of the Committee it would be impossible to appoint to this Board any person who is a party committeeman, or who has held or run for political office within five years.

DANGER OF "FOURTH BRANCH"

The Committee on Administrative Management also condemns all other boards and commissions when used for management, and recommends that they be abolished and their work transferred to the regular departments, in which there would be set up, wherever needed, a commission or board to deal exclusively with the judicial phases of the work. The Committee points out that the independent commissions have been created one by one over the past 50 years, and that they threaten in time to become "a headless fourth branch of the Government, not contemplated by the Constitution, and not responsible administratively either to the President, to the Congress, or to the Courts."

MANAGERIAL AGENCIES NEEDED

The budgeting and planning are together with personnel, the three managerial agencies which should be strengthened, in the opinion of the Committee. It is pointed out that the Bureau of the Budget was by law supposed to engage in efficiency research and to promote economy, but that the whole Budget Bureau spends only $187,000 a year though it is responsible for dealing with budgets of billions. The Committee recommends that the staff of the Bureau be expanded immediately, particularly through the development of its efficiency research division, which will advise the President in reassigning and reorganizing the work of the Executive Branch under the recommended program.

Planning has been carried on thus far through a temporary National Resources Committee and through many interdepartmental, State, and local planning commissions and committees. The Committee insists that this should be made permanent by the establishment of a National Resources Board. This board would be advisory only, and would work directly under the President to assist him in thinking broadly about the "state of the Nation," dealing particularly with problems which cut across departmental and jurisdictional lines. The board would continue to rely on interdepartmental committees and would encourage State and local planning bodies. The Committee believes that the main purpose of planning in America should be to bring into the center of government more intelligence, research, and long-range thinking about all our related problems, especially those dealing with water, land, and natural resources, so that the Congress and the President may, in determining policy and carrying on the Government, make a better job of it, and so that the Federal Government and the States and localities may work together more effectively in dealing with common problems.

EXECUTIVE ACCOUNTABILITY TO CONGRESS

Accountability of the Executive Branch to the Congress, the Committee maintains, has been confused and ineffective in the past because of the fact that the Comptroller General has endeavored to control the spending policy of the departments. This the Committee regards as "an unconstitutional usurpation of power" and recommends the abolition of the office and the establishment of a new office of Auditor General to do what the Comptroller was supposed but failed to do for 15 years, namely, give Congress an independent annual audit and a report on illegal transactions. The Committee does not blame any person for this failure, but says that the system as set up by law was impossible from a business standpoint, and certainly unconstitutional, if what has happened under the law was actually contemplated. The Committee points out that before its adoption the dangers of the law were recognized by Governor Frank O. Lowden, Secretary of the Treasury Carter Glass, and other experts, and since its enactment by President Hoover and by the Committee on Federal Expenditures of the United States Chamber of Commerce.

In line with these criticisms the Committee recommends that there be a postaudit, by an independent auditor (taking no part whatsoever in making administrative decisions) reporting illegal and wasteful practices directly to the policy-determining body, that is, the Congress, as would be done in any American business concern. Current administrative audit is transferred to the Treasury, under guidance on legal matters by the Attorney General, and the business of keeping the accounting system

680

up to date is entrusted to the Treasury where it may be related to the Budget system.

CONCLUSION

In its conclusion, the Committee on Administrative Management summarizes its five-point program for modernizing the Executive Branch and says:

"These changes cannot be adopted and maintained unless the American people itself fully appreciates the advantages of good management and insists upon getting them. The need for reorganization rests not alone on the idea of savings, considerable as they will be, but upon better service to society. The times demand better government organization, staffed with more competent public servants, more free to do their best, and coordinated by an Executive accountable to the Congress, and fully equipped with modern tools of management."

MEMBERSHIP OF PRESIDENT'S COMMITTEE ON ADMINISTRATIVE MANAGEMENT

The President's Committee on Administrative Management, which today submitted its report to the President, was appointed last May. It is made up of: Louis Brownlow, of Chicago, Director of the Public Administration Clearing House, Chairman; Luther Gulick, of New York, Director of the Institute of Public Administration; and Charles E. Merriam, of Chicago, Chairman of the Department of Political Science of the University of Chicago. Its Director of Research is Joseph P. Harris, of the staff of the Committee on Public Administration of the Social Science Research Council.

(See Items 43, 43A and 241 of this volume.)

242 ⟨ Statement on the Kidnapping of Charles Mattson, January 13, 1937

THE murder of the little Mattson boy has shocked the Nation. Every means at our command must be enlisted to capture and punish the perpetrator of this ghastly crime.

Attorney General Cummings informs me that he has offered a reward for information leading to the arrest of the criminal; and that the special agents of the Federal bureau of investigation of the Department of Justice are engaged in a search which will be pursued relentlessly and will not be terminated until the murderer is caught.

I bespeak for the agents of the Department of Justice the continued and wholehearted cooperation of the local police and all other law enforcement agents in this necessary work.

A crime of this kind is renewed evidence of the need of sustained effort in dealing with the criminal menace.

243 ⟨ The President Urges Extension of Authority to Negotiate Reciprocal Trade Agreements. January 14, 1937

BY THE Act of June 12, 1934 (Public No. 316, 73d Congress), the Congress authorized the Executive to enter into foreign trade agreements for the purpose of promoting the foreign commerce of the United States. This authority was conferred for a period of three years. I am very happy to learn that you have introduced in the House of Representatives a resolution (H. J. Res. 96), providing for an extension of this authority for a further period of three years. Such an extension is highly desirable in the interest of our Nation.

At the time of the original enactment, the world was moving in the direction of a progressive destruction of international commerce. Trade barriers had risen to unprecedented heights, and exclusive preferential arrangements were supplanting the rule of equal treatment in commercial relations. As a result of enhanced obstructions to trade and of increasing adverse discrimination on the part of other Nations, our foreign trade had suffered an even more drastic decline than the catastrophic fall in world trade as a whole.

ACCRUED BENEFITS CITED

If our agricultural and industrial interests, which had been severely injured by the contraction of their foreign markets, were to regain their deserved place in the international trade of the world and to expand foreign outlets for their products, it was necessary for our Government in a time of such emergency to be in a position to bargain with other governments by means of energetic and decisive negotiations. The executive branches of virtually all other important trading countries already possessed power to act promptly. By the Act of June 12, 1934, the Congress placed a similar authority in my hands.

Through the exercise of that authority, foreign trade agreements have been concluded with fifteen nations. Improved opportunities for our trade have been secured in such important markets as those of Canada, Cuba, Brazil, France, Belgium, The Netherlands, Switzerland and Sweden. Through our policy of demanding and granting equality of treatment we have obtained removal of discriminations where they existed in the trade agreement countries and guarantees of equal treatment in the future. At the same time our policy has served to reduce discriminatory practice in many other countries.

RESISTANCE TO ISOLATION

In the process of obtaining improvement in our export positions, the interests of our producers in the domestic market have been scrupulously safeguarded. This was made possible by painstaking effort on the part of the government agencies concerned with the negotiation of trade agreements and by the helpful

683

cooperation of the business community and the general public in making known to the Government their views and desires in the matter and in supplying valuable pertinent information.

Our vigorous initiative in the field of liberalization of commercial policies has been an important factor in arresting the world trend to national economic isolation, which seemed almost irresistible three years ago. Striking evidence of this is furnished by the actions of the industrial countries and by the discussions and recommendations of such international gatherings as the recent Buenos Aires conference.

But while accomplishment has been substantial and gratifying, the task is by no means completed. In international trade relations emergency conditions still exist. Barriers operating against our trade are still excessive. The reduction continues to be an essential requirement of a full and balanced economic recovery for our country. In the period which lies immediately ahead, our ability to act swiftly and effectively in the field of commercial policy will be indispensable, if the present favorable and promising trend toward a normalization and expansion of international trade, upon a friendly and constructive basis of fair-dealing and equal treatment, is to go forward.

ECONOMIC STRIFE INVOLVED

The development of liberalized trade practices has another effect, which transcends in importance even the material benefits conferred by trade improvement. Economic strife, resulting from inordinate or discriminatory trade barriers, is one of the most fruitful sources of political animosity and military conflict. A policy designed to reduce the excessive trade barriers and to establish equality of trade rights is a powerful instrument of economic appeasement and stability.

In the present unfortunate state of world affairs, we dare not, in justice to ourselves, relax our effort to abate the vigor of our leadership, in a world-wide movement for durable peace through economic prosperity.

NOTE: The Trade Agreements Act of 1934, and the general policy pursued by the Government to carry it out, were an important political issue during the Presidential campaign of 1936.

The Act was to expire in June, 1937. The Democratic platform pledged the continuance of the agreements, and the Republican platform condemned them. The issue became most acute in the States along the Canadian border and in the cattle-raising and dairying States, because of the trade agreement which had been entered into with Canada.

Many speeches were made by candidates and public officials on both sides, including the statement of my own views in favor of a continuance of the policy in addresses at Chicago, on December 9, 1935 (see Item 177, Vol. IV), in Canada, July 31, 1936 (see Item 93, Vol. V), at Chautauqua, August 14, 1936 (see Item 97, Vol. V), and at St. Paul, Minnesota, on October 9, 1936 (see Item 151, Vol. V).

In view of the fact that those who were considered strong supporters of the program were returned, almost without exception, to the House and the Senate, while some outstanding opponents of the program were defeated, it is safe to say that the American people approved the general program in the election of 1936.

The foregoing letter was sent by me urging the continuation of the program. A resolution continuing it was passed by the Congress, February 25, 1937, and approved by me on March 1, 1937 (Public Res. No. 10, 75th Congress).

244 ❡ A Greeting to the National Public Housing Conference. January 14, 1937

My dear Mrs. Simkhovitch:

WE HAVE come to realize that a Nation cannot function as a healthy democracy with part of its citizens living under good conditions and part forced to live under circumstances inimical to the general welfare. I recently called the attention of Congress to the fact that millions of Americans still live in habitations which not only fail to provide the physical benefits of modern civilization, but breed disease and impair the health of future generations.

Your organization has the opportunity effectively to carry this issue before the people. You will not be alone in your efforts.

Through the Public Works Administration the Federal Government has carried the fight directly to the slum. Today families taken from sub-standard housing are living happy, healthful lives in our first public housing project, Atlanta's Techwood development, which replaced eleven blocks of noisome slum with good housing at low rents. The Public Works Administration is now opening four more developments and has forty-six others under way.

Ten years ago public erection of fifty-one big, carefully planned community projects, replacing festering slum areas, would have seemed incredible. Yet we are doing this, and it is substantial evidence that the long fight against the slum finally is bearing fruit. If, indeed, the deeper purpose of democratic Government is to assist as many of its citizens as possible, especially those who need it most, then we have a great opportunity lying ahead in the specific field of housing.

Sincerely yours,

Mrs. Mary K. Simkhovitch,
New York, N. Y.

(This letter was read at the opening of the fourth annual meeting of the Conference, January 22, 1937.)

245 ❨ White House Statement on Appointment of Committee to Recommend Legislation for the Bonneville and Other Power Projects. January 18, 1937

The President has appointed an informal committee consisting of Secretary of the Interior Harold L. Ickes; Frederic A. Delano, Vice-Chairman, National Resources Committee; Robert E. Healy, Commissioner, Securities and Exchange Commission; Morris L. Cooke, Administrator, Rural Electrification Administration; Frank R. McNinch, Chairman, Federal Power Commission, to make recommendations to him with respect to legislation for the Bonneville and other power projects. Secretary Ickes will act as Chairman.

The following letter was addressed to Secretary Ickes, and similar letters were sent to the other members of the committee:

Dear Mr. Secretary:

POWER from the Bonneville project will be available for distribution this year. Therefore, legislation is immediately necessary. At the same time, it is highly advisable that such legislation conform to a national power generating, transmitting and distributing policy, such policy to be uniform as far as practicable or advisable. This does not mean identical rates in every part of the country but it does mean uniformity of policy. This policy once established will apply to existing projects, such as Boulder Dam and portions of the T.V.A. and to all new power developments as they are completed during the next few years.

Instead of asking the National Power Policy Committee of last year to reconvene, I am asking you to serve as Chairman with the following gentlemen as an informal committee to make recommendations to me with respect to legislation for the Bonneville and other power projects: Mr. Delano, Judge Healy, Mr. Cooke and Judge McNinch.

Inasmuch as all of you are in general familiar with the subject, I hope that you can let me have recommendations within a couple of weeks.

Yours very sincerely,

Hon. Harold L. Ickes,
Secretary of the Interior,
Washington, D. C.

NOTE: The Committee convened pursuant to the foregoing letter was somewhat different in membership from that of the National Power Policy Committee of 1934 (see Item 126, Vol. III).

Pursuant to my instructions, the Committee immediately proceeded with a study of the Bonneville project and made recommendations which I transmitted to the Congress on February 24, 1937, and which became embodied in legislation submitted to it.

687

246 ❪ A Greeting to the Dinner of the Electoral College on the Eve of the Inauguration of 1937. January 19, 1937

IT GIVES me great pleasure to send hearty felicitations and warmest personal greetings to the Presidential electors of the United States who are dining at the Mayflower Hotel on the eve of Inauguration. Yours was a special participation and the overwhelming victory which your votes registered is a measure of the responsibility which goes with so overwhelming a popular mandate.

We shall assume that responsibility cheerfully and in full faith that democracy can be made to function in the world of today as effectively as it did in the simple world in which our Nation was born a century and a half ago.

I trust that the dinner will be the rousing success which loyalty and fidelity to the principles merit.

Invitations to attend the Inauguration ceremonies to be held on January 20, 1937, in Washington, D. C., were sent by the Inaugural Committee to many persons throughout the United States. Through inadvertence, one was sent to the President himself.

He jestingly prepared the document reproduced on the opposite page, declining the invitation; but wrote on it a postscript in his own hand as indicated.

THE WHITE HOUSE
WASHINGTON

The President
regrets, that because of the
rush of official business
he is unable to accept the
courteous invitation to be present
at the ceremonies attending
the Inauguration of the
President of the United States
January twentieth
Nineteen hundred thirty-seven

I have re-arranged my engagements &
work & think I may be able to go —
Will know definitely Jan. 19 —

F.D.R.

Index

Aberdeen, S. D.
  Drought inspection trip, Item 106, p 307-308

Adams, John
  Item 190, p 521

Adams, Samuel
  Item 191, p 523

Adjusted Compensation Payment Act
  Item 29, p 103; Bankers requested to cooperate in cashing bonus checks, Item 61, p 193; Expenditures of Government increased by, Item 114, p 316-317; See also Bonus

Adjusted Service Certificates
  Exchange for bonds authorized by Congress, Item 14, p 68-69

Administrative Management of Government
  Summary of report of President's reorganization committee, Item 241A, p 674-681

Agricultural Adjustment Act
  Repeal of amendment to — recommended, Item 2, p 24; Cooperative idea its foundation, Item 151, p 420

Agricultural Adjustment Administration
  Placed under control of Bureau of Budget, Item 2, p 25; Made regular activity; Appropriation recommended for, Item 2, p 32; Parts of — declared unconstitutional, (Note) Item 39, p 139; Distributes food and feed to 19 states in drought area, (Note) Item 90, p 266; Income of farmers raised through programs of, Item 176, p 484

Agricultural Policy
  Must be a national, Item 169, p 467

Agricultural Problems
  Drought area, (Note) Item 99, p 294-295; Recommendations to correct situation, Item 104, p 301-305; Item 111, p 313; Item 153, p 425-426; Not for farmer alone, Item 156, p 433; Item 163, p 453-454; Item 165, p 455-457; Item 166, p 461-463; Item 167, p 463-465

Agricultural Program
  Should include crop insurance, Item 120, p 335; Compared to automobile industry, Item 180, p 498

Agricultural Prosperity
  During 1932-1935, (Note) Item 39, p 138

Agriculture
  Effect of subsidizing export crops, Item 4, p 45-49; National problem, Item 4, p 45-50; Gains in conservation and restoration of soil fertility by adjustment, Item 6, p 52-56; Closely linked with world economic situation, Item 33, p 115; Future plans for — will depend upon outlet abroad, Item 33, p 115; Recovery of — contributed to general recovery, (Note) Item 39, p 138; Greater part of world's population engaged in, Item 58, p 190; Proposed plan of Republican leaders for, Item 156, p 435-436; In 1932 was on road to pauperism, Item 156, p 432-433; Relation to industry, Item 156, p 433; Seven great accomplishments in behalf of, Item 156, p 434-435; Plans for future program of, Item 156, p 437-439; Item 169, p 467; Illinois, Item 174, p 477; State action alone impossible, Item 235, p 638; See also Agricultural Adjustment Act; Agricultural Problems; Agricultural Program; Agricultural Prosperity

Agriculture, Department of
  Diet survey by, Item 153, p 425; See also Agriculture, Secretary of

Agriculture, Secretary of
  Charged with execution of Migratory Bird Treaty Act, (Note) Item 30, p 108; Member of Committee on Industrial Analysis, Item 46A, p 152; Chairman of Interdepartmental Drought Committee, (Note) Item 90, p 265; See also Agriculture, Department of

Aiken, Governor George D., Vermont
  Letter re child labor amendment to Constitution, Item 237, p 657

Alamo
  Item 65, p 204; Address at, Item 66, p 206-207

Albany, N. Y.
  Remarks at, Item 188, p 515-516

Allred, Governor James V., Texas
  Item 67, p 208; Letter re child labor amendment to Constitution, Item 237, p 657

Altoona, Pa.
  Visit in flood area, (Note) Item 95, p 282

American Labor Party
  Pledges full support to President, Item

689

At home, Item 1, p 12-14; Economic, Item 1, p 16

Automobile Industry
Need of better relationship with employees, Item 180, p 498

Baker, Jacob
Assistant Works Progress Administrator to study cooperatives in Europe, Item 76, p 226

Bank Deposits
Efforts to make — safe, Item 175, p 479; Guaranteed, Item 176, p 481

Bank Failures, National
First year free from — in 55 years, Item 143, p 400-401; Item 175, p 479; Item 176, p 481; Item 202, p 555

Bankhead, Hon. John H.
Letter asking him to help prepare recommendations for legislation on farm tenancy situation, Item 133, p 373-374; Special committee on Farm Tenancy urged to confer with, Item 218, p 590-591

Bankruptcies
At a new low, Item 176, p 481

Barrows, Prof. Harlan H.
Member of Committee on Utilization of Resources of Great Plains Area, Item 131A, p 369

Battleships
See Capital Ships

Becker, Mrs. William A.
Letter to D.A.R. on national defense, Item 51, p 173-175

Belgium
Adherence to principles of tripartite declaration declared by, (Note) Item 135, p 378

Belligerent Countries
Proclamation placing embargo on export of arms, ammunition and implements of war to — revoked, Item 75, p 225

Bennett, Dr. H. H.
Member of Committee on Utilization of Resources of Great Plains Area, Item 131A, p 370

Berry, Major George L.
Greeting to Labor's Non-Partisan League, Item 94, p 280-281

Bill of Rights
Item 207, p 576

Binghamton, N. Y.
Visit in flood area, (Note) Item 95, p 282

Birthday Balls
Radio address on occasion of 3d Birthday Ball, Item 18, p 75-76

Bismarck, N. D.
Remarks at, Item 103, p 299-301

Bituminous Coal Conservation Act
Receipts accruing under, Item 2, p 31

Black, Dr. A. G.
Member of Crop Insurance Committee, Item 131, p 366

Blackwell, Dr. Elizabeth
First woman in America to receive a doctor's degree, Item 136, p 381

Bloomingburgh
Reference to Bloomington, Ill., as, (Note) Item 174, p 478-479

Bloomington, Ill.
Remarks at, Item 174, p 477-479

Bolton, Chester
Item 96, p 283

Bonneville Dam
White House statement on appointment of committee to recommend legislation for — and other power projects, Item 245, p 686-687; Congress passes legislation setting power policy, (Note) Item 245, p 687

Bonus
Vetoed by the President, Item 12, p 67; White House Statement on expediting payment of, Item 14, p 68-69; White House Statement on advisability of preserving — Bonds, Item 15, p 69-70, Item 29, p 103; President requests all bankers to cooperate in cashing — checks, Item 61, p 193; See also Adjusted Compensation Payment Act

Bonus Bill
Item 6, p 51

Bonus Bonds
White House Statement on advisability of preserving, Item 15, p 69-70

Boondoggling
President's comments on, Item 7, p 58; Item 113, p 316; Item 142, p 400; Item 143, p 401; Item 179, p 495; Item 184, p 507

Index

Couzens, James
Letter to — drafting him to head the Maritime Commission, Item 128, p 360-361; Item 179, p 494; Tribute to — on the occasion of his death, Item 193, p 531

Credit
Of Government in sound condition, Item 2, p 23

Creston, Ia.
Remarks at, Item 152, p 423-424

Crippled Children
Radio address on occasion of President's 3d Birthday Ball for benefit of, Item 18, p 75-76; Work of Kiwanis re, Item 77, p 228

Crop Curtailment
Program of, Item 83, p 247

Crop Insurance
In drought area, Item 104, p 301-305; Benefits to nation, Item 131, p 367-368; Item 156, p 431-439

Crop Insurance Committee
Creation and duties of, Item 131, p 366

Crop Production Loans
President vetoes a bill for, Item 25, p 87-89; Amount loaned; Total amount collected, (Note) Item 25, p 87-89; Allotment of funds for, Item 32, p 114

Cross, Governor Wilbur L., Connecticut
Letter re child labor amendment to Constitution, Item 237, p 657

Cuba
Platt Amendment abandoned, Item 97, p 287

Cummings, Attorney General
Offers reward in Mattson kidnapping case, Item 242, p 682

Curtis, Charles
Presidential statement on death of, Item 22, p 80

Czechoslovakia
Committee to study cooperatives in, Item 76, p 226

Dallas, Texas
Address at Texas Centennial Exposition, Item 68, p 209-214; Unveiling of Robert E. Lee memorial statue at, Item 69, p 214; Remarks at, Item 70, p 214-217

Davis, Chester C.
Letter to — authorizing survey of trade conditions in Europe, Item 33, p 115-116; Presidential statement on the survey by, Item 33A, p 116-117

Daughters of American Revolution
Letter to — on national defense, Item 51, p 173-175

Debt, National
Cost of program and increase of, Item 144, p 401-408; Increased by recovery program, Item 152, p 424; Increase of — outweighed by increase of national income, Item 155, p 428; Item 176, p 488

Deficiency Appropriation
Approved, (Note) Item 36, p 132; Immediate consideration requested of Congress, Item 235, p 634

Deflation
Stopped, Item 176, p 484

de Kruif, Dr. Paul
Item 18, p 76

Delano, Frederic A.
Member of committee on legislation for power projects, Item 245, p 686-687

Democracy
Andrew Jackson and, Item 64, p 198; Quotation of Abraham Lincoln re, Item 72, p 222; War for survival of, Item 79, p 236; Real struggle to continue and preserve, Item 170, p 473; Still hope of world, Item 224, p 609; Item 235, p 641

Democracy in Taxation
In 1776 the fight was for —. In 1936 that is still the fight, Item 191, p 523

Democratic National Campaign Headquarters, New York City
Remarks to workers of, Item 205, p 563-565

Democratic National Convention
Acceptance of renomination for Presidency, Item 79, p 230-236

Democratic National Platform of 1936
Item 79, p 234; Pledged continuance of reciprocal trade agreements, (Note) Item 243, p 685

Democrats
Comparison of leadership and philosophy of Republicans and, Item 137, p 383-392; Item 208, p 578

696

697

for vocational, Item 62, p 193-194; Imposition of new taxes for — prevented through Federal assistance; Stimulation of — through Works Program, Item 136, p 381

Election, 1936
Results of, (Note) Item 209, p 582

Electoral College
Greeting to dinner of, Item 246, p 688

Electric Home and Farm Authority
Placed under control of Bureau of Budget, Item 2, p 25

Electric Power
Need for public policy for promotion of; Construction of reservoirs for generation of, Item 123, p 354-355

Elkins, West Virginia
Campaign address at Mountain States Forest Festival, Item 141, p 396-400

Emergency Conservation Work
Additional funds allotted to, Item 45, p 151

Emergency Council, New Jersey State
See N. J. Emergency Council

Emergency Drought Areas
Designation of, (Note) Item 90, p 265-266

Emergency Railroad Transportation Act, 1933
Unsatisfactory to both companies and employees, Item 31, p 110; Labor protection provisions of, (Note) Item 31, p 112-113

Emergency Relief Appropriation
President's estimate and recommendations re, Item 36, p 126-131

Emergency Relief Appropriation Act of 1935
Number of persons to provide employment for under, Item 240, p 661

Emergency Relief Appropriation Act of 1936
Amount of; Approved, (Note) Item 36, p 131

Employment
Increases, Item 1, p 17; Problems of, Item 53, p 181-182; Item 64, p 201

Emporia, Kansas
Remarks at, Item 168, p 465-466

Engineering Schools
Letter to — of Nation on social respon-

sibility and problems of engineering, Item 192, p 530-531

England, King George V of
Messages of condolence on death of, Item 9, p 65, Item 93, p 278

Enochs, H. A.
Joint statement with George M. Harrison regarding Railroad Agreement, (Note) Item 31, p 113

Ethiopia
Presidential statement against profiteering in war between Italy and, Item 26, p 89-91; Exporting of arms and ammunition to — prohibited, Item 27, p 92-94; Presidential statement on revocation of neutrality proclamations in war between Italy and, Item 75, p 225

Erie, Pa.
Visit in flood area, (Note) Item 95, p 282

European Trade Conditions
Survey of, Item 33, p 115-116; Item 33A, p 116-117

Evans, John K.
(Note) Item 174, p 478-479

Executive Assistants
Message on government reorganization, Item 241, p 671-674; Item 241A, p 675-681

Executive Order
6147, Authorizing work on Indian reservations and enrolment of Indians in C.C.C., (Note) Item 50, p 173; 7252, Transferred records of N.R.A. and Department of Commerce, Item 46A, p 153; 7305, Re crop production loans, (Note) Item 25, p 89; 7323, Creating Committee of Industrial Analysis, Item 46A, p 152-158; 7421, Places postmasters of first, second, and third class under Civil Service Regulations, Item 91, p 269-271

Expenditures
See Budget

Export-Import Banks
Placed under control of Bureau of Budget, Item 2, p 25

Export Markets
Lost because of Smoot-Hawley tariff, Item 39, p 136

Fahey, John H., Chairman, Federal Home Loan Bank Board
Letter suggesting application of Civil

Index

A Treasury statement on, Item 135, p 376-378

Interstate Commerce Law
Abuses of railroads curbed by, Item 68, p 212

Intracoastal Waterway
Completion of — from Trenton, N. J. to Miami, Fla., Item 139, p 393-394

Iowa
Part Louisiana Purchase, Item 64, p 196

Irish
Have borne notable part in American history, Item 52, p 175-176

Isolation, National Economic
Discussed at Buenos Aires Conference, Item 243, p 682-685

Italy
Presidential statement against profiteering in war between Ethiopia and, Item 26, p 89-91; Exporting of arms and ammunition to — prohibited, Item 27, p 92-94; Presidential statement on revocation of neutrality Proclamations in war between — and Ethiopia, Item 75, p 225; Battleships under construction, Item 239, p 659

Jackson, Andrew
Item 1, p 13, Item 3, p 39-41, Item 64, p 197; Effect of — on American political life, Item 64, p 198; Item 130, p 362

Jackson Day Dinner
Address, Item 3, p 38-44

Jacksonville, Illinois
Drought inspection trip, Item 116, p 325-326

Jamestown, North Dakota
Drought inspection trip, Item 105, p 306

Jefferson Dinner
Address at, Item 53, p 177-182

Jefferson, Thomas
Item 1, p 13; Re Louisiana Purchase and Constitution, Item 64, p 196; Address at home of —, Monticello, Va., Item 82, p 240-243; Quoted on democracy, Item 176, p 486

Jensen, Governor Leslie, South Dakota
Letter re child labor amendment to Constitution, Item 237, p 657

Jersey City, New Jersey
Address at dedication of Medical Center, Item 145, p 408-410

Joffre, Marshal
Item 191, p 523

Johnston, Governor Olin D., South Carolina
Letter re child labor amendment to Constitution, Item 237, p 657

Johnstown, Pennsylvania
Flood conditions at, Item 41, p 142

Joliet, Illinois
Remarks at, Item 175, p 479-480

Jones, Jesse
Item 65, p 206

Jones, Marvin
Item 133, p 373-374; Special committee on Farm Tenancy urged to confer with, Item 218, p 590-591

Julesburg, Colorado
Drought inspection trip, Item 112, p 313-315

Jusserand Memorial
Address at dedication of — in Rock Creek Park, Washington, D. C., Item 212, p 584-585

Justice, Department of
Prevented violations of embargo of arms, (Note) Item 75, p 225; Mattson kidnapping case, Item 242, p 682

Justo, President Agustin P.
Suggestion to — for an Inter-American Conference, Item 17, p 72-73; Item 222, p 599; Item 224, p 604; Informal speech at luncheon for —, Buenos Aires, Argentina, Item 225, p 610-612

Kansas
Part Louisiana Purchase, Item 64, p 196

Kansas City, Missouri
Campaign address at, Item 170, p 469-473

Keegan, Rt. Rev. Msgr. Robert Fulton
Greeting to National Conference on Social Work, Item 57, p 188-189

King, W. MacKenzie
Active in negotiations for Great Lakes-St. Lawrence Treaty, (Note) Item 34, p 122-124; Invitation to visit White House, Item 93, p 279

705

706

Index

Index

Works Program
Usefulness of, Item 7, p 58-59; Time to reduce Federal expenditures on, (Note) Item 36, p 131; Employment on — decreased during 1936, (Note) Item 36, p 131-132; Usefulness of — depends upon the individual community, Item 89, p 261-263; All projects of local origin, Item 159, p 445; Investment, Item 159, p 445-446; Number of employable persons provided for under, Item 240, p 661

Works Progress Administration
Appropriation necessary for destitute unemployed, Item 36, p 129-131; Workers assist in flood relief work, (Note) Item 37, p 133, Item 41, p 141; Allocation for repairs and replacement of public property damaged by floods, Item 42, p 143; Allocation to — for flood relief work, Item 47, p 159; Administrator member of Interdepartmental Drought Committee, (Note) Item 90, p 265; Double purpose of work projects in drought areas, (Note) Item 90, p 268; Item 176, p 485; Large number of unemployed remain on, Item 219, p 594; Letter on appropriations for, Item 240, p 660-662; Physical accomplishment on — projects, (Note) Item 240, p 663-667

Works Progress and Relief, Federal Administrator of
Memorandum re prevention of losses by spring floods, Item 37, p 133

World Peace
Address at Chautauqua, N. Y., Item 97, p 285-292

World War Memorial, St. Louis, Missouri
Address at dedication of, Item 172, p 474-476

World's Fair, New York
Greeting to sponsors of, Item 221, p 596

Wright, Bishop R. R.
Letter to — on 74th Anniversary of Proclamation of Emancipation, Item 126, p 357-358

Wyoming
Large portion of — from Louisiana Purchase, Item 64, p 197

Young Democratic Club, Baltimore, Maryland
Address to, Item 48, p 159

Y.M.C.A.
Greeting to, Item 98, p 292-293

Young, Owen
Interested in possibilities of Bay of Fundy as tidal power development, Item 92, p 273

Youth
Destiny of, Item 3, p 44; Objective of, Item 48, p 160; Rehabilitation of — under C.C.C. program, (Note) Item 50, p 171-173; Recommendation re unemployment of, Item 74, p 224; Efforts in behalf of, Item 170, p 469-473

Index by Miss K. C. Blackburn